CONCHIES

Andy Ward

CONCHIES

The
Uncomfortable Story
of the
Payne Brothers:
Conscientious Objectors
in the
First World War

Matador
9 Priory Business Park,
Wistow Road, Kibworth Beauchamp,
Leicestershire. LE8 0RX
Tel: (+44) 116 279 2299
Fax: (+44) 116 279 2277
Email: books@troubador.co.uk
Web: www.troubador.co.uk/matador

ISBN 978 1784621 384

British Library Cataloguing in Publication Data.
A catalogue record for this book is available from the British Library.

Printed and bound by CPI Group (UK) Ltd, Croydon, CR0 4YY
Typeset in 11pt Aldine401 BT Roman by Troubador Publishing Ltd, Leicester, UK

Matador is an imprint of Troubador Publishing Ltd

For Sharon, Michael and Sarah.

CONTENTS

FOREWORD

As we reach the centenary of the Great War, we hear and read of valiant and heroic stories: the suffering of the troops in the trenches and the inhuman environments which the young men of the world endured in the name of 'victory' and the 'glory' of war. There is another story, one less spoken of. It is an unpopular story about individuals who, if living today, would be the focus of internet trolls but in their own day elicited an equally vehement reaction from their communities. These were the people who refused to fight for their country.

Many took this course of action because of the belief that killing their fellow man was a sin in the eyes of God. Some refused to fight because they felt unable to attack working men on socialist principles. There were many motives but each man felt compelled to follow the dictates of his conscience. Such individuals were vilified by their communities and many sought the company and support of like-minded groups, such as the Quakers, Christadelphians and other religious and humanist networks. Society did not differentiate between the reasons for refusal to fight and called them all 'conscientious objectors'.

The author of this book, Andy Ward, was a talented Historian and teacher with a passionate interest in the First World War. When preparing for his retirement, he was offered access to a collection of letters which had been discovered in the attic by a local family. They record a correspondence from 1916 to the end of the war between two brothers, Leonard and Roland Payne and their friends and family. The brothers chose to become conscientious objectors and the letters follow their journey through the system as the authorities sought first to dissuade them from that course, then to punish them and finally to place them somewhere where they would be useful. Andy's wide ranging research uncovered the stories behind the letters using evidence in the National Archives, the Quaker Library and local archives in the Leicestershire Record Office. He also made sure that every family holiday enabled visits to every place where the Payne brothers had been held around the country! His approach was meticulous and thorough and the result is an academic work of both local and national importance but it is also a very human story which Andy treated with balance and thought. His enthusiasm for the subject shines through and the account is both readable and enthralling.

Sadly, Andy died before he was able to see his book in print. His family are pleased to make his dream a reality.

Sharon Ward, 2014

PART ONE

HOME TOWN

*I*n our mind's eye and in our imagination we see them: two boys – brothers – well-dressed, smartly turned out in the fashion for boys in Edwardian England. It is Sunday and today is Christmas Day. The year is 1904: this year Christmas Day falls on a Sunday.

We see the boys as they trudge their way through the deep snow this cold Christmas morning, the scene familiar to us from a million Christmas cards, on their way to chapel in their small home town, deep in the English Midlands, to sing carols – for they are musically gifted – and to celebrate the birth of their Saviour, Jesus Christ. Perhaps they will sing Edmund Sears' great Victorian Nonconformist hymn 'It Came upon a Midnight Clear' with its lines 'And man at war with man hears not/ The love-song which they bring:/ O hush the noise ye men of strife,/ And hear the angels sing.' The hymn, and the Christian faith which underpins it, are taken seriously and literally by the boys and their family.

The older boy, a good looking nine-year-old, is wearing his chapel clothes, a long jacket with a button-up waistcoat and straight trousers down to his sturdy boots; his brother, two years younger, wears a similar jacket with stiff Eton collar beneath, and knickerbockers to the calf with dark stockings below. He also will be wearing hefty boots, for these are no barefoot urchins – far from it.

They are Leonard and Roland Payne (Roland already known as Bill, or 'Puffing Billy' to his friends), respectable, middle class boys, sons and grandsons of basket weavers, of successful, small businessmen selling what they make, catering for the needs of small town rural south Leicestershire: efficient, industrious, socially ambitious. Their father, John, has moved up in the world: he has for some years past acted as Assistant County Court Bailiff, serving summonses mainly for debt, and, where necessary, accompanying the unfortunates the dozen miles to Leicester Gaol. It is not a job he relishes and he often organises collections among the debtors' friends to pay off the creditors.

The new twentieth century is now safely underway, filled with hope and boundless possibilities, but also promising profound changes, some already in train. For Leonard and Roland the future looks bright and secure, their family well established, staunch members of the chapel and well respected among their neighbours. Roland has just this last year joined his brother as a pupil at the town's Sherrier Elementary School. They are strong boys, not particularly big for their age, but well able to fend for themselves in the hurly-burly of a boyish childhood, playing their summer games down by the river or in the recreation ground behind the churchyard. Leonard is already a keen rugby player, a member of the local rugby club juniors – a connection that will, in future years, stand both of them in good stead. Do they in the winter snows join in snowball fights? Probably, though not, perhaps, in an aggressive way. And in the wake of the South African War, had they played a boyish game of 'Britons' versus 'Boers', we wonder; it would be fascinating to know, either way.

3

For, though they do not yet know it as they make their way through the heavy snowdrifts this Christmas morning, Leonard and Roland have been born into a cursed generation, the last of the nineteenth century, the generation of the Great War. The lives of many of those who sit next to the brothers at their elementary school desks or share the children's pews with them in the Congregational Chapel, will be brought to ruination and, for some, a violent and squalid death far from home when they are barely full grown.

Not these brothers, though. Their fate will be different. For they will refuse to fight when war comes, and that refusal will mark and haunt them for the rest of their lives.

Let us for the moment leave the boys to their Christmas goose, their modest presents and their singing round the Christmas tree, as we seek first to understand something of the lost world they inhabit and the community of people of which they form a part – the same community which will reject them with a violence and anger they could not have anticipated and we can scarcely imagine: imprisoned, assaulted, their home attacked, their livelihood destroyed, they then forced to flee for their lives from this sleepy little market town.

Theirs is a remarkable – and surprising – story.

HOME TOWN

'SOMNOLENT RESPECTABILITY'

One observer, writing just before the First World War, characterised Leicestershire as a 'commonplace' county: if we remove the sneer from the voice, what remains is essentially true.[1] Its county town, too, lacks the extraordinary: 'the only praise that I ever heard visitors give to my native town of Leicester,' wrote the journalist Henry Nevinson, 'was that it was clean. They always said that, and they said no more'.[2]

In the south of the county, fourteen or so miles from Leicester and close to the border with Northamptonshire and Warwickshire, lies the small market town of Lutterworth. Every Thursday since 1214, the High Street had been lined with market stalls selling all kinds of produce, the pavements left wide enough to accommodate them. Lutterworth was commonplace and clean, a 'typical English town'[3] as some called it, 'neat and well-built'[4]: never a pretty place, but workmanlike and worthy. It was a town built by and for shopkeepers with the odd flourish of grandeur. A small town, characterised by its own local historian, writing just before the First World War, as wearing 'the same air of somnolent respectability which it wore in the early days of the last century'.[5] The 'last century' was, of course, the nineteenth.

Lutterworth was not the sort of place where anything of much consequence happened. True, the famous John Wyclif had been Rector of the place, the John Wyclif who was supposed to – but did not actually – translate the Bible into English there; the same John Wyclif who would be hailed by later Protestants as the 'Morning Star of the English Reformation'. Wyclif died in 1384. There was a bit of excitement forty-four years later when his heretical bones were dug up and ceremoniously burned and scattered in the River Swift as posthumous punishment.[6] After that… nothing much.

★

Lutterworth stands on the high ground above the River Swift, a lesser tributary of the Avon, in the gentle countryside of south Leicestershire. Lutterworth belongs in this place. The best approach to the town today is from the south, along the new road from Rugby, the magnificent vista suddenly revealing the town clinging to the hillside, the parish church of St Mary appearing to be lifted up out of the hill top, seemingly floating in a bed of great trees. It is surely one of the most extraordinary and dramatic approaches to any town in England, made all the more so in recent years by the remarkable half-size replica of a Gloster aeroplane in flight, which marks the entrance to the town – a tribute to one of the town's few other claims to fame, Sir Frank Whittle who, the town insists, did the essential work on his jet engine in the disused Ladywood Foundry buildings.

In outline, Lutterworth resembled a ragged crescent, perching on the high ground above the Swift. The whole town could be walked easily within fifteen minutes, even allowing for the occasional stop. Were we able to stroll through medieval Lutterworth, half a millennium ago, we would be struck by the continuity in the street pattern of this town, its shops gathered along that crescent, one horn pointing to Leicester heading north and the other, called Woodmarket, heading west, a wide and airy street lined with poor cottages and a handful of grander dwellings of the better-off.[7] Had we followed this road westward out of the town in 1900 or so, we would have passed the Union Workhouse set apart just beyond the edge of the town, out of sight and out of mind, and have been led thence out across the rolling Warwickshire countryside to Coventry, some fifteen miles to the west. Thus, for centuries, Lutterworth was linked to the two great medieval Midland towns of Leicester and Coventry, cradled inside that crescent of roads, shops and houses.

Lutterworth was a small town of innkeepers and shopkeepers; its main role was trade, supplying the neighbouring agricultural villages with the necessities of modern life[8]. It was a small market town with the commercial, legal, social and cultural paraphernalia of modern town life: bankers, insurance agents, educators, doctors, nursemaids, hairdressers and the rest, all serving a wider rural region.

Around it lay its inner ring of satellite agricultural villages, members of Lutterworth's extended family: Dunton Bassett, Gilmorton, Walcote, Swinford, Cotesbach (pronounced 'coats-batch') and Bitteswell (pronounced 'bitters-well'). Each of these small communities of a few hundred people depended on Lutterworth for many of the essentials of everyday modern life. A little further away lay an outer ring: villages like Ullesthorpe and Leire, with their railway connections; the Ashbys , Claybrookes and Peatlings (all Magna and Parva) and the Kilworths – North and South. The deserted medieval village of Misterton –

comprising a church, an absurdly grand vicarage, a big house and a handful of cottages – lay a couple of miles to the east, while another ancient settlement, Bittesby, also closed down for sheep in the fifteenth century, lay just off Roman Watling Street (the A5) cresting the high ground above Lutterworth in the opposite direction, to the west. These intensely rural communities were connected by their own enclosure roads, their ninety degree bends preserving the outlines of the medieval furlongs, roads set out before the coming of the motor car, linking Lutterworth to this agricultural hinterland, the wagons of no less than seventeen separate carriers shifting stuff weekly to and from all these nearby villages.[9]

In a wider perspective we can see Lutterworth standing at the centre of a network of longer, grander roads than those filaments stretching out to the local villages, big roads connecting it to the world beyond. For, as well as being a market town with local importance, Lutterworth had been a road town in the eighteenth century and the first half of the nineteenth. The big, long-range turnpike roads, the first instalment of the so-called 'Transport Revolution', set out in the eighteenth century with verges wide enough to turn a stage coach with its team of horses[10], studded at intervals by toll cottages to collect the money which paid for it all, linked Lutterworth to the outside world in all directions. A lot of business passed through the town off the ancient Watling Street, still the main road from London to Chester and Holyhead and thence Ireland, running along the high ground a mile or two west of the town. The old coaching inns – still eighteen of them at the start of the 1840s[11] – with their characteristic arched entrances, wide enough and high enough to allow a stagecoach passage, still line the High Street, though only one, 'The Greyhound', remains an inn today.

★

Lutterworth's population was modest. In 1841 it had numbered two and a half thousand – though it served a village population of a further ten thousand – twelve and a half thousand in all. Throughout the Victorian period, however, these numbers fell, and fell considerably. By the time the census was taken in 1901, the population of the town was eight hundred fewer than when Victoria had come to the throne, a fall of a third, and the numbers living in the catchment area had reduced by well over three thousand, a fall of a quarter. The sad fact was that Lutterworth was locked – or had locked itself – into its own time bubble and Victorian England simply passed it by. Isolated and alone, it was exposed unmercifully to the impact of external changes.

The first of these was a missed opportunity. In 1839 swarms of navvies, working for the Midland Counties Railway, had laid a new rail line from Leicester south to Rugby, and thence on to London, but had routed it three miles to the west of Lutterworth, through the villages of Broughton Astley and Ullesthorpe[12]: Lutterworth was literally bypassed. One observer in 1890 gave this dismissive explanation of why: 'Rugby accepted the railway in the beginnings of the railway movement but Lutterworth rejected it. It seems strange that landowners and graziers should have fought against the proposal on the grounds that the smoke of the passing engine would seriously discolour the wool of the sheep and that the continuous rush of the locomotive would so disturb the cattle as to interfere with the process of their fattening. So Rugby became a noted railway centre and Lutterworth was left to its bovine sleepiness.'[13] Clearly, 'bovine sleepiness' trumps 'somnolent respectability'.

The new line was opened in 1840 and, with the advent of the railway age, horse-drawn road transport, from which much of Lutterworth's income derived, went into decline. This was the second blow to the town's fortunes as the coaching trade slowly died out, unable to compete with the railways, which charged half as much, got there quicker and were more comfortable to ride in.[14] Innkeepers and hoteliers of Lutterworth also saw much of their business disappear, the decline insidious and relentless.

The third blow had already hurt the town and would continue to bleed it for decades to come. Framework knitting, traditionally an essential cottage industry across Leicestershire, had been in steep decline since the 1830s, so Lutterworth was hit hard yet again.[15] With fewer jobs and no railway to generate more, the most enterprising – or those most desperate to evade the clutches of the workhouse – left the town, many making for the new opportunities on offer in Leicester. By the end of Victoria's reign Lutterworth had only a small handful of framework knitters left, supplying a niche market using the modern Griswold circular knitting machines.

The 'Great Agricultural Depression', which stretched from 1875 to the Great War and robbed the pastoral farmers and their labourers of much of their livelihoods, was the fourth and, possibly, the greatest blow of them all. Unable to compete with cheap wheat from the great American prairies and, from the 1880s, with refrigerated imports of meat from New Zealand and Australia, the U.S.A. and Argentina, the welfare of the farming community was sacrificed to the interest of free trade and cheap food for the cities. Lutterworth's surrounding region was cattle rearing and sheep grazing country, land divided into smaller farms than anywhere else in the county, and with a strong line in pig breeding.[16] But as the market for expensive English meat declined, and the prosperity of the farmers and graziers fell, so Lutterworth's fortunes declined too, with fewer and poorer farmers and agricultural workers in the surrounding villages to buy its goods and services.[17]

More striking and more serious in its way than the absolute decline in Lutterworth's population was its composition as the Great War approached. The town was by now dependent on an immigrant flow to maintain even its already shrinking population. In 1891, at the time of the census, a fraction over 50% of those living in Lutterworth had been born there; by 1901, it was below 45%[18] and, by 1911, it was below 40%. While a third of the population had originated in the adjoining regions (Leicestershire, Warwickshire and Northamptonshire) the remainder had come from further afield. Almost every county in England was represented in the town, from the Channel Islands to Durham, from East Anglia to the West Country, few of them migrating from the big industrial areas, but most coming from places not too different from Lutterworth itself, small towns in rural areas. Among them were the Paynes. Reuben, the boys' grandfather, had shifted the fifteen miles or so from Market Harborough, en route to Lutterworth from Braybrooke in Northamptonshire. And in Lutterworth there existed small but noticeable contingents of Welsh, Scots and Irish, as well as the 'exotics' from far-flung places like Brooklyn in New York and Rapid City in Winnipeg, from Melbourne in Australia, and from New Zealand; moreover, there were a few service families, their children born in the Indian subcontinent, and a boy boarding at the grammar school who had been born in Barbados. The town must have been a veritable Tower of Babel of regional accents.[19]

The Earl of Denbigh's seat at Newnham Paddox near Lutterworth.
[Via Lost Heritage: a memorial to the lost country houses of England – matthewbeckett.com.
The house was demolished in 1952.]

Lutterworth, though, was an integral part of the wider rural society of south Leicestershire. And the surrounding countryside was dotted with grand houses, the dwelling places of those of money and status, on a level no Lutterworth tradesman could even dream of. At the pinnacle of the local social order were the true aristocrats, highest of all Rudolph Feilding, 9th Earl of Denbigh (the title dating back to James I) a man of minor national importance and a significant influence across the whole country during the Great War, living just over the Warwickshire border in his magnificent pile of Newnham Paddox. The management of his estate lands had effectively become its own cottage industry, devoted solely to maintaining the earl in the manner to which earls had grown accustomed to live. His family had been Lords of the Manor of Lutterworth since the seventeenth century[20] and his influence in the town, though indirect, was still a force to be reckoned with.

On an altogether more modest scale, a mile south of Lutterworth lay the village of Cotesbach. It was ruled by Charles Marriott, its Lord of the Manor, who was sixty-six years old when war broke out in 1914: a barrister and High Sheriff of Leicestershire when he had been only thirty, he was descended from a long and distinguished line of Anglican clergy with an admixture of gentry along the way. He owned almost the whole of the parish of Cotesbach, and was an influential leader of local society.[21]

Corbet Smith was also 'old' money. His inherited wealth, land and status dated back at least to the eighteenth century, even though by now he and his peers owned less of it than some of their social inferiors. Corbet Smith occupied both Walcote House, a mile or two to the east, and Bitteswell Hall, a mile to the north of Lutterworth. Well connected and with a decent pedigree, Corbet Smith was a military man, a Captain in the Royal Dragoons and then, on his retirement, an honorary Major in the Leicestershire Imperial Yeomanry. Sixty-nine in 1914, Corbet Smith is invariably referred to as '*Major* Corbet Smith'.[22] While the others were away with their regiments, he would play a key role in defining the local community's response to the Great War.

Families like these were recognised in Burke's *Landed Gentry* at the time. Other local families whose wealth derived blatantly from trade, such as the Hobsons who occupied the big house in Misterton, the Entwistles, who built a grand house at North Kilworth with wealth derived from their Rochdale textile mills, and the Murray Smiths of Gumley, who grew rich from railways and publishing,[23] were not, presumably because they were not perceived to be, gentry. Everywhere there were hierarchies.

South Leicestershire was a place particularly attractive to the aristocratic bourgeoisie of the Industrial Revolution because Lutterworth lies in the heart of the traditional gory battleground between the scarlet hunter and the fox. This was hunting and horse-riding country *par excellence*, and no safe place for wildlife. Blood sports, hunting, shooting and fishing were taken for granted as an essential part of the rural way of life.[24] The landscape of south Leicestershire was ideal country for fox-hunting with scattered small but conspicuous areas of woodland, deliberately left or specially planted after Enclosure as fox-covers where the fox could breed unhindered to provide a plentiful future supply of quarry, appropriately distributed to meet the needs of the hunts.[25] Hunting was about sport, not, of course, about vermin control.

While the 'new' and 'old' money families might become integrated through their schooling, clubs and military service, one distinction between them remained clear: their commitment to their local communities. It is striking that the 'old' money families (the Feildings of Newnham Paddox, Lord Braye of Stanford Hall, a handful of miles east of Lutterworth, the Marriotts of Cotesbach, and Corbet Smith of Bitteswell and Walcote) all involved themselves in local affairs in and around Lutterworth, as magistrates, school governors, Poor Law Guardians and the like and even on the sports field. In contrast, the 'new' money families generally did not, beyond the odd status giving stint on the magistrates' bench, preferring to create their own little worlds in their own big houses, feeling little obligation to pay their social dues to their less fortunate neighbours.[26]

★

Lutterworth town's hierarchy as the Great War approached was not clearly fixed and was more open to impromptu change; in a sense it was more volatile. There certainly was a hierarchy within the town's inhabitants. One only has to notice who lived in the bigger houses in town, who employed the greatest numbers of live-in domestic servants or scan the local newspapers or glance at the composition of local institutions like the Bench, the Parish and Rural District Councils, the Board of Workhouse Guardians, Overseers of the Poor, the various school governing bodies. The same men of influence appear again and again. However, it was a constantly shifting hierarchy: the men of substance in 1914 were not the same as the men of substance in 1900.

On the whole, the leaders of local town society were not men of inherited rank, as rural Lords of the Manor or local squires in the traditional sense, such as were to be found in the surrounding villages, although they did fulfil many of the same social obligations. These men formed more of a professional class, a meritocracy based on successful careers in law or medicine. Lupton Topham was the most

Lupton Topham photographed in 1900 (far right). The Rector, the Rev. Montague Alderson,
photographed in 1900 (second from right).
Lutterworth Museum.

august of the town's inhabitants. He lived in the very fine Lutterworth House, just off Woodmarket, and owned some valuable properties in the town[27]. His status in local society was amply confirmed when he was appointed High Sheriff of Leicestershire in 1914. Topham also had associations with the market town of Middleham, in North Yorkshire, owning another fine house there.

His brother Harry was the Rector, living next door. For all his divided interests, Topham gave a huge amount of his time, energy and money to Lutterworth: his name crops up over and over again in the archives of virtually every local institution. He was a man of very firm views, seeing the town rather in the way a medieval lord saw his fief, and uninterested in social improvement. To many, his influence was that of a dead hand on local life.

Not far below him in status was James Darlington, by 1914 an old man well into his eighties, but a man of distinguished record, a former High Sheriff and (unsuccessful) Conservative Parliamentary candidate in Rugby, as well as a lawyer and man of business in the coal mining industry. Like Topham, Darlington was active in local town affairs: so we find him graciously allowing his garden to be used for the Rose Show and garden fete held just as war was breaking out in the summer of 1914, to raise money for an alteration to the church organ. The show was opened, it goes without saying, by Lupton Topham.[28] Darlington had bought the house on the high ground which overlooks the southern entrance to the town, appropriately called 'The Hill', and more or less on the spot where, in medieval times, the town gibbet had stood[29]. There he lived a life of sumptuous luxury, employing more domestic servants than worked in most of the town's commercial businesses.[30] The house was later sold on: these grand houses were rarely inherited.[31]

Alongside them, inevitably high up in the pecking order, was the Rector, Montague Frederick Alderson, descended from a long line of lawyers and Anglican clergy, remarkably well-connected for a Midlands' English parson; his father had been Rector of Lutterworth before him.[32]

So, characteristic of England at that time, the oligarchy at the top of Lutterworth society was Anglican. They had more in common than that, though, for they all inhabited a *mental* world which was founded on notions of patriotism, of King, Country and Empire, a Britishness based on shared cultural values and a common history. It was one of the pillars on which their civilisation rested, and they were anxious that their society be given stability and cohesiveness through the promotion of these same values. The teaching of British History in schools was an essential vehicle for transmitting this agreed sense of identity.[33] Empire Day, May 24th, was one high point in the patriotic calendar of the country, in Lutterworth no less than elsewhere. The girls and boys of Sherrier School came together to be fed with patriotic speeches by the town's leading dignitaries, before singing patriotic songs, patriotically saluting the flag and being then dismissed to enjoy a patriotic half day holiday.[34] That the Empire Day speeches should be delivered by those at the top of the local tree, notably Lupton Topham of course, and that the annual prize giving ceremonies of Sherrier School and the grammar school held in the Town Hall (designed by Joseph Hansom of hansom cab fame and built in the 1830s, much to the town's pride) should be equally honoured by the presence of the same dignitaries, only served to reinforce the social hierarchy, to underline the demand for willing, enthusiastic and grateful deference.

Lutterworth paid a great deal of attention to the respectable upbringing of its children. They were bound to their local community through the Agricultural Show and the annual feast, both in the school holidays, and were allowed time off school for purely local occasions such as when the circus arrived in town, when the hunters and the hounds held a meet in neighbouring Bitteswell, when May Day garlands were carried through the town, and on the day in 1904 when the foundation stone of the new Wesleyan Chapel was laid.[35] The children of Lutterworth were made to feel part of the local community and its doings, but were, as well, taught of their place in the national community and beyond that within Britain's far-flung Empire, which gave them a defined – and important – pride in their status in the world simply by virtue of having been born British. This was no mere passing fashion, no whim or light fancy, but a defining – perhaps *the* defining – characteristic of their lives.

In a town like Lutterworth the promotion of these cultural values was a relatively easy task, for small town rural south Leicestershire had largely escaped the vast social changes the Industrial Revolution had brought, isolated as it was from so many of the profound changes through which Victoria's Britain was passing.

At the opposite end of the scale from the likes of Topham and Darlington and Alderson came those whose physical labour, largely unrecorded, got things done. These people lived in the smaller houses in the more crowded locations – Dixon's Court, Regents Street or Baker Street. Several years later this scathing verdict would be delivered on 'those snug little houses off Station Road, with two sweet little rooms; or those around that quaint yard called Dixon Square; or, again, those dinky little places tucked behind Woodmarket, how secluded and mellow they are! No gardens to till, scarcely any windows to clean, no absurd privacy, all life shared and its intimate details known to all.'[36] Those who lived there were those whose lives were overshadowed by the threat of the workhouse, sitting ominously at the edge of town and waiting for them should they fall sick or disabled, or simply grow old. Some were employed on the land as agricultural labourers, but more worked in the building trades, a neat demonstration of the urban over the rural character of the town. But Lutterworth remained in many respects a pre-industrial little town, a town without a self-conscious working class. When local historian Arthur Dyson likened it to Lutterworth a century earlier, he hit the mark more accurately than perhaps even he could have imagined. Domestic service in its various forms – that most socially divisive and class bound form of occupation – accounted for almost one in ten of the whole population of Lutterworth in 1901, the number of domestic servants a family employed an index of its wealth and status.[37]

In between came the 'middling sort', the most important of all being the shopkeepers who were the economic backbone of the town, its *raison d'être*. Not all shopkeepers were, of course, equal. They themselves were arranged in subtle

14

financial, economic and social hierarchies. As one informal indicator of money and status, two of the local grocers, Egbert Lavender on High Street and Ebenezer Chesterfield on Church Street, were among the first in Lutterworth to have a telephone installed – Egbert's phone number was Lutterworth 2 (number 1 being at the post office), with Ebenezer hurrying to catch up as Lutterworth 9.[38] Then there were the rival stationers, the Bottrills and the Abbotts, both on Church Street, and each producing its own local almanac. In addition, Abbotts were offering for sale 'books by all authors', as well as expensive writing papers, photographic services, picture framing and a range of fancy goods.[39] Frederick Bottrill competed by offering such luxuries as: 'Toilet paper, 500 in packet, 4d., 4½d.[40]; Japanese & very smooth, tough, soft, satin surface Paper, 4d. a Packet'.[41] An eye to comfort. And so it went on: butchers, bakers, and if not candlestick makers, at least candlestick sellers. In a vibrant, competitive commercial market – even on such a relatively small scale as this – anything to keep ahead of the competition. On Church Street there was Joseph Handford, offering 'fancy goods' of all sorts, including a range of china bearing a variety of Lutterworth photographs 'from Twopence each'.[42]

On a level less elevated than would allow telephone owning and the like was the Payne family, who were basket makers. They were comfortably placed as the middling of the 'middling sort'. John Payne, the head of the family, had married Jessie Handford, Joseph the fancy goods seller's daughter, and the two boys, Leonard and Roland, were their sons.

★

At the centre of the town lies the Parish Church of St. Mary's. This was where John Wyclif, a Yorkshireman and Oxford scholar, the so-called 'Morning Star of the English Reformation', had presided as Rector for ten years and where he had died on the last day of 1384. To Protestants across Britain, Europe and America, 'Wyclif's town' became a place of pilgrimage. 'A recent official report', we are told by proud locals during the First World War, 'shows that it is visited annually by some 10,000 persons. These people, as the Visitors' Book attests, hailed from every part of the English-speaking world.' One of them was David Lloyd George, the Chancellor of the Exchequer and future war leader, who visited in 1912.[43] Perhaps he patronised Joseph Handford's shop, purchasing a souvenir china plate marked with the name of Lutterworth. However, all of the so-called Wyclif relics the town had so proudly displayed to its visitors had been discredited, such as 'the most cherished of all Lutterworth's possessions', the very table at which Wyclif had sat as he had translated the Bible into English: so cherished in fact that the town had turned down an offer of £40,000 from American Christians. They should have taken the money, for the wooden table was very clearly an Elizabethan communion table, probably dating from the 1560s: a pleasing object and a valuable antique in its own right, but with no possible Wyclif connection. To add insult to injury, in later years even the claim that John Wyclif had translated the Bible was rejected by scholars.

At the same time, Lutterworth had a long tradition of Christian Non-Conformism, with Baptists and the Particular Baptists in Lutterworth since 1839, and the Primitive Methodists and a Salvation Army barracks (worshipping four times each Sunday, and on Wednesday evenings as well[44]). The Band of Hope (given special permission, at the request of the school managers, to give science lessons in Sherrier Elementary School from 1904 onwards), the Congregationalists and, of course, the Wesleyans (here since the year of Waterloo, and now in their new chapel opened in 1905) all in opposition to the Roman Catholics, established beyond the edge of the town on the Bitteswell Road since 1881. In addition, there was an array of discussion and self-help groups, a vocal Temperance Society, a couple of juvenile clubs, and a 'People's Club and Coffee House' on Bank Street, proprietor Joseph Banner.[45] There was no shortage of ideas circulating round Lutterworth in the last years of peace.

The drive to improvement through education shot through all the religious denominations, carried forward in the Mechanics Institution or Literary Institute, created in the 1840s by the parish curate John Gurney, and Thomas Dicey, Chairman of the Midland Counties Railway, whose new line ran through Leire and Ullesthorpe, and who lived in nearby Claybrooke Hall.[46] Their object was 'to provide healthful instruction and rational entertainment' through wholesome literature, along the lines of Samuel Smiles and his doctrine of 'self-help' (1859). Though it built up a fair collection of books, and was widely used – especially after it moved to its new home next to Sherrier School by the gates of the parish church in 1876 – it could not escape its Anglican origins. Rev Gurney refused to allow the institution to provide newspapers since they might contain items detrimental to the public's morals, and it was only after some time that *The Times* and some local newspapers were allowed. By 1914 it was 'used chiefly as news-rooms',[47] with the ubiquitous Lupton Topham as president.[48]

Most interesting, perhaps, was the adult school, which the Payne brothers would avidly attend when they grew older and which would profoundly affect their beliefs and their actions when the Great War came. The adult school movement, a hybrid of Bible study group and discussion forum, had had its origins at the end of the eighteenth century, founded by a Quaker and a Methodist, and was at the peak of its popularity in the first years of the twentieth century. In 1907 the movement declared its aims as being: '(a) The reverent study of the Bible as the central feature; and (b) Democratic, unsectarian, and non-party methods of working'.[49]

In Leicestershire there were thirty-six such schools, with some 3,600 members in 1897, rising to 119 schools with over ten thousand members in Leicestershire by 1905. The Lutterworth Adult School met at 8.45 on Sunday mornings in the Town Hall Assembly Room before the normal time for religious worship, so that members could go on to their respective churches and chapels, for the adult schools were non-denominational. One of its Vice-Presidents was John Payne, father of the brothers.[50] Increasingly, its Bible studies were supplemented by discussion of moral and social issues.[51] Its 1914 Social Service Handbook included a long list of areas in which members might become active: 'housing, blind, crippled, police courts, prison and after-care, allotments, smallholdings, mothers' guilds, ambulance and nursing classes, free holidays for children, handicrafts and exhibitions, boys' and girls' clubs, etc.'[52] On Sunday August 2nd 1914, as Europe was sliding into war, all the autonomous adult schools in Leicester and the county, including Lutterworth's, passed resolutions against the war.[53] The Christian and specifically the Quaker influence were clear to see.

RENAISSANCE

Just as the railway which bypassed Lutterworth in 1840, had dashed hopes of a bright Victorian future for the town, it was another railway which transformed the town's prospects sixty years later as Victoria's reign was drawing to its end. In 1899 the Great Central Railway came to Lutterworth. The new generation of farmers – better educated and more economically literate than their grandfathers (and chastened by decades of rural decline) – embraced the railway, and the town saw that new forms of economic activity and new business opportunities could now open up. Lutterworth experienced something of a renaissance as the pace quickened and new men and new money arrived. The Great Central Railway linked Lutterworth directly to Leicester and Sheffield in the north, southward to Rugby and beyond to the heart of London. As Jim Dodge put it, 'Lutterworth joined Victorian England sixty years late'.[54] For local people this allowed cheap, quick and easy contact with the rest of the country in a way never possible before. 'Due to the intense competition between the Midland Company and the new Great Central Railway, for the next forty years Leicester [and by extension south Leicestershire] enjoyed… a better express train service to and from London than any other comparable town'.[55] For the local economy, however, it offered more than simply the prospect of cheap travel: it offered the possibility of change as all kinds of prospects now opened up. After years of decline, the railway threw a lifeline to many local farmers in and around Lutterworth, allowing them to concentrate on dairy products and transport their milk churns to Leicester or Rugby or even to London, where the customers were.[56]

The greatest single impact on the town came with the arrival of George Spencer in 1902. Born in Nottinghamshire and coming from a textile trade background, Spencer, with two brothers, Herbert and Frank Barrowcliff, set up business in Lutterworth in 1902 producing knitted cloth, some of which was used by the Symington Company in Market Harborough to make their liberty bodices. Their factory was on New Street, at the north of the town. By 1908, though, the company seemed on the point of folding and it was then that luck came George's way. After a chance meeting with W.H. Revis, a former Sunday School acquaintance from Nottingham, on board a ship bound for America, Spencer set up a new company on the northern edge of Lutterworth, on Crescent Road, making hosiery. Things then moved quickly. Land on the other side of the Leicester Road was bought and a new and much bigger works, known as the 'Vedonis' works was erected there, equipped with the latest American 'Interlock' technology for hosiery production, and the business took off.[57] Lutterworth produced none of the raw materials nor the machinery used in the factory, and the town accounted for only a tiny proportion of the sales, but it was the excellence of the railway connection which had brought the company there, and with the factory came the workforce.

Spencer's works brought the Industrial Revolution to Lutterworth. For the first time in over sixty years, the population of the town started to grow, and new council housing had to be built along the Leicester Road and Crescent Road, close to the Spencer factories, to house them.[58] A photograph taken on the eve of the Great War shows the almost entirely female workforce of Spencer's works, all neatly dressed in civvies, outnumbering the males in the picture by eighty to just five, most of the men wearing the working class badge of the cloth cap, though a smartly dressed manager, hand on hip, stands apart from them, his suit, white shirt and dark tie marking out his higher status.[59]

Next came the foundries, again drawn by the railway. The 'Wycliffe Foundry' was built just off the Gilmorton Road, right next to the railway tracks, making castings for use on the railways, everything springing from its more or less central location in the rail network.[60] Raw materials had to be shipped in and finished products out, and part of the workforce commuted in from Leicester or Rugby, but the railway provided for this as well. It is noticeable that the foundry workforce, and in contrast to George Spencer's works, was predominantly male. A staff photograph taken in 1908 shows cloth capped, grubby faced workers, evidently not in their Sunday best, the managers still distinguished by their shirts and ties and their bowler hats and trilbies (the headgear of class distinction), while the women workers, who were a quarter of the workforce of about a hundred, are uniformly dressed in overalls, complete with hair covering and practical boots above the ankle, as befitted people working with hot metal. Another photograph, taken at the same time, shows the inside of the foundry, a group of women gazing unsmilingly at the camera, their surroundings dark and dingy and decidedly unfeminine.[61] We can readily understand that Lutterworth had never experienced working conditions as depressing looking as these before.

When a second foundry, the 'Ladywood Iron Works', was built next door to the

Wycliffe works along the Gilmorton Road, it looked for a time as though Lutterworth might develop into a small industrial centre, but nothing more came of this, and the two foundries remained like interesting appendages on the side of Lutterworth, in the town but not really part of the town, until war came when the demand for uniforms and shell casings changed the economic landscape.

For all that, the foundries and, to a lesser extent, George Spencer's 'Vedonis' works, did begin to alter the social structure of the town. While the women found jobs making hosiery and underwear for George Spencer, the men went to work in the foundries. At the time of the 1911 Census thirty-six men (no women) living in Lutterworth were working in the foundries. Of these, all but three of them were incomers from towns and cities with long traditions in metalworking; a quarter of them had moved from Walsall in Staffordshire. While these men provided the skilled workforce, all of the surrounding villages contributed manpower to the new labour pool and the railway itself provided transport for those who lived along its line. With these men came new attitudes and different relationships between worker and employer to those which somnolent, deferential, rural Lutterworth had ever seen before. There were now signs of movement, of a new desire to improve and adapt to change in ways much of the rest of the country had already adopted during Victoria's reign. There was a new mood of optimism in the town and a sense that while things were looking up, even more should be demanded.[62]

★

In part the new mood was caused by the appearance of those new men as leaders of local society: a tentative democratisation was taking place in Lutterworth, though not in the surrounding villages where the older rural and landed establishment still held sway. George Spencer was one of the new men. The new Minister at the Congregational Chapel, Arthur Massey, was another, as was Peter Rourke who built or rebuilt a considerable part of the town after arriving in Lutterworth in about 1907.[63] It was a sign of the times when, in the 1910 election for the Rural District Council, George Spencer polled more votes than Lupton Topham,[64] a symbolic shift from the old towards the new. The new men were not from the class of inherited land and wealth, such as Charles Marriott of Cotesbach or Corbet Smith of Bitteswell and Walcote, nor wealthy men from legal or medical backgrounds, like Lupton Topham or James Darlington, but men of humbler origin – self-made entrepreneurs who were possessed of a different outlook and mentality. What was more, Spencer and Massey were Non-Conformists (members of the Congregational Chapel at which the Paynes also worshipped) and not part of the Anglican clique, which had been used to running the town. Times were indeed changing.

★

What of the Payne family, whose two sons would be the focus for so much anger in years yet to come? Like much of Lutterworth's population, the Paynes were migrants.[65] The boys' grandfather, Reuben, had migrated to Lutterworth in 1864 from Market Harborough with his wife Catherine, their first-born daughters Mary and Caroline and their son John George, and set up business on Church Street making and selling baskets.[66] As the only basket weavers in Lutterworth their business thrived on a modest scale,[67] and Reuben fathered five more children in Lutterworth before his wife's death at the age of fifty-nine in 1894. John George Payne, the boys' father, met his wife, Jessie Handford in Lutterworth. Jessie's family owned the fancy wares shop selling Lutterworth crockery a few doors away on Church Street. They had four children before John inherited the basket weaving business on Reuben's death in 1903[68] – a daughter Jessie and the two brothers, Leonard and Roland, followed by a second daughter, Dora, born in 1901.

The Paynes were industrious people, hard working and on the lookout for new enterprises which would earn them extra income or grant them a higher social status. By 1908, John had taken over control of the family's basket weaving business from his younger brother, Frederick, and an advertisement placed in *Bottrill's Almanac of Lutterworth* in 1911 shows basket weaving to be the core of the business: 'Basket, Chair and Table Maker', it proclaimed. 'All kinds of fancy baskets kept in stock. Chairs re-seated in Cane, Wicker and Skein, Wicker furniture a speciality.' John also advertised himself as 'District Secretary and Expert to the Leicestershire Beekeepers' Association', offering 'Hives and Appliances to order. Bees bought and sold. Apiaries promptly attended to', with 'Good Workmanship Guaranteed'. And as if that were not enough, John was touting for business as the local agent for a London company, 'Foster's Parcels and Goods Express, Ltd.'.[69] The industrious Paynes were creating a small but enterprising local business empire in small town Lutterworth.

John was eager to establish himself in the local community by investing in landed property: he was co-owner of a clutch of half a dozen modest houses and cottages on Regent Street, one of Lutterworth's less affluent areas, where he also had a 'warehouse' or storeroom used to keep their stocks of raw materials.[70] This was in addition to their own house and basket shop, along with its neighbouring property rented to the cobbler Vincent Ward,[71] the field out of town along the

Rugby Road, where they kept their poultry and pig, and their garden and store shed on the Bitteswell Road.

More significantly, we also find John Payne acting as deputy Registrar of Marriages covering the whole area of the Poor Law Union, as well as holding that more significant role as Assistant Bailiff to the County Court's Office on Bank Street[72]; and, when he had dictated his entry for the 1901 Census, he had proudly given his occupation as 'County Court Bailiff', although, more accurately, he was Assistant Bailiff. By this time, the basket weaving business was being quietly relegated with a new address on Woodmarket, more prestigious and more comfortable than living over the shop on Church Street as his father had done. Both were indications of social ambition and a self-perceived rise in status.[73]

However, by 1911, though, the family's fortunes appear to have declined somewhat: filling in his own census form, John entered himself as a 'Basket Manufacturer', that last word perhaps a touch pretentious as he was back living above the shop on Church Street. Within the household it seems it was John's wife Jessie who kept the wheels turning. A deep and devout Christian, Jessie's moral sense was made of iron, a moral rectitude commonly found among strong women from that time who became used to holding family and household together in difficult times. Her son Leonard displayed much of the imprint of her personality, the same certainty of purpose and determination. Their first-born, Jessie, was a key member of the family: energetic and active like the rest of them, she was musical and artistic and she brought her own income to the family, working for George Spencer in his hosiery factory. Jessie was a fine letter writer and a good communicator. It is to her that we owe much of what we know of the brothers when their lives were turned upside-down by war. Not surprisingly, their most consistent contribution to the local community was through the Congregational Chapel, where the family worshipped and where they found a spiritual home. It was there that Leonard would learn to play the organ and where his older sister Jessie sang in the choir.[74]

★

So this was Lutterworth on the eve of the Great War. A small town like a thousand others scattered across Britain; a rather quiet, even dull, conservative little market town serving an intensely rural hinterland. It was a town on the way up, passing tentatively through great economic and social changes after years in the doldrums caused by its failure to attract the railway three generations before. The population was starting to recover, the town now had its own hospital,[75] George Spencer's hosiery business and the two foundries were bringing new and important sources of income to the town and also a new type of worker. There was a sense of things moving forward, albeit modestly and slowly. Arthur Dyson, writing in Lutterworth in 1913, said that 'in spite of the rush of express trains through its outskirts and the vibration of motor cars though its streets, it wears to-day much the same air of somnolent respectability which it wore in the early days of the last century'.

Despite the changes which were beginning to encroach upon daily life in the town, and despite that dependence on an inward flow of people from outside to keep up numbers, it remained a stable place, a place where crime levels remained relatively low and the townspeople could go about their business unmolested. As a community, it worked. But the signs were clear that Lutterworth was beginning to awake from its long sleep and realise that the world had moved on around it. Should it try to catch up or not? It was not the first time, and it would not be the last, that Lutterworth would have to resolve that dilemma.

The Payne family was an integral part of that community. Wherever we turn we seem to see the father of the family, John Payne, an energetic and socially conscious member of Lutterworth's commercial community. He was by no means 'somnolent', but an entrepreneur in his own right and a man set on making himself useful to the town: occupied in running things, being involved, making the wheels of the community turn. A minor local dynasty was in the making; his elder son, Leonard, was being groomed to inherit the family business just as John had inherited from his father, Reuben. Leonard was not sent to the local grammar school, although his younger brother Roland was,[76] because his destiny was to be in the family business. Such plans, for the Payne family and countless others like them, were about to be severely disrupted. It is perhaps a good thing that they did not know that.

NOTES & REFERENCES

1. *The Court Guide and County Blue Book of Derbyshire, Nottinghamshire, Leicestershire, Rutland and Northamptonshire*, pub Charles William Deacon, London, 1908, p.67.

2. Henry W. Nevinson, *Fire of Life*, James Nisbet, London, 1935, p. 1. Nevinson went on to say of Leicester that 'all [visitors] could see was a collection of dull streets with little, red-brick, slated houses for the workers in hosiery, elastic-web, and boot factories; a few old ruins, not very picturesque; a few old inns and churches; a Temperance Hotel for dreary meetings; a pitiful Museum of stuffed birds and Roman "remains"; and an unusual number of Nonconformist chapels.'

3. A.H. Dyson and S.H. Skillington, *Lutterworth Church and its Associations, with a Chapter on John Wycliffe*, C.H. Gee, Leicester, 1916, p. 9.

4. So it was described in *White's Directory of Leicestershire and Rutland*, 1877 edition.

5. A.H. Dyson (ed. Hugh Goodacre), *Lutterworth: John Wycliffe's Town*, Methuen, London, 1913, p. 1. Hereafter referenced as Dyson. A re-print was produced by Lutterworth Local History Group in 2001 and can be obtained through Lutterworth Museum. The text of Dyson's book is available on-line through Internet Archive at www.archive.org. See Dr John Goodacre's Preface to the 2001 reprint on the actual authorial origin of the book. His grandfather, Hugh Goodacre of Ullesthorpe is credited as the 'editor' of Dyson's history, though he appears to have written most of it himself.

6. James Crompton, *John Wyclif. A Study in Mythology*, Transactions of the Leicestershire Archælogical and Historical Society, Vol. XLII, 1966-7, pp. 25-6. Michael Wilks, *Misleading Manuscripts: Wyclif and the non-wycliffite bible* (1975), reprinted in Anne Hudson (ed.), *Wyclif: Political Ideas and Practice. Papers by Michael Wilks*, Oxbow Books, Oxford, 2000, p. 160. On the strength of the Wyclif connection, the Gideons later established their base in Lutterworth. Wyclif could still, on the eve of the Great War, arouse the most viciously hostile religious and social passions: 'Lutterworth…' wrote the author of the 'Court Guide', 'is by some esteemed to be the most famous place in Leicestershire, for it was here that John Wyclif, "the morning star of the Reformation" spent many years of his stormy life, translating the Bible and disseminating those curiously mixed religious and anarchical doctrines, which in his own day led to the Lollard rebellions, and in modern days to the various forms of socialism, which threaten the very structure of society… At this day of rapid disintegration of Christian belief and practice, it cannot

be said that the Church of England is as devoted to the turbulent Rector of Lutterworth's memory as are his logical descendants, the Nonconformists and Secularists.' *The Court Guide and County Blue Book of Derbyshire, Nottinghamshire, Leicestershire, Rutland and Northamptonshire*, pub. Charles William Deacon, London, 1908, pp. 80-82. One Catholic writer in 1884, for example, had described Wyclif as the 'messenger of evil', and 'a breeder of insurrection and insubordination in the State, of impurity and immorality in the household'. See Crompton, pp. 25-6. A useful summary of Wyclif's life and significance can be found in Margaret Deanesly, *The Significance of the Lollard Bible*, the Ethel M. Wood Lecture at the University of London, 1951, via http://www.medievalchurch.org.uk.

7. Terrier of Lutterworth 1509, Warwickshire Country Record Office, CR 2017 E.42. See *The Leicestershire Historian, Vol. 2*, No. 7, 1976. That there was ready contact between Lutterworth and Coventry is demonstrated by the unfortunate case of Robert Knottesford, a yeoman of Lutterworth. Visiting friends in Coventry in November 1535 – at a time of political and religious tension in England the like of which had not been seen before – the party got blindingly drunk and in the market place were caught short. 'They all untrussed them and did their easement at the cross', as their subsequent court appearance recorded. One of the party, called Apreston, tore down a nearby notice 'and cast the same to the said Heynes and bid him wipe his tail with them'. What they had not realised in their drunken – and possibly illiterate – state was that their toilet paper was a Royal Proclamation from Henry VIII. Tracked down to Lutterworth, Knottesford had to plead his case before the Mayor, the Recorder and eight Aldermen of Coventry: sadly, the outcome of the case is not known. (G.R. Elton, *Policy and Police. The Enforcement of the Reformation in the Age of Thomas Cromwell*, Cambridge University Press, 1972, p. 134.) Elton also recounted the story of a man called Harrison from Lutterworth who was accused of spreading the rumour that Henry VIII was dead in 1538 by telling the tale to one Petyfer who was passing from Leicester through the town and on into Northamptonshire, again a reminder of Lutterworth's central place in a wider communication and transport network. ibid., p. 74.

8. *Kelly's Directory of Leicestershire and Rutland*, London, 1904, p. 502.

9. ibid., p. 504. Rainbow's carrying cart, which did the Lutterworth-Leicester run every Wednesday and Saturday, can be seen in the Snibston Discovery Park at Coalville in north Leicestershire. In the late eighteenth century Lutterworth's tax payments on wagons and coaches was the third highest in Leicestershire. (Holger Th. Gräf, *Leicestershire Small Towns and Pre-Industrial Urbanisation*, in Transactions of the Leicestershire Archaeological and Historical Society, Vol. LXVIII, 1994.)

10. …as can still be seen in the Harborough, Coventry, Bitteswell and Leicester Roads out of the town. There is a fine example of a toll cottage on the border between

Lutterworth and Bitteswell. See Arthur Cossons, *The Turnpike Roads of Leicestershire and Rutland*, written in the 1950s, but published 2003, launched by Sir Neil Cossons, Chairman of English Heritage.

11. *Cook's Directory*, 1842, p.104. See Nikolaus Pevsner, *The Buildings of England. Leicestershire and Rutland*, revised by Elizabeth Williamson, with Geoffrey Brandwood, Penguin Books, Harmondsworth, 1984, p. 301.

12. Michael Foster, *The Railway at Ullesthorpe*, compiled by the Ullesthorpe Book Group, n.d., pp. 66-73. Exploiting its advantage Ullesthorpe even developed its own weekly market to rival Lutterworth's, ibid., p. 30. On the building of the railway through the village of Leire (which did not get its own 'Halt' until the 1920s), see *A Brief History of Leire'*, Part 2, Ian Burn, et. al., Leire History Group, 2000, pp.10-21. See Leicester Museum's, *The Last Main Line. An Illustrated History of the Building of the Great Central Railway*, 2nd edn., 1973; L.T.C. Rolt, *The Making of a Railway*, Hugh Evelyn, London, 1971; John Healy, *'Great Central Memories*, Baton Transport, London, 1987.

13. At the time of its publication, Lutterworth still did not have a railway. Cited in *200 Years of Methodism in Lutterworth*, published by the Lutterworth Wyclif Memorial Chapel, 2004, p. 7. While it would be all too easy to mock this as small-town ignorance and stupidity, it would only be fair to remember that there were still learned authorities who were uneasy about the new form of transport. This from J. Francis's *A History of the English Railway*, published in 1851: 'What was to be done with all those who have advanced money in making and repairing turnpike roads? What was to become of the coach-makers and harness-makers, coach masters, coach-men, inn-keepers, horse-breeders and horse-dealers? The beauty and comfort of country gentlemen's estates would be destroyed by it. Was the House aware of the smoke and the noise, the hiss and the whirl which locomotive engines, passing at a rate of ten or twelve miles an hour, would occasion? Neither the cattle ploughing in the fields or grazing in the meadows could behold them without dismay. Lease-holders and tenants, agriculturalists, graziers and dairy-men would all be in arms.' Quoted in Richard Tames, *Documents of the Industrial Revolution, 1750-1850*, Hutchinson Educational, 1971, pp. 42-4. In contrast to Lutterworth, Rugby developed as a railway and manufacturing centre, its population growing from 1,487 in 1801 (smaller than Lutterworth's 1,652) to almost 17,000 by the end of the century. *Victoria County History of Warwickshire*, Vol. 2, ed. William Page, Archibald Constable, London, 1908, p. 190.

14. J. Simmons, *Railways*, in *Victoria County History of Leicestershire* ed. W.G. Hoskins and R.A. McKinley, Dawsons, London, Vol. III, 1955, p. 116. It is no surprise that 1836 was the peak year for revenues on Leicestershire's toll roads, though local traffic about the county prevented a sudden or catastrophic decline. ibid., p. 83.

15. 'The Framework knitters here are now mostly employed by the Leicester

manufacturers', *White's Directory of Leicestershire*, 1846. On the sufferings of the framework knitters in Leicestershire see the evidence presented to the Royal Commission in 1844.

16. J. Philip Dodd, *The Agriculture of Leicestershire in the Mid-Nineteenth Century*, in Daniel Williams (ed.), *The Adaptation of Change. Essays upon the 19ᵗʰ Century History of Leicester and Leicestershire*, Leicestershire Museums Publication No. 18, 1980, p. 130. As a well informed observer noted: 'You could ride over most of Leicestershire and never see, let alone cross, a ploughed field'. (Guy Paget and Lionel Irvine, *Leicestershire*, Robert Hale, London, 1950, p. 197.) For a more 'scientific' way of saying much the same thing, see A.J. Herbertson and O.J.R. Howarth (eds), *The Oxford Survey of the British Empire: The British Isles*, Clarendon Press, Oxford, 1914, p. 164.) Or, as one less charitable local had it, a landscape of 'monotonous or slightly undulating fields... divided by hedgerows with hedgerow trees, and appreciated by foxhunters alone'. (Nevinson, p. 9. His view of Leicestershire's landscape should be set alongside the work of the late Professor W.G. Hoskins, who taught us how to look at the County's 'monotonous fields'.)

17. *Kelly's Directory of Leicestershire and Rutland*, London, 1904, pp. 502-4.

18. The statistics are even more alarming if we consider only heads of household: in 1901 only 40% had been born in Lutterworth (compared with 43.5% ten years before), with 60% originating elsewhere (when the corresponding figure for 1891 was 56.5%) Whether this was developing into a local demographic crisis is a moot point.

19. Censuses of 1891, 1901 and 1911. The 1891 Census for Lutterworth was computerised by Roger Little of the Lutterworth Local History Group in 2001. An accompanying Name Index was published in booklet form.

20. The Earl of Denbigh owned properties in Lutterworth of real estate value slightly above £15,000 in 1910, or about 10% of the total for the town. *Duties on Land Values ('Domesday') Book under the Finance Act 1910*, LRO.DE2972/149. Unfortunately the accompanying map appears to be no longer extant. The *Return of Owners of Land 1873* showed the Earl owning over 5000 acres worth just under £10,000 a year in rents in Leicestershire. (City Ordnance Agency, London, 1875.) See also Dyson, esp. Chapters XV and XXI. In Leicestershire as a whole the seven largest landowners owned 19% of the county. See John Bateman, *The Great Landowners of Great Britain and Ireland*, 1883 edn., David Spring, Leicester, 1971, pp. 506, 508 and passim. Neighbouring Rutland was one of the most aristocratically-dominated counties in England, with 70% owned by half a dozen landowners. J.V. Beckett puts these figures in context in *The East Midlands from A.D. 1000*, Longmans, London, 1988, p. 198.

21. *Burke's Landed Gentry*, 1906. Charles was a very keen cricketer and 'devoted a lifetime to the support of Leicestershire Cricket, took a prominent part in the formation of the

modern County Cricket Club in 1879 and [was] three times President of the Club. A first class bat, a good fielder, a member of the Oxford University XI, played for Gents of England v. Oxford and Cambridge in 1872 and 73 and for Leicestershire until 1893, also for M.C.C. and served in the Committee of that Club. [He was] also a keen supporter of the Lutterworth Club.' (Information supplied by L.G.D. Ogden in a letter to the Rector, Canon Good, dated 16th February 1977, held in Lutterworth Museum. (See also Dyson, p. 169.) In 1910 he owned properties worth almost £52,000, though in July 1916, for reasons which remain unclear, he sold off more than £7,500-worth of land in Cotesbach and Shawell, withdrawing a further £15,000-worth from sale. (*Duties on Land Values ('Domesday') Book under the Finance Act 1910*, LRO.DE2072/149, and *Rugby Advertiser*, 3rd July 1916.) He died in 1918.

22. Corbet Smith's father had been Sheriff of Leicestershire as long ago as 1845, the year of Corbet's birth. (LRO.QS.86/12.) When filling in his own form for the 1911 Census he gave his own 'occupation' as 'Retired Army Captain', while on the cover sheet he is called 'Major Corbet Smith'.

23. George Murray Smith, head of the family, had been Chairman of the Midland Railway since 1911, and was the eldest son of George Smith, a publisher and founder of the *Dictionary of National Biography*. See *Victoria County History of Leicestershire, Vol. 5*, 1964, p. 118. His wife, the Hon. Ellen Murray Smith, was a Strutt, a great-grand-daughter of the famous Jedediah Strutt of Industrial Revolution fame. See Burke's *Peerage*, 57th edn, 1895; and DNB, 1898. To sample the later fortunes of the Murray Smiths, see Ulricha Murray Smith, *Magic of the Quorn*, with a Foreword by H.R.H. The Prince of Wales, London, 1980, passim. Ulricha was a Thynne, related to the Marquis of Bath. Between Misterton and Gumley stands the magnificent Victorian Kilworth House, built and inhabited by John Entwistle and his wife Sophia, who were childless; another 'trade' family, their money coming from the woollen mills of Rochdale. http://www.kilworthhouse.co.uk/history.htm.

24. The best brief account of fox hunting in Leicestershire is Colin B. Ellis's article in the *Victoria County History of Leicestershire*, Vol. 3, London, 1969, pp. 269-81. See also J. Otho Paget, *Memories of the Shires*, London, 1920; Siegfried Sassoon, *The Complete Memoirs of George Sherston*, London, 1937; Colin B. Ellis, *Leicestershire and the Quorn Hunt*, Leicester, 1951. See also Charles Simpson, R.I., *The Harboro' Country*, John Lane the Bodley Head, London, 1927, pp. 138-144; Michael Clayton, *Foxhunting in Paradise*, John Murray, London, 1993. (The 'paradise' was Leicestershire.) Lutterworth had its own, humbler but no less bloody form of sport within living memory of the Great War – duck hunting. Large crowds would gather and contestants would come from far afield to take part, bringing their dogs and ducks with them: the ducks were released down by the mill race at the southern entrance to the town, to be hunted and killed by the

dogs. The dog which killed the greatest number of ducks was declared the winner, after which everyone retired to the local pubs to complete a good day of jolly sport.

25. W.G. Hoskins, *The Making of the English Landscape*, Penguin Books, Harmondsworth, 1970, pp. 197-8.

26. See, for example, the list of County Magistrates in *Kelly's Directory of Leicestershire and Rutland*, 1904. After the Great War the Hobsons at least began to play a more active role in local affairs. See for example *Lutterworth Guardian and South Leicestershire Advertiser*, 30ᵗʰ November 1923.

27. In 1910 his land holdings in Lutterworth were valued at nearly £6000: considerable, but less than half that owned by the Earl of Denbigh. (*Duties on Land Values ('Domesday') Book under the Finance Act 1910*, LRO.DE2972/149.) In Leicestershire as a whole the seven largest landowners owned 19% of the county. See John Bateman, *The Great Landowners of Great Britain and Ireland*, 1883 edn., David Spring, Leicester, 1971, pp. 506, 508 and passim. Neighbouring Rutland was one of the most aristocratically-dominated counties in England, with 70% owned by half a dozen landowners. J. Bateman, *The Great Landowners of Great Britain and Ireland* (1873), ed. D. Spring, Leicester University Press, Leicester, 1971. J.V. Beckett puts these figures in context in *The East Midlands from A.D. 1000*, Longmans, London, 1988, p. 198. Lupton's brother, Henry, was Rector of Middleham in North Yorkshire and Rural Dean of Catterick. (*Lutterworth Guardian* and *South Leicestershire Advertiser*, 28ᵗʰ February 1925.) Closely connected with the Parish Church, Topham presented the church with a new lectern in 1895, and then ensured everyone knew it by reading the lesson from it each Sunday for the next twenty-five years. (Dyson, pp. 126-7; Lutterworth Parochial Church Council Minutes, 1ˢᵗ November 1920. LRO.DE4336/34.)

28. *Leicester Daily Mercury*, 16ᵗʰ July 1914.

29. James Darlington died in February 1918; see the *Leicester Daily Mercury* 30ᵗʰ April 1918. On the gibbet see the Terrier of Lutterworth, 1509, WRO.CR 2017 E.42. An interpretation appeared in *The Leicestershire Historian*, Vol.2, No.7, 1976. See also John Goodacre, *The Transformation of a Peasant Economy. Townspeople and Villagers in the Lutterworth area, 1500-1700*, Scolar Press, London, 1994, pp.16-17.

30. In 1911 no less than nine live-in servants were employed in the house itself, while his coachman lived down the drive in his lodge with his wife and five children.

31. J.S. Dodge, *A Look at Lutterworth 2000 or Thereabouts*, pub. Lutterworth Grammar School and Community College, Lutterworth, 1999, p. 36.

32. The Aldersons give us an incidental but illuminating glimpse into the lives of the elite of local society, for on the last day of 1914 – in wartime – the Rector's sister Mary, already thirty-nine years old, married Lieutenant Colonel Charles Kindersley Porcher, late of the Coldstream Guards, in Lutterworth Parish Church, the marriage solemnised

by the Bishop of Peterborough. Though not quite top drawer by English aristocratic standards, it was a grand enough event, numbering many lords and ladies and 'hons.' among the guests. The bride wore cloth of gold with an old Brussels lace veil, and there was a guard of honour from the King's Royal Rifle Corps, the groom's present regiment. Among the guests was Lord Hugh Cecil M.P., who, in three years' time would courageously speak out in Parliament in defence of the conscientious objectors like the Payne brothers who were at that very moment at work in their basket weaving shop just a couple of hundred yards away. It is when we see the long list of wedding presents that we understand the social privilege of these people. Gifts included a range of silverware, a sable coat, a diamond and ruby ring, and a diamond brooch for the bride, an old Chinese ivory figure, a pearl and diamond pendant from the Darlingtons of 'The Hill', a diamond and turquoise ring from the Earl and Countess of Bessborough, with a matching bracelet from Lord and Lady Oranmore and Browne, and a cornucopia of diamonds and sapphires and rubies and pearls and furs and gold and silver, all the way down to a travelling clock from the Parish Church's St Mary's Guild, and silver spoons from the nurses at the Cottage Hospital. There was even an anonymous gift of a motor car. It is possible that when the *Rugby Advertiser* printed this huge list of lavish gifts alongside a list of gifts of tobacco and tea and sugar and a few crackers given as Christmas treats for the inmates of Lutterworth Workhouse, it was striving for ironic contrast, but that seems inherently unlikely. (*Rugby Advertiser*, 2nd January 1915.)

33. The report on teaching in Lutterworth Grammar School written by inspectors from Birmingham University in 1911 paid a great deal of attention to how History was taught in the school. Minutes of Governors, 1910-1929, LRO.ES/MB/211/3.

34. Sherrier School Log Books, e.g. LRO.DE3614/7, Girls' School Log Book. On the origins of Empire Day see Steve Roud, *The English Year. A month-by-month Guide to the Nation's Customs and Festivals, from May Day to Mischief Night*, Penguin Books, London, 2006, pp. 256-7.

35. ibid., 22nd November 1901, 27th October 1905; 6th December 1901; 1st May 1906; 28th September 1904.

36. Letter by 'Noah' published in the *Lutterworth Guardian and South Leicestershire Advertiser*, 26th October 1923.

37. Very few of these domestic servants were locals: only five of the live-in servants in Lutterworth had been born in the town, with only a further ten from nearby villages. One exception had been John Payne's sister Mary who had worked as nursemaid to the two daughters of Dr. Coleman on Oxford Street when the 1871 Census was taken.

38. *Bottrill's Almanac of Lutterworth*, 1910. Egbert Lavender could clearly afford a telephone since he was a significant landlord in his own right, owning houses and shops valued

together at well over £4000, putting him almost on a par with the town's top dogs. *Duties on Land Values ('Domesday') Book under the Finance Act 1910*, LRO.DE2972/149.

39. *Abbott's Illustrated Almanac of Lutterworth*, 1914.

40. 'd.' = old pence. There were twelve pennies in a shilling and twenty shillings in a pound: hence 240 old pence made up £1.

41. *Bottrill's Almanac of Lutterworth*, 1910.

42. Lynda Hill and Roz Bailey, *Butchers, Bakers and Candlestick Makers. Trades in a Victorian Street, Lutterworth, Leicestershire*, Volcano Publishing, Dunton Bassett, 1995, pp. 85-6.

43. A.H. Dyson and S.H. Skillington, *Lutterworth Church and its Associations, with a Chapter on John Wycliffe*, C.H. Gee, Leicester, 1916, pp. 9 and 49. See also G. Clarke Nuttall, *Guide to Leicester and Neighbourhood*, pub. Edward Shardlow, Leicester, 1905; and *A Guide to Leicester and District*, prepared for the British Association for the Advancement of Science; chairman of the Publications Sub-Committee, J. Mentor Gimson, Leicester, 1907. In 1984 the town enthusiastically celebrated the 600th anniversary of his death and produced a glossy guide, *Wycliffe Six Hundred*, pub. John Abbott of Lutterworth, 1983.

44. In 1901 James Preston, living in Georges Square, was the Captain. 1901 Census. 1.15.

45. Lutterworth had a noticeable Roman Catholic presence, not only through the church out on Bitteswell Road, but also *Kelly's Directory of Leicestershire and Rutland*, 1912 edn. notes the presence of a convent of the Poor Clares on Bank Street. It must have been of recent foundation because it was not shown on the 1911 Census. J.S. Dodge, 'Lutterworth Banks', in Lutterworth Local History Group Journal, 2002, p. 4, refers to it as being 'a Belgian nunnery during the Great War', though it was clearly there before: it is feasible that it sheltered Belgian refugees or nuns during the war. At least Lutterworth was spared the embarrassment of one distinguished visitor to the town in the 1720s, Daniel Defoe. In his *Tour through the Whole Island of Great Britain* he described how en route to Leicester from Boughton 'curiosity turned us west a little to see an old town called Lutterworth, famous for being the birth-place of honest John Wycliff, the first preacher of the Reformation in England... When we came there we saw nothing worth notice, nor did the people, as I could find, so much as know in general, that this great man was born amongst them'. Penguin edition, edited by Pat Rogers, 1971, p. 407. We can visualise the delicious encounter: Defoe's incredulity at the ignorance of the people of Lutterworth that they did not know Wyclif was born in the town; their bewilderment that Daniel Defoe, this famous and educated man, should believe that Wyclif was born (rather than died) in Lutterworth, no one quite willing to comment on the great man's ignorance. In fact, no one of distinction was ever born in Lutterworth.

46. Foster, p. 68.

47. *Kelly's Directory of Leicestershire and Rutland*, 1904, p. 502.

48. Dyson, pp. 176-7. Lutterworth Museum holds an undated printed table issued by Bottrill's bookshop for its 'Periodical Society', by which books could be circulated among the ten subscribers listed.

49. Smith, M. K. (2004) *Adult Schools and the Making of Adult Education*, the encyclopedia of informal education, at www.infed.org/lifelonglearning/adult_schools.htm.

50. *Abbott's Almanac of Lutterworth*, 1914.

51. *Victoria County History of Leicestershire*, Vol. III, p. 256.

52. W. Arnold Hall, *The Adult School Movement in the Twentieth Century*, University of Nottingham, Nottingham, 1985, p. 18.

53. *Leicester Daily Mercury*, Monday August 3rd 1914.

54. J.S. Dodge, *A Look at Lutterworth 2000 or Thereabouts*, pub. Lutterworth Grammar School and Community College, 1999, p. 71.

55. J. Simmons, in V.C.H., Vol. III, p. 125. There is a fine collection of photographs of the construction of the Great Central Railway in Gary Boyd-Hope and Andrew Sargent, *Railway and Rural Life: S.W.A. Newton and the Great Central Railway*, jointly published by English Heritage and Leicestershire County Council, 2007. Ullesthorpe's station was known as 'Ullesthorpe and Lutterworth'; see Photograph 49 in Brian Lund, *Leicestershire Railway Stations in Old Picture Postcards, Yesterday's Leicestershire Series* No. 2, pub. at Keyworth, Notts, 1996.

56. George Thorpe, *A Sketch of Lutterworth*, typescript in Lutterworth Library, 1969, reproduced by Leicestershire County Library, p. 4. In 1907 a farmer named Barnett from Swinford planned to sell the milk from his farm in London, a hundred miles away. Lutterworth Rural District Council Minutes 29th August 1907, held in Lutterworth Museum, ref. LUT.LM91/547. The railway offered cultural opportunities as well with rail excursions into Leicester to see the latest plays and musicals. In 1915, for instance, posters advertising Jack Hulbert's latest show, *The Cinema Star*, playing at the Royal Opera House there, gave train times from Lutterworth. (Helen and Richard Leacroft, *The Theatre in Leicestershire. A History of Entertainment in the County from the 15th Century to the 1960s,* pub. Leicestershire Libraries and Information Service, Leicester, 1986, p. 119.)

57. J.S. Dodge and Peter Spencer, *Notes for a Brief Life of George Spencer, 1868-1946*, published by J.S. Dodge, Lutterworth, 2001, pp. 3-4; typescript in Lutterworth Library.

58. J.S. Dodge, *The Leicester Road Council Estate, Lutterworth, 1913-2000,* pub. by the author, Lutterworth, 2006, pp. 1-3; and his *Peter Rourke. The Builder of Lutterworth*, 1966, pp. 126-7. Copy in Lutterworth Museum.

59. Geoff Smith, *Around Lutterworth. A Second Selection*, Tempus, *Images of England* Series, Stroud, 2002, p. 54.

60. In later years Lutterworth's position close to the M1 and M6 motorways would attract the massive Magna Park distribution centre just outside the town. Lutterworth lost its railway station and line in 1969.

61. Geoff Smith, *Around Lutterworth*, Chalford *The Archive Photograph Series*, Stroud, 1997, p. 65.

62. Money was spent on improving the appearance of the town when the Town Hall was refurbished in 1910, another sign of a growing self-confidence. See the photograph in Geoff Smith, *Around Lutterworth*, Chalford *The Archive Photograph* Series, Stroud, 1997, p. 90. Having said that, the Town Hall itself had come close to being the victim of the town's growth when detailed plans had been drawn up for its demolition in 1904 to make way for the widening of Station Road. 'Lutterworth Proposed Demolition of Town Hall &c.', LRO DE1379/736/17. The Town Hall was not the only place to be improved in the years before the Great War. In 1910 ten cottages on Station Road were demolished, and seven new and presumably more spacious houses built on the site. *Duties on Land Values ('Domesday') Book under the Finance Act 1910*, LRO.DE2972/149, entry dated 30th November 1910.

63. See J.S. Dodge, *A Look at Lutterworth 2000 or Thereabouts*, pub. Lutterworth Grammar School & Community College, 1999, pp. 81-7. Also Jim Dodge's biography of Rourke, copy in Lutterworth Museum.

64. Spencer was elected with 188 votes while Topham was re-elected with 181. This was one of the few contested elections in the district. Twenty-four local village elections were uncontested, including Misterton with Walcote (Corbet Smith) and Cotesbach (Charles Marriott), and there were contests in only five, including Lutterworth, where Spencer and Topham, together with the brewer Thomas Buck, were elected. Beyond the purely parochial, the politics of the Harborough Division, which included Lutterworth, were skewed by the growth of Leicester spreading into what had once been rural territory. In the 1906 Election almost a quarter of the voters lived in Leicester's suburbs, and if we add in those who voted in the division on the basis of property owned in Leicester, the figure rises to just below 40%. This goes some way to explaining how a Liberal of 'pretty advanced Radical' opinions came to be elected. In 1910 Harborough was retained by the Liberals with a reduced majority, while in Melton Mowbray Colonel Yate, a Tory of jingoist views who would in future years come to clash with the Great War conscientious objectors, was elected by a narrow majority. It was not until 1918 that the Labour Party made any significant showing in the Harborough Division. (*Victoria County History of Leicestershire*, Volume 2, pp. 139-41.) In November 1918 the Food Control Committee in Lutterworth deliberately co-opted two Labour members, Walter Williams of Bitteswell and Mrs E.A. Dalby of Lutterworth, but the first branch of the Labour Party in Lutterworth was not formally

established until the Summer of 1919. (*Rugby Advertiser*, 16th November 1918 and 13th June 1919.)

65. Reuben was one of the seven sons of Robert Payne and his wife Mary, all trained up as basket makers in the small village of Braybrooke, fifteen miles or so from Lutterworth on the far side of Market Harborough, across the Northamptonshire border. This over-production inevitably resulted in migrations – with a population of 450 or so how many basket makers could Braybrooke sustain? – as one son after another left home in the 1850s and 60s. Reuben moved first to Market Harborough, and when Isaac Woodward, the basket maker in Lutterworth retired in 1864, a further migration was called for and the Paynes ended up in Lutterworth.

66. They were not the only ones to leave Braybrooke. The village had lost a quarter of its population by 1871. *Whellan's Directory of Northamptonshire*, Whittaker's publishers, London, 1874, p. 823.

67. …though their daughter Mary had had to be put out to domestic service at a relatively early age.

68. Catherine's burial on January 12th 1894 and Reuben's burial on 20th June 1903 are recorded in the *Records of the Congregational Church of Lutterworth: Burials*. I am grateful to Irene Moore and the Elders of the Lutterworth United Reformed Church for allowing me access to their archive. An advert which appeared in *Bottrill's Almanac of Lutterworth* in 1911 claimed the business had been 'established upwards of ninety years'. It is not easy to decide exactly when the shift into Lutterworth from Market Harborough took place: the Lutterworth entry in *White's Directory of Leicestershire and Rutland* of 1863 contains no reference to the Paynes, while *Buchanan's Postal Directory for Leicestershire* of 1867 shows Reuben established as a basket weaver on Church Street, possibly taking over the business of Isaac Woodward. His brother remained in Market Harborough, weaving baskets there, where the family had been since the early 1850s: they appear in *Melville's Leicestershire Directory*, 1854. Reuben Payne does not appear in the Poll Books of 1868 or 1870, though Joseph Handford does. (LRO)

69. *Bottrill's Almanac of Lutterworth*, 1911. John, a former Salvationist, was a member of the Independent Order of Rechabites, a Friendly Society which upheld the values of thrift and abstinence from alcohol. Local historian, the late Joyce Mason, remembered the Paynes as busy people who were always active.

70. *Duties on Land Values ('Domesday') Book under the Finance Act 1910*, LRO.DE2072/149.

71. *Leicester Daily Mercury*, Wednesday 29th May 1918.

72. *Kelly's Directory of Leicestershire and Rutland*, 1904, p. 503. As Assistant County Court Bailiff, John was responsible for serving summonses, mainly for debt, and where necessary accompanying the unfortunates the dozen miles to Leicester Gaol. It was not a job he relished and family legend has it that he often organised collections among

the debtors' friends to pay off the creditors. When John moved up in the world for a time he left the business in the hands of his young brother Frederick.

73. 1901 Census, Enumeration District 1, Schedule 168. John used the Woodmarket address in his capacity as Bailiff, but the Church Street address when acting as deputy Registrar of Marriages; *Kelly's Directory of Leicestershire and Rutland*, 1904. Having said that, when John came to fill in his family's Census form in 1911 he filled in some of the information in the wrong columns and had to make some fairly obvious corrections.

74. Leonard's application to 'have use of our organ to receive lessons' was noted by the Congregational Church Meeting on April 1st 1914, and Leonard played at his first service on the morning of April 25th 1915. Lutterworth United Reformed Church archives, Minutes of Church Meetings, and Leonard to Harold Buck, 2nd May 1915.

75. Lutterworth's Cottage Hospital had been built in 1899, paid for from the will of Mrs Feiling Palmer, nobles oblige from a relative of the Feilding Earl of Denbigh. The idea that a town like Lutterworth might have its own hospital was at first greeted with a distinct lack of enthusiasm from some of the townspeople chiefly because the Christmas gifts to the poor which had come from Mrs Feilding Palmer were stopped in consequence. (*Rugby Advertiser*, 6th April 1901, quoted in Jean Keogh, *Feilding Palmer Cottage Hospital, 1899-1999*, privately printed, Lutterworth, 1999, p. 16.) The poorest were not expected to pay towards their treatment. Then, in 1911 James Darlington stumped up half the money needed to build an additional surgical wing onto the hospital, a symbolic shifting of roles from the old money and old families that had paid to build the hospital to the new money and new families which extended it. The patroness of the hospital was Queen Victoria's third daughter, Helena, known as Princess Christian of Schleswig Holstein. This may have caused some embarrassment in 1914 after war broke out against her husband's native Germany. *The Daily Chronicle* on November 27th 1914 published a photograph of the princess's son, Prince Albert, who was of course a cousin of George V, in German Army uniform under the heading 'German or English?' George V, upset by comments about the Royal House's German name, changed it to 'Windsor' in July 1917.

76. Fees at the grammar school were not excessive – £2 4s. 6d. per term ('inclusive of text books, stationery and games'), payable in advance – but the money had still to be found unless a child qualified for a free place. (*Bottrill's Almanac*, 1917.) There is no record that any of the Payne children were admitted on scholarship terms.

PART TWO

HOME FRONT

*I*t is now, shall we say, the legendary 'Golden Summer' of 1914. Leonard and Roland are now young men: Len is nineteen and his brother seventeen.

It is early on yet another warm sunny Sunday morning and we see the two of them, smartly dressed as befits the occasion, accompanying their father, John, on the short walk to the Town Hall at the top of High Street where John is keyholder. He is a leading figure in the local adult school, that interdenominational Christian discussion group which meets here every Sunday early enough to allow the participants to go on to their own churches for Sabbath worship. He arrives early, in time for the first arrivals.

Sunday remains an important day for the whole Payne family. Bible classes have always been an important part of their lives. The mother, Jessie, is a woman of strong traditional Christian values, a dedicated and active member of the Congregational Chapel, and she and her daughters, Jessie junior and little Dora, are even now getting themselves ready for chapel, dressing up in their Sunday best. The whole family is committed to their God. Mother, daughters and the two brothers have long been members of the Band of Hope: Leonard has been learning to play the organ for the past three months; he has been a Steward for the past five years and Roland for eighteen months. Little Dora is an enthusiastic Sunday School child: musical like her older sister, she sang a solo at the anniversary just a few weeks ago – much to the delight of those who heard it.

Leonard is the leader – strong-minded, energetic, organised, efficient, determined and stubborn. A young man who knows his own mind and is not to be deflected from a course he has decided upon, whatever may be the consequences. He has outlets enough for his energies. Leonard is already his father's 'right hand' in the business (as a friend described him). He is a regular member of the rugby club first XV, an important part of the local community and local life in Lutterworth. He is a keen student of the Bible, following courses in scripture study as an outlet for his intellectual capacities, and , like his older sister Jessie, musical, rubbing shoulders with some of the leaders of local society, like George Spencer's wife who is teaching him to play the Congregational Chapel organ. He is a sociable young man, secure in his generation in the town, imbued with that small town awareness of who had been in his year group in primary school, that cohort of children who had come through the same system, sharing many of the same memories and experiences. And it would appear he has something of the ladies' man about him, a characteristic he will carry through his life.

Roland is different. Roland follows where Leonard leads. While no one, it seems, has thought of giving Leonard any sort of formal extended education, Roland had been a grammar school boy – valuable in its own right, but also a sign of a family on the rise. For these are people who value education for its own sake and, in due course, their younger daughter Dora *will follow Roland to the grammar school, an enlightened move at a time when many still saw the education of girls as a waste of time and money since girls were destined for home, kitchen and nursery, none of which callings would require extra years of schooling. Of the two brothers, Leonard is the more natural scholar. (Roland's written English sometimes makes one doubt his extended education, but that is the way with dynasties.)*

So, in Lutterworth this is just another hot 'Golden Summer' Sunday morning. Adult school, then chapel, then home for Sunday dinner. But this is, in point of fact, not an ordinary Sunday morning. It is Sunday the 28th of June, and at the opposite end of Europe, where the day started much earlier than here, events are already unfolding in a town called Sarajevo which will, in the twinkling of an eye, sweep away forever the comfortable, familiar, secure world in which these two young men have grown up. Their lives are about to be turned upside-down.

HOME FRONT

At first there was indifference. Of course, the assassination in Sarajevo had flitted across the consciousness of most as they had read the terrible tale in their daily newspapers: yet another family tragedy for the aged Austrian Emperor Franz Josef, sad but far away. But that was now weeks ago, at the end of June. People had read it, shaken their heads and moved on. To most in Britain, the only threatening shadow on the horizon was the trouble, civil war even, which seemed to be looming throughout July to the west, in Ireland. Few eyes were looking the other way, to the east, to the heart of ancient Europe, where rivalries and hatreds even older were lying in wait to ambush the rulers of the Continent. Then, one after another, Austria, Serbia, Russia and Germany tumbled headlong into war as July of 1914 moved into August. It was a magnificent and terrible sight as the great and ancient Empires of Eastern Europe, like slumbering dinosaurs, roused themselves and mobilised for war: men in palaces deciding the fate of millions with the mere flourish of a pen.

But none of that trouble, of course, was thought to be any business of Britain's. Like a later conflict, it was all 'a quarrel in a far-away country between people of whom we know nothing'. While the conflict was localised in Eastern Europe, the British public looked on with mild interest, concern even, but there were far more pressing distractions at hand. For one thing there was the August Bank Holiday weekend to look forward to; the carnival atmosphere of that glorious weekend marked in Leicester by a multitude of pastimes and entertainments.

In the fine weather Leicestershire's County Cricket team was caught up in a tense championship match at rival Northampton that weekend. Bowling out the home side for 131 after Brown had destroyed their middle order, the Leicestershire batsmen set about building a solid first innings total of their own. The match swung in their direction and they amassed a useful lead of ninety-three before their last wicket fell. It seemed all over when the Northants second innings produced a meagre 175 runs. Eighty-three would win it for Leicestershire. But then an overnight downpour made the wicket virtually unplayable, and the war got in the way as their star player A.T. Sharp had to leave his Leicestershire team mates to join his regiment. After a delayed start, the remaining Leicestershire batsmen were all out for seventy-nine. A sensational loss, which rated headlines as big as those devoted to that troubling but distant conflict which was spilling over on the Continent.[1]

For those not sporting minded, there were the cinemas: Leicester was plentifully provided with 'picture palaces' – as many as twenty in the city, and well attended at that.[2] *Lost through Greed* (the 1914 equivalent of a James Bond movie) was packing the audiences in at the Grand Electric Palace and the same film was showing at The Picture House in Granby Street. Ace detective Joe Wilkins was called in after the poisoning of a wealthy banker and the false arrest of his son; our hero identified the true villain and pursued him across the rooftops, the chase reaching its climax when a balloon raced an aeroplane before Joe finally got his man. Thus virtue triumphed and evil was defeated, and all was well with the world. Innocent pleasures in a world now lost.

Or there were the music halls, criticised by some moralists as the cause of most of the social ills in the land. The Palace Theatre of Varieties in Belgrave Gate, managed (on an acting basis) by the splendidly named Trueman Towers, was the grandest.[3] There, that Bank Holiday weekend, the 'Great Comedian' Alfred Lester was topping the bill with a routine he called 'The Village Fire Brigade' and no doubt he had the audience in stitches. Supporting was Oswald Williams, 'the Great English Illusionist', who dazzled his public with such tricks as 'the homing bells', 'the flying chest', 'the water babe', and, most thrilling of all, 'the chair of death'. Lower down the bill was 'Du Calion and the Tottering Ladder', an act which was presumably self-explanatory.[4] We are told that the National Anthem was sung with especial fervour that Bank Holiday, an echo inside the theatre of intimations of what was closing round in the world outside. By Tuesday August 4th, reality set in and the concert by the Band of the Grenadier Guards, who been booked to play at the great Abbey Park Flower Show, was cancelled.[5]

Those who could afford it had made their escape that Bank Holiday weekend, unaware that for many it would be their last. Bookings were up as the better off sought their own place in the sun, a few days away from the dull grey humdrum of life and work. Some saw this as a sign of British sanity. 'It is remarkable how coolly people view the situation,' said one railway official. 'They give one the impression that whatever happens they do not intend to be deprived of their holidays.'[6] Thomas Cook's railway excursions to Skegness, Scarborough and Yarmouth were proving popular. And Dean and Dawson, of Gallowtree Gate in the centre of Leicester, were even now advertising 'Continental Holiday Tours' of France and Belgium. Ironically, many would be taking such a trip, all expenses paid, before long. A tour to Berlin (optimistically, given the circumstances) was also on offer.[7] The outbreak of hostilities on the Continent was unfortunate for those who had already handed over their money: the fortunes of war…

*

It was, in part at least, an illusion. In retrospect that last summer takes on the sadness of an insubstantial pageant, faded and lost on the far side of the great divide which is the Great War. But there *was* something frenetic, even desperate, about the determination of the British people that last weekend to enjoy themselves, not only because of the threat of war. What we are seeing is a society at play, or, rather, people trying to escape from the intractable realities which were threatening to tear their society apart. Britain in 1914 was a nation in turmoil: a society in conflict. Women were fighting men for the vote and the equality of life opportunities some thought that would bring; labour was fighting capital; Left was fighting Right; Catholic Irish were fighting Protestant Irish as Victorian England, past its time, was dying on its feet and the future was both unknown and unsettling. It is small wonder that some would turn shining eyes to a war, which offered, if not redemption, then a great simplification of troubles which seemed too complex to comprehend.

Even in Lutterworth, not usually noted for its carnival atmosphere,[8] 1914 was different. The Darlington family opened the grounds of their big house, 'The Hill', that weekend and held a garden fete in aid of the church organ fund. There was tennis and garden golf, table skittles, bowls and hoop-la. Even a rummage sale was held off the premises at the top of Regent Street. The highlight of the afternoon was a Ladies v. Gentlemen Cricket match, the result not recorded. The Town Band played through the afternoon and evening as the dancing went on into the night.[9]

*

But already the German Army was on the move. Before anyone seemed able to stop it, as if at its own behest, it mobilised itself. 'An amazing organisation is revealed,' a neutral American naval officer reported from Berlin. 'The mobilisation order puts six million men in the field under arms and affects the daily occupation of some twelve million, yet at the War Department all is serene.' The planning had been completed years before and thinking was no longer required. Officers and men were quietly recalled from leave, mobilisation rosters appeared overnight in all newspapers and were posted on public buildings in every hamlet, village and city of the German Empire, while heralds went round the towns blowing trumpets to summon reservists to the colours.[10] 'Public and private business is absolutely at a standstill,' reported one Leicestershire man who found himself in Frankfurt when war broke out, 'and the country, apart from the war areas, is a desolation.'[11]

The numbers, the logistics, the organisation, the forethought, the detail were staggering as the German Army assembled, grouped itself, reassembled itself into ever bigger units, clambered on board trains by the thousand and was borne at a constant nineteen miles per hour to its preordained destinations: small rural stations near the French and Belgian borders built years before with platforms a mile long to accommodate them.[12] 'Automatism displaced policy'[13]: this truly was war by timetable and this was no drill, no exercise, no parade ground rehearsal; the German Army came out fighting. Suddenly, the abyss opened.

For instead of mobilising to the east, against the Russians in support of Austria, the German Army was mobilising to the west, towards peaceable, neutral, little Belgium. At seven o'clock on the evening of Sunday August 2nd 1914, the German Ambassador in Brussels, von Below Saleske, delivered an ultimatum to the Belgian government which had been drawn up in Berlin a full week before. It demanded free passage through Belgian territory for the German Army *en route* to France on terms of 'friendly neutrality'. The independence and integrity of Belgium and its possessions would be maintained after the end of hostilities, it said. And, just to make certain that the Belgians understood what was being said to them, it gave them twelve hours to respond satisfactorily, after which Germany would regard and treat Belgium as an enemy – and would come anyway.[14] The Belgians duly responded twelve hours later, at seven o'clock on the morning of Monday August 3rd, with an undiplomatic and uncomplicated 'No'. At the same time, King Albert asked Britain for her diplomatic, but not her military support. Belgium was not yet invaded and Britain was not yet at war.

★

Was this any of Britain's business? Some thought so, [15] but most of those who spoke out did not. On Saturday August 1st, a letter of protest against British involvement was copied in the local Leicestershire newspapers, signed by a group of Oxbridge academics.[16] The Left wing 'Labour Leader' called for workers' demonstrations: 'war must be stopped and we must stop it'. The political Left in Leicester, in a last fleeting moment of unity, the Labour Party and the Independent Labour Party (I.L.P.) for once joining forces, organised a rally in the Market Place on that Sunday morning, August 2nd, to demand British neutrality. The President of the National Council of the Evangelical Free Churches called upon a higher authority, urging all Christian churches to 'pray without ceasing that God of His infinite mercy will turn from us and from the peoples of Europe the dread evils of pitiless war'.[17] Every one of the adult schools in Leicestershire in their Sunday morning meetings passed resolutions against war.[18] In the Wycliffe Congregational Chapel on College Street, off the London Road in Leicester, was the Rev. F. Seaward Beddow, who publicly declared his 'dismay and horror at the present prospect of a general European War' and called for British neutrality. Beddow would maintain his position throughout the war[19], and would prove one of the staunchest supporters of the conscientious objectors of Leicestershire.

The women had their say as well. Catherine Gittins, of Salisbury Road in Leicester, wrote to the *Leicester Mercury*: 'I would be grateful if you would allow me, as one of those at present debarred from exercising any direct influence on national affairs, to utter in your columns my individual protest which I am sure represents also that of thousands of my fellow women in Leicester against the foolish and wicked incitements to war now spread abroad by so large a portion of the European press. We had begun to hope that the good sense and right feeling of the mass of industrious and law-abiding people in every country would suffice to prevent the possibility of such a wanton stirring-up of the un-Christian passions of men as may lead, if unchecked, to the destruction of our own civilisation.'[20] Catherine Gittins and her sister would also have a significant role to play in the Payne brothers' defiance.

However, it was already too late. Early that morning German troops had forced their way into the neutral Grand Duchy of Luxemburg, seizing telegraph and railway facilities before moving south towards the capital. Belgium next – then France. And then… Britain?

★

Parliament met that Bank Holiday Monday, August 3rd. At 3 p.m. the Foreign Secretary, Sir Edward Grey, rose to speak. It was a speech which would change everything. Calmly, methodically, and with frequent references to the historical precedents, he explained why British interests required that the country support France in this conflict, and why Belgian neutrality must be defended. It balanced the tangible and the intangible, the defence of Britain's coasts and sea-borne trade and the defence of Britain's honour. A potentially hostile power commanding the Channel coast would leave Britain vulnerable to attack and possibly even invasion. But 'the real reason for going into the war,' he wrote later in his memoirs, 'was that, if we did not stand by France and stand up for Belgium against this aggression, we should be isolated, discredited, and hated; and there would be before us nothing but a miserable and ignoble future.' To many who heard it, it came down simply to a matter of honour – that word which would be used throughout this war, over and over again, all the way to the war graves and the memorials to the dead.[21]

But would Parliament or the nation follow him? One Foreign Office mandarin doubted it: 'There is a good deal of active opposition,' he said, 'and the crisis has come so rapidly that the country does not know what it is all about.'[22] And in his speech Grey recognised as much: events had moved so rapidly that 'the country... has not had time to realise the issue.'[23] Many who heard Grey's words in the House, and many, many more who read them in their newspapers next morning, caught only one word: 'Belgium'. It was not that anyone cared very much for Belgium,[24] but Belgium could be so easily visualised as the brave little boy in Bernard Partridge's celebrated cartoon which appeared in *Punch* within days of the declaration, defying the big bully Germany. The British sense of fair play and decency was outraged and the moral case was thus made.

Grey's speech was more compelling than he imagined, for next, John Redmond, leader of the turbulent Catholic Irish, rose and declared that 'the coast of Ireland will be defended from foreign invasion by her armed sons, and for this purpose armed Nationalist Catholics in the South will be only too glad to join arms with the armed Protestant Ulstermen in the North.'[25] The opposing forces in Ireland, until this moment poised on the verge of civil war, had thus done the unimaginable. When Ramsay Macdonald, leader of the Parliamentary Labour Group, rose to oppose he was already defending a lost cause. His position should have been buoyed up by that wave of anti-war sentiment, which had appeared in so many of the newspapers and from labour organisations, churches, chapels and adult schools across the country over the past couple of days, but he was left speechless and bewildered when the high rhetoric of International Socialism and Working Class Solidarity from *all* the belligerent countries just forty-eight hours before now evaporated leaving nothing behind. He was a man standing on sand.

MacDonald was on his feet for little more than five minutes, five misjudged minutes, in which he scarcely put forward any argument at all except recrimination. It was true that his party's view on the matter was clear: Sir Edward Grey had for years past pursued an anti-German foreign policy which had undermined Labour efforts to cultivate in Germany a socialist opposition capable of challenging the entrenched power of the Kaiser and the military, and at the same time had deliberately antagonised the Germans, provoking confrontation, conflict and a dangerous arms race. In 1912 Keir Hardy had told the Labour Party Conference that Grey's anti-German foreign policy was 'the cause of increasing armaments, international ill-will, and the betrayal of oppressed nationalities'.[26] But all that now seemed strangely irrelevant. Ramsay later wrote: 'It is a diplomatist's war, made by about half a dozen men. Up to the moment that the Ambassadors were withdrawn the peoples were at peace. They had no quarrel with each other: they bore each other no ill-will. A dozen men brought Europe to the brink of a precipice and Europe fell over it.'[27] That was undoubtedly true, but it too meant nothing now.

So, those like the Payne family in Lutterworth, who looked to MacDonald to present a clear and reasoned case *against* British involvement in the war that afternoon, were left disappointed. The pacifist Fenner Brockway was not the only one dismayed by MacDonald's impotence: 'My chief concern was about the attitude of the Labour Party and particularly Ramsay MacDonald, the Leader of the Parliamentary Group,' he later wrote. 'Then came the newspaper headlines about his speech in the Commons – "MacDonald says the Government is Wrong". I felt ashamed of my distrust. But the next day I read the speech in full and the distrust returned... He proceeded to declare in favour of war in certain circumstances'.[28] As Manny Shinwell shrewdly observed: 'The whole speech was based on suppositions about the situation, and on admissions that if his suppositions were wrong then war might be justified'.[29] Later that week MacDonald would tell his constituents in Leicester: 'Never did we arm our people and ask them to give us their lives, for less good cause than this'.[30]

★

German troops entered Belgium at 4pm on August 4th 1914. Britain had first to deliver an ultimatum demanding the Germans withdraw from Belgium: fair play required that at least. And when Germany refused, Great Britain declared war. It was 11pm on Tuesday August 4th, 1914: midnight, Berlin time.

As Asquith's government took Britain into the First World War, overwhelming public consent would follow in its wake: Grey had won the argument, and now, instead of Britain, it was Ramsay Macdonald – and by implication and association all those who opposed the war – who were 'isolated, discredited, and hated'. A couple of days later a majority of Labour M.P.s refused to support Ramsay MacDonald and he was forced to resign the leadership of the Parliamentary Party, which went to Arthur Henderson, leader of the so-called patriotic Labour M.P.s in the Commons[31] who had lent their support to Britain's participation.

Thus, Britain entered the First World War with barely a whimper.

★

Lutterworth's initial response to the outbreak of war was moulded by three factors and influences: the view of the leaders of local society, the attitude of the churches, and the wider picture of national news and events on the Continent, as the German Army continued its charge through Belgium and France.

First reactions were confusion, distraction and varying degrees of anxiety as the news spread: war had broken out on the Continent, though its meaning was still unclear. So there was bewilderment as the implications began to be glimpsed, a nervous quickening of the pace, but certainly not the immediate eager outburst of patriotic fervour or jingoistic rejoicings which some claim swept the country. Perhaps Lutterworth was too small for that. It was certainly cautious, more down-to-earth, more quizzical, more practical, more fearful of the unknown, as befitted this conservative little town of shopkeepers.[32]

Tuesday the 4th of August had been the first day of Lutterworth's Annual Agricultural Show, the most important date in the local calendar. Then, it had still been possible to ignore, or at least defer, the worrisome news and enjoy the day, but by Wednesday it was not. A heavy shower of rain overnight dampened some spirits, but Wednesday dawned clear and the day seemed set fair. Would the show even go ahead for its second day, some asked? But too many arrangements had been made, too much time and money committed, too many people with their livestock were already in Lutterworth, to simply cancel. The show was a great success, we are told, the best for years, though the mood was depressed and the committee, in response to a letter from Mr Cross of nearby Catthorpe, agreed to cancel the musical contribution of the Town Band to the carnival afternoon and the evening's scheduled dancing.[33]

At the end of the rather grand lunch the ubiquitous Lupton Topham felt constrained to say a few words, to set the right tone. To cheers he told his audience that Britain had done everything possible to preserve the peace, and that Germany was the aggressor: 'England could not, under the circumstances, remain neutral,' he said. 'What it meant for their country no one could tell; but they did know that it entailed upon them self-denial, self-restraint, courage, hope, and patience, and above all, an avoidance of panic'. This was followed by a rousing singing of the National Anthem.[34] In the event the band only got to play the first verse – hardly worth their trouble. It is reported that during the show a number of horses were commandeered by the army under the noses of their owners. [35]

For all Lupton Topham's words, there *was* panic – or panic buying at least – as fear of the unknown took hold. Since the end of the previous week the price of bread had been rising[36] and now, as soon as the shops reopened after the holiday, and with the prices of bread, butter, bacon, cheese and eggs all expected to rise[37], there was a run on food shops in Leicester, which led to their closure on the Wednesday afternoon. High moral principles were one thing, but practicalities were practicalities. In Rugby, half a dozen miles south of Lutterworth, at eleven in the morning on August 5th, the Co-op had to close its doors to prevent having its shelves stripped by anxious shoppers. Social divisions were exposed, some blaming the selfish rich for stockpiling food, while others blamed the wholesalers and shopkeepers who it was said were profiteering from the crisis: a traders' conspiracy.[38] One Rugby resident complained bitterly that 'almost before the declaration of war was published certain wholesale traders raised their prices. This had the effect of starting the desired panic, and large dealers were enabled to dispose of their existing stock at a handsome profit by placing the new prices on the old stock. One shopkeeper is reported to have sunk so low in his greed for profit as to issue "revised" bills to purchasers who omitted to pay the first bill on the day the goods were delivered. The patriotism of this class of people who regard a national crisis as a means of filling their own pockets is nauseating in the extreme.'[39]

Within days the message became sharper. Lutterworth's own local aristocrat, the Earl of Denbigh, was quick to state the case for war. In an open letter to the press within days of the outbreak, and reproduced in the local newspapers, he conceded that 'events have moved so quickly that the large majority of our friends and neighbours, so accustomed to peace, are stunned and bewildered at being suddenly brought face-to-face with that war which they never would believe was possible.' But it was the invasion of Belgium which had 'in a flash' transformed the whole situation and given Britain a cause to fight for: altruism in defence of Belgium, self-preservation from a rampant German militarism. He then briefly castigated 'the short-sightedness of those well-meaning but unpractical people who lived on the "brotherhood of man" and protested always against British armaments.'[40] It was a theme the Earl would pursue throughout the war with only the loaded word 'pacifist' inserted.

Alongside the words there was action. On Tuesday evening, even before the formal declaration, there had been a perceptible flurry of activity across the county as urgent messages were sent out to the men of the Leicestershire Yeomanry to report to headquarters the following morning; posters were put up for those who could not be contacted.[41] The Yeomanry's 'D' Squadron was based in Lutterworth, and there it assembled, probably allowed temporary accommodation in the classrooms of Sherrier School; the schools had, fortuitously, just broken up for their summer holiday, [42] until the assemblage was complete. Most moved off from Lutterworth station at the end of the week, seen off by Lupton Topham, the Rector and miscellaneous members of the Parish Council, with the Town Band on duty to play 'lively airs' to accompany the cheers. We are told that some members of the crowd that lined the streets to see them off were in tears.[43] They would not be the last tears shed in Lutterworth.

In the big houses that studded the countryside around Lutterworth anxiety and pride came together as word of mobilisation spread. In London, south Leicestershire men, professional soldiers as befitted their social standing, were already leaving. Alwyn Chadwyke Hobson of Misterton Hall, a mile from Lutterworth across the Rye Hills, was one, twenty-two years of age and a 2nd. Lieutenant in the 2nd Life Guards. His was one of those 'new' money families, originating in Manchester, their money made in brass founding, only recently joining the county set, taking over the hall from another military family, the Stewarts. Alwyn's brother Gerald was head of the family, a military man, a Lieutenant Colonel who would win for himself the D.S.O. in 1915.[44] That was also the year in which Alwyn would die. Arthur Murray Smith of Gumley Hall was in the same regiment. He was among the first cavalrymen sent to the Continent, part of the 'Composite Regiment' made up of the elite Squadrons of each of the Household Brigade Regiments, which went across with the B.E.F. He would not be returning home either.[45]

★

The Christian churches had a lot to think about as Britain went to war, in multi-denominational Lutterworth as much as anywhere else. Many Christians had difficult choices to make: to act and fight perceived evil with its own weapons, or follow the harder Christian path of peace, of turning the other cheek, of refusal to meet physical force with physical force, of loving thine enemy. It was a dilemma as old as Christianity itself, all the way back to Peter's sword in Gethsemane. Before the dramatic turn round in public opinion, which followed the declaration and the fact of war, all the Christian denominations had led prayers for peace. But in the new situation prayers for *peace* became, in most cases, prayers for *victory*. So, in Lutterworth, the Christian churches played their own decisive part in moulding popular opinion as the nation entered the Great War.

The Church of England led the charge. Lutterworth's Rector, Montague Alderson, was typical. While deeply regretting the fact of war and of Britain's involvement in it, he echoed the now familiar line that the war had to be won for the sake of 'civilisation' and 'Christian values' against an enemy which had repudiated both. 'It is no time to find fault or to indulge any pet theories', he wrote at the end of 1915, a clear rebuke to those like the Paynes whose pacifist principles got in the way of the demands of war. As the war went on, the Church would try to use it as a springboard for a spiritual missionary effort in Britain. In 1916 it would launch its 'National Mission' revival. The Rector of Lutterworth, Montague Alderson, explained: 'It is an effort to bring back God to His rightful place of pre-eminency in our national life. We have forgotten Him; ignored Him, and treated Him as non-existing in this world. In consequence we have starved our souls and brought our spiritual vitality to a very low ebb. We are seeing the error of our ways, and are now offering to Him a tardy act of reparation for our past years of neglect. The spirit of worship and adoration, of fellowship, of unity, and brotherly love, is manifesting itself; and if it purges out of our midst the deadly sins and low ideals of the past, this war with all its huge sacrifice of life, limb, and treasure will have indeed proved itself a blessing in disguise.'[46] As Professor Millman has pointed out: 'if the dissenters could appeal to Christian pacifism, the fact remained that most Christians were not pacifists. Many considered the interests of nation and church, in this fight, to be virtually identical. Christian duty… could easily be set against Christian conscience.'[47]

That the Anglican Church as a whole threw itself enthusiastically behind the war effort is too well documented to need embellishment here: this rather shocked reaction from one pacifist to a visit to the parish church in Houghton on the Hill in east Leicestershire in 1917 illustrates the point:

'It was a lovely day and as I arrived early I had a good look round the church. I picked up a book of *Prayers for use in Wartime*, they were all depicting us as the righteous defenders of truth against a very wicked and mistaken foe whom we much desired would repent. There was one cutting from a magazine in the book which began Lord God of Battles and rambled on in a spirit worthy of its beginning! There was also a picture of Britannia bending over a dying soldier and numerous small hand illuminated Rolls of Honour – churches do seem a queer mixture in these days. Afterwards when May and I went down together we were looking through the thirty-nine articles that come at the end of the prayer book and at the end of article thirty-seven it says something like this 'It is lawful for a man at the command of a magistrate to wear arms and to take part in wars'.[48]

It was a picturesque scene which could have been repeated almost anywhere in wartime Britain. If the Church of England was the Conservative Party at prayer, it was now unquestionably the English People at war.

The alliance of local leaders and the Anglican Church was, to many, irresistible. In Cotesbach, outside Lutterworth, Charles Marriott, the head of the family, encapsulated the unconscious blend of patriotism and God in his own verse, written for the occasion, couched in suitable archaic language, entitled (and probably written in) 'August 1914':

> 'England awake! The noble sons who made thee
> Call from the vast invisible, and say
> "Strengthen then thine arms! If enemies invade thee,
> Lift up thine heart, Fall on thy knees and pray.
> Just is thy cause, the cause of injured nations,
> True is thy heart, thy dauntless sons are true.
> Staunch thy response to longing expectations,
> Firm thy desire that peace might yet ensue.
> Great was thy patience, great is thy endeavour,
> Strong be the faith that tempers thy command;
> Grateful the love that flows to thee for ever,
> Wrung from the valiant by thy succouring hand.["]'[49]

The third factor in shaping local perceptions of the war came from outside: the near unanimity of the nation's politicians and press, and the monstrous conduct of the German Army in Belgium and France. These, combined with the concurrent attitudes of local leaders and the Christian churches, left no room for doubt that it was not only morally *right* but also morally *necessary* for Britain to be in this war. And much older visions were resurrected so what was seen from the outset as a just war became a crusade. Images of crusading knights abounded, giving heart to those who would send sons to the war, and consolation to those who would lose them. [50]

Cynicism about the motives of those who shaped the public's perception of this conflict – locally and nationally – would be misplaced. This document, dated November 16th 1914, was found among Charles Marriott's papers, written in his own hand:

> 'We believe that this war is the barbarous onslaught of the enemies of humanity and Christianity, and that the first is proved by the acts and the second by the writings of the Germans
> 'We further believe that our armies are engaged in a crusade as holy as any that has ever been undertaken, and that the lives that are being daily sacrificed by our heroic and devoted sons are not only being given in defence of their country, their homes and dear ones but are literally bestowed on the side of the Cross of Christ, and in opposition to the works of the devil. God alone knows the truth, but that is our belief...

'The tendencies of German philosophy have been to weaken the foundations of the Scriptures, and especially the narratives of the Gospels of such miracles as Our Lord's dealing with demoniacs and those possessed with evil spirits.

'But we believe we see an actual example of the leaders of a nation being possessed by the devil through the means of that very spirit of ὕβρις [hubris] or pride which led to his fall & will lead to their destruction.

'O Lord our God, let us learn our lesson, and turn away from all dealings with the hateful spirit of hostility, malice and anger, ~~and~~ to the blessed paths of Peace, Purity and Prosperity, through Jesus Christ our Lord.'

It is likely that this manuscript exhortation was intended to be read out in church. Its sincerity is self-evident.[51]

As Charles understood – and would understand more before a twelvemonth was out, on the other side of the coin of crusade were the twin concepts of 'sacrifice' and in its extreme form 'martyrdom'. That the comforting aura of 'sacrifice' would surround the names of those who died in the least comforting of circumstances is a sleight of hand, necessary in face of the vastness of the loss every town and village in the land would suffer – in every land that was drawn into the Great War. The vocabulary of loss – 'heroes', 'glory', and 'sacrifice' itself – and the use of a higher, more antiquated form of language, were attempts to elevate the squalid into the magnificent.[52] Crusade. Sacrifice. Martyrdom. A clear and necessary progression.

★

On the other hand, not everyone was an Anglican and the Church of England did not necessarily speak for all Christians. So the different Christian groups and individuals aligned themselves in accordance with their own moral values, their own understanding of the international situation, the latest news reports from the Continent, and their own interpretations of Scripture. There was no simple, consistent Christian response in Britain to the outbreak of war. Some responses were Biblical: Father Stephen Jarvis of the Roman Catholic St Marie's Church in Rugby, saw the war in Old Testament terms: 'We should ask ourselves whether we ourselves may not have deserved the evils from which we shall have to suffer through our sins. For God allows evils to happen to us in punishment of our sins.'[53] Some responses were worldly: the Rev. Norman Faid, from the Melbourne Road Primitive Methodist Chapel in Leicester, thought the war a capitalist conspiracy in which the workers of Europe would be called upon to lay down their lives for the profits of the plutocrats. (This would become standard fare for the Left throughout the war, and all demands for conscientious objection status on political grounds would be based on it.[54])

Some, indeed, blamed the Christian churches themselves for the fact of war through their failure to create a society in which war was impossible. One conscientious objector, Slater Wilson, expressed this anger: 'A great responsibility lies at the door of the professing Christian churches. A Staff Captain in the army, interviewed by the *Daily News* said, "…we feel that the Church is much to blame for the whole horrible affair. What in God's name has it been doing for centuries?" This is an assertion that if the Churches had been faithful to the Prince of Peace, whom they call Lord, war would be an impossibility. I believe this.'[55]

One relatively small religious group which took a dissenting view was the Christadelphians, whose pacifism was clear and absolute. Their fundamental opposition was straightforward enough: of American origin, they had secured conscientious objection rights in the U.S.A. as far back as the Civil War there in the 1860s. In Britain in 1903, in the wake of the Boer War, they had considered petitioning Parliament, pleading for recognition of their conscientious objection to military service, based on Scripture: '[Christadelphians] are conscientiously opposed to the bearing of arms, on the ground that the Bible, which they believe to be the Word of God, commands them not to kill; not to resist evil; to love their enemies; to bless those that curse them; to do good to those that hate them; to pray for those who despitefully use them and persecute them; and to do to men as they would do to them. Consequently, your petitioners entertain the conviction that they are debarred from taking any part in the conflicts that arise between nations. They recognise and discharge the duty of submitting to the laws enacted by the governments, where these laws do not conflict with the laws delivered by the Deity to His servants in His Word; but where human laws conflict with those that are divine, they feel themselves compelled to follow the example of the apostle Peter, who, before a judicial tribunal in such a case, declared that he must obey God rather than man.'[56] It was as clear a statement of the religious reasons for conscientious objection to military service as was ever produced. After a long and complex struggle the Christadelphians succeeded in getting their pacifist status recognised by the government.

Even the Quakers, whose 'Peace Testimony' was, to outsiders and many members of the Society of Friends itself, a key defining tenet, at first betrayed some uncertainty as to how to respond to the war. The editorial of their journal *The Friend*, on September 4th 1914 expressed support for the war itself and Britain's participation in it, using language which could have come from any 'patriotic' source of the time: 'We have been the unwilling witness,' it said, 'of atrocity and outrage by some parts of the German Army upon innocent men, women and children and upon their defenceless homes; we have seen the wanton and barbarous destruction of Aershot and Louvain; we have read of the sowing of the sea with mines (and the consequent disasters to neutral shipping) and of the dropping of bombs from airships upon Antwerp; and we have seen the neutral State of Belgium covered with terror, devastation and misery... We know now what a pernicious and soul-destroying thing is German military despotism!... [M]ost of us have probably come to the conclusion that Great Britain could not remain neutral, and that she had to fulfil her solemn obligations to others as well as defend her own country.'[57]

The Quakers faced a dilemma in how to respond to the new situation. First, they must recognise that the outbreak of war had created a novel situation. 'It is perfectly clear that our Peace Testimony cannot at present take its usual orthodox form of protesting against all war,' it said. 'We are in the midst of war. Though we are Quakers we are also Englishmen, and brave men are laying down their lives for us on the old battlefields of Flanders and France. Duty as they see it has called them. For that conception of duty they have sacrificed all. We cannot recall them, even if we would. Their very devotion compels us, holds us, and marks our own lives with the blood-red sign of worth. What shall we render them? How shall we prove we are worth fighting for? How can we translate, or at least represent our peace testimony in time of war? The answer to these hard questions must be made by each man for himself.'[58]

While that call for each man to reach his own decision was *intended* as a call to Quakers to support peaceable actions, such as the Friends' Ambulance Units in France, much of the editorial could almost be construed as a call to arms. And that was how some young Quakers saw it. A week later *The Friend* printed a letter from Bevan Baker of Harlesden, which must have sent shockwaves through many a Quaker heart. 'There appears to be,' wrote Baker, 'a growing feeling of uncertainty among young Friends as to whether this war is not one which may justify us in relaxing our principles against fighting. The fact that England has entered into the war in order to protect a small nation from the unjustifiable encroachments of Germany and the fact that the nature of the circumstances makes it difficult to see how our country could honourably have maintained her neutrality, have led many of us to wonder whether it is not right for us to fight for our birthright and whether any other course would not be a cowardly sheltering behind others.'[59] This was not a lone voice. The historian of the Society of Friends in peace and war, Margaret

Hirst, writing in 1923, told how 'a section of the Society' called for 'the temporary and permanent abandonment of what they described as the "traditional testimony" against war. A few went further, trying to prove that the testimony was not even traditional, and had never been held by the majority of the Society.'[60]

In November 1914, in an attempt to clear up the situation, the Quakers' 'Meeting for Sufferings' issued its own declaration on the war, reiterating the view that 'all war is utterly incompatible with the plain precepts of our Divine Lord and Lawgiver, and with the whole spirit and tenor of His Gospel, and that no plan of necessity or of policy, however urgent or peculiar, can avail to release either individuals or nations from the paramount allegiance which they owe unto Him who said "Love your enemies"...' It then continued: 'Whilst reaffirming this statement of our faith we cannot shelter ourselves behind any traditional tenet. We are in the presence of living issues. Today many of our fellow countrymen are impelled to enlist by a sense of chivalry towards the weak and by devotion to high national ideals. Today again members of our Society, especially the younger men, are entering upon a time of testing. We can well understand the appeal to noble instincts which makes men desire to risk their lives for their country. To turn from this call may seem to be a lower choice. In many cases it means braving the scorn of those who only interpret it as cowardice... The highest sacrifice is to contribute our lives to the cause of love in helping our country to a more Christ-like idea of service. Those who hear the call of this service, and who respond to it, will be helping their nation in the great spiritual conflicts which it must wage... We see danger to principle in undertaking any service auxiliary to warfare which involves becoming part of the military machine.'[61]

Others, too, had to tread a fine line, albeit on the other side. Typical of many was the dilemma faced by the Rev. Dr. John Clifford, who had trained at the Midland Baptist College in Leicester, and was perhaps the most influential of the Nonconformist campaigners in Edwardian England. A pacifist back to the Boer War, Clifford nevertheless threw his weight behind the 1914 war, convinced that the Germans had acted so outrageously that the use of force was not only necessary but morally justified. The Germans, 'deliberately and of express purpose and according to long prepared plans, had broken into Belgium, flung to the winds as veriest chaff her solemn treaty obligations, flouted public law, and trampled underfoot with ineffable scorn the rights of small nationalities as not even the small dust of the balance,' he wrote in 1917.[62] At the same time, though, Clifford maintained his support for those conscientious objectors whose personal beliefs forbade them to take part. He was not alone in occupying this narrow ground, forced to opt for supporting a war he loathed, feeling that it was God's will and the right thing to do and, therefore, the only course open: violating his own pacifist principles, but supporting those who disagreed.

And even within the Anglican Church itself there were a few dissenting voices, among them Canon Donaldson of Leicester's St Mark's parish, who preached in November 1914 that: 'War betrays the innocent, crushes the weak, violates purity, destroys and devastates fair and noble cities and wrecks their habitations'[63]. That last presumably was a reference to the sack of the peaceful and beautiful Belgian city of Louvain at the end of August 1914 which had horrified the nation and the world.[64] Sincere as Donaldson's pacifism was, it failed to address what for many was the decisive question: given that Britain was actually *at war*, what could or should pacifist Christians do to *stop* the war? Donaldson's claim that 'the real sin of the Church is not that she allows war, but that she tolerates the state of things that leads to war,' fudged the issue; the horse of war had already bolted, and belatedly to preach that the stable door should not have been left open sounded by now at best redundant, or at worst smacking of an 'I told you so' self-righteousness. As one Anglican vicar was quoted as saying, 'It is very awkward for anybody who has anything to do with Christianity.'[65] Just so.

★

Of more immediate moment to the Payne family, though, was the attitude of their own Congregational Church, and particularly its minister in Lutterworth, the Rev. Arthur Massey. As with all other Christian groups, attitudes to the war had to be resolved, policy had to be defined, especially in a loose and largely autonomous organisation like the Congregational Church, torn as it was between the demands of patriotism and the equally powerful demands of a Nonconformist radical non-violent Christian tradition. On 24th September 1914, the Congregation Church Union of Leicestershire and Rutland held its annual autumn get-together in Enderby, to the south of Leicester, the war forcing its way onto the agenda. It was asked, how many young men from the different Congregational Churches were already in the armed forces, as Regulars or Territorials? An incomplete survey conducted by cautious church leaders had so far discovered over 200 from the two counties. And many, many more would join up when called upon. It seems there was little reluctance to take up arms among young Congregationalists.

Perhaps encouraged by this fact, the chairman, the Rev Robert Veitch, of the London Road Chapel in Leicester, who was a significant local figure, described as 'a choice spirit and a great force in the social and educational life of Leicester',[66] proposed a carefully worded statement. The minutes recorded that: 'This assembly of Congregationalists of Leicestershire and Rutland deeply deplores that at this point in our national and Christian history we should be engaged in European war. It mourns the fearful loss of human life and the destruction of property, together with the devastation of fair cities. It nevertheless holds that every consideration of honour bound us to maintain the sacredness of international engagements and to oppose wanton aggression. It therefore earnestly prays for the decisive success of our arms and that this war may prove the end of war and the heaping up of armaments. May God so over-rule all events, as to bring about a speedy peace on conditions favourable to the establishment of permanent international goodwill? This assembly urges on our churches the steady continuance of their spiritual ministries, now needed now [sic] than ever. May the Christian Church prove to be in this crisis the courageous and trustful heart of the nation, as well as the active promoter of all philanthropic efforts for the alleviation of distress? This assembly finally prays that the experience through which the nation is passing may only produce a deeper religion, a greater patriotism, a finer character, and a more supreme devotion to national well-being.'[67]

The opening words of the Enderby statement, deploring the outbreak of war and the lives it would cost, are to be taken at face value. First the German invasion of Belgium, followed by the terrible news of German atrocities there – embellished by propaganda – cemented the *moral* case in the minds of many: aggression and savagery had to be opposed by whatever means were necessary, and, given that the Germans were not going to apologise and withdraw, that meant war.[68] Inevitably, there was dissent. At the Enderby meeting itself there were voices of opposition. Mr Hancock, while agreeing with most of the statement, felt that it failed in the highest Christian duty of 'non-resistance to evil'. That, at least, was how the secretary originally minuted the remark, though, interestingly and significantly, he later had to amend it to 'non-resistance to evil *by armed force*' – a necessary correction to an error which surely should not have been made. Hancock then proposed a procedural motion, seconded by the anti-war Rev Beddow from the Wycliffe Congregational Chapel in Leicester, that 'we pass to the next business'. The amendment was defeated, and the original statement was passed 'with enthusiasm', by sixty-seven votes to four.[69] The majority is all the more impressive given the defining feature of Congregationalism, that each congregation made its own autonomous decisions without any necessary reference to any other congregation.[70] The Enderby statement contained no reference to conscientious objection. On the national stage the picture was different only on that one issue of individual conscience: 'The [National] Congregational Union accepted the war as the only course "consonant with national righteousness" but declared its respect for those members who sincerely embraced pacifism.'[71] 'Respect', but not 'support'. Once passed, the Enderby statement defined the official attitude to the war of the Congregational Churches in Leicestershire and Rutland, and the issue was not debated again at this level. The statement was sent to the Prime Minister.

One man not at the Enderby meeting[72] was the Lutterworth minister, Arthur Massey, a man who would come to play an important part in the story of the Payne brothers. By all accounts, Massey was a popular and successful minister in Lutterworth, described by the historians of the church as 'inspiring'.[73] Incumbent since 1910, he had put the Congregational Church in Lutterworth, previously in a parlous state, onto a firmer footing. He was an active and progressive member of the local Lutterworth community, a moderniser, like George Spencer, seemingly with a finger in every social pie – Parish Councillor[74], governor of the grammar school[75] and overseer of the poor.[76] He was highly active in the usual important trivia of a Parish Council's responsibilities – having his say on everything from the provision of public conveniences in the town[77] to the management of the local fire brigade[78] and to the need for platform tickets on Sundays at the railway station[79]. He had also led those calls for a public mortuary for Lutterworth[80] in alliance with that other leader of progressive local society, George Spencer.

It seems certain that Massey would have wholeheartedly supported the stance taken at the Enderby meeting; that the war and its consequences were truly deplorable, but now Britain was at war, that war had to be fought vigorously and won, and the sooner the better. This meant pursuing the conflict resolutely whilst doing everything possible to minimise or at least alleviate the inevitable and terrible effects and those effects would, of course, grow more and more terrible as the war dragged on. The Congregational Church in Lutterworth gave its young men who went off to war what spiritual comfort it could, sending them a special pocket book which had been prepared by the Baptist and Congregational Unions, presumably containing inspiring and uplifting Christian thoughts. Eight were purchased.[81] Many soldiers accepted New Testaments supplied by the Scripture Gift Mission and Naval and Military Bible Society, and measuring not much more than 2½ inches by 4 (7 x 10 cm.). In the back they included a statement headed 'My Decision' which they were invited to sign, presumably to help God know his own. It said: 'Convinced of my sinful condition, and believing that Christ died for me, and rose again, and will save to the uttermost all who come unto God by Him (Heb. 7.25), I now receive Him as my personal Saviour, and with His help intend to confess Him openly'. To men about to go into the trenches, this 'Active Service Testament' was, no doubt, a great comfort.[82]

A man of principle, Massey would not flinch from the implications of Britain's involvement in this war. Before it was over he would leave his ministry in Lutterworth to join another 'ministry', as Secretary to the Leicestershire Local Committee of the Ministry of Pensions. 'I am conscious,' he said in September of 1918, 'of no change of atmosphere between that work and that in which I have hitherto laboured, and I feel that I have been as truly called to this form of service as I was to the pastorate. It is a ministry of restoration and uplifting. My duty and desire is to bring help to the helpless, hope to the hopeless; to bring light into the lives of those who by reason of disablement caused by their service to their country and of humanity, are finding life grey and hard.'[83] The Rev Massey walked a narrow path, but a clear one. It was a path that would bring him into direct confrontation with the Payne brothers when they decided the only option open to them was the even narrower path of conscientious objection.

★

In Lutterworth, everywhere we look, we see a huge infusion of energy, a quickening of the pace as everyone leapt forward eager to 'do their bit' and join in the national effort. War enthusiasm took hold as 'somnolent' Lutterworth woke up. The volunteering started with James Miller who claimed to be the first, recruited into the Leicestershire Regiment (the 'Tigers'), then surviving the Somme and Passchendaele, and eventually returning home more or less in one piece. Just over the county border at Monks Kirby, Tom Ward was desperate to join up: he had joined the army, under age, in 1904 and was in the reserve until he re-volunteered as soon as war broke out – in the hope of getting a better uniform! Whether he got a better uniform is not recorded, but his prospects did not look good: he was, on being sent rapidly to France, issued with a rifle, which lacked a bolt. The villagers of Monks Kirby clubbed together to buy him a silver medal to mark the fact that he was their first. Like James, he survived the war and returned home. The fact that Tom's precedence was claimed by him and his family, and was then passed down through the generations, carries echoes of the spirit of 1914.[84] In the first months a tally was kept of those who had gone, a list called the 'Roll of Honour' published in the *Lutterworth and District Almanac*, though it is not possible accurately to distinguish between those who were Regulars, the Territorials and those who volunteered after the outbreak of war. For Lutterworth the initial list showed 117 names. A further ninety-five would be added by the end of 1915.[85] This amounted to a little over 11% of the town's total population, an impressive figure when compared to Leicester's 2.6% recruitment.[86]

In Lutterworth's surrounding villages, its extended family, the picture was more mixed. Generally, the leaders of local society set the tone, starting with Lupton Topham's rousing speech at the Agricultural Show when war broke out. Eleven men went from Peatling Parva, out of only 120 villagers, while tiny Cotesbach, where the Marriotts lived in the big house, had produced eight men by the end of 1915, from a population of little over a hundred – and by the end of the war would have produced four more.[87] Charles sent his own sons: five in all joined the armed forces, including Fred, who received his commission before August was out, and Digby in September. Both served in the Rifle Brigade and both were killed at Ypres in 1915. Neither were the family of the Earl of Denbigh slow to volunteer: the boys in the army and navy, the Earl's daughters doing their bit as well – Lady Dorothie in the Munro Ambulance Corps, Lady Marjorie nursing in northern France, Lady Clare working with the Canadian Red Cross; even part of their house at Newnham Paddox was turned into an Auxiliary Home Hospital. They were indeed a family at war.[88]

More typical of volunteering among Lutterworth's extended family of villages were Gilmorton (6½ % of the total population) and Leire (4½ %). But by far the highest ratio came from Lutterworth's neighbouring village of Bitteswell, a mile down the road. This tranquil little farming community sent no less than thirty-seven men in the first seventeen months of the war, 12% of its total population – so many indeed that the Church Council had to call for more volunteers of its own to join the church choir.[89] The reason for this striking level of 'volunteering' is not difficult to see, for the loudest voice in village life came from Major Corbet Smith of Bitteswell Hall, a keen militarist whose attitudes were encapsulated in a letter he wrote to the local press in 1916: 'I was talking to a wounded boy of the Hampshire Regiment on the platform of Rugby station the other day,' he wrote. 'I asked him what his wounds were? He replied: "My right arm is shattered, three fingers off my left hand," and he also had a large gash across one cheek. He had been at Loos, Hulluck, and Ypres; and, as he termed it, had had the biggest part of a shell. He added: "I am no more use, sir; *but I am glad I went.*" A little thing like this, I think, helps to show the spirit of our men and the stuff they are made of.'[90] The Major used his position on the Executive of the County Relief Committee to further the cause of recruitment by speeding up the process: the District Relief Committees themselves should 'register the applications of intending recruits in districts where there is any delay in completing the formalities of enlistment', it decreed.[91] *'Squire nagged and bullied till I went to fight...'*[92] So again, the leaders of local society in and around Lutterworth played a decisive role in shaping the local response to war.

It would be another three weeks before Major Corbet Smith's Relief

Committee would get round to discussing how the families of the dead and wounded might be assisted – presumably it was thought that before they could be assisted, they must first be recruited – and even then the issue was farmed out to the 'Patriotic Committee'. And, just to be sure no one slipped through the net, the Major and his committee called for a distinctive badge to be worn by intended recruits. While no doubt protecting men out of uniform from those who were prepared to tackle anyone they saw as a 'shirker', the badge system also helped isolate those who, like the Payne brothers, had no intention of joining up by making them even more conspicuous.[93] In nearby Husbands Bosworth special cards were printed in April of 1915 to be placed in front windows 'to show that they have someone in their home who is fighting for his King and Country'.[94]

None of this prevented a meeting of the Rural District Council, chaired by the Major, from appealing strongly for exemption from military service for three of its workers when conscription was introduced in 1916. The Sanitary Inspector was one, accompanied by the council's steamroller driver and its bricklayer, who was apparently responsible not only for sewer repairs but also for operating the steam disinfector. It was recorded that the two latter were aged thirty-nine and thirty-eight and were both married, though by that time married men in their late thirties were being called up as a matter of routine. Major Corbet Smith was successful in his claim on behalf of the Sanitary Inspector, even though he had already been passed as medically fit, and the other two also evaded military service.[95] When it came to the demands of local government it would appear that some were more equal than others.

Everyone, it seems, wanted to be seen to be doing their bit, if only to ease the passage for others to join up. The County Councils Association in its *Official Gazette*, as one example, announced that 'those trained teachers who are under an obligation to serve in approved schools for not less than seven out of the ten years following the completion of their training, and who now proceed on military service will be allowed to count the period of their military service during the continuance of mobilisation towards the fulfilment of this period of seven years.'[96] There is an unconscious irony here which teachers will, no doubt, appreciate. The motives of those who did offer themselves in 1914 were inevitably mixed. For many we suppose it was a matter of patriotism, or the call of adventure in foreign parts, or the desire to cut a dash, or simple peer pressure fostered by the creation of those 'Pals' battalions, individual responsibility subsumed within the collective enthusiasm.

In Lutterworth Mr Tate, chairman of Lutterworth's Wycliffe Foundry, earned the headline in a local newspaper 'More Recruits: A Good Example', by promising on a visit to the foundry not only to keep open the jobs of men who volunteered but to 'look after the married men's dependents in their absence'. Thirty of his workers promptly marched off to the Glen Parva Barracks outside Leicester to volunteer their services.[97] A 'good example' it may have been, but, given that the foundry would soon be deluged with orders for munitions essential to the war effort, necessitating a huge expansion of the works, its wisdom may be questioned.

Others, too, had personal reasons for joining up: war as redemption. William Goulden, a farm hand from Misterton, a mile to the east of Lutterworth, volunteered after serving a month in jail at hard labour for theft: he had stolen £2 from his employer. Perhaps his criminal record had simply made him unemployable anywhere else, but he made amends by joining the 3rd Battalion of the Leicestershire Regiment; he survived the war.[98] More private, and more obscure, was the agony a young man from Great Dalby, near Melton Mowbray in north Leicestershire, confessed in a letter from hospital some months later. 'No doubt after my departure for foreign service', he wrote to a family friend, 'the busybodies would get hold of all my doings and pull me and mine to pieces. No doubt, to you it would appear a rash thing to do, but now after other developments you can see my reason. It was the most honourable thing I could do after making a slip; a slip which in an unguarded moment has caused the blot on my career.' That word 'honour' again. What terrible sin R.K. Peers had committed we do not know. He volunteered for the Leicestershire Yeomanry and was wounded on the terrible day for the Yeomanry outside Ypres in May of 1915, so presumably his self-sacrifice had served its personal purpose; we hope that a mangled foot provided a sufficiency of expiation for whatever it was that he had done.[99]

★

Setting the pace for volunteering in Lutterworth was a woman – Mary Marriott, from the big house in Cotesbach, head of the Women's Voluntary Aid Detachment which had been formed in Lutterworth in the spring of 1914.[100] While the first soldiers were being mobilised, and long before any British soldier had set foot on foreign soil, the redoubtable Mrs Marriott was seeking permission to use the little isolation hospital attached to the workhouse for the treatment of the wounded.[101] With commendable efficiency, spurred on no doubt by the fact that her husband was a prominent member of the Board of Guardians, her written request had, by Thursday August 6th, been received and acted upon. Mrs Marriott, it would seem, had no illusions about the fact that war meant suffering and wounds and death: the woman's touch.

With the outbreak of war the Feilding Palmer Hospital had been put on alert to receive the wounded, and then the new Methodist Chapel's schoolroom was set up as a V.A.D. hospital,[102] and, in light of all this activity, Mrs Marriott withdrew her request to use the workhouse facilities.[103] At a public meeting held in Lutterworth to organise things, the call went out for fifty-two carpenters, joiners and plumbers to adapt the buildings for medical use, plus other men willing to act as stretcher bearers. Perhaps ashamed of lagging behind the women of the town, some 200 men offered their services.[104] The first wounded did not, in fact, arrive until the end of April 1915, in the wake of the opening of the Second Battle of Ypres, and soon all the beds were occupied. Alongside the professional nursing staff, the daughters of the leading local families did their duty as well: a Topham, an Alderson and a Goodacre (from Ullesthorpe), whose family had already opened up their spacious house there to serve as a hospital for the wounded, worked full time, a week at a time, while Miss Ffinch dealt with all the linen and pyjamas.[105]

A letter written in July 1915 by young Esther Marriott of Cotesbach Hall described her work at the hospital:

'I was on duty at the hospital on Tuesday from 1.30 till 9,' she wrote to her brother Fred. 'It was rather fun as six new patients came by the 4.15 from Leicester. We got through our usual work, washing bandages and dusters, giving medicine at two o'clock, and mending a few garments, in good time and prepared an excellent tea for them consisting of bread and butter, and cake, and strawberries. They turned up in motor cars a few minutes before 4.30 and looked *much too* well to be interesting. Except one who had both hands thickly bandaged and could do nothing for himself. They aren't nearly so superior or interesting as the last lot except two, a red-haired Scotch boy, and the man with the bad hands called Griffiths, an Irish Guardsman he has rather a nice chum who does everything for him and feeds him like a child!'[106]

This time the men did not lag behind, for the problem of how to transport the injured from the railway station to the hospitals was one they could solve through their own bit of voluntary effort. At the outbreak of war a call had gone out to the owners of motor cars and motor cycles to contact the Leicestershire Automobile Club to offer their vehicles to the war effort for just this contingency.[107] Typical was this, from the summer of 1915: 'A further batch of nine wounded arrived by Great Central [Railway] on Tuesday afternoon, and were met at the station by Commandant Pryce T. Taylor with his car; by Mr H.B. Ffinch (secretary) with his car; several other gentlemen also lending their cars; and were conveyed to the

V.A.D. Hospital on the Coventry Road [the Methodist Chapel schoolroom], where excellent accommodation is provided for them.'[108] In one of his letters, Leonard mentioned that there were 'ten wounded here in the prepared hospital, they came this week. Father went to sit up with them last night, people are taking it in turns there'.[109] There is no reference to Leonard or Roland visiting the wounded in the hospital. Perhaps they thought their views on the war would be a provocation to the wounded.

In 1916, as casualty numbers rose and the demands became greater, the Congregational Chapel was asked if it could provide the V.A.D. with a dormitory, presumably for nursing and medical staff, and the Deacons' Meeting gladly availed, like the Methodists, offering the use of their schoolroom for that purpose.[110] We would imagine that the Paynes, staunch Congregationalists, approved of the move, but by the time the offer was made both the Payne brothers would be in military custody, hundreds of miles from home.

★

If Lutterworth's initial response to the war was shaped by the local leaders of society, by the Christian churches and by the horrible news of German atrocities in Belgium and France, larded with propaganda inventions, the reality of war on the Home Front (as it became known) presented an altogether more down beat, more depressing and wearing face. The impact on those men who went away to war is well enough known – the horrors of trench warfare thoroughly documented – but we are less familiar with the grinding day to day hardships of those left behind, of their experience of the First World War.[111] 1915 saw 'the death of glory' and 'the death of innocence'[112] on the battlefield, and the corrosive and insidious effects of war on the civilian population back in Britain robbed those there of any sense of glory and innocence as well.

With prices rising and breadwinners lost to so many families – whether the loss was permanent, for the duration, or still in the balance – there were many in the county left in real need. While the men at the front might be the 'millionaires on 1s. 2d. a day', as some described them,[113] half their pay was supposed to be sent home and many of the necessities of life had to be paid for by the soldier himself out of what remained. Families did receive a Separation Allowance from the government – 12s. 6d. for the wife, and between two and three shillings for each child – but these sums were inadequate: 'starvation money, that's all you could call it', as one recipient remembered many years later,[114] and many found survival difficult. In Leicester, in a first flush of enthusiasm, the council proposed making up the wages of all corporation workers who went off to the war to their existing, pre-war civilian levels, but on referring the matter to the Finance Committee decided instead on the cheaper expedient of granting, for single men with dependants, five shillings per week, while married men were given six shillings with one-and-tuppence for each child; single men without dependants got nothing extra.[115] The families of men in private employment took their chances with their employers, though it seems generally that they went with the promise that their jobs would be held open for them until they returned[116]: but, then, it would be 'all over by Christmas' anyway, so that would not be a problem.[117]

The financial hardship experienced by many of the families who sent men off to the war was echoed by fears of a moral fragility, which was – potentially at least – even more corrosive. While not every man who did his duty by his King and Country did his duty equally by his wife and family, the suspicion was that not all those wives were doing their duty by their husbands either. In a society in which the prevailing political opinion was that women could not be trusted with the vote, it is hardly surprising that women as the 'the weaker vessel' should not be trusted morally either, and anyway, military efficiency demanded that men away from their families ought not to be worrying about the faithfulness of their spouses back home. The Chief Constable of Leicestershire, in December 1914, was alerting his superintendents across the county to the moral dangers to women who were allowed to wander near army bases, advising that a 'fatherly spirit' should inform their dealings with these women and girls, and that they be 'looked after' by the police. For all that, the heading to the agenda item was 'Cessation of Army Separation Allowance for the Unworthy.'[118] The issue of wives turning casually to drink had been raised at some very exalted levels, the Archbishop of Canterbury writing to Lord Kitchener in October of 1914 suggesting that it was a danger to be taken seriously, and it was even suggested that special legislation should be introduced specifically to control women's drinking. The War Office had warned dependants that if they spent their allowances on alcohol, those allowances would be stopped: the assumption seems to have been that without the watchful presence of their husbands, and without this threat, they probably would.[119] And in May of 1915 it was recorded that: 'The chief constable wants wives of married members of H.M. Forces to remain at home as much as possible,' though he did concede that they 'Can go away for holiday if desired.'[120] Coming from the chief constable, this presumably became policy.

Unmarried young women were, inevitably, seen as being even more vulnerable, and the churches as well as the police took preventive (or protective) action. The General Committee of the Congregational Union in Leicestershire reported in

September 1915 that 'in certain centres local ladies of high character were undertaking patrol work in the streets and speaking as occasion required to groups of young girls and soldiers'.[121] Their concern for the moral welfare of these young women was not entirely misplaced, as the case of two sisters from Wigston, just south of Leicester, indicates. It was alleged that the girls, with a female friend, were beguiled into a car by soldiers from the 125th Anti-Aircraft Battery, based at Carlton Clump near Kibworth Harcourt, on the evening of August 12th 1916, plied with drink in 'The Coach and Horses' pub in the village, taken to the camp and there raped.[122]

Some single women who found survival difficult sought relief in marriage, though it is impossible to know how far the urge was emotional and how far financial. In one of Jessie's letters to her brothers, written in the summer of 1917, we find a rare sour note:

> 'We are having a few weddings down here lately, Nellie Barlow married David Kemp on Sat. and Francis Buck was married today to Francis [sic.] Ridgeway. I think it is a great waste of money, all these soldiers getting married, and the government have to keep their wives, they only get married for the money, some of them'. [123]

★

Children too found themselves drawn in: 'we are boys and cannot yet show our loyalty by taking our place in the firing line'; the significance of that 'yet' running loud and clear and ominous. [124] At the grammar school, out on the Bitteswell Road, the military spirit percolated from the headmaster (whisked away at the outbreak of war to his Territorial Regiment) down, prompting the creation of a Cadet Corps in 1915, in conjunction with the new 1st Grammar Schools Cadet Battalion of the Leicestershire Regiment. That this was intended as serious training for a new generation of army officers was in no doubt, for this was not merely a school based recreational activity for military minded, middle class grammar school boys: it involved a special instructional school and army style camps. We are told that 'every eligible boy in the school was in fact a member', though whether this was by choice, pressure or compulsion we do not know: there is no hint of conscientious objection being offered or claimed here.[125]

But some young people would have none of it, and Lutterworth's Parish Council would be exercised by the increasingly unruly behaviour of some of the young as the war went on.[126] There had been problems before, complaints of bad language used by some youths in the town, and of children making noise at night and keeping Lutterworth's shopkeepers from their sleep. There had also been reports of vandalism at the Recreation Ground, blamed on the young, even of youths of fifteen and sixteen disrupting the Christmas morning church service by throwing snowballs into the church and hurling blocks of ice against the doors,[127] but by 1916 the council was worried by much more serious disorder, of 'street brawling and the hooliganism of youths just in their teens'. While much of this was confined to the Recreation Ground, the only area in Lutterworth where young people could gather in the evenings and at weekends free of charge, there was claimed to be a 'constant' flow of complaints from members of the public. Bad language seems to have upset most, and in particular that directed towards 'respectable ladies' who were walking out. The dark winter nights seem to have made things worse rather than better, presumably because it was more difficult to identify the culprits, especially after the blackout was introduced. The council was clearly shocked, and George Spencer said he had 'not heard anything to equal it'. Troublemakers should be prosecuted, they thought, as the 'only possible deterrent'.[128]

All this speaks of a growing lack of respect for authority among the young, of things threatening to get out of hand, of a perceived challenge to the social order in the town. It is possible to argue that for some young people this was an inarticulate form of protest, of objection to what the war was doing to their town and their country, or, alternatively, that the town fathers were more than usually anxious, given the circumstances. Warning notices about unruly behaviour had already been put up around Lutterworth on several occasions, and had been ignored. One councillor, Mr Taylor, blamed the 'depletion of the police force' for the problem and suggested that the special constables be instructed to take the matter in hand. We may ask, though, how much authority the special constables actually carried. Back in September the chief constable, addressing the Lutterworth Magistrates, had gone to great lengths to praise the specials and the work they did, particularly in face of the Zeppelin threat when they might be called from their beds in the middle of the night to supervise the 'adjustment of the lighting' and the enforcement of the blackout. The chief constable said that 'he mentioned this openly, because he felt it was his duty, so that the public might know when they saw any person wearing the badge that it was an honourable distinction, and one greatly appreciated by himself.'[129] The fact that the chief constable himself felt it necessary to speak out in defence of the specials suggests that there was a need to uphold and reinforce their authority.

But lack of enforcement cannot fully explain the perceived upsurge in teenage violence in Lutterworth. Behind it – and beyond the jurisdiction of Parish Council and chief constable alike – was the departure of so many of Lutterworth's men for the Front. Conscription during 1916 would compound the problem, taking older married men, husbands and fathers, away to the army and leaving many more mothers with the burden of coping with their children alone, often unwillingly. As Ben Beazley put it, 'for the first time in modern history, society was experiencing the creation on a grand scale of what were, to all intents and purposes, single parent families'.[130] For those families in which the father had been lost forever, the problem was, of course, even worse.

All this came on top of concerns over the sexual welfare of the young: the Ruri-Decanal Conference, meeting in Lutterworth in the spring of 1918, feared that 'the Church was winning the battle against intemperance, but losing it against impurity… It remains urgently necessary to raise public and private opinion on purity of life'.[131] 'Purity' had been the theme of the 1914 Ruri-Decanal Conference held in Lutterworth, *before* the outbreak of war, when Major Corbet Smith had blamed 'poor parenting': 'The responsibility for the greater part rested with the parents in allowing young people to roam about at night,' he was reported as saying then, and 'it was in this way much of the evil commenced'.[132] If that diagnosis was right, then by the latter stages of the war the moral peril for the young must inevitably have been all the greater – especially in view of the Major's own evident success in pushing men into the army and sending them away to France.

★

But violence and disorder were not confined to the young, the anti-German hysteria in the early weeks of the war fuelled sporadic outbursts of crowd violence across the country directed against anyone who stood out as 'different' or 'foreign'. To help whip up this atmosphere was the war's first great spy scandal. The activities of Karl Ernst, a hairdresser from Shoreditch, had been known to British Intelligence since 1911, and on the outbreak of war Ernst and several members of his spy ring, such as it was, were arrested. In all, twenty-one were rounded up and packed off to jail.[133] If further confirmation was needed, in October came the trial for espionage of the far more dangerous Carl Lody, a genuine spy with real naval knowledge. Unlike all the other spy trials in the First World War, Lody's case was heard in public and reported in detail in the press. Lody did not get off as lightly as Ernst: he was shot in the Tower of London on November 6th.[134] It was perfect food for spy mania and perfect food for a xenophobic fear of anyone with a foreign sounding name or background. Innocent people, hitherto accepted as a quaint addition to British life, now ignored the Home Secretary's reassuring observation that 'the great majority of Germans remaining in this country are peaceful and innocent persons from whom no danger is to be feared'.[135]

Suddenly, these harmless folk were seen as sinister, a fifth column even before the phrase had been invented. From the very outset of the war people with foreign sounding names had found themselves particularly vulnerable, as 'public opinion' or 'mob rule' took over in some places. In the first days of the war in nearby Rugby there were shades of things to come as a Dr. Krumbholz's friends had to publish the fact that he had not left the town to take his place in the *German* Army, as was widely believed, but that he was, in fact, *British*, born in London, and had been mobilised into his Territorial Regiment, the Royal Warwickshires.[136]

Worse was to follow. At ten o'clock on the evening of Tuesday August 11th 1914, a mob several hundred strong gathered outside a second-hand clothes shop in Warwick Street in Rugby, owned by a family with a 'foreign' name. The members of the crowd apparently believed the family to be German Jews. Only when the man came out of his shop, risking life and limb, and showed them a photograph of himself in his Russian Army uniform was the no doubt drunken crowd convinced that he was on their side. They went away singing 'For he's a jolly good fellow'.[137] (The potential for mob violence was there already. Two socialists who had attempted to speak against the war in the town's market place on the previous Sunday evening had had to be rescued from a hostile and violent crowd by the police.[138]).

Feelings would run higher yet. The sinking of the *Lusitania* on May 7th 1915 provoked a wave of anti-German riots across Britain, even though many of those attacked were as much innocent bystanders as those who had gone down with the great ship.[139] In the days after the sinking the press in Leicester, as elsewhere, did its best to incite hatred of all things German. Day after day there were headline stories, full of moral outrage and sound and fury at this extraordinary atrocity. Much play was made of the 'women and children' who went down with the ship and, in Leicester, of the few local men who had survived the sinking: Mr Harold Ramsbottom was interviewed at length by the local press about his experience. The anti-German riots in Liverpool, London and elsewhere were lovingly reported in all their detail, and on Monday the 10th the *Leicester Daily Mercury* published the heart-rending story of Mrs Booth, a former Groby school mistress, resident in Canada, who had been on her way home to visit her parents in Hugglescote on board the *Lusitania* and who was now listed among the missing. The brother and sister of the missing woman were reported *en route* to Queenstown to find Mrs Booth's baby and try to find Mrs Booth herself. The article was accompanied by a delightful photograph of mother and child. [140]

If this was not an incitement to violence, it did not fall far short. On Wednesday May the 12th a threatening crowd gathered outside the shop of Mr George Leeson, pork butcher, on King Richard's Road in Leicester. The pubs had just called time and a couple of women lobbed half-bricks through Mr Leeson's shop windows. More missiles followed. 'Feelings began to run high,' reported the *Leicester Daily Post*, 'without any particular cause being assignable to it.'[141] Why poor Mr Leeson? The answer seems to be that he had once entertained Ramsay MacDonald, and, the previous year, had thought of taking a holiday in Germany.[142] Mr Leeson was distraught. He'd never been to Germany and had spent last year's holiday in Jersey. 'Only last week,' he protested, 'I gave a couple of pounds to the Belgian Trade Unionists' Fund and I also sent off a parcel of bacon for the English prisoners in Germany.'[143]

There were other, more subtle indications of public outrage; 'Whites Jewellers, Granby Street, are All-British Jewellers', announced a notice in the *Leicester Mail*. 'British capital, British assistants, British goods; no foreigner of any nationality or naturalised German is connected with Whites in any way whatever.'[144] Others had made such declarations before; many more would yet. Not since the roasting of infants' feet in Belgium had the British propaganda circus had such fun or caused so much harm.

In Leicestershire the chief constable warned his men that 'Aliens, espec. Germans, [are] to be carefully observed, eyes and ears to be kept open,' and that 'even Englishmen may give help to the enemy',[145] and, from the outset, the Leicestershire Police were vigilant. A Mr Trawton from Coalville, to the north of the county, was identified as a 'possible German', and the local police were told to 'keep look out' on him.[146] Their hand had been strengthened by the 'Aliens Restriction Act', passed by Parliament on August 5th 1914, and the further legislation which followed. All aliens had to register; none could move more than five miles from their homes and any change of address must be notified; they were not allowed to possess any firearms or explosives without express written permission; they could not hold more than three gallons (about 13.5 litres) of petrol, though they were also banned from owning any motor car, motor cycle or aeroplane; they could not own signalling equipment, including carrier and homing pigeons; they were not allowed to use any kind of code or cipher in their letters. Everyone was expected to seek out these 'enemies of the state' and report any who had not registered or acted suspiciously, to the police.

One 'enemy alien' was the husband of Mrs Jessie Seebach, who had lived amicably enough with their neighbours in the village of Cotesbach, a mile down the Rugby Road from Lutterworth, the home of the formidable Mrs Marriott.

Jessie was married to Frank Gottlieff Seebach: whether he was German or Austrian is unclear, but Frank was interned under an order issued on May 13th, 1915. It was as much for the protection of people like him from the violent attacks made by British city mobs in the wake of the sinking of the *Lusitania* as for any reason of national security. Meanwhile, Jessie, who was forty-one, had to throw herself on the mercy of the Poor Law in order to survive, and so became enmeshed in the workings of government bureaucracy. Jessie was granted ten shillings a week, which she had to appear before the Poor Law Guardians to collect and sign for every week – no doubt a necessary but still a petty humiliation, the money then being deducted from the allowance paid to her husband in his internment camp.[147]

In 1916 a new shadow, a new fear, would appear over inland Leicestershire when a Zeppelin passed over, bombing Loughborough in the north of the county, killing ten and injuring eight more. The Zeppelin, the L20, was seen in the sky over Bitteswell and Lutterworth on the night of 31st January 1916, and the waves of panic it caused resonate through the documents. The Bitteswell Church Council met in emergency session and decided that the church must be insured for £5,000 against air raids, though with a hint of optimism, or meanness, the policy was to run only for six months, until the lighter evenings of the summer. Sunday evening services in the winter were moved to 3 p.m. and the choir was to practise in the afternoon, not the evening.[148] To the north of Lutterworth in the township of Blaby, the tops of the street lights were first painted black and then turned off completely; and the mother of a boy who 'unscrewed the pipe of a [gas] lamp on the church wall and lit the gas' was fined the not inconsiderable sum of five shillings – whether for wasting gas or endangering the blackout is not specified.[149]

The Magistrates' Courts had to deal with a steady trickle of those who had breached the regulations and allowed a light to show at night. John Whyment of Station Road in Lutterworth was one such, caught showing lights on one night in September of 1916. He and his female companions appear to have found the matter rather amusing, and even switched their lights back on after assuring Inspector Holland that they would comply. The inspector took a dim view of the case (or to the disrespect shown to his office): 'There was now far too much laxity in the district with regards to lights,' he was reported to have told the court, 'and whether it was a policeman or a special constable who complained it was absolutely necessary for public safety that their instructions should be attended to'. The magistrates concurred and, after reminding the defendant that the maximum penalty was £100, they fined him thirty shillings – still three times their normal punishment.[150] So now 'the lamps were going out' in Lutterworth as well.

If we were to search for one word to sum up the condition of the local community as the first year of the war dragged by it would be *anxiety*. It was not *fear* as such, for fear can be reduced or overcome if the right steps are taken. Anxiety is more a general, pervasive uncertainty of what the future might hold, difficult if not impossible to combat, a universal part of the human condition.[151] There was anxiety about the progress of the war as the first Christmas came and went with no resolution in sight: no one doubted that Britain would *win*, but when and at what cost? There was also anxiety among the family and friends of those who had gone to fight, a position which inevitably might lead to their loved ones' deaths; and, for the first time, anxiety about air raids. With the men away it was almost taken for granted that some women might lose their moral way, and some youths might run amuck, an anxiety about a possible social and spiritual breakdown. Behind it all was the grinding spectre of poverty and of families having to cope in straitened circumstances for the duration, however long that might be. All this brought with it the need to find scapegoats against whom all those anxieties could be focussed, scapegoats in the form of those suspected of foreign origin or connection, or those who were in some way different: people whose names sounded strange or foreign, or people whose attitude to the war was not that of the majority.

★

In the midst of such anxiety, how was the Payne family coping?

Basket makers, like the Paynes, now found their products in high demand for the safe transport of shells from Britain to France and Flanders and, in due course, to the Middle East and beyond. 'Shell baskets' were cylindrical containers into which larger shells could be placed for their journey to the ammunition dumps across the sea. Smaller shells could be moved in large wickerwork racks (rather like wine racks), which were light, disposable and, most important, spark free. In Leicestershire the Peach family had set up a kind of co-operative called the 'Dryad Company', which contracted out big orders to small local firms across the county, including the Paynes of Lutterworth. So it was that John Payne accepted a huge contract for making shell baskets for the army, an order which can only have increased following the 'Great Shell Shortage' of 1915 when Britain's failure at the Battles of Neuve Chapelle and Aubers Ridge was blamed on a shortage of explosive shells.[152] Wickerwork had other important uses in the Great War and the military demand was high. There were baskets to be hung below observation balloons on the Western Front to give intrepid observers a view of what was happening behind enemy trench lines. The navy saw only slowly the potential for airborne observation kite balloons for spotting enemy ships beyond the horizon and for the protecting of convoys by seeing submerged U-Boats through the water, but when it did, demand for the kind of wickerwork done by the Paynes rose again.[153] As the war went on the Payne family business readily accepted other government contracts. In July of 1916 Jessie Payne, the boys' mother, wrote to Leonard to tell him how:

'Dad is doing Areoplane *[sic]* seats for the Dryad. Dora is helping him she can manage very nicely ~~three~~ four lines across. My word she is excited, always telling us what she had earned. 3/6 this week'.[154]

Thus this, in every sense, *family* business was doing its bit towards the war effort. 'Doing their bit' of course, fell short of volunteering to fight.

★

The war came home to the Payne family for all that. Among the bundle of Payne letters is a fragment, undated, its last page or pages with the signature, missing, lacking a clear return address. The part we have reads:

'18th Apl / 15
Sunday
Dear Len,

I received your letter about ten days ago, and intended answering it before, but was very upset when I heard about Father's death that I did not feel like letter writing.

You can guess what a shock it was to me when I received the telegram telling me about it.

I tried to get leave to come home for the funeral, but could not get it. I should very much like to have got *[sic]* for a few days, but perhaps after all it was as well I didn't as I should not *[sic]* liked to have come out here again.

We came out of the trenches on Thursday night, and we now are a few miles behind the firing line for a short rest to recouperate *[sic]* our health.

We are billeted at a farm and sleep in a barn. We have to wash in the ditch water along the road-side, and the water for breakfast and tea we have to fetch from about ½ mile away.

Have just come back from church parade, which was held in the field, and all the Batt: *[Battalion]* attended.

We also had one last Sun: and also Palm Sunday, but we were in the trenches at Easter and got relieved on Easter Monday. *[Easter Sunday was on April 4ᵗʰ in 1915.]*

The trenches we have just come out of are only 100 yards from the Germans, so you see we have been pretty close to them. I don't know how long we are here for, or where we go to next, but suppose we shall take up a fresh position at some hot spot.

I saw in the Rugby paper that Edgar Chamberlain was at the Battle of Neuve Chapelle, so I expect he had a warm time of it.

I see by the casualty lists that several of our Coy [*Company*] from? Minster? were killed or wounded there.

Did you see in the *Rugby Advertiser* about Dale from Easenhall behind *[sic]* killed. He was in this Coy and was not far from us when he was killed.

The weather out here has been changeable, but the last few days have been grand, although it is very…' *[The letter ends here].* [155]

It is not very difficult to identify the author of the letter as Harold Buck. Harold's father, Thomas Buck, was buried on 10ᵗʰ April 1915, the service conducted by the minister Arthur Massey in the Congregational Chapel, a service which Harold had not been released to attend, the interment being in Lutterworth Parish Church graveyard.[156] Harold Buck, three years older than Leonard, had been a pupil at the town's Sherrier Elementary School but had moved up to the grammar school in 1906 (where Leonard did not follow him) when he must have been fourteen. The two boys grew up together, both at school and in the Congregational Church Sunday School, and it could be that they were among the boys whom the superintendent, Mr Bishop, had cause to complain of because of their unruly behaviour during services – though we imagine that parental discipline in both families would be powerful enough to stamp that out.[157] The Bucks, like the Paynes, were well-to-do on a modest scale, Harold's father Thomas supporting his wife, Annie, and his family of four children, of whom Harold was the youngest. After trying his hand as an accounts clerk with the British Thomson-Houston (B.T.H.) company in Rugby, Harold had joined the army. He was mobilised with his regiment, The Rifle Brigade.[158] Like the Paynes, the Bucks were stalwarts of the Congregational Church in Lutterworth, and the references to the church parades clearly suggest a shared interest. The Bucks lived round the corner from the Paynes, in Baker Street Yard, and Harold's father Thomas was, appropriately enough, a baker and confectioner.[159] Their friendship must have been close indeed. This is the only personal letter written to the Paynes by anyone in the armed forces; even Harold's chosen military profession, and the disagreements which this must have spawned, had not come between them. Harold's letter is matter-of-fact, stoical, moving quickly away from the intensely emotional response to his father's death and his inability to comfort his mother and siblings when they needed him most, refusing to dwell on that comment that if he did come home he would not want to go back, sparse in its details of his time in the trenches. It is a letter powerful for what it does not say, a communications between two friends who did not need or want flowery expressions, who perhaps did not quite know how to express their inner feelings.

Harold's letter also gives us insights into that small world these young men inhabited. Frank Dale[160] of Easenhall, a village across the Warwickshire border, half a dozen miles from Lutterworth, had been killed outside Ypres on March 22nd. Harold and Frank were members of the same military outfit, the 1st Battalion Rifle Brigade, and it is probable that both knew Len through the chapel. Frank was one of 'Kitcheners' Volunteers'; he had signed up on September 2nd 1914, presumably under aged, because he was reported as being not yet nineteen when he died[161]; certainly, the photograph of him which appeared in the *Rugby Advertiser* on April 10th 1915 (the edition which Harold must have read in the trenches) is of a boy barely old enough to shave.

Not that everyone out with the army reacted like that. Edgar Chamberlain lived within a few yards of both the Paynes and the Bucks, but his response to the experience of war was quite different, and helps us define a wider range of responses. The letter he wrote home after the Battle of Neuve Chapelle, and which was published in the same edition of the local newspaper which reported the violent death of young Frank Dale, was full of excitement, of the thrill and adventure of war, of post-battle euphoria. Chamberlain wrote:

'We have had a warm time this journey and I trust we struck a very effective blow for the Old Country, judging by the results we left on the battlefield. We made an attack on the German trenches in broad daylight, and actually succeeded in capturing several lines of them, and advanced quite a mile at the point of the bayonet. Our big guns started "the show", as the captain called it. After a terrific bombardment of their trenches the order was given for us to mount the parapet and charge (our platoon leading). All seemed quite eager. There was no hesitation. Our lieutenant took the lead, and soon we were all charging as fast as the nature of the ground would permit. Of course, our guns had done a lot of damage, but there were still many of the enemy to be dealt with.

After this had been done we set about making our position secure, as of course there was bound to be a counter attack. Well, we had not long to wait for it. Just before dawn the next morning a heavy rifle fire announced the approach of the enemy. On they came, and got pretty close, but were gradually repulsed. As the day broke we saw them lying literally in heaps, many dead, some moving about in agony, and others shamming death (as we found out afterwards). The only result of their counter attack was that they took possession of a length of trench which ran nearly at right angles to the one in which we were, and as we could get a glimpse of them occasionally we had a go at peppering them. Soon the place was too warm, and they began to creep out one by one and take to their heels. Very few, however, got away. As each man crept out hundreds of rifles were brought on him, and down he stumbled, never to get up again. This could not last long, and soon the white flag was raised, and out they came to the top of the trench. A more abject, craven looking lot I never saw as they stood or knelt with their hands up imploring mercy. Of course, there were exceptions, and I could not help admiring one or two men who carried wounded comrades on their backs to our lines. As the prisoners marched in some from among the heaps of apparently dead got up and joined them.' He added, almost as an afterthought: 'Of course, we had our casualties, and I have lost one or two of my pals.'[162]

Chamberlain was describing his part in the British attack launched on March 10th 1915, and which is known as the Battle of Neuve Chapelle, an assault which won spectacular success (in trench warfare terms at least) in its first few hours, as Chamberlain claimed, but which soon became bogged down with the loss of 13,000 British lives and a roughly equal number of sons of German mothers. Chamberlain's is not *the* authentic voice of the trenches, but it is certainly *an* authentic voice, and it comes from a man who was a part of the same community as the conscientious objectors who lived a hundred yards away.

Leonard's reply to his friend Harold gives us our first and only intimate glimpse of any of the Payne family at this stage of the war. With a postscript added at the top of the first page, this is Leonard's letter in its entirety:

'P.S. I have posted you off a small box *[?]* and little gift from home. I hope you receive it all right.

Church Street
Lutterworth
Sunday May 2nd, 1915

Dear Harold,
    Thanks for your letter received last Wednesday. I thought it had got lost or something seeing as I did not hear from you, but I quite understand how upset

you would be when you heard of your father's death. I felt very sorry for you, specially as you were so far away from home and in so dangerous a place too. I wished very much that you would get over so that we could see you again, and have a good talk, but as you say you and your people would have felt it very hard when you had to go back again so perhaps it was best. Things are about the same in the old town, a little better if anything now that the summer is approaching. But still it will not be like the old times it is miserable at the best of times with all the fellows away. I feel very lonely sometimes just as if I have not a friend in the world, I never see Bob above five minutes a week, and Nellie seems to have quite fallen out with me but what for I do not know, but still I must keep plodding along and looking forward to the time when all will be peace and quietness once more and may it not be long. I think ~~may~~ *[sic]* my only friend is my motor bicycle which I have bought, I can amuse myself a little by riding it and cleaning it etc, but I wish you were here so that you could have a ride on the back, it is fine. I played the organ at the Cong Chapel last Sunday in the morning, I felt very nervous being may *[sic]* first appearance in public but I got on fairly well and have played at the week-night service since. Miss Coles is going away for a nurse in a week or two so I suppose Mrs Spencer and I will take it in turns playing at the services. I went in for another Scripture exam in March and passed with a first class certificate the only one in the school. I am glad that you are having good weather it is jolly hot here but as you say cold at nights. I really don't know what else to talk about except Gladys, I am glad you still here *[sic]* from her I thought she perhaps had stopped writing to you after the little upset some time ago that I think I told you about, I see her sometimes but never have a chance of a talk with her. I suppose you have heard that Bill Phillips is wounded in the hand but not very serious,

Holland & Gunter are all right so far I think, Albert Everton has not gone to the front again he is in the Isle of Wight with the band so one of the wounded soldiers say *[sic]* that knows him and is at the hospital here. We have ten wounded here in the prepared hospital, they came this week. Father went to sit up with them last ~~Sun~~ night, people are taking it in turns there. Jack Holland saw Jack ~~Fisher~~ Fisher the other day he has been in battles since the battle of the Marne he says he looks nothing but a bundle of dirt and rags but is still smoking a cigarette, this was told me by Fred as I have not heard a word from Jack.

Goodbye for the present and good luck, good health, and a safe return we all wish you here. I remain

Yours Sincerely

Len.'[163]

P. S. I have posted you off a small box a little gift from home I hope you receive it alright.

Church Street
Lutterworth
Sunday May 2. 1915

Dear Harold

Thanks for your letter received last Wednesday. I thought it had got lost or something being as I did not hear from you, but I quite understand how upset you would be when you heard of your fathers death. I felt very sorry for you, especially as you were so far away from home and in so dangerous a place too. I wished very much that you would get over so that we could see you again, & have a good talk, but as you say you & your people would have felt it very hard when you had to go back again so perhaps it was best. Things are about the same in the old town, a little better if anything now that the summer is approaching. But still it will not be like the old times it is miserable at the best of times with all the fellows away. I feel very lonely sometimes just as if I have not a friend in the world, I never see Bob above five minutes a week, and Nellie seems to have quite fallen out with me but what for I do not know, but still I must

The first page of Leonard's letter to Harold,
2nd May 1915
(Original 200x250mm)

On the most superficial level, the letter gives us insights into Leonard's life in Lutterworth in wartime. 'It is miserable at the best of times with all the fellows away,' he writes, confessing to 'feeling very lonely sometimes just as if I had not a friend in the world' except his beloved motor bike. It is almost as if his friend Harold is the only one he can unburden himself to, especially since other friends, like Bob, have not kept contact, and Nellie 'seems to have quite fallen out with me'. The chapel, of course, gives him an important point of reference, and something positive in his life, his nervousness about playing the organ for services, but his apparent success, and that triumph in the Scripture exam ('first class certificate the only one in the school'). It would appear that of his contemporaries only Fred Holland, the son of the local police inspector, had spoken to him. Though he did not yet know it, Leonard's life and that of Fred and his brother Jack would become dangerously and horribly intertwined before this war was over.

What can we learn of Leonard's own state of mind from this letter? One word in twenty in this letter is 'I', which could simply reflect the nature of the letter, but also suggests a degree of self-absorption, a realisation of what his conscientious objection would cost him, extending even to self-pity. If we read those phrases again – 'miserable at the best of times', 'feel very lonely', 'not a friend in the world', 'never see Bob', 'fallen out with me' – we can see a young man wrapped up in himself and his own troubles. He talks about people other than himself, Harold and his family, and the chapel organists, Miss Coles and Mrs Spencer, only after that phrase, 'I really don't know what else to talk about' – a phrase which will appear regularly at this point in his letters. Those mentioned after that are there because they were mutual acquaintances, and as such Harold might find them interesting, not because they are central to Leonard's own life. In this intensely personal letter, he does not mention any member of his own family. He does, though, mention his motor bike, and it is not hard to understand the appeal of the freedom of the open road for a young man who needed, every now and then, to escape from his home town, if only for a short time. But even here the war threatened to impinge on his life: at the outbreak of war that call had gone out to the owners of motor cars and motor cycles to contact the Leicestershire Automobile Club to offer their vehicles for the war effort.[164] Presumably, Leonard did not respond. It had taken Harold's letter ten days to arrive with Leonard in Lutterworth; it was delivered on Wednesday April 28th. Leonard wrote his reply the following Sunday, May 2nd. It would appear that Leonard's letter was never posted, which is why it remains in the collection. Harold Buck had been killed in action at St Julien outside Ypres on Monday April 26th 1915.

For Harold's family, of course, it was a double tragedy. Thomas, Harold's father, had been buried on April 10th; then not much more than a fortnight later Harold had been killed. There would be no funeral for Harold; no remains were found to bury, and he would become one of those tens of thousands whose life and death would be recorded on the Menin Gate in Ypres. And, after the war was over, a special plaque would be put up in the Congregational Chapel in his memory. Little consolation really for his mother, Annie, and we do not know how well she coped although probably much the same as the tens of thousands of others – one day at a time. Deprived of her youngest son's comfort in the loss of her husband by the army's claim of precedence over his time and presence, she had now lost her son Harold as well, due to the army's superior claim of precedence over his life. Leonard must have been acutely aware of the Buck family's torment, for he was not only Harold's good friend, but he had also seen and met with the Bucks every week at chapel. He had even reminded Harold in his last letter that it was not only he who would have found it hard to return to the Front, but 'your people' would find his return hard as well.

Leonard had lost a friend. When he wrote his last, unposted, letter to Harold, he saw the war as a nuisance, an inconvenience. He wanted the war to end so 'the fellows' could come back; he wanted Harold to come home so they could 'have a good talk', and Harold could ride pillion on the back of his motor bike: 'it is fine', he wrote, anxious to share this new excitement with his pal. He looked forward to the time of 'peace and quietness once more', when his settled routine could be restored. The war was a temporary and passing inconvenience to him, not yet an unspeakable tragedy. Harold's death changed all that as, for the first time, the war had struck him personally. His inner thoughts are lost, for we see nothing of him until the following spring when the military came to get him.

We can perhaps gauge the impact of the death of Leonard's friend from the fact that these two letters are the only ones preserved from the time before Leonard and Roland's real troubles with the military began a year later. This last exchange had a very special meaning for Leonard and may have been a turning point for him in his self-imposed isolation; he now had to adjust to this new reality. It would be reasonable to assume that he blamed 'the military', an embodiment of which his religious principles already made him dislike and distrust, and which had now ridden roughshod over his and his friends' lives. 'The military' had forbidden Harold to return home to attend his father's funeral and comfort his mother and his siblings. He and his family had been refused that act of simple humanity by a 'military machine', which was, almost by definition, inhuman. And now that same 'military machine' had done for Harold himself.

★

Leonard was not the only one left bereft. In the beginning the war was carried to the Germans by the Regular Army, the professionals, the original 'Old Contemptibles', like Harold (though he did not live long enough to be classified as such), among them some who had not lived in Lutterworth for years past – their families known, their loss felt by those who remembered them, those who had possibly been to school with them. Frederick Shortland was the first. Though there is confusion about his army records,[165] it seems clear that he was sent into action against the Germans with the Northumberland Fusiliers in support of the 4th Royal Fusiliers near the River Aisne in northern France, at Vailly, east of Soissons, on a wet and miserable Monday morning, September 14th, 1914, and was killed in heavy fighting there.[166]

It is possible that another man with a (tenuous) local connection was killed in the first weeks of the war, for Elizabeth Smith, living in Dixon's Court, up before the Lutterworth Magistrates on a charge of drunkenness in October, pleaded in extenuation that she had two sons in the army, that one had been wounded and the other was dead.[167] It is not at present possible to verify this claim, nor to say how her son came to be dead. In neighbouring Bitteswell, Edward and Elizabeth Adams lost their son, Thomas, outside Ypres, a week after the First Battle of Ypres had petered out, on a day (November 17th) when not much was happening; no body was recovered, so perhaps he was unlucky enough to be caught by an exploding shell (no body to bury) or was killed out in No Man's Land on the kind of trench raid the soldiers hated (body not recoverable). There was Henry Cooke, born in Lutterworth, raised a few miles away in Peatling Parva, a Lance-Corporal in the 1st Battalion of the Leicester Regiment – the 'Tigers' – who also died outside Ypres, just before Christmas in 1914; and Harry Goodman of the Coldstream Guards, killed in January of 1915. Like Tom Adams, neither Henry, Harry, or Fred Shortland has a grave. Richard Pindar (or Pinder) had lived with his sister and her husband, who appears to have worked for Lupton Topham in the big house off Woodmarket; a professional soldier since 1907, he was killed south of Ypres in March 1915. At least Richard has a grave of his own.[168]

More certainly recorded was Edward Bond, not a soldier but a Leading Signalman on board the Dreadnought battleship *H.M.S. Bulwark*. His parents, Charles senior and Emily, like so many in Lutterworth, came from Northamptonshire, and had moved to Lutterworth from Holdenby, apparently following their Rector, the Rev. Frederick Alderson, when he had taken over the cure of Lutterworth in 1894. They had remained in Lutterworth, living in George's Square, under the shadow of Sherrier School in the middle of town, after Frederick Alderson was succeeded as Rector by his son Montague.[169] Edward had attended

Sherrier School and as such, despite his absence as a career seaman, would have been known about the town. Edward's death was tragically absurd. A sudden, unimaginably massive explosion on the morning of November 26th literally blew his battleship to pieces while moored off Sheerness in the Medway in Kent. Winston Churchill, First Lord of the Admiralty, told the House of Commons that 'the ship had entirely disappeared when the smoke had cleared away', and divers found only bits and pieces of twisted steel on the river bed. At first a German U-Boat was suspected or even enemy sabotage. The official enquiry came to a more mundane explanation: the explosion was caused entirely by the sloppy handling of high explosives combined with, probably, a carelessly dropped cigarette end.[170] Twelve of the Bulwark's 750 crew survived, but Edward Bond was not one of them. It was a sad death, a case of wrong place, wrong time although that was no consolation to his family.

The war had not yet finished with the Bond family. Their younger son, Charles, aged only twenty-three, was killed in Belgium near the village of Verlorenhoek at the beginning of May in 1915, caught up in what came to be called the Second Battle of Ypres. That dreadful and messy battle had begun on April 22nd with clouds of chlorine gas released against the French along the northern edge of the Ypres Salient – 168 tons of the stuff from 4000 cylinders along a four mile front[171]. On a gentle northerly breeze, on a beautiful spring evening, the yellowish cloud wafted across No Man's Land. And as it came it killed. It killed the spring leaves on the trees and the birds in the air. It bleached the grass yellow. In the trenches poisoned men and rats lay side by side. Not only did it kill; it killed in a particularly horrible way. Death was caused by asphyxia, though it was not as simple as that. The gas was a powerful irritant, which attacked the lungs and corroded all mucous membranes, causing spasms of the glottis and oedema of the lungs. The heart dilated and the skin turned blue. It caused a burning sensation in the throat, the nose and the eyes. It made men blind. And as the gas was heavier than air it settled most densely in low-lying places, such as trenches cut into the ground.[172] *Then* the burning cloud of gas, cold to the breath,[173] wafted on in the calm evening sunshine towards the French support lines. By seven o'clock the gas had created a gap four and a half miles wide in the Salient, a gap in which no one was left alive to resist. The unthinkable had happened. The Germans had broken the Ypres Salient. Only a desperate last ditch resistance saved the Salient around Ypres, but the desperate British Generals could only watch as it collapsed inward like a deflating football under relentless German assaults. This is why Charles Bond, in this tiny village of Verlorenhoek, originally safely behind British lines, came to die on Monday May 3rd 1915. 'Second Ypres' was not yet over; nor had it taken its last local life.

Thursday 13th of May, Ascension Day in 1915, was the fateful day for Leicestershire, the day the Leicestershire Yeomanry went into action for the first time, and were slaughtered outside Ypres. In what was to be the last day of 'Second Ypres', the Germans launched a violent assault in torrential rain against the middle of the Salient in a final attempt to break through and take the town itself. The part-timers of the Leicestershire Yeomanry, those local men who had been 'embodied' before war had been declared, held the trench line in the middle of the assault. Trapped in their front line trench, under furious German bombardment, the troops to their left deserting their own section of the line, leaving both front and support lines entirely empty and with no communication trench to withdraw through, German troops actually entered their own trench. The Leicestershire Yeomanry lost ninety-seven men, or ninety-eight if we include the unfortunate Belgian interpreter, Monsieur du Can, who was with them at the time.[174]

The first ominously fragmentary reports of what had happened on that Thursday morning did not appear in the local newspapers until Monday, May 17th. Details were few. The deaths of Percy Evans Freke, the commander, and Leo Burton, the Leicester football star, were reported in the *Leicester Daily Mercury* on that day, alongside vague reports that the Yeomanry had been in action and other casualties must be expected. On Sunday, a long list of wounded of all regiments newly arrived in Leicester the day before, included only five Yeomen.[175] By Tuesday the 18th a grimmer, darker mood settled over the county as hints of the scale of what had happened began filtering through. General reports appeared, given headline status in phrases such as 'Leicester Yeomanry's Glorious Stand: Colonel and six other Officers killed'. The public was given this garbled and worrying account,

> 'In the desperate fighting which lasted throughout the whole of Thursday last, the Leicestershire Yeomanry helped to save the British lines on the Menin-Ypres road, by holding up hordes of the enemy and massed artillery, until such time as reinforcements could arrive on the scene. In the process the Yeomanry lost over 200 men.'[176]

That the Yeomanry had done something very brave and very praiseworthy was clear, but an anxious county public needed a different kind of information. The message was, 'Awaiting further details.'[177] There was much confusion but a handful of names began to appear. Sergeant John Berry, a long-standing Yeoman, would now not marry his fiancée, Gertie Ellis. His death was reported by his friend Sergeant Christian. What became of Gertie in later years we do not know. Sam

Sleath from Ullesthorpe and Francis Matthews from nearby Gilmorton were both killed, 'for dear old England, and the loved ones at home', the news passed on in a letter from Albert Lyon to a friend in Sutton in the Elms, and then reported in the press.[178] There were survivors too. The two Bevin brothers from Ashby Magna had survived, though Roland was shot in the leg.[179] In some cases, relief bore the scars of tangible loss. Bob Strond wrote home to say he was well, 'but there is one fellow whom I shall miss terribly. He is Frank White, a young fellow from Quorn, who was in my section. He has been my pal all the way through. We always marched together. As a matter of fact we have been through everything side by side. On the day we were told to go up, he was asked with me to stay behind; we spun up a coin to see if we should go or not, and he went, and, poor chap, was killed whilst fighting. He was an absolute gentleman. Even his horse and mine are the greatest pals.'[180] Press reports like these must have had a massive impact on those who read them.

But then there were those, like William Smith from Lutterworth, the seventeen-year-old son of James Basil Smith and his wife Elizabeth of Baker Street, who were listed as 'missing'.[181] 'Missing' meant exactly what it said, and, given the nature of the action on Ascension Day, there were bound to be many men in this group. The initial list contained eighty-one names. The Horse Guards, who had gone through the trenches after the last counter-attack, had collected no identity discs, so the missing must include unknown numbers who were no longer alive. And since the new British front line had been dug further back than the original one, which was now out in No Man's Land, there could be no way of confirming or refuting individual identities; and there would be no way until that narrow strip of land was retaken by the British on the first day of the Passchendaele Offensive over two years away. By that time there would be little left to recover. The uncertainty must for the relatives and friends have been agonising. What were they to make of things when they read in the official list published on Wednesday the 19th of May that among the missing were Sergeant Wright and Troopers Fewkes and Rhodes, when the *Leicester Daily Post* had already published interviews with the two troopers alive and well and living at the North Evington Military Hospital in Leicester, and the *Leicester Mail* had published an interview with the sergeant, who was clearly not missing at all?[182] If these men were not in fact missing, then perhaps there was still hope for some at least of the other men posted in that agonising category of missing. Or what should they make of this report which they read in their newspapers on the 19th May the heading, 'Letter from "Dead" Officer'? The story was of a Lieutenant in the Durham Light Infantry who had been reported killed, but had now written home to say that he was in fact a prisoner of war. 'His supposed death may have arisen through him being left wounded on the battlefield after an engagement,' reported the *Leicester Mail*.[183]

Less helpful was the remark by the press baron Alfred Harmsworth, Lord Northcliffe, whose *Amalgamated Press* became such a major source of public information about the war, that 'it is more than possible that there is a considerable number of men who have been reported as missing and dead who are not missing or dead at all. One case was discovered, of a soldier who had been reported missing for more than a year but who was found in comfortable surroundings doing duty as an army cook in a totally different part of the field from that in which he had disappeared.'[184] Further hopes were raised in the hearts of stricken relatives when four privates, previously reported as missing, turned up alive and well, and no less than twenty-five other missing men were discovered among the wounded. Even locally, one of these miracles occurred: Sergeant Hutt was eventually able to return to his home in the village of Walcote outside Lutterworth, no doubt to the enormous relief and joy of his family.[185] Sadly, he would be one of the few.[186]

In small communities like these the missing and the dead were real people with families, school friends and 'pals', with all the power and emotion that word carried at that time, with networks of relationships, positive and negative, and histories of their own. They were not mere names carved on war memorial stones. Their mothers and their fathers lived next door or just down the street; their sweethearts, no doubt, were inconsolable. How much of a consolation could it have been that politicians and journalists, few of whom would ever get to confront the war face to face, tried to find a meaning to the conflict? One local newspaper wrote, under the headline 'More Yeomen Wanted' (to replace those slaughtered on Ascension Day), that 'in song and story the yeomen of England have figured as the flower of our manhood. They are the pride of our race, and represent the type of men who have fought and died in the long line of battles from Agincourt down through the centuries to the modern Armageddon'.[187] The comment appeared next to the column which contained a seemingly endless list of Leicestershire Yeomen 'Killed', 'Wounded' and 'Missing'.

Innocence and glory alike foundered in 1915 in the Flanders' mud and the disease-ridden squalor of the Dardanelles and Mesopotamia. And the death toll among local men continued to mount. In June 1915 Ypres claimed the life of William Foulkes: he had joined up, into the 1/6th Royal Warwickshire Regiment, on the same day as his friend William Wright from Bitteswell Road in Lutterworth. (William Wright survived the fighting at Ypres, only to be killed on the terrible first day of the Battle of the Somme, 1st July 1916, along with 19,239 others.[188]) Henry Pulman died at Ypres on September 25th, the same day that Edmund Day from

Station Road was killed, aged nineteen, at Loos, thirty miles away down the line to the south, close to where Charles Thorne would be killed in October. Less dramatic, but still a war death, was Alfred Carter who had lived near Edmund Day on Station Road, dead from liver and gall bladder disease at his base in Cheshire, and buried there. On Christmas Eve, in far-away Iraq, Arthur Corrall from Bank Street died of wounds in the 'filthy little Arab mud-heap'[189] of Kut on the Tigris in Mesopotamia, surrounded by Turkish troops, and with no real possibility of escape. The British garrison in Kut surrendered four months later on April 29th 1916 after a terrible siege.[190] At Gallipoli a month or so later, Wycliffe Sarson, a navy man fighting on land, was killed on June 4th, during an abortive assault against the Turkish defences.[191] So far, the town had lost fourteen sons not counting those lost to the surrounding villages and 1915 was only just out. The war had indeed come home to Lutterworth and it was nowhere near ending yet.

This was not the war those who had so enthusiastically joined in 1914 had expected. As Jay Winter has observed: 'A war that is supposed to have a beginning, a middle, and an end, had a middle and a middle, and then another middle, and then another year and another battle and another last push, and a middle that went on and on and on.'[192] So, a grimmer mood had now set in, far removed from the patriotic determination of just sixteen months earlier when there had been a tangible sense of doing something glorious and honourable and right. 'Brave little Belgium' and its sacred neutrality were now hardly mentioned and 'Flanders' became the preferred name. Those refugees were now seen as tiresome, unattractive and dull, no longer the point of the war. The vocabulary of 'glory' and 'patriotism' had given way to the much heavier, more serious; a language of 'duty', 'honour' and 'loyalty', but also of 'sacrifice' and 'redemption'.[193]

The generals had failed to win the war, and it was now plain to all, whatever gloss the propaganda machine might want to impose upon it, that this war would run and run until one side or the other dropped dead from exhaustion. This was now the principal assumption of the war. The war had taken on a momentum of its own which neither side could control any longer; the war would now devour its own children. Too much had been committed, too much already spent, too much sacrificed to end in anything short of total victory. Now the focus would shift a little, towards those who refused to 'do their bit' to help secure that final victory. The war was about to visit the Payne brothers, and the warning, spoken by William Green of the adult school movement in Leicester on the last Sunday of peace, that 'they would not have any option about going to war, but they would be fetched',[194] was about to be fulfilled. The needs of the nation now meant that Leonard and Roland themselves would come into the firing line, one way or the other.

Basket weavers in Castle Donington making shell baskets.
Photograph from Castle Donington Museum
http://www.castledoningtonmuseum.org.uk

NOTES & REFERENCES

1. *Victoria County History of Leicestershire, Vol. 3*, p. 284. E.E. Snow, (*A History of Leicestershire Cricket, Leicester*, 1949, p. 240) blamed the defeat on bad light during Leicestershire's second innings. Dennis Lambert, (*The History of Leicestershire County Cricket Club*, London, 1992, p. 86,) wrote that it was A.T. Sharp's departure for war service which 'in effect lost Leicestershire the match'. Excuses, excuses... 1914 was, in fact, Aubrey Sharp's sixth First Class season; he survived the Great War intact, and from 1921 captained the team with distinction. A long-standing Vice President of the club, he was killed in a road accident in 1973 at the age of eighty-four. (I am grateful to Pat Mannion for this reference.) Out in the county many local league games were being played out. Woodhouse beat Shepshed Town after bowling them all out for just forty-two. Blaby Village went one better, taking all of Earl Shilton Albion's wickets for thirty-five runs. Apparently, Leicestershire that season did not possess much depth in batting. (See for example, *A Century of Cricket: A History of Shepshed Town Cricket Club from 1869 to 1969*, Shepshed, 1969.)

2. Sidney E. Coleman, *Leicester as I Remember it*, in *The Leicestershire Historian*, 1978-9. It has been estimated that twenty million people went to the cinema each week in Great Britain by 1914. George L. Mosse, *Fallen Soldiers. Reshaping the Memory of the World Wars*, O.U.P., 1990, p. 147.

3. *Wright's Directory of Leicester*, 1914. On the Leicester Palace Theatre, see Helen and Richard Leacroft, *The Theatre in Leicestershire. A History of Entertainment in the County from the 15th Century to the 1960s*, pub. Leicestershire Libraries and Information Service, Leicester, 1986, pp. 99-102. Its bar was, apparently, one of its main attractions. The music halls were criticised by many moralists as the source of many of society's moral ailments. (Alfred Emmott (President), *The Nation's Morals, Being the Proceedings of the Public Morals Conference held in London on the 14th and 15th July 1910*, Cassell, London, 1910, p. 188.)

4. *Leicester Mercury*, 1st August, 1914.

5. *Leicester Daily Post*, 5th August, 1914, reported that they had been 'detained in London' – though they would not, of course, be there for long. The previous Wednesday the Congregational Sunday School had enjoyed its annual treat, a trip to Abbey Park in Leicester 'in breaks and wagonettes' rather than the more expensive but far more

convenient railway. Much of the day must have been spent in travelling, though no doubt they sang their way there and their way back – those who hadn't fallen asleep. *Rugby Advertiser*, 1st August 1914.

6. *Leicester Mercury*, 3rd August 1914. We can suppose also that some people from Lutterworth had gone to Leicester for a day out. Back in June the *Rugby Advertiser* had reported that Whitsun in Lutterworth was very quiet because so many people had gone away by train for the holiday – though Lutterworth had its own distractions that weekend. *Rugby Advertiser*, 6th June 1914.

7. *Leicester Mercury*, 1st August 1914.

8. A local newspaper observed, 'the town is invariably quiet on Bank Holidays, there being little out of the ordinary to attract visitors'. *Rugby Advertiser*, 8th August 1914.

9. *Rugby Advertiser*, 8th August 1914.

10. Robert B. Asprey, *The German High Command at War*, Warner Books, London, 1994, p. 47.

11. *Leicester Daily Mercury*, 3rd August 1914.

12. John Keegan, *A History of Warfare*, Hutchinson, London, 1993, p. 307.

13. The phrase is William McNeill's, in *A World History*, Oxford University Press, Oxford, 1979, p. 492. More recently Terence Zuber has questioned the very existence of the Schlieffen Plan: 'There never was a Schlieffen Plan,' he writes. (p. 9.) Instead he identifies a series of German war plans, continuously modified to meet changing circumstances in the years before 1914. Further, he argues that German planning did not envisage a deep invasion of France aimed at the annihilation of the French Army, such as what happened, but a more limited series of 'ordinary victories', which would free up troops to be sent east against the Russians. Seeking to contradict those who would use the Schlieffen Plan as evidence of German aggression and war guilt, Zuber argues that 'there was no such timetable [of invasion] in the German war plans – ever. If there was, as A.J.P. Taylor thought, a "War by Timetable", then that timetable was Franco-Russian.' (Terence Zuber, *The Real German War Plan 1904-14*, The History Press, Stroud, 2011, p. 184 and pp. 147-9 and 174-87.)

14. *War 1914: Punishing the Serbs*, Stationery Office, London, 1999, p. 192. The best account of the outbreak of war remains Barbara Tuchman, *August 1914*, Constable, London, 1962.

15. On Friday, 31st July, the *Leicester Daily Mercury* reprinted a piece from Lord Northcliffe's *Times* newspaper which concluded that: 'The instinct of self-preservation, which is the strongest factor in national life, therefore compels us – if the efforts of our government to keep the peace should fail – to be ready to strike with all our force for our own safety and for that of our friends.' *Leicester Daily Mercury*, 31st July 1914. The issue of whether the article was officially-inspired or not was deliberately and overtly fudged in the

newspapers which printed it. It was, in fact, a brilliant piece of sleight of hand, written by J.W. Flanagan, a journalist at *The Times*, to advance the newspaper's oft-repeated view that Britain must be prepared to go to war against Germany. (Henry Wickham Steed, *Through Thirty Years, 1892-1922. A Personal Narrative*, Heinemann, London, 1924, Vol. 2, pp. 6-7.)

16. Niall Ferguson, *The Pity of War*, Allen Lane, The Penguin Press, London, 1998, pp. 181-3. On the other side of what would become No Man's Land the great German writer Hermann Hesse took a similar view on the responsibility of artists when war broke out. In an article of September 1914 he asked: 'We artists, writers, and journalists – can it be our function to make things worse than they are? Is the situation not already ugly and deplorable enough?… It is absurd and wrong that any man who ever, in a lucid hour, believes in the idea of humanity, in international thought, in an artistic beauty cutting across national boundaries, should now, frightened by the monstrous thing that has happened, throw down the banner and relegate what is best in him to the general ruin… Precisely this wretched World War must make us more keenly aware that love is higher than hate, understanding than anger, peace than war. Or what would be the good of it?' (Hermann Hesse, *O Freunde, nicht diese Töne!* translated by Ralph Manheim, in *If the War goes on… : Reflections on War and Politics*, Picador, London, 1974, pp. 13-17.) Hesse's voice, like that of those Oxbridge scholars, was drowned out by the calls for war. Whoever listens to academics and artists anyway?

17. *Leicester Daily Mercury*, 1st August 1914.

18. *Leicester Daily Mercury*, 3rd August 1914.

19. ibid.

20. *Leicester Daily Mercury*, 4th August 1914.

21. Text reprinted in Grey, *Twenty-Five Years. 1892-1916*, Hodder and Stoughton, London, 1925. Vol. 2, Appendix D, pp. 294-309. It is interesting to note that Britain's insistence on defending the rights of small nations to live free and independent lives did not extend to the Irish, who were not, presumably, considered nation enough, nor to any other subjects of the British Empire.

22. Sir Arthur Nicholson, Permanent Under-Secretary, quoted by Henry Wickham Steed, op. cit. pp. 26-7.

23. A.J.P. Taylor commented on the Foreign Secretary, Sir Edward Grey, that: 'If there is criticism of Grey, it must be that he had not educated the British public enough in the previous years'.) Lloyd George testified to the lack of consideration of Foreign Policy issues throughout the government's life. (David Lloyd George, *War Memoirs*, Odhams, London, 1938 edn, pp. 27 and 33-4.) Some Germans blamed Grey for failing to use his influence to prevent Russian mobilisation. (See G. Lowes Dickinson, *The International Anarchy, 1904-1914*, pub. The Century Co., New York & London, 1926,

p. 457.) The French, on the other hand, blamed him for refusing to declare British support for France in the event of a German invasion, thus failing to deter German aggression. In a letter from Asquith to his special friend Venetia Stanley, written on August 2nd, he rehearsed the arguments and thus clarified his own thoughts: '1. We have no obligation of any kind either to France or Russia to give them military or naval help. 2. The despatch of the expeditionary force to help France at this moment is out of the question and would serve no object. 3. We mustn't forget the ties created by our long-standing and intimate friendship with France. 4. It is against British interests that France should be wiped out as a great power. 5. We cannot allow Germany to use the Channel as a hostile base. 6. We have obligations to Belgium to prevent her being utilized and absorbed by Germany.' (Quoted by Naomi B. Levine in *Politics, Religion and Love. The Story of H.H. Asquith, Venetia Stanley and Edwin Montagu, based on the Life and Letters of Edwin Samuel Montagu*, New York University Press, New York and London, 1991, pp. 228-9. As Naomi Levine points out, the Cabinet was divided over whether Britain's obligation to Belgium was one of policy or one of law, a crucial issue in defining Britain's freedom of action.) Gary Sheffield has emphasised the continuity in British foreign policy thus revealed: 'Substituting the names of the appropriate states, this summary of the situation on 2nd August 1914 would have been instantly recognisable to Palmerston, Castlereagh and even Elizabeth I.' (Gary Sheffield, *Forgotten Victory. The First World War: Myths and Realities*, Review Books, London, 2002, pp. 47-8.) Given this, some recent critics have gone much further than Taylor in criticising Grey by drawing attention to the failure to develop a big British Army, which could have fulfilled these continental obligations. On the other hand, this would have involved the introduction of conscription before the outbreak of war which (as we shall see) was politically too sensitive and anyway ran counter to the entire political philosophy of the Liberal Party and government. (See Niall Ferguson in Jay Winter (ed.), *The Legacy of the Great War Ninety Years on*, University of Missouri Press, Columbia and London, 2009, pp. 49-50.) Whatever arguments historians may have dallied with, the fact was that the members of the Cabinet had been caught unawares by the sudden crisis, as ill-informed as the rest of the country, as bewildered as everyone else. This was, after all, a Liberal Government, and the Liberal Party was not traditionally warlike and, indeed, contained a strongly pacifist element.

24. What most British people knew of Belgium came from the appalling colonial record in the Congo of the late, monstrous King Leopold, atrocities known through Conrad's *Heart of Darkness* (1902) and Arthur Conan Doyle's *The Crime of the Congo*, published in 1909. (See Adam Hochschild, *King Leopold's Ghost. A Story of Greed, Terror and Heroism in Colonial Africa*, Mariner Books, London, 1998, passim.) We note the Australian writer L.A. Carlyon's comment that 'Belgium indeed knew all about atrocities: it had been

committing them in the Congo for decades.' (L.A. Carlyon, *Gallipoli*, Bantam Books, London, 2003, p.141.) Leopold had died in 1909, to be succeeded by his nephew Albert who was a much nicer man.

25. Hansard, 3rd August 1914, col. 1829. See Herbert Asquith, *Memories and Reflections, 1852-1927*, Vol. 2, London, 1928, pp. 37-8. It was an extraordinary statement and its implications were as exhilarating as they were profound: there would be no civil war in Ireland – at least, not yet. (See George Dangerfield, *The Strange Death of Liberal England*, Macgibbon & Key, London, 1966, p. 338.)

26. David Boulton, *Objection Overruled*, Macgibbon and Kee, London, 1967, p.29. (A more detailed view of the German position is given in Jonathan Sperber, *The Kaiser's Voters. Electors and Elections in Imperial Germany*, C.U.P., Cambridge, 1997, p.40.) In reporting back to his constituents in the left-wing *Leicester Pioneer* the following Friday MacDonald wrote that: 'There is no doubt whatever but that when all this is over and we turn back to it in cold blood and read it carefully so as to ascertain why England has practically declared war on Germany, we shall find that the only reason from beginning to end in it is that our Foreign Office is anti-German and that the Admiralty was anxious to seize any opportunity of using the navy in battle practice'. (*Leicester Pioneer*, 7th August 1914.) The shot at Churchill, First Lord of the Admiralty, was well aimed – Churchill was pretty much the only member of the government enthusiastically to embrace war in August 1914 – but his attack on Grey and the Foreign Office was more problematical.

27. Quoted in Fenner Brockway, *Inside the Left. Thirty Years of Platform, Press, Prison and Parliament*, George Allen & Unwin, London, 1942, p. 45. Lloyd George in his *War Memoirs* borrowed the image, adding a Welsh flourish to trump MacDonald's Scots: 'The nations backed their machines over the precipice'. (*War Memoirs*, Vol. 1, Odhams Press, London, n.d., p. 34.) For a contemporary view of the 'democratisation' of foreign policy, see R.W. Seton-Watson, J. Dover Wilson, Alfred E. Zimmern and Arthur Greenwood, *The War and Democracy*, Macmillan, London, 1914, pp. 222-231.

28. *Brockway*, p. 44.

29. Emanuel Shinwell, *The Labour Story*, Macdonald, London, 1963, p. 87.

30. *Leicester Pioneer*, 7th August 1914.

31. David Nash and David Reeder (eds.), *Leicester in the Twentieth Century*, Alan Sutton with Leicester City Council, Stroud, 1993, p. 113. Even Keir Hardie, hero of the Left, was howled out of Merthyr Tydfil when he tried to speak against the war. (Adam Hochschild, *To End All Wars. How the First World War Divided Britain*, Macmillan, London, 2011, p. 95.) Thereafter the Parliamentary Labour Group's support for the war and the I.L.P.'s opposition split the Labour movement permanently. The bulk of the English conscientious objectors would come from the I.L.P.. And Leicester's voters

did not forget. In the immediate post-war election of December 1918, in which MacDonald stood in Leicester West on a policy of non-co-operation with Lloyd George's government he lost massively to the pro-co-operation Labour candidate. The *Leicester Mercury* wrote that 'at the beginning of the war he misjudged and misrepresented Sir Edward Grey and the policy of the government. In that course he ran counter… to the interests of the nation, just as it entered upon a tremendous conflict… [H]ad his advice been followed, and that of the organisation on whose platform he appeared, there would have been not a peace after victory, but a cessation of hostilities by negotiation. We cannot forget these things.' (David Marquand, *Ramsay MacDonald*, Jonathan Cape, London, 1977, pp. 234-5.)

32. Leonard recalled that 'when in 1914 the war came, I could not understand what was happening, it seemed so wrong to me that people should want to kill each other. It was such a blow to everyone that I think most people did not understand what was happening.' Leonard Payne, written statement to Peter Liddle, 1973, p. 3. As a precautionary attempt to damp down panic the government had raised the Bank Rate on August 1st from 4% to 10%, while the rich or financially astute rushed to withdraw their savings. (R.W. Seton-Watson, et al., pp. 304-311.)It would seem that even the criminals of Leicestershire were taken aback: the chief constable reported in October: 'County exceptional quiet'. (Minutes of Superintendents' Meetings, LRO.DE5491/104, 5th October 1914.)

33. *Leicester Daily Mercury*, 5th and 6th August 1914. *Rugby Advertiser*, 8th August 1914. An agricultural success, the show was a financial disaster, takings not even reaching £50, when twice that much had been expected, enough, it had been hoped, to wipe out the previous year's deficit of £35. It was indeed, 'rather hard lines on the society'.

34. Popular reactions to the outbreak of war have been the subject of some debate, the older view of a sudden and wild war enthusiasm bursting forth fully formed on the day war broke out replaced by a more nuanced and realistic understanding. In 1915 the psychologist Wilfred Trotter observed the public reaction thus: 'The first feeling of the ordinary citizen was fear – an immense, vague, aching anxiety, perhaps typically vague and unfocused, but naturally tending soon to localize itself in channels customary to the individual and leading to fears for his future, his food supply, his family, his trade, and so forth. Side by side with fear there was a heightening of the normal intolerance of isolation… The necessity for companionship was strong enough to break down the distinctions of class, to dissipate the reserve between strangers, which is to some extent a concomitant mechanism. The change in the customary frigid atmosphere of the railway train, the omnibus, and all such meeting-places was a most interesting experience for a psychologist.' (Wilfred Trotter, *Speculations upon the Human Mind in 1915*, reprinted in *Instincts of the Herd in Peace and War, 1916-1919*, OUP, 1953, pp. 110-

1.) Another psychologist, William Brown, sometime Officer in Charge of the Craiglockhart Hospital, later wrote: 'Some of us can remember the sudden war fever in 1914, the transformation which occurred in the imagination of the people on the eve of war and during the weeks that followed. We remember the changed mental outlook, the sort of things that people thought and said, the incredible things they believed, and how what they ordinarily kept under came uppermost. We realized then how thin was the veneer over our primitive instincts, how people seemed only too glad to release those instincts when they could do so in a communal way, with everybody about them sharing the same experience and with the whole matter apparently sanctified by the idealistic principle of fighting for King and Country, and for civilization.' (William Brown, *War and the Psychological Conditions of Peace*, Adam & Charles Black, London, 1942, pp. 7-8.) In 1916 Bertrand Russell put forward his ideas about the importance of *impulse* and *instinct*, claiming that 'to very many men, the instinct of patriotism, when the war broke out, was the first instinct that had bridged the gulf [between *thought* and *instinct*], the first that had made them feel a really profound unity with others'. (Lecture written in 1915 and delivered early in 1916, *Why Men Fight*, Routledge Classics, London, 2010, p. 140.)

35. *Leicester Daily Mercury*, 5th August 1914. *Rugby Advertiser*, 8th August 1914. Well-known breeders and trainers of horses, judges at horse shows, landowners, masters of foxhounds – anyone with an eye for a sound horse – were already being mobilised to select the most suitable horses for war. Each day, selected horses were sent to Clearing Stations for distribution. One of the biggest of these stations was in the market place in Market Harborough, lent for the purpose by the town council at a judicious rent of £10 per week. (See Basil Clarke in H. W. Wilson and J. Hammerton, ed. *The Great War: The Standard History of the All-Europe Conflict*, Vol. 9, London, 1917, pp. 454-5. Also J.C. Davies, *Town Affairs: The Making of Modern Market Harborough*, Market Harborough U.D.C., 1974, p. 37.) Davies records that the inconvenient and excessive accumulation of horse manure in the middle of town was resolved by an equitable distribution among local farmers.

36. *Leicester Daily Mercury*, 31st July 1914.

37. *Rugby Advertiser*, 4th August 1914.

38. From everywhere, it seemed, the same complaints were made. An individual signing him- or herself 'A. Parent' wrote to the *Rugby Advertiser* on 8th August complaining that 'people to whom a small rise would have made little or no difference, have by their inconsiderate actions caused such an inflation of the prices of absolute necessaries that the poor man with his large family and limited means is placed in a very serious position', while in Loughborough, to the north of the county, the Town Council expressed its outrage 'against the manner in which many of the wealthy and well-to-

do are laying in excessive stores, and artificially enhancing prices against the poor'. (*Leicester Daily Post*, 6th August 1914.) At the end of 1914 the Town Council there began a system of free food hand-outs to those in need, a provision continued daily until the end of March 1915. By then the number being fed had risen to thirty-seven. The thickness of the ledger in which the hand-outs were recorded suggests that someone in Loughborough believed the provision of food would be a very considerable long-term commitment. (LRO.DG9/2810.) By February 1915 the price of flour would rise by 75%, home meat by 6%, sugar by 72% and coal by 15%. As the war went on, and as the German U-Boat campaign developed, prices would rise higher yet. (Arthur Marwick, *The Deluge*, Penguin Books, Harmondsworth, 1967, p. 42.)

39. *Rugby Advertiser*, 29th August 1914.

40. *Rugby Advertiser*, 8th August 1914.

41. *Leicester Mercury*, 5th August 1914. Technically, the Yeomanry was 'embodied' rather than 'mobilised'. In Lord Haldane's mind the Yeomanry and the other Territorial Regiments had always been intended to be used overseas if necessary. They were Britain's voluntary answer to the compulsory systems of conscription used in Germany and France. Of course, he said that they were for home defence only, but he was a politician who needed to get his proposals through a suspicious Parliament – so he would, wouldn't he. (See A.J. Anthony Morris, *Haldane's Army Reforms, 1906-8*, in *History*, February 1971; Peter Dennis, *The Territorial Army, 1907-1940*, Royal Historical Society, London, 1987, pp. 10-13; George Codrington, *An Outline of the History of the Leicestershire (Prince Albert's Own) Yeomanry*, London, 1928, pp. 24-25.) The Territorial and Reserve Forces Act of 1907 is well summarised in *The Yeomanry Cavalry of Worcestershire, 1794-1913* by Q.L., Preface by Lord Cobham, privately printed, Devises, 1913, pp. 231-4. We suppose that all this was understood by those who signed up. The events of 1914 would certainly suggest that it was.

42. The school holiday had begun on July 31st, the Friday before the Bank Holiday. Other squadrons called in from their wide rural catchment areas used local schools in this way; *Leicester Mercury*, 4th August 1914. Some were luckier: at Loughborough the men of 'C' Squadron who also had to assemble in the town from the outlying farms and villages were distributed among the local pubs for accommodation; *Melton Mowbray Mercury* and *Oakham and Uppingham News*, 6th August 1914.

43. *Rugby Advertiser*, 15th August 1914. Among those from Lutterworth who went were William Smith, the son of James Basil, a shoemaker, and Elizabeth Martha Smith of Baker Street, just round the corner from the Paynes' shop; William was seventeen years old. Frank Matthews, twenty years old, the same age as Leonard, born in Lutterworth but living in nearby Gilmorton, made his way into Lutterworth as well; and riding or walking in the three miles or so from Ullesthorpe was Sam Sleath, a little older at

twenty-two. Beyond the odd brief period of leave, Frank, Sam and seventeen-year-old William would not be returning home. Four other Lutterworth Yeomen went on that day – Corporal L.A. Barrs, Trooper Percy John Measures, Sergeant Fred Porter, and S.Q.M.S. Frank Rose: they all survived. Roll Book of the Leicestershire (Prince Albert's Own) Yeomanry, held as LRO.DE3765/2; Roll Book belonging to 'A' Squadron, LRO.DE2472/27. The town's grammar school lost its headmaster when war broke out. Stuart Douglas was called to his Territorial Regiment (the 4th Wiltshires) when war was declared. Douglas would lose a leg in 1917 and return to the school in 1918, where he would remain as headmaster until 1930.

44. *Kelly's Directory of Leicestershire*, 1912. Burke's *Landed Gentry*, 18th edn, Vol. 1, 1965.

45. Sir George Arthur, *The Story of the Household Cavalry*, Vol. 3, London, 1926, pp. 71-2 and 226. There is a photograph of Arthur in H. Wilson and J. Hammerton, eds., *The Great War: The Standard History of the All-Europe Conflict, Vol. 6*, 1916, p. 396. Arthur's younger brother Jack was also at this moment mobilising along with his Regiment, the Royal Horse Guards. Geoffrey was with the Royal Fusiliers. Arthur was wounded on October 20th 1914 whilst serving one of the Regiment's machine-guns, and did not recover. 'Died of Wounds', they called it.

46. See his annual letters published in *Bottrill's Almanac of Lutterworth*, published through the war years. The veiled attack on the Paynes can be found in *Lutterworth Almanac*, 1915; the National Mission and its possibilities are reported in the 1917 almanac. By Christmas 1914 30% of all Anglican ordinands had already enlisted, and after Trinity Sunday 1915 the bishops refused to accept any candidate for ordination who was fit for military service. (Brock Millman, *Managing Domestic Dissent in First World War Britain*, Cass, London, 2000. p. 33.) Much the same applied in Scotland where 90% of the country's ministers sent their offspring to the Front. (See Trevor Royle, *The Flowers of the Forest. Scotland and the First World War*, Birlinn, Edinburgh, 2007, p. 31.)

47. Brock Millman, *HMG and the War against Dissent, 1914-18*, Journal of Contemporary History, July 2005, p. 418.

48. Marion Harper to Leonard, 3rd July 1917.

49. I am grateful to Sophy Newton, Charles Marriott's great grand-daughter, for generously allowing me access to Charles's papers and permission to quote from them. The Marriott family papers are held in Cotesbach Hall. Among Charles Marriott's papers is the original draft form of this verse containing several alterations and amendments to the text. Half a dozen fair copies of the verse exist, all in Charles's firm, strong handwriting, which suggests that this may have been written as an additional verse or verses to a hymn to be sung in Cotesbach's parish church in August 1914. The unusual metre suggests that this may have been divided into two verses sung to the tune 'Russian Anthem', with words by the early Victorian writer H.F. Chorley, a hymn

designated 'In Time of Trouble' in 'Hymns Ancient and Modern' (Hymn 742. 'Hymns Ancient and Modern Revised', Hymn 491, where it is classified as a hymn 'In Time of War'). Less likely is Hymn 538 in the English Hymnal, to be sung 'in time of trouble' to the tune L'Omnipotent'.

50. Roland H. Bainton, *Christian Attitudes toward War and Peace*, New York, 1960, p. 207. In another World War Nicholas Spykman would write that 'national struggles inevitably become struggles between good and evil, crusades against sin and the devil. Modern wars can be fought successfully only in an atmosphere of unreality and make-believe.' (Nicholas Spykman, *America's Struggle in World Politics*, Harcourt, New York, 1942, p. 37, quoted in Bainton, op. cit. p. 264.) Even more cynically – or realistically – the American theologian Culbert Rutenber wrote: 'It is difficult to avoid the conclusion that while all wars are coated with a moral veneer, the real reason for Christian support of them is something less than justice, something more akin to such human reasons as national pride, fear, [or] self-preservation.' (C.G. Rutenber, *The Dagger and the Cross: An Examination of Christian Pacifism*, Fellowship Publications, New York, 1958, p. 98.)

51. Charles Marriott papers, Cotesbach Hall. That is not, of course, to say that all those who attacked the Germans – the 'Hun' – with their pens were as moderate at Charles Marriott. The editor of the local newspaper in Hinckley, half a dozen miles to the west of Lutterworth, invited his readers to suggest what might be done with the Kaiser. A female correspondent thought that he should be locked in a cage in London Zoo, 'guarded with a few violent Suffragettes', before being blown up with one of his own bombs, while one John Harrison suggested: 'I should get a strong piece of string, tie the two ends to his moustache, and hang it on a nail. Then I should heat a poker, and after properly getting it red-hot I should put it in front of his face, so that when he pulled back sharply he would pull his whiskers out. Then I should get a razor and shave his hair off his head, and fairly make him look a silly ass.' The age and/or the mental condition of John Harrison are not divulged. *Hinckley Echo*, 17th February 1915. Not all anti-German writings of the First World War were so jovially creative: others were more sinister. One of the most outrageous examples of this pornography of hate engendered by the Great War was written by Henry de Halsalle in 1916 under the title *Degenerate Germany* (published by T. Werner Laurie, London, n.d.) Its opening passage, set bizarrely in mock-Gothic script, reads: 'Forevermore Remember, O ye Christian Nations of the Earth, the vile Germanic race. In your Schools teach ye your Youth the everlasting Iniquity of these impious and depraved barbarians. Above the Gates of your Capitals cut deep these words: *No German Enters Here*. In your Market Places, upon the portals, there engrave:- *No Wares herein came from the great Assassin's crimson hand*. Upon the doors of your Churches, ay, and above your Altars, let those who worship read:- *Father forgive them not, for they know what they do.*' There follow 260 pages of the

most outrageous national slanders set in print before the Nazis' anti-Semitic onslaught against the Jews. The book culminates in a breath-taking mix of racist hatreds with the claim that Germans are of Negro descent and are thus naturally barbaric, and that even Bismarck had Negro features. The book was republished in India by the Nabu Press in 2010.

52. Alan Borg, *War Memorials from Antiquity to the Present*, Leo Cooper, London, 1991, pp. 73-4. Gavin Stamp, *The Memorial to the Missing of the Somme*, Profile Books, London, 2007, pp. 82 and 99. The 'high diction' derived ultimately from the King James Bible and became, to many in England, the language of God. Medieval imagery came to the fore in Britain during and after the Great War, British soldiers being represented as upholders of medieval knightly Chivalry (however much this may have contrasted with the reality in the trenches), Christian warriors fighting for God against an ungodly and 'beastly' foe (and often drawn and painted as such in wartime propaganda images), Crusaders in an imagined and romanticised holy war (underlined on the ground with Allenby's capture of Jerusalem from the Turks in 1918), even the 'Agincourt archers' (later transmogrified into the 'Angel of Mons'), through to the iconography of memorialisation: the slaughter on the Western Front was portrayed as holy sacrifice, and was thus given meaning. (See Stefan Goebel, *The Great War and Medieval Memory: War, Remembrance and Medievalism in Britain and Germany, 1914-1940*, C.U.P., 2007; Allen J. Frantzen, *Bloody Good: Chivalry, Sacrifice and the Great War*, Chicago University Press, Chicago, 2003.) When considering the conscientious objectors, of course, all that imagery was reversed.

53. *Rugby Advertiser*, 8th August 1914.

54. *Leicester Pioneer*, 21st August 1914. It is not a coincidence that Faid's sermon was reported in the socialist *Leicester Pioneer*. This 'conspiracy theory' for the outbreak of war was standard fare on the Left, and would become a more widespread view as the twentieth century wore on. (See Boulton, pp. 29-30.) For a Second World War exposition of the position, see Fenner Brockway and Frederick Mullally, *Death Pays a Dividend*, Victor Gollancz, The Left Book Club, London, 1944, passim.

55. *For His Name's Sake. Being a Record of the Witness given by Members of Churches of Christ in Great Britain against Militarism during the European War 1914-1918*, W. Barker, Printer, Mansfield Road, Heanor 1921, p. 51.

56. Quoted in Frank G. Jannaway, *Without the Camp: Being the Story of Why and How the Christadelphians were Exempted from Military Service*, published by the author, 1917, pp. 19-20. My thanks to the East Coventry Christadelphian Ecclesia, and the late David Price for the loan of this book. In the front of Jannaway's book stands this extraordinary statement: '*Note to Subscribers.* 'Let it be remembered that nothing that is contained herein is intended to discountenance a Briton joining the army and fighting for his

country. The Author considers it not only the duty of a Briton, but his privilege so to do, and it is unpatriotic, to say the least, for such a one to stand idly by while such a ruthless enemy as Germany threatens his country. This book is only for Christadelphians, whose Kingdom is "not of this world"…; they are neutrals; they never vote; and, as such, the British Constitution says they are not liable to be called upon to fight. In all other respects they have to be subject to the laws of the country; and, thus, every bona fide Christadelphian, although not permitted by his Lord to fight, will do his best in civil life to help the land of his birth in its hour of distress.' The statement that the British Constitution exempted them from fighting because they did not vote is a novel and factually untrue one, the confusion possibly caused by proposals that those who refused to fight should be disenfranchised. The corollary did not apply. The Churches of Christ, like the Christadelphians, were an off-shoot of the American Evangelical movement, and boasted half a dozen congregations in Leicester by 1914. They also held strongly pacifist beliefs and had been prepared to expel any member who joined the armed forces. Yet even here there was division over the issue of military service, and 125 of its young members had volunteered by the spring of 1916, 10% of its total membership in the town. Though this must have been, at first, a great source of disappointment to Church elders, they soon fell in behind the national mood, and before the war was over one conscientious objector, Walter Crossthwaite, would bitterly complain that the Churches' 'leaders urged our young men to enlist and fight for King and Country, and scant sympathy was given to those who stood for the old attitude. With the coming of conscription, we saw our young men turned down by tribunals of which leaders in their own churches were chairmen. Brethren, some of whom were elders in the churches, sat on magisterial benches and handed their own Brethren over to their persecutors.' The words of the Master had almost a complete and literal fulfilment: 'And brother shall deliver up brother to death. … And ye shall be hated of all men for my name's sake'. See A.C. Watters, *History of the British Churches of Christ*, via www.simplychristians.eu. The mayor of Leicester through almost the whole of the Great War, Jonathan North, was a prominent member of the Churches of Christ, where he taught Sunday School. (See Derek Seaton, *Sir Jonathan North: Manufacturer, Politician and Philanthropist*, in John Hinks (ed.) *Aspects of Leicester. Discovering Local History*, Wharncliffe Books, Barnsley, 2000, p.63.) Lloyd George himself was a member of the Criccieth Church of Christ.

57. The name 'Louvain' appears over and over again in the documents of the time. In Cotesbach Charles Marriott wrote to his son Jem that 'the indignation and horror felt at the sacking of Louvain by the German Army gave an enormous impetus to the recruiting, and it immediately increased by leaps and bounds.' Father to Jem, 18th September 1914. Marriott family papers.

58. *The Friend*, 4th September 1914.

59. *The Friend*, 11th September 1914. Baker did then go on to distance himself from such views and reiterate the traditional Quaker peace testimony. The journal's editorial of the following week contained this extraordinary statement: 'We do not agree with those who urge that the business of the Society [of Friends], as such, is to assist the State in the prosecution of the war'. It is the 'as such' which leaps from the page, the implication that some Quakers thought it was. *The Friend*, 18th September 1914.

60. Margaret E. Hirst, *The Quakers in Peace and War*, Swarthmore Press, London, 1923, pp. 503-4. During the nineteenth century Quakerism had undergone significant changes, from the superficial (though significant) abandonment of their distinctive form of dress and their ban on marrying outside the Quaker community, to revisions of their emphasis on the 'Inner Light' in favour of a more Bible-based approach to the roots of belief. In this sense, they were growing closer to mainstream Nonconformity before the outbreak of the First World War. (See Ian Packer, *Religion and the New Liberalism. The Rowntree Family, Quakerism and Social Reform*, Journal of British Studies, April 2003, esp. pp. 243-4.)

61. Quoted in Boulton, p. 53. Unfortunately, Boulton ignored the divisions and uncertainty within the Quaker movement at the beginning of the war. By May 1915, when the Quaker Yearly Meeting was held in an atmosphere of 'uncertainty', at least 215 Quakers had joined the army or navy, including forty-three in the R.A.M.C. Fifteen Quakers were known to be members of recruiting committees or were actively engaged in recruiting; and two had already been killed on active service. Others were engaged in 'the manufacture of munitions and military supplies, and no one was certain what proportion of the whole membership was in agreement with these actions.' (Hirst, pp. 504-5.) Quoting an incomplete return from Quaker Meetings in 1917 Margaret Hirst wrote that 560 Quakers had enlisted in the armed forces (though presumably mostly in non-combatant roles) or 33.6% of eligible Quaker men. (p. 538.)

62. Quoted in Arthur Marwick, *The Deluge. British Society and the First World War*, Penguin Books, Harmondsworth, 1967, p. 32.

63. Malcolm Elliott, *Opposition to the First World War: The Fate of Conscientious Objectors in Leicester*, Transactions of the Leicestershire Archaeological and Historical Society, Vol. 77, Leicester, 2003, p. 83.

64. On the sack of Louvain, see John Horne and Alan Kramer, *German Atrocities 1914: A History of Denial* London, 2001, pp. 38-42. *The War Illustrated*, 19th September 1914 provides a good example of how it was used in the British media. Alan Kramer set the sack in a broader context in *Dynamic of Destruction. Culture and Mass Killing in the First World War*, O.U.P., 2007, Chapter 1, 'The Burning of Louvain'.

65. Quoted by Rev Beddow LRO.N/C/MB/11.

66. *Leicester. Its Civic, Industrial, Institutional and Social Life*, compiled by Chas Howes, published by The Midland Service Agencies, Leicester, 1927, p. 227.

67. Minutes of the Leicestershire and Rutland Congregational Union General Committee, 24th September 1914. LRO. N/C/MB/10.

68. Horne and Kramer, passim.

69. Minutes of the Leicestershire and Rutland Congregational Union General Committee, 24th September 1914. LRO. N/C/MB/10.

70. Gerald Rimmington, *Congregationalism and Society in Leicestershire and Rutland, 1916-1966*, Transactions of the Leicestershire Archaeological and Historical Society, Volume 8, Leicester, 2007. Having committed itself to supporting the war, the Congregational Church stuck to its guns. In his Presidential Address to the Annual Assembly in London in October 1917 the Rev. Bernard Snell said that 'some of the Churches had recognised the world was in travail but others, from their dugouts, gave sanctuary to those who were insensible to the tremendous issues of the war, and failed to realise the splendour of our cause. We are in absolute antagonism to Germany, for the foul character of her government was patent now to all the world. We are at war for right against wrong, and until right had won this is not the hour to listen to peace.' (*Leicester Daily Mercury*, 4th October 1917.)

71. John Rae *Conscience and Politics. The British Government and the Conscientious Objector to Military Service, 1916-1919,* O.U.P., Oxford, 1970, p. 79, with reference to R. Tudur Jones, *Congregationalism in England, 1662-1962*, London, 1962, p. 356. While some individuals held out against war the Nonconformist churches quickly followed the Anglican line: 'The ultra-patriotic response of the national church encouraged other denominations and sects to rally to the war effort to avoid seeming insufficiently patriotic. While many nonconforming denominations and sects were pacific-ist, none was willing to renounce recourse to arms in all cases... The First World War, most quickly concluded, was a just war, even a crusade.' (Millman, p. 33.) The first sentence in this passage is less than fair: the Nonconformists had minds of their own and had reached their own conclusions independently without being pressurised by the appearance of 'seeming insufficiently patriotic'.

72. Minutes of the Leicestershire and Rutland Congregational Union General Committee, 24th September 1914. LRO.N/C/MB/10.

73. *History of Lutterworth United Reformed Church 1689-1997*, compiled by Ron Gates, researched by Peter Bruce, edited by Barbara Gates, pp. 22-24.

74. Lutterworth Parish Council Minutes, 17th April 1913. LRO DE/2254/3.

75. ibid. 26th May 1913

76. ibid. 19th April 1915; and Minutes of the Board of Guardians, 29th April 1915. LRO G/8/8a/22.

77. Lutterworth Parish Council Minutes 30th November 1914

78. ibid. 20th April 1914.

79. ibid. 25th May 1914

80. ibid. 27th July 1914

81. *Minute Book of Church Meetings of the Congregational Church in Lutterworth*, 16th December 1914. Archive held by the Elders of the Lutterworth United Reformed Church.

82. The version issued in the Boer War was slightly larger, had hard covers (unlike the Great War edition), and bore on the back the words 'Peace through the Blood of His Cross' and 'My Peace I Give unto You', author's collection.

83. Quoted in *Leicester Mail*, 20th September 1918. LRO N/C/X/7.

84. *Lutterworth Mail*, 31st January 2008, reporting the unveiling of a bench in the middle of the town to the memory of James Miller. I am grateful to Mrs Eileen Derrick for telling me the story of her father, Tom Ward. At the big house at Gumley a poetry competition was organised among the staff by the lady of the house, Ellen Murray Smith. The head kitchen maid submitted this: 'A uniform is attractive and makes a man look smart, And oft a well brushed khaki suit will win a maiden's heart, But do not be discouraged, when the war is done, That your lovely boy in khaki is only the Dustman's son.' (LRO.DE1313/28)It is not known whether this offering won the prize or not. War as leveller!

85. *Bottrill's Almanac of Lutterworth and District*, 1916; undated 'Our Roll of Honour', LRO.DE3614/38.

86. By contrast, in urban Leicester volunteering was at first slow, much to the embarrassment of the city fathers. In the first flush of volunteering 6.7% of the population of Manchester and Sheffield joined up, while in Newcastle and in nearby Nottingham the figure was 18.5%, and in Leicester – 2.6. By the start of 1915 the reluctance of Leicester had become a public scandal. When the Recruiting Committee itself met, many of its members failed to attend. (Jack Simmons, *Leicester Past and Present*, Vol. 2, London, 1974, p. 63.) Taking the whole county, with Rutland added, the tendency was for men to join the Territorials rather than Kitchener's New Army. 40% of those who had enlisted by December 1914 had joined the Territorials, as opposed to 28% in Nottingham and Derby. (LRO, DE819/1, quoted in Glenn Steppler, *Britons, To Arms! The Story of the British Volunteer Soldier and the Volunteer Tradition in Leicestershire and Rutland*, Stroud, 1992, p.116.) It is a sobering comment on the general state of health of the men of Leicester that 12% of those who did try to join up failed the medical and were rejected. (Minutes of the Emergency Committee of the Territorial Association, 10th December 1914, LRO, DE819/1.) Explaining the sluggish pace of recruitment taxed Leicester's historian of the war, F.P. Armitage: the belief that the war was going better than it actually was; the lack of enthusiasm from the political Left in Leicester; the remoteness of the

war to people there; the demand for labour with so many military contracts coming in, especially to the hosiery and the boot and shoe industries; fears that jobs would not be held over for those who did join up. (F.P. Armitage, *Leicester, 1914-1918: The War-time Story of a Midland Town*, Leicester, 1933, pp. 24, 28, 30-2, 78. The phenomenon is further analysed by Adrian Gregory in *The Last Great War. British Society and the First World War*, C.U.P., 2008, pp. 88-9.) It goes without saying that almost all of these considerations applied to towns like Nottingham as well. Or perhaps it was just that the men of Leicester were not keen on commitment: the local newspaper just before the outbreak of war, reported that Leicester had the highest rate of bachelors of any county borough in Britain. (*Leicester Daily Mercury*, 31st July 1914.) On the one hand this was, after all, 'Radical Leicester' with its long tradition of left-wing politics, and its core of socialists and pacifists and Nonconformist Christians, but it was also, on the other hand, a down-to-earth working town with a living to make. So it came down to principles and money. The Leicester representatives of the National Union of Boot and Shoe Operatives, for example, at first shared the Left's lack of enthusiasm for 'the deplorable outbreak of war on the Continent', but soon changed their tune when the orders for army boots rolled in. In October the Union's President, T.F. Richards, reported 'I have been very busy during the month with government contractors. No less than eighteen firms in the town of Leicester have obtained such orders.' Employers were paying above agreed rates simply to attract workers. One Branch Secretary in Northampton put it more succinctly: 'every factory is a gold mine'. And who would willingly walk away from a gold mine? (Alan Fox, *A History of the National Union of Boot and Shoe Operatives, 1874-1957*, Oxford, 1958, p. 367.) Nearby Hinckley also profited from the war, as local historian Evelyn Henderson explained: 'In the hosiery industry, like the footwear industry, within weeks of the outbreak of war scores of firms were tendering for, and receiving, enormous orders from the War Office. By the beginning of 1915 the Board of Trade was reporting that in Hinckley almost every factory was working overtime on government contracts'. (Evelyn Henderson, *Milestones of Hinckley, 1640-1981*, Hinckley, 1981.) Another historian of Hinckley quoted the town's official guide of 1915: 'The town of Hinckley finds itself pursuing its usual avocations, and even more prosperous than before… Never were our factories more inundated with orders and never was labour more in demand.' (Quoted in Hugh A. Bevin, *The Book of Hinckley*, Barracuda Books, Buckingham, 1983, p. 81.) At the same time, other industries encountered difficulties as large numbers of their workers rushed to join up. For example, the building trade was hit hard when 4,000 members of the Amalgamated Society of Woodworkers flocked into the army in the first month, followed by another 13,000 by the end of the war. (S. Higenbottam, *Our Society's History*, published by the Amalgamated Society of Woodworkers, Manchester, 1939, p.191.)

87. Recruitment figures from *Bottrill's Almanac of Lutterworth*, 1916; Cotesbach complete figure from 'Roll of Honour' in the parish church. It would be a truly terrible war for Charles and Mary Marriott. Two sons, Frederick and Hugh, died just a few weeks apart in 1915, both outside Ypres, both on 'all quiet on the Western Front' days. Frederick has no grave, simply an inscription on the Menin Gate; Hugh is buried in the Reservoir Cemetery, north of the city, the temporary wooden cross, complete with his metal stamped identification marker, being returned to his parents, and now occupying pride of place in Cotesbach Church, just across the road from the house in which they lived. (George L. Mosse wrote of such crosses in *Fallen Soldiers. Reshaping the Memory of the World Wars*, O.U.P., 1990, p. 91.) Their brothers, three of them, were also in uniform, one in the army, one in the air force and one in the navy, as if to spread the risk, though the gnawing anxiety must have been terrible. In the event, all of them returned. Frederick and Hugh Marriott were the only two from their home village of Cotesbach not to return. For this reason, Cotesbach has no war memorial as such, though the parish church does contain a list of the twelve men from the village (population about 100) who were in the armed forces, and a new west window in memory of Frederick and Hugh was installed in the parish church. (On the Marriotts, see Burke's *Landed Gentry*, 1906 and 1925 editions.) On the Marriotts' landholding, see *Duties on Land Values ('Domesday') Book under the Finance Act 1910*, LRO.DE2972/149. In the summer of 1916 the Marriotts sold off a large proportion of their lands and properties in Cotesbach and Shawell, raising over £7,600, a further £15,000's worth of properties being withdrawn when they failed to reach their reserve price. *Rugby Advertiser*, 3rd July 1916.

88. Their letters can be read at WRO.CR2017: C582/1-109; C588/1-37; C604/1-50. Gerald Gliddon, *The Aristocracy and the Great War*, Gliddon Books, Norwich, 2002. The Earl's butler, James Swingler, would lose his son Francis to the flu pandemic of 1918 whilst serving with the Sherwood Foresters. (Lutterworth Local History Group, *Lutterworth War Memorial Names, 1914-1918, 1939-1945. A Preliminary Study*, 2005, p. 1-66.)

89. Minute Book. Bitteswell Church Committees, 1914-1919. LRO.DE759/43.

90. *Rugby Advertiser*, 29th July 1916. Emphasis in original. This soldier was not unique, though whether this was due to the traditional vision of the 'Blighty one' – the injury which would ensure no return to the Front, whatever he might have said to the Major – or whether it was more to do with a self-perception of masculinity, is open to question. The American feminist historian Nicoletta Gullace wrote that: 'If the outward signs of the willingness to brave death – a uniform, a medal, a stump – had become the new symbols of masculinity, the potential mutilation of the male body was the price to be paid for the preservation of the masculine soul'. (Nicoletta Gullace, *"The Blood of Our Sons": Men, Women, and the Renegotiation of British Citizenship During the Great War*, Palgrave Macmillan, Basingstoke, 2002, p. 38.)

91. Minutes of the Executive Committee of the County Relief Committee, 26th August 1914, LRO.14D35/1/3.

92. From *Memorial Tablet* by Siegfried Sassoon, November 1918. One Lutterworth Parish Councillor, Mr Brown, even urged the council to mount its own recruitment campaign, a proposal turned down on grounds of practicality rather than principle. (LRO.DE2254/3 Lutterworth Parish Concil Minutes, 31st August 1914.) In Ashby de la Zouch, in north Leicestershire, a particularly zealous recruiting officer named Captain Stevenson was seeking police assistance in drawing up a list of men between nineteen and thirty-eight in his area. The local superintendent inquired 'what he proposes to make of the information'. No answer is recorded. (Leicestershire Constabulary, Minutes of Superintendents' Meetings, 4th January 1915. LRO.DE5491/104.) It was a taste of things to come.

93. Minutes of the Executive Committee of the County Relief Committee, 16th September 1914, LRO.14D35/1/3.

94. *The Gartree Deanery Magazine*, quoted in the magazine of the Husbands Bosworth Historical Society, *Bygone Bosworth*, No. 9, September 1986. In 1916 the new National Service Department sold, for a shilling, a small heart-shaped medal, the 'pendant of service and sacrifice', to those women who could prove they had relatives serving in the armed forces. (Adrian Gregory, *The Last Great War. British Society and the First World War*, C.U.P., 2008, p.113.) On a better-known form of pressure, we are familiar with the tales of young women handing out white feathers to young men not in uniform, shaming them by that mark of cowardice, but more recent research has cast doubt on the prevalence and the popularity of this display of feminine power, however traumatic it undoubtedly was for those who received this unwelcome gift. (*Gulace*, Chapter 4.)

95. *Rugby Advertiser*, 27th May 1916. The appeal for the Sanitary Inspector was lodged by the council itself: the Sanitary Inspector was instructed to appeal for the other two – a nice example of local authority hierarchy in action. The Sanitary Inspector, A.J. Ross, continued signing documents for the council long afterwards; the other two are not named. None of the three men protected by Major Corbet Smith had, apparently, volunteered for military service in the first twenty-two months of the war. In November 1917, when the bricklayer and the steam disinfector operator applied for a raise in pay, they were both turned down. (*Rugby Advertiser*, 17th November 1917.) Perhaps it was thought they should be grateful for what they had got.

96. *Official Gazette of the County Councils Association*, *Vol.10*, September 1914, p. 157, at LRO.14DE35/1/11.

97. *Rugby Advertiser*, 29th August 1914.

98. *Rugby Advertiser*, 18th July 1914; *Bottrill's Almanac of Lutterworth*, 1916.

99. LRO. DE2051/7. Peers' record with the Yeomanry is outlined in the *Roll Book of the Yeomanry*, LRO. DE3765/2, p. 103.

100. *Bottrill's Almanac of Lutterworth,* 1916. In April 1915 Mary Marriott had been appointed to the Workhouse 'Institution Women's Committee'. (Board of Guardians Minutes, 15th April 1915. LRO.DE1909/353.) Late in 1917 Mary's efforts were recognised when she was summoned to Buckingham Palace to receive the Red Cross medal from the king. Marriott family papers, letter from Charles to Jem, 30th December 1917. George V himself saw the desirability of giving out medals to recognise civilian efforts and in 1917 created the OBE for just that purpose. By 1919 some 22,000 had been given out. Martin Pugh, *We Danced All Night. A Social History of Britain Between the Wars*, Vintage Books, London, 2009, p. 367.

101. Guardians' Minute Book, 6th August 1914, LRO G/8/8a/21.

102. Jean Keogh, *Feilding Palmer Hospital 1899-1999*, privately printed, Lutterworth, 1999, p. 26. A plaque inside the Methodist chapel schoolroom records that 539 war-wounded were treated there in the First World War.

103. Guardians' Minute Book, 20th August 1914, LRO G/8/8a/21. The Cottage Hospital Committee also sought thirty beds in private homes in the town for the use of the wounded, though these do not appear to have materialised and the idea was not pursued. (*Leicester Daily Mercury*, 7th August 1914.) Lutterworth Fire Brigade also did its part, its members brushing up on their first aid skills. (Minute Book of Lutterworth Parish Meetings, 1894-1967. LRO DE2254/13, 29th March 1915.)

104. *Rugby Advertiser*, 15th August 1914.

105. *Lutterworth Almanac* for 1915. On Ullesthorpe Court, see Wendy Priestley's contribution to 'Ullesthorpe', compiled by the Ullesthorpe Book Group, privately published, n.d., pp. 136-7, which includes two well-chosen photographs.

106. Esther Marriott to Fred Marriott, 1st July 1915. Marriott papers, Cotesbach Hall.

107. *Leicester Daily Mercury*, 4th August 1914.

108. Press cutting in anon scrapbook *Obituaries of Rugbeians*, Vol. 1 (photocopy in Rugby Public Library).

109. Leonard to (Harold Buck), 2nd May 1915.

110. Minutes of Lutterworth Congregational Church Meeting, Deacons' Meeting, 17th July 1916, document held by the Elders of the Lutterworth United Reformed Church. I am grateful to the Elders and Irene Moore for allowing access to their archive.

111. The balance has been somewhat redressed in recent years by books such as Steve Humphries and Richard van Emden's *All Quiet on the Home Front. An Oral History of Life in Britain during the First World War*, 2004; as well as through the work of historians like Adrian Gregory, especially *The Last Great War. British Society and the First World War*, CUP, 2008.

112. For example: Robin Neillands, *The Death of Glory. The Western Front, 1915*, John Murray, London, 2006; Lyn MacDonald, *1915. The Death of Innocence*, Penguin Books, 1997.

113. Wilson and Hammerton, eds., Vol. 6, 1916, p. 348.

114. Margaret Powell from Hove, quoted in Gregory, p. 286. 'A month into the war the left-wing Leicester Pioneer was campaigning for an increase in the family allowances, ironically so as to boost recruiting. (*Leicester Pioneer*, 4th September 1914.)

115. Minutes of Proceedings of the Leicester Borough & County Borough Council, 8th September 1914. The issue of what, if anything, to pay the widows of soldiers who were killed was debated in May 1915, but no agreement was reached at that time. ibid., 2nd May 1915.

116. For example, thirty-five companies in Rugby had made this undertaking by mid-August. (*Rugby Advertiser,* 15th August 1914.)

117. The National Relief Fund in Leicestershire had helped two and a half thousand dependants by the first Christmas of the war, grants or advances averaging 16s 6d. each. (Report on the Administration of the National Relief Fund up to 31st March 1915, Cd. 7756, Appendix I.) Stuart Hallifax has questioned whether the belief that it would be 'all over by Christmas' survived the first weeks of the war. (*Over by Christmas: British Popular Opinion and the Short War in 1914*, First World War Studies, Vol. 1, No. 2.) Few military men expected a short war, and within the Cabinet, Lord Haldane agreed: 'I thought,' he wrote in his memoirs, 'from my study of the German General Staff, that once the German war party had got into the saddle and the sword had been drawn from the scabbard, it would be a war not merely for the overthrow of France and Russia, but for the domination of the world.' (*Richard Burdon Haldane. An Autobiography*, Hodder and Stoughton, London, 1929, p. 274.) From the military establishment Kitchener and Haig agreed, the latter writing in his diary on August 5th of a War Council at 10 Downing Street at which he had asserted that 'Great Britain and Germany would be fighting for their existence. Therefore the war was bound to be a long war, and neither would acknowledge defeat after a short struggle... I held that we must organise our resources for a *war of several years'*. (Gary Sheffield and John Bourne (eds), *Douglas Haig. War Diaries and Letters, 1914-1918*, Weidenfeld and Nicolson, London, 2005, p. 54, emphasis in original; John Terraine, *Douglas Haig. The Educated Soldier*, Leo Cooper, London, 1990, pp. 72-75.)

118. Leicestershire Constabulary. Minutes of Superintendents' Meetings, 14th December 1914. LRO.DE5491/104/1. How far the chief constable was justified in his concern is uncertain. In Lutterworth the number of illegitimate births recorded in the Church of England's Baptism Register suggests that no illegitimate children were conceived during the war before the middle of 1916, and only three others thereafter, an average

over the war years not very different from both before and after. (LRO.DE4336/1 and /2.) In a sermon preached in Coventry in May of 1915 the Bishop of Worcester expressed his concern: 'No one could fail to see that there was just now in some directions a weakening of womanly virtue and purity of thought and action,' he was reported as saying, 'The cause was direct and indirect: direct because there were those who were now advocating such a loosening of the idea of marriage that in practice society was confronted with something approaching free love; and indirectly by those who, moved by excellent sentiments of pity and mercy, seemed unable to take the wider view of what was necessary for national purity and self-respect, and played into the hands of the destroyer because they were obsessed by individual cases of hardship which had rightly touched their hearts… They also endangered the sense of self-respect in our own girls if they led them to see that those who had parted with their womanly virtue were to be petted in their confinement, perhaps even more than the poor man's honourable wife.' The Bishop spoke of 'girls who are likely to become mothers through the dangerous system of billeting soldiers.' (*Rugby Advertiser*, 8ᵗʰ May 1915.) But, across the country police forces found they could use their wartime powers to enforce their own moral code, while denying that that was what they were doing. The *Wakefield Express*, for example, gave extensive coverage to a court case in which a local woman, Madge Owen, married to a soldier, had been caught *in flagrante* in a hotel room in Leeds with a soldier named as Jack Cooper from the mining town of South Kirkby. He had given the hotel-keeper his correct name and address but she had called herself 'Mrs Cooper' living at his address. They were prosecuted, along with several other couples, under the Aliens' Restriction Order which, as a means of catching spies, dictated that all hotel registration forms must be truthful. They were fined, and the magistrate recommended that her Separation Allowance be stopped forthwith. *Wakefield Express*, 11ᵗʰ November 1916.

119. Gregory, pp. 95-6; he also quotes the Bishop of London's view that some of the women left behind 'drink very much' (p. 169). Deborah Thom writes of the attempt to legislate against *women*'s drinking (which was successfully resisted by the Liquor Control Board's Women's Advisory Committee), and more broadly points out that 'war particularly encourages speculation about civic and communal responsibility, and particularly stimulates discussion about morality. The First World War saw a large expansion of such debates about where women could go safely and where they should be allowed to share all the experiences of men.' (Deborah Thom, *Nice Girls and Rude Girls. Women Workers in World War 1*, I.B. Tauris, London, 2000, pp. 168, 8.) In the autumn and winter of 1917 the *Leicester Daily Mercury* hosted a spirited correspondence about drinking among women and the young, provoked by a letter from one S.J. Mellor which referred to 'the appalling amount of drinking amongst women in

Leicester'. (*Leicester Daily Mercury*, 4th October 1917.) See also Ben Beazley, *Four Years Remembered. Leicester During the Great War*, Breedon Books, Derby, 1999, p. 37.

120. Leicestershire Constabulary. Minutes of Superintendents' Meetings, 31st May 1915. LRO.DE 5491/104/1.

121. Minutes of the Leicestershire and Rutland Congregational Union General Committee, 23rd September 1915, LRO.N/C/MB/10. The Suffragettes too were alert to the danger, not to the women involved, but to the men. Their journal *Common Cause* in several articles published in the autumn of 1914 called for 'the protection of our young soldiers, many of them only nineteen, from the solicitations of women' and described the women who drank and loitered near army camps as 'a real scandal'. (Cited in Kramer, p. 251.)

122. Letter from B.H. Thornton to the Chief Constable of Leicestershire, LRO.Misc.449/3.

123. Jessie to Leonard and Roland, 3rd July 1917.

124. *Young England. An Illustrated Magazine for Boys throughout the English-Speaking World,* 37th Annual Volume, 1915-1916, The Pilgrim Press, London, p. 116.

125. George Irving, *Lutterworth Grammar School Anniversary Book*, 1956, p. 39. Reprinted and extended, Lutterworth GS & CC, Lutterworth, 1980. The grammar school authorities apparently deemed it wise to bring home to the children – girls as well as boys – in another way that there was a war on by replacing the prizes traditionally awarded to outstanding pupils at Christmas with cheaper certificates, as the minutes had it, 'for the year of war'. The timing was to prove somewhat optimistic. Minutes of the Governors of Lutterworth Grammar School, LRO.ES/MB/211/3, 14th September 1914. Other children too could find themselves enrolled into service. Before the war the National Service League had attempted to take control of the Boy Scouts and incorporate them into a War Office scheme to turn all such youth movements into army cadet forces, but this had been blocked by Baden Powell, (see Allen Warren, *Sir Robert Baden-Powell, the Scout Movement and Citizen Training in Great Britain 1900-1920*, English Historical Review, 1986, esp. pp, 390-396) while other groups, like the Church Lads' Brigade, which 'incorporated concepts of Christian manliness and intense patriotism with military uniforms and drill' eagerly joined the scheme. (Thomas Kennedy, *The Hound of Conscience. A History of the No-Conscription Fellowship, 1914-1919*, University of Arkansas Press, Fayetteville, 1981, pp. 23-25.) Baden Powell had created the Scout Defence Corps in 1913 to aid the civil authorities in case of war; the first into action were the Scouts of Hertfordshire. (See the letter from Frank Brittain, archivist of the Hertfordshire Scouts, to the BBC History Magazine, February 2009.) At the outbreak of war Baden Powell called for a thousand Boy Scouts to volunteer to be useful by helping in 'collecting and distributing information re supplies, billeting, guarding culverts and telegraphs, assisting post

offices, police, fire brigades, ambulances, and poor relief distribution'. (*Leicester Pioneer*, 7th August 1914.) The local Girl Guides chipped in by making extra clothing for the sick and wounded, to be distributed by the Red Cross and the St John's Ambulance Brigade. (*Rugby Advertiser*, 8th and 15th August 1914.) Some confusion was – and is – caused by the Scouts' promotion of what might be called 'military values' such as loyalty, obedience, self-reliance and adaptability, and its emphasis on building 'character' (see Mark Freeman, *Muscular Quakerism? The Society of Friends and Youth Organisations in Britain, c. 1900-1950*, English Historical Review, cxxv, June 2010) but Baden Powell had already declared the Scouting movement 'non-militaristic', and we should not see it as a proto-military organisation: it was, indeed, accused during the war of harbouring youthful conscientious objectors who were reluctant to join the cadet training corps with their military drill and arms training. Every Scout must be prepared to 'do his bit' for King and Country – short of wearing military uniform and bearing arms. The German Boy Scouts, by contrast, were active in promoting drill and military-style training. (Kramer, p. 160.)

126. *Rugby Advertiser*, 2nd December 1916.

127. Lutterworth Parish Council Minutes, 30th November 1914 and 31st May 1915. *Rugby Advertiser*, 5th September 1914. The culprits in the Christmas Day events appeared before the magistrates (Lupton Topham in the chair) as reported in the *Rugby Advertiser* on January 9th 1915. Then there was the obscure case of fourteen-year-old Harry Elson, placed in the workhouse on February 4th 1915 by the police and released the same day: no reasons are given for his admittance or discharge. Suggested answers would be sheer speculation. Lutterworth Workhouse Master's Report Book, 4th February 1915. LRO.DE1909/441.

128. *Rugby Advertiser*, 2nd December 1916.

129. *Rugby Advertiser*, 7th October 1916. Despite this the chief constable had put on record his dislike of the specials. In May 1915, when the Police (Emergency) Act had allowed serving officers to join the army, counting their time in khaki against their police service and making up the wages of married men to their police pay, the chief constable had made it clear that he would rather their replacements were parish constables than specials. (Leicestershire Constabulary, Minutes of Superintendents' Meetings, 31st May 1915, LRO.DE5491/104.) We are also reminded of Marie Lloyd's music hall song, 'My Old Man said Follow the Van' (or 'Band' in some versions) with its line: 'You can't trust a special like the old-time coppers'.

130. Beazley, p. 37.

131. *Rugby Advertiser*, 25th May 1918. The theme of moral decadence had been taken up by H.G. Wells just after the outbreak of war: 'A new generation was growing up which had been too young to be chastened by the long-drawn humiliations of South Africa.

It danced an indecent dance called the Tango to express itself. "Tangoism" was not a chance phenomenon in British life; it was allied to a movement of irrational extravagance in art, to such phenomena as the diseased growth of night clubs in London, and to the violent last hysteria of the feminist movement... England in the beginning of 1914... had an extraordinary appearance of spent forces and intellectual despair; its life seemed to be divided between dense stupidity on the side of authority, venal muddle-headedness in politics, and an almost insane personal irresponsibility. Every idiot in the country was professing to be a "Rebel", and trying to do something more conspicuously mischievous and silly than the others.' (H.G. Wells, *Will the War Change England?,* in *The War Illustrated Deluxe* volume II, page 608.) War as catharsis.

132. *Rugby Advertiser*, 27th June 1914.

133. N. Hiley, *Counter Espionage and Security in Great Britain during the First World War*, English Historical Review, 1986, pp. 637.

134. Christopher Andrew, *The Defence of the Realm. The Authorized History of MI5*, Allen Lane, London, 2009, pp. 64-5. Leonard Sellers, *Shot in the Tower. The Story of the Spies Executed in the Tower of London in the First World War*, Leo Cooper, London, 1997, Chapter 2.

135. *Rugby Advertiser*, 15th August 1914. Throughout the war the British people were fed a constant diet of sentiments like these: 'The German governess in your home, the German hairdresser who clipped the heads of the Aldershot subalterns, the waiters in the restaurants, the clever German lad whom you helped along out of his poverty and to whom you gave a job, the dandy who flirted with your daughter in smart London drawing-rooms, all were creating this vast war-machine quite as keenly as Bertha Krupp's workmen were welding the molten steel for your annihilation.' Haldane Macfall, *Germany at Bay*, George H. Doran, New York, n.d. (1917), p.72.

136. *Rugby Advertiser*, 8th August 1914.

137. *Rugby Advertiser*, 15th August 1914. The crowd's linking of 'German' and 'Jew' is intriguing, reflecting a conflation in the public imagination of the two, as 'Jews' became increasingly identified with 'Germans'. In 1915, in the wake of the sinking of the *Lusitania* and the anti-German violence which followed, the *Jewish Chronicle* asked rhetorically whether 'people should be taught, day by day, to identify Jew with German'. (Quoted in Alyson Pendlebury, *Portraying "the Jew" in First World War Britain*, Vallentine Mitchell, London and Portland Oregon, 2006.) In this case we do not know whether the shopkeeper was Jewish or not, though his ownership of a second-hand clothes shop may have suggested to some that he was, but it was his supposed 'Germanness' which was the issue, and he was not asked to demonstrate that he was not a Jew.

138. ibid.

139. On the sinking, see J. Corbett, *Naval Operations*, Vol. II, London, 1921, pp. 393-4.

Corbett's tally of lost lives and the one generally accepted was 1,198, though Colin Simpson recovered three missing victims, stowaways who turned out to be Germans with a camera. They were locked in the ship's prison cells; when the ship was torpedoed no one thought to release them. (Colin Simpson, *Lusitania*, Penguin Books, Harmondsworth, 1974, pp. 104-9.) See also Diana Preston. *Wilful Murder. The Sinking of the Lusitania*, Corgi Books, London, 2003.

140. *Leicester Daily Mercury*, 10th May, 1915.

141. *Leicester Daily Post*, 14th May, 1915. His shop was at No. 117; Wright's Directory, 1914.

142. F.P. Armitage, *Leicester 1914-1918*, Leicester, 1933, p. 60.

143. *Leicester Daily Post*, 14th May, 1915.

144. *Leicester Mail*, 17th May 1915.

145. Leicestershire Constabulary. Minutes of Superintendents' Meetings, 6th August 1914, LRO.DE 5491/104/1. The chief constable's view was in line with and was informed by the security services; see Hiley, pp. 646-7. Professor Christopher Andrew reports that 'at least 32,000 (mostly men of military age) were interned, at least 20,000 (mostly women, children and non-combatant men) repatriated, and the remainder subjected to numerous restrictions'. (Andrew, p. 81.)

146. Leicestershire Constabulary. Minutes of Superintendents' Meetings', 6th August 1914, LRO.DE 5491/104/1.

147. See the file of letters in LRO.DE1379/23/1 to 29. Under the Naturalisation Act of 1870 Jessie was stripped of her British nationality and took on the nationality of her husband when she married, and in that sense was, in law, an 'enemy alien', despite her British birth. Professor Panikos Panayi explains the system: 'From November 1914 the Local Government Board took charge of the welfare of British-born wives of enemy aliens. The funds they handed out went through Boards of Guardians and they remained distinct from poor relief. To qualify for the Local Government Board funds a woman had to be the wife of an interned alien without "sufficient resources". Initially the scale of payment stood at 10s. per week for a wife and 1s. 6d. for each child for families living in London, and 8s. and 1s. 6d. respectively for wives and children living outside London… When a woman made a claim she had to produce proof of her English birth, her marriage, and her husband's internment. Investigation of cases by Poor Law Guardians took weeks.' Even then she received far less than the Separation Allowance paid to the wives of soldiers. (Panikos Panayi, *The Enemy in Our Midst. Germans in Britain During the First World War*, Berg, New York and London, 1991, pp. 260-1. See also Margaret E. Hirst, *The Quakers in Peace and War*, Swarthmore Press, London, 1923, p. 495, n. 1.) Jessie had, on marriage, acquired her husband's 'enemy' nationality. It is possible that another case can be found when Ilse and Fred Kleinschmidt who lived with their mother on Bitteswell Road appear in the record

when they fell victim to the 1917 Scarlet Fever epidemic in Lutterworth. (LRO.DE1379/826/1-6.) In January 1918 the police superintendent in Lutterworth, Walter Holland, reported to his chief constable that 'Trautmann, of North Kilworth, should be interned although he is naturalized': the chief constable replied that 'if he erred it would be on the safe side'. (Leicestershire Constabulary. Minutes of Superintendents' Meetings, 25th January 1918, LRO.DE 5491/104/1.) This came at a time of heightened anxiety, even panic, when the Northcliffe press was campaigning for the internment of all aliens. Trautmann was presumably interned, though no evidence is offered as to why. On the internment of 'enemy aliens', see Panayi, Chapters 3 and 4. See also Laura Tabili, *"Outsiders in the Land of their Birth": Exogamy, Citizenship and Identity in War and Peace*, Journal of British Studies, October 2005.

148. Minute Book, Bitteswell Church Committees, 1914-1919. LEO.DE759/43. See also F.P. Armitage, *Leicester, 1914-1918*, Backus, Leicester, 1933, pp. 129-30.

149. K.C, Clarke, *Blaby Parish Council: The First Hundred Years, 1894-1994*, no imprint, 1995, p. 4.

150. *Rugby Advertiser*, 9th September 1916. Whyment was not the only awkward customer. A farmer named Henry Jarvis from nearby Leire, when appearing before the Lutterworth Magistrates for showing a light a few weeks later, told the court that if the government wanted him to put up blackout, they should pay for it themselves. Lord Braye, presiding, was less than sympathetic and fined him £3. (*Rugby Advertiser*, 14th October 1916.)

151. Stimulating comparisons with an earlier period of history can be found in William G. Naphy and Penny Roberts (eds.), *Fear in Early Modern Society*, Manchester University Press, Manchester, 1997, esp. pp. 2-3 and 190.

152. See Adrian Bristow, *A Serious Disappointment. The Battle of Aubers Ridge 1915 and the Subsequent Munitions Scandal*, Leo Cooper, London, 1995. Thomas Ingram, a medical officer who had worked for Lutterworth Workhouse, wrote to the Guardians from the Front in 1915: 'what we need is shells and lots more shells to let our fellows get a chance of coming to close quarters with the enemy. I was pleased to hear you have started a munitions factory at Lutterworth and hope that you are working overtime. Get the girls and the physically unfit men to make shells and send the others out here and then it won't be very long before this war is over.' (LRO.DE1909/353, 28th October 1915.) Captain Ingram was killed a year later tending the wounded at the Front on the night of September 16th 1916. (C.W.G.C.)

153. Henry Newbolt, *Naval Operations*, (Official History), Vol. V, Longmans, Green and Co., London, 1931, p.121; R.D. Layman, *Naval Aviation in the First World War. Its Impact and Influence*, reprinted by Caxton Press, London, 2002, pp. 118-125.

154. Mother to Leonard, 14th July 1916.

155. (Harold Buck) to Leonard, 18th April 1915.

156. Lutterworth Parish Church Burials Register, LRO.DE4336/20. The Congregational Chapel had no burial ground of its own. The Buck family appears frequently in the records of the Congregational Chapel, now held in the United Reformed Church.

157. Archives of the Lutterworth Congregational Church, now held in the United Reformed Church.

158. Lutterworth Local History Group, *Lutterworth War Memorial Names, 1914-1918, 1939-1945. A Preliminary Study*, 2005, p. 1-19.

159. There were two Thomas Bucks in Lutterworth; the other was a brewer, very active in local affairs.

160. Full name George Frank Dale. A member of the 1st Rifle Brigade, he was killed near Ypres on March 22nd 1915; his name appears on the War Memorial inside Monks Kirby Church in Warwickshire.

161. *Rugby Advertiser*, April 10th 1915; C.W.G.C.

162. *Rugby Advertiser*, 10th April 1915. Lutterworth Museum holds a photograph of Edgar Chamberlain in church choir robes.

163. Leonard to Harold Buck, 2nd May 1915.

164. *Leicester Daily Mercury*, 4th August 1914.

165. Lutterworth Local History Group, *Lutterworth War Memorial Names*, 2005, p. 1/75. His name was added to his family's gravestone in Lutterworth Churchyard, identifying his date of death, but possibly incorrectly giving his place of death as 'Belgium'. It is not possible to identify him in the Commonwealth War Graves Commission records, but his name appears among the dead in *Bottrill's Almanac of Lutterworth* for 1916 and 1917, both giving the 14th September 1914 date.

166. Lyn Macdonald, *1914*, Penguin Books, London, 1989, p. 308.

167. *Leicester Daily Mercury*, 9th October 1914.

168. Lutterworth Local History Group, *Lutterworth War Memorial Names, 1914-1918, 1939-1945. A Preliminary Study*, Lutterworth, 2005.

169. ibid. p. 1.11 and 1.16.

170. Admiralty Staff History, CB1515(24), *The Technical History and Index, Volume 2, Part 24, Storage and Handling of Explosives in Warships*, October 1919; available via Dave Alton at www.1914-1918.invisionzone.com.; full version of the Naval Enquiry Report at www.gwpda.org/naval/thist24; see also www.nhcra-online.org/20c/bulwark.

171. Martin Gilbert, *First World War*, London, 1995, p. 144.

172. J.E. Edmonds and G.C. Wynne, *Military Operations, France and Belgium, December 1914 to May 1915*, H.M.S.O., London, 1927 (Official History), p. 177, n. 3.

173. *With the First Canadian Contingent*, letters by Canadian soldiers published on behalf of the Canadian Field Comforts Commission, Toronto, 1915, p. 86.

174. The Official History gives twelve officers and 175 other ranks killed or wounded. The Emergency Committee Minutes, Territorial Association, 1st July 1915 gave forty-seven killed, though no names were given. LRO.DE819/1. George Codrington, in his *History of the Yeomanry* gives slightly different figures: eighty-seven men and seven officers killed, giving a total of ninety-four. The discrepancy is accounted for by the three men who died of wounds after the 13th: Private Chester on the 15th, Sergeant Stafford in hospital in Nottingham on the 30th of May, and Henry Mason.

175. *Leicester Mail*, 17th May 1915.

176. *Leicester Daily Post*, 18th May, 1915.

177. *Leicester Daily Mercury*, 18th May 1915.

177. *Melton Mowbray Mercury and Oakham and Uppingham News*, 27th May 1915; the letter was also quoted elsewhere.

178. *Leicester Mail*, 19th May 1915.

180. *Leicester Mail*, 21st May 1915.

181. William Smith's name appears on the War Memorial in Bitteswell, though his parents lived in Baker Street in Lutterworth; Register of Electors, Southern and Harborough Districts, LRO.CC/C/1/84/1-2. 'List of Men Serving with the Colours', Bitteswell, undated MS., LRO.DE759/46.

182. *Leicester Mail and Leicester Daily Post*, 17th and 19th May 1915.

183. *Leicester Mail*, 19th May 1915.

184. Lord Northcliffe, *At the War*, London, 1916, p. 24.

185. *Leicester Daily Mercury*, 22nd May, 1915.

186. The strain on relatives has not always been sufficiently considered. On Saturday, 29th May 1915, for example, the *Leicester Mail* carried a story about the Annual Report of the Leicester Borough Mental Hospital. The number of patients had increased, especially males; and one woman had been admitted who had seven sons serving at the Front, five of whom had already been wounded. A connection to her mental state, though not proven, is suggested.

187. *Leicester Chronicle and Leicestershire Mercury*, 22nd May 1915.

188. Martin Middlebrook, *The First Day on the Somme, 1st July 1916*, Allen Lane, The Penguin Press, London, 1971, p.263.

189. The phrase is C.R.M.F. Cruttwell's, *A History of the War, 1914-1918*, 1936, Granada Publishing, London, 1982, p.347.

190. Lutterworth Local History Group, *Lutterworth War Memorial Names, 1914-1918, 1939-1945*, Lutterworth, 2005.

191. Sarson was a Stoker 1st Class, fighting on land as part of the Hood Battalion of the Royal Naval Division. The action in which he was killed, officially the Third Battle of Krithia, was brilliantly described by Robert Rhodes James in *Gallipoli*, Pimlico Books, London, 1999, pp. 210-5.

192. Jay Winter (ed.), *The Legacy of the Great War Ninety Years On*, University of Missouri Press and the National World War I Memorial Museum, Kansas City, Missouri, Columbia & London, 2009, p. 111.

193. See Bob Bushaway, *Name upon Name. The Great War and Remembrance*, in Roy Porter (ed.), *Myths of the English*, Polity Press, London, 1993, pp.142 and 152.

194. *Leicester Pioneer*, 7th August 1914.

PART THREE

AWAY FROM HOME

ASQUITH'S *SHIP OF LIBERAL VALUES*

At the start of House of Commons business on Wednesday, January 5th 1916 the Prime Minister, Herbert Asquith, stood up to propose the Military Service (No. 2) Bill – the 'Conscription Bill' – to Parliament. The voluntary principle, which had supplied all Britain's recruitment needs in the war so far, was about to be abolished.

> 'Single men of military age who have no ground whatever for exemption or excuse... shall be deemed to have done what everyone agrees it is their duty to the State in times like these to do, and be treated as though they had attested or enlisted.'

Put more bluntly, every unmarried man between the ages of eighteen and forty-one was liable to be called up for compulsory military service. There would, though, be 'exceptions' to the general rule: men not normally resident in Britain, men already in the services, and the clergy. More troublesome was the issue of those to be 'exempted': men whose work was regarded as being of particular national importance, surviving sons with dependent families, those too ill or infirm to be of military use and, finally, those with 'a conscientious objection to the undertaking of combatant service'.[1]

For Asquith, the inclusion of the 'conscience clause' was an important if forlorn attempt to salvage something of his Liberal values of individualism and personal liberty and, above all, *voluntarism* from the bitterness of his defeat at the hands of his pro-conscription rivals and from the ruthless demands of Lloyd George and Winston Churchill, Lord Curzon and the press baron Lord Northcliffe, from the bulk of the Conservatives in the Coalition government and the insistent demands of the army. Asquith detested the idea of compulsion to his very soul, but the failure of the Derby Scheme in October (by which men were invited to 'attest' or state their willingness to be called when the need arose) was sufficient to force the Prime

Minister to concede.[2] For all that, the inclusion of the conscience clause did mark 'a triumph for all that was best and most enlightened in British life'.[3]

Amidst cries of disapproval from M.P.s who rejected the whole idea of a conscience clause, Asquith patiently explained: 'I am rather sorry to hear those expressions of dissent, and even of derision from some quarters,' he said. '…Those of us who know the real facts of British life know quite well that there are a great many people belonging to various religious denominations, or to various schools of thought, who are quite prepared to serve their country in the war, but who object, on conscientious grounds, to the taking of life. They are, however, quite willing to perform many other military duties… [This] I am certain is all they would claim… exemption from military combatant duties only… [but] could take – as most of us can – military duties in the fullest sense of the term…'[4] 'It respects,' Asquith concluded, 'the scruples of those who on conscientious grounds, object to undertaking combatant service'.[5]

It was all very *reasonable*, and the mechanism by which the genuineness of each individual's claim would be assessed was also very *reasonable*. Local Tribunals in the man's home town would be the first point of referral. Or, as Lord Sandhurst put it when the issue of the Tribunals was debated in the Lords early in May, the genuine conscientious objector would be known 'in country districts' where the Tribunal would have 'intimate local knowledge of the man, his family, his upbringing, his general surroundings and atmosphere'.[6] What better safeguard could there be for the man whose religious convictions and civic involvement could not be doubted? Who would be better placed to come to fair and reasonable judgements about each man's claim than his neighbours and peers?

A further safeguard was to be the Appeal Tribunals, set up, generally, in each county and nominated by the government, which would ensure fairness in individual cases and achieve 'uniformity of decision in regard to the decisions of the Primary Body'. Finally, to prevent any possibility of miscarriage, there was to be a further and final appeal to the Central Tribunal in London.[7] These safeguards meant those who opposed the very principle of a conscientious exemption could feel confident that no 'slacker' or 'shirker' or 'coward' could slip through the net, while potential conscientious objectors knew that their cases would be thoroughly and equitably heard and a right decision reached. In other words, the Tribunals were there to not only make the system fair, but make it be *seen* to be fair.

Despite this, the system attracted widespread criticism at the time and it has been attacked even more vehemently since. Why? Let us visualise the 'conscience clause' system as a ship at sea: Asquith's *Ship of Liberal Values*. It was destined to founder upon four great rocks, some visible at the time of its launch, some more unexpected, and some out of reach of Asquith's reasonable and liberal vision.

THE FIRST ROCK

THE INCOMPETENCE OF THE TRIBUNALS

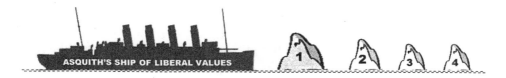

Image via http://www.titanicandco.com/cunard

Posterity has not been kind to the Military Service Act Tribunals of the First World War, largely because it has accepted without question the damning criticisms made by the conscientious objectors who appeared before them, compounded by the fact that almost all the records of their work were destroyed in the 1920s. In no other sphere would we be expected to accept the verdict of those who saw themselves as the victims of a system without hearing from the other side. This is unfair. The fact was that the number of men who applied for exemptions was immense, clogging up the system: as the historian Adrian Gregory suggests, as many as a million men appeared before the Tribunals, and 'it must have been a rare individual who did not make a claim for at least temporary exemption'.[8]

Therefore, it is worth reminding ourselves that the Military Service Act Tribunals were not *all* about conscientious objectors – far from it. The overwhelming number of cases dealt with came under the headings of economic or domestic hardship, cases which the Tribunals generally treated with consideration and generosity: the claim to a conscientious exemption was very rare indeed.[9] That the Tribunals dealt efficiently and effectively with those who claimed economic or personal exemption (or, more usually, the employers of men claimed to be economically essential) is ignored in the rush to condemn.

What they were not good at and were incompetent to handle, were claims for exemption on grounds of *conscience*. Nor, given the circumstances, could they be.

It was one thing to weigh the level of financial hardship the absence of a son or father might impose, or to decide whether a firm might go into bankruptcy without its key workers, or what the impact of the conscription of a widow's last son and only breadwinner might be, but weighing men's souls was a different matter. Claims based on individual conscience or, more accurately, the grounds on which they were made, usually fell beyond the normal competence or experience of the men who sat in judgement, so it cannot really surprise us when they failed to handle many of these cases in the spirit of the Act. It is clear that their performance in the more difficult cases fell far short of the ideal, and far short of the 'reasonable' judgement Asquith had envisaged from them. It was a consequence of devolved responsibility.

One writer sympathetic to the cause of the conscientious objectors, writing just after the First World War, explained the problem: 'Then was instituted the most extraordinary attempt to exercise spiritual insight ever handed over to bodies of amateurs. The task would have been essentially impossible, even if exercised sympathetically by bodies of men trained to understand the ways of sensitive souls, if such men there are.'[10] The Classical scholar, Gilbert Murray, had made much the same point in 1917: 'The first and most obvious fault about many of them was their lack of the necessary qualifications for dealing with questions of conscience, or for at all understanding the mind of an intellectual or religious man, not to speak of an eccentric or enthusiast.'[11] The Tribunals could not 'open windows into men's souls', as Elizabeth I had understood when faced with her own Papist conscientious objectors.

On the other hand, the evidence can be misleading. The accounts of many conscientious objectors and their supporters then and since, make it appear that it was harder to be passed by a Local Tribunal on grounds of conscience than it was for the Biblical camel to be passed through the eye of the needle. However, of the 16,000 men who claimed a conscientious objection to military service, 10,000 were passed by the Tribunals and given purely civilian jobs to do, mainly in agriculture, or they took up non-combatant duties at or near the front lines. In their cases the Tribunals attracted no complaint. The number rejected by the Tribunals was thus about 6,000.

At the Second Reading debate one week later, the former Home Secretary, Sir John Simon, put his finger on the nub of the problem: 'while I do not desire to see any man shield himself behind provisions for the conscientious objector unless he holds a really deep conscientious objection in his own heart, I find it very difficult to see how adequate provision is to be made for the genuine and conscientious objector, while at the same time you avoid making the meshes of your net too wide…' for then 'the class of person with whom I have no more sympathy than any man in this House; that is the shirker, who is so mean as to pretend that it is his conscience that prevents him taking part in his country's war,'[12] would slip through and be accepted as genuine. In the event, the meshes of the net were made too narrow, not too wide.

The problem lay with the composition of the Local and Appeal Tribunals: 'The Tribunals… were generally selected from such local notabilities as had shown great interest in recruiting under the Derby Scheme'[13], and, as one contemporary critic suggested, 'they were of course anxious to please the War Office, to satisfy the more turbulent newspapers, and to display their own patriotism by sending other people to the trenches'.[14] It was then, as John Graham observed, that 'the impossible became the tragic'.[15]

Lord Sydenham, speaking in the Lords, was worried about another problem, the variety of reasons a man might claim his conscience prevented him from military service: 'I can assure the House that you find in dealing with them that the number of classes and the natures of conscientious objection are infinitely varied. The only points which these men have in common are a rooted aversion to war—a most meritorious sentiment…' He went on. 'I will give your Lordships a few instances. The extreme objector will consent to serve in a civil hospital, but if three or four soldiers are put into that hospital he will decline to do anything. That is a difficult kind of man to deal with. Then, again, some will work at munitions, while others will have nothing to do with munitions because they say that this is the exact equivalent to doing combatant work. As the Right Rev. Prelate [the Bishop of Oxford, Charles Gore] pointed out, even the whole of the members of the Society of Friends do not see with one eye in this matter. Some of them are doing admirable ambulance work in France; others are fighting—though perhaps surreptitiously—while others will have nothing to do even with a military hospital; so that in dealing with a body like the Society of Friends you are faced with a great variety of differences. Then there are some objectors who will do most things provided they do not do them under any form of military authority. The objection is not to the work, but to the authority under which the work is done. Then there is a quite considerable class of objectors who will do no work of any kind on a [Sunday] unless it may be work of mercy, and they will not do work of mercy if they are to do it under orders from anybody else. There are also many who will do nothing which they think might release other men for combatant service. In some cases the objections are much more political than religious, and there are cases in which the objector himself is not quite clear whether his objections are political or religious. These are instances of the great variations of the forms of conscientious objection which come before the Tribunals.'[16] It is little wonder the Tribunals were confused.

As the weeks went by and the new system got under way, the difficulties multiplied as more and more uncertainty clouded round the Tribunals (despite new guidance sent out by the Ministry on February 3rd ('guidance' not 'instruction') and some astonishing verdicts were handed down. The Tribunals were given the power to grant any one of three degrees of exemption: absolute or unconditional exemption, exemption from military service on condition that the claimant did civilian work of national importance, and thirdly non-combatant service in the army as part of the Non-Combatant Corps, though many Tribunals seem not to have understood this. In Parliament the Minister responsible, the Tory conscriptionist, Walter Long, found himself increasingly embattled and embarrassed. But central government was reluctant to intervene. As Long told Parliament, 'The appointment of the Tribunal has been left to the local authority as containing the elected representatives of the people. I do not think it would be right for me to interfere with their discretion unless there are very strong reasons for doing so.'[17] Arguably, 'very strong reasons' did already exist, but, sensibly enough, the government declined to enter that particular minefield. All Long could do was to defend the name of the Tribunals as best he could: 'I have no reason to think that generally the Local Tribunals which have been appointed do not command general confidence,' he told Parliament, and in economic and domestic cases he was probably right.[18]

Meanwhile the anecdotal evidence was accumulating. At Market Bosworth, just a handful of miles from Lutterworth, during the same sitting in which a claimant on conscientious grounds was refused, the chairman asking him how long he had 'suffered with conscientious objection', the Tribunal granted a six months' exemption to six servants of the Atherstone Hunt, the given reason that 'the preservation of hunting was necessary for the continuation of the breeding and raising of eligible horses' for the cavalry.[19] From across the country there were reported attempts to exclude anti-conscriptionists from membership of Tribunals, of Tribunal chairmen who declared that they intended to grant no exemptions, of Tribunals which deliberately excluded representatives from labour, or which excluded women (though they were under no obligation to include them), which refused to allow claimants legal representation, and even of some Local Tribunals being unaware that they could grant absolute exemption on conscientious grounds at all.[20] At least one M.P. wanted all reporting of conscientious claims before Local Tribunals to be banned: Major Newman asked, early in March, 'whether, in view of the exhibition of lack of manhood and cowardice displayed before Local

Tribunals by young men seeking escape from military service on conscientious grounds, he will censor in the public Press all reports of such exhibitions?' Herbert Samuel, the Home Secretary, declined, though one of his colleagues, Hayes Fisher, did give the view that Tribunals could indeed, if they so wished, exclude the press from their hearings.[21]

Across much of the country, it seems, the conscientious objectors were regarded with incomprehension and bafflement by the Local Tribunals. They were treated with hostility, their beliefs and their claims, let alone their rights under the Military Service Act, ignored. This was not a simple lack of intellectual and moral competence in dealing with such cases. It was a positive rejection. The Local Tribunals seemed to be wilfully ignoring the official guidelines and Asquith's intentions of *reasonableness*, and were, by and large, refusing absolute exemption to those who claimed exemption on grounds of conscience, on their own initiative and according to their own definition of the rules. The Intermediate Tribunals which should have acted as courts of appeal, behaved in much the same way. If their function, as defined by the Prime Minister, was to ensure uniformity of treatment, they were doing that all too well – though entirely counter to the Prime Minister's cherished intentions.

Why the Tribunals should have been so uniformly hostile is not necessarily self-evident. Broadly, the Tribunals were confronted by two very different kinds of conscientious objector: the religious and the political. The Payne brothers fell into the former category. Unless they belonged to a recognised religious group with a tradition of pacifism, and sometimes even then,[22] they were not likely to have an easy time in convincing the Tribunal members of their genuineness. With very few exceptions the Christian denominations in Britain had declared themselves, either reluctantly or enthusiastically, *for* the war in 1914. So to many Tribunal members the equation was simple; if a man said he was, for example, an Anglican, and the Church of England had declared its support for the war and for the participation of its members in it, then the individual claiming conscientious objection to fighting *must* be wrong. Moreover, his motives must be suspect, if not downright mendacious.

Even more problematical for the Tribunals were those who objected on *political* grounds, men usually of a left wing socialist leaning who refused to participate in what they saw as a capitalist war of workers killing workers at the behest of industrialists and profiteers, or saw conscription as the unjustifiable intrusion of the State into the lives of individual free citizens, or both. These men formed the majority of those who claimed a conscientious objection in the First World War. They were generally not pacifists, for they believed in class war and many, in 1917, would applaud the coming of the Russian Revolution. We can guess at the attitude of many Tribunal members to men like these from this extract from a popular magazine published throughout the Great War and chronicling its progress. Commenting on the reluctance of some trade unionists to support the war, it told its readers that there existed 'a small, noisy minority of born "slackers" and canny working-class profiteers, [together] with hopeless cranks, fishers in troubled waters and agitators of a dubious sort…' which was 'ready to help Germany by preventing us from becoming a great military power on the continental scale' through conscription.[23]

When explaining the hostility of many of the Tribunals, it must also be said that simple stupidity played its part. The army complained that genuine conscientious objectors were being passed into its ranks when the Tribunals had been designed to save the military from the disruption which genuine conscientious objectors in its ranks would cause. When the army was in the midst of the greatest war the world had ever seen, frantically trying to train up civilians into soldiers who could be sent up against what was widely believed to be the best army in the world, every genuine conscientious objector the Tribunals failed to exempt was an additional and unwanted distraction. Yet the *military* representatives on the Tribunals generally took upon themselves the role of prosecutor whenever a claim of conscience appeared, and were the ones least likely to approve their appeals. Even Hayes Fisher of the Local Government Board confessed that sometimes he felt 'a little ashamed of some of the Tribunals'.[24]

★

It had been clear from the outset that Leonard Payne would decline to accept conscription. That Roland would follow him was rather less certain. In 1973 the brothers were interviewed together by Peter Liddle for his massive archive held in the Brotherton Library of Leeds University. Leonard told him that 'I didn't have any doubts about it at all', and his attitudes and actions from thereon leave no doubt about the truth of that. 'I never felt any different from the beginning of the war,' he said. 'We had been brought up in a very narrow circle… We had been brought up that way all our lives. All our people had always been opposed to war and I think it was part of that that was in our minds all the time. I don't think we ever forgot that… I don't say that the war was wrong,' Leonard concluded, 'I was convinced I was going to take no part in it at all.'[25]

Peter Liddle skilfully probed the nature and the strength of their rejection, putting questions very much like those in the minds of the Tribunal members.

'[When] you two brothers, who were then as close as you are now, were together outside the hearing of anybody else or indeed when you were by yourselves, I wouldn't be surprised if sometimes searching self-analysis took place in which without the pressure of other people being involved you tried to ask yourselves honestly if you were – and I use this word in inverted commas – "in a cowardly fashion avoiding the danger of being wounded or shot",' he asked. Again, 'England, for all the poverty and injustice, nevertheless had a way of life which many people – a majority of people – did not wish to see altered and believed (perhaps wrongly, I don't know) that it would be altered if German militarism was able to exercise a dominance over Europe and that there were numbers of people who were prepared to fight to preserve the English way of life and you would benefit by their efforts to which you were not contributing. Did you amongst yourselves ever ask these questions?' However cautiously put, the question was a valid one, one which many of the conscientious objectors found themselves asking. It is clear from Leonard's answer that these were matters which had not impinged in any significant degree upon his consciousness. The question about whether he ever considered his refusal to go might be motivated by cowardice was ignored completely, and the second part drew the response that, 'I think we realised what these fellows [who did join the army] were trying to do. I mean they were sincere about it and no doubt the country would benefit by what they were doing, but you see the point was we didn't agree with the way it was being done. That was the point, I think.' It is a curiously imprecise, inarticulate answer, and one which might have been probed further, the meaning of 'the way it was being done' remaining densely obscure.

Peter Liddle pressed both brothers on the issue of the rights and wrongs of the war. 'What would you do,' he asked, paraphrasing the famous question put to several of the conscientious objectors, 'if a German came into your home and attacked your mother?'[26] Leonard side-stepped the issue, first with a joke and then saying he could not remember being asked the question and then, 'I don't know, it is very difficult to say.' Roland's response was, in its way, more revealing. He told Peter Liddle, 'I can't definitely give answers, no, because I don't know what the state of my mind at the time'. *[sic.]* The interviewer interpreted this as meaning he could not possibly have given an answer to such a hypothetical question, but the incoherence suggests a deeper confusion in Roland's mind, even so many years after the war. His answer could plausibly mean 'I don't know how I would have answered that question because I do not now know what the state of my mind was *at that time.*' Here, Leonard showed some understanding that, *at that time*, they were very different people from what they had become: 'You see', he told Peter Liddle, 'we were young and I don't think we realised altogether what was going on.'

For Leonard, it was all very simple and though he denied it had anything to do with 'native obstinacy', it is clear that this was one element in his personality which was given every opportunity for self-expression when confronted by the call up. When asked the question: 'Can you tell me today with absolute honesty that at no stage did you have serious doubts about your stand?' Leonard's reply was absolute, 'No, I didn't have any doubts about it at all.' Again, Roland's answer was more revealing: 'I think I got more determined as things went on', which would suggest that at first he did have doubts about what he should do. What swept him along in these early days was without doubt the influence of his family, especially of his mother and of Leonard. Whatever personal reservations Roland might have had, the charge of cowardice or slacking, or an awareness of the dangers the country faced from German military might across the Channel, for good or ill, he threw in his lot with his brother.

★

When Leonard and Roland were called up for military service they naturally applied for exemption to the Local Tribunal in Lutterworth on grounds of conscience. In law and justice they were entitled to an absolute exemption from military service on grounds of religious belief, but in practice their prospects were not good. In theory they should have had a good hearing, the genuineness of their case was self-evident. The 'intimate local knowledge of the man, his family, his upbringing, his general surroundings and atmosphere' would all inform the local men who would sit in judgement. It did not work out like that.[27] Now, Asquith's *Ship of Liberal Values* and all that was said at the First Reading debate in the House of Commons about the safeguarding of the individual's rights of conscience, with those tiers of Local, Intermediate and Central Tribunals to safeguard the rights of men like Leonard and Roland Payne, would be put to the test.

Virtually the only record of the Payne brothers' call up and appearance before the Appeals Tribunals comes from the information they gave in 1973 in their interview with Peter Liddle. This presents us with problems; firstly, because there is no independent corroborating evidence save the verdict handed down; and, secondly, because of the great distance in time between the event and its recollection. So, given that we must treat it with a degree of caution, this is what Leonard and Roland Payne remembered. 'It was a local thing and they were mostly local men that were on it…' It was made up of 'a lot of local farmers, naturally, being a farming area and there was one representative from the foundries. He never said a word the whole time… It was the old [Poor Law] Board of Guardians really that ran things in Lutterworth and the biggest trouble was that there was a military representative, he was called and you couldn't put your case because he simply sat there and he snapped at everything and everybody. He wouldn't listen to any sort of reason at all and that is what went on. Then you were turned down there.'[28]

It would be easy simply to write off the Lutterworth Tribunal as yet another of all those Local Tribunals whose judgements were dismissive of claims of conscience, a Tribunal of the men of local power and influence; 'the old Board of Guardians', imposing their own world view on their social inferiors, as yet another kangaroo court, its decisions already made, ignoring the evidence of the Paynes' claims as well as its own local knowledge of them and their family, bullied by the military representative into delivering an unfair, unjust and false judgement. This was certainly how the Payne family saw it.

While we have little direct evidence of the prevailing attitude towards the Payne brothers among their neighbours in Lutterworth, their own Congregational Minister, Arthur Massey's, disapproval of and opposition to their conscientious stand, supported as it was by the vast majority of the Congregational churches of Leicestershire and of Britain, left them without the institutional support which groups like the Quakers and Christadelphians enjoyed. So if the Tribunal was looking for some sort of authentication from their church, it was not forthcoming – quite the opposite, in fact. It was much the same when they appealed to the county wide Tribunal in Leicester on April 15th 1916: 'the very same thing happened again. The military representative simply snapped and snarled at everything and everybody,' said Leonard. His conclusion was that 'the Tribunals were the biggest farce ever invented.'[30] So, as Sir John Simon had predicted from the outset, the Tribunals were failing, not in principle, but in their sadly deficient practice. Of all the official institutions which dealt with conscientious objectors in the First World War, the Tribunals were the only ones which proved incapable of learning and when the Tribunals failed, the whole system failed.

However, this does not entirely explain the rejection of their plea, first by the Lutterworth Tribunal and, then, by the County Tribunal (using the same evidence which had failed to convince the local members). In Lutterworth there had been at least one member sympathetic to the family's personal plight, the most important local businessman, George Spencer, who had gone out of his way to visit the family in their home in Church Street to try to talk them round. However, even if the Lutterworth Tribunal had been exclusively made up of tub-thumping jingoists, something more was needed. Something which would with absolute certainty scotch the brothers' claim to be conscientious objectors to military service; something which would force even George Spencer's friendly hand.

Unfortunately, for the Paynes, there was something: the shell baskets that they had spent months industriously creating, whose purpose was to make the transportation of explosive shells more efficient in the military's quest to kill Germans. This argued against their claim to be genuine Christian conscientious objectors and that was the position both Tribunals took.[29] It is possible that the Lutterworth Tribunal and the County Appeal Tribunal, sitting in Leicester, were acting in a better informed way than we suppose, in fact, precisely in the way the framers of the Military Service Act had envisioned. Were its members actually using the local knowledge they had in the way they were *supposed* to? Did they, in honesty and in justice, render a *true* judgement? Such questions are difficult to answer.

THE SECOND ROCK

THE MILITARY MIND

ASQUITH'S SHIP OF LIBERAL VALUES

The second great rock on which Asquith's *Ship of Liberal Values* foundered was the mentality of the British military: the military mind. Of course, if the Tribunals had done their work properly there would have been no conscientious objectors in the army at all, but the Tribunals, bent on doing what they saw as their patriotic duty, unwittingly passed on to the military an entirely unlooked for problem. Thus the military representatives on the Tribunals helped create the problem of the conscientious objectors, a problem their military colleagues would fail to resolve.

Just as it would be easy to caricature the Tribunals as jingoistic, clumsy and insensitive, so the military mind readily lends itself to satire, as David Low's later creation 'Colonel Blimp' showed most eloquently. Major Corbet Smith of Bitteswell with his war enthusiasm, his eagerness to push every young man he could into the army and promote recruitment to the full, his praise for young men who showed fighting spirit, even his arguably misleading military title, all pointed to a mind apparently designed and built for the First World War. But, while it was true that men like Corbet Smith encapsulated one particular manifestation of the military mind, the truth of the matter was that there was no single military mind or military mentality. Nor should we assume that stupidity was any more prevalent in the First World War British Army than in any other walk of life. General Hoffman's jibe that the British soldiers were 'lions led by donkeys' has long been discredited, at least so far as the officers' side of the equation is concerned.[31]

ARREST

Rejected by the Local and the Intermediate Appeals Tribunal, in law both Leonard and Roland Payne were now soldiers. In their own eyes, they were not. Therefore, when they were summoned to appear at the Glen Parva Military Barracks at Wigston, just south of Leicester, to begin their training, they refused to go. For the moment nothing would happen: they were not due to report for duty for a further fortnight. Did they, during that time, suffer any doubts? Leonard at least, seems to have been resolved. Roland, given that both his parents and his older brother were fixed in their determination, must have buried any misgivings he might have felt. To defy the authorities and the power of the state was not something to be taken lightly, but to defy his family would be on an altogether different scale.

May 16th 1916 was the day they were due to report to the army. Nothing happened. A week went by. Then came Wednesday the 24th.[32] Leonard had spent much of the day in Leicester before attending an N.C.F. meeting in the evening with a young woman called Marion Harper. It had been a day of glorious sunshine and warmth and Marion later recalled Leonard as saying, 'Fancy killing on a day like this'.[33] Leonard's absence in Leicester did no more, of course, than delay what was inevitable.[34] He recalled in 1973, 'I… was near home on my bicicle [sic.] when two policemen pushed me off and said that they had been waiting all day to get me.'[35] He was taken to the police station in Lutterworth while his bicycle was returned home and his family told what had happened. Roland was in their Church Street home when the police called: 'I said to them, what about me? They said we have got warrants for your arrest but we will leave you until the morning, but I said I might as well come with you now. So I went straight away because I didn't want us to be divided. So they brought me up to the police station.'[36] Leonard remembered that, 'they took all my clothes away from me and left me with a hard board to spend the night on.[37] Next morning I was taken before a magistrate, and the military escort was already waiting to take me to the Barracks at Glen Parva, Leicester', the depot of the Leicestershire Regiment, the famous 'Tigers'.[38] It was but a short journey by train from their home town, their family and the world they knew, into the alien and forbidding world governed by the military.

Army Form W. 3236.

NOTICE PAPER to be sent to men who belong to the Army Reserve under the provisions of the Military Service Act, 1916.

[In accordance with the provisions of Section 24 (2) of the Reserve Forces Act, 1882, "evidence of the delivery at the last registered place of abode of a man belonging to the Army Reserve of a notice, or of a letter addressed to such man, and containing a notice, shall be evidence that such notice was brought to the knowledge of such man."

Surname _Payne_

Christian Name _Leonard._

Address _Church Street_
Lutterworth

Number in Military Register (Army Book 414) _4. Butt._

Class Number _53._

You are hereby warned that you will be required to join for service with the Colours on the _16th May_ 1916.

You should therefore present yourself at _Glen Parva Barracks, Nr Leicester_ on the above date, not later than _9 a m_ o'clock, bringing this paper with you.

*This will be struck out if the man resides within 5 miles of the place at which he is required to present himself.

A Railway Warrant is enclosed herewith.*

_____ Signature.

2nd May 1916 Date.

LEICESTER. Place.

_____ Rank.

_____ Appointment.

N.B.—Particular attention is called to Section 15 of the Reserve Forces Act, 1882, which provides that where a man belonging to the Army Reserve is called out on Permanent service, and such man, without leave lawfully granted or such sickness or other reasonable excuse as may be allowed in the prescribed manner, fails to appear at any time and place at which he is required on such calling out to attend, he shall be guilty, according to the circumstances, of deserting, within the meaning of Section 12, or of absenting himself without leave within the meaning of Section 15 of the Army Act, 1881.

(S.O. 259) Wt. 16793—5846. 100,000. 2/16. Forms/W. 3236/1.

Army Form W3236:
Leonard is summoned to formally enlist at the Glen Parva Barracks, at Wigston, Leicester.

The brothers' experience was the formal process of 'handing over' from civilian to army control. Another objector who passed through the process was Edward Bonser. He left this description, 'Only those people who have experienced being "handed over" can understand the meaning of such a phrase, more especially when the term only applies to that type of manhood which is looked upon with contempt and even derision. "Handed over" is a crude, harsh, rough phrase, and to realise its meaning three parties are necessarily concerned. In this case, two mighty powers, the authorities of the civil law and the military on the one hand and an innocent individual deemed to have transgressed, on the other.'

The Payne brothers' arrival at the barracks must have been similar to Bonser's: 'Under an hour's time, we were moving in the train en route for the barracks, and again coming events occupied too large a sphere of our horizon which, in a degree, brought us to a state of despondency. On arrival at the barracks, among the busy stir of hundreds of recruits passing to and fro, with occasional bugle blasts and harsh voices here and there of "Shun", "Halt", "Quick March", "About Turn", etc., we were led before an army officer who required answers to a list of questions. "Married or Single?" was one question, and my reply was the former. (Since the "I will" was said after Nov. 2, 1915, I was deemed to be a single married man). [The Paynes were, of course, unmarried.] "Sign here for wife's allowance," said he in a stern authoritative tone. "That I cannot do," I replied gently, and added that if I did, my wife absolutely refused to accept any army pay. Whereupon the storm of his language arose, the wind of his temper waxed strong, and, after giving an exhibition of his innermost feelings and thoughts, he commanded the escort to confine me to the guard-room and to shoot me if he liked. The guard-room was reached, the door clanged, and the huge bolt shot home. I now realised that I had indeed been "handed over".'[39]

The forbidding exterior of Lutterworth Police Station
Via http://www.hinckley.netfirms.com/Hinckley

WITH THE TIGERS

'A MOST DISMAL PLACE'

So began Leonard and Roland Payne's time in the hands of the military. They found their new temporary home 'a most dismal place'. Leonard later recalled that 'we had a large wooden bed to sleep on, very dark and very damp too.'[40] They were segregated from the more pliant recruits in the married quarters of the barracks.[41] The official position of how the army was supposed to treat men like Leonard and Roland Payne was clear: '...once a man is handed over... to the military authorities as a soldier, it is not for the military authorities to consider the reasons such a man may have for refusing to do his work... the clear duty of every commanding officer [is] to do his best with the legitimate means at his disposal to make every man who is handed over to him an efficient soldier.'[42]

On Friday, their first full day there, Roland wrote home:

Dear Dad and Mother,

Just a line to let you know we are going on all right. We have just been locked in here again after going before the doctor. We have been passed for home service. They wanted to put us in the Non-Combative Corps which we did not accept.

We have been ordered to sign some papers two or three times but refused. I suppose the next thing will be to force kaki *[sic]* on us, so don't be supprised *[sic]* if they send our ~~clos~~ togs home. If they do we shall only wear just enough to keep us warm… We are having a fine time, plenty to eat bacon and tomatoes this morning the others having sausage. The fellows [i.e other conscientious objectors] are very good they share everything they get, cake or oranges.

Love to all,

Roland.[43]

Leonard later recalled how, 'arriving [at Glen Parva] I was taken to a clothes store and again all my clothes were taken away and khaki clothes *forced* on me' – though exactly how they were forced on him he did not say. 'I took these off except trousers which I had to wear.'[44] The wearing of the khaki uniform defined a man's new existence as part of a larger whole, his position in the rigidly structured hierarchy shown by stripes or stars (or lack of them), his 'family' unit identified by his regimental badge. It marked the first stage in the loss of his individuality. So the significance of the uniform was far greater to the conscientious objectors than merely keeping warm or physical decency. For the army khaki *had* to be worn: for the conscientious objectors it *had* to be resisted.

If Leonard felt as bereft as Edward Bonser had, his loneliness was in part ameliorated by the presence of his brother Roland and the other objectors already in the barracks. For the Paynes were by no means the only objectors to pass into the Glen Parva Barracks and a genuine sense of comradeship quickly developed between these young men who knew each other from their membership of the Leicester branch of the No-Conscription Fellowship. Leonard sent a pencilled letter card home from the guard room at Glen Parva on that first day:

'We are in the guard-room for refusing to sign papers which we were asked to sign when we arrived last night. There are nine of us here all members of the NCF Green, Linnel, Stevens, Dix, Adkins, Hassal and others. We slept on boards, with three blankets last night it was jolly hard but still we shall get use *[sic]* to it. Most of the fellows have been forceably *[sic]* dressed in khaki yesterday but they are only wearing part of their clothes. They refuse all orders and are on good terms with the soldiers. Allan Shoults is having a rough time of it he was the first here and has been given fourteen days solitary confinement the first twenty-four hours on bread and water. Still we are not downhearted we have some good fun… Adkins was making us laugh all night. Bill [Roland] says he is in the pink. So good bye for the present and good hope for the future'.[45]

The Regimental Depot: Glen Parva Barracks, South Wigston. Opened in 1881, the depot (also known as Wigston Barracks) was well known to generations of Tigers who undertook their basic training there.
www.green-tiger.co.uk/sitebuildercontent/sitebuilderpictures/.pond/glenparva.

Roland wrote again on Saturday, May 27th, his second day as a 'soldier', his cheerfulness intended to reassure the family at home in Lutterworth:

'Dear All,

We are still going on all right although we are on our own since the others were put in the cells. We had tomatoes and sausage for breakfast this morning and some very good tea in a bucket. Whilst having this a major came in, and told us that it was a very serious matter to disobey an order given by a superior officer, and then ordered us to sign that paper, which we refused. Then we were took *[sic]* before the company officer for disobeying and were remanded to go before the commanding officer. These papers which they wanted us to sign are nothing more or less than a Derby Recruiting Paper. They kept telling us we are in the Non-Combatent *[sic]* Corps but we tell them we are in nothing. I suppose we shall be put in the cells before long after we have seen the C.O. Have just seen Adkins he says it is better in the cells than in here, accept *[sic]* for being by yourself. Have just seen Sholts *[sic]* after being on bread and water for forty-six hours still as bright as ever. Thanks for your nice letter. We are still more determind *[sic]* than ever. They tell us we are mad because everything they give us, we only laugh.

Love

Roland'.[46]

Leonard too, wrote home that Saturday to ask his father to send them clean handkerchiefs and a Bible, '...which are the only things we can have'.[47] The same day he wrote again to his father, John:

'Guard room

We are still here. No doubt you will wonder why we are writing so many letters in a hurry, it is because they keep fetching us out and bringing us back here again... You see we cannot let you know anything now. We have had many good talks with the soldiers who are in sympathy with us and they listen very attentively while we explain our views. I expect Mr Beddow will be allowed to visit us in prison we should like him too [sic]. Then we can tell him news of how we are getting on. Cheer up we shall be quite happy under punishment'.[48]

This letter is shorter than any he had so far sent, more focussed, more businesslike, perhaps more urgent. The reference to the Rev Beddow also betrays anxiety, the need to mobilise the web of support which the conscientious objectors had woven round themselves long before the crisis had come through the post. There was to be disappointment, though, for the army restricted Beddow to visit his own congregation, but no one else's.[49] A supportive pastoral visit from Rev Massey from Lutterworth was, of course, out of the question.

The Parade Ground at the Glen Parva Barracks
From Matthew Richardson, 'The Tigers...' Pen & Sword Books, Barnsley, 2000, p. 38.
Acknowledgement to Mr R.J. Cattell

In the same letter Leonard asked his father to, 'Let the NCF know all the news possible…'[50] This reference to the No-Conscription Fellowship is significant in itself. The N.C.F. had been created in the autumn of 1914 by Fenner Brockway of the Independent Labour Party (ILP) and his wife, Lilla, to protest against Britain's involvement in the war and provide support for like-minded people. At first, while volunteering had provided the war's manpower demands, the organisation's title had appeared misjudged, or at least premature, but as the military's needs grew ever greater and more urgent the organisation's purpose had become more sharply defined, to help and support those young men who were caught up in the thing, especially those who fell foul of the law. Leonard's own account, given many years later, suggests that he and Roland had joined well before conscription had become a fact.

From its inception, the NCF was an umbrella under which conscientious objectors of all kinds could take what shelter they could. Membership reached 10,000 at its peak, two thirds of whom were members of the Independent Labour Party, the next largest group being the Quakers. But there were more than that as Howard Marten, a Quaker objector himself, recorded, 'You found the ranks of the No-Conscription Fellowship were made up of men from every conceivable walk of life. You had all sorts of religious groups, from the Salvation Army to the Seventh Day Adventists; Church of England, Roman Catholics; there was no limit. It was a sort of cross section of every type. Then you had in addition to that the more politically minded: the Independent Labour Party, and different degrees of socialists, and the ordinary political parties. Then a very curious group of what I used to call "artistically minded". There were a lot of men who were not in any way organized or attached, but I should call them the aesthetic group: artists, musicians, all that.'[51] Its leadership was drawn chiefly from men of the Left. Clifford Allen, a leading light in left wing Labour politics, friend of socialist luminaries G.D.H. Cole, Sidney Webb and Ramsay MacDonald, and, like Brockway, a journalist and publicist, came to play a leading role in the organisation, while the socialist C.H. Norman's uncompromising anti-war stance, aggressively pursued, would prove divisive as the war went on; moreover, the philosopher Bertrand Russell was a leading voice of the organisation.[52]

As membership grew the Fellowship's leaders faced the urgent problem of structure: to devise a form of organisation which would protect their work from the growing interest and interference of the police. Thus was revealed one of the NCF's most remarkable and impressive achievements: its astonishing degree of organisation. Organisation was certainly needed.

Fear of police and security service interference was not based on paranoia – at least not on the paranoia of its members. Fixated on the idea that the pacifist and anti-war organisations were, albeit unwittingly, being financed by the German Government in an attempt to undermine the morale of the British people and, more to the point, the British Army, the security services mounted a 'huge operation' to spy on them and hamper their work. In June 1916 special branch officers raided the headquarters of the NCF in London and seized all their records and papers, together with three-quarters of a ton of printed materials.[53] It was precisely against this contingency that the NCF had organised itself along lines similar to those of the Suffragettes and of Sinn Fein, who had also been the subject of close police surveillance. A 'shadow' system was set up by the NCF, striking in its complexity and scope, and all in secret. As the historian of the NCF explained: 'Special means of communication were devised linking the entire network of divisions, branches and single members into a grid system through which messages and instructions could pass rapidly and safely'.[54]

As Fenner Brockway later recalled, 'The NCF was never actually suppressed, but in readiness we had a duplicate organisation throughout the country.' At times this almost led it into playing something akin to a childish game of hide and seek, though the stakes were much higher than in any playground. 'On one occasion, owing to a terrifying mistake on my part, the entire plans of our "underground" organisation were within a hair's breadth of falling into the hands of the police; indeed, they were actually in their hands, and then returned innocently to us!'[55] The plans had been left in a taxi and, after the taxi driver had handed them over to the police, it took luck, good connections and subterfuge to get them back unopened.

In Leicester the hub of the NCF's operations was a small, unassuming eating place in Leicester, the Café Vegetaria, run by a woman (as many NCF branches were) called Ella Stevens.[56] The café was an established business before the outbreak of the Great War, run by Albert Broadbent, and was on Leicester's Market Place, next door to the Anti-Socialist Union and just across the square from the Leicester Free Church Council and the offices of Chief Constable Edward Holmes.[57] Its location, therefore, put it at the heart of things. Ella acted as the conduit for information about all things to do with the conscientious objectors in Leicestershire, linking the local to the national organisation. A pair of letters in the Payne collection identify 'Ella Stevens care of the Café Vegetaria' in Leicester as the post office for information about Leicestershire objectors: Marion Harper told the Payne family in Lutterworth that there was a letter from one Green to a Mrs Goddard still waiting for him at the café, presumably expecting the Paynes to pass the information on, further filaments in the network.[58]

It was here that Leonard had attended numerous meetings before being called up: 'We used to hold a lot of meetings in Leicester and we were hounded about quite a bit. We had to go from different places because the police tried to break up the meetings. We used to go to a vegetarian café in the cellar and we used to meet in the cellars. When we started the meeting we would get hounded out of it and would have to go somewhere else.' Though the police never used direct violence against them, their purpose was clear enough, obliging the group to follow NCF security procedures, as Leonard remembered: 'We used to keep a duplicate copy of the minutes so that if one lot got taken by the police we had another lot to refer to. One night, when the police raided the place one of our members was at the door and knew what was going on and he came with a whole lot of papers under his arm selling newspapers to put the police off. So we got rid of the literature and everything like that out of the way.'[59] It was a game of cat and mouse.

★

The NCF gave to people like the Paynes whatever support it could and support they certainly needed; behind the joviality and reassurance of his first letters home, the strain was telling on Leonard's mind. A few weeks later he confessed that:

> '…it was jolly hard the first week and I shall never forget the first Sunday here. Bill and I were put in rooms in a different block of buildings to the other chaps and I happened to get in a back room where I could see nothing. I felt all right until the bells began to ring for church and if you remember it was anniversary day at home. I thought of home and wished I was there for the anniversary. I could not get it off my mind. Then Bill shouted through the wall that _____ come home. And if ever Satan tempted me it was that day, I could almost hear him saying "Chuck it up and go home it is silly being shut in here".'[60]

★

The officers at the Glen Parva Barracks were as perplexed as their NCOs by these new recruits who refused to be recruited. Asquith's *reasonable* assumption had been that conscientious objectors would 'take the form of exemption from military combatant duties only' and that 'he could take, as most of us can, military duties in the fullest sense of the term,'[61] and some at least of the officers at Glen Parva seem to have believed that that was a *reasonable* course too. On their arrival at Glen Parva Barracks, 'We have been passed for home service. They wanted to put us in the Non-Combative Corps which we did not accept'.[62] Later, 'They kept telling us we are in the Non-Combatent [sic] Corps but we tell them we are in nothing'.[63] Leonard remembered that 'they knew that we were interested in the Quakers and they wanted us to go to the Friends' Ambulance Unit... but at the time we didn't approve of the Friends' Ambulance Unit because we felt by going to the Friends' Ambulance Unit we were pushing people out of the RAMC into the army to do things we wouldn't do ourselves.'[64]

Asquith's whole scheme for using conscientious objectors in non-combatant roles and the creation of the Non-Combatant Corps were problematical, the hull of his *Ship of Liberal Values* dented, though not breached by it. The Bishop of Oxford, addressing the House of Lords in May 1916, went to the heart of the difficulty: 'I can hardly conceive any conscience – certainly not the conscience of those with whom we are dealing in this matter – which would refuse to allow a man to wear and use arms, but would allow of his doing all that work which is part and parcel of the same operation, such as the digging of trenches and barbed wire work. That kind of work does seem to me to be so absolutely part of the military operations that people whose conscientious objection is against taking part in military operations would hardly be expected to be willing to accept that work... I believe it has been universally rejected by the whole body of conscientious objectors.'[65] This certainly rang true for Leonard Payne: when challenged by Peter Liddle in 1973 over the veracity of his claim that every man who joined the Friends' Ambulance Unit was pushing another man into the army, albeit the Royal Army Medical Corps, he retreated to his second line of argument: 'At that time we didn't agree with the Friends' Ambulance Unit because they were posted to a French unit in France and we understood that they were helping to move munitions about and things like that which we didn't think was right.'[66] The contradiction is too obvious to dwell on: it was all right to *make* the baskets in which the shells were being moved, but not all right to *use* them! Such was the moral complexity in which they found themselves enmeshed.[67]

THE (MILITARY) DAILY ROUND

A very long letter from Leonard, dated Wednesday 14th of June 1916, gives us a clearer idea of their daily routine in the Glen Parva Barracks. It was written in pencil on seven small sheets of very dark coloured paper, which could even have been toilet paper, and is very difficult to read in places, faded pencil strokes in Leonard's miniscule writing.[68]

'We get up at 6 a.m., fold our three blankets, wash, _____ out, and then wait until 8.30 for breakfast. Then, we sometimes take back the dirty pots, or _____ a few _____, peel onions, potatoes, or something like this for about an hour. Then we have time spare until 11.15 when we go out for exercise on the barracks square until twelve fifteen. Then about 1.15 we have our dinner and then a wait again until 3.15 when we have another wait round until 4.15. Tea at 5, bring us our blankets at 6, come round for our boots, trousers [?], socks, etc about eight oclock [sic], then in bed until morning. We have nothing to eat from five oclock [sic] tea until 8.30 next morning so you see it is a jolly long time to wait'.[69]

Food was very much on his mind:

'The food is good but very scarce. I could eat what we get all day in one meal. For breakfast we get different every morning, sometimes bacon and tomatoes, sausage and tomatoes, and kipper. We also get _____ _____, two rounds of bread with a decent bit of butter to them [?] the bread is the biggest portion of the breakfast.

Dinner. The meals are much the same. Meat, beans, peas, cabbage and potatoes sometimes Yorkshire pudding or rolly polly or _____ but not much of any.

Tea. Two rounds of bread and butter a lettice [sic] leaf or a bit of jam or sometimes a bit of cake.

We get tea to drink _____ _____ _____ ____, and nothing else to drink at all.'

Indeed, in their early days at Wigston the brothers got into a row with the guards over their food. Leonard explained that he and Roland had been separated after sharing a cell for a time because of 'a bit of trouble':

> 'You see all the food here is sent down to us in one lot and the guards share it out. Mine and Bill's got very much less [*sic*] and they stopped bringing us pudding. I should not have known that it was the guards that stopped it only one day I went to the cookhouse and the man said to me should you like some of that stewed rhubarb for your teas, of course, I said yes I have not had any such thing lately. He said you should have done it has been sent down to you. So you see what brutes some men are to stop our food and eat it themselves. So when this guard came round I told him about it and told him I should tell the sergeant if it was not altered. He swore and made various excuses, but still it was better afterwards. So for spite he made a bother about me talking to Bill so I was moved to the other end of the building.'

That the brothers would not stand by and be exploited by individual soldiers, even appealing to the NCO for help, had now been established! However, the crux of the issue would be their attitude towards those in command, those issuing military orders.

SPANKED

It was now that the folly of the Tribunals in passing men like Leonard Payne and his friends from the Leicester NCF into the army became all too apparent. If they had thought that the objectors were not genuine and would give in, when put in khaki under military command, they had misjudged the men before them. If they had thought that the objectors *were* genuine, but were so weak and cowardly that they would surrender and put on uniform when faced by a full-time sergeant major, they were equally wrong. Just how wrong was about to be demonstrated, for now the problem was firmly in the hands of the army: and the military mind struggled to cope with a quandary like this. Its first resort was 'spanking'.

We can readily understand that the officers and NCOs of the Glen Parva Barracks were, to say the least, perplexed by the influx of 'conscientious objectors'. Many of the sergeants and sergeant majors had long military experience, but limited education and a narrow world view. They were men used to obedience and authority and who found it hard to cope with those who refused to obey, defied their authority and punishments and who cheerfully called their bluff. Some, at least, were long serving NCOs, veterans of Victoria's Army, called out of retirement to meet the need.[70] What they had not yet learned was that military discipline 'ultimately relied on the consent of the governed' in a citizen army.[71] To add to their perplexity, the men before them on the parade ground were not even genuine conscientious objectors (if such things existed!), but shirkers and slackers and, moreover, hypocrites, wilfully and in cowardly fashion avoiding the call to defend their King and Country in its hour of greatest need. They could not be genuine, for had the Tribunals not said so? The tactic habitually employed by the NCOs across the British Army was simple bullying, for authorised bullying was systemic, an essential part of how the army went about its normal business.[72]

When the academic Gilbert Murray enquired about one particular undergraduate who had been called up despite claiming conscientious objection, he was told: 'Well, we'll see when we get him in the barracks. It's him against us, and I think we shall get the best of it.' 'Do you want to shoot him?' I asked. 'No,

147

we won't shoot him. We'll spank him. We'll make him wish he had never been born.'[73] 'Spanking' took many forms,[74] but clear patterns of brutality emerged and there are too many individual cases to be written off as isolated incidents. Non-Commissioned Officers in the First World War British Army, when at the Front, come across as men who were often sympathetic to their men, father-figures mediating between the man and his distant officer and the orders which linked the two. Those involved in the initial training of recruits, on the other hand, often had a reputation for sternness amounting sometimes to cruelty when confronted by what they could not understand. They might well be stern and unbending, for their task was to turn raw civilians into front line soldiers in a matter of a few months at most, and gentleness was not going to achieve that. In their own eyes, and in the eyes of their officers, they were doing a necessary job well.

Others disagreed, and a stream of questions in Parliament highlighted individual cases. The following samples (and by far the least lurid), are some of those raised on just one day, 10th May 1916: Sir W. Byles asked the Under-Secretary for War, Harold Tennant (who happened to be Asquith's brother-in-law), 'whether he is aware that Oscar Gristwood Ricketts, a conscientious objector to military service, was arrested, charged at Brentford Police Court, fined two guineas, and handed over to the military authorities, and that in conveying him to Felixstowe they exposed him to the shame of being handcuffed in the public streets and railways; whether he is now in the Harwich circular redoubt, confined to a cell, and his only food dry biscuits and water; whether this young man has resigned a good post in a city bank and offered himself for any work of national importance that is consistent with his religious and moral convictions; and whether he proposes to take any action in the matter?'

On the same day Philip Snowden asked Tennant '(1) if he will make an immediate inquiry into the treatment of a number of conscientious objectors who belong to Darwen, Lancashire, who were taken to the military barracks at Preston and there subjected to the grossest ill-treatment, being forcibly stripped and marched round the barrack square practically undressed, and after being put in uniform one of them was taken into a room and, on the testimony of a person there, brutally kicked around the room until his groans could be heard outside; in view of the fact that statements of similar and worse treatment of conscientious objectors are coming from many other districts, will he take immediate steps to have this brutal conduct on the part of the military stopped and proper punishment meted out to those responsible for it; and (2) what action he has taken upon the allegations of D. S. Parkes, a conscientious objector to military service, who has been convicted by a district court-martial at Winchester on charges of refusal to obey military orders; that on his arrest under the Military Service Act, 1916, he was placed in the guardroom at Whitehall and informed that he would be shot at dawn for refusing to give information demanded; that he was insulted by the non-commissioned officer in charge of the guard-room, who also placed a bayonet to his heart; that he was then taken into another room, where a rifle was pointed at him, and then he was told that he was graciously pardoned; that this action was repeated later, a rifle being loaded in his presence and an order given to a soldier to fire; and, if no action has been taken upon these serious allegations, will he order a thorough inquiry at once into the alleged conduct of the non-commissioned officers and soldiers who tortured this man?'

Mr Jowett asked the Under-Secretary for War '(1) concerning an absentee under the Military Service Act, 1916, named Alan J. McDougall, who was handed over to the military authorities on 25th April last, and who afterwards, at Scotland Yard, refused to sign attestation papers and was, notwithstanding this refusal, passed for general service and sent to the depot of the 4/3rd London Regiment, where he was mishandled by some soldiers and who afterwards forcibly put khaki clothes on him, if he will say... what has been done with him; (2) if he is aware that Norman Gaudie, a conscientious objector, of Sunderland, who was fined £2 at Jarrow Police Court and handed over to the military authorities on 19th April and was subsequently taken to Newcastle Barracks and from there to Richmond Castle, has been subjected to severe treatment, his own clothes torn off and khaki clothes forced on him, and afterwards put in irons on account of his resistance and handcuffed; whether he will cause inquiries to be made into the conduct of the military authorities concerned with the object of preventing the continuance of this method of treating conscientious objectors; and (3) what has become of W. Hammond, a conscientious objector, who was arrested on 17th April last, tried on 18th April, fined £2, and handed over to the military authorities, was afterwards taken to Mill Hill Barracks and from there to Northampton, where he was put in the guard-room for seven days, was on hunger strike and without food for five days, as the result of which he had to be removed to a military hospital, and was due to be tried by court-martial on 2nd May?[75]

All this kind of treatment did was create martyrs (in the eyes of their supporters at least) and provoke the army into taking action. We see an example in a letter written by Marion Harper to Jessie Payne, in June of that year, reporting on an address given to the NCF in Leicester by the saintly Alfred Salter, the Bermondsey G.P. and leading light of the Fellowship:

'Dr Salter repeated what I think all of us know so well, that the men are fighting in the spirit of love, and what is more are conquering. He told of those three

Bermondsey men who had nothing but blankets to wear for a week, how they were taken out and asked to drill, how the roughest and worst element amongst the soldiers threw mud at them, but they never resisted. When the news reached the head office of the NCF, Dr Salter went to the war office and obtained an order that this treatment must cease. Armed with this order he went to the camp. The COs were called together and asked to name the men who had abused them, being told that these men would be punished. They all three said, 'we do not wish you to punish them, they did not understand, else they would not have done it'.[76]

'Father forgive them for they know not what they do'!

★

The two great symbolic sticking-points were uniform and drill. As they refused to wear the one, so they refused to do the other. In part physical training and basic military drill were intended to mould the body and mind of the new recruit, promote the required physical fitness and to instil a mentality of unthinking obedience, of the surrender of free will. One soldier, Private Noakes, told how 'we sloped, ordered, presented, trailed, reversed, piled arms and did everything possible with them except fire them. With rifles we marched, counter-marched, wheeled right and left, inclined and formed squads and about turned until we were streaming sweat and weak in the knees with exhaustion'. But it was more than physical training. Stephen Graham wrote that 'all private soldiers were passive. NCOs were active and drove privates to do what was required. The real driving power lay in the brutal word and thought and act. I noticed that men who in themselves were not brutal, cultivated brutality to get the army tone. The characteristic word of command was not merely enforced by firmness, by loudness, by peremptoriness. The vital thing in it must be menace. It must be an intimidating bawl; it must act on the nerves. Soldiers must be driven by frightening them all the way.'[77] Men about to face the trenches where they would be expected to overcome all their instincts of survival must be taught to obey without questioning, without thinking. That, for the army, was why drill *had* to be performed (by men in uniform): it was also why the conscientious objectors *had* to resist it (without uniform).

Leonard Payne not only set out *not* to follow this path, but to disrupt it, to undermine its fundamental principles, to openly mock its most powerful weapons of fear and menace. He told his family back home:

'Shortly after we were here we were asked to go down for exercise. I went down but bill *[sic]* would not dress to go to see what it was. When I got down I found it was drill so I refused to drill and went back. I think only six stayed down for drill. They soon get *[sic]* fed up of drilling six so they came and told us it was the doctor's orders that we should do it, so we all went down this time to see what was going to happen. The six that would drill were put in the first line and the rest behind. When the order for quick march was given six moved on and the rest stood as if they were stuffed. Then they fetched a lot of soldiers out and we had two each pulling us round the barracks square for the hour. But now we have agreed to walk round for exercise without marching. I had four soldiers all one afternoon. I would not move an inch. They took it in turns pulling me round and they didn't half sweat too. I got put in irons two hours for this but it was worth it for it stopped them trying to force us again. Bill had two big soldiers at him pulling him round but they did not rough us very much... You would laugh to see us on parade all out of step, coats unbuttoned, hats on all ways but the right, some with no hats at all. All the soldiers turn out to see us go round and they laugh like anything we look so funny'.[78]

Leonard later remembered that, 'we sat on the floor and if they said go right, we went left. If they said go forwards we went backwards... they put the old soldiers behind us to give us digs in the back and that sort of thing. They used to drag us around with our feet at times... They were quite cruel,' he went on, but 'they weren't brutal. Of course, the fellows couldn't help themselves. They had to do it. I don't think the soldiers liked it.'[79] If this was Leonard's revenge against the military for the death of his friend Harold Buck, he was learning that individual soldiers were, like him, men caught up in the throes of the thing.

The military's attempt to isolate them, to stop them talking when out of their cells, was equally fruitless:

'We all talk when we get outside. They tried to stop us talking, but we told them we were not soldiers and we would not stop until they put handcuffs on our tongues... Bill is quite well so am I. We see each other and have a talk every day when we go out for anything. He has been very brave and has stuck it well, he is always smiling I think he rather enjoys the fun'.

Leonard described other acts of defiance, 'One morning we refused to carry some blankets, etc so they hung them on us and pushed us along. We got irons for two hours again for this but we can stand them we lay down and go to sleep with them on so you can tell they do not hurt us much. It is to frighten you more than anything else'. Army regulations prescribed 'Field Punishment No. 1 for those who did not obey. Such field punishment shall be of the character of personal restraint'.[80] This was interpreted as tying the man to the wheel of a gun carriage for a certain number of hours each day, and leaving him to his discomfort and humiliation for all to see. The Payne brothers were sentenced to twenty-eight days of this 'Field Punishment No. 1'. However, the Glen Parva Barracks did not possess a suitable gun whose wheel could be borrowed for four weeks. There were probably suitable fences available, but the disruption which a vocal conscientious objector could cause – especially since the commanding officer seems to have had more than his fair share of them to handle – was probably seen as a price too high for the punishment of recalcitrant non-recruits. So, ever resourceful, the army came up with its own solution: 'They used to bring round handcuffs and they used to put them behind our backs and chain us with these handcuffs for so many hours a day.'[81]

For all that, individual relationships did prove possible, in spite of the official military disapproval:

'I have a good friend here one of the guards, he use [sic] to lodge at Mrs Greens Peacock Yard and he worked at the foundry. He knew me when he knew I came from Lutterworth he asked me if I was the basket maker's son. He said I remember you said at the start of the war you would not be a soldier. The other night he came to see how I was getting on and I said I felt cold and hungry, he went away and when he was the only one on guard I heard someone gently open my door and it was him with a round of bread and butter for my supper. Jolly good of him I shall not forget such a kind action in a hurry. He is coming over to Lutt soon so I shall try to get him to call he is a very nice chap the best guard we have. The other night my door was left unlocked all night, I went along the passage and took Hassal a pencil and had a talk to all the chaps while the guard was away.'

He was not the only one:

'Do you remember that young fellow of the three in the room that day you were here, well he was named Tomlinson and a great friend of Tomlinson the old Lutterworth Station Master, although no relation. He was a nice chap, but he has gone to Newcastle now. Mother asked me why I was in the guard-room again, well the detention room is full up, so I have been given the priviliage [sic] of being in the guard-room again. It is much better than the detention room was.'[82]

NOT ALONE

The days became weeks and, as time passed by, the impasse remained as unresolved as ever. The presence of other conscientious objectors at Glen Parva Barracks made their predicament tolerable, but without doubt it was the outside support they received which gave them hope for the future and strengthened their resolve. First and foremost, of course, was their family, whose unquestioning loyalty and encouragement never wavered. Close behind the family were Thomas Harper and his daughter Marion. The Harper family originated in the high Pennines of Yorkshire, where Thomas's father Samuel had farmed fourteen acres of the remote and barren land of Deepdale, above Dent. Mary Harper, Thomas's mother, had made a living as a commercial traveller dealing in groceries and drapery, living in what must have been a harsh and difficult environment. Hit by the same agricultural depression which was casting its shadow over Lutterworth and south Leicestershire, and which would ruin the finances of Charles Marriott of Cotesbach Hall, the Harpers left their valley in the 1860s and moved to Manchester. It was there, in 1866, that their third child, Thomas, was born. We can readily imagine the shock it must have been to move from the silent, isolated rural environment of the high Pennines into dirty, noisy Manchester, and for reasons we can only guess at the family moved back into the high Dales, to Sedbergh, before the 1860s were out. The 1881 Census shows Thomas, now fifteen, following his mother's lead as a draper's apprentice, but ten years later he was listed as 'visiting' a fifty-year-old widow called Ann Holmes, whose daughter Mary Jane he was about the marry. It was now that his career led him in a fresh direction as well, for he was listed as not only a draper, but also a 'machine agent'. He had found his niche. It was this mechanical link which would provide him with his future prosperity for by 1901, still living in Settle in the Yorkshire Dales, he was shown as a 'cycle maker / agent repairer'. It was there that he and Mary Jane had their first child, a daughter whom they called Marion – the Marion Harper who would give the Payne brothers so much essential support.

By 1909 Thomas and his growing family had moved to the easier cycling country of Leicestershire and Thomas was prosperous enough to set up a cycle shop of his own in the prestigious Belgrave Gate in the city centre and later to buy a spacious house, called 'Penelve', on the Wanlip Road in the comfortable suburb of Syston, just north of Leicester.[83] Thomas had had the foresight, the business acumen, the capital, and the luck to catch the boom in cycling which swept the country between the achievement of greater leisure time in the 1880s and the coming of the motor car, another example of Victorian economic and geographical mobility: another Victorian success story.

Although his and his family's material way of life had changed, his core beliefs and values had not, for he had brought with him from Yorkshire a deep and passionate brand of Nonconformist Christian faith. By the outbreak of the Great War he was well known in and around Lutterworth and willing to make the twenty mile journey even for small scale events like the Sunday School anniversary party held in the village of Walcote, close to Lutterworth. The Hamilton family of Walcote told Leonard that:

'We had an S.S. Anniversary last Sunday everything went off a treat, considering its [sic] such a small affair. Mr Harper took both services and was very good'.[84]

The first surviving letter written by Thomas to the brothers is full of that Evangelical spirit:

'First of all let me say how very much we all appreciate the stand you are making for *true* freedom you are in the line with all those who have stood for God and righteousness down all the ages therefore boys count it *all* joy you cannot stand in your own strength but the everlasting arms of God are underneath you and He is able to do for you above all that you can ask or think therefore dear ones *stand* in His strength alone.

Our prayers go up for you frequently and you can rest assured we are doing all we can to bring this wicked business to a close'.[85]

It was his daughter Marion – twenty-three years old in 1916 – who would act as the brothers' most important link to the outside world through the No-Conscription Fellowship, and she was, after their family, their most important support. She was also a vital support to their family in Lutterworth, and a strong bond developed between them all.[86] Leonard had spent his last evening before his arrest with Marion at an NCF meeting in Leicester.[87]

Marion is a fascinating character. Her family was clearly well-to-do, living in a large late Victorian semi-detached house in Syston, her father a successful entrepreneur. Her background in Northern Nonconformism helped draw her towards the more radical wing of politics through the I.L.P. and Ramsay MacDonald's war resistance.[88] During the war Marion became increasingly interested in that great Russian icon of pacifism, Leo Tolstoy, recommending books to Leonard like *Father Sergius*, a short novel exploring the inner meaning of the Christian life and finding it in self-abnegation and personal annihilation before God and his people.[89] Whether Leonard read the book is not known. A woman of some education, she does, in her way, typify what strange bedfellows the anti-war movement spawned. When, for example, a conference of left wing groups in Britain was convened in Leeds in June of 1917 in the wake of Russia's first Revolution, Marion waxed enthusiastic in a letter to Leonard, 'From what you say I gather that you were not at the Leeds Conference, it must have been a great time. Dr. Hodgkin was there and he said that if the spirit of Christ was not there he did not know where it was'.[90] In retrospect it seems ironic that this same Leeds Conference endorsed the setting up of Russian-style 'Soviets of Workers' and Soldiers' Delegates' in Britain, the left wingers seeing this as a move towards a socialist society, the NCF and the Christians seeing it as the kind of revolutionary upheaval which 'would ultimately end the war and sweep away European militarism'.[91] A few weeks afterwards Marion was writing that, 'It is the I.L.P. Garden Party next Saturday, and in the afternoon the District Conference organized by the Workers & Soldiers Council [i.e. 'Soviet'] is to meet. I rather want to be elected a delegate but don't know whether it will come off. In any case I shall go to the Garden Party and hear MacDonald'.[92]

Before the year was out the militantly atheist Bolshevik Party would seize power by armed force in Russia in the name of the Soviets there, immediately announce its withdrawal from the First World War, launch itself into unimaginably brutal civil war, invade a neighbouring country with the aim of spreading Communism by force into the whole of Europe, and begin one of the most ruthless persecutions of Christianity the world has ever seen. From Tolstoy to Lenin: strange bedfellows indeed.

Confinement with no obvious end in sight was playing on Leonard's mind and depression was threatening to set in:

> 'After dinner I felt as bad, when suddenly I heard a voice outside my door and I at once recognised it to be Mr Harper. Wasn't I glad to see him that day. I was ____ _____ I had nothing to say to him, I have thought since it seems as if he was Divinely led to come in our weakest moments to bring us cheer and hope for the future. When he shook hands to go I felt a lot more cheerful, and about a quarter

of an hour later we were moved to the rooms of those who had gone home. This was better and we could see the other fellows. Tea soon arrived and shortly the bells began again for evensong. This seemed to inspire all the fellows _____ and heads appeared from many windows and next I heard was someone's voice strike up 'Oh God our Help in ages Past' and at once the yard was ringing with the sound of many voices. The hymn was sung through and *[?]* the next I remember was from the next window _____ Mr Gulson *[??]* was reading his Testament out loud to everybody round. This was fine and I went to sleep quite in good spirits. This was the worst and hardest day, I shall never forget it as long as I live'.[93]

Meanwhile, support was rallying. The family was allowed to visit them[94] and their presence was drawing in the oxygen of publicity, albeit with the expected result as Leonard recalled:

'We were a nuisance and the people who were on the road could see what was going on, on this parade ground. They wrote articles in the Leicester paper about this and they sent the Mayor of Leicester to come and interview us individually to know if it was true. We told him what was going on and he said well, if you disobey orders you must expect it and that was as far as we got with him…'[95]

'The Seargent *[sic]* Major has come in and caught me writing this but did not say anything to me, only he asked me if I had changed my mind yet. He said "I think you are very foolish to be shut in here *["]*. I have not heard any more [about] C[ourt] M[artial] but expect to each day. I am still going on in the same way plenty of food, etc. I felt a bit rocky yesterday but am quite all right again now… Have you heard from Bill lately I hope he is still doing well. I have nothing much to say…'[96]

At this point the letter as it exists ends abruptly. The final pages are missing, the story yet unfinished. We cannot escape the feeling that the army itself was giving up on them, understanding that it had been defeated in the field of mental and moral battle by a force too strong.

WHITBURN ARMY CAMP, COUNTY DURHAM

'IT IS VERY MONOTONOUS IN HERE' [97]

When the move came, it came, as in the fashion of the military, very suddenly. On Friday June 16th, after three weeks of supposed 'basic training' in Glen Parva Barracks, the brothers were assigned to their new Regiment and moved out. We can follow them through the next days in the self-conscious 'diary' written by Roland a week later:

> [Friday June 16th 1916.] 'Fetched out of cells. Took up to Guards [*sic*] Room. There given letters, the money, and writing material that was left. Then took from our comrades, and put in amongst some soldiers. From there we were taken to Wigston Magna Station and put in train'. [98]

The No-Conscription Fellowship is famed for the efficiency with which it monitored the movements of all the conscientious objectors, and Marion Harper and Dorothy Gittins were watching out for the move, as Dorothy told their mother:

> 'I saw your two boys yesterday, with all the others, going off to various places. I

cycled over to the barracks and got there by eight o'clock. Very soon after, as I was waiting in the station booking office two were brought along – Hickman and Stanyon – due for Aldershot. After I had talked to them and they went to the train, I walked with the others to the furthest station. There were twelve with all their full kit. They looked very fit and cheerful. When we got to the station I handed out chocolates and writing paper and money etc! And while talking to them, your two boys arrived and came running up to shake hands. The elder one – Leonard? (I get mixed) looked very well and was full of spirits – the younger looked rather pale, but seemed quite cheerful and undaunted. They told me of course that as far as they knew they were going to Sunderland, but you will hear when they arrive.' Also, Marion told Leonard, 'If we had been sure you would travel on Friday I would have come over to Wigston and then trained it back to Syston and the others would have met you at Syston station. However I am glad some of our members were on the alert. D.E.G [Dorothy Gittins] is splendid is she not?'[99]

As the train passed through Sheffield on its way north Leonard was able to write a hasty postcard home:

'We are off to Sunderland with ten more men who are passed for home service the same as we are. They say we are attatched [sic.] to the Sherwood Foresters but that does not matter to us we shall do nothing at all we feel well and are eagerly waiting events. Bill and I are lucky to be together. We went through Syston station and could see Mr Harper's house I wished I could get at it. We are the only two C.O.s here but these men are very nice and quite in sympathy with us'.[100] Roland's 'diary' recorded, 'We got as far as York and then changing [sic], and also getting some tea and cakes from a Red Cross canteen. Then we got to Durham after being nearly baked and getting off there. Then we have to wait for half and [sic] hour and get in a slow train for Sunderland. At last we get to Sunderland, so we get on the tram cars and rides [sic] for about two miles. Then we get off and walk about two miles to the Headquarters of the 3rd Sherwood Foresters. Here we wait a short time and are then handed over to a soldier to take us to Whitburn. On arriving at our destination no one knew we were coming or anything about us, so we made some tea with some tea we had got and also had some bread and fat as they had ~~got~~'.

The small town of Whitburn stood then, as it stands now, on the rugged north-east coast of England. Twice the size of Lutterworth, its mining and seafaring legacies are clear to see.[101] This is a hard and bleak coast, livings made in hard ways, coal mining and fishing with a bit of bleak farming and rows of small terraced miners' cottagers speaking of a working class almost unknown in far off Lutterworth. In Lutterworth the biggest houses were owned by professional men, lawyers and doctors: here there was the odd landed family, but most were built by ship owners, railway engineers and the like, self-made men of the Industrial Revolution building comfortable homes for themselves. When one, Thomas Barnes, tried to stop the common people walking in front of his new flamboyant mansion the people of Whitburn took him to court and won. This is a no nonsense sort of a place.[102]

A huddle of wooden hutments by the road north out of Whitburn village, the road to South Shields and beyond that Newcastle, marked the army camp as it stood in 1916.[103] Sloping away was a huge area of open ground marked by the massive man-made earthen butts and the smaller spotting shelters which marked the firing range; ships at sea and walkers along the coastal path were warned to keep well clear when the infantry was learning how to kill Germans. The land stretches down for a good mile to the earthen cliffs and beyond them the flat rocky outcrops reaching out into the cold waters of the North Sea. For this is a treacherous coast, the twenty-six miles between Newcastle to the north and Sunderland within sight of Whitburn to the south once among the busiest along the British coast: it records forty-four shipwrecks for every mile of coastland here. In bad weather, which is not infrequent on this coast, Whitburn can appear a bleak and inhospitable place, especially when the winds whip across it from the exposed north and east, the town's windmill standing behind the army camp an ominous reminder of how windswept this coast can be. The army camp resembled a military island isolated on the cold north-east coast. The 7th D.L.I had criss-crossed the seaward zone with a maze of trenches exactly paralleling the trench lines in Flanders and France – the scars still visible today – 'with a Greek-key pattern of firing bays and communication trenches. This was the firing line; behind this came the support and reserve lines. The system was linked to similar trenches on either flank, with the heavy guns of Frenchman's Fort and Tynemouth covering the seaward approaches.'[104] Reminder enough that these trenches were no mere training exercise: the country was at war and a German invasion or raid by sea was a possibility at any time, the coastline needing to be defended.

By 1916 the military had taken over parts of the town itself, including a large residential building called Hill House, adjoining the vicarage, on the main road out of Whitburn, inland towards Cleadon. As its name implies, Hill House stands on high ground set back a little from the road, a large and imposing structure which the 3rd Sherwood Foresters took over as their headquarters in the town. Today, Hill House is divided into two substantial homes, constituting the left-hand two-thirds of the whole building.

Hill House in Whitburn, Headquarters of the 3rd Sherwood Foresters.
Photo by the author.

It was there that Leonard and Roland went to see the officers in charge of the Sherwood Foresters to impress on them that they were not ordinary squaddies. 'Then we rest until bed time after going to see the company officer to tell him we were conscientious objectors and should refuse all orders. We did not have a very good night it was too ~~noisley~~[?] noisey.[105] Roland had been assigned to the school building in Whitburn itself. Just how 'noisey' it was is clear from a letter Roland wrote home a few days later, 'The first night I was here I had a man turned in with me for fighting with a shovel and another for being absent. The fighting man was called 'Ginger', and was orderly over Jack Holland's mess. He got quite pally with me and said he was going to be a C.O. if he did not get off so they let him off'.[106]

The reference to Jack Holland would immediately have struck a chord with his family at home in Lutterworth for he was the son of the Lutterworth Police Inspector and had been well known to both Payne brothers since school days. Jack's brother Fred was also in the 3rd Battalion Sherwood Foresters. But the situation had changed: Jack and Fred Holland were now officers in the King's Army, and Leonard and Roland Payne were conscientious objectors to military service, so things were much more complex now than a shared home town would allow.

[Saturday June 17th 1916] 'Next morning we were up at 5.30 and ordered to go out to parade at 6.15. This we refused. Sergeant Major comes in to separate us. Then we demand to see the C.O. Then we were took *[sic]* to the Orderly Room to see him. Leonard sees him first and while I was seeing him Leonard was packed off to R Company leaving me at H Company'.[107] This changed their situation and now that this was understood by the military authorities at Whitburn, their treatment changed. The brothers had been assigned to different companies within the battalion, and this effectively separated them for much of their time.

Until now, Roland's diary had been about 'we'; from here on it was chiefly about 'I'. 'After this I was left for the soldiers to do as they liked with me, being in a room with the ruffist *[sic]* lot possible, all old reservists'.[108] A few days later, in a postcard home he filled out the picture, 'We slept with the soldiers, hearing fearful language… It is an awful place here just like a hell on earth. The soldiers keep on telling me awful tales about what ~~we~~ I *[?]* shall have to go through and keep on telling me to give in. This morning a soldier locked me in a dark coal cellar but I pulled the door down and got out'.[109]

How to handle these two men who refused to play the army's game? The problem was in the hands of Major Wise. If any man by his everyday character contradicts the stereotype we have of the 'donkeyish' army officer of the First World War, it was the appropriately named Major Wise. It is possible that he had some foreknowledge of Leonard and Roland, knew someone who was familiar with Lutterworth and the Payne family, though, if that was true, he kept the details from them,[110] but his attitude towards them throughout was exemplary in its

The Whitburn Coast. On the left part of one of the huge earthen embankments which mark the end of the rifle range, on the right the cold North Sea. The whole of this coastline was entrenched against possible German attack.
Photo by the author.

161

sympathy and wisdom.[111] First, though, things had to be brought to a head, their simple statement to the officers in Hill House that they were conscientious objectors was insufficient grounds for the military to act against them. Roland's diary described what happened next. 'Sunday morning [June18th, 1916] I refuse to have equipment, and also to go on parade for chapel, one lot going to church and the other lot going to chapel. After church and chapel parade I am ordered to lay my kit out for inspection and to take my boots and socks off for foot inspection. When the officers come round to inspect I told them I was a C.O. and refused to obey any orders, also I refused to stand to attention'.[112] Roland's terse description does little to convey the drama of the confrontation between the conscientious objector and the representatives of military authority. In a barracks hut full of new squaddies, fresh from their basic training, the open and apparently careless defiance of these two brothers must have come as a shock. Some, perhaps, had been sent up from Glen Parva with the Payne brothers and knew of their antics on the parade ground there, were all too aware that they had refused even to carry their own kitbags, knew that they were wearing at best a token kind of khaki uniform and that there might be trouble now they had arrived with their new regiment, but none of them had seen much of them while they had been kept in isolation there, handcuffed in their rooms, undergoing that token Field Punishment No. 1.

Roland again. 'About half an hour after this Major Wise comes to see me, begging me to give in, telling me ~~we~~ they were fighting for Christianity and we were fighting against it. This was of no use.'[113] There is no doubting the major's sincerity for, like many in the army, he was personally and deeply convinced of the rightness of Britain's cause, that this war could be likened to a crusade of good against evil, Christian truth against wickedness. As a thoughtful Christian he tried to reconcile the opposing views on the issue of military service and Christian values. A few days later Leonard told his sister Jessie. 'Major Wise who is a very nice gentleman actually took the trouble to go before the C.O. when we were there and tell him there was no doubt that we were sincere in all our belief, and not like many of the conscientious objectors. I had a talk with him before and he is a treat to talk too [sic]. He takes services in the church here and he is so sorry he has had to send us to C.O. to be remanded for court martial'.[114] Perhaps Major Wise did not know it, but his argument was already familiar to the brothers and already unconvincing to them.

Their sergeant, a man called Chart, used cruder, though no more effective, tactics. 'On going down to the lawn [sic] for dinner Sergeant Chart gave an order that I was to have nothing to eat until I did something to earn it. The soldiers on hearing this, those that came from Leicester, told me to come with them and they would see that I did not go short, so I had my meals with them until being moved'.[115]

Monday morning, June 19th.

'At 9 am I was brought before the company officer and remanded to see Major Wise. Then I was took [sic] to him, seeing Leonard there for refusing to stand to attention. He then remanded us to see the colonel, the commanding officer. Then we were took to Guards Room [sic] at R Company where Leonard had just left, me being put in there, and Leonard in a dark room'. Leonard, in a letter to his sister Jessie written a few days afterwards, gave a few more details about the 'dark room' incident, which probably occurred that night. 'I was in a dark cell from 5 pm on [Mon]day until 8 am the next. The cell door had two little bits of glass in door [sic] which were boarded over to make it dark so I pulled on [sic] lot of boards off to get a bit of light, so they hung a bag on the outside side [sic] so it was as bad as ever'.[116]

Major Wise had not given up yet though. Having failed to convince them to abandon their conscientious objection, he called in reinforcements whom he thought might have a better chance of success, a Congregational minister from Sunderland who was prepared to make the trip to Whitburn that Monday afternoon:

'At the request of the major he came right down from Sunderland about two miles to the lieu[tenant's] house and had us over there for about half an hour talking to us. He was a fine gentleman to talk to, a bit different to Massey, he would not persuade us in anyway [sic] but he said he was sorry we had to go to prison if it could be prevented. It was jolly good of him to come and also good of the major to allow him to come to his private house to see us there. But still I have come to see that some of these officers are good Christians although soldiers, they do not like to have to punish us at all.'[117]

Roland's account of the meeting was terser:

'In the afternoon we were sent for one last time to see a Congregational Minister from Sunderland, at the company officer's house. He told us that the war was right and wanted us to give in and be forgiven. This was refused. About five hours afterwards I was sent for to see the company officer. He said he was going to give me until tomorrow morning to think about what the minister had said.'

Roland, Tuesday June 20th and Wednesday 21st June 1916:

'The next morning I go to him [Major Wise] again and tell him I am not going to give in. He then tells me he will be very sorry to have to send me to prison being so young and wants to give me another day to think about it. This I refuse and so we are brought up before the commanding officer the next day and remanded for district court marshial *[sic]*. My crime is for refusing to lay kit down for inspection and for refusing to accept equipment. Then we are led away, me being left at K Coy Guards Room and Leonard taken back to his dark room. Since then I have been passed by doctor for court marshial *[sic]* and have remained here since.'[118]

A last unavailing attempt was also made to talk Leonard round:

'The lieu. that is charging me called me to oneside *[sic]* to see if I still held to my belief an *[sic]* if he should stop my case going before C.O. of course it was on condition I started to be a soldier. Of course I told him I should go through to the end and he was sorry. They do not like convicting us but it is there *[sic]* duty so they have to do it.'[119]

What of the ordinary squaddies, conscripts themselves, as they encountered what were probably their first fully-fledged conscientious objectors? If we believe the testimony of both brothers they understood the fight they were putting up, perhaps secretly even envying their refusal to follow the crowd in defying the government's and the military's claimed right to force men to kill. Leonard recorded these examples of support from the other ranks:

'We have made a marked impression on the men since we have been here they think we are bricks to stand what we have stood without flinching… I heard a voice shouting into my cell last night, 'How are you getting on, Sunny' *[sic]* I said all right, and he said Stick to it you'll get out soon. I don't know who it was but it was a soldier of some sort… I wish I had all the money you sent me. I could get a few extras such as chocolates, oranges, etc. The guards would get it for me.'[120]

Roland, too, found some supportive soldiers. He wrote on Thursday 29th June that, 'I am having a bit of peace now I am here, because the soldiers seem in sympathy with me'. Similarly, Leonard even found some common ground with a soldier fresh home from the front. He wrote, 'A young fellow here is very good to me he is a Roman Catholic, he has been to the front and he told me he never neglected to say his prayers night and morn and he thinks through this God has brought him safely back although wounded'.[121] However, there is no case we know of in which either Leonard or Roland persuaded any soldier, by word or example, to throw down his rifle and join them.

However, not all the soldiers reacted in such a congenial manner. Leonard had complained before about his clothing being stolen, and now he reported to his family about one military policeman. Unfortunately, this letter is damaged, but the sense is still clear:

> 'One young policeman here is a regular thief, they are allowed anywhere they like [...] when they are on duty with their badge on their arm. I mean on anybodys [*sic*] [...] the mornings he puts his badge (M.P.) on his arm, when he is [...] round a little farm a short distance from here and pinches eggs, he came [...] this morning. The farm people do not say anything to him because they think he [...] and joking about this and fried some with bacon for lunch.'[122]

We can readily understand Leonard's feeling of moral indignation when he saw men of such woefully inferior character holding him in custody. For Leonard, as a poultry keeper himself, the fact that eggs were being stolen by the miscreant M.P. must have added to the outrage.

While the officers and some of the privates, at least, appear to have been as sympathetic as far as their duty would allow, the response of the NCOs was less understanding. Leonard commented, 'You always find here the officers are all right, it is the corporals and sergeants that are the bullies'.[123] It was probably one of these NCOs who was behind a cruel prank played on Leonard, reported in a letter home on Wednesday June 28th: 'One day I was fetched out with a man with a rifle to be shot. I walked boldly out and they seemed quite surprised'.[124] It was a crude echo of the treatment of the 'Frenchmen' and a heavy-handed joke which, on Leonard's evidence, backfired although he says nothing about how he had felt at that moment. Was this the action of bored NCOs with a victim they could bully at will?

We might, though, without excusing it, ponder the words of the most Christian of all the conscientious objectors, Corder Catchpool: 'When I see so many men about the barracks with one, two or even three or more of the little vertical gold stripes on their sleeve, hobbling about on sticks, or with arms hanging useless, I hope to myself that if any C.O.s should meet with contempt or abuse in the army... they may have the grace quietly to understand.'[125] The 'little vertical gold stripes' were Wound Stripes. In the military scale of values a Wound Stripe could be seen as a would not have been.

We are miss the motor bicycle very much. Marion Harper has been to our house for the week end and said how quiet is was without you. I do not like it when I'm in bed not to say good-night to you but never mind we shall be able to see you when it is all over which I hope will be very soon. Dada brought the cake on Thursday but said he could not leave them. Dada was very disappointed because you could not have them but will save you some cake when you come home.

Heartfelt as they clearly were, letters from home must sometimes have made life harder for the brothers. Here, their young sister Dora writes to Leonard and Roland, 22nd June 1916 (Original 160x210mm) sign of manliness, a 'red badge of courage' to which conscientious objectors could never aspire. The absolute contrast between the 'manliness' of the soldier and the 'unmanliness' of the conscientious objector is characteristic of a society in which for generations the warrior had been held up as the ultimate sign of male virtue.[126]

★

The army had tried its best to talk the Payne brothers into conforming, without result, but this could not go on. As yet, no charges had been laid against them, but that was about to change. Leonard was first. On Saturday June 24th 1916 the pantomime of disobedience of the previous week was acted out again, this time for the record:

Lieutenant Shelley's statement in evidence.

'At Whitburn on the 24th June 1916 about 11 am I was inspecting company billets at Sinclairs Cottage, Whitburn, accompanied by the Orderly Sergeant of Letter "R" Company. The sergeant called the room to attention, and the accused took no notice of the order.

The orderly sergeant gave the order to accused to stand to attention and he again failed to do so.

I then gave the order myself to the accused. The accused, whom I now identify, folded his arms and said, "I shall not stand to attention".'

Sergeant Frederick Treadgold confirmed the lieutenant's evidence, adding only that there there was 'a party of men in the room' where the confrontation took place.

Leonard did not cross-examine either witness (what would have been the point?) and reserved his defence. He was to be tried by district court martial.[127]

Leonard sent a letter card home that Saturday afternoon which added detail to the plain military record:

'Dear Mother

I have been put in the guard room this morning for refusing to obey orders. I was taken before a captain or something of the kind this morning *[sic]* of course he tried to convince me I was a soldier and tried to make me drill but he did not succeed. He was very wild because he did not succeed and he addressed the soldiers saying that I was the sort of men *[sic]* they had been fighting for. He called me all sorts of names and he has been to me twice more since and tried to make me stand to attention by kicking my heels together and holding my hands by my side but he got sick of it and sent me to *[sic]* here… I have to wait here until Monday then I shall be taken before the commanding officer so I understand.'[128]

He wrote again to his parents on Sunday lunchtime:

'I am having a good time in the guard room so far, more food, papers to read, and can write when you like. I shall be before the commanding officer in the morning I expect my charge is refusing to obey an order by an officer. We have a good fire and make toast etc. The military policeman here is a decent old chap, he shaved me this morning and he lets me do as I like when ~~now~~ nobody is about.'[129]

The 'old' military policeman, whose name was Dawes, took Leonard under his wing, treating him almost as though he was his own son, so far as military circumstances would allow.[130]

Meanwhile, Roland wrote home that Saturday afternoon, unaware that his brother had been charged and confined:

'This morning we were separated, Leonard being took *[sic]* to another company. I saw him soon after that and he told me he was all right, and had wrote *[sic]* home. After dinner I went down to his quarters and was informed that he had been put in the guard room for disobeying orders. I can't understand why I have not, for I have disobeyed a major, captain, lieutenant, and loads of Non-Coms [i.e. NCOs].'[131]

He did not have to wait long. The following day, Sunday June 25th, it was Roland's turn. The specifics were different; Roland was charged with refusing to lay out his kit for inspection, but the offence was the same, refusal to obey a lawful order. The charge was under Section 9.2 of the Army Act: 'Every person subject to military law who… disobeys any lawful command by his superior officer, shall, on conviction by court martial… if he commits such offence not on active service, be liable… to suffer imprisonment, or such less punishment as is in the Act mentioned'.[132]

It was their tenth day at the Whitburn Army Camp.

2.30 a.m.   Guard Room.   Saturday   all Hill house

Dear mother   Whitburn nr Sunderland

I have been put in the Guard Room this morning for refusing to obey orders. I was taken before a Captain on something of the kind this morning of course he tried to convince me I was a soldier & tried to make me drill but he did not succeed. He was very wild because he did not succeed & he addressed the soldiers saying that I was the sort of men they had been fighting for. He called me all sorts of names & he has been to me twice since & tried to make me stand to attention by kicking my heels together & holding my hands by my side but he soon got sick of it & sent me to here. I have seen Bill since I wrote you the letter from the billet which I hope you will receive alright. He is quite alright & in the best of spirits & I have just heard again that he is quite well. I have to wait here until monday then I shall be taken before the Commanding Officer as I understand. I don't know if Bill will be taken before him then or not, but I hope he has written to you & told you what is happening to him. There is a pen & ink here so I am making use of it. I had a walk out this morning so that was the reason I saw Bill I went back to where I left him. If you send me a letter please put in a few stamped envelopes & writing paper they are better than P. Cards & letter cards. I should not be surprised if we get a court martial from here. I should not come up for a little time if I was Dad, I will try to let you know if I get any sentence at all. I suppose you could have to write for permission to see us if we get detention here or put into prison. Cheer up. Love to all
Leonard.

Leonard's miniscule handwriting on the postcard to his mother, 24th June 1916
(Original 90x140mm)

THE WAITING GAME

The weather had changed. After the glorious weather which had marked their arrival, the wind shifted and within a few days Leonard was complaining that, 'It is terribly cold up here we are right on the sea coast and you can hear the hooters of the ships every minute. It's a very rocky coast and it is nearly always raining'.[133] In these conditions they were forced into wearing khaki, but 'only enough to keep us warm', as Roland assured his parents.[134] So, now they had to wait. They had been charged, and they now expected it would be 'a week or two' before their formal court martial[135], but they had underestimated the army's ability to drag its feet when it wanted to. Court martial would mean inevitable conviction, and that would mean inevitable imprisonment, albeit in a civil prison,[136] which was something the officers at Whitburn wanted to avoid if they could. Perhaps, then, they might be able to talk them round, given a little more time and perhaps a little more pressure.

However, the delay gave the brothers' supporters time to organise their own lines of defence, though the communication and logistical problems so far from home were enormous. As soon as it was known the brothers had been sent to the north-east, Marion Harper used her contacts in the FoR and the NCF to compile a list of people in the Sunderland area able to help. Her father, Thomas, told the Payne family in Lutterworth on Saturday the 24th that, 'I think Herbert Corder would be [sic] of the best person to call on if you go to Sunderland he has himself been in prison in Australia through the military service out there... Marion wrote Herbert Corder this morning'.[137] There were others too... 'Miss Stevens [of the Café Vegetaria in Leicester Market Place] was saying yesterday that Mr Robertson the local treasurer of the NCF has a brother who lives in Sunderland and is treasurer of their NCF so they are hoping to get help from him'.[138]

Within a few days the brothers had received visitors, though the army was hardly helpful.[139] Roland wrote to his parents. 'Yesterday afternoon [Wednesday 28th June] two young fellows came to see me from Sunderland and they said they had heard from you. They went to see Leonard and were allowed to see him through a window but not to speak to him. They said they were going to write back'.[140] The first outside glimpse of the brothers in their army camp at Whitburn

Marion Harper's support and encouragement never wavered.
At the top of the page her embossed address in Syston, 5th July 1916.
(Original 200x250mm)

comes in a letter Thomas Emmerson of New Silksworth near Sunderland wrote to Miss Gittens in Leicester (at her request) and which was subsequently passed on to the family in Lutterworth:

> 'The elder of the two [brothers] is stationed at Whitburn Schools. Comrades have tried to obtain an interview with him, by seeking permission from the officer in charge, who, however, refused, stating that he was awaiting court martial, while a serg. major informed us what he would do if it was left to him. You can imagine the rest? When inquiring for Payne from the corporal in charge, he said he was in the adjoining room, had been examined for court martial, was fit. At this stage a face appeared at *[sic]* window, whom it was stated was prisoner. He acknowledge *[sic]* salute, and he was looking well and seemed to be all right, as far as appearances go.'

Roland seemed to be faring better:

> 'The younger Payne, it was learned was at the "Hutments Camp" about a mile away. Comrades went there and were fortunate enough to be taken to *[sic]* hut where he was prisoner. Called out to door and a few minutes conversation ensued. He is well, looking well, pleased to see friends, has been examined and fit for court martial sentence. Treatment fairly good, better than where his elder brother is and was.'[141]

★

Now the brothers were split up, leaving Leonard feeling acutely anxious and isolated, the separation from his brother pushing him towards crisis as his near paranoia grew increasingly intense. It is not easy at first to discern the reasons for Leonard's concern. In part it had to be a natural anxiety over the forthcoming court martial and what would follow it. Civil prisons, though less harsh than military prisons, were an unknown environment for him and after imprisonment there was the prospect of return to the military so the whole cat and mouse cycle could repeat itself endlessly. But this on its own cannot fully explain Leonard's state of mind, his depression and anxiety and the crisis it provoked. The fact was that an appalling thought had occurred to him, a terrifying possibility weighing heavily on his mind. This was that his younger brother might be *about to give up*. It was a horrifying prospect, for if Roland gave up, Leonard must have known that he would be unable to continue with his stand alone. But again, there was more to it than that. The relationship of the two brothers was an extremely close symbiotic relationship of mutual dependence. Roland followed where Leonard led. Leonard needed someone

172

to dominate while Roland needed someone to lead him. For Leonard to lose his brother would be to lose a part of his own personality. We see Leonard's psychological need to dominate those around him at every stage, never more than when he was at the Whitburn camp; the fear that his brother might give in and leave him isolated among men he could not dominate provoked something close to panic.

Roland's perceived fragility was no secret in the family, his mother encouraging him on in a way she rarely did with Leonard; 'I have every faith to believe that you will be all right... Stick to it, my lad'.[142] Even Marion Harper's mother in far-away Lancashire was aware of uncertainties about Roland. She was writing to Leonard just a couple of weeks later reassuring him: 'I feel that Roland will be firm, though he may be sorely tempted being so young'.[143] Even Roland himself had had his doubts, for his mother said that Roland is 'doing better than he expected'.[144]

Despite all this, there seems no possibility that Roland might throw in the towel. It was not just that he faced the same subtle pressures from home that had helped shape Leonard's conscientious objection, but also that it stemmed from his relationship with his brother. We saw this at the outset when Leonard had been first arrested in Lutterworth on his way back from Leicester: the police were prepared to wait until the following morning to take Roland into custody, but he had gone voluntarily to the cells, 'because I didn't want us to be divided'. This was more than fraternal loyalty. Roland could not conceive of life apart from his brother, even for one night. In an inverted sort of way, he was asserting his own identity by following where his older brother led. He was always the junior partner. At times he seems almost to be the 'invisible man', and we can scarcely make him out in Leonard's shadow, always the 'kid brother'. Even in the 1970s, when they were both old men, interviewed by Peter Liddle, Leonard's voice is the dominant one, Roland content to add a few comments of his own, but nothing more. It was inconceivable that in 1916 he might strike out on his own, assert an individuality apart from Leonard's, give up his conscientious objection and desert his older brother.

Leonard's fears about his brother were compounded by the army's treatment of Roland, which he thought was far too lenient. On Sunday 25th June he sent a postcard to his parents complaining:

'They are letting him run about as he likes and do as he likes as far as I can see. I do not think he is stern enough with them and does little things that they ask him to do and I think they will gradually try to work it on him if he is not careful. They can be too kind with you here. If you write him let him know this... I feel in the best of health and spirits but am rather concerned about Bill taking it so easy. I have written him a letter and shall try to post it here if I can.'[145]

We might see behind this a classic military tactic, as old as war itself – divide and rule. Another conscientious objector, Edward Williamson Mason, at precisely the same time but in Catterick Camp, experienced the same ploy. Two other objectors called Pawlet and Garston, had just been sentenced to detention by their colonel. 'After the two had got their twenty-eight days and refused all duties, the officers tried to separate us by preferential treatment. I had a good breakfast today, and the sergeant spoke less gruffly to me. He asked me what I thought of the other two refusing duty. I replied that it was their affair. He gave me my letters and kept back those of the other chaps because of their refusal to obey'.[146]

Roland himself, in trying to reassure those at home, unwittingly added to their concern with positive words, 'I am still as well as ever, in fact it is as good as my summer holidays. I am up and out for a wash at 5.00 in the morning, which means of course 4.30 ordinary times. I have to walk about a hundred yards for a wash so I get a good early morning's sea breeze. The sea is beautiful here. The navy is not far away and when I am out I see lots of destroyers…'[147] A day or two later he told them, '…I had nearly two hours on the sea front yesterday afternoon'.[148]

Even allowing for Roland's propensity to put a brave face on things, the discrepancy between his freedom and Leonard's confinement is striking. Years later Roland still remembered that period of freedom, and the 'official' reason for it. 'I was allowed to run about freely for about a fortnight. Nobody bothered with me whatever. I didn't know that anybody was watching me but I understood afterwards that there was some man watching me the whole time. He was a Catholic chap, he was a very nice chap. He told me afterwards that he had been appointed to keep his eye on me. Well, then they couldn't keep me in the guard room where Len was and they didn't want to put us together'.[149]

★

Leonard too, came to believe he was being spied on though not by some lone soldier dogging his footsteps in this amateurish way. Rather, it was the power of the State which Leonard felt weighing him down. He wrote a stern, almost petulant letter to his parents a few days after being charged, insisting that they write to each brother separately and frantically demanding that they keep track of all their correspondence:

> 'You see I do not know if you have written to the military to know anything. You say so little in your letters and we get them so irregular. Enclosed you will find the only two letters I have received from you as you will see I do not know much news… Have you addressed any letters to Hillfield House I have not received any.

In your next letter to this address state how many letters you have written to me or Bill if you can remember then it will give me some idea how many are lost.'[150]

His distrust extended particularly to the military and the post office. From their time in Wigston he had been methodically dating his postcards and letters home, often recording when they were received as well as when the last letter had been delivered. In an extraordinary letter written by Leonard on July 5th, he set out the procedures he wanted his family to follow. Was this Leonard trying to control those around him, Leonard feeling alone and paranoid, or merely the mind games of a man with nothing much to do?

'I did not receive any letters last night and they are always late in the morning (eleven o'clock) so I shall perhaps have to post this before I get one from you. I hope you have put some news in this time… I have put the date of the last letter I sent home, the date that marked on the letter, and I want you to do the same on mine. By this we shall know if you get all mine and I get all yours. But you will want to keep a seperate [sic] slip of paper with all the dates of letters you write or else if one gets lost it would spoil it. If you keep a record of every letter you send and I give you the dates of those I receive you will see if we lose any. I will also keep the dates of mine and you let me know the dates you receive then I shall know if you get all I send you. Cross them off your list when you know I have them and I will when you have got mine.'[151]

How important this lifeline of communication was to him became clear when its existence was threatened. He wrote to his sister Jessie in a letter which gives us disturbing insights into his state of mind:

'It is very silly to send P.C.s, this morning the corporal told me I should get my letters but should not be allowed to write to anyone. You see they read p. cards and they find out people are looking after us so they will try to stop letters going out with information… I shall get them out quite easy if they leave me writing paper and a pencil, but if they take away what I have I shall buy some more. If I suddenly cease writing you will know what has happened, they might take my money as well, but I shall beat them I shall hide some in my boots or somewhere. And you could put me a bit in my letters too (What What) [sic]. There are plenty of ways if you make your mind up.'[152]

If proof were needed that their letters were being read, Roland found it inadvertently but he could not, of course, warn his brother. (Or are we ourselves falling into the paranoid trap?) This is what Roland told his family at home in an easily opened letter card:

'Since I wrote you the P.C. that you will receive at the same time as this, I understand that I can't receive any letters. I have not heard anything from you yet, so the guard told me that if you sent the letters for me to him he would open them and give me them. He is a very nice fellow to take such a great risk of getting into trouble as this and he will get my letters out in the same way...

This fellow stayed at Bitteswell when that 15,000 came through [in March 1915]. He has been to the Dardanelles since and says only 4,000 got back, and they were wounded.'[153]

It was Private J. Kirk of K Company who had acted as postman, got this card of Roland's into the post, and had offered to act again. Roland gave Kirk's own return address to his parents.[154] A few days later Private Kirk was transferred from the Whitburn camp to Newcastle for reasons we are not told, but might be able to guess. Thus we have a cautionary tale about Roland's naïveté and the efficiency of military censorship![155]

A few days later a letter to each of the brothers from Rev. Seaward Beddow, the Minister of the Wycliffe Congregational Church on Prebend Street in Leicester, served to raise further Leonard's feeling of insecurity. Beddow was well known as an outspoken opponent of the war and an ardent pacifist. His letter was dated July 1st,[156] but did not arrive for several days and when it did it provoked a flurry of suspicion from Leonard. He wrote to his family back home, 'Of course he had to be careful what he put in the letter for fear of it being opened. I could see that by the way he had worded it. I know that his letters are watched at [sic] Leicester end'.[157] Whatever Leonard saw in 'the way he had worded it' is not now evident.

How far did Leonard's growing paranoia about security service surveillance and mail tampering have any substance? From the outset, assuming that anyone who opposed the war must be in the pay of the Germans,[158] the introduction of conscription had offered the security services the opportunity to clamp down on anti-war, anti-militarist and pacifist groups of all kinds – quite apart from its work in tracking down enemy spies.[159] Only a week or two before the Payne brothers were formally charged an MI5 officer had reported to his superiors in a secret memorandum about one anti-conscription group that: 'It may be fearlessly stated that the real aim of the National Council Against Conscription and others in their fanatical opposition to compulsory military service, is to work up feeling, especially in the workshops, against measures necessary for the successful prosecution of the war... If they are not for the success of our country it is not unreasonable if they are classed as pro-German. That, at any rate, is what the mass of the public consider them; and the public is substantially right'.[160]

The Defence of the Realm Act (DORA), passed at the outbreak of war and subsequently expanded and amended, gave the government powers 'which were contrary to any idea of parliamentary accountability and which affected the independence of the judiciary'[161], in fact 'powers close to martial law'[162], and subsequent legislation went further and further down the road of repression. Herbert Corder himself had already been intimidated by DORA. 'My public actions on behalf of these young men [i.e conscientious objectors] has, I fear, been misunderstood and I have only just escaped arrest under the Defence of the Realm Act'.[163]

It does not come as a surprise, therefore, that in just sixteen months (June 1916 to October 1917) no less than 5,246 people in Britain were investigated by the security services purely because of their association with pacifist or anti-militarist groups.[164] The security services in the First World War had become 'the first official body in Britain specifically dedicated to political policing'[165], or, as one other historian has argued, 'the Home Office... became not merely an instrument of government but also an organ of political repression'.[166]

★

Repression on its own would not, though, resolve the problem of the conscientious objectors.[167] On June 29th 1916, as the Payne brothers awaited their court martial on the cold Durham coast, the Prime Minister, Herbert Asquith, announced a new system to Parliament, a system which would remedy the blunders of the failed Tribunals, and do justice to the genuine conscientious objector, salvaging some remnant of Asquith's *'Ship of Liberal Values'*. Conscientious objectors who failed to convince their Local Tribunals, who were conscripted into the army and who then refused orders would first be court martialled and then transferred to a civilian prison. On the one hand, this confirmed the transfer to civilian control, while at the same time giving a sop to those who argued for 'equality of sacrifice', that the objectors should also have to suffer, as those who went into the army suffered.

It was what followed which was new. For their cases would then be reviewed by the Central Tribunal which would decide, case by case, whether each man's objection was genuinely conscientious or not. Where it was deemed not genuine the man would be returned to prison and ultimately returned to the military, but where the man's objection was genuine he would be placed under the direction of a committee chaired by a Home Office official, William Brace, which would assign him to carry out civil 'work of national importance' under civilian control. Technically, the man would be put into section W of the Army Reserve, set up for 'all soldiers whose service is deemed to be more valuable to the country in civil more than military employment'.[168] There would, as we shall see, be unforeseen complications as the 'Home Office Scheme' came into operation, but it was an obvious and reasonable attempt to reconcile the conscientious objectors' demands with those of a nation at war.

To do 'work of national importance' had been Leonard's aim from the outset. It was the kind of civilian work those passed by the Tribunals had been offered. Leonard was sceptical whether the government's new offer was genuine, remarking, '…surely it is not going to be another Tribunal trick, or else we shall be as bad as ever'.[169] His mother reinforced his caution, advising Roland that, '[You] should not take it unless it is quite under civil control and [you are] allowed to wear private clothes. They will claim you while in soldier's clothes'.[170] Marion Harper too was doubtful. She wrote, 'I am afraid you won't find the work of 'national importance' much to your mind, because I understand you would only get army pay, would have to work in gangs and would not be allowed to have a say in politics, or help with peace propaganda… I hope I have not damped [sic] your hopes only I thought you did not know you might be glad to be put on your guard'.[171]

But what concerned Leonard most was something rather surprising: would the scheme become a shirkers' charter, allowing men whose conscientious objection was not genuine to abuse the system, to the discredit of those whose conscientious objection was genuine? He asked, 'What is going to be the thing to pick out the genuine man from the other[?] [It] would be quite easy for a man to say he was a c. objector and go to civil prison about a month or two and then get work of national importance, [so] there would be thousands do it'.[172] This was not the first time the thought had occurred to him as some days before he had written that we are, '…sincere in all our belief, and not like many of the conscientious objectors'.[173]

How should we interpret this? After all, it was only reasonable that he would desire that he and the other men of genuine conscientious objection be respected as men of principle, acting out of firm and true beliefs, possibly even as martyrs for their faith. If men were passed through whose claimed conscientious objection was evidently insincere, it would bring the whole concept of conscientious objection into disrepute and confirm the public's view that the system was nothing more than a haven for anyone who wanted to shirk their responsibilities. Behind this we might glimpse the implication that men who did *not* have a genuine conscientious objection *should* be in the army, fighting and killing Germans.

On the other hand, perhaps this indicated a self-obsessed self-righteousness. In Leonard we occasionally catch a glimpse of that unedifying element in his character, a readiness to criticise what he saw as the shortcomings of others, especially where religion was concerned. This exchange, for example, comes, first, from a letter from his mother giving some local news. 'Mrs Turner [wife of the Mr Turner who ran the adult school in Lutterworth] has had an accident, fell off her machine will not be able to use her arm for six weeks so her posting is done. She went to see the flying at Lilbourne Sunday afternoon'.[174] Leonard's response was, 'Mrs Turner should not go to see flying on Sundays, then she would not get hurt'. Almost as an afterthought, he added, 'but still I am sorry for her'.[175]

With a family to support and a business to run, John George Payne clearly missed the help his sons had provided. Here he shows his awareness of the error in accepting the contract for shell baskets for the government.

(Original 200x250mm)

COURT MARTIAL

Throughout, it had been John's intention to be present at his sons' Court Martial. Court Martials were notionally held in public, so John, especially with his legal background as Assistant County Court Bailiff, could have usefully attended, and he wrote to the Commander of the 3rd Sherwood Foresters, Colonel Heath, seeking permission to visit his sons and to be notified in advance of the date of their military trial. Leonard's mother wrote, 'If he gets to know he will be there distance and money is nothing to him'.[176] Meanwhile Jessie also assured Roland that, 'Dad has written to the colonel and asked him to let him know when the court martial is and the time and place, and if he lets him know, nothing will stop him coming up'.[177]

However, John's ambition was to be frustrated. Leonard wrote to his mother on Friday July 7th 1916:

'By the time you receive this we shall be on our way to court martial, (Sat 8th. 10.30am I think is the time). I shall be looking out for Dad hoping that the colonel let him know in good time. I knew late last night, but doubted if the fellow that told me had the right tale. If I had been certain I should have sent a letter Fri morning, but then I would not have given you a chance to get here, if you had received the letter. I do not know now where it will be held, but I think it is Cleaden Camp about a mile and a half from here. I went to headquarters, Mayfield, this morning to receive a copy of the charge against me, they read it out to me and told me I should be tried by district court martial on Saturday, but I am not sure of the time he said. But I trust you will have this news through all right. On returning from headquarters I met Roland going up for the same thing, I suppose. I could not speak to him but just gave him a smile and nod as I went by. I know if Dad cannot get [sic] it will not be want of trying, but if you do not get news of course it is impossible. If this is the first news you get, I shall feel although Dad is not here, you will not forget us about this time.'[178]

Leonard, writing on printed headed paper, 'Whitburn, Near Sunderland', then filled three further pages with news and requests for news. But the letter seems disjointed, almost rambling, like a letter written from the condemned cell on the last night:

> '…Oh, when my mind will be filled with the strains of music again, it will be a bit different to the oaths and curses here. The war as you say is horrid I am sick of reading about it, it makes one's blood boil to think people read it and smile when they read of thousands of dead, especially Germans, poor beggars.'[179]

Yet alongside these lofty ideals we again catch a glimpse of that strange mixture inside his head as more small-minded thoughts could not be kept out: Aunt Lucy, his mother's older sister, was in the firing-line this time, accused of spreading rumours in Lutterworth that John was planning to close the shop.[180] And he said he was 'glad to hear Dad "chalked" you[ng] Smith off he wanted it and ask for it too'. It seems a nervous, edgy letter, as well it might, and he clung to his mother and his Bible. She had written to him the previous Monday, stiffening his resolve in time of trouble: 'Stick to it lad. God is on our side, if God be for us who can be against us. I am glad you have got your Bible I read that chapter this morning once again, so pleased that it has been such a consolation to you. I have pointed it out to Roland and ask him to read it. I am sure it will help him'.[181] Her reference was to Chapter 4 of Peter's First Epistle, the 12th and 13th verses of which read: 'Beloved, think it not strange concerning the fiery trial which is to try you, as though some strange thing happened unto you: But rejoice, inasmuch as ye are partakers of Christ's sufferings; that, when his glory shall be revealed, ye may be glad also with exceeding joy'. Leonard took the point, saying, 'Those few verses suit the position of today A.1. I read them as soon as I finished reading letters this morning'.[182]

Towards the end of his long letter, Leonard returned to what must have been in the forefront of his mind for he only made reference in his letters to Biblical texts or religious teachings when he was sorely tried:

> 'I am still hoping to see Dad in the morning, if not tomorrow later on perhaps. Well I feel fit for it, you know what the scriptures tell us, words shall be given us in that hour, and that we are not to trouble what we shall say when we are brought before judges and princes. Well I must close now and get ready for morning.'

Their father raced up to the north-east as quickly as he could, but did not manage to get to Whitburn on time, arriving on Sunday the 9th July. The previous day, on the 8th July 1916, Leonard and Roland Payne were tried by Court Martial. It was an open and shut case under Section 9 of the Army Act of 1913. Roland's Charge Sheet read:

'The Accused No: 49292 Private Roland Payne, 3rd lion The Sherwood Foresters (Nottinghamshire and Derbyshire Regiment), a Soldier of the Regular Forces is charged with:-

DISOBEYING IN SUCH MANNER AS TO SHOW A WILFUL DEFIANCE OF AUTHORITY A LAWFUL COMMAND GIVEN PERSONALLY BY HIS SUPERIOR OFFICER IN THE EXECUTION OF HIS OFFICE, in that he, at Whitburn on the 25th day of June 1916 when personally ordered by No: 6070 Sergeant W. Chart, 3rd Battalion The Sherwood Foresters (Nottinghamshire and Derbyshire Regiment) upon Company Officer's Kit Inspection to lay down his kit did not do so saying 'I cannot do so, I have conscientious objections to obeying any Military Orders'.

(sd) E.C. Heath Lieut. Colonel.

Commanding 3rd Bn: The Sherwood Foresters.

Roker, Sunderland.

30th June 1916.'[183]

They were found guilty. In many ways, the trial was a decided anticlimax. Leonard wrote to his sister Jessie the day after his court – martial, Sunday July 9th:

'Yesterday we were before court martial as I expect you know by the letter I sent you. It was not much to face, and I had nothing much to say. I think the thing was settled before we went before them. The court consisted of a colonel and two captains. We were marched out a good many times, swearing witnesses, etc. The colonel was very nice, some of the things I said in my statement, he said, I should not put down if I were you, I don't think it will help you at all. You see he said, I'm here to help you. Of course he may be, or he may not but I think he was sincere. We do not know our sentence until it is read out that may be this week.'[184]

Peter Liddle's interview with the brothers in the 1970s elicited a few more details. It seems they were formally tried at Mayfield, a large house in Sunderland which was the depot for the Sherwood Foresters in that area. They were asked, for the record, about their beliefs and the grounds for their conscientious objection to serving in the army, the sort of questions they had been asked so many times before.[185]

On Tuesday July 11th Leonard wrote home to say that he was 'very pleased to see Dad and was very sorry that he had been so put about to get to us. He looked very tired on Sunday, but better on Monday. I expect he will tell you all the news… I expect Dad has arrived home by now. I was very sorry he could not see Roland to talk to him, but he was very lucky to see me as he did. I am sure I admire him very much for his pluck getting to us as he did. It was good of him to come right up here such a distance to see us… Tell Dad that chocolate was jolly good'.[186] In fact, John did see his younger son even though they were not allowed to speak to each other, for Roland wrote home, 'I did not think Dad looked very well on Sunday or perhaps he was very tired. Tell him not to worry himself about us, for we shall be all right, it won't be for long'.[187]

This occasion was the first time John had seen his sons since they had been taken from Wigston Barracks and the first time they had seen him. It seems that John had driven to the north-east by motorbike[188], a prodigious undertaking, though his fatigue must also have been caused by the weeks of worry and strain, which had preceded that long journey. Leonard and Roland in their letters home rarely asked how the family in Lutterworth was bearing up. If they had it is doubtful they would have received an honest reply.

What *should* have happened at this point was the formal proclamation of their sentence to the regiment and their immediate transfer to civilian custody. However, this did not happen. The 'reading out' of court martial sentences was a formal and elaborate ritual with its own customs and traditions, and the new system for dealing with conscientious objectors was barely set up, so they would have to wait in the hands of the military until the appropriate arrangements could be made. So the brothers spent the following days in limbo, convicted of a serious military offence, but not yet sentenced and with no idea what the sentence would be; anxious to discover what was happening to other conscientious objectors in the same position; unsure about whether they would actually be sent to a civil prison or would be offered work of 'national importance' straight away or at all; whether that work would be acceptable to them or would involve them making munitions, which would not. They heard rumours, Chinese whispers, and tales, positive and negative, helpful and frightening, from their guards who knew no more than they did. Leonard told his mother that 'they think up here that work of "national importance" is nothing but making munitions. I have had arguments with soldiers about that, they told me we had got to make munitions'.[189] Meanwhile, Roland was told a different tale. 'The soldiers tell me here we shall almost get off. I hope we shall, I should love to go to the field again. It is very monotonous here'.[190]

Bewildered, both brothers needed clarification, as Leonard told his family back home:

'I have asked to see Major Wise to see what he says about this work [of "national importance"]. I understand he can recomend [sic] any of us for it if he thinks we are genuine. I shall perhaps be before him this afternoon and shall make him understand already that I am not afraid of any punishment, but yet I am willing to accept work of N.I, under civil power. What I mean is, I am not going to be a soldier whatever happens, but if the terms are suitable for this work it would be better than prison. I shall want a very clear understanding before I take any steps because I am not going to be tricked into anything. But Major Wise is a gentleman who will do his best for me I am sure.'[191]

Outside support came also from Herbert Corder, the Sunderland Quaker[192], who brought good news about the evolving government policy towards conscientious objectors. Leonard wrote home, breathlessly adding an extra page to an already completed letter:

'Since I started this letter I have been talking to Mr Corder… He came up with a lady named Miss Smith from Fritchley Nr Derby to see the new C.O.s. … Mr Corder said all C.O. sentences were to be served in civil prison so it won't be so bad. And he said those that were willing to accept work of N.I. would be released from civil prison. So there is great hope I think.'[193]

At this point, Roland told his mother that, 'my three pals are still in here with me. They had a lady named Miss Smith to see them last night, bringing them soap, towels, knives, forks, writing material, stamps, etc. She is a Quakeress, and came with that Mr Corder from Sunderland. She went and saw Leonard and wanted to see me but was not allowed, because she hadn't got a permit to see me'.[194]

It was a reminder that his position had altered since his court-martial. He was no longer the favoured one and the rules now applied to him as well.

★

For Leonard, living conditions after the court-martial seem to have improved: he was putting on weight[195], but his general health had suffered during the past weeks of strain. His main physical problem was constipation, which quickly turned into diarrhoea – without the aid of the 'health salts' he had felt obliged to buy.[196] Roland

Church Street
Lutterworth
June 30th 1916

My Dear Leonard.

We received your letter to Jessie this morning she had gone to work so we opened it. We have sent you several letters One letter with a Postal Order for 5/-. I have enclosed the counterfoil it was made out to you. I think I sent it guard Room Whitburn Nr. Sunderland. We are hard at work outside for you. We have written to a Gentleman in Sunderland reccomended by Mr Harper and he has promised to see you if he can get Permission to come in Dad as written to Mr Heath as you wished & ask him to give him permission to see you. also when you were to have a C Mar. if he gets to know he will be there distance & money is nothing to him. We had a letter from Roland. Wednesday & Thursday he is alright & was sticking to it. We feel Proud of you. that you are willing to suffer for the course of Peace. stick to it. my boy it will all come right in the end. you may feel assured. we are looking out after you as much as possible

A typical blend of practical help and uplifting exhortation from their mother Jessie to Leonard
30th June 1916
(Original 200x250mm)

too was suffering physical symptoms, writing that, 'I have not been quite so well lately… Last Thursday night I woke up with awful pains in my inside, I must have caught a cold or something'.[197] That was not his only worry for it was now his turn to feel the weight of military authority. After the Court Martial, the generous treatment he had received at Whitburn was abruptly halted. 'Divide and rule' hadn't worked, so there was now no point, though the change in his treatment perhaps had more to do with personal factors, the arrival of a new sergeant major for K Company, as Roland told his father:

'The S.M… is a big enemy of mine. He came in yesterday morning bullying and swearing awful at me, and tried to tell me Len was going on parade today. He ordered the police to stand me on my head and put on my putties, because I refused, also to cut down my rations. These things the police won't do, but put them on properly. It nearly broke their hearts to keep me back from seeing [i.e. making human contact with] you and Leonard on Sunday. This S.M. only started duty yesterday and has given orders to keep me locked in always and when on exercise not to go outside the camp or have longer than an hour. This makes it much worse, but if he comes again like he came yesterday I shall report him to Colonel Heath. The soldiers have all got to here [sic] about all these things and say they are going to shoot him when he gets out to the front for he treats them the same… I don't take any notice of the S.M.'s tale. He wanted to know if I should give in… and I told him 'no'.'[198]

His food ration had also been reduced:

'We have now been put on prison diet, but I don't know whether this is for regular or not…[199] My food will now be, bread and dripping for breakfast, a bowl of soup for dinner, and bread and dripping for tea, with a bowl of tea for breakfast and tea.'[200]

…and the Sergeant Major had found an ingenious way of turning his exercise period to the common good:

'I am… making footpaths. For my hour's exercise I have to walk up and down an ash footpath about twenty yards long. The sergeant m told me he wanted a footpath making. The police are very good to me though they let me have a good rest when there is no one looking.'[201]

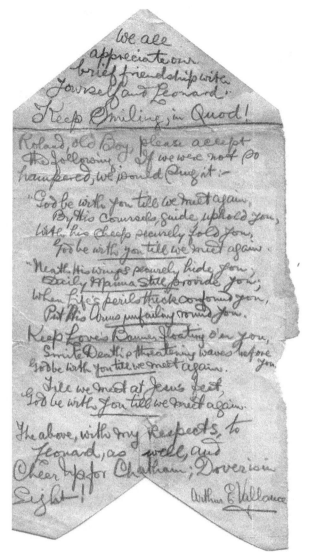

Some ingenuity was needed at times as conscientious objectors communicated with each other. Here, Arthur Vallance uses the inside of an envelope in writing to Roland. Postmarked 7th July 1916. (Original 120 x 230 mm.) Written on the inside of an envelope.

The sergeant major's claim that Leonard had been on parade was, strictly speaking, untrue. It was all a matter of interpretation, as Leonard explained in a letter to his sister Jessie on Sunday July 16th:

'It is all not what they have been telling him about going on parade. I tell you what they have got hold of, yesterday morning (Sat) [July 15th] the order came that everyman *[sic]* was to be on parade, prisoners as well. At first I said I should not go, but thought it no good kicking because I should only have to get dragged there. I and three more prisoners were taken under escort and put behind the troops on parade ground. Then we were marched to Cleaden Camp about two and a half miles from here to their parade ground, here we were lined up just the same with some more troops. I thought at first it was for our court martial sentence to be read out but it was not. It was to see the presentation of the D.C.M. to one of the Sherwood Foresters. It was presented by General English, the band played and it was quite a smart affair. There was to be a march past but the prisoners were taken away before this happened. So that is all the parade I have done, which was nothing.'[202]

The mood in this letter is more positive, less anxious, now that the watershed of the Court Martial was passed. While Roland's treatment was tighter, the period after the Court Martial, ironically enough, saw something of a liberation for Leonard. His attitude to the soldiers at the camp was becoming more nuanced as he gained a better understanding of the military system which governed their lives, and he was also becoming more aware of the impact his own actions were having on the soldiers around him. The Saturday of the parade, July 15th, was an eventful day.

That evening: '…there was five more C.O.s arrived here from Derby, they have been c[ourt] m[artialled] and have just finished fifty-six days in a military prison. Fine chaps they are too and they look well. I had a talk with them last night and tell you how this happened. I have to go upstairs to the lavatory and of course I have a policeman with me. We had three fresh men on the police yesterday so two of these went upstairs with me. They did not know their duty, or they would have stopped me talking to them. On our way upstairs we met two fellows who didn't have *[sic]* want a shave with a lance cpl. The lance cpl said to me, "Here are some of your pals" so of course I stopped and had a talk to them and shook hands with them. Next we advanced up the stairs and as the lavatory was engaged we had to wait outside, of course, the other three came and had a good talk to me. This talking kept on for about five minutes until an officer came and made a scene. He put one policeman under arrest and brought a charge against the other for allowing me to talk to these others. When we got back into the guard room the policeman that was under arrest fainted away and we had a terrible job to bring him round, we got water and unbuttoned his clothes, and at last carried him outside in the air. Then a stretcher was brought and he was taken to hospital, he is better now. You see he was a new recruit put on the job and he was frightened to death. So you see what trouble I get people into if I am not very careful… The C.O.s asked me for writing paper and I promised to give them stamps, paper, towel and soap for a wash, but this affair upset the lot and I could not get the things to them. The poor chaps had no money or anything, I should have given them plenty if this lot hadn't have happened. Just my luck, though, getting caught talking to them. I expect to see them again no doubt they will get in *[sic]* guard room in a bit. They tell me they expect to get court martialled *[sic]* again and put in civil prison this time, then they will be willing to accept work of n[ational] importance if they get a chance to'.[203]

Here was a new role for Leonard Payne and one which he relished enormously: elder statesman for the conscientious objector community in Whitburn Army Camp. Roland also wrote about meeting some of these new objectors a few days later. 'I have now got three other conscientious objectors come to me. They have been in the same place as Leonard for a short time, and have been in some military prison at Wakefield. They are remanded for a second court martial. They seem a nice lot of chaps, and have been in a military gaol fifty-six days'.[204]

Leonard was now an old hand at the Whitburn camp and he enjoyed his new role as he took the newest arrivals under his wing:

'I think I told you we have a lot of C.O.s here now, seven here and five a little way off at Cleaden, beside Bill and I. Yesterday morning [Monday July 17th] about 6 am we were awakened and saw five brought into for refusing to parade. I got up and had a good jaw to them and found them in *[sic]* paper, pencil, stamps, towel, soap, and I don't know what else. I lent one chap some money to get some with when he was parted from us and put on his own. They about cleared me out of writing stuff. They were taken before Major Wise and this morning they have gone before Colonel Heath to be remanded for C.M. This is their second C.M., that *[sic]* got fifty-six days at the last, part they served at Derby and some in a military prison at Wandsworth. Three are in guard room with me and two in police room and two that arrived last night in the bath room. We all went out for an hours *[sic]* exercise yesterday morning and afternoon. This was in a field and we had to walk round and round the field about ten yards from each other. It has caused quite a panic this lot arriving here and I have heard there are some more to come on Sat. One chap in my room belongs to the International Bible Students Association, and I think the other two are socialists or something of that. One belongs to Plymouth Brethering *[sic]*, one a Methodist and I don't know what the others are. Two of them are very willing to accept work of N.I. and the major is going to see what he can do for them... They call me the head man over the new C.O.s that have arrived. I look after them and show them how to get on a bit.'[205]

READING OUT

hings now happened suddenly. On Wednesday July 19th Leonard had been told by a corporal that he should expect to be moved on Saturday[206], though nothing could happen until their sentences had been officially 'read out'. This happened at 9.30 a.m. on Thursday the 20th, as Roland reported home:

> 'I have just sent a postcard telling you the result of the court martial. There were two company's [sic] of soldiers, one from Whit[burn] and one from here [Seaburn Huts], lined up in two lines, at the reading out. Leonard's was read out first, and mine sec, both of us getting one years imprisonment. They did not say any more, where we were going to, or anything about it.'[207]

Many years later, when interviewed by Pete Liddle, they gave some more details of the procedure: 'We were court martialled and then we were taken to a camp where there were thousands of troops and people reading out the results of the courts martial. They called out for private so and so to step forward and we didn't taken any notice. You were supposed to walk so many paces forward when they read out the court martial. So one of these soldiers gave me a good shove in the back and pushed me forward. So I thought, well that is all right, I will have a little walk. So I walked right across the parade ground to the other side much to the disgust of the officers and everybody else'.[208]

The prospect of a year's imprisonment did not daunt them, in part because of their ignorance of the prison system (even the civilian prison to which they should be consigned) and partly because they did not think they would have to serve it. All the talk in conscientious objector circles was of a relaxation of the system. In his postcard he had written, 'It has not been commuted as yet, but my pals think it will be, when out of the way of the soldiers. I am still cheerful as ever, it is not possible to get downhearted, with pals like these and the *conscience*'.[209] His mother also believed her sons would not have to spend the coming year in gaol: she wrote to Leonard to say, 'We went to the NCF meeting last night, it was a grand meeting… they all said it would be commuted, you would never have all that lot.

Mr Harper was there and he said you would never serve it all'. [210] On the other hand, 'Mr Harper said the war would be over soon, and then there would be an end to it'.

Even Mr Harper was not right all of the time.

★

After the reading out of the sentence, the brothers' status changed again, though to *what* was unclear. Had they started their sentences yet? If so, they *should* have been in civilian custody, not military. Leonard believed he had started serving his time, and noticed the change with some pleasure. He wrote, 'I have to work now, you see I am doing my twelve months and so have to work the same as prisoners do. I have to do work in the cook house such as, washing up, scrubbing and all sorts of things. We work from nine to twelve – two to five, so it is not so bad. It is better than being shut up all day'.

His work there has a curiously ambiguous feel to it. Was he actually *aiding the military* in performing these domestic tasks about the camp? A strict absolutist would say 'yes', but in his own mind, he was not. Uncertainty remains, however. Technically, since he ought to now be in *civilian* custody, in a *civilian* prison, he could argue that he was not really in *military* custody at all – even though, in fact, he was. He was in a kind of *pretend* civilian gaol, and caught in another of those intricate conundrums into which the conscientious objectors were frequently thrust, and to which each found his own solution. He was even looking forward to civilian prison life, as he told his mother: 'So Mr Twilly is in Durham prison is he, what a lark if we get there, we shall meet our old pals once more'.[211] As events would show, it is a comment of breathtaking naïveté.

Roland, by contrast, appears to have had no work to do, which goes some way to explain his apparent flatness of spirit. During this waiting time, he had little to say that was positive, qualifying the phrase, 'I am going on all right' by adding, 'only always hungry'. The only brighter note was a further visit from Mr Corder, accompanied by his wife, on the previous Sunday. Since then, though, nothing had happened. Boredom and uncertainty were taking their toll: 'the same things happen every day, week in, week out'; and he added 'it seems as if I am to remain here always'. The loss of liberty a prison sentence implied, even as uncertain a one as this, was affecting him.[212] His conditions had clearly tightened, his letters home, he believed – at long last! – now subject to censorship and delay. He complained of feeling isolated: 'I dont [sic] get any news here, being dead to the things outside'. Being unable to see his brother added to the isolation.

Leonard, too, noticed a tightening of the rules, though he was able to find a way round them: 'I have not yet got permission to receive letters but the Cpl told me he would give me those that had come for me, and he told me to write home and tell you to stop writing me. But send through the address I gave you until I let you know if I can get them direct to me'.[213] The mysterious contact seems to have been an individual, presumably a soldier, called Whitehouse.[214] Leonard's resourcefulness plus the kindness of an ordinary serviceman were enough to circumvent the power of the military machine. Corporal Whitehouse would not be the last.

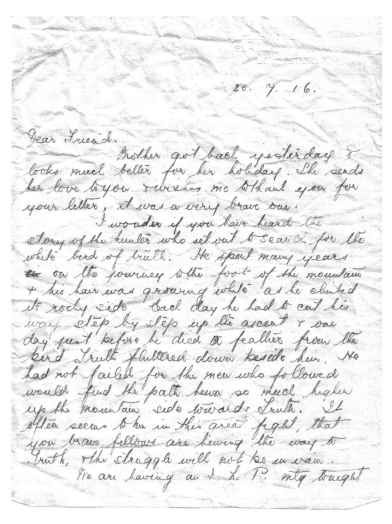

Marian tells Leonard the inspiring story of the White Bird of Truth, 20th July 1916
(Original 180x250mm)

THE THIRD ROCK

THE UNIMAGINABLE SCALE OF THE GREAT WAR

Of course, it is entirely possible that there was another, darker, reason for the hardening of the military's official attitude towards the Payne brothers at Whitburn and the other conscientious objectors scattered in army bases up and down the country, for the war situation was looking altogether more dangerous, more threatening as the summer of 1916 ground on. The sheer scale of the war as it developed through 1916, as the whole nation geared up towards Total War (out of necessity, not choice), meant Asquith's liberal cast of mind appeared less and less relevant against the overriding need to win the war – at whatever cost.

In the spring the Germans had launched their massive attack against the French fortress city of Verdun. The German commander, Falkenhayn, had spelled out his strategy: 'Our enemies, thanks to their superiority in men and material, are increasing their resources much more than we are. If that process continues a moment must come when the balance of numbers itself will deprive Germany of all remaining hope', he wrote. 'Within our reach behind the French sector of the Western Front there are objectives for the retention of which the French General Staff would be compelled to throw in every man they have. If they do so the forces of France will bleed to death'.[215] Thus the terrible Battle of Verdun was launched and France was bled white. Then, at Easter, Irish Nationalists had rebelled against the British in Dublin: though the rising was put down with relative ease, it showed up the dangers to which this war was exposing the social and political fabric of the countries involved – as all of them would discover before the thing was over. Then, on the last day of May and the first day of June in 1916, the Royal Navy had clashed with the German High Seas Fleet off Jutland[216], and Britain's faith in its Grand

Fleet to protect it from harm suddenly seemed vulnerable. The British lost more ships and men, and the German Fleet was not defeated. Perhaps there was some cause for optimism in the east, where the Russian General Brusilov was securing the first and last great Russian victory over the Austrians in Galicia, and it looked for a time as though Germany's principal ally might be knocked out of the war. But the Russians ran out of steam and the attack petered out. As the year went on the political situation in Russia would slide inexorably towards Revolution and after that mass desertions, and, in 1917, Russia's withdrawal from the First World War.

To many in Britain, though, the most shocking setback in the early summer of 1916 was the loss of the great iconic hero of the nation when Lord Kitchener went down with *H.M.S. Hampshire* off the Orkneys on June 5th 1916. In Lutterworth the schools were closed at 11.30 a week later so that children and teachers could attend a memorial service in his honour.[217]

But for the British even these events, traumatic as they were, paled in comparison to the effects of the great offensive launched by Douglas Haig on the Somme in northern France on July 1st. So much has been written about the Battle of the Somme, and especially its first day, on which 20,000 British soldiers lost their lives, that it needs no reiteration here.[218] Initial reports of great British successes could not hide from the military itself the vast scale of the losses and inevitably men of the Sherwood Foresters were among those fatally caught up in the tragedy. In the army, a regiment is a family, and that is how we should understand the impact of so many losses on the Sherwood Foresters, nominally Leonard and Roland Payne's regiment.

In graphic style Arthur Conan Doyle gave this description of what befell the 5th and 7th Battalions of the Sherwood Foresters, described by Haig himself as 'a fine keen looking lot of men'[219]: 'The fate of the right attack was bad, but that of the left [outside Gommecourt at the northern end of the twenty-mile-long line of attack] was even worse, for at this point we had experience of a German procedure which was tried at several places along the line with most deadly effect, and accounted for some of our very high losses. This device was to stuff their front line dug-outs with machine-guns and men, who would emerge when the wave of stormers had passed, attacking them from the rear, confident that their own rear was safe on account of the terrific barrage between the lines. In this case the stormers were completely trapped. The 5th and 7th Sherwood Foresters dashed through the open ground, carried the trenches and pushed forward in their fiery career. Instantly the barrage fell, the concealed infantry rose behind them, and their fate was sealed. With great valour the leading four waves stormed their way up the communication trenches and beat down all opposition until their own dwindling numbers and the failure of their bombs left them helpless among their enemies. Thus perished the first companies of two fine Battalions'.[220] A dozen miles to the south the 11th Battalion was at the same time suffering the loss of 437 officers and men as casualties from an active complement of about 730.[221] Whether we follow Conan Doyle's dashing style or the more clinical statistics of the battle, the outcome remains the same – and its impact on the Sherwood Foresters just as devastating.

A few days later, Leonard wrote to his parents saying, 'Isn't the war awful, the thousands that are being killed, and mostly men from up here in the British Army. And the Germans and French must be losing a terrible lot. Draughts *[sic]* of men keep going from round here to the front, in fact nearly every day some go. They have nearly cleared all the Notts and Derby camps out round here, so they must be losing a lot… Nearly all the officers of the 'Sherwoods' have been sent to France to fill up the gaps made by recent fighting'.[222] Roland was made more directly aware of the departure of men for the Front. He wrote, 'About the worst night I have had here was last Tuesday [11th July]. I had a lot of drunken men put in here, being pay night, and one was being sick all the time on the floor. I could hardly get any air we were so crowded, this place being so badly ventilated. There was a lot sent to France from here last night also a lot of absentees'.[223]

★

On Tuesday morning, July 25th, Major Wise visited Leonard with the news that the following day he was to be consigned to prison, and that Roland was to be sent with him. He added: 'I hope when you come out the war is over'. As Leonard then commented, 'He was a real gentleman'.[224] Leonard wrote home with the news:

'By the time you receive this letter I shall be in Newcastle, I don't know if we are going to prison there but I expect that it what it is. I and Bill have been examined by the doctor this afternoon to see if we are fit for punishment. Of course I could not speak to him as usual, but I get *[sic]* one word in, he asked me if it was civil prison and I said yes. I am not certain that Bill is going with me but it looks like it, all I know is I am going to Newcastle… I do hope Bill goes with me, but I expect he will… I wish I was certain I was going to prison, I would post all my old letters home to you… I have no idea when I shall be able to write you again, but if you don't hear from me you will understand and also if you don't hear from Bill you will know he has been moved too. If you don't hear from us where we have been put, you must write Major Wise or Colonel Heath, Headquarters, 3 Sherwood Foresters, Mayfield, Sunderland. But you may be sure I shall do my best to let you know where I am, but if I can't of course you will understand, I shall have no chance of answering the letters I have received so if you will thank Mr Thompson very much for his, I greatly enjoyed reading it. Write Kit and Marion a P.C. and tell them I can't possibly answer, but I thank them very much for their kind letters… Just give my Kind Regards to all friends I know, I would like to write them all but it is impossible.'[225]

It is all overstated, nervous, edgy, rather like a last letter from someone about to face certain death, his anxiety heightened because he did not know where he was going. And yet he managed to rally his spirits, saying, 'I feel ful [sic] of excitement and wonder of what will happen next, but I do not see any fear, I have forgotten how to fear. I feel that God is with me wherever I go and he will help me in the worst possible dangers and in the darkest hour'. [226]

A Corporal Lockton, in an unofficial act of humanity in defiance of military regulations, wrote to the Payne family in Lutterworth. Undated, the letter read:

'K. Coy. 3rd Sherwood Foresters
Seaburn Hutments Sunderland
Dear Sir,
    I am writing to tell you that your two sons R and L Payne have gone to H.M. Prison Newcastle and one of them asked me to write to you and tell you where they were I had to take them that is how I know but don't [sic] tell anyone who told you where they were as I may get into trouble.
    Yours Sincerely,
    10518 Cpl. G.R. Lockton.'[227]

The same day, Wednesday 26th July 1916, Leonard managed to get a letter card home, postmarked Newcastle on Tyne. Addressed to his mother, it read:

'Sunderland
26 [July] 1916
Dear Mother,
    We are just off the Newcastle to prison [sic] civil prison. I can't tell you the address or anything but you will find out if you write where I told you. It is just one oclock [sic]. We have our soldiers' kit with and I expect they will take it away from us when we get there. Bill is with me and I am glad. I hope you receive all my old letters which I have sent home to you. I feel in the best of health and spirits

and I hope you will soon see us again. I received a letter from a girl friend of mine from Cotesbach, you might guess who it was. Give my love to all friends and the best of love to you all. Excuse writing the train rocks.

Leonard' [228]

From Lutterworth, John wrote to Major Wise. He received this handwritten reply, formal and courteous, but lacking embellishment or human comment. It was dated Friday August 4th, over a week after the brothers had left Whitburn Camp.

'Dear Sir,

In reply to your letter asking about your sons I have to inform you that they have been committed to the civil prison at Newcastle on Tyne to undergo a year's sentence. They were quite well when last I saw them just before they were taken to prison.'[229]

PRISON

For those who went through it, imprisonment was the most traumatic event of their whole conscientious objector experience.

Newcastle's massive old gaol dated, like Leicester's Welford Road Gaol, from the 1820s, the time when a wave of prison building was under way, not because there were so many new prisoners to accommodate, but because the newest theories said that if prisoners were kept in isolation from each other they could better contemplate the error of their ways. This meant one prisoner to one cell: in other words, for the first shocking weeks at least, solitary confinement. Those theories still applied in 1916.

They would be applied to the conscientious objectors when they entered the prison system. This was a problem. It was a system designed to recover the evildoer, the delinquent and, in its broadest sense, the sinner. Ironically, it had been the Quakers of Pennsylvania who had, in the nineteenth century, developed the idea of solitary and silent imprisonment to make the criminal confront his own conscience, so he could thereby understand the error of his ways, and thence find enlightenment from within himself.[230] It was not a system designed to confront the righteous prisoner, and its relevance to men who were there *because of* their consciences, and some of whom were anyway Quakers themselves, remains hard to fathom.

Confinement in the Whitburn Army Camp, even in the guard room, had not prepared them for this. At Whitburn there had at least been some human contact: sympathetic soldiers willing to pass on letters; a kindly old military policeman who had treated Leonard as though he were his own son; a major who was understanding and prepared to give them a hearing; a corporal willing to pass news to their family;

inexperienced military policemen who would allow them to chat to other prisoners when they happened to meet in the corridor whilst waiting to go to the toilet; even that sergeant major who made them walk up and down to make a footpath. But Newcastle Prison was not like that. Built on the pattern of wings radiating out from the centre, it was vast, friendless and impersonal. That was how it was meant to be: a place specifically and skilfully designed and managed to *punish*.

Prison regulations were stern and the brothers now found themselves in the hands of a system which would allow no leeway. To the prison authorities they were merely convicted criminals: that their crime was refusing to be soldiers rather than theft or assault or rape, made no difference at all. There would be no 'give' here, no sympathetic ear to listen to their case and protect them. This was no 'lark'.

A brief and unscientific survey of the dozen or so men admitted to Newcastle Prison immediately before the arrival of the Payne brothers is suggestive of the type of prisoner the warders were more accustomed to dealing with. Apart from one man on remand for embezzlement, there were a couple of drunks locked up for a week and a beggar who got twenty-eight days of possibly welcome shelter. Sentences tended to be measured in days. There were some whose crimes would not today be regarded as criminal. A labourer called Edward Jackson was locked up for twenty-five days for using indecent language, and the prison's Nominal Register records William Harold Smith, a soldier from Leicester, whose crime had been to attempt to take his own life: no details were given. Then there were two young soldiers, Hyman Cantor and George North, their offence at first entered in the register as 'Buggery', but then crossed out and 'Gross Indecency' written in its place. Homosexual acts were criminal acts in 1916: Cantor got three months and North, the younger of the two, got six months, which must have seemed like a lifetime. Several were war related: a seaman from neutral Denmark, who had come ashore and neglected to register himself, was gaoled for a few days and a handful of navy sailors late back from shore leave, most classified as 'stragglers' though one as a 'deserter', were locked up before being handed over to military custody, and no doubt further punishment, when they got back on board. Then, of course, there were the two conscientious objectors, Leonard and Roland Payne, who passed through the forbidding gates and walls of Newcastle Prison on Wednesday July 26th 1916.[231]

They were not the first conscientious objectors to enter Newcastle Prison – far from it. Arthur Askwith Craven had been the first, gaoled on June 8th after using insubordinate language in the Newcastle Barracks, and twenty-four others had followed before the Paynes arrived – not that the Paynes were aware of them. The system made sure of that.

NEWCASTLE GAOL, 1825.

First they were bathed. Fred Tait, a schoolteacher from Gateshead, experienced the joys of prison bathing there a few weeks before the Paynes: 'My first introduction to prison bathing was at Newcastle', he wrote, 'where the baths were in a very dark part of the prison. I began by losing the soap, quite an easy matter as it is generally about one inch long by a quarter inch square, and having found it was proceeding to give my attention to my right toe when the warder yelled "Plugs out". I continued on the toe, but not for long. "Come on out of that, get your clothes on." "But I haven't finished yet," I said. "Ain't finished. How long do ye want? You ain't in the Ritz Club, me boy". So I got out without my bath'.[232]

It was now time to exchange the makeshift khaki they had been brought in for prison uniform: a green vest with a red stripe round its middle, with similar socks, and cotton shirt also with a red stripe but with the small black broad arrows which have become the traditional symbol of prison gear. Then a waistcoat, coat, buttoned down the front, trousers and conical shaped hat, all in grey and all marked with the black sign of the broad arrow, and finally a pair of shoes. None of it, of course, was new, and much was well-worn and probably ill-fitting as well, the shoes 'so worn down you couldn't walk' in them.[233]

Leonard later recalled: 'I saw these clothes beside the bath which I was supposed to put on. Well, I got dressed and a warder came in and he said what are you going to do with those? Aren't you going to put those on? I said I thought they were pyjamas and he said you don't get pyjamas in prison. They were the pants and vest and they all had a red line down and they had three rows of buttons on which you buttoned up if you were fat'.[234] One size, it would appear, ill-fitted all.

As Leonard and Roland passed through the admission procedure and were taken off each to his cell, they now understood the terrifying truth that each was to be put into his own cell so that even the tenuous and irregular contact between the brothers at Whitburn camp was broken. Solitary confinement and silence. The 'Abstract of the Regulations Relating to the Treatment and Conduct of Convicted Prisoners' gave as its very first rule: 'Prisoners shall preserve silence'; while the second rule stated that 'They shall not communicate, or attempt to do so, with one another, or with any strangers or others who may visit the prison'. Among offences which would make them liable to punishment was 'singing, whistling or making any unnecessary noise'.[235] Mark Hayler, an objector who was repeatedly imprisoned, recalled when interviewed by the Imperial War Museum in 1974: 'What the silent system means is known only to those who have experienced it. To see all around you human beings like yourself and not be able to speak to them is the most inhuman punishment that can be meted out to any person. It is cruel and heartless'.[236] Robert Price, a conscientious objector in another gaol, went through the same experience: 'I then began to collect myself, and I realised that this was solitary confinement. In other words, I was deprived of my elementary rights, vouchsafed to all creation, of associating with my kind. I know no worse or more brutal form of punishment. I have seen men driven stark mad by it. On men with a highly strung nervous temperament it is disastrous. If a man has a moral weakness it drives his weakness within him and weakens what strong points he may have'.[237] It was something all the imprisoned conscientious objectors remembered with horror and it was what would lead many of them in later years to campaign for prison reform.[238]

We can gain some insights into the mechanics of prison life as the Payne brothers experienced them in those weeks when they were not allowed the privilege of writing home, from an unexpected source – a man who identified himself simply by his prison cell number 'B-2-15', who wrote in the early 1920s a remarkable account of his time as a convicted criminal (for he was no conscientious objector) in Leicester's Welford Road Gaol, to which many of the Leicestershire objectors were sent, though not as it happened the Payne brothers. B-2-15 was a recidivist with a wide experience of the English prison system, including Newcastle, Durham and Wormwood Scrubs Prisons (all three of which Leonard and Roland would come to know at firsthand before long), so although his background was very different from the Paynes', he can be called upon as an expert witness on how the system worked.[239]

'Prisons are all alike', wrote B-2-25, and it rapidly becomes clear in reading the prison memoires of the various conscientious objectors that their experiences were in many ways interchangeable. Robert Mennell, like all the rest, was deeply affected by the first experience of imprisonment: 'Who will ever forget the first puzzled survey of the cell utensils in the dim light', he wrote, 'the tentative taps through the walls, half enquiry, half welcome from the men on either side, and then the taking down of the "bed", sans mattress, sans mailbags, sans everything that would entitle it to the pleasant name of bed; and then the hours of heartache and intermittent sleep',[240] B-2-25 was better able to recall and describe what he found in every English prison cell: 'Here was the small narrow stool, the little table in the corner near the door, the three-plank bed-board, with a couple of blankets thrown over the top, reared up against the wall. In the far right-hand corner was fixed the small shelf made to hold the prisoner's Bible, Prayer Book, library book, hairbrush and comb, slate, tin knife and spoon, peculiarly shaped pint pot, and small receptacle for salt'. Prisoners who asked were supplied with a toothbrush: those who did not were not.[241] Inevitably, the first thing a prisoner did was to stand on his stool to see what he could see out of the window, small, barred and high up, which immediately broke the rules but was necessary for the sake of morale, even though the sight was often grim with no cheering or colourful sight to gaze out on. From their cells in Newcastle the Paynes' only view was of the prison yard and the exercise rings where prisoners could be seen walking round and round, enjoying perhaps the one short period in each day when they were allowed out of their cells. Leonard was shocked by his new surroundings: he later remembered Newcastle as 'a terrible prison. It was a very old prison and it was terribly dark. Horrible little tiny windows and everything. It was a wicked old prison'.[242]

What of the mental impact of this new environment on men like Leonard and Roland Payne? They were, it is true, under civilian rather than military control, but for all that they were men in prison. Robert Price, in a similar position, said: 'There was now no buoyancy left. The outlook was changed… You are driven within yourself. You ask yourself: "Is it worth the candle? Whatever has made me take this step? To where will your sufferings lead?" So I stood still; looked round, ruminated a little; realised my isolation and well-nigh choked with emotion, for I thought of home. I knew that somewhere in that same building was my only brother. I longed to speak to him; to signal that I was there, if only I could convey the word by telepathy! But I hadn't faith in that. Could he be in the next cell? I tapped at the wall. There was no response. I tapped again. The only answer was the echo from the empty halls. How near was the next man? How far? Just then the corridors echoed with the tread of some unknown person. Who could it be? My cell door opened and the warder handed in my first prison meal, a pint of porridge and an eight ounce loaf of brown bread, but sans butter, sans sugar, sans tasty bits – and sans appetite also'.[243]

This was far from the 'lark' Leonard had anticipated, anticipation based on a profound ignorance of how the prison system in Britain actually worked. One conscientious objector, Corder Catchpool, in letters written at the time, summed up his shock as he passed from the *anticipation* of prison – 'I feel this is a challenge to us, and we are trying to accept it as such; it is a big adventure... It sounds so funny to speak of prison as being in any sense an adventure – but, it really is when thought of in the light of that challenge – much more so than going out to the front; for example, the dangers are so much subtler, more insidious, incalculable. The equipment must be so entirely spiritual' – to its *reality*: 'It is the cold, calculated system of inhumanity that strikes one about prison. A few weeks after entering prison for the first time, I asked a friend how he was getting on. "It's *organised hell*," he replied – and I thought he could not have described it better'.[244]

So Leonard and Roland Payne, each alone in his own stone cell, spent their first restless night in Newcastle's old gaol. 'Many and various were the positions I assumed during the dark hours of those first few nights', said B-2-15. 'Sound, unbroken sleep was unknown to me at that time. Nothing but dozings; and then the familiar ache to awaken me to the consciousness that I was a prisoner'.[245] At five-thirty they were awakened by the sound of a shrill shrieking bell, 'loud enough to awaken the dead', said B-2-15: 'for a few minutes after the ringing of the bell, silence – the silence of the graveyard that has reigned through the night – continues'. Fred Tait remembered those first moments of waking: 'I am usually awakened by the watchman tramping around and putting the lights on. Then I feel particularly sleepy and by the time he is ringing the bell, I am dozing off into a sweet slumber. But beauty sleeps are not allowed in prison'.[246] 'Then there are sounds', said B-2-15, 'some distant, some near at hand – sounds of men moving about, of windows rattling and bed-boards being hoisted up against the wall. They are all commencing another day, each with his own hopes, fears, misgivings, delusions, and unknown anticipations'.

The Payne brothers now had to learn the arcane rules of this new world into which each had been thrust alone. Leonard later told how, 'when I wanted to go to the lavatory first time, I rang the bell in the cell which shows the number outside the cell which the warder is supposed to see and come and see what you want. Well, I rung and nobody came for a long time. In fact nobody came at all. So I had to use the chamber pot which was in my cell... It was an earthenware pot with a lid on and that was what we had to use all the time we were there. We never went to a lavatory at all'.[247] In prison they were not allowed razors, for obvious reasons, and therefore could not shave so it was a feature of all men serving sentences that they wore beards. This must have been a novel and unaccustomed experience, and Roland 'had curls down my back', he remembered.[248]

In the Prison Cell.
Line drawing from 'Among the Broad-Arrow Men of Leicester Gaol, 1920.
A Plain Account of English Prison Life' by 'B-2-15'.

ABANDON HOPE, ALL YE WHO ENTER HERE !

The conscientious objectors' macabre sense of humour.
The view appears to be of the execution chamber, possibly even in Wakefield Gaol,
with trapdoor and lever. Leonard was shaken when he was shown the gallows.
Thanks to John and Margaret Payne

A set of 'Regulation Cards' was suspended from a small hook on one side of the cell, just so no one (at least, no one who could read) could be in any doubt about the strict rules under which they would spend the coming days, months and years. The 'Silence Regulation' governed all prisoners, not only forbidding spoken contact between prisoners, but blocking *any* kind of human contact. Slopping out in the morning had to be done one prisoner at a time to prevent contact with anyone except the prison staff. Being newly convicted, Leonard and Roland, each of course in his separate cell, were then shown by the hall warder how to fold their bedding and how to arrange everything they were allowed to have in their cells.[249]

Time was to become a preoccupying principle. The stereotype of the convict chalking off the days in 'farm-gate' groups of five on his cell wall is well enough known, but it was the passing of the minutes and the hours of each day which was the most wearing. 'We had no clocks,' Leonard remembered. 'We didn't know the time. We only estimated the time,' though it later came to his mind that they could hear the church clocks out in the town chiming, punctuating their day, perhaps reminding them how time was speeding by – or dragging.[250]

The other guiding principle of prison life was helplessness: no man in control of his own destiny, nor even able to influence it. Those Prison Regulations were open-ended, of course. 'The official card of rules which hangs in every cell,' wrote Fred Tait, 'mentions twenty-two groups (mark the word) of offences for which a prisoner can be punished and then in order that nothing should be omitted adds, "In any other way offending against good order and discipline". In other words a prison warder can have any man punished whom he dislikes and beside a prison governor, the Sultan of Turkey is a mere puppet, and the Mikado a model of a constitutional monarch.'[251]

That said, Tait found the prison warders a fascinating species, bound by a rigid set of rules and regulations themselves, and yet in some cases, at least, with some human instincts miraculously intact: 'Their notions or ideas, if they possess any, are cut and dried to the official formula. The warder is continually thinking of his book of instructions... Many are old soldiers and sailors and strangely enough I have always got on well with them, or most of those who have been in the army. They seem to have a lot of sympathy for C.Os. But while a superior officer is about a warder is not a man, but a machine. He is bound by an iron discipline to do everything in a certain manner... The wonder is not that some warders are bullies, but that any dare to show any signs of human feeling or sympathy whatever. It says a great deal for human nature that men can live for years under such a pressurised system and still be men'.[252] Much the same might be said of the prisoners too.

Bullying was hardly necessary anyway, in such a rigidly controlled environment, the carrot more effective than the stick. Prisoners who co-operated passed through an arcane and complex system of 'marks' and 'stages' which earned them privileges such as access to library books and 'school instruction', and, above all, the right, for those who reached the dizzy heights of Stage 4, to send and receive letters and visits. One prisoner who fell foul of the system told *The Tribunal*, the newspaper of the conscientious objectors, that he had been 'put on punishment diet and confined to cells, reduced 112 marks, and therefore, needing 224 marks (one month) to earn privilege of letter or visiting', the 'punishment diet' amounting to '8ozs. [227 grams] bread and mug of water twice a day'.[253]

Having few other distractions, food became a major preoccupation of those in gaol. Breakfast was, of course, given to each prisoner in his own cell by a warder, the convict who carried the large can of gruel kept out of sight. A pint of gruel or thin porridge (known to the prisoners as 'skilly') and a hunk of bread with half an ounce of margarine constituted breakfast. It was hardly a promising start to the day. Leonard recalled that 'most of the meals had beans in them. We used to have a metal thing come with the meat course, if it was called a meat course, in the bottom of this thing, and a little deep lid on the top which held potatoes in'.[254] B-

A spoof postcard produced in support of the conscientious objectors.
The caption reads: 'AN APPEAL TO REASON'.
Thanks to John and Margaret Payne.

2-15 said convicts were given a pint of soup on Saturdays and Wednesdays, always beans on Mondays, 'cooked meat without bone' on Fridays, suet pudding on Tuesdays and Thursdays, and four ounces of corned beef on Sundays.[255] No doubt the brothers thought longingly of the Sunday dinners their mother had prepared for them at home and which the family would even now be enjoying.

After a time they could tell the day of the week from the food they were given. Leonard was unimpressed: 'The potatoes had never been scraped, they were simply in their skins with eyes and bits of the ground still on them'.[256] The last meal of the day was a bowl of porridge with a hunk of bread, doled out at four o'clock in the afternoon. We can gauge something of the quality of the food they were given from Leonard's recollection that 'one day we had a little bit of bacon in these baked beans. This bacon was so terribly tough you couldn't possibly eat it. So I asked the warder, what about this bacon, you can't eat that. He said, you are not supposed to eat that, you use that to clean your shoes with'.[257]

Complaints, though, were not encouraged, and 'frivolous and groundless complaints, repeatedly made' were 'dealt with as a breach of prison discipline'.[258] What constituted a 'frivolous' or a 'groundless' complaint about the food was, of course, a matter of taste. One objector, held in Pentonville, said that 'the low diet which we had during the first week weakened all of us,'[259] and even experienced convicts found that the meals left a 'ready for more' feeling in their wake.[260] Roland, as usual, put a positive spin on things later, when writing home, telling his mother:

'It is very bad diet, more porridge than anything else, but I have found it plenty always. We get porridge for breakfast + supper always, but very good dinners.'[261]

At this point, we might quote from *The C.O. Clink Chronicle*, a small publication which contained extracts – all light-hearted – from half a dozen unofficial objector leaflets. This comes from the 'Literary Outlet' of those who had been held in Birmingham and Hull Prisons:

CAUTION! DANGER FOR C.O.'S!
On release, beware of retaining prison habits, and remember:
When invited out to dinner, DON'T demand to have your bread weighed. They may not have scales handy.
DON'T keep one handkerchief a whole week. They are not rationed outside.
No more free travelling. When journeying by rail, DON'T forget your ticket. You will only get back here in drab otherwise.
DON'T wash your tablecloth in the bath – it dirties the water so.
When visited by ladies, DON'T have a policeman present, or a long table between the fair ones and yourself.
DON'T wear your address on your jacket. You may be taken for a cabby or a hawker.
DON'T wink instead of saying 'How-dye-do?' Nice people will not understand sufficiently, and nasty ones will understand too much.
DON'T get up at 5:30 a.m. It is impious, for if you were meant to get up the sun would be shining.
DON'T put blacklead pencils into the seams of your waistcoat, or put newspapers down your socks. You'll find a pocket in a civilian coat.
DON'T knock on a wall with a spoon. That will not please that kind of neighbour.[262]

Before they could be set to work they had to be medically examined: for such was the rule. Fred Tait recalled what happened to him on his entry into Newcastle Prison: 'When I first made acquaintance with a prison cell, and was wondering what on earth would happen next, and feeling miserable, the door suddenly opened. "Take yer shirt orf," said a warder, putting his head in. Then the doctor entered, looked at me, talking all the time, but whether to me or not I do not know, and walked out again with a hope that I would not get my position again (as a teacher) when I was released.'[263]

The Paynes' medical examination would have been no less cursory – hence their failure to remember it had happened – but the prison doctor had on that basis approved them for the labour of sewing mailbags. This was classified, in prison terms, as 'light' labour.

So now an officer, known as the 'Taskmaster', brought a bundle of canvas and rope, wax, scissors, needle and thread to their cells for the day's work.[264] Even though Leonard and Roland were both used to working with their hands, with dextrous fingers and strong wrists, they did not at first find the work easy. Roland recalled many years later how 'they used to bring us a pile of mailbags into the cell and my job was sewing the little tabs and rings on that they put the rope through to make them tight, and I was supposed to do a certain task every day. Well, I wasn't able to do the task for a bit because it took me a long time to thread a needle in the first place, but I eventually got so I could do more than my quota'.[265] Their material reward for completing their daily task was a mug of cocoa in the evening, an unappetizing brew which Leonard likened to mud. 'Horrible,' he said.[266]

But, in a curious and unexpected way, it was the work itself which was the true reward: making mailbags at least broke the mind-numbing monotony of prison life, confined to their cells alone for twenty-three hours of every twenty-four. Another conscientious objector, J.J. Pendry, held in Lewes Prison expressed the point well: 'When I consider what prison life would be like without work I am thankful that I have work to do; it relieves the tedium immensely. Most of my waking time is given to work, but I don't think that is a trouble to any of us.'[267]

The system decreed absolute silence, but the reality, inevitably, was different. Men in confinement are bound to find ways round the rule, and the ways were many, varied and mightily ingenious. Whatever the efforts of the Newcastle Prison authorities, communication between prisoners, though irregular, was possible, even when the pipe-phone could not be used. Our expert witness, B-2-15, told how convicts would scratch messages, often containing 'adjectives not found in any dictionary',[268] into the underside of the tin utensils their meals arrived in in the hope that sooner or later they might arrive with the desired recipient.

More experienced convicts mastered the art of undetected speaking out loud whilst in the exercise yard, carrying on ventriloquist style conversations with their neighbours, the warders completely unable to identify the culprits: 'I have seen them looking searchingly at men as they travelled round', said convict B-2-15, 'when voices were quite audible, and being puzzled as to whom the offenders were'.[269] Leonard himself described another vocal outlet: 'In Newcastle there was a warder there. He was an Irishman and you could ask to fall out [from exercise] if you wanted to and stand to the side of him if you thought you had had enough walking. Well, he was such a good fellow he would let somebody else fall out the other side as well that he knew you wanted to talk to and you could hold a conversation behind his back, and he would let you do that. He was the only warder I ever knew that would let you do that. Another thing was there was a water tap beside one exercise ring and we used to go to this tap, wait until your friends came by you and you could talk to him while he was in front of you, but you must not move your head because the warder would see you in a minute.'[270]

More reliable opportunities for contact came during the Sunday chapel service when surreptitious notes could be passed: since prisoners were not allowed any writing materials, other methods had to be found. Leonard recalled how 'we liked going to chapel for one reason. We used to use the toilet paper in the cells and we used to prick letters with our needles so that you could hold them up to the light and read them. Well, we then used to put these in the prayer books, go to chapel, give everybody the understanding where you wanted your book to go. If I wanted to send Roland the letter I would make the chap understand how many more along the row I wanted it to go and this was the way we could communicate with each other because we had plenty of time to do these letters'.[271] We know that Leonard was able to communicate by a primitive sign language with Ron Long, another conscientious objector, for Ron was put on bread and water for three days when caught.[272]

None of this could, of course, compare with letters home. The sheer number of letters written to and from their home in Lutterworth during June and July testifies to the importance of that moral lifeline and now it was cut. There are no letters from or to Leonard and Roland until the end of August – a month of isolation. While in Newcastle, his younger sister Dora had celebrated (if that was the word) her fifteenth birthday, which of course her brothers were not allowed to mark, the first they had ever missed: when Leonard was allowed to write he could only, belatedly, assure her that he had not forgotten.[273] We hope that Dora understood.

★

Their father, meanwhile, on a more practical level, was trying to find news about them. On August 14th, almost three weeks into their time in the gaol in Newcastle, John wrote to the governor:

Dear Sir,

Could you kindly let me and my wife know if the health of my two boys Roland and Leonard Payne is satisfactory as we are anxious.

Yours Respectfully,

John G. Payne [274]

The reply was written on the reverse of the letter:

'These prisoners are in their usual health.' [275]

...that was all, the signature – 'F.W. Gibson' – produced by a rubber stamp (a necessary precaution for a prison governor to avoid the danger of forgery).

It was not only the boys' physical health, but also their spiritual welfare which was troubling their family at home. Exactly how their next request came about is unclear, but a week later their mother wrote to the governor with a different request:

Dear Sir

I should like my two sons Leonard and Roland Payne to be visited by the Quaker chaplain.

Your's [sic] Sincerely

Mrs J.G. Payne. [276]

On the same day she wrote to the Quakers' 'Visitation of Prisoners Committee' at Ethelburga House in London. They replied promptly on the 23rd:

'Dear Friend,

With reference to your letter of 22nd inst., I have written to our visitor at Newcastle, telling him that you have written to the governor and asking him to be sure and ask specially to see your sons the next time he goes there. When I hear from him I shall at once let you know.'[277]

The typewritten letter was signed by W. Frederick Douglas, the organising secretary of the committee.

In his 1973 interview Leonard gave details, probably unknown to his family at home, of his attempt to secure a Quaker visitor: 'We were booked in as Congregationalists and the chaplain at Newcastle came to see me and he seemed so terrified that he didn't know what to say or what to do. I tried to persuade him to get in touch with my parents at home but he said he couldn't do that. So, of course, he was pretty much useless really. So I asked permission to change my religion and I asked if I could have a Quaker chaplain. So they said, well to do that you have to go before the governor. So they took me down next day before the governor. I was placed in one cage and the governor was in another so I wouldn't be able to throw anything at him I suppose, and I said to him that I wished to have a Quaker chaplain to visit me. He replied, well that would mean you would have to change your religion and he said prison is no place to change your religion in. So it wasn't allowed.'[278]

The governor gave the same reply to their mother, a reply which must have dashed her hopes:

> 'On reception into this prison your sons Leonard and Roland Payne declared their religion as Congregational and cannot therefore be visited by a minister of any other denomination, excepting the Chaplain of the Prison.'[279]

Again, the stamped signature. So the silence, the isolation, continued.

But, as good as their word, the Quakers did contact Herbert Corder who again travelled from his home in Sunderland this time to Newcastle to visit the prison, and who gives us our only contemporary sighting of the brothers in Newcastle Prison. He reported to their father in a letter dated August 30th, that:

> 'I saw Roland last week and had a glimpse of his brother but the warder took them away again as he said they were to see a Congregational minister and not a "Friend". I told him that the minister had only been once and that he wished to see me instead but it was no use.'[280]

The Prison System was proving a brick wall.

★

By the time Corder's letter was written, though, their situation had changed dramatically and the brothers were no longer in prison in Newcastle. On August 29th things moved and the change was sudden and dramatic. While the brothers had been defying the military at Whitburn and serving the time at Newcastle, the politicians had been moving to find a solution to the problem of the conscientious objectors.

But the path was not an easy one. Amongst military historians of the First World War it has become a commonplace in recent years to talk of a 'learning curve' among Britain's army commanders. Though at first as nonplussed as any other country's generals when confronted by the extraordinary demands of trench warfare, they did in time learn how to use new technologies and new tactics, new ways of thinking. Haig's reputation (among professional military historians at least) has been largely rehabilitated in light of the successes achieved in the autumn of 1918 which led to Germany's defeat in November.[281] It has to be conceded, of course, that before that curve had achieved any sort of significant altitude huge numbers of lives had been thrown away in futile and frustrating assaults against formidable German positions along the Western Front, but the British commanders, though not the fastest learners in military history, were not the stubborn and stupid 'donkeys' of myth.

We can see in this an analogy with the way the British Army tried to handle another entirely novel problem: that of the conscientious objectors thrust into their ranks through the incompetence of the tribunals. While Leonard and Roland Payne and their companions in the Glen Parva Barracks were persisting in their defiance, the military was deciding that the issue must be forced, and in doing so was proving the hollowness of the 'Non-Combatant Corps' solution to the conscientious objector problem. On Friday 2nd June 1916 four men were sentenced to death by court martial for disobedience. Their names were Jack Foister, Howard Marten, Jonathan Ring and Harry Scullard. All four belonged to the Non-Combatant Corps, and all four were conscientious objectors. Between then and Thursday the 13th a further thirty-four conscientious objectors were condemned to death for the same offence.[282]

At its crudest, an exasperated army had decided to call the bluff of the conscientious objectors. Section 9 of the Army Act of 1913 clearly laid down that anyone who wilfully disobeyed an order 'shall be liable to suffer death or such less punishment as is in the Act mentioned'.[283] To impose a sentence of death on men who were still in Britain, in their army bases but claiming not to be in the army, would have seemed extreme and created all kinds of difficulties with the press, the public and the politicians, so the idea was to take them over to France where it might – stretching a point – be said that they were on active service, in a sense in the face of the enemy, given that the enemy's face was still a long way away. In military terms the charge was serious. Sixty-eight men in the British Army were sentenced to death for disobedience during the First World War, of whom five were actually shot by firing squad, three of them on the Western Front. Only a few weeks before the conscientious objectors' sentencing two soldiers, Private James Cuthbert of the Cheshire Regiment and Driver John Hasemore of the Royal Artillery, had been shot by firing squad on charges of disobedience. Cuthbert was executed as an example to others, while Hasemore had displayed the kind of absolute defiance of military authority shown by the conscientious objectors, except (the fatal phrase) 'when on active service'.[284]

The sentencing of the objectors can be seen as nothing more than a charade, a cynical attempt to bully them into falling in, and, after a suitably dramatic pause the sentences of death were commuted to ten years' imprisonment. To have shot these men would have been entirely unacceptable: the army was not a complete law unto itself. Even so, ten year sentences were severe enough even when served in a civilian rather than a military prison, though the popular perception was that they, like military service, would only be 'for the duration'. It was a tactic destined from the outset for failure: not only did it fail to intimidate the conscientious objectors, but it threatened to upset the very fine balance the government had struck between meeting the demands of the war, on the one hand, and the maintenance of public support for the war on the other.[285] Creating martyrs was exactly what the government did *not* want.

But something more was signalled by the episode. Very slowly, the army was raising itself up its own learning curve, coming to terms with the fact that it was now becoming an increasingly conscript army. To shoot regular soldiers was one thing; even the execution of volunteers could, in the view of the generals, be justified. But executing pressed men was a different issue altogether and shooting conscientious objectors was something different again. The army as an institution was bewildered, unable to work out what to do with men who refused to obey orders and who were not afraid of the punishments available; it was something beyond its previous experience. As the war went on the number of their soldiers executed would fall in recognition of the changing structure and character of the army as it responded to conscription, but that was in the future.[286] Meanwhile, official attitudes to the conscientious objectors were changing as well, with more immediate effect. On June 22nd the Labour M.P. George Barnes raised the matter of the 'French' objectors in Parliament, to be told by the Minister, Harold Tennant, that he had no knowledge of the case, dismissing it as an unfounded rumour.[287] Four days later, things were different.

The House of Commons Order Paper for June 26th featured a string of questions aimed at the Prime Minister about the 'Frenchmen', as they became known. By now it was clear that this was one incredible wartime rumour that was absolutely true. Asquith, who found the army's actions indefensible, wisely delegated the issue to Harold Tennant, his Under-Secretary for War, who found himself having to play a straight bat on a sticky wicket. In a bad-tempered exchange, he confirmed that thirty-four men had been subjected to this latest military novelty (not the four Barnes had been aware of), but then had to concede that the only way he could investigate such cases was through the army's own chain of command. 'That is to say, then,' said Philip Snowden, 'that the only evidence the War Office takes is the evidence of the incriminated parties themselves?' – a comment which drew no response from the minister.[288]

Two days later the Prime Minister acted to head off what could have been a 'public relations disaster'. Men imprisoned as conscientious objectors were to have their cases reviewed by a War Office committee or by the Central Tribunal and, if their objection was deemed to be genuinely based on conscience, they were to be offered 'work of national importance' under civil control. It was not a new idea; since March those conscientious objectors who had been allowed absolute exemption by the Tribunals (mainly Quakers and, since April, the Christadelphians) had been put to work by the Pelham Committee, for the most part in agriculture.[289] This new application of the principle became known as the 'Home Office Scheme' and William Brace would head a Home Office Committee to find the suitable work required. Asquith's proposal can be seen as a *reasonable* attempt to salvage his *'Ship of Liberal Values'* from the incompetence of the Local Tribunals and the brutality of the military, both of which had threatened to sink it without trace. The mock deaths of the 'Frenchmen' had not been in vain.

★

The offer of the 'Home Office Scheme' giving conscientious objectors 'work of national importance' to do had been announced to Parliament by Asquith on June 29th. It was a product of the far bigger discussions which ravaged the government and the military during 1916 – and for the remainder of the war. But the conscientious objectors were never more than a detail – albeit a troubling and troublesome one – little more than a footnote to the much more urgent and competing demands for manpower (and womanpower) to sustain both the military and civilian demands of something which was moving inexorably in the direction of Total War.[290]

Through 1916 and 1917 the scale of the army's call for more and more manpower exceeded all previous levels and it was already clear that the demands of this war would extend in one way or another to everyone of working age in the country, and that a massive increase in state power would be needed to implement and control it. At issue was the mobilisation of the nation's entire manpower resources, either into military service or by direction into essential industries through a system of civilian national service, a proposal fiercely resisted by the

Trade Unions. By November 1916 the military was demanding that the age for civil and military liability be raised to fifty-five, with some politicians suggesting sixty as the upper age limit; and in February of 1917 – ahead of the Passchendaele offensive – the army was demanding that between 100,000 and 170,000 men be called up every month, and was complaining bitterly of the 'excessive powers to exempt men conferred... on Tribunals and government departments'.[291] A few conscientious objectors here and there did not make a great deal of difference in the bigger scheme of things.[292]

Though there would be many problems in the implementation of the policy, leading one historian to comment that 'the so-called Home Office Scheme probably caused more frustration for those involved than any other aspect of conscription'[293], it was a brilliant solution to a problem the government and the army might otherwise have found increasingly disruptive, for it had the effect of clearly splitting off those men who would refuse to accept the Scheme and would elect to remain in prison – the uncompromising 'absolutists' – from the more moderate objectors who were prepared to do civilian work under civilian control, whatever other conditions this might imply. The wheels of the scheme would be oiled by the Central Tribunal, acting on the request of the army, which would grant exemption in 1916 to over 85% of those who appeared before it.[294]

The solution of offering those who claimed a conscientious objection 'work of national importance', such as had already been offered to those who had been accepted by the Local Tribunal, at a time when the principle of 'work of national importance' for all was being touted as an answer to the nation's wider manpower crisis, did little more than apply the solution of one problem to another: it would preserve the self-respect of the compliant objectors and allow them to do *something* useful, which is what most of them wanted to do, and both sides would save face. The government believed that no one would be humiliated who took up its offer and the nonsense of brute force and mock death sentences would be forgotten.

★

Leonard's scepticism had been evident throughout, as also had been his readiness to accept the Home Office Scheme if there were no unacceptable strings attached. Was the government's offer genuine? At the very least the offer of 'work of national importance' had provided a pragmatic solution to a practical problem using ideas already to hand, and 'work of national importance' became little more than a euphemism for 'any work the objector was willing to accept': virtually anything could count as nationally important work – given enough imagination. It was as satisfactory and appropriate a solution as could reasonably be found; it is difficult to think of better in the circumstances.

However, for many conscientious objectors this was no simple question. Doing 'work of national importance' at a time when the overriding national priority was to win the war must inevitably involve compromises difficult to reconcile with the demands of conscience: would 'nationally important' work not inevitably have some connection to the demands of Total War?[295] If they accepted some purely civilian task unconnected with the military, did this not free up some other man, a man already doing the 'work of national importance' to which they would be assigned, to be put into the army? Were they not thereby indirectly aiding the military in its recruitment drive and was it right to help, however passively, send some other man into the war to kill or be killed when they would not go themselves?

DURHAM

O n the morning of Tuesday August 29th all the conscientious objectors held at Newcastle were hastily shaved, changed out of their broad-arrow suits, and bundled together to be transported to the railway station where they were put on a train to Durham, twenty or so miles to the south.[296] Whether they were in a position to appreciate the spectacular view of Durham Cathedral and Castle the railway affords is not known, but it was already growing dark so perhaps that was an experience they could not as yet enjoy. Nor do we know whether they welcomed the beauty of the city as they were paraded down North Street before crossing the River Wear at Framwellgate Bridge (the cathedral and castle towering over them, those greatest symbols of the power of Medieval Church and State), thence on up the steeply sloping Silver Street to the Market

Durham Prison
The site of the former execution yard.
http://www.thenorthernecho.co.uk

218

Place in the neck of the peninsular formed by the river, before crossing the steeply descending Elvet Bridge, spanning the upstream arm of the loop, and thence up the street called New Elvet to the prison on the high ground to the east. As well as being a very beautiful place, Durham is very much a three-dimensional city.

Leonard had other priorities: 'It seems so peculiar', he wrote, 'seeing people after being shut up for so long'.[297] But for all their temporary respite they were still prisoners and their new cells might have made them long to be back in Newcastle Prison. The plan was to hold them in Durham for one night initially before sending them off to London to be interviewed by the Central Tribunal, the arrangements made at short notice and no particular provision having been made for them. Leonard, speaking in 1973, remembered:

> 'When we first arrived at Durham, half the prison had been shut down: the whole of the top wing, and I have never seen anything like it in my life. The windows had been left open and in every cell there had been crows in and you never saw such filth in all your life in these cells, and they put us straight in them. They shoved us in these cells one night in the dark. There were no beds in or anything... I think they'd been shut because of air raids or something like that. We hadn't any food for a good many hours and we thought surely they will give us some food but they didn't. But to our surprise in the morning there was a pot of porridge on the table which we didn't know was there. We hadn't seen it because it was so dark.'[298]

As the party set off at 8.20 the following morning to be marched under military escort back through Durham city to set off to London,[299] that extraordinary network of information and support set up by the NCF was already swinging into

Durham Prison

action. A flurry of letters passed to and fro as the impasse was ending. The Payne family received a letter dated August 29th from Ella Stevens at the Café Vegetaria in Leicester, full of optimism. Seaward Beddow had been in the north-east and had telegrammed the café that morning, telling her that Leonard and Roland were being moved from Newcastle to Durham, under escort[300], en route for Wormwood Scrubs Prison in London and their appearance before the Central Tribunal. Thirteen of 'our men' had already been told that when their sentences expired they would be released under furlough 'under the new Scheme'. She continued, 'I cannot think, however, that your sons will have to go back to Newcastle to finish their sentences'.[301]

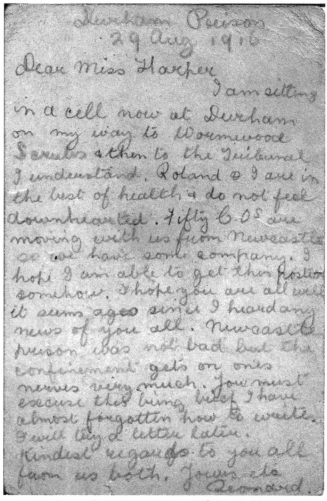

Leonard to Marian Harper, 29th August 1916
(Original 87x140mm)

This was the breakthrough the family had been waiting for, and a letter arrived in Church Street, possibly by the next post, from Leonard confirming the change:

'We are just off from here [Newcastle Prison] to Durham and then to London we hear, to meet Tribunal *[sic]*. Fifty C.Os are leaving here all together so we are lively… I expect we shall get work of n[ational] i[mportance] this time but if we do not I don't know what will happen then I suppose it will be more prison for us.' [302]

Their movements were being tracked by the NCF and on their way to the station through the centre of Durham that morning they were accompanied by a group of women who collected everyone's name and home address and then spent the rest of the day writing to their relatives to tell them the news. Among them was Mrs Haigh from Low Fell near Gateshead, whose only son Thomas, a nineteen-year-old postman, was among the group.[303] The poor woman had been to the prison in Newcastle the previous afternoon, only to be told that they had all been moved; she reached Durham in time to see them leave the next morning. 'They are all so bright, happy, determined', she wrote to the Payne family. 'My heart was full of delight at the sight of sixty boys that are not afraid to show the world what they are out for, The *[sic]* boys who are going to build the England of the future'. The group of fifty from Newcastle Prison had been joined by ten others already in Durham Prison for the trip to London, this time changed out of their prison clothes and into military khaki[304], perhaps the army's last gesture of control over them. Certain they would be *offered* work of national importance, Mrs Haigh was still uncertain about whether they would all *accept* it. Perhaps most important for the Payne family was her final comment, 'The boy who gave me this adress *[sic]* looked very well indeed and was so anxious for you to know that he was all right'.[305]

The train journey to London was long, but clearly not long enough for the prisoners. Roland wrote of their journey, 'This time we had a military escort and also marched to and from the stations. It was a very long train ride, from early in the morning till dark at night, but we liked that, we should have liked it longer, because we were having such a good time, and it was such a change from being by ourselves always'.[306]

Leonard, more practically minded, took better note of the view outside their carriage. A fortnight later he wrote to his father that:

'I enjoyed the ride to London very much as you will guess after the short spell of imprisonment at Newcastle. It was quite a treat to see the cornfields and the orchards once more, and made one long more than ever to be free again. It was a long ride you must know from here and took about twelve hours.

I expect you are now in the midst of Harvest Festivals at the chapels and churches? This being the month for them. I noticed the fruit and the corn and I thought it looked a very good season this year. But I suppose it will look better to me when I get outside again.'[307]

Unsurprisingly, bureaucracy lagged behind reality. A cyclostyled letter from the Central Tribunal in London, evidently a copy of the written notification given to Leonard, was sent to Mrs Payne in Lutterworth, dated August 30th but not posted until two days later, on September 1st, informing her that Leonard was to go before the Tribunal which would be held in Wormwood Scrubs Prison. By that time, of course, the process had already been completed. The letter threatened that failure to convince the Tribunal would see them returned to their army units, but it continued:

'If, on the other hand, after consideration of your case, the Tribunal are satisfied that you have a conscientious objection to military service based on religious or moral grounds, you will be transferred to Section W of the Army Reserve, whereupon you will cease to be subject to military discipline and the Army Act, as also to draw pay from army funds; and your case will be sent to the civil committee which has been appointed by the Home Office, in order that you may be placed on civil work under civil control and under conditions to be determined by that committee.'[308]

We can easily imagine the joy with which this letter – the first official confirmation of the change – was received in the Payne household.

WORMWOOD SCRUBS

John Hoare, a better connected conscientious objector than the Payne brothers, and already in 'the Scrubs', recalled his own appearance before the August Central Tribunal: 'That same afternoon we were marched down and stood in the main courtyard between the main gateway and visiting magistrates' room (where the Tribunal sat), looking towards the green lawn and gay flower beds that lie in front of the chapel. The Tribunal were over an hour late... In came a nice looking old man with rather a long face and side-whiskers (Lord Salisbury, the Chairman, I was told), a middle-aged man with pince-nez and a tail-coat, looking very brisk but rather worried, and a third man who made no impression on me at all. One of the two was G.N. Barnes, the Labour M.P. We waited in an ante-room in the corner of which there was a door with two large panes in it through which

Inside Wormwood Scrubs Prison, c. 1890
http://www.photohistory-sussex.co.uk/BexhillPhotgrsC.htm

a warder looked into the room, out of earshot but in sight. Through this door I was pushed at last and found myself in a closely railed and wired-in dock. "You are Joseph Edward Hoare?" asked the Chairman. "Yes." "Your age?" "Twenty." "You were granted non-combatant exemption by the Oxford Local and Appeal Tribunals?" "Yes." "Did you produce any testimonials?" "Yes, from Mr Temple." "What, William Temple?" [the future Archbishop of Canterbury] "Yes." "Thank you, that will do." Exit, adjudged sincere!'[309]

The Payne brothers' appearance before the Tribunal – presumably in similar circumstances, but without the magic name of William Temple, proved even more of an anticlimax. Held on Thursday 31st August, the Tribunal members showed little apparent interest in Roland's case. 'They never asked us many questions at all, or at the finish tell us any result. It seemed very strange'.[310] For many of the religious objectors like the Payne brothers it had been clear from the outset that non-military work under civilian control would be acceptable as an alternative to service with the army including work with the Friends' Ambulance Unit or the Medical Corps. It was, after all, similar to what they would have been offered had they been accepted by the Local Tribunals – as they should have been. The circumstances now, though, would be different, for, if the Central Tribunal accepted them, it would be up to the Brace Committee, rather than the Pelham Committee, to find them appropriate work and define the conditions in which they would be expected to do it.

We can gauge the reactions of the two brothers since both wrote from the train which carried them back from London to Durham the next day. Their letters were 'illegal', and when Leonard first tried to post a letter home he had been stopped by a guard.[311] Roland's letter revealed his ebullient mood:

'We have had a very good time these last two days, enjoying ourselves fine. We have been before the Tribunal but have not heard the result yet… We are not going back to Newcastle again we are going to stay at Durham. Wormwood is a nice place, close to the White City London, could see it from my cell window.'[312]

Roland Payne was possibly the only person ever to describe the prison at Wormwood Scrubs as 'nice'.[313] Perhaps it reflects better treatment there, though more likely it betrays a kind of euphoria now that he was within sight of being released from the prison system, bravado suggestive of how much strain he had actually been under during those stressful months in Whitburn and Newcastle. 'I expect we shall get work of national importance soon', he wrote.

Leonard's reaction could not have been more different. While the train passed through Market Harborough on its way back to the North, just a dozen or so miles from home, on railway toilet paper, punched 'N.E.R.' (North Eastern Railway) and 'Satine', an ironic echo of their own secret communication in prison, Leonard explained his depression:

> 'We have been before the Tribunal which consisted of two men which had our Tribunal papers and of course the old subject of Shell Bas *[sic]* came up again. I did my best to explain my reason for doing them, but I am very doubtful as to the result. I don't expect we shall be proved genuine so if we are not we shall be in prison till next May and then handed back to the military again. I feel rather downhearted when I think of this but must not lose hopes yet. We may be offered work if they think we are genuine… Bill and I are in good health although rather downhearted as to the future.'[314]

It is in this letter that we catch our first hint of what was weighing on his mind. 'Shell Bas' – those shell baskets they had spent the early months of the war weaving, had come back to haunt them, now threatening to compromise their whole claim to conscientious objection. How could they be pacifists and object to military service if they were making baskets for the safe transport of explosive shells, which would be used to kill other human beings? Could the individual go so far in furthering the conduct of the war and still claim to remain conscientiously aloof? Apparently Leonard understood the implications of this, the tell-tale traces of their and their family's actions in those papers the Tribunal members had before them, while his younger brother did not.

> 'We hear such reports of this work of N.I. we do not know what to do at all we all seem at sea. I think we shall accept if we are given a guantee *[sic]* that it is under the ~~Military~~ civil control. But there seems a doubt if it is under civil or military. But whatever the work is it can't be worse than prison. I do hope we are offered some work it will prove that we are genuine if nothing else… It is an awful position to be placed in not knowing what to do, and being kept in the dark as well. But we must hope that we shall be rightly guided and take the right step… We had a paper given to us in Wormwood Prison telling us that if genuine we should be placed in Army Reserve W and then put under a Civil Commitee *[sic]* for civil work under civil control and that if we gave up this work we should be sent back to prison to finish our sentences and then be handed over to the military again. It seems a muddle all the way through.'[315]

Leonard's depression went beyond the legal or administrative or even the moral questions – would the work offered be acceptable, and, equally important, would the Central Tribunal accept *him* as a genuine conscientious objector? For, no matter how willing the spirit, the flesh was also demanding to be heard. In 1973 Leonard confessed that: 'I think we had had enough punishment... we had the rough of it and we weren't going to have any more of that prison because I think it would have killed us eventually if we had stayed much longer';[316] and he reminded us that 'as I was so young I had really had enough of this prison life'.[317]

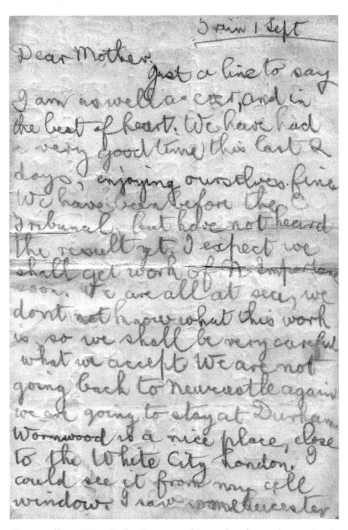

Perpetually positive, Roland wrote to his mother from what evidently
was a jerky train ride back to the north, 1ˢᵗ September 1916
(Original 112x180mm)

DURHAM – AGAIN

The forbidding walls of Durham Prison
Copyright http://ww2.durham.gov.uk

In the meantime they were returned to the prison system, to Durham Prison. Mrs Haigh, who had witnessed their departure, was there also for their return. She told the boys' mother:

'Well they came back (as probably you will have heard by now) on the Friday night [1ˢᵗ September]. I went to Drh to meet them… I walked from the station to the prison with them they were in good spirits singing all the way and cheered heartily before entering the gates… I took as much as I could carry to eat for them but it seemed so little among so many… I was so pleased that all the relatives that I had wrote to of those 'boys' answered by return of post and I just handed them the replies I got and it cheered them so… Your 'boy' was pleased to have the note you sent me the military does not give you much chance of speaking to them when they are moving like that. They all seemed to have enjoyed the little liberty more than one said to me "Freedom is sweet".'[318]

The family at home in Lutterworth must also have been reassured by a letter they received from the brother of the Roughtons, Quakers from New Basford in Nottinghamshire who had been on the same train to London and at the Central Tribunal, as the network of supporters and informants grew denser by the week.[319] Leonard had met up with the elder of the two whilst with the army on the coast

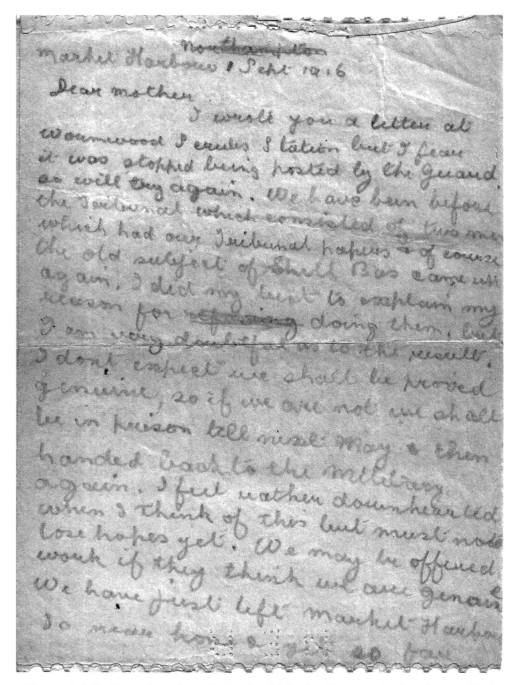

Characteristically, Leonard was less optimistic than his brother. Here he writes from the train North to his Mother on three sheets of toilet paper, perforated 'N.E.R.', and still joined. 1 September 1916.
(Original 125x170mm)

and had at that time written to their widowed mother, so now their younger brother, himself awaiting arrest as a conscientious objector and identified only by his initials 'H.L.', was returning the gesture of friendship:

> 'I do not think they will find Durham Prison as bad as they think,' he told them, 'because a Mr Stone from Nottm. went to Newcastle and Durham to see some of his boys and he told me that Durham was the best of the two'.[320]

★

After their London trip the conditions of their imprisonment were eased. Under standard Prison Regulations their good conduct had earned them extra rights. On the 12th of September the brothers were each allowed to write a letter home, this time on official blue prison paper, the first page of which contained a long series of printed rules setting out what could and could not be said. 'The permission to write and receive letters,' it told them, 'is given to prisoners for the purpose of enabling them to keep in connection with their respectable friends *and not that they may be kept informed of public events*' – the underlining in red ink. All letters would be read by the prison authorities: 'Any which are of objectionable tendency, either to or from prisoners, or containing slang, or improper expressions, will be suppressed' it warned in another sentence underlined in red ink.

The brothers and their family were now left in limbo. Leonard wrote home, 'I am quite in the dark as to what is likely to happen'.[321] The fact, though, was that a government anxious to get the conscientious objector business buried once and for all was not going to put further obstacles in the way of men who were willing to accept their offer of work under civilian control. The Central Tribunal passed as genuine the overwhelming majority of objectors who came before it, and over four thousand men accepted the offer of 'work of national importance' as an alternative to imprisonment or military service.[322] On September 12th both brothers wrote home to give their family the good news that their unlooked-for appeal had been successful: they had been offered 'work of national importance' to do[323] and had accepted it, the indiscretion of the shell baskets apparently ignored.

However, to Leonard's suspicious mind, that was not necessarily the end of the story for it still did not resolve the issue of whether the work they were *actually* given would be acceptable to them. He wrote home:

> 'I have accepted [the offer of work of national importance] although rather in the dark as to what it is, but I hope it is all right and that I have taken the right step. I

thought it right to accept this, as I had offered to take such work before when in the hands of the military you will remember. If this work is against our conscience, or it is proved to be helping the military we shall still be at liberty to give it up and come back to prison to finish our sentence.'[324]

What he did not say was that after completion of their sentences they would be returned to military custody and the whole business of defiance, arrest, Court Martial and prison would begin all over again. While Leonard was cautious, still distrustful, Roland was characteristically more optimistic: not only did he tease his family by not revealing the success of his appeal until half way through his long letter, but he expected to be released 'any day'.[325] His message to his mother from Durham Prison that, 'I have'nt [sic.] felt unwell since I entered prison, it must suit me'[326] has to be taken with a large pinch of salt, for even he showed signs of the stress of imprisonment as the days passed by and nothing happened. Three weeks later he wrote home to his family in Lutterworth, the letter marked by the prison authorities 'In lieu of visit':

'Thanks very much for your last letter. I was so pleased to hear from you again after such a long time. I am so glad you are all keeping so well, and I hope you are all quite well know. It is supprising [sic] how a letter cheers one up who has been so long away from home. I was getting very anxious about you all, such awful things kept passing through my mind. I quite think you have done the right thing in not coming all this long way to see us, it is not worthwhile when a letter will answer the same purpose. Of course if you should wish to visit us next time, just put who can come in your answer back, and I will apply for the visiting forms of the same next when the time comes. I shall be allowed to write and recieve [sic] a letter also a visit this time of thirty minutes again in about a fortnights time if all goes on all right, but I have no doubt I shall be allowed to write and receive a letter again if you do not come instead. I am going on just as well as ever, still smiling, although I have had rather a bad cold lately, but it is quite well now. The weather begins to get a bit like winter now up here, being very cold at nights and early in the morings [sic]. We have all been out on exercise about six oclock [sic] in the mornings here until this week, before breakfast, but now it gets too dark, so you may depend it was rather cold. The temperature up here seems so much colder than down in the midlands. I don't remember ever being too warm all the summer even. I have been very patiently waiting to be released this last week or two, but now I have about given up all hopes… I quite expected to be out before now, and doing that work. What has happened? Has the Scheme broke down or what? Do you think there is any possibility of our sentences being commuted?'[327]

The acceptance by Leonard and Roland Payne of the alternative service option of the Home Office Scheme, had ensured their eventual release from detention in Durham Prison once suitable accommodation and work had been arranged, and the start of a happier period in their lives. They would not be allowed to return home, nor would they be allowed to weave baskets, logical and sensible as that may have been, for the original Pelham Committee had recommended that 'in a number of cases men who are not available for active military service may, with some advantage to the nation, be employed in the class of work in which they are already engaged, but as a general rule it may be expedient that an applicant should not be allowed to remain under the same employer and in some cases, a change of locality may be advisable'.[328]

cells, The Tribunal seemed to me to be a worse tribunal than the last two. They never asked us many questions at all, or at the finish tell us any result, it seemed very strange. Well the next day we returned after having another very good time. We were in khaki for this trip, but we changed again into prison clothes as soon as we arrived. A day or two after this I had a paper come, to say that the tribunal had found me genuine, which I filled up answering the questions. They wanted to know if I was willing to do work of national importance under civilian control and nothing to do with the military. This I promised to do. I stated what my occupation was, but I don't know what work I shall get or where it will be. I expect you know more about it than I do, by reading about it in the papers. I am now expecting to be released any day, and am anxiously waiting. Of course we don't know anything here. We expect we shall be allowed to come home for a day or two first before we are sent to this work, but we dont know. If I was sure of coming home within a week or two it would not matter about you coming up here to see me, but of course please yourselves. I am allowed to see three of you each visit as you will understand by the names on the bottom of this letter. Dont forget to write a good long letter in return as soon as you can because I might be gone from here any day now, because that paper said I was to be released if I accepted that work. I hope you are all well and that you are not troubling yourselves about me, because I am quite alright, and safe and sound. I haven't felt unwell since I entered prison, it must suit me. I understand now that I am in some Army Reserve

A sign of their new more privileged position as Roland writes to his Mother on blue prison notepaper,
12 September 1916.
(Original 190x240mm)

THE FOURTH ROCK

THE INTRANSIGENCE OF THE 'ABSOLUTISTS'

The Home Office Scheme split the community of conscientious objection from top to bottom and brought to a kind of prominence those conscientious objectors who came to be known as the 'absolutists'. The seaworthiness of Asquith's *Ship of Liberal Values*, already grievously damaged by the incompetence of the Tribunals and the brutality of the military mind, would be most sorely tested by the simple intransigence, the *unreasonableness*, of the absolutist conscientious objectors.

While objectors like the Paynes saw the Home Office Scheme and the Central Tribunal as a lifeline, others, including the socialist schoolteacher Fred Tait, dismissed the Central Tribunal and all its works: 'The C.Os (some sixty) were taken from [Durham] prison in order to make a pilgrimage to the shrine of the Central Tribunal at Wormwood Scrubs', he wrote contemptuously (this party being the one containing Leonard and Roland Payne). He then rejected its offer of work of national importance.[329] Many others followed Fred's intransigent line, for the fact was that there were almost as many reasons for conscientious objection as there were conscientious objectors. The political Left – itself divided into scarcely fewer denominations and sects than the Christian Churches – provided the bulk of the conscientious objectors. These were young men, strong-minded and opinionated, many with views and habits of thought that put them on the edges of the society of their day, the religious and the political objectors both tending towards dogmatism and fragmentation.

Membership of the NCF reached 10,000 at its peak, from every social background and habit of mind, as Howard Marten recorded: 'You found the ranks of the No-Conscription Fellowship were made up of men from every conceivable walk of life. You had all sorts of religious groups, from the Salvation Army to the

Seventh Day Adventists; Church of England, Roman Catholics; there was no limit. It was a sort of cross section of every type. Then you had in addition to that the more politically minded: the Independent Labour Party, and different degrees of socialists, and the ordinary political parties. Then a very curious group of what I used to call artistically minded. There were a lot of men who were not in any way organized or attached, but I should call them the aesthetic group: artists, musicians, all that'.[330]

What was at issue was the *purpose* of their conscientious objection. To the Paynes it was purely personal and individual, a matter between them and their God. They were not *'thinking'* conscientious objectors, brought to their stand through rational thought and argument, men of deep philosophical or theological insight. Their religion was a simple one, based squarely on Bible teaching: 'Thou shalt not kill' from the Old Testament and 'Love thy neighbour' from the New. It was a world view taken in with their mother's milk and thereafter immutable. In that sense they were *'conforming'* conscientious objectors and all the more stubborn for that. When asked directly by Peter Liddle in 1973 whether accepting the Home Office Scheme had compromised his basic principles, Len immediately replied, 'No it didn't at all.'[331] Other religious objectors took a different view. While it was undoubtedly true that, as Margaret Hirst pointed out, 'very few conscientious objectors on religious grounds took up the "absolutist" position',[332] some did. One of these was Corder Catchpool. Sharing most, if not all, of the Payne family's religious convictions, he nevertheless believed that men who accepted the scheme must have been left with 'a haunting sense of having chosen a spiritual "second best". I am not sure that Christ's agony in Gethsemane was not essentially a struggle to refuse "alternative service" to Calvary.'[333] Was this suffering for Christ's sake or the aura of martyrdom which many conscientious objectors were drawing round themselves? However we look at it, it was a blow somewhat below the Christian belt.

Stephen Hobhouse was another, his view a different one again. 'It was often objected at the time,' he wrote in the 1930s, fending off criticisms which had rankled with him down the years, 'that the religious or moral objector, however genuine, was out for a more or less selfish individualism, for the saving of his own soul, for the keeping of his own hands clean at the expense of the nation to which he owed so much. From a fairly wide experience of the movement I was able to maintain with confidence that both the leaders and the main body of the conscientious objectors, whether professed Christian or not, had not only an individual objection, of a deep moral or religious kind, to becoming, under the Military Service Acts, a cog in the great machine for slaughtering Germans into which the nation had been transformed, but an equally deep conviction, stronger and more outspoken, no doubt, in some than in others, that what was spiritual salvation for themselves must be the only salvation, spiritually and therefore materially also, for the nation as a whole; and that to persist, whether now or in future crises, in the idea that we must ward off aggression by organised war would involve the ultimate ruin of all that is worth living for, both in our own or in other countries. It is true that we felt that to take part in killing operations would involve us individually in definite sin; but most of us felt too that we were out to save society, to save our country and mankind, quite as much as to save our own souls.'[334] Society could be saved by the actions of individuals.[335] There is no evidence whatsoever that Leonard and Roland Payne ever entertained such altruistic notions. It is doubtful whether they would have understood or even recognised them.

Those who became known as the 'absolutists' held that the Home Office Scheme should not be accepted under any circumstances. Many of these men stuck firmly to their belief that they were fighting against *war itself* and that there should be no co-operation whatsoever with 'militarism'. When Lloyd George had made it plain – as if it were not plain enough already – that anyone who refused the offer of alternative non-military work risked being handed over to the military authorities[336], it merely added fuel to the flames and strengthened their resolve yet further. When the scheme was discussed by NCF members at Mill Hill, for example, it was unanimously agreed that the Home Office Scheme must be rejected outright. '[It] is in spirit and effect subversive of all freedom and justice in that (a) it perpetuates a form of punishment beyond the term of imprisonment, and (b) it fixes a rate of remuneration and existence which are best expressed as a condition of slavery, and (c) that it is in essence a bargain with the government to facilitate the working of the Conscription Acts.'[337] Moreover, to accept compulsory employment under the Home Office Scheme as an alternative to military service or imprisonment was a betrayal of the fundamental principles of individual freedom of conscience for which the leaders of the NCF believed they were the fighting.[338]

And yet… the majority of conscientious objectors *did* accept the Home Office Scheme. After the war the NCF's own figures showed that 3,862 of its members (out of 6,312 arrested) accepted the alternative of 'work of national importance'.[339]

Therefore, the Payne brothers found themselves in the middle ground, a kind of moral 'No Man's Land'. They 'had to face a double-edged charge of shirking; from their country in the eyes of the public and from their principles in the eyes of their pacifist comrades'.[340] As Leonard said, 'A lot of people thought we had let them down' on both sides.[341]

★

The Payne brothers, Leonard and Roland, remained languishing in Durham Prison and the days, then weeks, dragged by. Conditions – by design or familiarity – appear to have eased somewhat, albeit never reaching the level of the 'lark' which Leonard had anticipated before his first traumatic encounter with prison life in Newcastle's grim old gaol.[342] Years later, in interview, Leonard reminded his brother of the occasion when he had been caught speaking to him through the cell window: 'We used to shout out of the window and you could hold your hand to your ear so we could hear what each other was saying'. When caught he was moved to a different cell, on the bottom landing, but 'it wasn't long before I looked out one morning and he was there as well. This warder had found out that we were brothers and he shifted you [Roland] down as well. Not only did he do that but he sent me off to collect the sanitary things and sent it to his cell. He opened your door and left me for a long time with you to talk. Then he came back and said "I'm sorry but I will have to get you out now. I have let you be in long enough", and he used to regularly send me with this thing to see you and have a talk with you in that bottom landing'.[343] For all that, Leonard reminded his sister Jessie in early October that a month had now passed since they had been offered the alternative route and that nothing had so far happened. They were still unsure of their fate, the prospect of transfer to some different regime the nature of which they could not yet understand still being dangled in front of them, but so far not activated.

They had to rely on outsiders to give what news they could. Rev. Seaward Beddow from Leicester was able to see them, but Thomas Harper, though in Durham, had been refused a pass. Mother wrote to them on October 3rd with what little news she had:

'You ask us to tell you about work of national importance. I do not know much about it there are a good few accepted it but some have not. Just over one hundred have been sent to Aberdeen, they did not get very comfortable quarters but it has been looked into and I think it is much better now. Some have been sent to Wales they are doing well and seem to be enjoying themselves and now we have just heard some are at Coventry, but what work they are doing I do not know, some have been sent straight to work and others have been sent home on furlough so you see it is quite uncertain which way it will be. Allen Shoults is at home still, he has answered some questions and sent it up to London but has not heard anything yet so I expect he will soon be at work. Mr H. Adkins got work on a farm but they would not let him have that he must do their work. There are a few atheists home who have finished their sentence but they have all got to go before the Central Tribunal so I expect they will all have to work in some way or other.'[344]

The following day she wrote a more motherly letter to Roland, containing more news of family members, of Aunt Alice who had given up her shop in London because she was afraid of air raids – modern war in action. She wrote, 'You must not loose [sic] hope yet it must take time to get things into working order. I do not think you will have to finish your sentence before you get work you know there are some who had ten years sentence they are at work in Aberdeen some of them… Lutterworth is still about the same not altered a bit only a few men less. I do wish as you say we could hear of peace but we must wait patiently peace will come sometime. Now don't worry if you can help it and when you get anxious and think all sort of things don't dwell on them no more than you can help we are still hoping for you to be released. I hope it will not be long'.[345] Her hope was to be fulfilled.

WAKEFIELD

On Thursday, October 12th 1916 John Payne posted a letter-card to Leonard at his new address:

> 'Work Centre,
> Love Lane,
> Wakefield,
> Yorks.' [346]

The 'Work Centre' at Love Lane was, in reality, the former Wakefield Prison, hastily converted for them to carry out their 'work of national importance'. As we might expect, the move had come suddenly. Marion Harper confessed she was 'surprise[d] to hear about your release' after receiving a postcard from the brothers, and we can easily imagine the rejoicing when the Harpers met up with John and Jessie junior on the Friday evening, October 13th.[347]

The Exercise Yard, Wakefield Prison/Work Centre.
Photograph courtesy of John Payne.

237

Inevitably, the wheels of bureaucracy ground slower, and the official letter to John confirming the change in his sons' circumstances lagged several days behind. Tardy or not, it must have been well received by the family. Bearing the embossed address: 'Home Office, Whitehall, S.W.', and the reference 'C.O. 1095', it read:

'Sir,

I am directed by the Committee on Employment of Conscientious Objectors to acknowledge the receipt of your letter of the 11th instant addressed to The Right Hon. Herbert Samuel, and to say that your sons have been released from Durham Prison and have been sent to take up work under this Committee to at the Work Centre at Wakefield.

Yours faithfully,

W.E.S. Tyler.'[348]

A handwritten postscript gave the address of the Work Centre. The letter was dated October 16th, several days after the brothers had actually been released from Durham Prison. John's letter-card to his sons gives the clearest possible indication of their new and changed circumstances:

'We were so delighted to hear you was moved. I shall come up on Saturday with your clothes. I will try and be up about midday but will let you know later as to train. Could you meet me if I let you know what time I arrive also station, do not mind your present clothes we will soon change this. Best wishes to you both shall see you soon. From your Loving Father and Mother.

J.G. Payne.'[349]

On the same day Jessie wrote a short letter saying much the same. Their father would be coming up to Wakefield two days later, on Saturday morning, and would bring their civilian clothes with him. Presumably they were still wearing prison clothes, an important symbol to them, just as the wearing of khaki had carried a more than literal meaning. The ever practical Jessie thought ahead: let the family know, by wire if necessary, if they couldn't meet him at the station, and John would make his way to the prison to see them there. Either way, she reassured them, 'he will be there in time for you to wear them in the afternoon'.[350]

We know nothing of John's trip to Wakefield except that it took place without any apparent hitch and from that day, Saturday 14th October, Leonard and Roland wore their prized civilian clothing. Perhaps more than anything else, this symbolised their final escape from the clutches of the military and the prison system as well. They were now civilians doing *work of national importance*, doing their bit towards the collective effort without compromising their religious principles. It was true that they would have to live in the Work Centre and to that extent were not free men, but they would be allowed free association with other objectors of like mind: the authorities had abandoned any attempt to isolate them. 'It was an open prison,' Leonard remembered later. 'The only restriction we had was that we had to sign a book when we went out and when we came in again. We were allowed out after about six o'clock in the evening and we had to be back by half past nine.'[351] Hence his matter-of-fact announcement that he was 'just going out for a walk', and that he 'had an invitation to go to Leeds [some ten miles away] tonight', but which he planned to defer until 'next week'. He had regained an element of control over his own life again.

On a wider scale the Brace Committee was encountering difficulties which had not – though perhaps should have – been anticipated. There had been particular problems at the Dyce Quarry outside Aberdeen[352] where conscientious objectors were housed in a tent village in atrocious conditions and expected to do hard manual labour to which many were physically unsuited. The death of one of them, Walter Roberts, was blamed, reasonably enough, on the barbarity of the conditions there and, in a flurry of government embarrassment, it was closed down after just ten weeks, in October 1916.[353] While it would certainly appear that there was a distinct lack of care shown by those responsible for the conscientious objectors, we might reasonably agree with the academic G.G. Coulton, writing at the time, who suggested that 'the worst hardships of which conscientious objectors complain are due to the haste and disorganisation of our present emergency measures'.[354] The British Government, with no experience of conscription and conscientious objection to fall back on, was having to make it up as it went along.[355] To the victims, of course, brutality, carelessness or ignorance were all the same.

This brings us back to the paradox of why so many conscientious objectors, including those committed to the No-Conscription Fellowship, accepted the Home Office Scheme. The religious objectors usually had no objection to working in the national interest in wartime on civilian projects, and some of the non-religious ones had no desire to submit their bodies further to prison regimes, but others had a different motive.

The truth is that many of the men who accepted the Home Office Scheme did so because they wanted to break the Home Office Scheme. They could not do this if they were locked in a prison cell and anyway the scheme offered a more congenial way to fight their own particular war. We might take note of this comment which appeared in *Punch* magazine in 1919 in a review of Harold Begbie's pro-conscientious objector novel *Mr Sterling Sticks it Out*:[356] 'I emphatically dispute [Begbie's] assumption that the matter [of the conscientious objectors] was a simple one. It was not the saintly, single-minded and sweet-natured C.O.'s of Christopher Sterling's type that made the chief difficulty. There were few of this literal interpretation and heroic texture. The real difficulty was created by men of a very different character and in much greater numbers, sincere in varying degrees, but deliberately, passionately and unscrupulously obstructive, bent on baulking the national will and making anything like reasonable treatment of them impossible. It would require saints, not men, to deal without occasional lapses from strict equity with such infuriating folk.'[357]

We might remember that many of the socialist objectors in no way shared the Payne brothers' Bible-based pacifism nor any philosophical form of pacifism, but were dedicated to the idea of class war, with all the conflict, even violence, which that implied.[358]

Problems were encountered with some of the objectors at the Warwick Work Centre where they refused to work, and those employed by Llanelly Rural District Council, which had offered to take them on, were accused of 'slacking and malingering'. These were men who had no intention of co-operating with the scheme they had nominally accepted and were prepared to make things as difficult as possible for those in authority. The concentration of so many committed socialists in one place, out to hamstring the Home Office Scheme, was proving a poisoned chalice. The Payne brothers saw this for themselves in Wakefield where there were men 'with very strong political beliefs that I couldn't share. You would put them down as communists these days'.[359]

It was clear before the end of 1916 that the government was losing control of the conscientious objectors and ninety-two of the most uncooperative were sent back to gaol. This did not, of course, solve the problem, for after the completion of their sentences they were supposed to be returned to military control – when the army did not want them and had supported the Work Centre solution as a way of getting these awkward and disobedient men off their hands.[360] The Central Tribunal's necessary generosity – like the Local Tribunals' lack of it – had backfired badly. The problem of the conscientious objectors was not going away.

★

In appearance their new home was not at all different from the Newcastle and Durham gaols. Built in the 1840s Wakefield Prison was a grim, forbidding place, the same high walls, the same plan based on wings radiating out from the centre in a semicircle[361], the same echoing galleries with the necessary 'suicide netting', the same small cells, the same rudimentary facilities. B-2-15, who lived there for a time, praised its vegetable gardens and its 'refreshing green plots'[362] – small comfort, one would have thought.

Immediately before its conversion to Work Centre, the building had been used by the army as a detention centre and several of the conscientious objectors Roland had met whilst at the Whitburn Army Camp had been held there in military custody.[363] Before that it had been a civil prison. One thing, which Leonard would remember for the rest of his life, was the guided tour he was given and the visit to the Condemned Cell: 'We saw all parts of the prison we had never seen before, but to see the gallows where the men were hung was a terrible shock. The Condemned Cell just near to this horrible trap on which the rope hung above I have never forgotten. I had a talk to one of the warders who had been connected with this terrible business, and he told me that people who talked about the prisoner walking bravely to the gallows was absolute rubbish, nine times out of ten they were dragged out.'[364] Now there was one fundamental difference: all the locks had been removed. The atmosphere was almost carnival as the first contingent of conscientious objectors arrived at Wakefield, including Leonard and Roland Payne. They knew many of their companions already from their long journey to the Central Tribunal at Wormwood Scrubs and in Durham Prison, and a party atmosphere must have prevailed, initially at least. Old friends reunited. There was no solitary confinement or silent system here!

The men here were not prisoners as such. As William Marwick, who would become one of the Paynes' closest friends, later recalled, the new regime could hardly have been more different from the old: The 'C.O.s were… accommodated in cells from which locks were removed. Considerable latitude was allowed, in respect of freedom to go outside after working hours, limited travel and periodic home leave, and a measure of self-government in house meetings and committees.'[365] Even so, it was a grim looking place to live. In the New Year of 1917 the brothers were able to send photographs of the prison to Marion Harper, who was suitably impressed:

> 'The place doesn't look over-inviting to say the least of it! As to the recreation ground it looks awful, fancy walking round and round 'spuds' for an hour with those awful chimneys and that doleful looking building to cheer you up on your way! I wonder all prisoners don't go entirely mad in melancholy.'[366]

It would seem that this was the photograph Marion was looking at:

Payne papers, Liddle Collection, Leeds

An awful place.[367]

Of course, like Newcastle and Durham gaols, Wakefield had been built for the silent, separate system, assuming that every man would spend most of his time in solitude or in small and tightly controlled groups. So the walkways were narrow and inconvenient, the ground floor space inadequate for such large numbers, the sheer noise of so much shouting, laughter and horseplay with all the doors open, echoing off the walls and galleries, cheerfully deafening.

Inside the Galleries at Wakefield Gaol.
Payne papers, Liddle Collection, Leeds

242

For their first five months or so in the Wakefield Centre, Leonard worked making rope, while Roland was assigned to the mat making workshop. Roland later recalled that 'one of us did rope making and I was making mats for gymnasiums and they found out I had been in the basket business, so they put me in charge of teaching the new ones that came in.'[368] Whether Jessie's comment that, 'I should think they will make you foreman over the mat making soon'[369] literally came true is not known, *de facto* perhaps, if not *de jure*. They kept their heads down and got on with the jobs assigned to them, though some conscientious objectors would find reasons not to comply: what would the ropes be used for when the military was such a large consumer? What if those gym mats were used in the training of soldiers? Even if those specific ropes and those particular mats were not for military use, their production in the Work Centre was freeing up some other man to go into the army. It was, again, a fine line and a fine compromise.

There was another problem, too, about the *nature* of the work they were doing, for making mats and ropes was stretching the concept of 'work of national importance' to its limits. William Marwick, in matter-of-fact style, told how the 'C.O.s were engaged in the ordinary *prison* tasks'.[370] But was this what they *should* have been doing? Robert Mennell afterwards wrote that: 'The nature of the work on which these men [in the Work Centres] were placed was very wasteful, in that no attempt was made to utilise the undoubted high average capacity available in the settlements',[371] and Howard Marten questioned 'the economic wastefulness of the greater part of the work, conducted as it mostly was under the old penal tradition'.[372] Would it not have made more sense to have allowed skilled workers like the Paynes to use their basketry skills in the national interest? As Marwick had perceived, making rope or mats – like sewing mailbags – were useful tasks in their own right, but their original purpose had been to harness cheap convict labour to do unskilled jobs to meet government needs and thus pass the time in gaol by keeping convicted criminals appropriately busy, and, at heart, it still consisted in doing jobs which could just as easily have been done by those too old, too young or too infirm for the armed forces, or by women. It had the taint of convict labour about it, a message which would not be lost on those living in prison buildings.

This is not what Asquith's government, nor Lloyd George's from December 1916, intended, the whole philosophy behind the Home Office Scheme being that it was an *alternative* to prison, not a replacement of it, a means of enticing in the *reasonable* objectors and isolating the *unreasonable*. Only thus, they believed, could the conscientious objector problem be encouraged to go away, leaving the isolation of prison only to those absolutists who *refused* the alternative, neatly putting them out of circulation behind real prison walls and thus silencing them and their influence. The moral certainty and stubborn courage of the absolutists would in that way play into the government's hands. The absolutists had cornered themselves.

★

Thus, the accepting conscientious objectors settled into their new lives in the Wakefield Work Centre. William Marwick's diary gives us interesting insights into this new daily environment:

'Tuesday October 24th 1916: Arrived Wakefield from Wormwood Scrubs. House in 'Work Centre' (former Jail).

Wednesday October 25th: Started work in ropery. [with Leonard]

Saturday October 28th: Half-day. Took car [tram] to Leeds, visited J.R. Taylor (former fellow student, now W.E.A. Tutor); returned by train.

Tuesday October 31st: Went in evening to social at 'Quaker' Friends Meeting House, used as social centre for C.O.s.

Wednesday 1st November: General House Meeting. Constitution carried, officials elected; put on Education Committee.

Thursday November 2nd: Lecture by J.R. Taylor in Centre on 'Economic Reconstruction after the War'. Small but keen attendance, good discussion.

Friday November 3rd: House Meeting in evening.

Friday November 10th to Sunday November 12th: Orderly duty.

Tuesday November 14th: Education Committee Meeting.

Wednesday November 15th: House Committee Meeting.

Thursday November 16th: Pay during work. House meeting in afternoon. Strike declared.

Friday November 17th: Out on strike all day. Evening meeting decided by ballot to resume work.

Saturday November 18th: Back to work.'[373]

Even these few entries encapsulate much of the life of the Wakefield Work Centre: the men's freedom to leave at weekends and in the evenings, the internal self-management through its own properly constituted committees with regular democratic meetings, the visiting speakers and the educational opportunities provided by the inmates themselves, the mix of religious interests with political education, even the organisation of short-term strike action, democratically controlled, when the men felt there was something to protest about.

These were young men, gathered together in one confined space, away from home, in some ways not very different from university or college students, or even from their young contemporaries called up into the army. Like all young men of the time they played music and formed their own band[374], and enjoyed kicking a football around.[375] Inevitably, perhaps, some strayed into the area of amateur dramatics, and later in 1917 put on a variety show. One of their friends described it:

> 'We had a concert on Mon and Tues night of this week. Did we tell you that the H[ome] O[ffice] has forbidden the use of the chapel for concerts. The old convict prison chapel has now been fitted up as a theatre and as it is so much less than the other, concerts have to be held twice. Hence one concert Mon and Tues. Charlie Botham took part in it dressed as a lady. It was a light music hall style, but pretty decent all the same, except in parts. They finished off with a sketch 'Phipps'. J. Roper, Runacres & Evill, and all three were really fine. Roper as the lady of course. The place is very much better for the hearing than the other place was. It looks as if there was going to be a concert every week, as there are two or three concert parties. The news has just come from Dartmoor that they have just performed *A Midsummer Nights Dream*. They must have some talent there.'[376]

The Paynes, though, remained insecure and aloof on the fringes of much of Wakefield Work Centre social life, keeping themselves to themselves and to their small circle of friends. When interviewed in 1973 they showed little awareness of either the political debates in the centre or its social activities, Leonard's feeble excuse being that 'we were so glad to get our freedom we didn't want to tie ourselves down'. His comment that 'it was a universe in itself was Wakefield' applying just as much to him and his brother as to the Work Centre as a community.[377] Leonard and Roland, after six months in the all-male environment of military and gaol, had now found other preoccupations, as we shall see.

★

One thing that is clear is that the inmates of the Wakefield Centre were an argumentative bunch. These were men who generally came from a higher than average intellectual and educational background[378], and given that it was their stubborn beliefs and determination of purpose which had landed them here, we should not wonder that the arguments were heated indeed. Leonard later wrote 'you can imagine the arguments etc that went on, people with all different religious views, socialists, agnostics, etc. Men with great talents, doctors, actors, judges' sons, people from all sorts of universities'[379] – a comment which betrays his own uncertainty, his own feelings of insecurity, even inferiority. He had, after all, progressed no further than Lutterworth's – albeit very competent – elementary school. One of his new friends had to reprimand him in order to encourage:

'I'm sorry to hear that you are 'absolutely brainless'. I should never have imagined it if you hadn't told me, but I suppose I must take your word for it. Seriously, however, don't you mistake academic training or even brilliance for intelligence. Some people get so highly educated and so brainy in their own line that they seem to have no room left in there and that accounts for some learned professors being so crazy about the war etc.'[380]

Among the educated men in Wakefield was one who would become a firm friend, William Marwick, an Edinburgh graduate and the last person the Paynes would have met, let alone become friends with, in the normal course of their lives as basket weavers in Lutterworth. Born in Nigeria to Christian missionary parents, Marwick had graduated with First Class Honours in History from Edinburgh University, his call-up in 1916 being delayed so he could sit his final exams, his Evangelical upbringing and his commitment to Christian socialism obliging him to seek conscientious objector status. His appeal rejected, Marwick was held for a time in Stirling Castle before being court martialled for his refusal to put on khaki and was sent to Wormwood Scrubs Prison, like the Paynes, a long way from home. Like the Paynes, he had been held in solitary confinement, though his response was rather different: it 'came as some relief from the congested guard room, but was becoming tedious from lack of company', he later recalled. By now the Home Office Scheme was up and running, and Marwick was sent straight to Wakefield. He arrived a few days after the Paynes, on October 24th 1916.[381]

For young men like Leonard Payne the Wakefield Work Centre opened up educational possibilities that would never have come their way otherwise: it became their university. Distinguished speakers like the philosopher Bertrand Russell, the social historian G.D.H. Cole and the journalist Ivor Brown, came and gave supportive talks to the 'residents'.[382] Leonard recalled that 'there was a chap called Howes, who was one of the professors at either Oxford or Cambridge, and there was another fellow from Durham University who was there with us too'.[383] A bewildering array of courses of study became available as the educated men there, evenings free and time on their hands, started up classes in their own specialist areas. William Marwick taught History, while Leonard availed himself of the chance to learn French[384] – ironic perhaps since he would not be going to France, at least not while the war was on. But it worked the other way as well, giving the more highly educated objectors the chance to mix with people from very different social backgrounds to their own and, for some, a new audience to proselytize. William Marwick could not have been the only one who found that 'these experiences of manual labour and of the society of industrial workers influenced my later professional and political career'.[385]

★

As for the Paynes, now they were no longer caught in the machinery of the prison system, they were allowed home visits. They were quick to seize the opportunity, for Marion wrote of this in that first letter to them, hoping the brothers would soon be able to come home to Lutterworth. John called in on the Harpers on his way back from Wakefield, giving them their formal invitation to join the celebrations.[386]

So preparations now got under way for the brothers' visit home the following weekend. The logistics of the thing would not be easy. It was not until Wednesday October 18th, that Leonard was able to find a way of doing it. In the days of multiple railway companies, each with its own lines and stations, it would be a complicated business, involving changes in Sheffield and Leicester, before finally arriving at Lutterworth's own station at 5:21 p.m. on Saturday, October 20th 1916.

★

But what of the Lutterworth the brothers were returning to, however briefly, in the autumn of 1916? While the fortunes of the brothers were now on the rise, the same cannot be said of their home town.

This small market town, noted (if that is the word) for its somnolent respectability, was experiencing stress in its otherwise bland façade. Though Jessie senior had told Roland that the town was much as before: 'Lutterworth is still about the same not altered a bit only a few men less'[387], the changes to the local community in the past six months had been clear and distressing. 'A few men less' did not only mean that men had been called up to military service and so were absent from the town's streets, shops and houses, but that 'a few men less' would be a permanent matter, for what was happening during those last few months of the brothers' absence from Lutterworth was the Battle of the Somme, still not over when Leonard and Roland came home on their first visit from Wakefield.

The slaughter on the Somme could not long be kept secret from the British public – the long and growing lists of men missing or dead filled increasing inches of column space in local newspapers across the country. Lutterworth, too, suffered losses on the Somme in those first few days of the 'Big Push'. William Wright did not live beyond the first day, one of the twenty thousand who died on July 1st 1916, killed in the disastrous attack on Serre at the northern end of the battlefield. Alice Barlow lost her boyfriend, 'sweetheart' in the terminology of the time, Douglas Gauld.[388] Originally from Lancashire, Douglas had lived in North Kilworth, a few miles east of Lutterworth on the old turnpike road to Market Harborough. His Battalion, the 10th Worcestershires, was supposed to have been sent, like William Wright's Battalion, over the top on the first morning, but were granted a reprieve – for forty-three hours at least. Attacking the remnants of the village of La Boisselle, at 3 a.m. on July 3rd, he and his fellows had been sucked into desperate hand to hand fighting in the ruins of the village itself. Exactly where and how he died can never be known, but wherever and however it happened, it must have been terrible. 'Eight hundred and ten men went in. Four hundred and forty-eight came out.'[389]

There was then a pause. Not in the battle, but in the procession of local Lutterworth men killed in it, until John Herbert of Baker Street, serving in the 7th Battalion of the Leicestershire Regiment, lost his life in the Bazentin-le-Petit Wood near Mametz on July 14th and William Herrick, of the 9th Battalion, died in the same place on the same day, their remains never recovered. Claude Taylor was next, killed at Delville Wood on the high ground above the Somme on August 24th. Alfred Drake, a year older than Leonard Payne, was killed at Gueudecourt on September 25th; Harry Matthews in an assault against the near impregnable Schwaben Redoubt beside Thiepval three days later.

If the posted forms of official notification and the seemingly endless casualty lists in all the local newspapers day after day, some accompanied by photographs to add to the pathos, were not reminder enough, there was the constant stream of wounded and mutilated ferried in great haste from the railway station to the Cottage Hospital or the Methodist schoolroom, some with parts missing. With the Somme, the war was coming home to Lutterworth.

★

In the local community the strain was telling too, the Parish Council, exercised by the unruly behaviour of the young, discussing the problem at great length. There had been problems before, from children making noise at night and keeping

Lutterworth's shopkeepers from their sleep, and there had been some vandalism at the Recreation Ground, blamed on the young[390], but now the council was worried by much more serious disorder, of 'street brawling and the hooliganism of youths just in their teens'. While much of this was confined to the Recreation Ground, which was the only area in Lutterworth where young people could gather in the evenings and at weekends free of charge, and around football matches, there was claimed to be a 'constant' flow of complaints from members of the public about the conduct of its youth. Bad language seems to have upset most and in particular that directed towards 'respectable ladies' who were walking out. The dark winter nights seem to have made things worse rather than better, presumably because it was more difficult to identify the culprits, especially in black-out conditions. The council was clearly shocked, and George Spencer said he had 'not heard anything to equal it'. Trouble-makers should be prosecuted, they thought, as the 'only possible deterrent'.[391]

All this speaks of a decline in respect for authority. Warning notices about unruly behaviour had already been put up around the town on several occasions – and had been ignored. One councillor, Mr Taylor, blamed the 'depletion of the police force' for the problem and suggested that the special constables be instructed to take the matter in hand. We may ask, though, how much authority the special constables actually carried. Back in September the chief constable, addressing the Lutterworth Magistrates, had gone to great lengths to praise the specials and the work they did, particularly in face of the Zeppelin threat when they might be called from their beds in the middle of the night to supervise the 'adjustment of the lighting' and the enforcement of the black-out. The suspicion that he protested too much was confirmed when he went on to say that 'he mentioned this openly, because he felt it was his duty, so that the public might know when they saw any person wearing the badge that it was an honourable distinction, and one greatly appreciated by himself'.[392]

But lack of enforcement cannot fully explain the perceived upsurge in teenage violence in Lutterworth. Behind it – and beyond the jurisdiction of Parish Council and Chief Constable alike – was the departure of so many of Lutterworth's men for the Front. Conscription during 1916 compounded the problem, taking husbands and fathers away to the army and leaving many mothers with the burden of coping with their children alone. For those families in which the father had been lost forever, the problem was, of course, even more desperate.

★

This first home-coming had been, as we would expect, eagerly awaited, and Jessie had so many questions to ask that she and her father had to stay up late putting together a list.[393] But what actually transpired in that first gathering, and what was said on both sides, what news, feelings, opinions, experiences, emotions were exchanged, is not known; nor what silences there were. Tears were presumably shed, but no one wrote anything down. We can presume but not know.

Ever since their departure in the spring there had been speculation in Lutterworth about their whereabouts, 'No one hear [sic] says anything about you and in fact I do not think they know were [sic] you are except [what] they have learned by the post and we say very little we keep our own counsel' [394], as their mother told them in July while they were awaiting court martial in Whitburn. That their neighbours were curious is attested by Dora, 'Lutterworth is just the same everyone wanting to know your business'[395], while Jessie was exercised by those who shared the pews with her in the Congregational Chapel, 'They are just the same lot of hypocrites [sic] especially the old girl (Em) you know'.[396]

What did their neighbours make of their arrival back home? A letter written by Jessie to Leonard ten days after their visit gives us two tantalising glimpses of the reaction when the two brothers, in civilian clothes and free, arrived suddenly in the town on a dark Saturday evening, 'The people here have just about got over their shock in seeing you. When Dad and Mother got home from the station that Sunday night they found "Slackers' Rest" chalked cross [sic] the shutters, I guess it was those boys'.[397]

Why should local people have been so surprised to see the brothers in town? Certainly, they had been away for some seven months and their imprisonment as conscientious objectors must have been known, as also presumably must the new arrangements based round 'work of national importance' and the Work Centre system, but what was probably not fully understood was the freedom which the new system gave the brothers to come and go with such relative ease. According to their aunt, C. Drake, their return had 'set people talking a bit', though, when she was writing a week afterwards, she said 'it is all over now'.[398]

Perhaps the chalked 'Slackers' Rest' message on the shop's shutters hints at an accompanying disapproval, if not outright anger. There are many messages which could have been put there, but the choice of the word 'slacker' is significant, suggesting not merely that the brothers were failing to do their bit towards the communal national effort by putting on uniform and joining in the fighting, but that their reluctance was due to selfish and dishonourable motives. Clearly, the notion that they were doing work of importance to the nation as an appropriate and commensurate substitute for military service had failed to convince those whose fingers were chalk stained on that Sunday evening.

However, caution is necessary. We could dismiss Jessie's explanation that it was simply 'those boys' – 'those', rather than 'some' or 'a few' – the implication being that the family had been troubled by a specific group of local boys too young for military service, a group probably mentioned within the family while the brothers had been at home. Identifying the boys is now no longer possible and it may be that Jessie's phrase was intended to trivialise the local hostility to the brothers and thus reassure them. So did these 'boys', if indeed it was boys who had perpetrated the act, reflect a wider critical attitude towards the Paynes? The phrase 'Slackers' Rest' is not a childish one. Children may have chalked the slogan up, but they must have been mimicking a phrase heard from their elders. There was something distinctly ominous in all of this.

★

If there was a library inside the Work Centre we hear nothing of it, for the men instead used their evenings to go down into the town to use the library there. They did not have borrowing rights, but were able to read what the library had to offer, especially the newspapers – much to the disgust of some of the locals. Tensions within the town were evidently rising. Wakefield City Council, in its meeting on January 2nd 1917, debated at length what could be done about the Work Centre inmates who were spending their evenings cluttering up the town's Free Public Library. Councillor Graham set the ball rolling when he asked 'if the members of the Public Library Committee had taken into consideration the over-running of the reading room by the conscientious objectors from Wakefield Jail, and if so, what steps had been taken to mitigate the evil?' 'Evil' was a strong word and it was not long before the councillor showed his true colours, and the underlying issue came to the fore: 'There is a strong feeling in the city about the way these men parade the streets in the evenings, and going away on week-end leaves,' he said. 'There is a strong feeling about these men getting such splendid treatment, with loads of sugar and any amount of jam, whilst our soldiers' wives and families are very hard put to get hold of these things.' Councillor Jackson concurred: 'I think it is a disgrace and a scandal that we should have to rub shoulder to shoulder with such a lot of contemptible curs,' he said. The Mayor proposed writing to the Home Office requesting that the doors of the Work Centre be kept locked, but, since that offered little hope of success, the Library Committee was instructed to work out ways and means of keeping the 'horde' from its reading rooms.[399]

The library issue was but the latest in a running battle between a town which felt itself swamped by hundreds of young men suddenly planted in its midst, with no apparent consultation with the good people of Wakefield, men with nothing much to do during evenings and weekends, and Work Centre inmates who were very often not the most co-operative of men. It may be that the citizens of Wakefield felt put upon enough already since the huge Entertainment Park at nearby Lofthouse had been taken from them to serve as an internment camp for enemy aliens – though the internees there were, at least, kept behind barbed wire.[400]

At first there had been bewilderment in Wakefield when the prison, in the middle of the town, suddenly took in this new influx and then *opened its doors*. Bewilderment slowly turned to anger when it was realised exactly who these men were, who were appearing in increasingly and alarmingly large numbers on the streets of Wakefield.[401] Like the whole of Britain in 1916, the prevailing attitude was of support for a war which none wanted but which, it was believed, had to be fought and won. When a sermon preached by Canon Welch, the Vicar of Wakefield, in the cathedral in November, appeared to suggest that after the war Germany should be treated fairly and without rancour or revenge, the local newspaper had no compunction about flatly contradicting him, thundering that 'no sane person would dream of leaving it in the power of Germany to bring about a cataclysm at any future time such as the one the world is now experiencing'.[402] There was to be no suggestion of moral equivalence between the contesting parties in this war. Nor would there be much toleration shown towards those who refused to take part.

What had stirred up the particular controversy in Wakefield was the visit of Dr John Clifford, the Leicester trained Baptist prophet, who had so reluctantly decided in 1914 to give the war his support as the lesser of two evils. His address, given to mark the anniversary of the Zion Brotherhood and Sisterhood in Wakefield, on November 20th 1916, was enthusiastically reported in the local press and was evidently well received. Extra seating had to be put out to accommodate all those who wanted to attend. The local newspaper reporter gushed with pride that such an august figure should have visited his home town.[403] It was fairly straightforward fare from Clifford, speaking of the brotherhood of mankind and the desirability of peace, nothing that would cause alarm to the guardians of the state. A couple of weeks later, though, a short letter was published in the local paper from someone signing him or herself 'Anxious'. It read: 'There are in Wakefield at the present time some hundreds of those strange *criminals* known as conscientious objectors. At a recent meeting at Zion Brotherhood, when Dr John Clifford visited Wakefield, these C.O.s attended in large numbers, and from the applause with which they greeted certain statements by the speaker it would seem that they conceive of their actions as in some way connected with Brotherhood and the teaching of Jesus. I ask you, how can members of a *real* Brotherhood stand aside when they hear Dr

Clifford tell them that this war is, so far as Britain is concerned, a war waged on behalf of the Kingdom of God? I pause for a reply!'[404]

'Strange *Criminals* known as conscientious objectors' was bad enough, but it paled in comparison with what was to follow. It is not clear exactly what provoked the new Wakefield onslaught, but it may well have been word that the objectors housed in the Work Centre would be allowed to spend Christmas at home with their families. Two days before Christmas 1916, and with a distinct shortage of 'Christmas spirit', the *Wakefield Express* published a letter from 'Disgusted' under the heading '"Conscientious Objectors" in Wakefield', the inverted commas a deliberate statement: 'Please permit me through the medium of your columns to voice the feelings of many with regard to that tribe now housed in Wakefield (temporarily, heaven), and known as "conscientious objectors", although probably many of them do not possess a conscience at all. It makes one positively ill to see these brazen-faced, thick-skinned, pigeon-hearted *criminals* walking about the streets as if they had bought the earth… Wakefield Jail has been occupied by all sorts of persons in its history but the present occupants must be regarded as the limit. Just imagine any person who thinks he is entitled to be called a man object to defend his country under circumstances so well known! But they are not men, and better *criminals* can be caught with a piece of cheese and a penny trap.'[405]

If that wasn't enough, the *'Express'*s editorial went into all out attack. It read: 'Amongst the "objects" at present enjoying hospitality in the Shirkers' Shelter, Love Lane, Wakefield [i.e. Wakefield Prison/Work Centre], are several of the familiar type of tub-thumping or street-corner orators. The pity is that they are not dealt with in the manner they certainly would be dealt with if they were actual subjects residing in the country which is their "spiritual home". At times these unwelcome visitors have attempted to air their pro-German views in the streets of the city, but the authorities promptly stepped in, and by so doing undoubtedly prevented a breach of the peace. Free speech is one of our greatest heritages, and a liberty of which we are rightly jealous. But there are obvious times when the diatribes of avowed traitors and the vaporings of individuals who are friendly to every country but their own are a positive danger to the Commonwealth. Certainly the present is not a time when the great majority of loyal citizens will quietly listen to men who have sunk so low as to palliate the atrocities committed by the Huns, and beg that they should be treated with the respect and consideration which we should only be too glad to extend towards a humane and honourable foe.'[406]

★

The Paynes took advantage of their new found freedom to spend Christmas of 1916 at home, though this time their transport arrangements proved complicated. Under the original Home Office Scheme the objectors were allowed not only generous 'holiday' time, but also free transport. Just a few days before Christmas, however, their rights to rail travel were withdrawn and at short notice their supporters, notably the indomitable Harpers, had to make their own arrangements to get them home for the holiday.[407] It was an astonishingly elaborate arrangement which Marion organised at almost no notice:

> 'I wrote to Mr Searle's mother [in Sheffield] but she is full up so the son is willing to help you along… The point is, would you care to leave Wakefield on bikes on Friday night, [Christmas Day in 1916 was on the Monday] go to Mr Searle's and then be ready for Mr Allen on Sat. mg. Mr Allen says he will meet you with the motor at Mr Searle's house, on Sat. mg. at 11, he may be a little later in case of anything going wrong, but he wants you to be sure to be ready by then because of getting here by daylight. Then the other proposition is, will you stay at the Work Centre over Friday night and cycle straight to Mr Searle's on Sat. mg. I don't know of course how you are fixed for getting breakfast etc. early You would have the morning light for your ride instead of the night, but be at 56 Brunswick St. by eleven sure.
>
> Enclosed is also a diagram from Mr Searle showing how you are to find their house. I hope I have made it clear that you meet the motor at Mr S's house whether you go on Friday night or cycle there on Sat. Mg… we don't want a hitch if we can help it.'[408]

Nothing speaks so eloquently of the sheer efficiency of the supporting system for the conscientious objectors as this. But it was all in vain. Marion's hope that 'all is clear and that a thaw will soon make the roads free from snow' was not to be fulfilled and the brothers, determined to get home by any way possible, broke the rules and caught the train. Allen, meanwhile, had driven up to Sheffield through the heavy snow, only to find that the brothers were not there.[409]

It would appear that there were no repercussions from their breach of the travel regulations at the season of goodwill and in the New Year Jessie was able to express her relief, 'I am glad you have not heard anything about using the trains and I hope you won't'.[410] Like their earlier visit, we know nothing of the details of that Christmas at home in 1916. Being that time of year it was probably a traditional affair, though limited by wartime conditions. Their farmstead on the outskirts of Lutterworth no doubt provided the centrepiece of the Christmas dinner, father carving the goose (if goose they had) as he always did, decorations on the Christmas tree, modest gifts exchanged, sad thoughts of the boys' plight and their uncertain future. We know nothing of the reaction of their neighbours at their sudden arrival back home, especially those neighbours with sons in the army who were not at home that Christmas. But of overt tension we hear nothing. Their cousin, Kit Ball, had written with heavy irony that 'I daresay the Lutterworth people are very complimentary. They are noted for it. If I were you I should not take any notice, they'll get over it the same as everyone else'.[411] If only that that were true!

★

Lifelong friendships were forged in the Wakefield Work Centre. William Marwick, the Edinburgh graduate and Christian socialist, never forgot the Payne brothers[412], but there was also Eddie Beaton, a clerk by trade, born in London but living (when at home) at Potternewton outside Leeds, Joe Todd, a Cumberland farmer's son, and Ron Long from Newton Aycliffe in County Durham. Ron had been with the Paynes since their time in Durham Prison, where, according to Leonard, he had taught them to communicate by signals across the prison gallery: Leonard later described how 'all the prison clothes were the same size as each other and [Ron] was such a short man he had to turn the trousers right up his legs to make them short enough so he could walk'.[413] We might, in fanciful mode, think of these as 'The Wakefield Six' – William Marwick, Eddie Beaton, Joe Todd, Ron Long, and Leonard and Roland Payne. Until the end of Leonard's life he kept their names in his address book.

As disparate a bunch as one could imagine in other ways, they were all bound together by their shared religious bent. Not, of course, that they always saw eye to eye – that would have been too much to expect. The Paynes, for example, saw Seaward Beddow of the Wycliffe Congregational Chapel in Leicester as a lifeline, helping to keep them in touch with the world outside – especially that small portion which supported them – yet Ron Long, when he heard of Beddow's attempt to release Ewart Long, would have none of it:

> 'My many thanks for your action re Seward *[sic]* B[eddow] & Ewart, but Leon I am rather against what I call particularly *organized* efforts and did not join the FOR or NCF – FOR THAT reason… You see we preferred faith in God to bring things all right, *in accordance with **His**** will, for by seeking his release we might perchance have been acting against God's purpose and will.'[414]

Eddie Beaton, too, was not shy about banging the religious drum, as his admiration – in a letter damaged over time – clearly shows:

'He is proving to be a very [★ word missing] little chap refusing all [order]s even in military prison. [Inde]ed his steadfastness to the [trut]h marks an epoch in his life [whi]ch is but a stepping stone to [tha]t Better Land, promised [to] the children of God.'[415]

Sometimes, we catch unmistakable glimpses of another common Christian characteristic, an astonishing self-righteousness. So Ron Long told Leonard in a letter shortly before Christmas 1917:

'Yes, I agree with you re the real Xmas message and feeling but we must remember even whilst sympathizing with the people, that they have rejected Jesus Christ and his message and despite the condition that rejection has brought them to, still remain selfish, proud and even refusing to hear His Words.'[416]

So, the war was God's punishment on a world which had rejected Him. An Old Testament prophet could hardly have put it better.

★

On the other hand, when we remind ourselves that, in the midst of the occasional flurry of self-righteousness and martyrdom talk, these were young men away from home, treated as adults under minimal supervision except that which the Scheme required, it is inevitable that sex would come to play a significant part in the lives of some, at least, of those in Wakefield. The good people of the town were certainly aware of the impact the presence of so many young men – 'conchies' or not – was having on sections of the female population of the town, especially when virtually all of the eligible males of Wakefield were away in the army. Insult was being added to injury as the *Wakefield Express* was not slow to point out: 'Another matter, which certainly does not add to the credit of Wakefield is the fact that girls – a positive disgrace to their sex – can be seen inviting the attentions of these male curios, and Love Lane [the location of Wakefield Prison] is now the rendezvous for misfits in both sexes'.[417] Not that such thunderings had much effect, for in the summer of 1918 we find the same complaint: 'The disgraceful manner in which certain Wakefield girls flirt about with those very peculiar people excites the utmost contempt on the part of decent women', a comment made, we presume, by a male journalist.[418] It is clear enough that this touched a raw nerve. We have seen that all over the country police forces were on the alert, keeping a watchful eye on the women in their areas, fearful they might slip into drunkenness, infidelity or worse, their attitude one of vigilant paternalism, protecting the female as much from herself as from the attentions of the male. They saw this as their duty and their responsibility. That young women in Wakefield might be consorting with the inmates of the Wakefield Work Centre – the despised conscientious objectors – added insult to injury.

Henry Kissinger famously said that power was the great aphrodisiac. It would seem that being a conscientious objector in the First World War had much the same effect. Or perhaps it was simply that these just happened to be available males; feast in time of dearth. What is clear is that Leonard and Roland Payne made their own contribution to the feast and Leonard in particular took advantage of what was on offer, though we might imagine that the moral inhibitions imposed by his upbringing and the time in which he lived would have kept him on the purer side of chastity. Perhaps we can presume that his female acquaintanceships were of a casual nature; 'playing the field' as a later expression would have it. External constraints were one thing: we do not know for certain what constraints he put upon his own behaviour, if any. What we do know of Leonard's sexual adventures comes from the letters of the 'Wakefield Six' after they had been split up and sent to different destinations: his friends at the centre would tease him about his prowess with the ladies. After Leonard left Wakefield, Ron Long would write to him about Joe Todd. 'Joe tries to take your place in kissing etc but no go. He is no good at it at all'.[419]

From his later location in mid-Wales, William Marwick would also make play of Leonard's sexual proclivities, 'Last night Prof. Howat gave us a discourse on a subject which would have provoked you to eloquence (privately I mean) – viz. the Relations of the Sexes'.[420] The precise meaning of his 'private eloquence' is less than clear, though again speculation might fill in the gaps. Equally suggestive is a comment made in an undated letter to the brothers by William Deas, a friend though not one of their inner circle: 'I expect you are still carr[y]ing your free love principles out in Birmingham or elsewhere. I expect you have both, between you, had about all the girls not engaged, and one or two that are'.[421] 'Engaged', but at least not 'married', as far as we know.

On occasion what might be taken as youthful banter went beyond the boundaries of good taste, as when a bored William Marwick spent Christmas Day 1916 penning a verse which included the couplet:

'When the boys are in the trenches
And Leonard 'mid the wenches...' [422]

We are reminded that there was no Christmas Truce in 1916, and on the Western Front snow lay on the ground.[423] The usual rule of kill and be killed still applied there, Christmas Day or not... and there were no wenches in the trenches.

★

Whatever Christmas goodwill they had found in Lutterworth – in their own home if not in the town – lasted no longer than the turkey, for arriving back in Wakefield after the holiday the brothers found that trouble had again erupted there, the issue of travel rights providing another flashpoint of conflict between the inmates of the Wakefield Work Centre and the local population. At dispute was the issue, not of train fares, but of tram fares. Five objectors – Percy Horner (a Labour member of Leeds City Council), Arthur Emmett, Norman Daniels, and Abraham and Solomon Pearce[424] – had evidently seen in the New Year of 1917 in Leeds, and were returning by tramcar very early on the morning of January 1st. They asked for and were issued with workmen's three-penny concessionary tickets at half price by the conductress, one Kate Sewell, but they were then told by an inspector that they were not *bona fide* workmen and must pay the full fare. They refused. To them this was an issue of principle and these were men of principle: that was why they were there.

They appeared in the West Riding Police Court in Wakefield in the middle of January. Their argument, well presented by the group's leader, Percy Horner, was that they *were* workers and were thus entitled to the reduced fare, and that the prosecution would not have been brought had they not been conscientious objectors living in the Wakefield Work Centre. He was probably right, but the magistrates none the less found against them.[425] The affair attracted the attention and the concern of the family back at home in Lutterworth. On January 19th Jessie was writing to Roland:

> 'Dad is very anxious about the bothers you are having at Wakefield, and he says you are not to get mixed up in them, he says that bother about the workman's ticket is not worth fighting for, he said he would rather pay the full fare and so say nothing about it. We shall look out for it in the *Labour Leader* but be sure and tell how you settle it.'[426]

The Work Centre inmates did not ignore the storm of abuse directed against them in the *Wakefield Express*. After one particularly venomous diatribe by Driver C. Crowther of the Royal Field Artillery in which he asserted that 'It is owing to there being so many of these "objects" at home that we cannot have more leave, so there is no wonder that soldiers hold them in such contempt'[427], Howard Marten, from within the wall of the prison/Work Centre, decided to respond. It was hardly a letter calculated to win friends, its tone superior and patronising. 'Personally, I have very great sympathy with Driver Crowther and thousands similarly situated, who through a blind adherence to the dictates of military domination are enduring daily hardship and privation', he wrote. As one of those who had been to France and then sentenced to death, Marten claimed to speak from experience: 'I can truthfully say that in the case of the vast majority of the soldiers with whom I came into contact in that country, I found that they fully appreciated the ideals which prompted the attitude of the conscientious objector'.[428]

If the objectors hoped to get a fair hearing in the town – the local paper did, after all, print Marten's letter in full – they had only to read on to the next letter in the same edition, printed under the heading 'An Ex-Soldier's Opinion of Conscientious Objectors'. The writer, signing himself 'Once a "Tommy"', gave his full backing, not to Marten, but to Driver Crowther, and broadened the attack: 'If the "Love Lane Men" were left to be dealt with by the soldiers, I have an idea where they would all soon be! They seem to nurse the idea that they have a right to monopolise the whole town, and cause all the mischief they can, what with refusing to pay tram fares, obstructing the footpaths, and other little things calculated to cause annoyance. It aggravates one to see them walking about grinning like monkeys because they are still here, despite the war, and being kept far better than the lads who have gone across the sea in defence of our mothers, wives, and children. Why not send them out? They would get plenty of cheap rides there, with a nice sail on a big ship thrown in! If they won't fight for their country, why should they be allowed to live in it?'[429]

The debate, such as it was, had ground to a halt. The following week another letter from a Work Centre inmate, James McMurdo, re-asserted that soldiers had in his experience, like Marten's, been supportive: 'They applauded the stand we C.O.'s were making, and constantly expressed a wish to join us', which did not advance the case at all.[430] Assertion simply followed assertion and the newspaper's editor grew tired and moved on to other matters, the choice of a new mayor, teachers' pay in the town, and other pressing issues of the day.

The Paynes themselves were not immune from the local resentment. It may well have been sometime around now that this event happened, told years later by Leonard Payne: 'A chap came up to me in the centre of Wakefield one afternoon and made some silly remark. He wanted to know if I could tell him the time or something or other and he simply put his fist up and smashed me straight in the face. Things were getting very bitter in Wakefield at that time.'[431]

BRADFORD

But if Wakefield was proving less than congenial, the Paynes found friendlier contacts elsewhere, we presume through that remarkable network of anti-conscriptionists of the NCF which put them in touch with supporters in Bradford, a dozen miles from the Work Centre. It was from there that they were contacted by Harry Hainsworth, a Quaker who lived on Oxford Street in the Undercliffe area of the city, and the Graham sisters, nineteen-year-old Alice and Edith two years younger, living half a mile away in one of the comfortable but not over-spacious terraced houses on Beech Grove in the north-east part of Bradford. Their older brother Frank was a conscientious objector who had also accepted the Home Office Scheme. This new freedom of movement gave them the chance to exploit the opportunity of personal contact, which they were not slow to seize. Harry wrote to the brothers on November 6th in 1916:

> 'Though we have known each other so short a time, I feel there is a good deal in common between us, that our friendship will grow and develop into a living fire. At the present time old friends are being shed, and at some personal cost, but believe me new one's [sic] are being found that will stand the test, for in our movement now we are going through the fire in which the worthless are destroyed and only the real article comes through unscathed.'[432]

The language does not surprise, nor does Hainsworth's belief that everything possible was being done on the 'outside' in 'breaking down prejudice and removing misunderstandings regarding our attitude towards war'. Both were entirely typical of the mentality of those who supported the religious conscientious objectors, as was his ardent desire to be of practical help:

> 'I also trust you will let us know how the comrade is going on whom you said was cast adrift by his parents we should be pleased to offer him hospitality at Christmas if no other arrangement is made, as I feel it is our duty who are on the outside to make the task as light as possibly for you who are in the first line of defence.'[433]

The language is strikingly military with its references to comradeship, duty and 'line of defence', neatly turning the prevalent military jargon on its head.

It was in Bradford that they met the Graham sisters on a cold, rainy, West Yorkshire winter's day. The welcome was warm, but rainy days in Bradford have always been rainy days in Bradford, and Leonard was less than impressed by what he saw: Edith had to assure him that 'Bradford really isn't a bad place when you know it'.[434] Whatever impression Bradford had made on them, they, it seems, made a good impression on the Graham sisters. Jessie told Leonard, in a letter dated October 31st 1916, 'I have heard all about you [from Roland] at Bradford a girl name Alice Graham where you stayed sent me a fine letter... she says you can go any weekend you like, it is very nice of her'.[435] Even through the shortage of punctuation, we can still see that Leonard had made a good impression on these girls as well.

The Bradford contact also gave the brothers their first glimpse outside the shelter of military camp and prison in which they had been cocooned for the past six months. Whether what they saw shocked them is not recorded, but they might well have modified the idea of 'equality of sacrifice' by comparing their working and living conditions with those of ordinary civilians, including these two teenage girls. We do not know what kind of work the Graham sisters were doing and it may well have been that they had jobs in Bradford's textile factories, where by 1916 production was running at a very high level and which had taken on more new workers than any other British industry. Edith told Leonard that she had not written to him more often because: 'We have been so busy at work, working until eight o'clock every night that I was too tired when I got home'.[436] Things would not improve, for on Christmas Day 1917 she told Leonard, 'As you guess I was working until nearly 11 p.m. last night, it being Christmas Eve, but we have next Thursday [December 27th] holiday all day'. [437]

Her normal working week included Saturdays and even when she was due to sing in Bradford's Channing Hall, she had to take time off work to go there.[438] It was just over a week later, on Wednesday November 15th, that Edith wrote to Leonard again:

'Dear Leonard,

Thanks for letter received this morning. As it is Wednesday and a half day holiday for me, I am writing back straight away, otherwise you might not get an answer for weeks and weeks. I am like you not particularly fond of letter writing. I had quite a large post this morning, as it is my birthday today. I wish you many happy returns of your birthday. Jessie said it was your birthday when she wrote.

Better late than never. You must come on Saturday as arranged, I will see Dad is at the station to meet you.'

It is a beautifully naïve letter which Edith ends by saying: 'Please do not call me *Miss Graham* it is just *Edith* (plain English) to all my friends. I hope you will forgive me for not calling you *Mr* but really I cannot'.[439]

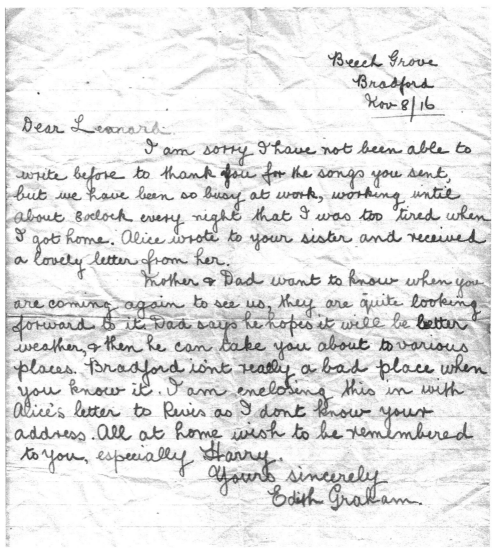

Edith Graham writes to Leonard 8th November 1916.
(Original 180x250mm)

The other objectors are invariably referred to as 'Mr'; only Leonard was on first name terms. She found him shy, which is surprising.[440] That seventeen year old Edith was rather taken by Leonard seems clear and not only because of their shared musicianship. How far her attitude to him was coloured by their common religious beliefs and how far by personal attraction, nor how far Leonard reciprocated, are not so clear. More than a year later, in January of 1918, we find Edith repeating her admonition, added as a P.S. to a letter to Leonard, 'Please will you do me a favour and not call me Miss Graham, we are all *C.O.s.*'[441] Perhaps it was a necessary distancing on Leonard's part? That the relationship between Leonard and the Graham sisters was not straightforward becomes increasingly clear, though the nature of the difficulty remains elusive. On January 22nd 1917 Jessie had to admonish her brother:

> 'I had a letter from Alice Graham and she said she does not hear from you (bad boy). You just write… I should go to Bradford if I were you.'[442]

Because we have none of Leonard's own letters from this time, it is impossible to be certain, but the clear inference is that he had raised with his sister whether he should visit the Grahams or not. Edith wrote to Leonard on Thursday January 25th, a short note complaining that Leonard had not written and the Grahams wanted to know if he and Roland were going to visit them on the coming Saturday. A reply by return of post was, understandably, requested.[443] In the event, Leonard did go to Bradford for that weekend[444], though one is left wondering why it had been the subject of such soul-searching. We get further hints that relations were not quite as they might have been three weeks later when Edith Graham wrote a very brief – even curt – note to Leonard. Evidently Leonard had written to her sister Alice, but, 'Alice hasn't had time to answer your letter. She is working at a new place, and hasn't time for letter writing now'.[445]

'Hasn't time for letter writing'. Not 'Hasn't time to write to you just now but will do as soon as she gets the chance' and there is no apology. Surely even a brief, hastily scribbled note from Alice explaining her situation would have served, but instead it was her cross sounding older sister who wrote to Leonard. Later in the same short letter (and occupying half of it), we perhaps are given a clue as to the cause of the Graham girls' ire. Edith wrote, 'By the way didn't I see you in Bradford on the Sunday after you had been to our house [i.e. 4th February 1917]. I was in the Bradford Moor barrier waiting for a car and couldn't get out, or I should have run across. I did whistle but you didn't look round'.[446] If it really was Leonard she saw and her behaviour would suggest she was certain it was, one can understand why she might feel offended that he had been in Bradford without telling her, especially when in the same letter she told Leonard that her father had just incurred expense on his behalf, sending a package to Lutterworth by post. All kinds of innocent explanations occur and we do not have Leonard's reply, if indeed he made one, but the suspicion of avoidance remains.

After this there is a long silence. In November 1917 – by which time Leonard and Roland had been away from Yorkshire for the best part of a year – Alice Graham sent Jessie a birthday present[447], and on Christmas Day 1917 Edith wrote to Leonard in very friendly terms, her letter suggesting that there may have been contact during the year and suggesting that, 'One of these days you will be seeing Alice and I down there touring round. We have to go to Scotland, Ireland, and Wales after the war to see different C.O.s. Really it will take us all our lives to visit everybody'.[448] Evidently Leonard replied and for a time their correspondence was renewed, though Leonard still showed an uncharacteristic reserve, and Edith had again to admonish him for calling her 'Miss Graham' rather than 'Edith'.[449] There is one further letter from Edith, written on the last day of February 1918, and then nothing more.

★

Meanwhile, back at Wakefield, relationships were growing complicated, possibly connected to Leonard's deep interest in matters of gender. If he needed a warning of the dangers of more serious relationships it was provided by his friend Joe Todd, the farmer's son from Penrith who was 'no good' at kissing. The story of Joe's love life is tortuous indeed, but it is the supposed connection to Leonard which catches the eye.

Long before his arrival at the Wakefield Centre, Joe had been in a serious relationship with a girl called Annie Dawson: whether they were engaged or not is unclear, but at one point Joe Todd did talk of himself as 'married'[450], and engagement amounted to much the same thing by the conventions of the time. Their relationship, though, was doomed to founder. Ron Long, in a letter to Leonard in September of 1917, explained the breakdown of the relationship between Annie and Joe Todd. The two lovers had entered into a pact:

'A mutual agreement was made that nothing definite should be done and said for three years and those three years elapsed (I believe) at about Xmas [1916] or March last [1917]. At the end of this time (circumstances having separated them for a while) they met again and she found out that he had not the regard for her that formerly overcame his heart or that he *thought* he had.

What did he do. He worried a great deal and finally nearly six months later broke the news to his girl and I might say almost if not quite broke her heart.'[451]

The Todd family, and possibly the Dawson family too, had assumed that their relationship would turn into something more permanent, and in August Joe was lamenting that:

'I have got into hot water over it from all over. It was a case last week of dreading every post that came, and the trouble was there were nearly always two or three letters came. My people are very much cut up about it, as they thought a tremendous lot of Annie. I don't know what her people think. I haven't heard much.'[452]

There was even talk at one point that Leonard's father with Thomas Harper might visit Annie, though why they – of all people – should have wanted to intervene and to what purpose is unclear, but Joe scotched the thought straight away:

'Mr Harper and John Payne may be visiting... As to him calling on Miss A.D. well ___ ___ ___ *[sic]*. That's all I can say on the matter.'

As one might expect, the break up was traumatic on both sides and Joe himself told Leonard that:

'I really couldn't see my way to do anything else to be honest with the girl. I didn't care for her as I should. I used to do so once, but I don't now. The trouble is that she cares... It has cost me something to do it, as I knew what it would cost her, and also I knew what a really fine girl she is... It's a rotten thing for me to do, but I cannot help it. I have to write here *[sic – her]* tonight, as she wants to know again ~~that~~ if it's really true, so you can imagine what a job I've got.'[453]

The change of 'that' to 'if' speaks volumes for the agony it cost both of them. When Ron made the point to Leonard, he laid it on with a trowel:

'Poor Annie, I have seen some of her letters to Joe, Leon and to try and express the love, unselfish, thoughtful only of him, and yet the terrible pain of heart she felt, is beyond my powers of imagination. A love forgiving every fault, putting the blame only on its own shoulders, yet wondering why, painful, crushed, yet looking every post for some note, card, or letter to ease its dullness and to fulfil and satisfy that spark of hope that love clings too *[sic]*... Poor girl, she may be ruined for life, her faith in man maybe broken… Strange is't *[sic]* it Leon, these things occur every day I suppose and no one notices. You never know what an aching heart is behind a smiling face. I have often noticed a drop of the lips when people have smiled and wondered what was wrong.'[454]

Joe Todd did not walk away scot-free: the trauma turned his hair white.[455]

Joe Todd's heartfelt letter to Len and Bill
29 August 1917
(Original 200x240mm)

Yet the relationship between Joe Todd and Annie Dawson, and its collapse, raises some intriguing points about these young people and their lives during the First World War. In trying to explain things to Leonard, Ron Long said this:

'AD [Annie Dawson] as you know being a religious, high minded young lady, has very strict and what may seem rather strange views of what should and what shouldn't be, in the relationship of the sexes and their friendships, and I need scarcely add she does not believe in platonic friendship. Previous to meeting with the inevitable other party (J.[Joe Todd]) she had nothing to do with boys and had firmly resolved only one or none. In proper novel style the *right one* came along and that one firmly believed he had love for her, but she knowing his extreme liking for ladies' company rather suspected him.'

There follows an intense, but rather long and rambling analysis, full of underlinings (sometimes four deep) of his friend's relationship and the causes of its ending. Perhaps inevitably, the letter ends with a brief homily:

'Yet Leon there was something far deeper than human love for human: her love for God. It was marvellous, wonderful, glorious, and beautiful in its expression. A kind of asking God, why?! Yet trust and faith. The faith that wrote that famous hymn "Oh, Love that would not let me go".'[456]

What makes the affair of interest for us is the suggestion that Leonard was in some way responsible for the break up of Joe's engagement to Annie Dawson. When Joe Todd ruefully wrote to the two brothers after the break up, he said that, 'Strange to say she is inclined to blame you, Len, for it to a certain extent, as she thinks that you didn't think much of her for being such a quiet girl, and therefore not your sort. I have assured her she has nothing to blame you for...'[457] It is carefully denied, but the suspicion lingers and Ron's protestation a couple of weeks later that 'I know there is nothing cross or angry between you...'[458] makes one think that there might have been, or perhaps there ought to have been. So what might Leonard have done to attract such a suspicion? Whether Annie was Leonard's 'sort' or not, as Joe Todd suggested, is irrelevant, unless Leonard had in some way turned Joe against her. But why would he have done that? Ron Long hinted that Leonard had 'encroached upon' Joe's feelings, though, 'I think it next to impossible that your friendship had interfered with the game of progressive love as played by AD & JT'.[459]

At first sight the phrase, 'the game of progressive love', leaps from the page, its meaning and significance unclear. Does it mean 'progressive' as in 'modern' or 'forward looking' and can we place it alongside Ron's remark that Annie 'does not believe in platonic friendship'[460] to build the image of a relationship based on unrestrained sexuality, perhaps along lines which their contemporary D.H. Lawrence might have recognised? Or is the relationship more respectable and conventional than all that: did 'progressive' simply mean a love which was meant to *progress* or *develop* in stately manner from one chaste stage to another until the climax of the wedding night? For evangelical Christians like Joe and Annie, the latter seems more likely than the former: more Marty Robbins[461] than Harold Robbins.

Perhaps, viewed in that light, we can understand that Leonard might well have made tactless remarks to Joe about his rather prim and proper girlfriend, in contrast presumably to the girls Leonard was consorting with in Wakefield, and in light of what Ron described as Joe Todd's, 'extreme liking for ladies' company'.[462] Ron Long agreed with Leonard's apparent assertion that they had said nothing that could be misconstrued as offensive towards Annie: '...the only *[time]* you remember discussing AD was with me and I am sure our remarks were very complimentary'.[463] ...But there are hints that, whatever might or might not have been said between Leonard and Ron Long, remarks were directed towards Joe Todd as well, for it is certain that the topic of his relationship with Annie did enter their conversation. When writing to Leonard and Roland in August telling of his break up with Annie, Joe said, 'Perhaps Len won't [be surprised] though, as I believe I dropped a hint or two' ...and in the same letter comes the disturbing remark that, 'I suppose Len will crow a bit now'.[464]

It is difficult to see what he could have meant unless Leonard had in some way anticipated or predicted that their relationship would founder – or had even helped make it founder. We can suppose that, though Leonard had no desire to break up Joe Todd's relationship with Annie Dawson – a relationship apparently on the verge of deep and lifelong commitment, probably even engagement, seeds of doubt may have been sown in both their minds: in his about the desirability of a marriage with such a strait-laced woman, and in hers about how far she could trust her boyfriend's fidelity in the company of people like Leonard Payne. If in his mind there were already doubts, this could only have accentuated them and hastened the breakdown of their relationship. It is also quite possible that there was here an element of resentment by proxy if Leonard saw Joe Todd's commitment to Annie as standing in the way of his own friendship with Joe – and Joe's position as part of the 'inner circle' of friends at Wakefield – and of Joe's enjoyment of life in Wakefield in the way Leonard was enjoying it. Perhaps that was what Joe Todd meant when he told Leonard and Roland that, 'Incidently *[sic]* as the only married man in the six has now turned bachelor again, I suppose the group will be perfect'.[465]

2 the sexes & their friendships, & I need scarcely add she does not believe in "Platonic friendship. Previous to meeting with the inevitable "other party" (If she had nothing to do with boys & had firmly resolved only1 or none, In proper novel style the right one came along. & that one firmly believed he had. love for her, but she knowing his extreme liking for ladies company, rather suspected him. However a mutual agreement was made that nothing definite should be done & said for 3 years & those 3 years elapsed (I believe) at about Xmas or March last. At the end of this time (circumstances having separated them for a while) they met again & He. found out that he had not the regard for her that formerly overcame his heart or that he thought he had.

What did he do. He worried a great deal & finally nearly 6 months later broke the news to his girl & I might say almost if not quite broke her heart.

This is it. He loved the girl & later found out he did not so broke everything up. I had an extreme sense of unworthiness of her (& well he might for she is splendid. Now I argue this way. She rather mistrusted him all along. He knew & mistrusted himself & partially lost his self respect, & consequently calling himself unworthy his feeling of love might have turned to admiration & reverence. Then again Leon a person whom you know trusts you in a vital question gains your respect. (not reverence) but an equal kind of feeling, & sometimes your love, For I cannot imagine liking anyone who mistrusted me, & I believe (sub-consciously not consciously felt rather like a man after his first sentence — otherwise damned once, perhaps for all —. & he realized it but not in his conscious self until very much later. Now that is only one theory Leon

He says so

Think this over Leon it is true.

Ron Long's analysis of his friend's relationships in a letter to Leonard dated 13th September 1917
(Original 200x240mm)

★

Roland's experience of the opposite sex in Wakefield was very different from Leonard's, for Roland found a wife there – though not at once. Her name was Edith Marsh. Clearly not one of the girls about town, Edith Marsh was from a staunchly Quaker family living in Garden City just outside Wakefield, off the Dewsbury Road, and it was through her support work with the conscientious objectors in the Wakefield Centre that she met the Payne brothers. By the spring of 1917 the families were in contact with each other on a more or less formal basis[466], the Paynes visiting the Marshes on a trip to the North in June. Edith's mother even offered to take in the brothers' washing.[467] Though the genesis of their connection was a formal one through the Quakers' network, there was from the outset a personal element as well. But it was Leonard who first attracted her, not Roland, and the two developed a relationship the nature of which remains unknown.[468] What is clear is that, whatever Edith's feelings for Leonard may have been, they were not reciprocated or not sustained.

Edith Marsh's relationship with Roland grew more slowly and it was only when she realised that Leonard was not available to her as a marriage partner that she switched her attention to Roland, though perhaps, love working in mysterious ways, she came to see in Roland's personality things which Leonard lacked and which attracted her more. For all that, the romance was slow burning and it was not until 1926 that they eventually married.[469] In 1928 they would move into their new home built on the family's land by the Rugby Road in Lutterworth.

HORBURY AND BEYOND

The Home Office Scheme was, meanwhile, running into difficulties, expected to cope with larger numbers than were anticipated, with only the Work Centres at Wakefield and Warwick and a handful of outside placements for conscientious objectors on their release from prison.

The managers of the scheme, the Brace Committee, were caught in an invidious position. On the one hand, they were in charge of a scheme which was supposed to meet the requirements of the conscientious objectors, providing them with 'work of national importance' which they could do as an alternative to military service, a system which had to be seen by the objectors as decidedly *not* punitive. Most of the religious objectors, like the Paynes, had few difficulties with this, even though, in truth, some of the tasks they were given could only marginally be regarded as being of importance to the nation and they accepted that they would be kept away from their homes for the duration. But the political objectors, who formed the great majority of recognised objectors, had more diverse views, ranging for co-operation with the scheme to an apparent determination to smash the system altogether. At the same time the Brace Committee was trying to cope with these problems, it had to recognise that public opinion lay much closer to Lloyd George (Prime Minister in December 1916) and his Home Secretary George Cave, in demanding a tougher line with the 'conchies', especially those 'politicals', and a more punitive approach altogether.[470]

Dartmoor Prison, renamed 'The Princetown Work Centre', was emptied of the last of its convicted criminal population and turned over to the Home Office Scheme. The choice was tactless in the extreme for, as John Rae explained, 'the process of "deprisoning", however well meant, could not remove the flavour of the penal institution, particularly when the only work available was quarrying, reclaiming land for the Prison Commissioners and the Duchy of Cornwall, and "ordinary prison industries"… [with] the inescapably overtones of punishment'.[471] With the dread name 'Dartmoor' and its profoundly inhospitable location, it could not be other, but much the same might be said of those other converted prisons, including of course Wakefield. So when the summer of 1917 saw the first hints of

271

an easing of the system, it was driven by force of circumstance, not by a change of policy or heart. Thus the out-working scheme was introduced to ease the crowding in the Work Centres and to drive a further wedge between the co-operating and the non-co-operating objectors, by treating the former with greater leniency in reward for their co-operation and further isolating the latter. It was not very different from the wedge which had successfully hived off the absolutists from those who had accepted the Home Office Scheme and gone into the Work Centres.

In January 1917 a printed letter from War Office Contracts Department was sent to the Payne brothers notifying them that it might be possible for them to work outside the Work Centre for a private employer, if their skills were needed there[472], and in February Marion Harper, too, as well informed as ever, had got wind that changes were on their way, 'They seem to keep getting fellows away from the Centre'[473].

Given the slow pace of things we should not be surprised that it was not until March of 1917 that Leonard, Roland and twenty or so other conscientious objectors were put onto new work, outside the Work Centre, at Horbury, two or three few miles from Wakefield, in a gravel quarry.[474] This carries with it the implication that the Paynes were judged good and reliable workers, men compliant with the demands of the scheme. No doubt the extra freedom, working outdoors in the spring air, was welcome and it seems that they settled well into their new work environment, though it did involve a tram ride out to Horbury and back each day, for which they paid the full fare after that spat at the beginning of the year over tram fares.[475] Though the nature of their work there remains frustratingly obscure, it was

A group of the Horbury conscientious objectors. Roland Payne is on the back row, fourth from the right. (Photograph courtesy of John Payne, Roland's grandson.)

clear that the work there would only be temporary and Jessie hoped that any new outside work might bring them closer to home even though the rules of the Home Office Scheme were clear: no one should be less than fifty miles from their home.[476]

As the Horbury work drew towards its close, another move was on the cards for the Paynes, one which would be brought about by the new agent set to run the Work Centre, Edwin Gilbert. Gilbert arrived to take over the centre in the spring of 1917, at a time when the Home Office Scheme was refined so only the hard core of absolutist objectors – those who refused to accept 'work of national importance' *and* refused to accept the pardons that were on offer on the grounds that they had done nothing to be pardoned for – were still in prison, alongside, illogically and paradoxically, those who were new cases referred by the Tribunals.[477] These tended to be those whose objection was political: religious objectors of whatever stripe were by now being passed more or less automatically into the Work Centres, adding to the increasing pressure. This does not, however, fully explain the departure of the Payne brothers from the Wakefield Centre in the summer of 1917. The Paynes' attitude towards Edwin Gilbert is unclear. In May 1917, not long after he had arrived to take over the Wakefield Centre, Marion Harper replied to a letter from Leonard by saying that: 'I am glad you have got such a fine impression of Edwin Gilbert, it makes life so much more worthwhile living with such men… [with] his great sense of justice'.[478]

In interviews over half a century later, however, Leonard told Peter Liddle that 'Gilbert the agent wasn't very popular at Wakefield… He was an old man. He was a Quaker and would have sympathies with conscientious objectors but he was a man who wanted to keep to the letter of the law. He was very strict.' He then told the story of how Gilbert had alienated many of the conscientious objectors in his previous Work Centre, at Warwick, over the issue of home visits at Christmas 1916 – when Leonard and Roland had managed the journey only by surreptitiously taking seats on the train home. At Warwick, Leonard said, 'he questioned each one individually if they had used the trains and the fellows that were really honest and said they had, he sent them back to prison and he got a bad name for that. He could have overlooked it because it was nothing really.'[479] Perhaps more perceptively, William Marwick thought that, 'I would quite expect Gilbert to make himself very agreeable in private life: he had that look about him, and always seemed a bit uncomfortable in his place as agent'.[480] What perhaps counted for more was that John Payne was already acquainted with Edwin Gilbert. He told his sons that, 'I know Mr E Gilbert who is to be over you when he was in Leicester he took a big part in adult school work I expect he does now.'[481]

At first there were the inevitable delays and confusions, the date of their departure and their destination unknown. Several places were mooted through the spring and into the early summer of 1917 and all was confusion, confusion caused by the Brace Committee's difficulty in finding companies – and their workers – willing to take them on. In June Jessie was worried that her brothers might be pushed into working for the military, as she wrote to Leonard, 'I hope you do not get on a list for that war work, because you do not want to go back to prison, anything is better than that, I expect you would have to go back if you refused to go where they wanted you to… It will be nice to go to Wales, I hope you can get there, it is not so far away'.[482]

On the 3rd of July Jessie wrote, 'I should not be in a hurry to be moved, until you can see a nice place. We thought about you coming home for a night, if you go down south…'[483]

…While on the same day Marion was writing:

'I remember you said you would finish at Horbury early this week so I wonder whether you will receive this, in case you have departed from the beloved Work Centre! I am sorry the chance of getting to Ingleton seems cut off, however perhaps something better will turn up.'[484]

But nothing happened and a fortnight later Jessie was writing to Leonard, 'I am glad you are going to stay at Wakefield a bit longer, you may get to a worse place, so stay as long as you can'.[485] …While a week later Marion wrote, 'I wonder if you will work in the new quarry if it is opened. It will be rather strange if you go to Brecon'.[486]

★

A week later they were in Birmingham and would never return to the Wakefield Work Centre. On July 25th Father wrote to Roland, overjoyed that his sons would be moving closer to home:

'We received your letter this morning quite safe and was so glad to hear we was going to see you both so soon, how good of Mr Gilbert. I would like you both to thank him and all Wakefield friends for all their kindness to you both.'[487]

…Again with that implication that Gilbert had pulled some strings on their behalf, however unlikely that seems given his supposed martinet track record. At the end of July 1917 a letter to Leonard and Roland from William Marwick was addressed to:

'c/o Mrs Raynor, 121 Mary Vale R., Bournville.'[488]

The letter was initially posted in Wales to Lutterworth (suggesting William knew they had moved but did not know where to), but then, on request, forwarded to the Birmingham address. Their move had been made.

We know very little about their time in Birmingham (chiefly of course because we have none of their own letters from that time), but in his written statement made in 1973 Leonard remembered his time there with relative fondness. 'My brother and I were offered work in a chemical works near Birmingham, and as it was much nearer our home we accepted. Chalk was produced for the base of toothpaste, metal polish, etc. It was very hard work and long hours, but we were more free than the Wakefield Centre. All we lacked was money, we were paid 4/8 per week by the Home Office. They also paid our board and lodgings. We were quite near to Bournville Chocolate Factory and as you may know the owners were Quakers, and much in sympathy with our cause, so we had many friends at this time.'[489] Later in the year Marion Harper reinforced the point: 'It is good you are having so many invitations from friends in B'ham, you'll know a fearful squash of folks'.[490] Late in November 1917 they must have been cheered when two other of the Wakefield objectors, one called Bale and the other their old friend, the lovelorn Joe Todd, came to work with them.[491]

★

Gradually they were able to establish links with the local community, for in October William was talking of the possibility of teaching in the local Sunday school: 'I shall be interested to hear how your S.S. teaching project comes off. There is some suggestion that some of us help in that way in the independent church here'.[492] At the same time, in Bournville Leonard and Roland were doing much the same thing, working there with the children of Quakers, for their father wrote early in November: 'We are thinking about you tonight at your class I could just see you with them boys and Leonard hope you both will do your best'.[493] A few days later Marion was asking: 'How did the first venture at the model S.S. go off? There is one thing about it, it struck me they were very model children as well as having all the conveniences'.[494] Of course sport was a good ice breaker, as a note from one G. Herick testifies: 'If possible will you and your brother turn up to play for 'Fircroft' on Saturday. It has been arranged to kick off at *2.30* so will you meet us at the Loft at 2.15. If unable to play please write me'.[495]

★

2

his music. I do not know what it is for yet, but I think it is something to do with the soldiers.

On Sunday afternoon we are having our prizes, Mr Massey is giving the address, and Mr Bishop as superintendent is making the presentation, we have got forty nine books, and mine is called The Heiress of Wylmington by Evelyn Everett Green. I have made the highest marks in the school one hundred and two. We are going to have prizes for good conduct, Mother says I shall come last now I am in Mrs Massey's class. I shall keep my book nice so you can read it. Mother has got twelve new scripture pictures for the Infants.

(Tom) Emily has got a little son. The fowls do not lay any eggs I shall have to run then round. I hope you received the mufflers safely.

On Wednesday Feb 7th there is to be a Co-op concert, Jessie and I might go, a costume party called The Jays have been engaged.

Dora writes a news filled letter to her big brother Leonard, 30th January 1917. She was apparently under no illusions about the position her brothers' stand had placed her in with the congregational minister Arthur Massey, but life went on…
(Original 200x250mm)

Being as close to home as Birmingham offered the possibility of more frequent home visits, which they exploited to the limit. An indication of how lightly they were supervised came in August when they went home for Dora's birthday – they had missed her last birthday whilst in prison in Newcastle – without seeking official permission, a fact which the Agent Edwin Gilbert chose to ignore.[496]

As the year went along, the brothers' freedom of movement grew and Christmas 1917 was, like Christmas 1916, spent at home. Not all the Home Office Scheme conscientious objectors were so lucky: Alice and Edith Graham's older brother Frank was on Dartmoor and couldn't get home, although his wife was able to spend time in Devon, at her own expense, of course.[497] Eddie Beaton in mid-Wales had had to spend Christmas away from his home. He was curious as to how Leonard and Roland were welcomed in their home town: 'How do Lutterworth people take your so frequent home going? I hope reconciliation has been the order of the day and that you are good friends with all'.[498]

We do not, of course, have the brothers' reply, but it is clear that all was not well with the family at home in Lutterworth. They kept up a cheerful face when talking to their sons and even made the journey up to Yorkshire to visit them while they were in Wakefield[499], but their troubles could not help but spill over into words. Reconciliation with the Congregational Chapel was never likely while Arthur Massey was there. While we are suspicious of Leonard's later statement that 'the Minister of the Congregationalist church told us to clear out of the place, he wouldn't have such people in the place', it is clear that that was indeed how Leonard understood the situation, even if that was not literally what was said.

Meanwhile, Massey remained absolutely fixed in his hostility to the brothers' conscientious objection. The minister's relations with the rest of the family, who continued their attendance at chapel, were inevitably uneasy. Little Dora had written to Leonard early in the year telling him, in excited terms, about the musical concert she was in rehearsal for:

'We are having a concert children from all denominations are taking part, Sunday schools, day schools, Roman Catholics, Scouts, and the Cadet corp. Miss Darlington is the head of it. I am singing in some glees called ("The Bell Ringer") and ("Land to the Leeward Ho") *[sic]* Mr Haswell is training us, he is so strict, he makes us open our mouths about two inches. If you were here you would be able to play for me as Mr Haswell lets me have his music. I do not know what it is for yet, but I think it is something to do with the soldiers.'

Yet even here in this joyously childish letter there sounded a sad note:

'On Sunday afternoon we are having our [Sunday school] prizes, Mr Massey is giving the address, and Mr Bishop as superintendent… We are going to have prizes for good conduct, Mother says I shall come last now I am in Mr Massey's class.'[500]

We do not know whether this dire forecast proved correct.

More important, except perhaps to Dora, were the family's financial difficulties. It was not that no business was coming in: there were plenty of orders, but with his two sons away and his temporary workers unreliable, John could not take on the contracts which would have secured the family's position.[501] If John was struggling, so too was Lutterworth in that summer of 1917 due to the financial crisis which threatened the town's most important employer, George Spencer's Vedonis hosiery works. In July Jessie told Leonard that:

'I am still very short of work, I only work about three days a week, this last three weeks I have only drawn 10/-. I think *Spencer* is about done up, there is a report about that the place has been advertised for sale, but I do not know how true it is and some say he is closing down. I am about fed up with it, I shall have to leave if it does not alter.'[502]

She told Roland that:

'I have not got any more work, Mr Spencer has told a lot of the girls to get a fresh place, they have only got to work there another week, so I expect I shall be the next. What do you think of my wages this week 1/9, not so bad. I go down to the shop and do cane chairs when we have any in. I can do them very well now. I am thinking of going on dress baskets, do you think I could manage it.'[503]

Dora, meanwhile, who was already adept at simple basket weaving[504], had started work for Johnson's Grocer's shop, weighing out the goods and keeping the shelves full, as well as serving the customers. For this she was able to bring six shillings and six pence per week of much needed new money into the family.[505] In June she was given a raise in pay to 7/6 per week, a creditable rate for a girl of her age.[506]

In March of 1917 Mother, her anxiety for the family's plight all too evident, was tempted by the possibility of taking over Lutterworth's Telephone Exchange:

'We have got the offer of the Telephone Exchange. Mr Phillips giving it up what do you say about it shall we put in for it it will bring us in about £20 per year. But of course we should not be able to leave the house at all someone would always have to stay in, 8/6 a week it would be a nice little income, we should have to take it in turns staying in. Let us know as soon as you can, what you think about it, there will not be much work but it will be a big tie, you only have to put them on the trunk when they ring up.'[507]

John had his doubts:

'Poor Mother has put in for the Exchange but I am afraid it will be a big tie for her it is open all the week nights as well you are liable to a call any hour through the night but this does not often occur.'[508]

We hear nothing more of the Telephone Exchange proposition, so presumably second thoughts prevailed, or perhaps, for reasons unknown, someone else was chosen in preference to the Paynes. The Paynes even thought of displaying an advertising board on their land to raise a little extra cash.[509] All the signs are there of a family struggling financially.

In addition to the family's money troubles there was the failing mental condition of Joseph Handford, the brothers' maternal grandfather, during 1917. In February their mother told them that, 'Granddad is just about the same. His mind is not a bit better but he looks well. He is always worrying about his garden of course everybody is taking his things. He is going to the police station we have to tell him all sorts of rubbish to passify [sic] him'.[510] A month or so later, in April, she signed off a letter to Leonard with, 'Here is poor Old Granddad coming in. He wants Dad to do something to his garden and how is it possible he cannot do much at his own. I must stop now he is asking all manner of questions'.[511]

Lutterworth's woes were increased when a virulent strand of scarlet fever spread across the town from contaminated milk from Arthur Lee's Woodbrig Farm just outside town on the Coventry Road. As the disease flared up in February and March of 1917, the Deputy Medical Officer reported fifty-eight cases in Lutterworth, with an average age of twelve years; the isolation hospitals were full and one person already had died. The County Council blamed the Rural District Council for the debacle and the Rural District Council blamed the County Council; the Medical Officer of Health was absent on war work at the crucial time and farmer Lee just wanted to sell his milk again.[512] It was as if God himself had turned his back on this small town of shopkeepers.

★

It is unfortunate that we know so little about the brothers' time in Birmingham, but their friends kept in touch by post and through their correspondence we can gain insights into the lives of those other conscientious objectors. For Joe Todd and Ronald Long there was at first no change: they remained in the Wakefield Work Centre (though Joe would join the Paynes in Birmingham later in the year). The departure of their friends hit them hard; Joe wrote to them from the Work Centre in July 1917:

> 'It's rotten here without you, Ron and I are feeling very lonely… Don't start telling anyone off for a week or two yet…
>
> Best love to both of you from Ron and I.
>
> Yours affectionately,
>
> *Joe*
>
> X X X X'[513]

The summer of 1917 was a time of growing discontent among the men on the Home Office Scheme. At Wakefield the trouble for a time focused around the election of the objectors' representatives. Under the Code of Rules for the scheme the men were allowed to 'elect representatives for such purposes relating to their communal life as may to them seem proper'.[514] How seriously they took these elections is unclear, but Joe Todd's letter to Leonard written on August 29th 1917 leaves the impression they got the representatives they deserved:

> 'I've no doubt Ron will have told you about the elections. The results were declared this afternoon. *Stott* 116. Crammer 111. Runacres 98. The rottenest thing that has happened in the history of Wakefield Centre. It has been done more in the way of a joke than anything else, but I'm afraid it will be an expensive joke, as Stott won't do I'm afraid. The committee seems to be a pretty good one though. There is a danger they will all resign. I don't think we have seen the finish of this election, long though it has been on. We had rather a good joke from the hospital last night. We decided that for a bit of fun we would carry a man across to the polling booth on a stretcher. It had all to be done in Watson's office, and as a man voted he was struck off the list. Anyhow, Craven, Botham, Bullard and I got the stretchers and put a man (Lawrence) (dressed in his pyjamas) on it, also a placard 'Vote for Crammer or Runacres'. Why we put both it so happened two (Craven & I) were Runacrites and the other two Crammerites. It made quite a sensation marching up the centre with the chap.'[515]

It is not a joke which carries well across time. Exactly what was the problem with Stott is not explained, but the juvenile atmosphere is clear enough to see, especially when in the same letter Joe told how:

'…The agent had a prowl round the landings at 11.30 last night, and they made a bit of an ass of him – making noises as soon as his back was turned. So he has stopped all priveleges [*sic*] from Sept 3rd to 15th. As to whether it applies to hospital or not we are not yet sure, but I hope it won't, and if not I'll try and get a permit for your dad as well as Mr Harper.'

Making 'a bit of an ass' of the agent: a bit of harmless horseplay or making a mockery of the Home Office Scheme and all it stood for? The agent clearly saw this as the latter and the hard line conscientious objectors would have seen it in the same way.

We have one other glimpse into the politics of the Wakefield Work Centre in an undated fragment of a letter about a conflict between the inmates and the agent. The agent, it seems, had decided to call the inmates' bluff. Ronald was the writer, and the fragment reads:

'…informed us that if the list [?] was refused and the house [?] maintained its attitude he would [be] obliged to hand in his resignation and had in fact already written the telegram out. After discussion Green of the Cook-house and a man named Wilson advanced superheated argument *against* the agent being allowed to have the list. A lot of rash talk and bitterness ended with no bottom. The most sensible arguments were advanced by Stott, Wardropper, [*sic.*] Boxall, Benson & Whichels, all of them in favour of meeting the agent in a fair square and trustful manner and as the agent asked placing all cards on the table. Thanks to their speeches, reason, sense and good feeling prevailed and eighty per cent of men voted in favour of the agent. So good.'[516]

At least Stott came out of this tale rather better.

★

Joe Todd and Ronald Long seem not to have engaged with the war fought by the hard line conscientious objectors against the agent and the system he represented; instead, they made the best of it and at the end of August Joe was writing enthusiastically to Leonard and Roland and painting a very comfortable picture of their life there:

'I am flitting from my cell M1/7 to and [sic] officers room on N3 – the old women's prison. It is on the top landing, which is a slight disadvantage in some things, but it has two big windows and a fireplace, is well ventilated, has two cupboards and plenty of books, and there is a fine view out of the windows. It is a very cosy room too. I have got a decent table – (about 5ft x 3ft) and table-cloth, also a fire lit and its almost (?) like home. At any rate it is as near like home as anything can be here.

Abe Pearce, Ron and I had a good supper up here last night. They got hold of some onions, and I fried them, and we had coffee, onions, lettuce, radishes and bread and margo. It wasn't bad at all. Ron and I still sleep up here, and in case I should sleep in in a morning, I have fitted up one of the landing bells so that they can ring it from the bottom to wake me up. So far I have been all right, as Ron is a very good riser in a morning and can do all the 'waking' business necessary…

I only wish I had you two up in my snuggery on N3. It's a perfect treat. I've got my pictures on the walls and with the fire, a good light and a nice hearthrug its A1. Abe Pearce is up here doing a bit of swotting as its very cold in the cells. It only wants you two to make the thing all right and of course if Brecon chaps were here too, all the better.'[517]

The 'Brecon chaps' were William Marwick and Eddie Beaton.

Eddie had been the first to be sent to Talgarth in mid-Wales, which was surely the most beautiful place where any conscientious objectors could be sent in the First World War. He and his companions were housed in the unfinished sanatorium hospital there and his first impressions were close to ecstatic:

'The 'San' Lodge Box,
    Talgarth,
    Nr Brecon,
    Wales.
    Dear Len and Bill,
We arrived here at ten o'clock last evening just after the golden sun had sunk. The Black Mountains are only about ten miles away and the Brecon Beacons about five. Words cannot describe the beauty of this country – it is really lovely. There are no huts and we are living in a sanatorium, a spotlessly clean set of little villas. We sleep on prison bed-boards, mattress, pillow, three blankets but no sheets.

Things are very primitive, the water supply is not yet kept on so we have to draw the water from the well.

The present job is excavating the water mains to be laid; we started at 1.30 today and the work is no harder than Horbury. I am told that only one more draft is coming from Wakefield and that the camp of eighty men will be completed on Wednesday of next week, so I am hoping to see you both down here soon along with William, Ronnie and Joe. Of course we are a bit isolated but it is a lovely spot.

Some of the rooms hold two beds and others as many as eight. Each room is filled with electric light but the globes and dynamos have not yet arrived.

Lovely French windows are to each room and I think things will run very smoothly and well.

The job of excavation will last for a few weeks and as all the men will be here tomorrow week (as already mentioned) I am unable to say what the next job will be. The natives seem quite sympathetic, many were at the station to meet us in and bade us 'Good evening' in quite a friendly manner.

The hours of work are from 7 a.m. until 6 p.m. with an hour's break at noon for lunch. We have dinner at the close of the day's work. We have had a general meeting tonight and elected John Young and Tom Williamson as temporary chairman and secretary. The agent resembles a prosperous publican but seems a fairly reasonable man. He says we will get the best of food but we are endeavouring to do all the catering ourselves. Accept my fondest love yourselves and give same to William, Ronnie and Joe. I will write to them in turn, and do hope you will come down here with me.

Your ever true friend,

Eddie.' [518]

William Marwick, the Scot, was moved to Talgarth a couple of weeks later and on July 29th sent a postcard to the Paynes' Lutterworth address, which was forwarded to them in Bourneville:

'Arrived safe in Friday night, to the effusive joy of E.J.B. *[Eddie Beaton]* This is a case of roughing it – the place is a holiday and health resort. I shall be glad if it serves the purpose for me – I don't want it for the duration. A larger contingent of rebels – of whom Bob Wright is one!! Wonderful what the agent has under his hat – physically; like Gilbert swollen double, temper ditto. Bark seems to be much worse than his bite. Delighted to hear plenty Scots accents. Four out of five in my room Scotsmen. This is only a few preliminary remarks, until the Correspondence Circle gets in order. Best wishes from Eddie and myself.

Yours truly,

W.H Marwick.' '[519]

Though in mid-July Eddie Beaton had expected the Paynes' arrival in Wales at any time – and it seems they thought so too – it was not to be. The authorities were content to leave them making toothpaste in Birmingham.

Remote as Talgarth may have been the young men made themselves at home there and in October William was telling the Paynes:

The "San" Lodge Box
Talgarth
Nr. Breé'on,
Wales.

July 14'. 17

My dear Len & Bill,

We arrived here at ten o'clock last evening, just after the golden sun had sunk. The Black Mountains are only about 10 miles away and Brecon Beacons about 5. Words cannot describe the beauty of this country. it is really lovely. There are no huts and we are living in the Sanatorium, a spotlessly clean set of little villas. We sleep on prison bed-boards, mattress, pillow, 3 blankets but no sheets.

Things are very primitive, the water supply is not yet put-in so we have to draw the water from the well,

The present job is excavating

Eddie Beaton to Len and Bill (Roland) 17th July 1917 from Wales
(Original 115x180mm)

'The main items of interest here since I last wrote are these. We have three classes now going steady, with lecturers or debates twice a week… We had a concert the other night. These functions have taken place in our new 'communal room' which has now been in use for a week, and boasts a coke-store, table and benches. We have our dailies and a few weeklies which the Friends send, also some games from the same source.'

These young men shared the soldiers' knack of making a home wherever they found themselves, even to the point of fraternising with the local females, as William Marwick told the brothers from mid-Wales: 'This nice wild young man [Eddie Beaton] is well in at least, and seems quite *epris* with a certain young lady'.[520] It would appear that here too the fact that the available males were conscientious objectors did not prevent the local girls associating with them unchaperoned.

At Christmas 1917 they were not able to get home (unlike the Paynes), but certainly made the most of where they were, as Eddie reported:

'We had a fine social at the house of kind friends in the village at Bronllys on Boxing Day and what with a scrumptious feed, songs, recitations, etc we had a royal time. My contribution to the programme took the form of a 'Humourous Recital' and I am glad to be able to say without the slightest boast on my part that I kept the company in roars of laughter for some considerable time.

I left the social at eight to meet my lady friend in Talgarth and so terminated my Christmas with a pleasant 1½ hrs. in the company of one I think the world of. I was again favoured with her company last evening and on walking up the Bronllys reverse was startled at the spectacle which met my gaze, to wit, Willie Marwick and Dan Davies in the company of two fine girls. It is something strange to see Dan so engaged, but William, why I nearly fainted. I don't half 'pull his leg' especially as the girl he was with is a school teacher who has spent some time in Scotland.'[521]

Eddie and William may have kept clear of the political game being played by the hard line conscientious objectors but, no matter how idyllic the surroundings and how congenial the locals, politics were never far from the surface and in August, as active discontent spread throughout the system, trouble flared in Talgarth too. William wrote to tell Leonard about it:

'Though my orderly job has been very monotonous the camp as a whole has had a lively time this week. It began last Sat. with the men knocking off at twelve instead of one because of their lunch ration being withheld. The agent refused their pay and a letter from the H[ome] O[ffice] confirmed this, and also decreed that the men were to work full ten hours next Sat. On both Mon. and Tues. there were excited meetings, all in the dark as to what was to be done, as we did not get the H.O. letter till Friday. The chief action was to draw up a stiff letter to the H.O., making all manner of charges (quite justifiably) against the agent's character and conduct. Then on Friday night when no answer to this had come and the other letter was before us, another meeting took place and red revolution was talked, with the usual irrelevance. On Sat. Major Terrell and Capt. Stevenson turned up to investigation [sic] the whole situation. The men had to work the ten hours but got their pay for the previous week and the lunch ration was confirmed. They promise also to give the agent a telling off about his ways. Bob Wright is to be sent back to Wakefield, two men, Hutchinson and Parsley arrested for 'slacking'. The former was an absolutist and had done eight months, coming out only because of the serious illness of his wife, and all his time here has just been asking for it. He is just like a big romping schoolboy; he came running into quarters the other day, and called out to me jubilantly "I've got the sack, I'm off home." I asked why and he said "I had a row with the agent and called him 'Old Pot belly' and he said he didn't need my services any more." Then he packed up and off he went and hasn't been seen since. He is a wholesale draper in Cardiff and seems well to do.'[522]

By October, there had been an improvement in the situation in Talgarth but, with winter approaching, trouble still lurked just below the surface. William told Leonard:

'Today we have got a new agent, though whether temporarily or permanently we do not know. Some say it is only to allow P. Williams to go on holiday. He is one Hunt, said to be Gov. or ex-Govr. of Usk Prison. He is elderly, with something of Keywood in his features and got up like a nonconformist parson with bibulous tendencies on holiday. He has made a good impression for a start by giving late leave for a concert in Talgarth tonight. Any change is a relief from old "Ponty".

The weather here is bitterly cold, and it is a cruel job getting up in the morning, especially as the breakfast here is nothing to enthuse over. I think we shall all be out for red revolution if it lasts much longer. I shouldn't be surprised if there was a change in our position, but I don't expect one for the better unless as a result of our own acts.'[523]

The pessimism continued at Talgarth into the winter, not helped by the continuing rapid turnover of agents:

'We are certainly having "some choice agents" (EJB's expression[]) just now – boozy old swearing ex-military men. The present one seems quite harmless, but unfortunately is very much under the thumb of Pierce Williams. He seems unable to think for himself, has to follow somebody's advice or printed regulations. No wonder, after forty years in the army.'[524]

The monotony of life in the Talgarth Centre was getting on Eddie Beaton's nerves. He wrote to Leonard just after Christmas of 1917:

'Well dear boys, in spite of absence from home we have spent a happy Christmas and look forward to the New Year to the new Scheme and to a world rebuilt and peace everlasting... I do hope the new Scheme soon comes into operation, I'm feeling "fed up" absolutely and it would take a little now to make me repudiate. We in H.O. Camps get very little news and have to trust to our kind friends such as you who are happily placed under more favourable conditions.'[525]

But no relief came to Eddie that winter and he was still in Talgarth as the spring of 1918 approached. His situation was all the more painful since his hopes for transfer out of Talgarth had been raised in November 1917 when a Cabinet Committee had decided that after twelve months of good behaviour and industry on the Home Office Scheme objectors would be eligible for a transfer out of the restrictions of the scheme and into a freer work regime out in the world, as close to their own homes as they could arrange.[526] It was a major triumph for good sense, but for Eddie it did not come and his frustration grew. In April 1918 he told Leonard that:

'A fortnight has now elapsed since I was qualified and I have not found any work in Leeds or near my home... Birmingham's the place I mean is very attractive after so many long and weary months at that very dry little hole of Talgarth. I wrote to Alternative Service Guild but there was nothing doing in Leeds and at the foot of their list appeared the name of your firm so I wrote and recd. their offer of 48/= per week + 3/= war bonus, and a 5/= production bonus...

I am absolutely "fed up" with Talgarth and it is very irritating and annoying to know you are qualified yet cannot get away. Joe has been staying with my people, and he and you both strongly advise me not to go to B'ham, so I must hang on here I suppose, until something else turns up.

I do sincerely hope that you and Bill will be able to get home on the new Scheme – it will be fine for you.

I am so glad your letter came, as I might have been silly enough to accept, as I am absolutely driven to despair with being so "fed up" and sick of life on the "Scream".'[527]

★

*His initial euphoria having vanished in a
Welsh winter, Eddie Beaton writes to
Leonard, 7th April 1918
(Original 115x175mm)*

The strain was telling on the Payne brothers too. Marion had put it into words the previous summer:

> 'I am sure you must be heartily sick of the Scheme. I have often thought lately that we are entering upon the hardest phase of our peace testimony, the glamour of the first venture against militarism has gone and we are up against what seems to be the all powerful hand of militarism.'[528]

Even though Leonard was able to live freely out in the community, close enough to home to make frequent and unmonitored visits, he still felt the weight of his predicament bearing down on him and in a letter to Marion – now lost – he must have poured his heart out. In December 1917, in reply, she tried to reassure him:

> 'Many thanks for your letter… I do not wonder that you feel as you do about the past eighteen months, in one way I do expect you feel as if your lives were being wasted and yet I feel as if the time must have been a wonderful one, for the friendships you have made and the deep religious experiences through which you have passed.'[529]

★

What Leonard may not have fully realised was that those on the 'outside' were working hard to secure his release: until the government changed its policy, though, there was little chance of further relaxation. But then, in the autumn of 1917, the government, it seemed, was shifting its position, coming round to the view that the moderate objectors might be released from their Work Centres and allowed to return to their homes – though not the absolutists. The cost of keeping them in expensive centres and the rule that they should not work at their own trades had always defied logic and now a more sensible and less punitive (or bloody minded) approach was mooted in government.

On November 2nd 1917 John Payne, with his usual disregard for punctuation, wrote to his younger son, '…enclosing a cutting or two out of the papers there seems a fair chance of you all being released soon look at the Labour Leader this week there was a strong letter in *The Times* one day last week as I do hope something may be done'.[530]

The managers of the Dryad cane furniture works in Leicester were not slow to understand the significance of these developments and at the end of October had already written to John in Lutterworth:

> 'I have several hundred eighteen pdr shell baskets to place out, and should be glad to know if you could make some for us. It occurred to me that by doing so you might be able to get your boys home again. I could promise several months work.'[531]

The temptation to seize any opportunity to get his sons home must have been great indeed to John, not only for the obvious personal reasons but also because he was trying to run the family business without his two sons to help him and with a wife and two daughters to feed in the increasingly difficult conditions of wartime. The prospect of a fat government contract to fulfil was alluring, but…

Of course, it was not as simple as that. Those shell baskets were coming back to haunt them again! We may ask how could two men who had so consistently defied the military, refusing to have anything to do with war work, declining to put themselves under military control, now return home to make a comfortable living making what were in effect war materials for use by the army, albeit only wickerwork baskets for transporting shells? The issue of whether the shell baskets were 'war materials' or not had long ago been resolved: whatever their purpose, they certainly had no civilian use. Had their father understood the problem? He sent his sons a copy of the Dryad offer, adding that, '…this work would not preduice *[sic – prejudice]* us at all as far as I can see…' He urged the brothers to contact Mrs Peach, the manager in charge of the cane weaving department at the Dryad works. Later in the week he would take the opportunity '…to call at the Dryad and again explain my position and see what can be done… but think it over and let me know'.[532]

★

But relief and release came, as usual, suddenly and without warning. Leonard and Roland Payne were passed out of the Home Office Scheme on April 15th 1918, two years to the day since their appeal against conscription had been rejected by the Leicester Tribunal. They could now return home and live freely under the nominal supervision of their father. Their ordeal at the hands of the army, the Prison Service and the Home Office Scheme was over.

HOME OFFICE
WHITEHALL
S.W. 1

17-4-18

E.E.9.

Sir,

 I am directed by the Committee on Employment of Conscientious Objectors to say that they have authorised the employment under you of *Leonard* *R Payne* a Conscientious Objector who has been for 12 months employed under them, and has shewn himself by good conduct and industry to be qualified for Exceptional Employment under their Rules. The man has been informed that his employment under you has been authorised, and that he must take up that employment on *the 29th of April* and I am to ask that you will be so good as to fill up and return the enclosed form within a week from that date.

 I enclose a copy of an undertaking which has been signed by the man, and am to ask that you will endeavour to see that it is faithfully observed. The Committee wish to call your special attention to paragraph 6 of the undertaking.

 Each month from the date of his taking up his employment you will be asked to furnish a report on his industry and conduct, and the Committee request that such reports may be punctually and faithfully rendered. They would be further obliged if you could give at least a week's notice if at any time you should wish the employment to cease, giving your reasons and stating particularly whether you have any complaint or charge to make against the man.

 Yours faithfully,

 Secretary

4H9.

John Payne is notified that his sons will be coming home, in a letter from the Home Office, 17th April 1918
(Original 200x250)

★

Before we follow them home let us pause to consider their treatment at the hands of the State power during those two years away. While it would be crass to attempt to construct a 'hierarchy of suffering', it cannot be denied that there were many different experiences of the First World War, some more comfortable than others. To try to understand that hellish war and its varying impacts on individuals, we might invoke Dante's great medieval vision of the Circles of Hell with its subtle gradings of horror and suffering. The metaphor is not outlandish. 'Hell' was for many who experienced the war at first hand the only image they could find to conjure up the unexplainable when ordinary, everyday language failed. But the Hell of 1914-1918 is not some divinely ordained inferno, in which eternal punishment is justly heaped on those who have erred. For, as in some monstrous cosmic inversion, it is not the sinners but the righteous who are tormented. Or, rather, the Great War revealed a Hell blindly indifferent to good and evil.

In the lowest and deepest Circles of Hell were the men who fought this war in the trenches and on the battlefield – in Flanders or France, in Italy, the Dardanelles or Mesopotamia, in Africa, on the high seas, in the air. A parish priest from Leamington, attached as military chaplain, Bernard McNulty, wrote powerfully to his parishioners in a letter widely printed in the local press: 'Try to imagine what I see this day, and what I have seen for weeks past, and I think that you will not wonder that I speak of it as Hell. All around me, as far as the eye can reach, it is the very "abomination of desolation"… Just miles of liquid mud! There is literally nothing left standing, not a village, not a barn or shelter – churches, houses, all have been swept off the face of the earth…

'Shall I tell you more, my readers? Why not? It is well that you should try to realise it all. Then, in imagination, walk with me across the deserted plain. There are poor little graves by the score to be seen – graves of *unknown* British soldiers. A cap marks one, a rifle stuck in the ground reveals another; whilst yet others are marked by a broken bit of wood, for there has not yet been time to put up crosses on the battlefield… and for every grave you see there are hundreds unseen in the parapets of those endless lines of destroyed trenches which we must cross as we walk… Oh, the horror of it all! Are you beginning to agree with me that this district is Hell on earth?'[533]

We might remind ourselves that in 1916 – when the Paynes were in their barracks and in their prison cells – the slaughter of the Somme was taking place only a few hundred miles away and that in 1917 – when they were in the Wakefield Work Centre and living free lives in Birmingham – men their own age were drowning on the endless upward slope to Passchendaele. The men who fought and died there really did die 'in Hell' as Sassoon's famous poem had it.[534] While Leonard and Roland were 'carrying out their free love principles' among the young ladies of Birmingham[535] and William Marwick was tramping the Welsh hills with his new found 'fine girl'[536], and at Wakefield the inmates were making a mockery of the elections which were supposed to give them a mature voice in the running of their own affairs, young men of their own age, from their own home towns, were going over the top in France and in Flanders and not coming back.

Some in those lower depths of Hell were pushed even lower, even further down into the deeps, for they were driven mad: their bodies survived the war, but their minds did not. Ivor Gurney, musician and celebrated war poet, wrote that 'There are strange Hells within the minds war made'[537], and wrote from firsthand experience: Gurney was to die in a mental hospital after his mind was broken by war. His mother, seeing him in the City of London Asylum years after the end of the war, wrote in anguish: 'I wish I could do something to make him better or that we could get him to a smaller place tis like a lot of cattle there he says it is Hell… They will never have their names on the roll of honour but I don't think that they ought to be crowded up like a lot of cattle but be treated honourably their whole life ruined'.[538] Though official attitudes towards shell shock and mental illness did improve during the war, one civil servant in the Ministry of Pensions as late as March 1918 could still write that 'There are some men who "funk" or dislike military service to such an extent that it sends them off their heads. It is a "tall order"… for the State to take on the liability to support, possibly for life, a man who becomes a lunatic because he is a coward and fears to undertake the liability which falls upon him as an Englishman'.[539] Hell was not only to be found at the Front.

Some men were unable to cope in other ways. Arthur Earp of the Warwickshire Regiment was but one, chosen at random. Towards the end of June 1916, in the build-up towards the terrible first day on the Somme, Earp left his post, turning up again just behind the lines twenty-four hours later, saying he had been unable to stand the incessant noise of his own side's week long bombardment of the German positions and the intensity of the German counter-bombardment directed towards him.[540] There is no overt suggestion of shell-shock or any other mental disturbance here, only of a boy who had reached his personal limit, who could not stand it any longer. Arthur Earp had been one of those who had volunteered in the first flush of patriotic enthusiasm in 'that strange year' of 1914, the year in which hundreds of thousands of young men across Britain rushed to sign up for a war they could not have begun to comprehend. Court martialled in the aftermath of the 1st of July, Earp was found guilty and sentenced to death by firing squad, though the court added: 'Recommendation for mercy. The Court recommends the accused for mercy *owing to intense bombardment to which the accused had been subjected to* and on account of his good character'. In rejecting the recommendation, Sir Douglas Haig wrote: 'How can we ever win if this plea is allowed?'[541] Not to be taken literally, of course, but it can reasonably stand for all those killed or maimed in the Great War. Arthur Earp was shot by a firing squad of his own countrymen on July 22nd 1916 at Bouzincourt. He was twenty-five years old. His whole life was ruined with the afterlife of his reputation as well.

We must place those absolutist conscientious objectors who remained in prison rather than accept the Home Office Scheme in a Circle of Hell somewhat above those terrible Lower Depths in which the generic 'Tommy' and Ivor Gurney and Arthur Earp found themselves stranded. The lot of the absolutist was not an easy one – far from it – as they were ground down by the endless circle of 'cat and mouse'. Absolutists from Clifford Allen[542] to Fenner Brockway[543] and on to Fred Tait, for whom, as we have seen, it was all too much in the end, suffered the mental torment of the absolutists' treadmill.

There were conscientious objectors who accepted the scheme but still died, of natural causes, exacerbated sometimes by neglect and sometimes by brutal official indifference. At first sight the case of Henry Firth provides as clear an example of what could happen as we might wish to find – or not wish to find.[544] After serving nine months' imprisonment in Wormwood Scrubs and Maidstone Gaols, Firth surrendered his absolutist stand and was sent to the Work Centre at Princetown in what had been Dartmoor Prison. Much of the work demanded of men like him on Dartmoor consisted of the pointless punitive 'hard labour' which had been given to convicted criminals there for generations past, as when one group of prisoners was set to pile up stones while another group was set to clear them, the groups endlessly changing places. In the House of Lords Lord Parmoor summed up the mental effect: 'these men are going downhill on a very steep gradient. The speed is accelerated, health is broken, nerves are unstrung and their mental vision is clouded'.[545] But Henry Firth provides us with a particularly sad case study: his health was very poor and he was described as 'a mere bag of bones' when he arrived on the moor. In theory under the same rules as the Paynes or the Talgarth or Wakefield objectors, Firth was set to work in the quarry breaking up rocks, which he was barely able to do. An appeal to the doctor was rejected, though it must have been evident that he was diabetic and that the work regime there could have serious consequences. After six days he visited the doctor again and was told that he was being selfish, that his condition was nothing compared to what the men in the trenches were suffering. Daily calls on the doctor produced the same result, and on January 23rd 1918 he was put on all night white-washing duties, and, even though unable to work, was put on the same the following night. On January 28th, in the teeth of the Dartmoor winter, he was returned to the quarry, and on the 30th was at last admitted to the hospital where he was given cod-liver oil. After a delegation of his fellow inmates pleaded with the doctor Henry Firth was put onto a milk diet. A request for eggs was turned down on the grounds that eggs were for the men fighting in France. On the morning of February 6th one of his friends grew so alarmed that he asked permission to send a telegram to his wife: permission was refused. He died that afternoon.

Edith Graham in Bradford was well informed about the events in Dartmoor for her brother was also being held there and towards the end of February she wrote to Leonard:

'My brother is still at Dartmoor, and no prospects of being moved anywhere else… Have you heard that C.H. Norman and ten of the Committee at Dartmoor have been arrested. I think it is because they have demanded an inquiry into the death of Firth who died a week or two ago.'[546]

The Men's Committee had called a one day work and food strike. Eddie Beaton at Talgarth was also disturbed by the news from Dartmoor:

'I suppose you heard of the death of Firth at Dartmoor and the strike, the arrest of C.H. Norman and [I.P.] Hughes. Poor Firth, he is the seventeenth C.O. to pay the supreme sacrifice, like a hero, as indeed a martyr he is, he goes the silent way of the rest to the Great Beyond.'[547]

The scandal of Henry Firth's death had, in the first instance, no consequences. Major George Terrell, one of the dominant voices in the treatment of conscientious objectors, hurried down to Dartmoor where he ordered the inmates confined to their quarters after work for fourteen days and saw to the arrest of Clarence Norman and I.P. Hughes. The doctor was exonerated: 'on the very smallest foundation they built a superstructure of oppression and improper conduct on the part of the officials', he said. The coroner's inquest concurred. Precisely which Circle of Hell Henry Firth had found himself in is imprecisely known.

The case also reminds us that, for all the government's restrictions and controls, the opening of mail and the harassment of opponents of the war – draconian and brutal as that could be – Britain held on to its democratic values. We are reminded that the NCF 'had a press department which constantly sought to draw the attention of the public to what was happening to C.O.s and the ill-treatment and brutality many were subjected to'[548], and the publicity given to the Firth case reopened the issue of how the objectors should be treated, and especially of what work they should be called upon to undertake, to public debate. Voices like that of Philip Snowden could still protest freely, albeit from his privileged position in Parliament.

Even here the complaints fell largely on deaf ears. Coming as it did on the eve of the great German Military Offensive on March 1918, news of the Dartmoor strike gave those who regarded the conscientious objectors with contempt a further stick with which to beat them. That was the other side of the democratic coin – the side of public opinion – one less welcome to the conscientious objectors and their supporters. If we were to attempt to draw up a 'Hierarchy of Resentments' generated by the First World War we would have to place the conscientious objectors among those most resented by their neighbours, alongside such bogeys as military brass hats, soldiers who were in uniform and away from their homes and families but who never saw a German or a Turk, their service confined to cookhouse or pay corps[549], war profiteers, the women who threatened male dominance in the workplace and were tolerated only for the duration, and those male munitions workers who worked alongside the women, all stirring deep resentment among the men in uniform.

It was a tangled web, but it was based on a simple belief in fairness and equality of sacrifice: was it equitable that fit, young, healthy men should be free to claim a conscientious objection to military service and thus evade the horrors of Hell? Many thought it was not, especially when the Home Office Scheme, for necessary reasons, began accepting men whose sincerity was at the very best questionable or whose purposes were less than constructive.

Some of the conscientious objectors themselves recognised that these things were relative. As Frank Jannaway wrote to one of his Christadelphian 'brothers' who had complained bitterly about the 'agonising' treatment of those sent to the Dartmoor Settlement:

'I would like you to come with me on my weekly visit to Wormwood Scrubs Prison. It adjoins the "Orthopaedic Hospital", where the broken soldiers are patched up; some hopelessly crippled, almost beyond recognition, other sufficiently mended to go again "to the Front". As I watch these poor "convalescents" (!) in some cases with both legs gone, I feel not only indignant, but disgusted that any Christadelphian should murmur because our Heavenly Father in His all-wisdom has permitted a brother here and there to suffer for conscience sake!…

'Returning to the case you describe as "agonising". Such language is monstrous; a gross exaggeration. What he and others are experiencing at Dartmoor is a mere picnic compared with what their late shop-mates and fellow-clerks are having to undergo in the trenches. Would either of those at Dartmoor be willing to change places with those in France or Mesopotamia? I am positive they wouldn't, altogether apart from the question of conscience.'[550]

Nothing we have heard here accords with the Payne brothers' experience of the First World War beyond perhaps their short stay in Newcastle Prison. Perhaps the Paynes' war experience was akin to the prisoners of war, some held for years on end – far longer than any conscientious objector – in enemy hands and subject to enemy control, victim to the food shortages which racked Germany in the last years of the war?[551] Or what of those 'enemy aliens' interned in Britain, including those interned, as in some vindictive joke, in the pleasure grounds outside Wakefield, whiling their time away in lectures and amateur dramatics and terrible fears for their families back home? But no prisoner of war and no internee was allowed out of camp in the evenings, or allowed to go home for weekends, or to spend Christmas with their families. They had to bear their separation with whatever patience and fortitude they could muster, isolated in the midst of their nation's enemies.

We could argue that the Paynes should not have been in that position in the first place and they would not had the Tribunals done the job Asquith had entrusted to them. Perhaps that is how we should argue: no parade ground, no court-martial, no prison cell, no Work Centre with its charade of 'work of national importance'. The brothers could and should have been given absolute exemption and allowed to go about their normal lives as though there were no war on, but that in the circumstances of the time would have been difficult, Congregationalists disowned by their own minister, living in a small town and increasingly distressed and disturbed. We do not know what their lives would have been like, how their neighbours would have responded to them, had they been given the right to remain at home throughout the war, weaving baskets under absolute exemption from military service, because that did not happen. Or they might have been granted a conditional exemption from the outset by their Local Tribunal, living away from home and labouring on the land. However, these things did not happen, and we can only evaluate their experience for what it was, not for what it might have been or even what it should have been.

If we were to attach the label 'prisoners of conscience' to the Payne brothers, that would in one sense be truthful, but misleading. Especially when we consider their treatment at the hands of the State in their own day with the twentieth century's later 'prisoners of conscience' under less benign regimes. The world since the Great War has sadly seen a massive increase in the numbers of prisoners of conscience as oppressive regimes have proliferated and as public sensibilities have responded through organisations like the (governmental) United Nations and (the independent) Amnesty International. The experience of the British First World War conscientious objectors cannot, for instance, be compared to those conscientious objectors who quietly fought wars of peace against the Nazi regime in Germany – Dietrich Bonhoeffer, Martin Niemöller, Sophie Scholl, Otto and Elise Hampel and others – nor those who defied the Soviet power – Andrei Sakharov, Aleksandr Solzhenitsyn, Andrei Sinyavsky, Vladimir Bukovsky, Natalia Gorbanevskaya and many more – nor those whose quiet defiance has consciously put their own lives in danger under a hundred dictatorial regimes across the world since the First World War. The register in which we would be evaluating these people's experiences would be wrong if applied to the Paynes and the other Great War conscientious objectors, the scale inappropriate to *their* time. The Wakefield Work Centre and the civil prisons in Newcastle and Durham were not Dachau, nor yet the thousand camps of Stalin's landlocked 'Gulag archipelago' with their hundreds of thousands of prisoners of conscience. It is a question of scale and degree.

So, we find ourselves with the Paynes, in the uppermost layer of the abyss, in the First Circle of Hell. Not really Hell at all but the 'Limbo' defined by Catholic theology and Dante's imagination: not punished but allowed to live in relative comfort, a state almost of suspended animation where they were held in loose chains to await the conclusion of the war, a conclusion to which they made no contribution whatsoever. It is only when we peer downward, into the lower Circles of that Hell, that we understand how privileged and fortunate they were. Indeed, we might ask whether Leonard and Roland Payne were ever more than inconvenienced by their treatment at the hands of the State. There seems little doubt that they were genuinely traumatised by their time in the prison system, but during their short stay in gaol they were treated no differently from other convicts who had broken the law and under the Home Office Scheme they were treated a great deal better. They clearly thought they had been treated badly and Roland's grandson, John, recalls that he 'would only mention it [his experience as a conscientious objector] to me when I was down or feeling sad, almost as a comparison of how bad things really were for him'.[552]

Certainly, they complained: they were not allowed to live at home (though from Birmingham and even from Wakefield they could visit more or less at will); they weren't paid enough; the agents set over them were not to their taste; they were expected to pay full fare on the trams; or they complained about their boredom and that their lives seemed to be drifting away. But they and their friends, Eddie and William in rural mid-Wales, Ron and Joe in Wakefield, Leonard and Roland in Bourneville working in their chemicals factory, Christians and conscientious objectors all, at least had the freedom to form associations, establish friendships, play around with the girls and enjoy themselves. Above all, Leonard and Roland Payne had been kept together. If they were indeed 'martyrs', men who suffered for their beliefs, as they liked to think of themselves, it was indeed a strange kind of 'martyrdom'. It was one in which those who chose not to be 'martyred' in this way suffered far worse horrors and indignities than those who did. It has to be said that, on the whole, while in the hands of the State in its various manifestations, Leonard and Roland Payne had had a very cushy First World War.

★

What of Asquith's *Ship of Liberal Values*, that high aspiration that a modern war could be fought whilst maintaining the best of English liberal values? It had been grievously damaged by the first rock, the incompetence of the Local Tribunals in dealing with those men who claimed exemption from military service on grounds of their conscientious values. The rigidity and brutality of the military mind had dented it further until more humane and politically astute and liberal minds prevailed and the conscientious objectors were rescued from the worst excesses of an army with other priorities. This had been the second rock. The third rock was the most tragic of all, for as the sheer scale of the war and the losses and damage it inflicted on every level of society became more evident, attitudes hardened as a kind of desperation took hold of the country and allowing the luxury of conscientious objection came to seem more and more undesirable. Already low in the water, the *Ship of Liberal Values* was all but scuppered by the fourth rock, its inability to cope with the intransigence of those absolutist conscientious objectors who regarded those liberal values as a sham and set out to expose and sink them.

But the *Ship of Liberal Values* was still afloat – just, although Asquith himself was no longer at the helm. It finally foundered not through any governmental attitude or policy, though Lloyd George's single-minded and ruthless determination did stir the waters greatly.

What finally sunk it was the hidden fifth rock, a largely submerged rock, the *Rock of Public Opinion* – as we and the Paynes were about to discover.

NOTES & REFERENCES

1. Hansard, 5th January 1916, col. 957. Conscription in Britain did not spring into existence out of nowhere in 1916. We can trace its evolution through books. In modern times the issue of conscription went back to the overwhelming German victory in the Franco-Prussian War of 1870-1 and the publication in *Blackwood's Magazine* of 'The Battle of Dorking: Reminiscences of a Volunteer', a story which told, with great verisimilitude, of a successful German invasion of Britain. The punchline, or moral, of the story comes at the end. After denouncing the passing of political power from 'the class which had been used to rule, and to face political dangers, and which had brought the nation with honour unsullied through former struggles, into the hands of the lower classes, uneducated, untrained to the use of political rights, and swayed by demagogues,' Chesney reached his point: 'Politics had become a mere bidding for Radical votes, and those who should have led the nation stooped rather to pander to the selfishness of the day, and humoured the popular cry which denounced those who would secure the defence of the nation by enforced arming of its manhood, as interfering with the liberties of the people.' (The complete text is printed in I.F. Clarke, *The Tale of the Next Great War, 1871-1914. Fictions of Future Warfare and of Battles Still-to-Come*, Liverpool University Press, Liverpool, 1995, pp. 27-73.) A runaway popular success, the story spawned a flood of 'invasion-scare' fictions over the coming years, including Erskine Childers' *Riddle of the Sands* (1903) and John Buchan's *The 39 Steps* (1915). In the world of reality, rather than parable, peacetime conscription was a live political issue in the years immediately before World War One, and in 1910 one of the most popular and able of the British Generals, Sir Ian Hamilton, published a book called *Compulsory Service* which, despite its title, set out the case against conscription. Behind the scenes the army had been exploring the idea of compulsory conscription and had set its face firmly against it. (*Richard Burdon Haldane. An Autobiography*, Hodder and Stoughton, London, 1929, pp. 195-7.) With the navy to defend the coastline, a small, highly trained and flexible professional army to do any serious land fighting, and Haldane's Territorials, like Lutterworth's Leicestershire Yeomanry, newly-reorganised and revitalised, to secure the homeland, a mass army of unwilling conscripts would not only be superfluous but positively harmful, diluting the regulars into training Battalions, taking workers out of the economy (anything above 60,000

would be positively harmful he believed) and, more to the point, it would be extremely expensive; so Hamilton argued. Only in the direst emergency, such as the need to fight a prolonged war in Europe, would compulsion be contemplated as a 'Third Line' behind the Regulars and the Territorials. (John Lee, *A Soldier's Life. General Sir Ian Hamilton, 1853-1947*, Macmillan, London, pp. 105-7.) The politicians favoured Hamilton's view as being not only properly 'English' and truly 'liberal' in spirit, but, more importantly, cheaper. Then Field Marshal Lord Roberts of Kandahar, V.C., Hamilton's former chief, and a national hero, weighed into the debate with a book he partly authored but which went out under his name, called *Fallacies and Facts. An Answer to "Compulsory Service"*. The book is an all-out attack on Hamilton and Haldane, his political master, by name; a strenuously argued case for compulsory military service in peacetime. (Earl Roberts of Kandahar, *Fallacies and Facts. An Answer to "Compulsory Service"*, John Murray, London, 1911, especially pp. 1-51.) The section penned by Roberts himself is called 'The Nation's Peril', and the argument is along the lines that wars are not won by navies defending coastlines, but by armies going out to confront and defeat the foe, as they had not done in Europe since the Crimea and, before that, Napoleon, a century before. Roberts pounced on Hamilton and Haldane's concession that a conscript army might, in certain extreme circumstances, be needed: 'It comes, then, to this,' wrote Roberts, 'that Sir Ian Hamilton deliberately recommends that this country's small fighting forces should be maintained in the field, abroad as well as at home, by men compelled to fight, but not permitted any training prior to the outbreak of hostilities. And this Third Line is to be utilized when the nation and the Empire are "fighting for bare life"!' (Roberts, especially p. 43.) It should not surprise us that this arcane debate about the technicalities of military recruitment was carried into the public sphere; it was an age of mass communication, mass literacy, mass (male) democracy, an age in which military spats were conducted in public. Even the children were not immune from the arguments. In 1901, for example, Edmund Francis Sellar had produced *The Story of Lord Roberts* in *The Children's Heroes Series*, placing Roberts firmly into the context of Britain's great (military) heroes and past glories: the closing words of the book are: 'Under his fostering care a spirit of patriotism has been awakened, and it is to be hoped that the day is not far distant when every able-bodied man in the country will have learnt to be able to shoot, and to fight, if necessary, for his hearth and home'. (Edmund Francis Sellar, *The Story of Lord Roberts* in *The Children's Heroes Series*, published by T.C. and E.C. Jack, London, 1901, p. 120.) The ideas contained in the book formed part of the socialisation of the generation of boys who became the men of 1914, shaping their attitudes and moulding their values. One historian specialising in German history has suggested that 'the "civility" and anti-militarism of British society were perhaps more a matter of self-perception than a faithful representation of reality'. He points out that the National Service League attracted some 100,000 members, including 177 members of the House of Commons. (Christopher Clark, *Iron Kingdom. The Rise and Downfall of Prussia, 1600-1947*, Allen Lane, London, 2006, p. 601, with reference to the work of Anne Summers and John M. Mackenzie.) A radical view on the matter of war and peace came from Norman Angell in his book *The Great Illusion. A Study of the Relation of Military Power in Nations to their Economic and Social Advantage*, first published in 1909, and going into a series of new editions thereafter. (A revised edition was even published as a 'Penguin Special' in December of 1938, under the title *The Great Illusion – Now*, arguing against British involvement in war against Hitler.) Angell argued that in war there could be no victors. He offered a non-religious basis for pacifism, and the idea caught on with remarkable speed. In the first part of the book Angell argued on purely practical and rational grounds that it is an illusion to believe that any country can gain materially from winning a war. He then sought to refute the notion that war and violence are integral parts of human nature. In summary: '1. That the alleged un-changeability of human nature is not a fact, and all the evidence is against it (e.g. the disappearance, or at least the attenuation, of the temper which leads us to enforce our religious beliefs on others, and of the temper which produced the duel); 2. That warlike nations do not inherit the earth; 3. That physical force is a constantly diminishing factor in human affairs; that this involves profound psychological modifications; and 4. That the increasing factor is co-operation, and that this factor tends to attenuate State divisions which in no way represent the limits of that co-operation. (Norman Angell, *The Great Illusion. A Study of the Relation of Military Power in Nations to their Economic and Social Advantage*, Heinemann, London, 1910 edn., p. 144.) When war came Lord Kitchener, the most popular military folk hero of the Great War, affirmed his faith in the voluntary principle to which he had lent his face in the most famous and successful poster campaign in British history, 'Your King and Country need you'. In 1916, addressing a meeting of Parliamentarians, he asked: 'Why did not the War Office demand compulsory service? I think that is easily answered. The question of a social change involving the whole country and running counter to the ancient traditions of the British people is not a matter for a [government] department to decide. So long as sufficient men came in, it was not my duty to ask for special means of obtaining them.' (Quoted in Asquith, *Memories and Reflections 1852-1927*, Cassell, London, 1928, Vol. 2, pp.123-4. For the overview see R.J.Q. Adams and Philip P. Poirier, *The Conscription Controversy in Great Britain, 1900-1918*, Macmillan, London, 1987, passim.) 1915 changed all that. The debate on conscription even reached Lutterworth, safe and cosy in its Midlands greenery. For many years Lutterworth had had an evening school, providing a boost for about thirty boys of ambition, teaching them elementary book-keeping, business correspondence, English composition, basic arithmetic, decimals, percentages and the mysteries of interest, together with the essentials of grammar using *Pitman's Practical Primer.* On the evening of Tuesday 24th November 1914 the boys were given an essay to write: the title 'Is Conscription necessary in England?' Sadly, none of their essays have survived. (Evening School Log Book. LRO: DE/3614/6. The evening school closed in February of 1915 without explanation.)

2. Trevor Wilson, *The Downfall of the Liberal Party, 1914-1935*, Collins, London, 1968, pp. 76-83. For the Prime Minister's version, see H.H. Asquith, *The Genesis of the War*, Cassell, London, 1923, pp. 138-9. James Cameron memorably described Asquith as 'the able, reflective, cautious and monumentally reliable man who was secure on all things and passionate on none: the moderate.' (James Cameron, *1914*, Cassell, London, 1959, p. 8.) And the Prime Minister's wife, Margot Asquith, discussing birth control issues with Cynthia Mosley, told her that 'Henry always withdrew in time, such a noble man!' (Quoted in Martin Pugh, *We Danced all Night. A Social History of Britain between the Wars*, Vintage Books, London, 2009, p. 165.) It might serve as an appropriate epitaph for his Premiership.

3. The phrase was used by A.J.P. Taylor in *The Origins of the Second World War* (Penguin Books, Harmondsworth, 1964, p. 235) of the Munich agreement of 1938.

4. Hansard, 5th January 1916, cols. 957-8.

5. Hansard, 5th January 1916, col. 961. Asquith's wording was designed to beguile and disarm those critics on the Tory benches who opposed the idea of any kind of conscientious exemption. He was following the examples of both Germany and France, which, while refusing to recognise conscientious objection to military service as such, accommodated claimants in non-combatant roles. There, conscription had been part of the culture for decades: in Britain, without such a tradition, the situation was very different. As Henry Nevinson argued in 1916, the whole edifice of the conscience clause was founded on a misunderstanding, on the mistaken belief that all conscientious objectors would be like the Quakers, willing to accept non-combatant work of Christian charity such as they were already doing through their Friends' Ambulance Unit. 'Who else could object, where Quakers made a compromise?' But some Christians, together with the bulk of the socialist objectors, would have nothing to do with non-combatant duties or any offered alternative to military service. (Henry W. Nevinson, *The Conscientious Objector*, typescript article in Friends' Library, London, Box L207/39, p. 4.)

6. House of Lords Debate, 4th May 1916, col. 917.

7. Hansard, 5th January 1916, cols. 959-960.

8. Adrian Gregory, *The Last Great War. British Society and the First World War*, C.U.P., 2008, pp. 101-8. This provides indirect evidence for the extrapolated figure of a million

applicants, which Gregory gave in the *Journal of British Studies*, July 2004, p. 411. The apparent prevalence of claims for exemption not only suggests a reluctance to join up – a reluctance which had made conscription necessary in the first place – but also the muddying of the waters when genuine conscientious objectors appeared before the Tribunals. (See Lois Bibbing, *Telling Tales about Men. Conceptions of Conscientious Objectors to Military Service during the First World War*, Manchester University Press, 2009, pp. 179-184.)

9. David Boulton's claim of an 'avalanche of conscientious objectors who made application to appear before' the Tribunals is hardly borne out by the facts. Just over 16,000 claims were made on grounds of conscience before just under 2,000 Tribunals, on average eight each. With (based on a rough and ready calculation) each Tribunal encountering a claim of conscientious objection once every four months, this was a modest avalanche indeed: more a trickle really – and a trickle which gave the Tribunals little experience of dealing with such cases. (David Boulton, *Objection Overruled*, Macgibbon & Key, London, 1967, p. 124.)

10. John W. Graham, *Conscription and Conscience*, George Allen and Unwin, London, 1922, p. 68.

11. Gilbert Murray, introduction to Mrs Henry Hobhouse, *"I Appeal Unto Caesar". The Case of the Conscientious Objector*, George Allen and Unwin, London, 1917, p. vii. The text of the 4th edition is available online via http://www.archive.org. We might question the implied claim that conscientious objectors were men of uniquely delicate sensibilities. All that said, some Tribunals were recognised for their fairness by conscientious objectors themselves. (See Bibbing, pp. 170-1, and the references given there.)

12. Hansard, 12th January 1916, cols. 1648-9. Simon was an absolute opponent of the principle of conscription. See Brock Millman, *Managing Domestic Dissent in First World War Britain,* Cass, London, 2000, p. 49 and pp. 65-6, n. 4.

13. Graham, p. 68.

14. Murray, ibid., p. vii.

15. Graham, p. 68.

16. House of Lords Debate, 4th May 1916, cols. 914-5.

17. Hansard, 24th February 1916, col. 791. See also Viscount Long of Wraxall (Walter Long), *Memories*, Hutchinson, London, 1923, pp. 224-5.

18. Hansard, 24th February 1916, cols. 789-91.

19. *Hinckley Echo*, 15th March 1916. The man replied that he 'did not know he suffered at all. He held views.' The case was taken up in Parliament by Philip Snowden and his comments printed in his *British Prussianism. The Scandal of the Tribunals*, National Labour Press, London, 1916, p. 9. See Bibbings, p. 180, where Market Bosworth is rendered

'Market Boswell'. Though critics of the Tribunals immediately seized on this case as an arbitrary injustice, the Tribunal was acting, in the case of the Hunt servants if not the conscientious objector, precisely in line with government policy as stated in a Circular issued by Lord Derby in December 1915 in response to demand from the War Office Director of Remounts. Hunt servants were exempted from the call-up to help secure a continuing flow of cavalry mounts. The decision was later reviewed but not finally withdrawn until December 1917. One correspondent complained: 'A young married man recently told me he would not volunteer while the War Office could spare thousands (?) of unmarried men to foster hunting... This favouritism is causing general discontent especially among parents who have given their all to the cause. (My only son joined at the outbreak of the War)'. Letter to the War Office from W. Long of Bournemouth, 13th March 1916, in Ian Beckett, *Home Front 1914-1918. How Britain Survived the Great War*, The National Archives, Kew, 2006, pp. 131-3.

20. Philip Snowden, Hansard, 24th and 29th February 1916, and persistently over the following weeks and months.

21. Hansard, 8th March 1916; see also 14th March. Another M.P. raised the issue from a South Yorkshire Tribunal, where 'two reporters representing newspapers known to be unsympathetic to conscientious objectors were admitted' to the hearing, while others were excluded, and 'the Tribunal permitted the reporters already referred to to remain whilst the case was being discussed, although the applicant himself was asked to withdraw'. (Hansard, 16th March 1916.) See also Cyril Pearce, *Comrades in Conscience. The Story of an English Community's Opposition to the Great War*, Francis Boutle, London, 2001, Appendix III.

22. See, for example, Frank G. Jannaway, *Without the Camp. Being the Story of Why and How the Christadelphians were Exempted from Military Service*, published by the author, London, 1917, passim.

23. H.W. Wilson and J.A. Hammerton (eds), *The Great War. The Standard History of the All-European Conflict*, Amalgamated Press, Vol. 7, London, 1916, p. 38.

24. Hansard, 25th October 1916, col. 1262. A nice caricature of the Tribunals in action can be found in Lily Tobias' 1933 novel, *Eunice Fleet*, which adds to the mix the notion that partiality was shown towards friends and business associates of Tribunal members. *Eunice Fleet,* Honno Classics, Wales, 2004, pp. 89-99.

25. Leonard, Liddle interview, 1973, Tape 70 transcript, p. 7. The recorded interview and a transcript are held in the Special Collections of the Brotherton Library, University of Leeds.

26. One M.P. had already complained about this kind of question in Parliament: 'Mr Outhwaite asked the President of the Local Government Board whether, in view of his instructions to Local Tribunals that they should confine their inquiries to

ascertaining facts, he will discourage the putting of hypothetic questions to the conscientious objector, such as those as to what he would do in the case of his mother being attacked by a German, such questions having no relation to fact, in view of the recent statement of the First Lord of the Admiralty that enlistment is for a cause which does not involve invasion or even the serious danger of invasion of our hearths and homes?' Walter Long replied that: 'I cannot undertake to issue such instructions as are suggested'. (Hansard, 9th March 1916.) This satirical version comes from an anonymous 'chronicle' published under the title *The [First] Book of Artemas*, in mock-Biblical style: '1. And when the fighters had gone forth unto the war, there yet remained *certain men* that were strong and sound of limb. And every man that went not forth, *he had* his reason. 2. And some said, To kill men in battle is a wicked *thing*. Would ye therefore have us *to go* against our consciences? 3. And when the people questioned these, they replied unto them, saying, The wise man giveth obedience unto his conscience lest it torment him; neither *is there* any escape from it. And we are men of wisdom. 4. And if one of the men of Hu shall ravish our eldest daughter, *then* shall we offer unto him she *that is* next unto her that he may ravish her also; for so it is written. 5. And they that questioned them forbore to ask them more, deeming a conscience *such as this* was assuredly come from the devil.' (Published by W. Westall, London, 1918, Chapter XII.)

27. In his 1973 interview with Peter Liddle, Leonard made no reference to George Spencer being on the Tribunal, though earlier the local industrialist had tried to persuade the brothers to answer the call to military service: 'Two of the leading people in Lutterworth came to see us and told us if we didn't register we should be made conscripts and they tried to threaten us with that… Spencer [was] one of the big hosiery manufacturers and of course these people carried a lot of weight in a place like Lutterworth… [He came to see us] and he told us what would be done with us if we didn't do so and so and he was a [Congregational] chapel man. He also tried to use our mother because he had been a big friend of our mother's for many years and he wanted it for her sake.' (Liddle interview, 1973, Tape 70, p. 3.)

28. Liddle interview, 1973, Tape 70, p. 5. We might even speculate that the army shoved its less intellectually gifted officers into the Tribunals and away from more pressing and important military duties. In the Second World War the Tribunals did not contain a military representative.

29. Others faced with the dilemma of whether they could fulfil war contracts came to a different conclusion. Later in 1916 Edmund Harvey, in an adjournment debate in the House of Commons, raised the issue of a conscientious objector called Malcolm Sparkes, 'a lifelong member of the Society of Friends, and highly esteemed by the members of that society. He was managing director of a firm making woodwork for

the building trade, or builders' fittings. On the outbreak of the war his firm, in which he had not a controlling interest, decided to do war work and make packing-cases for the Ministry of Munitions. He resigned his position as managing director as a protest, not feeling able to keep it in the new circumstances.' Hansard, 25th October 1916, col. 1251. In their 1973 interview the issue of the shell baskets did not get a mention.

30. Liddle interview, 1973, Tape 70, p. 5.

31. The best known statement of the 'donkeys' theory was put by Alan Clark in *The Donkeys*, Hutchinson, London, 1961; the stage show and film *Oh! What a Lovely War* (1969), and the BBC's *Blackadder Goes Forth* (1989) were based on this interpretation. It is today a view which military historians, by and large, dismiss. For a recent assessment see Gary Sheffield, *Forgotten Victory*, Review Books, London, 2002, pp. 1-3.

32. There is some confusion as to the exact date on which Leonard Payne was arrested. In his written statement in 1973 he gave the date as May 16th, but this cannot be correct, for on Friday the 26th he wrote a postcard to his parents saying he had arrived at Glen Parva Barracks the previous evening, Thursday the 25th (Leonard to Father, Mother and all, 26th May 1916.); and in one of her letters Marion Harper explicitly said that he had been arrested on a Wednesday, which would have been late on the evening of Wednesday the 24th. (Marion to Mr Payne [Leonard], 13th July 1916.)

33. Marion to Leonard, 3rd July 1917.

34. Marion to Mr Payne [Leonard], 13th July 1916.

35. Leonard Payne, MS notes for Peter Liddle, 1973, p. 4.

36. Liddle interview, 1973, Tape 70, transcript p. 8.

37. Leonard Payne, MS notes for Peter Liddle, 1973, p. 4.

38. ibid.

39. *For His Name's Sake. Being a Record of the Witness given by Members of Churches of Christ in Great Britain against Militarism during the European War 1914-1918*, pub. W. Barker, Printer, Mansfield Road, Heanor 1921, pp. 43-47. via http://www.netcomuk.co.uk/~pdover/fhnsidx.htm. Extract from *Handed Over* by Edward Bonser. Since the original call-up under the Military Service Act had been for single men only, the army was worried about men they believed had married just to avoid service; so marriages solemnised after the date Bonser mentioned were deemed not to have happened: hence Bonser's 'single married man'.

40. Leonard Payne, MS notes for Peter Liddle, 1973, p. 4.

41. Liddle interview, 1973, Tape 70, transcript, p. 9.

42. Minutes of the Imperial War Cabinet, 15th May 1916, quoted in Bibbings, p. 124.

43. Roland to Dad and Mother, 26th May 1916.

44. Leonard Payne, MS notes for Peter Liddle, 1973, p. 4.

45. Leonard to Father, Mother and all, 26th May 1916.

46. Roland to All, 27th May 1916.

47. Leonard to 'Mr J.G. Payne', undated, postmarked 27th May 1916.

48. Leonard to J.G. Payne, undated, postmarked 27th May 1916.

49. Leonard to Father, Mother and all, 14th June 1916.

50. Leonard to J.G. Payne, undated, postmarked 27th May 1916.

51. Quoted in Felicity Goodall, *A Question of Conscience. Conscientious Objection in the two World Wars,* Sutton, Stroud, 1997, p. 4, with ref. to IWM Sound Archives 383/6.

52. See Thomas C. Kennedy, *The Hound of Conscience: A History of the No-Conscription Fellowship, 1914-1919,* University of Arkansas Press, 1987. See also University of Hull, Pressure Group Archives Subject Guide: No Conscription Fellowship (Willesden Branch), via www.hull.ac.uk/arc/collection/pressuregrouparchives.

53. N. Hiley, *Counter Espionage and Security in Great Britain during the First World War*, English Historical Review, 1986, p. 651. John Buchan set part of his novel *Mr Standfast*, written in 1917 and 1918, in an improbable colony of conscientious objectors which had been infiltrated by a German agent and thus inadvertently posed a threat to national security.

54. Kennedy, p. 65. Something of the atmosphere is captured by Pat Barker in her novel *The Eye in the Door*, Penguin Books, Harmondsworth, 1993.

55. Fenner Brockway, *Inside the Left. Thirty Years of Platform, Press, Prison and Parliament*, George Allen & Unwin, London, 1942, pp. 70-1.

56. Ella H. Stevens was Secretary of the Leicester Branch of the No-Conscription Fellowship. Kennedy, p. 297. Ella signed a printed letter to Leonard as Branch Secretary of the NCF, dated 3rd July 1919.

57. The café appears in *White's Directory of Leicester* in 1911 and 1914, but not in 1909.

58. Marion to Mr Payne, 13th July 1916; and Marion to Jessie, 14th July 1916.

59. Liddle interview, 1973, Tape 70, transcript p. 4. Among the Payne documents in Leeds is Fenner Brockway's reply to Leonard's request for information about the NCF. It is dated 17th December 1915.

60. Leonard to Father, Mother and all, 14th June 1916.

61. Hansard, 5th January 1916, cols. 957-8.

62. Roland to Dad and Mother, 26th May 1916.

63. Roland to All, 27th May 1916.

64. Liddle interview, 1973, Tape 70, transcript, p. 9.

65. House of Lords Debate, 4th May 1916, col. 906.

66. Liddle interview, 1973, Tape 70, transcript, p. 9.

67. For all the Bishop's words, and all the difficulties involved, the Non-Combatant Corps had attracted by the end of 1916 over 3,000 conscientious objectors who did see it as a morally acceptable alternative to taking up arms themselves. (Rae, p. 194.) Others were prepared to join the Friends' Ambulance Unit and the Royal Army Medical Corps,

involved in non-combatant military support services, yielding a total in such work of, by one estimate, 5,344. (Cyril Pearce, *Comrades in Conscience. The Story of an English Community's Opposition to the Great War*, Francis Boutle, London, 2001, p. 177.) The Bishop of Oxford's judgement that: 'I venture to say that the Non-Combatant Corps has been from every point of view a great failure,' proved premature.

68. In fact, Leonard later referred to this letter: 'Surely you did not read that letter I wrote on brown paper at Wigston, did you copy it out again or something. I had a job to read it myself, so I don't know how you managed it.' Leonard to Father and all, 6th July 1916.

69. Leonard to Father, Mother and all, 14th June 1916. Paragraph structure added.

70. A copy of an advertisement for such men which appeared in the *Leicester Evening Mail* in September 1914 is printed in Matthew Richardson, *The Tigers. 6th, 7th, 8th and 9th (Service) Battalions of the Leicestershire Regiment*, Pen & Sword Books, Barnsley, 2000, p. 40.

71. Richard Holmes, *Tommy. The British Soldier on the Western Front, 1914-1918*, Harper Perennial, London, 2005, p. 348.

72. So, at any rate, was the view taken by the Bishop of Oxford when addressing the House of Lords on May 4th 1916: 'I presume that it is true to say that the very object of military discipline is to break the man in, to break his insubordination, and that therefore the business of the military authorities is conceived to be the breaking of his spirit. I suppose that is true. At any rate, they act on that principle', though this did bring a stout rejoinder from Lord Sandhurst on behalf of the War Office: 'I confess that, having been mixed up with soldiers all my life and having for a few years myself been a soldier, this is the first time I have ever heard that the object of discipline was to break a man's spirit', a reply which left ample scope for day-to-day bullying on every parade ground in Britain. (House of Lords Debate, 4th May 1916, cols. 910 and 919.) None of which, of course, can begin to explain, let alone condone, the brutality experienced by many everyday soldiers at the huge army base known as the Bullring, near Étaples, with those enduring military prison in the worst position. One conscientious objector, Robert Price, wrote that 'My knowledge of is based on a month's stay at Étaples, the remainder at Les Attaques No. 5 Military Prison. It was here I witnessed and experienced the most barbarous treatment. I will content myself by giving an extract from a letter by me on my return to Wandsworth Prison. On the "compound" at Étaples we were horse-whipped, half-choked by sandbags slung round our necks, and thrown into dark cells. Later, for an hour and a half, ten or twelve of the army's biggest bullies set about five of us, for refusing to obey the order to "double" – and we were whipped, struck and kicked, with fists and boots, thrown down, kicked whilst down, thrown against the railings, shaken as a dog would shake a rat, pushed and dragged about until totally

exhausted, and we were all on the point of collapse.' And he had worse tales to tell about others. (Robert Price, *For His Name's Sake: Being a Record of the Witness given by Members of Churches of Christ in Great Britain against Militarism during the European War, 1914-1918*, published by W. Barker, Heanor, 1921, quoted in Peter Brock (ed.), *These Strange Criminals. An Anthology of Prison Memoirs by Conscientious Objectors from the Great War to the Cold War*, Toronto, 2004, pp. 85-6.)

73. Gilbert Murray, ibid., p. ix.

74. Roland later remembered that one conscientious objector had given up because he was not allowed to smoke. Liddle interview, 1973, Tape 70, transcript, p. 10.

75. The minister's response was less than helpful, pleading that 'the labour involved in procuring answers to such inquiries is enormous. No such staff is available at present, and, if the House considers that answers to inquiries of this kind should be secured, a special staff will become necessary. I am reluctant any further to ask officials, not only in the War Office, but in the various commands, to undertake work of this kind in addition to that with which they are already overburdened,' to which Snowden retorted: 'Are these men then to continue to be tortured because inquiry may involve a little trouble at the War Office?'

76. Marion Harper to Jessie, 27th June 1916.

77. Noakes and Graham quoted in Denis Winter's, *Death's Men. Soldiers of the Great War*, Penguin Books, Harmondsworth, 1979, pp. 39-41.

78. Leonard to Father, Mother and all, 14th June 1916.

79. Liddle interview, 1973, Tape 70, transcript, p. 9. One NCO responsible for ill-treating conscientious objectors later expressed his regrets: 'We had to do it, I suppose that was our excuse. But ever since then I've admired these men intensely. I would take off my hat to them any time, because I realise that what they did in defying the British military might – and they defied it in every way possible – they had far more guts than we did who were doing these things to them.' (Sergeant Charles Lippett of the Queen's Royal West Sussex Regt., quoted in Arthur, Max (ed.), *Forgotten Voices of the Great War. A New History of WW1 in the words of the Men and Women who were there*, Ebury Books, London, 2003, pp. 109.)

80. *Manual of Military Law*, War Office, 1914, p. 417. Archibald Baxter, a New Zealand conscientious objector who by some bizarre twist of military logic was shipped to Britain in 1917, left this harrowing description of Field Punishment No.1: 'He [the NCO] took me over to the poles, which were willow stumps, six to eight inches in diameter and twice the height of a man, and placed me against one of them. It was inclined forward out of the perpendicular. Almost always afterwards he picked the same one for me. I stood with my back to it and he tied me to it by the ankles, knees and wrists. He was an expert at the job, and knew how to pull and strain at the ropes

till they cut into the flesh and completely stopped the circulation. When I was taken off my hands were always black with congested blood. My hands were taken back behind the pole, tied together and pulled well up it, straining and cramping the muscles and forcing them into an unnatural position. Most knots will slacken after a time. His never did. The slope of the post brought me into a hanging position, causing a large part of my weight to come on my arms and I could get no proper grip with my feet on the ground, as it was worn away round the pole and my toes were consequently much lower than my heels. I was strained so tightly up against the post that I was unable to move body or limbs a fraction of an inch... The mental effect was almost as frightening as the physical. I felt I was going mad.' (Archibald Baxter, *We Will Not Cease. The Autobiography of a Conscientious Objector*, Victor Gallancz, London, 1939, pp. 155-6.)

81. Liddle interview, 1973, Tape 70, transcript, p. 9. Regulations stated that a man should be subjected to Field Punishment No. 1 for no more than two hours per day, usually one hour in the morning and one in the afternoon. We suppose these timings were imposed on the conscientious objectors in the Glen Parva Barracks.

82. Leonard to Father and all, 14th June 1916.

83. His first appearance in a Leicester directory is in *Wright's Directory* of 1909 where he warrants two entries: as a 'representative' – of what is not specified – operating from his home address at that time on Kirby Road in the west of Leicester, and as Managing Director of Harper's Cycle Co. Ltd., on Belgrave Gate.

84. E. & A. Hamilton to Leonard, 21st June 1916.

85. Thomas Harper to Leonard and Roland, 22nd June 1916.

86. 'We all like Marrion [sic] very much, I think she is lovely.' Jessie to Leonard, June 1916.

87. Thomas's sister, Marion's aunt, was Secretary to the Burnley branch of the NCF. Mother to Leonard, 22nd July 1916.

88. Marion to Mr Payne, 20th July 1916.

89. The most conveniently available translation is by Paul Foote in *Master and Man and other stories,* Penguin Classics, Harmondsworth, 1977. Her choice of this story for Leonard to read is intriguing, for in Tolstoy's story Sergius is brought down by his inability to control his sexual urges. It may have been unintentional, or it may have been a subtle warning to Leonard about his own behaviour, or could there have been a barely decipherable sub-text in Marion's choice of reading for Leonard? We have no evidence of any inappropriate contact between them.

90. Marion to Leonard, 19th June 1917 (misdated 1919 in original).

91. Kennedy, p. 236.

92. Marion, incomplete letter, July/August 1917.

93. Leonard to Father, Mother and all, 14th June 1916.

94. Leonard to Father and all, 14th June 1916.

95. Liddle interview, Tape 70, transcript, p. 10.

96. Leonard to Father and all, 14th June 1916.

97. Roland to Mother and Dad, 15th July 1916.

98. Roland's 'Diary since leaving Wigston Barracks until now', written Friday morning 23rd June 1916.

99. Dorothy Gittins' letter to Mrs Payne, in among the Payne documents in the Liddle Collection, Brotherton Library, University of Leeds. Marion to Leonard 26th June 1916.

100. Leonard to Mother from the train in Sheffield, 11.30 a.m. 16th June 1916.

101. *Kelly's Directory of Durham*, 1914, p. 545.

102. Sybil Reeder (compiled by), *Memories of Whitburn in Words and Pictures*, Whitburn, 2007.

103. According to a plaque which used to stand there the camp buildings were rebuilt in brick in the 1950s; it was shut down at the end of March 2010.

104. From the plaque referred to above. An interesting explanation of home-based training trench-systems to be found on Cannock Chase can be seen at www.staffspasttrack.org.uk.

105. Roland's 'Diary', written 23rd June 1916.

106. Roland to Mother and Dad, 29th June 1916.

107. Roland's 'Diary', written 23rd June 1916.

108. ibid.

109. Roland to Mother and Dad, postmarked 24th June 1916.

110. Liddle interview, Tape 70, transcript, pp. 12-13.

111. In November 1916 Wise was promoted Lieutenant Colonel of the 3rd Battalion, Sherwood Foresters. (Army List 1918.)

112. Roland's 'Diary', written 23rd June 1916.

113. ibid.

114. Leonard to Jessie, 28th June 1916.

115. Roland's 'Diary', written 23rd June 1916.

116. Leonard to Jessie, 28th June 1916.

117. ibid.

118. Roland's 'Diary', written 23rd June 1916.

119. Leonard to Jessie, 28th June 1916.

120. ibid.

121. ibid.

122. Leonard to Dora and all, 2nd July 1916. Richard Holmes, 'Tommy', pp. 555ff. is illuminating about the unofficial side of military conduct.

123. Leonard to Jessie, 28th June 1916.

124. ibid.

125. Corder Catchpool, *On Two Fronts: Letters of a Conscientious Objector*, George Allen and

Unwin, London, 1918, 3rd edn., 1940, p. 117. Letter dated 23rd January 1917. Wound Stripes were normally worn on the left forearm and denoted a wound sustained in combat.

126. The conscientious objector Edward Williamson Mason pondered the influence of this definition of 'manliness' on the army. 'I thought what a good effect women would have were they allowed to assist in the administration of the army,' he mused in 1916, whilst in military custody at Catterick. 'I am sure their presence in the guardroom, for example, would alter its coarse tone into something finer and more sympathetic. Men together – and women together for that matter – dwelling away from the other sex, deteriorate and develop characteristics which society, through the intermingling of the sexes, has come to taboo or reprehend... Womanly influence would soften the rigidity of the army and make it more comfortable... Of course the army scorns the womanly influence. The Regimental Sergeant Major, after he had exhausted all his powers of persuasion and all the force of his personality, exclaimed as a final, heartfelt appeal: "Surely, surely, Mason, you are not going to act the woman?" "Aye, yes, I'll act the woman if I can be as kind and as gentle as the lady who has just visited me – Mrs Thompson, a Quaker lady from York. What a pleasure to talk to such a body." She was with me for about fifteen minutes. I have not had such a glow of pure joy since my arrest.' E. Williamson Mason. *Made Free in Prison*, George Allen & Unwin, London, 1918, pp. 62-3. The issue of 'manliness' has attracted a lot of attention from historians, for example Bibbings, *Telling Tales*, pp. 90-103 where the 'manliness' of the soldier is contrasted with the 'unmanliness' of the conscientious objector; see also George L. Mosse, *Fallen Soldiers. Reshaping the Memory of the World Wars*, O.U.P., 1990, esp. pp. 60-64. Much of the wartime propaganda made use of this gender dichotomy, the role of the male to protect the female emphasised throughout, from Belgian women to Edith Cavell. See Nicoletta Gullace, *"The Blood of Our Sons": Men, Women, and the Renegotiation of British Citizenship During the Great War*, Palgrave Macmillan, Basingstoke, 2002, p. 100. This is not a purely European, let alone British, attitude, and examples can be found in a wide range of cultures. The anthropologist Maurice Davie, for example, wrote of the 'manliness' v. 'womanliness' dichotomy that 'when the Iroquois denationalized the Delawares and prohibited them from going to war, the latter were, according to the Indian notion, "made women" and were henceforth to confine themselves to pursuits appropriate to women. Among the Pomo of California, when a man became too infirm to be a warrior, he was made a menial and required to assist the squaws. This is true in Cuba and Greenland, with the additional degradation of wearing female dress.' Quoted in Barbara Ehrenreich, *Blood Rites. The Origins and History of the Passions of War*, Granta, London, 2011, p. 126, and the other examples given there. The concept is well enough known to anyone familiar with the

'women and children first' evacuation of the *Titanic* and the castigation of Bruce Ismay for allegedly dressing as a *woman* to escape with his life.

127. The typescript is held in the Liddle Collection, Brotherton Library, University of Leeds.

128. Leonard to Mother, 24th June 1916.

129. Leonard to Father and Mother, 12.30 p.m., Sunday 25th June 1916.

130. Roland to Mother, 19th July 1916.

131. Roland to Mother and Dad, postmarked 24th June 1916.

132. *Manual of Military Law*, War Office, London, 1914, p. 387.

133. Leonard to Jessie, 28th June 1916.

134. Roland to Mother and Dad, postmarked 24th June 1916.

135. Leonard to Dora, 26th June 1916.

136. Army Order X of May 25th 1916 had decreed that all men convicted but claiming a conscientious objection should be confined in civil prisons under Home Office control, rather than military prisons under the War Office. Liaison with the civil prison authorities may also have been a factor in delaying their court martial.

137. Thomas Harper to Mr and Mrs Payne, 24th June 1916. Corder had had experience of imprisonment for defying the military call-up in Australia where the compulsory military training scheme in force since 1911 made no allowance for conscientious objection and had young men imprisoned and sometimes subjected to solitary confinement. (Australian Parliamentary Library website at www.aph.gov.au/library/pubs.) He was the author of a pamphlet entitled *Compulsory Military Service in Australia and New Zealand*, published by Burtt Bros., Hull, n.d., catalogued in the Friends Library in London under 'Northern Friends Peace Board', Vol. 1, 1916-1928: 'Under the fair-sounding name of Citizen Service,' Corder wrote, 'there has been set up in our Dominions a system of military training which contains in it the germ of all the evils of European conscription. It has placed its grip on the mere child, enrols him as part of the military machine, and puts him under military control to mould his character and fashion him to its will.' That John and Jessie wrote to Herbert Corder is confirmed in Mother's letter to Leonard dated 30th June 1916. Ironically, Australia's Defence Act of 1903 had recognised conscience as grounds for exemption from military service.

138. Marion to Jessie, 27th June 1916. Among the Payne papers is a list of 'Members of the F.o.R. in Sunderland. It is undated and unsigned. It is not in Marion's handwriting. It contains five names and addresses, all in Sunderland: 'T.R. Blumer, 3 The Elms. Herbert Corder, 1 Carlton Terrace, (a leading Quaker). O. Gibson, 6 Worcester Terrace. Mrs. K.W. Jones, 14 St. Bedes Terrace. Mr. J.H. Wilkinson, c/o Mrs Arneson [?], 7 Lorne Terrace (probably a C.O.).'Another was Dick Heil from an address in nearby

Monkwearmouth, who sent the brothers a postcard dated the 29th June:Dear Comrades, Can you communicate with me at the above address, letting me know when would be the best time, and how to get to see you. Is there anything particular that you want? Yours fraternally Dick Heil. But Dick Heil's letter took the best part of a week in getting to Leonard, just a few miles away, and by that time it was hardly worth replying: 'they would not let him see us,' Len told his sister, 5th July 1916.

139. Thomas Harper to Mrs and Mrs Payne, 24th June 1916.

140. Roland to Mother and Dad, 29th June 1916. Their identity is not revealed, though it is possible that they could have been Herbert Corder and/or Mr Robertson's brother. Leonard was aware of their presence, and wrote home to his family a few days afterwards that 'I do not think it would be any good me writing to the address you have given me because they would not let him see us unless he got special permission from Major Wise 3rd Sherwood Foresters he might get it if he wrote to him. You see that may have been the gentleman that came up the other day to see me. I cannot tell.' Leonard to Father and all, Friday (June 30th) 1916, six o'clock.

141. Thomas Emmerson to Miss Gitten [sic], 1st July 1916.

142. Mother to Roland, 22nd July 1916.

143. Mary Harper to Leonard, 6th July 1916.

144. Mother to Leonard, 3rd July 1916.

145. Leonard to Father and Mother, 25th June 1916.

146. E. Williamson Mason, pp. 46-7. Entry for 26th July 1916. Garston would, in fact, give up his conscientious objection when threatened with the military prison at Wakefield. ibid. p. 72.

147. Roland to Dad and Mother, 30th June 1916.

148. Roland to Mother and Dad, 1st July 1916.

149. Liddle interview, 1973, transcript, Tape 70, p. 11.

150. Leonard to Father and all, Friday (30th June) six o'clock.

151. Leonard to Jessie, 5th July 1916.

152. ibid.

153. Roland to Dad and Mother, undated. Bizarrely the card is postmarked on both June 27th in Sunderland and June 28th in Wolverhampton. It seems unlikely that this signifies anything sinister: though the letter and the envelope are written in pencil, there is, for instance, no sign of a Wolverhampton address having been written first, then rubbed out and Roland's home address substituted. And anyway, the Lutterworth address is clearly in Roland's own handwriting. Paranoia had here been taken too far! On the troops passing through Lutterworth in 1915, evidently the source of some local excitement, the *Rugby Advertiser* reported on a two-night billet by a 'considerable body of troops from one of the huge preparatory camps, some thousands of whom

will shortly be trekking through Leicestershire,' adding that 'the schools, Town Hall and all public rooms are bring requisitioned, the villages in the neighbourhood also coming in for their share.' *Rugby Advertiser*, 27th March 1915. It would appear that other soldiers passed through the town, for the Workhouse Guardians' Minutes in April reported 'the receipt of and payment to the Treasurer of 11/8d for 70 soldiers billeted in the [Workhouse] Hospital on the 7th inst.' (Board of Guardians Minutes, 29th April 1915. LRO.DE1909/353.)

154. J. Kirk is not an uncommon name, but a Company Sergeant Major John Kirk, 1st/5th Sherwood Foresters, died on 1st July 1917 and is commemorated on the Arras Memorial. (C.W.G.C.) Edward Williamson Mason, at Catterick Camp, also found a friendly soldier willing to smuggle a letter out for him. op. cit., letter dated 27th July 1916.

155. Roland to Mother and Dad, 1st July 1916.

156. Seaward Beddow to 'Dear Friend', 1st July 1916.

157. Leonard to Jessie, 5th July 1916.

158. For example a security service document dated 20th July 1915, declared that 'Many people are asking where the funds are coming from to carry on this Peace propaganda. There is little doubt there is German money in it, but it is impossible to find out the source through which it percolates.' Quoted in Hiley, p. 650; see also the slightly different quotation from the same document in Christopher Andrew, *The Defence of the Realm. The Authorized History of MI5*, Allen Lane, London, 2009, p. 94.

159. For a full account see Millman, esp. pp. 78-82.

160. Major Victor Ferguson to Vernon Kell, head of MI5, 14th June 1916, quoted in Hiley, p. 651.

161. Hew Strachan, *The First World War*, Pocket Books, London, 2006, p. 230.

162. Andrew, p. 53.

163. Herbert Corder to 'My Dear Friend', 27th July 1916. Presumably Corder's support for conscientious objectors had come too close to advocating refusal of conscription, which was illegal under the Defence of the Realm Act. Corder's caution is entirely understandable since in Australia he had been in prison for his defiance of the Australian Military Service Act.

164. This in addition to those suspected of spying. Hiley, p. 651.

165. ibid., p. 660.

166. Tania Rose, *Aspects of Political Censorship, 1914-1918*, University of Hull Press, Hull, 1995, p. 4. In fact the massive expansion in the role of the security services 'had come without any direct political review of the matter; it had been determined solely by the officials of the departments concerned.' Hiley, p. 660.

167. The details of the wider debate on the use of man- and woman-power can be found in *Adams and Poirier*, Chapter 9.

168. Rae, p. 161.

169. Leonard to the family, 2nd July 1916.

170. Mother to Roland, 21st July 1916. On the same day she wrote to Leonard referring to a letter John had written to him the previous day telling him about the scheme: this letter is not in the collection.

171. Marion to 'Mr Harper', 22nd July 1916.

172. Leonard to Dora and all, 2nd July

173. Leonard to Jessie, 28th June 1916.

174. Mother to Leonard, 3rd July 1916.

175. Leonard to Father and all, 6th July 1916.

176. Mother to Leonard, 30th June 1916.

177. Jessie to Roland, undated.

178. Leonard to Mother, 7th July 1916. In fact the Adjutant of the 3rd Sherwood Foresters sent a terse typed note to John dated Thursday July 6th informing him his sons' court martial would take place at Mayfield, Roker, on the Saturday morning at 10.30. Even with the best will in the world (which he had) John could not have got there in time. The letter is among the Payne papers in the Liddle Collection, Brotherton Library, Leeds University.

179. ibid.

180. 'I didn't think Lutterworth had altered much, and it doesn't seem as if Aunt Lucy has, she starts tales like that herself, she is "fishing" trying to catch news without asking.' Leonard to Mother, 7th July 1916.

181. Mother to Leonard, 3rd July 1916.

182. Leonard to Mother, 7th July 1916.

183. The original of this document, originally in the Payne family's collection, is now in the Liddle Collection in Leeds University's Brotherton Library. See also *Manual of Military Law*, War Office, 1914, p. 387.

184. Leonard to Jessie, 9th/11th July 1916.

185. Liddle interview 1973, Transcript, Tape 70, p. 11.

186. Leonard to Jessie, 9th/11th July 1916.

187. Roland to Mother and Dad, 11th July 1916.

188. Leonard to Mother and all, 13th July 1916.

189. Leonard to Mother, 7th July 1916.

190. Roland to Mother and Dad, 15th July 1916.

191. Leonard to Dora and all, 18th July 1916.

192. On his trip to the north-east, in his failed attempt to attend the boys' court martial, John had tried to call in on Mr Corder in Sunderland, only to find him out – another frustration. ibid.

193. ibid.

194. Roland to Mother, 19th July 1916. It is a tribute to the speed of communication that on the following Saturday Marion was able to report that she had met a lady who might be the mysterious 'Miss Smith'. Marion to 'Mr Payne', 22nd July 1916.

195. Leonard to Father and all, 6th July 1916.

196. Leonard to Mother and all, 13th July 1916.

197. Roland to Mother and Dad, 15th July 1916.

198. Roland to Mother and Dad, 11th July 1916.

199. Roland to Mother, 19th July 1916.

200. Roland to Mother, 20th July 1916.

201. Roland to Mother and Dad, 18th July 1916.

202. Leonard to Jessie, 16th July 1916.

203. ibid. It is possible that among the newly arrived conscientious objectors was W.J. Roughton, a Quaker from New Basford in Nottinghamshire. Leonard wrote to his widowed mother from Whitburn. See H.L. Roughton to Mrs Payne, 2nd September 1916.

204. ibid.

205. Leonard to Dora and all, 18th July 1916. The International Bible Students Association changed its name in 1931 to the Jehovah's Witnesses. See *Jehovah's Witnesses. Proclaimers of God's Kingdom*, Watch Tower Bible and Tract Society, New York, 1993, p. 149. I am grateful to Anna Slater for this reference.

206. Leonard to Mother, 1st July 1916.

207. Roland to Mother, 20th July 1916.

208. Liddle Interview 1973, transcript, Tape 70, p. 12. The details of their court martial, conviction and sentence were published in *The Tribunal* on July 27th, 1916, p. 4. There is no corroborating evidence for their conduct during the reading out.

209. Roland to Father, postmarked 20th July 1916.

210. Mother to Leonard, 22nd July 1916.

211. Leonard to Mother, 24th July 1916.

212. Roland to Dad and Mother, 24th July 1916.

213. Leonard to Mother, 24th July 1916.

214. ibid. He is mentioned first in a letter from Leonard written that Monday.

215. Quoted in Alistair Horne, *The Price of Glory. Verdun 1916*, Penguin Books, Harmondsworth, 1964, pp. 43-4. Ian Ousby, *The Road to Verdun. France, Nationalism and the First World War*, Jonathan Cape, London, 2002, pp. 40-41, suggests that Falkenhayn was in fact planning nothing very different from other Great War Generals, though his statement of attrition was worded more bluntly than most. See also Malcolm Brown, *Verdun 1916*, Tempus Books, London, 2003, p. 34. The evidence,

though, is not clear-cut, and some historians now believe that the 'attrition' claim was merely a screen to cover the fact that he tried to capture Verdun in 1916 and failed. (Hew Strachan, *The First World War. A New Illustrated History*, Simon and Schuster, London, 2003, p. 184.) Whatever the truth of that, what Falkenhayn had stumbled upon – a war of attrition in which 'the balance of numbers' of those remaining alive at the end would be decisive – chills the blood. By the end of the Battle of Verdun some 377,000 Frenchmen were dead, wounded, captured or missing. The comparable German figure was 337,000, so the Germans could, on the balance of numbers' theory, count this a success. (Brown, pp. 230-1.) Such was the madness of this war.

216. An acquaintance of the brothers, Billy Ball, was at the battle on board *H.M.S. Benbow*. Leonard to Dora and all, 18th July 1916.

217. Tuesday 13th June, 1916. LRO.DE 3614/7.

218. Useful are Martin Middlebrook, *The First Day on the Somme*, Allen Lane, London, 1971; A.H. Farrar-Hockley, *The Somme*, Batsford, London, 1964; Lyn Macdonald, *Somme*, Michael Joseph, London, 1983; Peter Liddle, *The 1916 Battle of the Somme. A Reappraisal,* Leo Cooper, London, 1992.

219. Gary Sheffield and John Bourne (eds.), *Douglas Haig. War Diaries and Letters, 1914-1918*, Weidenfeld & Nicolson, London, 2005, p. 110.

220. Arthur Conan Doyle, *The British Campaign in France and Flanders*, 1916, Hodder & Stoughton, London, 1918, pp. 41-2.

221. A.H. Farrar-Hockley, *The Somme*, Batsford, London, 1964, p. 117.

222. Leonard to Mother and all, 13th July 1916.

223. Roland to Mother and Dad, 15th July 1916.

224. Liddle interview 1973, Tape 70, transcript, pp. 12-13.

225. Leonard to Mother and all, 25th July 1916 (incomplete). Roland drew a brief pen portrait of Colonel Heath in one of his letters home: 'He is a very stern and harsh man, also a bit of a German just like the Kaiser, and has served a lot of time in Germany on the Secret Service Staff for our government.' Roland to Dad and Mother, 6th July 1916.

226. ibid.

227. Cpl. G.R. Lockton to 'Dear Sir', undated.

228. Leonard to Mother, 26th July 1916. The letter from the girl friend in Cotesbach is not in the collection.

229. Major Wise to John Payne, 4th August 1916.

230. See Michel Foucault, *Discipline and Punish. The Birth of the Prison*, trans. Alan Sheridan, Peregrine Books, London, 1979, esp. pp. 236-9.

231. Newcastle Prison Male Nominal Register. DRO P/1/8, Vol. 107. Leonard's name appears at entry number 524 and Roland's at 525. There were, of course, more serious

offenders admitted to the prison at this time, including thieves and several convicted of child cruelty. No one had been hanged in Newcastle Prison since the demented triple-murderer John Amos in 1913. Peter Wilson, *Twentieth Century Hangings*, Blackie, London, 2002, pp. 159-60.

232. Fred Tait, *Diary of a Conscientious Objector, 23 March 1918 to 26 April 1918*, Quaker Library, London, Temp. MSS 907, pp. 17-18.

233. Leonard, Liddle interview, 1973, Tape 44. See also *Among the Broad-Arrow Men of Leicester Gaol, 1920. A Plain Account of English Prison Life* by 'B-2-15', reprinted by David Dover, Loughborough, n.d. (2008), p. 2.

234. Leonard, Liddle interview, 1973, Tape 44.

235. A copy of the document is among the Payne brothers' documents held in the Liddle Collection, Leeds University.

236. Quoted in Lyn Smith (ed.), *Voices against War. A Century of Protest*, Mainstream Publishing, Edinburgh & London, 2009, p. 37.

237. Robert Price, 'Prison' in *For His Name's Sake. Being a Record of the Witness given by Members of Churches of Christ in Great Britain against Militarism during the European War 1914-1918*, W. Barker, Printer, Mansfield Road, Heanor, 1921. Fred Tait, in his unpublished *Diary of a Conscientious Objector*, written between 23rd March and 26th April 1918 while he was in Leicester Prison as a kind of retrospective of his twenty-one months of imprisonment, wrote that 'in solitary confinement thought becomes torture, and life is an unbearable burden. A man is thrown absolutely upon himself and most men are unable to be sufficient for themselves.' Quaker Library, London, Temp. MSS 907, p. 18. A schoolteacher before conscription, Tait noted the decline in his own mental faculties with bewildered mystification: close to the point where he would give up his resistance and, by implication, allow himself to be drafted into the military, he wrote in his 'Diary' that 'Even now I cannot express myself properly, as soon as I begin to talk my vocabulary disappears… I doubt if I could count properly at tennis, I am certain I couldn't at billiards, my chess is in a mist, and I am not quite sure I could repair a puncture properly… Two years sewing mail-bags and pasting books has wiped out all the important facts with which I used to spoon feed about fifty small boys and girls.' pp. 11 and 62-3.

238. For example, Stephen Hobhouse and Fenner Brockway's influential 1922 book *English Prisons Today*. Hobhouse's *An English Prison from Within* is reprinted in Peter Brock (ed.), *These Strange Criminals. An Anthology of Prison Memoirs by Conscientious Objectors from the Great War to the Cold War*, Toronto, 2004, pp. 14-29.

239. 'B-2-15', *Among the Broad-Arrow Men of Leicester Gaol, 1920. A Plain Account of English Prison Life*, reprinted by David Dover, Loughborough, n.d. (2008). The specific experiences of those imprisoned in Leicester can be usefully traced through this book.

240. Robert O. Mennell, *The Conscientious Objector in Prison*, in *The No-Conscription Fellowship. A Souvenir of its Work during the Years 1914-1919*, London, 1919, p. 55.

241. 'B-2-15', pp. 9 and 121.

242. Leonard, Liddle interview, 1973.

243. Price, ibid. According to one Scottish objector, Eric Dott, held in Wormwood Scrubs, the porridge there was cooked unsalted, and was virtually inedible to the English prisoners: only the Scottish prisoners knew how to salt it. (Quoted in Trevor Royle, *The Flowers of the Forest. Scotland and the First World War*, Birlinn Books, Edinburgh, 2007, p. 248.) Fenner Brockway, in his memoir *Inside the Left*, referred to the limited form of communication provided by walls and water-pipes as the 'pipe-phone'.

244. Catchpool, pp.119 and 151. It would have been interesting to have heard Catchpool's comments on life on the Western Front in the trenches, if he had ever experienced that. Without in any way trying to out-do Catchpool, one un-named objector commented that: 'Men are animalised here… The reforming zeal of John Howard surely did not intend the solitary system to become (I cannot describe it better otherwise) a human dog-kennel.' (Quoted in Peter Brock (ed.), *These Strange Criminals. An Anthology of Prison Memoirs by Conscientious Objectors from the Great War to the Cold War*, Toronto, 2004, p. 17.)

245. 'B-2-15', p. 11. The conscientious objector Fred Tait found the same even after months in gaol: 'Sleep refuses to be wooed in prison at reasonable times… As soon as I get into bed my brain becomes extraordinarily active… A film of events over which I seem to have no control, is displayed before me… I try my left side, thump the very hard pillow, turn on my right side, try on my back, try tying my legs in a knot… But it is no use.' Tait, p. 35.

246. Tait, p. 36.

247. Leonard, Liddle interview, 1973.

248. Roland, Liddle interview, 1973, Tape 70.

249. 'B-2-15', pp. 12-13.

250. Liddle interview, Tape 40, transcript, p. 2.

251. Tait, p. 24.

252. ibid. pp. 24 and 27. Stephen Hobhouse's reflections on prison warders, written in 1919, can be found in Peter Brock (ed.), pp. 22-3.

253. *The Tribunal*, 3rd August 1916.

254. Liddle interview, Tape 40, transcript, p. 2.

255. 'B-2-15', p. 30. Leonard too remembered the Sunday corned beef, served with a chunk of bread. In April 1917 prison rations were reduced due to food shortages caused by the war. (ibid., p. 14.) Stephen Hobhouse, in prison at that time as a conscientious objector, said that: 'There is good evidence to show that many men are suffering seriously from

under-feeding. Nearly all of us constantly knew what hunger means; and an extra crust of dry bread would be to most a great prize.' (Quoted in Brock (ed.), p. 19.)

256. Leonard, Liddle interview, 1973.

257. ibid., Tape 40, transcript, p. 2.

258. 'Abstract of the Regulations Relating to the Treatment and Conduct of Convicted Prisoners', rule 5.

259. *The Tribunal*, 3rd August 1916.

260. 'B-2-15', p. 30. The complex *Dietary for Prisoners in Local Prisons* can be found among the Payne documents in the Liddle Collection, Leeds. Hubert Peet left a detailed account of the prison diet – and of his own reactions to prison life – in his *112 Days' Hard Labour: Being some Reflections on the First of My Sentences as a Conscientious Objector*, published by 'The Ploughshare', London, 1917 and quoted in Brock (ed.), pp. 38-49.

261. Roland to Mother, 1st September 1916.

262. *The C.O. Clink Chronicle*, pub. National Labour Press, London, Manchester & Leicester, n.d., p. 10, found among the Payne brothers' papers.

263. Tait, p. 43. He later encountered the same doctor who 'came round for a medical inspection… He walked into each cell, "Pull yer sleeve up" said a warder. The M.O. touched me on the wrist and walked out. I was satisfactory.' ibid., p. 43.

264. B-2-15, pp. 3, 27 and 29.

265. Roland, Liddle interview, 1973.

266. Leonard, Liddle interview, 1973.

267. Letter quoted in *The Tribunal*, 29th June 1916. The 14th September issue of *The Tribunal*, however, reported that six men held in Lewes Gaol were refusing work and were accordingly being put on bread and water for three days each week. The prison doctor, described in the piece as a 'brute', reportedly told them they would 'go mad in less than six weeks'. (*The Tribunal*, 14th September 1916 among the Payne brothers' papers in the Liddle collection, Leeds University.)

268. 'B-2-15', p. 31.

269. ibid., p. 61.

270. Liddle interview, Tape 40, p. 15.

271. Leonard, Liddle interview, 1973. 'B-2-15' described a similar form of communication, p. 123. Len, in his written statement to Peter Liddle prior to the 1973 interview, described another form of illicit communication: 'Chapel was one of our main sources of making contact with the person we wished to speak with. This was done by singing the words we wished to convey into the ear of the person directly in front.' This was not referred to in the interview itself. 'B-2-15' described this form of communication in more detail: 'A congregation of bawling men and an organ can cover a multitude of forbidden words, and the voices behind sang to the tune of the organ, first one man,

then his neighbour, but instead of "And behold from henceforth," came the question, "What are you in for?" Then followed the reply, which should have been, "All generations shall call me blessed," "I'm in for shop-breaking"; and, again, during the singing of "For He that is Mighty hath magnified me," "How long have you got?" and the reply "Six months' hard labour" substituted for "And Holy is His name." p. 62. The similarity of these two passages raises the suspicion that Leonard's recollection on this point may have been a false one, given nearly sixty years after the event; it is possible that he had heard of this way of communicating messages from other imprisoned conscientious objectors later, or even that he had at some point read 'B-2-15's book, since its subject matter could not but have been of interest to him, given his own experiences. His use of the word 'we' in his written statement does not convey personal involvement, his failure to mention such a striking form of communication in the interview which followed, and the intrinsic unlikelihood that he would have used divine service for such a purpose, all make his claim seem unreliable.

272. Leonard, Liddle interview, 1973.

273. Leonard to Mother, 29th August 1916.

274. John Payne to the Governor, Newcastle Prison, 14th August 1916.

275. The reply was dated August 15th 1916.

276. Mother to the Governor, Newcastle Prison, 22nd August 1916.

277. Quaker Visitation Committee to Mother, 23rd August 1916.

278. Leonard, Liddle interview, 1973, Tape 44. What might have been: the Quaker conscientious objector Stephen Hobhouse characterised his 'fortnightly half-hour of united worship and our fortnightly ten minutes with our visiting minister' as 'brief glimpses of Heaven.' (Quoted in Brock (ed.), p. 17.)

279. Governor, Newcastle Prison, to Mother, 23rd August 1916, on reverse of Mother to the Governor, Newcastle Prison, 22nd August 1916.

280. Herbert Corder to John Payne, 30th August 1916.

281. See, for example, Gary Sheffield, *Forgotten Victory. The First World War: Myths and Realities*, Review Books, London, 2002, passim; Michael Howard et al, *A Part of History. Aspects of the British Experience of the First World War*, Continuum, London, 2008, esp. Gary Sheffield's essay which forms Chapter 1.

282. Gerard Oram, *Death Sentences passed by Military Courts of the British Army 1914-1924*, (ed. Julian Putkowski), Francis Boutle, London, 1998, p. 35. Another member of the Non-Combatant Corps, Alfred Evans, was sentenced to death on June 24th. ibid., pp. 35-6.

283. War Office, *Manual of Military Law*, 1914, p. 387.

284. Julian Putkowski and Julian Sykes, *Shot at Dawn. Executions in World War One by Authority of the British Army Act*, Leo Cooper, London, 1992, pp. 76-78 and 79-80;

Cathryn Corns and John Hughes-Wilson, *Blindfold and Alone. Military Executions in the Great War*, Cassell, London, 2001, pp. 128-132; Gerard Oram, *Death Sentences passed by Military Courts of the British Army 1914-1924*, (ed. Julian Putkowski), Francis Boutle, London, 1998.

285. The ploy did not fool the other conscientious objectors, though Jessie, in a letter to Leonard dated July 5th, did refer to 'that bit of [news]paper you sent, it said that thirty-four had been sentenced to death, and then it does not say any more.' But she continued: 'That is not right, their sentence was commuted to ten years imprisonment, and they are back in England, but of course that only means for the duration of the war. Miss Gittins wrote and told us it was a gigantic bluff.' It is not clear what cutting Leonard had sent home, but one is left wondering why he would have sent such an incomplete version. Did he really believe the death sentences would stand (though he must have known they had been immediately commuted), or was he trying to frighten his family back home (when he must have known they knew the capital sentences had been commuted), or was he trying to make a point about the brutal treatment of the conscientious objectors by the military (when he must have known that these men were not actually going to be executed), or had he actually found an incomplete news report which he sent home to make a point about not trusting the press?

286. Gerard Oram, *Worthless Men. Race, Eugenics and the Death Penalty in the British Army during the First World War*, Francis Boutle, London, 1998, p. 42.

287. Boulton, pp. 173-4.

288. Hansard, 26th June 1916, cols. 521-8. To show that the old 'military mind' was still alive and well, a Colonel Griffiths asked: 'If these thirty-four men are sentenced to death for disobeying the orders of their superior officers, why are they not shot like other soldiers?' col. 524.

289. See Jannaway, pp. 142-228.

290. The details of the debate can be found in *Adams and Poirier*, Chapter 9.

291. ibid., pp. 186 and 199-200.

292. When the Quaker M.P. T. Edmund Harvey had suggested in late July 1916 that the conscientious objectors were 'neither numerous enough nor important enough, in the eyes of statesmen' to be the subject of intricate government subterfuge, he was fiercely condemned in a prickly editorial in *The Tribunal* on 27th July 1916; see also Kennedy, p. 159.

293. Rae, p. 162.

294. ibid., Appendix G.

295. Clifford Allen himself came up against the same barrier when questioned at his own Tribunal hearing: 'It is impossible to do anything at the present moment without assisting in the war,' he told a Tribunal member, 'If I eat I help the revenue. If I travel

by train or bus I help the revenue. If I forego smoking and left my money in the bank in current or deposit account, it would be used to assist the country. The only alternative is to leave the country, but that the government will not permit.' Quoted in Arthur Marwick, *Clifford Allen. The Open Conspirator*, Oliver & Boyd, London, 1964, p. 30. Allen here raised the more difficult question of taxation for war. The issue is explored in *Quaker Statements of Conscience. Documents from Britain Yearly Meeting and New York Yearly Meeting in support of war tax resisters in the UK and USA*, published by 'Peace Tax Seven', London, 2009.

296. The forty-nine men from Newcastle Prison who were transferred to Durham that day were, in alphabetical order and with their Newcastle Admission Numbers: Alexander Bain 465, Albert Bateman 399, A. Boyce 376 and 530, C. Bristol 585, Alfred Brocklebank 356, Fred Cocking 400 and 623, Arthur Askwith Craven 289, A. Daniels 610, S.J. Daniels 619, Norman Daniels 475, Alfred Herbert Dobbing 299, Arthur Dykes 476, C. Dykes 487, C.E. Fawcett 611, R.P. Flint 582, Aaron Ernest Gompertz 470, William Graham 332, Thomas Haig 388, Henry Hodgson 540, P. Horner 402, G. Horwill 614, H. Horwill 617, David Caradog Jones 327, J.R. Long 606, A. Marks 477, E. McEllin 613, J.H. McEllin 620, L. McEllin 615, P.J. McEllin 616, Percy Motham 624, Robert Pallister 297, Leonard Payne 524, Roland Payne 524, Abraham Philip Pearce 403, Soloman Pearce 404, Henry [sic Hy] Perceval Peart 561, Wilfred Purvis 584, R.N. Roughton 605, W.J. Roughton 581, William Shew 478, A.J. Statham 607, David Fleming Stephenson 354, Henry Stoddart 318, Walter Summerbell 298, Frederick Tait 413, W.H. Thompson 612, A.E. Vallance 580, H. Wall 618, and William Thomas Whitehouse 698. Newcastle Prison Male Nominal Register, Vol. 107. DRO P/1/8. There may have been others held in Durham Prison, but the corresponding Register for Durham is not in the Durham County Record Office.

297. Leonard to Mother, 29th August 1916.

298. Leonard, Liddle interview, Tape 44. Though this suggests that Leonard and Roland (or others) were held together in a shared cell, this could not have been the case. Solitary confinement was still the rule.

299. Roland to Mother, 12th September 1916.

300. ibid.

301. Ella Stevens to Mr Payne, 29th August 1916.

302. Leonard to Mother, 29th August 1916.

303. The Newcastle Prison Nominal Register (entry 388) spells his name without a final 'h', but his mother spelt it with one. Perhaps the Prison Officer's spelling was influenced by the name of the Commander of British Forces in France and Flanders, an understandable if somewhat inappropriate error.

304. Roland to Mother, 12th September 1916.

305. Mrs Haigh to Mr and Mrs Payne, 30th August 1916.

306. Roland to Mother, 12th September 1916.

307. Leonard to Father, 12th September 1916.

308. Central Tribunal to Mrs Payne, 30th August 1916. There is no mention in any of the Paynes' documents about what happened to their army pay.

309. Quoted in Brock (ed.), p. 57. William Temple nevertheless believed firmly in the State's right to use military force and the individual's responsibility to comply. He wrote in 1928, when Anglican Bishop of Manchester: 'The right of the State to employ force is derived from the fact that it alone acts for a community of such a kind that actual membership of it cannot be repudiated… If I am opposed to the requirements of the State, made in the name of the national community, I can only put myself outside their scope either by transferring myself to the territory of another state or by forgoing the advantages of civilisation altogether. Thus the State has a universal authority over its members such as is not elsewhere to be found. The force with which the State is entrusted is the means of making actual and effective this universality of Law.' (William Temple, *Christianity and the State*, Macmillan, London, 1928, pp. 112-3.) Temple went on to become Archbishop of Canterbury.

310. Roland to Mother, 12th September 1916.

311. Leonard to Mother, 1st September 1916.

312. Roland to Mother, 1st September 1916.

313. Fenner Brockway, who spent some time in Wormwood Scrubs, later described his own first reactions: 'We passed through arched cloisters along the edge of a green lawn overlooked by a chapel built in the Gothic style; this gave the appearance of a college rather than a gaol.' So far, so good – until he was taken to his cell: 'But inside the prison halls were of the same pattern [as other gaols] – long buildings with five storeys of cells, and spidery gangways and stairways'. op. cit., p. 90.

314. Leonard to Mother, 1st September 1916. It seems that this was one of the letters he smuggled off the train at York: 'We had a crowd of friends waiting at York for us with refreshments which were good. I have sent two letters home and given my address to a lady who will write you I expect so I hope you will hear in the end.' (Leonard to Jessie, undated, 'York 8.15'.)

315. ibid.

316. Leonard, Liddle interview, 1973, Tape 44.

317. Leonard, MS autobiographical notes, 1973.

318. Mrs L. Haigh to Mother, 11th September 1916. The delay in writing was caused by Mrs Haigh's mislaying the Paynes' address.

319. W.J. Roughton and R.N. Roughton appear in the Newcastle Prison Nominal Register at entries 581 and 605, and were among those sent to Wormwood Scrubs with the Paynes on August 29th.

320. H.L. Roughton to Mrs Payne, 2nd September 1916.

321. 12th September 1916. On September 5th their family had been officially notified that they were being held in Durham Prison and that they would now be allowed to send and receive letters, and that a visiting order would be sent to them in due course, effective on or about the 22nd.

322. 89.1% of those interviewed were accepted as genuine conscientious objectors. (Kennedy, p. 161 and nn. 19 and 20.) Numbers have to be treated with caution, their precise meaning ascertained. David Boulton wrote that overall, some 5,000 objectors were interviewed in prison, 3,750 of whom accepted the Home Office Scheme. About 1,350 rejected it as 'absolutists', 158 were deemed not to be genuine conscientious objectors, and a further 127 remained in prison because of their misbehaviour. (Boulton, p. 219.) According to figures produced by the No-Conscription Fellowship, by war's end 3,612 men had accepted the Home Office Scheme after serving a time in prison, from a total of 6,312 men who were arrested as conscientious objectors, or 57%. (*The No-Conscription Fellowship. A Souvenir of its work during the years 1914-1919*, p. 5.) The case is confused by men like Edward Williamson Mason who at first accepted the Home Office Scheme, but then gave back their word and became 'absolutists' instead, preferring to return to prison.

323. Leonard to Father, 12th September 1916.

324. ibid.

325. Roland to Mother, 12th September 1916.

326. ibid.

327. Roland to Mother, Dad, Jessie and Dora, 3rd October 1916.

328. Quoted in Jannaway, p.146. Jannaway quoted verbatim the list of approved occupational areas in which conscientious objectors could be employed. A summary is given in Boulton, p. 133.

329. Tait, p. 43.

330. Quoted in Felicity Goodall, *A Question of Conscience. Conscientious Objection in the two World Wars*, Sutton, Stroud, 1997, p. 4, with ref. to IWM Sound Archives 383/6.

331. Leonard, Liddle interview, 1973, Tape 44. At no point in their letters did the Payne brothers make the nature of their pacifism explicit. In part, it arose from an emphasis on rules, which by their written nature are open to variations in interpretation. As the American theologian John Yoder put it: 'The giving and receiving of communication, even if it be in the name of God, is subject to shadings of meaning which the habit of thinking of a limited number of absolute principles fails to respect. This is well exemplified by the very case of the Ten Commandments, where the strictest translation would probably read not, "Thou shalt not kill" but rather "Thou shalt do no murder".' (John H. Yoder, *Nevertheless: The Varieties and Shortcomings of Religious*

Pacifism, Scottdale, Pennsylvania and Kitchener, Ontario, 1971, pp. 30-31 and n. 12 on p. 136.) But the Paynes seem to have gone beyond this, relying on the Beatitudes: 'You have heard that it hath been said, Thou shalt love thy neighbour, and hate thine enemy. But I say unto you, Love your enemies, bless them that curse you, do good to them that hate you, and pray for them which despitefully use you, and persecute you.' (Matthew, 5, 43-44; Luke, 6, 27-28.) The texts here allow for no linguistic ambiguity, address not simple actions (whether 'kill' or 'do murder'), but the inner spirit of faith which lies behind Christian conduct. 'Here is the wisdom of God,' as Culbert Rutenber put it, 'for this emphasis on principles rather than rules insures the relevancy of the New Testament for every age.' (Culbert G. Rutenber, *The Dagger and the Cross: An Examination of Christian Pacifism*, New York, 1958, p. 46.)

332. Hirst, p. 520.

333. Quoted in Kennedy, p. 161.

334. Stephen Hobhouse, *Fourteen Months' Service with the Colours*, in Julian Bell (ed.), *We Did Not Fight, 1914-1918 Experiences of War Resisters*, Cobden-Sanderson, London, 1935, pp. 167-8. We must bear in mind that Hobhouse was writing in the mid-1930s, when the delayed shock of the Great War, the impact of the Great Depression, and the rise of fascist dictatorships across much of the world had led to the birth of a 'peace movement' in Britain. To call those who opposed the Great War at the time a 'movement' was premature.

335. We might pause to consider an opposing point of view – not 'idealism' over 'realism', but 'realism' over 'idealism' – most ably put by the great medievalist G.G. Coulton in 1917: 'If the non-resistant party, now clearly marked out from the rest by law and by legal registration, differentiates itself with anything like the same clearness in moral and intellectual qualities, we shall have gained one of the greatest steps forward towards world-peace. If their business-capacity, their probity, their self-sacrifice, their breadth of view and intelligent sympathy with adverse opinions, if their fortitude in face of the ordinary hardships and burdens of life makes it possible that conscientious objectors could preserve through adversity, by sheer moral force, something of that unity and determination which the soldier shows in the face of the enemy, then the world will begin to believe in the possibility of a non-resistant State. If their indifference to worldly goods proves equal to their dislike of the forcible methods by which alone the possession of worldly goods has ever been defended, here again their good example will effect what no mere words can ever do. They will show us how essentially false is the conception of the strong man armed, keeping his goods in peace. Few, however, really believe in the possibility of civilized existence without self-defence.' (G.G. Coulton, *The Case for Compulsory Military Service*, Macmillan, London, 1917, p. 248.)

336. Quoted in *The Tribunal*, 27th July 1916, p. 3. Lloyd George's famous – or infamous – statement on the treatment of the absolutists has gone down in conscientious objector folklore: 'With that kind of man I, personally, have no sympathy whatsoever. I do not think that they deserve the slightest consideration. With regard to those who object to shedding blood, it is the traditional policy of this country to respect that view, and we do not propose to depart from it; but in the other case I shall only consider the best means of making the path of that class as hard as possible.' (Quoted in Boulton, pp. 186-7.)

337. *The Tribunal*, 14th September 1916, p. 3.

338. Kennedy, pp. 159-60.

339. *The No-Conscription Fellowship. A Souvenir of its Work during the Years 1914-1919*, pp. 37-8. This amounts to 61%. Not all conscientious objectors were members of the NCF.

340. Kennedy, p. 161.

341. Leonard in Liddle interview transcript, Tape 44, p. 6.

342. Leonard to Mother, 24th July.

343. Leonard, Liddle interview, 1973, Tape 44.

344. Mother to Leonard, 3rd October 1916.

345. Mother to Roland, 4th October 1916.

346. Very few letters from the brothers during their time in Wakefield – apart from a few on strictly practical matters – have survived in the family's collection. It is certain that they wrote letters, for we have the family's replies, and we have plenty of letters written to them from home and from the Harpers, but the family appears not to have saved their letters home. We also have their own recollections of the nine or ten months they lived in Wakefield, given over half a century later, together with a handful of incidental documents. But their own reactions to life in the Wakefield Centre remain frustratingly sparse.

347. Marion to Leonard (?), 13th October 1916.

348. W.E.S Tyler (Home Office) to John Payne, 16th October 1916.

349. John to the 'Boys', 12th October 1916.

350. Jessie to Leonard and Roland, 12th October 1916.

351. Leonard, Liddle interview, 1973, Tape 44.

352. Alluded to in Mother's letter to Leonard, 3rd October 1916; and Mother to Roland, 4th October 1916.

353. Boulton, pp. 211-2. To suggest, as Boulton does, that Dyce was a 'prototype concentration camp' is absurd, an abuse of language and history.

354. Coulton, p. 297.

355. The doleful experience of the Boer War 'concentration camps' had created such a scandal that the government now was sensitive to the potential for bad publicity. See

Thomas Packenham, *The Boer War*, Weidenfeld & Nicolson, London, 1979, esp. Chapter 39.

356. Begbie was himself too old to be called up, but drew on the experiences of the conscientious objectors and then added the novelist's eye to graphically portray the ill-treatment of conscientious objectors in this novel, the publication of which was banned by the government's Press Bureau until after the war. His main character, the significantly named Christopher Sterling, dies in prison at the end of the novel. (Harold Begbie, *Mr Sterling Sticks it Out*, Headley Bros., London, 1919, esp. pp. 276-7 on prison conditions.) The published book contains documents relating to its ban during the war. His earlier pro-war writings led Henry Nevinson to describe him as 'that energetic christian', a rebuke whose sting can be felt still. (Henry W. Nevinson, in *The Conscientious Objector*, a typescript article in Friends' Library, London, Box L207/39, p. 3.)

357. Quoted in a piece by George Simmers via http://greatwarfiction.wordpress.com, which contains useful comments on Begbie's novel.

358. Kennedy, pp. 51-2. Many of the left-wing objectors and could not accept the original NCF creed that 'human life [is] sacred': hence the need for Clifford Allen and the others to re-write their statement of belief omitting the offending phrase.

359. Leonard, Liddle interview, Tape 40, transcript, p. 7.

360. Rae, pp. 180-1.

361. See R.S. Duncan*, Here We Go Round the Mulberry Bush. The House of Correction 1595 / HM Prison Wakefield 1995*, published by the author, 1994.

362. 'B-2-15', pp. 25-6.

363. Roland to Mother and Dad, 18th July 1916.

364. Leonard Payne, written statement to Peter Liddle, 1973. We might ponder this harrowing description of men forcibly dragged to their deaths with the men serving on the Western Front who were climbing up out of their trenches to go over the top to face a scarcely less certain death. The most recent man to be hanged here had been a forty-year-old soldier called William McCartney for the murder of his bigamously-married wife Charlotte, executed four days after Christmas in 1915. Wilson, p. 183.

365. Undated typescript statement by William Marwick, Liddle Collection, University of Leeds.

366. Marion to Friends, 31st January 1917.

367. It would seem also that they sent Marion a photograph taken inside one of the cells, though this has not survived. These photographs, however, were found among their papers in the Liddle Collection in Leeds.

368. Liddle interview, 1973, Tape 44, p. 5. Since the middle years of the nineteenth century Wakefield Prison had developed a reputation as a progressive prison in which convicts were put to useful work in place of the pointless and punishing treadmill and crank,

and considerable revenues were raised accordingly, out of which the prisoners were paid a small amount. Its conversion to Work Centre was thus within the traditions of the gaol. See: http://freepages.rootsweb.ancestry.com/~wakefield/prison/histpris.html

369. Jessie to Roland, 31st October 1916.

370. Undated typescript statement by William Marwick, Liddle Collection, Leeds. Emphasis added.

371. Robert Mennell, 'The C.O. in Prison', in *The No-Conscription Fellowship. A Souvenir of its Work during the Years 1914-1919*, London, 1919, p. 55.

372. ibid., p. 72.

373. Marwick typescript, Liddle Collection, Leeds.

374. 'It was a very good thing you took your Fiddle and I hope you will be a professional player at Christmas. What is Leonard going to play in the band, is he learning to fiddle.' Jessie to Roland, 31st October 1916.

375. 'I am sorry you got hurt at football but you cannott allways *[sic]* help these things what position does Bill play in would he like those large guards he had when at G School.' Father to Leonard, 7th December 1916.

376. Joe Todd to Len and Bill, 29th August 1917.

377. Liddle interview, Tape 44, p. 7.

378. A brief survey of the Newcastle Prison Nominal Roll Register suggests that the objectors' educational level was consistently above average, with a good proportion of men said to be of 'superior' education, while the average for the more common criminals was almost invariably given as average or below. Durham CRO.P/1/8.

379. Leonard Payne, written MS statement to Peter Liddle, 1973.

380. William Marwick to Leonard, 30th November 1917. For all that, a week or two later Leonard told Marion Harper that he was enjoying Browning's poetry, and she responded in kind, recommending 'Rabbi Ben Ezra' and 'The Flight of the Duchess'. Marion to Leonard, 6th December 1917.

381. Typescript autobiographical notes and *Transcript of Manuscript Journal, 1916*, both in the Liddle Collection, Brotherton Library, Leeds University.

382. William Marwick, typescript notes, Liddle Collection, Brotherton Library, Leeds University.

383. Liddle interview, Tape 40, transcript, p. 7.

384. Father to Leonard, 7th December 1916. In an undated letter from relatives in Rothwell, Leonard was asked: 'Please would you mind lending me your French book, the one you were showing me when you were home?' Reuben to Leonard, undated. On the reverse of some letters, e.g. 10th January 1917, Leonard had practised writing out numbers in French.

385. William Marwick, autobiographical notes, Liddle Collection, Leeds.

386. Jessie to Leonard and Roland, October 1916.

387. Mother to Roland, 4th October 1916.

388. Jessie to Leonard, 15th July 1916.

389. Lyn Macdonald, *Somme*, Michael Joseph, London, 1983, p. 99; Lutterworth Local History Group, *Lutterworth War Memorial Names, 1914-1918, 1939-1945: A Preliminary Study*, Lutterworth, 2005, from which all reference to individual local men are taken.

390. Lutterworth Parish Council Minutes, 30th November 1914 and 31st May 1915.

391. *Rugby Advertiser*, 2nd December 1916.

392. *Rugby Advertiser*, 7th October 1916.

393. Jessie to Leonard and Roland, 19th October 1916.

394. Mother to Leonard, 3rd July 1916. She wrote a very similar letter to Roland on the same day.

395. Dora to Leonard, 5th July 1916.

396. Jessie to Leonard, 5th July 1916.

397. Jessie to Leonard and Roland, 31st October 1916.

398. C. Drake to Leonard, 7th November 1916.

399. *Wakefield Express*, 6th January 1917.

400. See Peter Wood, *The Zivilinternierunglasger [sic] (Zivilinternierungslager) at Lofthouse Park*, in Kate Taylor (ed.), *Aspects of Wakefield. Discovering Local History 3*, Wharncliffe Books, 2001, pp. 97-107.

401. John Graham denied that there was hostility towards the conscientious objectors in the town: 'For a long time the efforts of the local press did not produce any hostility among the townspeople; later on a gang of roughs was organized to attack the C.O.s as they returned to the prison in the evenings'. (Graham, p. 233.) Late in the Wakefield Centre's life, in 1918, its inmates wrote to the Home Secretary to complain that the *Wakefield Express* was urging its readers to intimidate those men sent there from the Knutsford Centre. (Kennedy, p. 176, n. 73.) Graham's conspiracy theory is somewhat undermined by the fact that the press in Warwick printed similar sentiments in similar language from its own readers when the old prison there was converted into a Work Centre at the same time. (See the correspondence columns in *The Warwick and Warwickshire Advertiser* and *Leamington Gazette* between November 4th and 25th 1916.) It would appear that the local press was reflecting as much as moulding local public opinion.

402. *Wakefield Express*, 18th November 1916.

403. *Wakefield Express*, 25th November 1916.

404. *Wakefield Express*, 9th December 1916.

405. *Wakefield Express*, 23th December 1916.

406. ibid.

407. Jessie to Leonard, 19th Dec 1916. 'We are not doing anything in the way of making arrangements for you to come home we are leaving it entirely to Mr Harper, so you must fix it up with him...'

408. Marion to Leonard and Roland, 19th December, 1916. See also Jessie to Leonard, 19th Dec 1916.

409. Liddle interview, 1973, Tape 44, p, 11.

410. Jessie to Roland, 8th January 1917. The epic story of the Christmas of 1916 remained part of family legend, and Marion's prediction that 'You won't forget this 1916 Xmas adventure in a hurry I'm sure' proved true: Leonard recalled it in great detail in his manuscript autobiographical notes in 1973.

411. Kit Ball to Leonard, 21st July 1916.

412. See his typescript autobiographical notes in the Liddle Collection, Brotherton Library, University of Leeds.

413. Leonard Payne, interview with Peter Liddle, 1973, Tape 70. It is possible that the friends visited the Payne family in Lutterworth in 1917, for Jessie wrote to Leonard on June 21st that: 'It will be very nice if the six of you can get together, you are so used to each other'. (Jessie to Leonard 21st June 1917), and on 3rd July she told Leonard: 'We thought about you coming home for a night, if you go down south, before you mentioned it, we had even arranged where the six of you were going to sleep, and we had got you all fixed up.' (Jessie to Leonard 3rd July 1917) – though it seems inherently unlikely, and anyway there is no evidence the visit ever took place.

414. Ron Long to Leonard, 13th February 1918. Ewart and Ron may have been related.

415. Eddie to Leonard, 4th March 1918. It is not clear exactly who 'he' is.

416. Ron Long to Leonard, 13th December 1917.

417. *Wakefield Express*, 23rd December 1916. We have seen how Leicestershire's Chief Constable was keeping a paternalistic eye on the 'weaker sex' in his own county, acting not only as moral police but also to protect men away at the Front from the anxieties surrounding unsupervised wives and daughters at home.

418. *Wakefield Express*, 4th May 1918.

419. Ron Long to Leonard, undated letter fragment.

420. William Marwick to Leonard, 12th October 1917.

421. Will Deas to 'Lenard & Will' (i.e. Roland aka Bill), undated letter, October 1917.

422. William Marwick, fragment dated 25th December.

423. Captain J.C. Dunn, *The War the Infantry Knew, 1914-1919*, Abacus Books, London, 1994, p. 287.

424. All but Emmett had accompanied the Paynes from Newcastle to Durham and thence to Wakefield. Newcastle Prison Male Nominal Register, Vol. 107. Durham CRO, P/1/8.

425. *Wakefield Express*, 27th January 1917.

426. Jessie to Roland, 19th January 1917.

427. *Wakefield Express*, 27th January 1917. It goes without saying that the relatively small number of conscientious objectors would have had virtually no effect on the leave serving soldiers were granted.

428. *Wakefield Express*, 3rd February 1917.

429. *Wakefield Express*, 3rd February 1917. 'Once a "Tommy's" letter missed the point that Howard Marten had, in fact, been sent to France and sentenced to death but had still refused to comply and had stuck to his pacifist principles. All that was explained in Marten's letter, but since that letter was published in the same edition, it may well be that 'Once…' was not aware of the fact… if he had cared.

430. *Wakefield Express*, 10th February 1917.

431. Leonard Payne, Liddle interview transcript, Tape 40, p. 8.

432. Harry Hainsworth to 'My dear Friend', 6th November 1916.

433. ibid.

434. Edith Graham to Leonard, 8th November 1916. There may have been a family connection between the Grahams and the Hainsworths. Edith told Leonard that 'all at home… especially Harry' wished to be remembered to him.

435. Jessie to Leonard, 31st October 1916.

436. Edith Graham to Leonard, 8th November 1916. For the employment of women in the textile industry, see Deborah Thom, *Nice Girls and Rude Girls. Women Workers in World War 1*, I.B. Tauris, London, 2000, p. 35.

437. Edith Graham to Leonard, 25th December 1917.

438. Edith Graham to Leonard, 15th November 1916.

439. ibid.

440. Edith Graham to Leonard, 6th December 1916.

441. Edith Graham to Leonard, 23rd January 1918.

442. Jessie to Leonard, 22nd January 1917.

443. Edith Graham to Leonard, 25th January 1917.

444. Dora to Leonard, 30th January 1917.

445. Edith Graham to Leonard, 20th February 1917.

446. ibid.

447. Dora to Leonard, 7th November 1917.

448. Edith Graham to Leonard, 25th December 1917.

449. Edith Graham to Leonard, 23rd January 1918. Early in March 1918 Eddie Beaton wrote to Leonard from his work base at Talgarth in mid-Wales, and from this letter we learn that Leonard was 'fed up with Friends'. Eddie presumed that this meant Quakers, but 'those with whom you are working and not with the society in general'. Eddie to

Leonard, 4th March 1918. One wonders whether Leonard had the Grahams in mind as well?

450. Joe to Len and Bill, 29th August 1917.

451. Ron to Leonard, 13th September 1917.

452. Joe to Len and Bill, 29th August 1917.

453. ibid.

454. Ron to Leonard, 13th September 1917.

455. ibid.

456. ibid.

457. Joe to Len and Bill, 29th August 1917.

458. Ron to Leonard, 13th September 1917.

459. ibid.

460. ibid.

461. Marty Robbins, 'Progressive Love' lyrics, 1962.

462. Ron to Leonard, 13th September 1917. In a later fragment Ron wrote that 'since he broke off relationships with AD he has shown a decided tendency for female company, unfortunately to the extent of leaving me to myself.' Ron to ? Undated fragment.

463. ibid.

464. Joe to Len and Bill, 29th August 1917.

465. ibid. Joe, it seems, was the marrying kind, for a brief exchange of letters at Christmas 1924 refers to his wife Lucy. (Joseph A. Shipley to Leonard, 17th December 1924); 'Lucy and Joe' to 'Mr and Mrs Payne', 24th December 1924.

466. Father to Leonard 5th March 1917: (as post script) 'Remember me to all kind Friends *Mr Marsh included.*' Underlining in original.

467. Jessie to Leonard 4th June 1917: 'Now about your pyjamas, when we were up at Mrs Marsh's, we told her you were going to send them home to be washed, and then she said she would wash them for you with pleasure, so we think it would be as cheap if you took them to her.'

468. It appears that during the summer of 1917, as the Paynes' relationship with the Marsh family was growing, the Grahams in Bradford – and especially Alice – were fading from sight. (Jessie to Roland, June 1917; and Jessie to Leonard, 4th June 1917.) To add to the obscurity of these relationships, Joe Todd included an enigmatic passage in a letter written to both Payne brothers in August 1917. 'I am very glad that the long expected is not absolutely a paragon of perfection as far as personal appearance is concerned. It is probably better for both you and her. As to her not understanding your remark re "sloppy" people, I could hardly hope she would, though she might in a month or two. I often wonder how you are getting on with her.' (Joe to Leonard and Roland, 29th August 1917.) The meaning remains indecipherable, especially since

we do not know which brother it is addressed to. Could it be a reference to Edith Marsh, directed to Leonard?

469. I am particularly grateful to Nancy Lord, Roland's niece, and also to John and Tony Payne for insights into their grandparents' relationship. The family holds a copy of their Quaker wedding certificate. Roland's parents both signed the certificate as witnesses, but no one else from Roland's immediate family. Their names appear in the Electoral Register for Misterton (in which parish their new house lay) in 1929. (LRO.)

470. Rae, pp.181-4; Millman, p. 194.

471. Rae, p. 184.

472. Printed letter from War Office Contracts Dept., 10th January 1917.

473. Marion to Friend, 25th February 1917.

474. Leonard, MS autobiographical notes, Liddle Collection, Leeds, 1973.

475. Father to Leonard, 5th March 1917: 'Glad you like your new work we do hope you will be able to get *Bill* with you. I shall be glad to send on your bycicles [sic] if you find you need them and save tram fares.' There is no evidence that their father's offer was taken up. Also Jessie to Roland, 8th March 1917: 'We were pleased to hear you were working with Leonard and that you like the work. When you write again, we should like you to describe the work, how you do it, what the gravel is for, and where it goes when you have done with it, and everything you know about it.' Because none of Roland's letters from this time survive, what could have been a modest window into their world at Horbury remains firmly shut.

476. Jessie to Roland, June 1917.

477. Millman, pp. 194-5.

478. Marion to Leonard, 5th May 1917.

479. Liddle interview, 1973, Tape 44, p. 10. After Leonard and Roland had travelled home by train that Christmas they admitted that 'We did break the law but we weren't asked to confess it'. (ibid., p. 11.) In a letter from William Marwick, written in August 1917 he referred to Gilbert in rather uncomplimentary terms, using the phrase: '"pot-bellied" as our old agent here.' William Marwick to Leonard, 19th August 1917. (cf. n. 488, below.)

480. William Marwick to Leonard, 30th November 1917.

481. Father to Roland and Leonard, 29th March 1917.

482. Jessie to Leonard, 21st June 1917.

483. Jessie to Leonard, 3rd July 1917.

484. Marion to Leonard, 3rd July 1917.

485. Jessie to Roland, 15th July 1917.

486. Marion to Leonard, 22nd July 1917.

487. Father to Roland, 25ᵗʰ July 1917.

488. William to Leonard and Roland, 30ᵗʰ July 1917. It would appear that one of their fellow-lodgers was African – something of a rarity in Britain at that date: 'What part of Africa does your fellow-lodger come from? I wouldn't agree with you that all Africans are smart on their feet: some are as "pot-bellied" as our old agent here.' William Marwick to Leonard 19ᵗʰ August 1917. (cf. n. 479, above.)

489. Leonard's MS autobiographical notes, Liddle Collection, Leeds, pp. 9-10.

490. Marion to Leonard, 7ᵗʰ November 1917. In October they moved to new digs at 269 Fordhouse Lane, Stirchley, Birmingham. (Joe to Leonard, postmarked 27ᵗʰ November 1917.) 'I was very glad to get yours of 3ʳᵈ, and to hear that you found you *new* abode so much to your liking.' (William Marwick to Leonard, 12ᵗʰ October 1917.) At a later date Leonard moved to 22 Ashmore Road, Cotteridge, Kings Norton in Birmingham; April 1918.

491. 'We (Bale and I) will be down as soon as your firm send word they have got digs for us, so we will likely be down Thurs. or Fri.' Joe to Leonard, Postmarked Tuesday 27ᵗʰ November, 1917. 'It is nice that Mr Todd [Joe] is coming to you, you well have a jolly time. I hope Mr Bale is with you as well if he is fit for the work.' Marion to Leonard, 6ᵗʰ December 1917. (The discrepancy of dates may be due to the fact that Marion was not at home in Syston but staying at Bentham near Lancaster at that time.]

492. William Marwick to Leonard, 12ᵗʰ October 1917.

493. John to Bill, Friday 2ⁿᵈ November 1917.

494. Marion to Leonard, 7ᵗʰ November 1917.

495. G. Herick, 246 Beaumont Road, Bournville, Bham to Leonard at 269 Fordhouse Lane, Stirchley, 27ᵗʰ November 1917.

496. 'Gilbert told me he was over at your digs and that the landlady told him you were at home as it was your sister's birthday, but of course he did not look upon it as a crime at all, so you need not bother yourself at all.' (Joe [in Wakefield] to Len and Bill, 29ᵗʰ August 1917.)

497. Edith Graham to Leonard, 23ʳᵈ January 1918.

498. Eddie to Leonard and Roland, 28ᵗʰ December, 1917.

499. Sid Collins to Leonard, undated.

500. Dora to Leonard, 30ᵗʰ January, 1917. George Haswell was the choirmaster of the parish church.

501. J G Payne to Leonard 7ᵗʰ February 1917: 'I have any amount of contracts come through but I simply have to lay them aside'.

502. Jessie to Leonard, 3ʳᵈ July 1917.

503. Jessie to Roland undated fragment, July 1917. '1/9' presumably means £1-9 shillings.

504. 'Dora is helping [Dad] she can manage very nicely ~~three~~ four lines across. My word

she is excited always telling us what she has earned. 3/6 this week.' Mother to Leonard, 14th July 1916.

505. Father to Leonard, 5th March 1917 17.014; Jessie to Roland, 8th March 1917.

506. Father to Leonard and Roland, June 1917.

507. Mother to Leonard and Roland, 26th March 1917.

508. Father to Roland and Leonard, 29th March 1917.

509. Jessie to Leonard, 12th April 1917.

510. Mother to Leonard and Roland 15th February 1917.

511. Mother to Leonard, 30th April 1917.

512. Correspondence re. Scarlet Fever, Lutterworth, 1917. LRO.DE1379/826/1-6.

513. Joe to Leonard and Roland, 29th July 1917. Again we catch a hint of Leonard's character in that 'telling off' remark. It falls entirely within the scope of what we know of him – the way he organised his family's letter-writing so a complete record could be maintained, the relationship with his brother, the threatened breaking of which pushed him into crisis whilst at Whitburn.

514. Quoted in Rae, p. 182.

515. Joe to Len and Bill, 29th August 1917.

516. Ronald to (?) Leonard, undated fragment, p. 5.

517. Joe to Len and Bill, 29th August 1917. 17.043

518. Eddie to Len and Bill, 17th July 1917. There is some uncertainty as to where exactly they were staying. It seems most likely that they were housed in a miners' sanatorium in Bronlly, just across the valley, and, as Talgarth's local historian informs me, 'The views as described would be the views from Bronllys, although I think he got the two mountain ranges the wrong way round. The Black Mountains are about five miles away and the view of them from the "San" is one of the best in Wales.' I am grateful to Jan Hughes and 'Jan the Library' of Talgarth for this information. We may here note the words of Sid Collins, who had been with the Paynes at the Horbury Quarry, and found himself in the Princetown Centre on Dartmoor. Like Eddie, he was able to stand back and, quite literally, enjoy the view: 'We are having magnificent weather and the country all about here is lovely, it would be an ideal spot for a holiday.' But reality intruded into his meditations: 'Although it is so pretty, one cannot appreciate the scenery quite as much as we should like owing to knowing that we are *still* prisoners although among such beautiful country. There is always that feeling within us that tells us we are exiles.' (Sid Collins to Leonard, undated.)

519. William to Leonard and Roland, 29th July 1917.

520. William Marwick to Leonard, 12th October 1917.

521. Eddie to Leonard and Roland, 28th December 1917. Ron Long, from Wakefield, told Leonard about his own arrangements for Christmas: 'Re Xmas my good friends at

Emley have invited me over for Xmas and Boxing days.' Ronald (Wakefield) to Leonard, 13th December 1917.

522. William Marwick to Leonard, 19th August 1917.

523. William Marwick to Leonard, 12th October 1917.

524. William Marwick to Leonard, 30th November 1917. Pierce Williams, it would appear, had been on holiday, though his precise status is not clear.

525. Eddie to Leonard and Roland, 28th December 1917.

526. Rae, p. 188.

527. Eddie to 'My dear Leonard', 7th April 1918.

528. Marion, incomplete letter, July/August 1917.

529. Marion to Leonard, 6th December 1917.

530. John to Bill, 2nd November 1917.

531. A.H. Crampton of the Dryad Cane and Metal Works to John Payne, 30th October 1917.

532. John Payne to Len and Bill, 3rd November 1917. For all that, John was well aware of the difficulties which had stemmed from their earlier shell-basket work. He had written to Roland in July of 1916 about another offered contract for work for the military, saying that 'I should not accept work of that sort (certainly no) the same trouble would take place as when we made the shell Bas.' John to Roland, 6th July 1916.

533. *Rugby Advertiser*, 16th December 1916. This was the Hell in which Leonard's best friend, Harold Buck, had died in 1915. Some historians have contemptuously spoken of what they call the 'boo-hoo' school of history which dwells on the horrors of the trenches and the losses of the men who were there. Even war can appear an abstract thing when viewed from a lofty enough ivory tower – or helicopter gun-ship?

534. Frequently anthologised, Siegfried Sassoon's *Memorial Tablet (Great War)* can be found, for example, in E.L. Black (ed.), *1914-1918 in Poetry*, University of London Press, London, 1970, p. 122.

535. Will Deas to 'Leonard and Will' (i.e. Roland aka Bill), undated letter, October 1917.

536. Eddie to Leonard and Roland, 28th December 1917.

537. Quoted in Brian MacArthur, *For King and Country. Voices from the First World War*, Abacus Books, London, 2008, p. 431.

538. Quoted in Peter Barham, *Forgotten Lunatics of the Great War*, Yale, London, 2007, pp. 264-5.

539. Quoted ibid.,'Epigrams'. (Original ref. is to TNA/PRO PIN 15/864.) The sentiment was not isolated: George Mosse argued that shell shock was used as a metaphor for the unmanly behaviour of outsiders to normal society, of incomplete men. (*Shell Shock as Social Disease*, Journal of Contemporary History, 2000, p. 104, quoted Barham, p.

132.) Specifically on 'shell-shock' see Wendy Holden, *Shell Shock. The Psychological Impact of War*, Channel 4 Books, London, 1998. The stigma persisted. Soldiers who had suffered mental breakdown were not invited to participate in the remembrance ceremonies at the Cenotaph, and when George VI was crowned in 1937 his personal message to every individual ex-serviceman still undergoing medical treatment was not conveyed to those with mental illnesses on the insistence of the Ministry of Pensions. Barham, p. 300.

540. We are reminded of Yossarian's plea that the enemy's sole purpose was to kill him personally in Joseph Heller's Second World War novel *Catch 22*, in Chapter 2: a not uncommon sensation, and one with tragic consequences for Arthur Earp.

541. Quoted in Cathryn Corns and John Hughes-Wilson, *Blindfold and Alone. British Military Executions in the Great War*, Cassell, London, 2002, p. 143. In the view of Gerard Oram the High Command was not simply out to make examples, but to weed out those who it saw as 'worthless men', including some at least of those who claimed shell shock as a defence. Writing of two officers who were executed, 2nd Lieutenant Eric Poole in December 1916 and Sub-Lieutenant Edwin Dyett in January 1917, Oram concluded that 'Far from evoking a sympathetic response, the shell shock defence had in both cases attracted a condemnation which ultimately proved lethal. Military commanders were not prepared to tolerate soldiers who, in their opinion, did not have the strength of character to withstand trench warfare. Such men were branded "worthless" without considering whether there were other duties they might be fit to perform.' Both men – like Private Earp – had to be swept away. (Gerard Oram, *Worthless Men. Race, Eugenics and the Death Penalty in the British Army during the First World War*, Francis Boutle, London, 1988, p. 101 in the context of pp. 89-101.) Eugenic thinking was commonplace in Britain before and during the Great War. In Leicester, for example, Leonard Darwin, the youngest son of the great Charles and President of the Eugenics Education Society, had lectured the Junior Constitutional Club in the days before the outbreak of war in 1914 on the subject of 'Eugenics and Legislation': prevention of unsuitable breeding was the key to the future, he believed. 'The incurably mentally deficient should be segregated, because if they went on breeding the breed of our race would be tarnished. Habitual criminals should be segregated,' he argued, 'but the segregation or period of preventive detention should be made as pleasant as possible.' The report was buried deep in an unexceptional page in the middle of the *Leicester Daily Mercury*; it attracted little attention and passed without comment. It was, frankly, pretty unremarkable stuff for 1914. But had Major Darwin and his audience known what we know; that for some the future did indeed lie in blood and breeding and race and a willingness to suppress those of undesirable blood stock, perhaps the assumptions behind his address might not have passed by

unchallenged. See also G.R. Searle, *Eugenics and Politics in Britain, 1900-1914*, Leyden, 1976. British eugenicists were divided on the issue of whether war was a good thing or a bad thing. The former view was that military training kept young men fit and healthy, and thus helped strengthen the 'race' [nation]; the alternative, and the official E.E.S. view espoused by Darwin, was that since war tended to kill the fittest young men before they had finished their breeding duties, it tended to weaken the blood stock. (See Searle, pp. 36-8.) On the application of eugenicist thinking in the Great War, see Gerard Oram, *Worthless Men: Race, Eugenics and the Death Penalty during the First World War*, London, 1998, esp. pp. 89-101. Many more men attempted to desert, such as William Palmer from the village of Walton by Kimcote, two or three miles to the east of Lutterworth, who claimed that a doctor had declared him unfit for military service. He had failed to inform his regiment, the Durham Light Infantry, and was returned to military jurisdiction by the Lutterworth Magistrates. (*Rugby Advertiser*, 5th August 1916.) More clear-cut was the case of an Ullesthorpe man, James Bird, of the 4th Berkshire Regiment, spotted by an alert police constable who arrested him and brought him before the magistrates, thus earning a reward for his efforts. Bird had hidden his uniform and clearly intended to deprive the army of his services. Like Palmer, he was handed back to his Regiment. (*Rugby Advertiser*, 26th August 1916.) The reasons why men deserted are not necessarily self-evident but are beyond the scope of this present work. And we recall the case of Leonard's friend Harold Buck, refused permission to return to Lutterworth for his father's funeral, who reflected that: 'perhaps after all it was as well I didn't as I should not *[sic]* liked to have come out here again'. (Harold Buck) to Leonard, 18th April 1915.

542. Arthur Marwick, Clifford Allen, p.35.

543. Fenner Brockway, p. 103.

544. What follows is from Boulton, p. 281; and Rae, p. 188.

545. Quoted in Rae, p. 189.

546. Edith Graham to Leonard, 28th February 1918.

547. Eddie to Leonard, 4th March 1918. The self-perceived standing of the conscientious objectors in the long tradition of Christian martyrdom is a recurring theme. This, for example, comes from the autobiographical writings of J. Scott Druckers: 'If a Catholic lawgiver commands his Protestant subjects to profess their belief in transubstantiation they should be prepared to suffer any punishment rather than obey the law; and, conversely, a sincere Catholic should refuse conformity to Protestant doctrines established and imposed by law. The early history of Christianity, of Protestantism, of Non-conformity, and the whole course of the struggles for freedom of thought, freedom of speech, and the free expression of political ideas would furnish innumerable illustrations of this principle, and in thinking of them we must remember

that in their own day these rebels would not appear as they do now. The very fact that they were persecuted so cruelly shows that public opinion was against them almost unanimously. They were misunderstood and misrepresented; falsely accused; their ideas distorted and caricatured; derided as fanatics and fools, as madmen, as enemies to society and persons whom it was dangerous to permit to live. Only after much struggle and suffering were these different classes of "non-conformists" able to establish their claim to be unrestrained by law.' (J. Scott Druckers, *Handed Over: The Prison Experiences of Mr J. Scott Druckers, Solicitor, of Chancery Lane, under the Military Service Act*. Written by himself. Foreword by T. Edmund Harvey MP, C.W. Daniel, London, June 1917, pp. 2-3: full text via Internet Archive www. Archive.org)

548. via Peace Pledge Union website. The contrast with Germany is striking, for there the military took dictatorial command of the nation in 1916 in the guise of Ludendorff and Hindenburg – 'the rule of an independent military machine which had escaped from the control of its authors.' (A.J.P. Taylor, *The Course of German History*, Methuen, London, 1961, p. 196.) Britain never suffered that fate.

549. Frank Richards was dismissive of such 'lead-swingers', men who were still drawing pensions years after the war, still wearing their medals on Armistice Day, convinced they had 'done their bit'; one had 'contracted several dangerous complaints through shaking the Crown and Anchor dice down at the Base'. (Quoted in MacArthur (ed.), pp. 429-30.)

550. Jannaway, p. 286.

551. Robert Jackson, *The Prisoners, 1914-1918*, Routledge, London, 1989, esp. Chapters 3 and 8 on the PoW Camps, and Chapter 4 on the civilians interned in Germany.

552. John Payne, e-mail to the author. It would be facetious to suggest that, with his track record among the ladies, Leonard might more appropriately have been assigned to Dante's Second Circle of Hell – that reserved for the Lustful.

PART FOUR

HOMECOMING

HOMECOMING

Joyous as the brothers' homecoming undoubtedly was to the family, others held a different view.

At first there was only verbal abuse, the family subjected to 'booing and hooting' in the street.[1] One of the local newspapers told how 'each night a crowd gathered outside the premises where the young men resided; and "booings" and rough horseplay took place on the appearance of either of the youths or their parents, this being accompanied with threats. The crowds became bigger and more determined in attitude each evening'. It was said that some in the town had decided that the brothers must be driven out and were holding informal meetings to orchestrate their campaign.[2]

We have no evidence of how the family reacted to this, but can well imagine the shock and distress it must have caused, especially to the brothers' younger sister Dora who, no doubt, had to endure torment and bullying in the school playground as well, the attitude of her teachers possibly ambivalent. While Leonard and Roland had been away, out of sight for most of the time in Whitburn, Newcastle, Durham, Wakefield and Birmingham, they had drawn little attention, 'out of mind' – attracting curiosity and suspicion, but nothing much else. We remember that the phrase 'Slackers' Rest' had been chalked across the shop's shutters after the brothers had paid a brief visit home in October 1916 – an incident Jessie blamed on local boys.[3] Now they were back at home permanently, living there freely and going about their business just as though there was no war on and as if they were just like everyone else.

But, of course, they were not 'just like everyone else' – as 'everyone else' was acutely aware. Public hostility towards conscientious objectors since conscription had been introduced in 1916 is well enough documented – a hostility which grew more intense as the war went on. But this was something more than the mere handing out of white feathers to passing strangers. The Payne brothers' return was closer to home, more personal, and in a small town there was nowhere to hide.

The brothers, away from home for two years, had been living in their own bubble, surrounded by like-minded people there to support and encourage them, living in places where their own beliefs were the norm, only occasionally subject to disapproval, as when Leonard had been punched in the face in Wakefield (attributable, as usual, to drink). They had been given little information about what reception they might expect from their neighbours back home. Years later they would blame the hostility of their reception on 'drunken hooligans', a necessary and sensible reticence absolving their neighbours of responsibility, but a long way from the truth of the matter.

For five weeks things went on like this and then, one evening at seven or eight o'clock, Roland set out to cycle to the family's field off the Rugby Road, about half a mile from their home and shop on Church Street, to collect the eggs from their hens, a straw lined bucket slung from his handlebars. It was a part of their daily routine – ordinary, everyday, necessary. Turning into the top of High Street he relished the glide down the steep High Street, gathering speed as he went. Swinging round the wide bend at the bottom of the hill, without losing momentum, he needed to start pedalling again only when he passed 'The Fox Inn' on his right and then continue across the bridge over the modest River Swift before climbing up the far side of the valley to their field on the high ground where they grew their fruit trees and kept their hens, livestock and beehives. It was a trip he had made any number of times. Perhaps he noticed a group of young men, his old school friends, gathered near the bridge as he passed by. They watched, but did not acknowledge him.

It would not have taken him very long to check the goats and the beehives, gather in the harvest of eggs and stow them safely in the bucket for the ride back home. As he cycled down the slope towards the bridge, he noticed that a sizeable group of young men had gathered on the bridge, spilling across the road. For some time past Lutterworth had been troubled by groups of youths causing obstructions, blocking pavements and forcing people into the road, but this was different. There were twelve, perhaps fifteen of them and they had formed a sort of road block with their bodies. Roland knew them, had been at school with many of them, but their look was far from friendly. Should he turn back? Or should he carry on and see what happened? There was no other practicable way to get back home so on he went.

Of all people, it was Jack Holland, the son of Police Superintendent Walter Holland and the stepson of his wife Ada[4], from the police house by the Gilmorton Road at the top of High Street who seemed to be the leader of the group. Jack had encountered the Payne brothers whilst they were in Whitburn, he then an officer in the Sherwood Foresters, they prisoners refusing to obey orders.[5] The group blocked Roland's way. He was pushed off his bike, the bucket sent flying, the eggs smashed. He was seized by the arms, possibly pushed to the ground, and from somewhere a bag of blue dye was produced, his face roughly smeared until it was bright blue. What was said is not recorded, but we can easily imagine the insults and the catcalls and the general merriment at Roland's expense – not fun, but with an edge of violence, even hatred. For this was not simply a bit of rough horseplay. This had been a carefully planned and vigorously executed ambush; one might almost say with 'military precision', well worked out in advance. The group had not finished yet, though: Roland found himself picked up bodily, carried round the side of the bridge and down to the waterside, where he was hurled into the narrow but fast flowing river.

There he was left, struggling to extricate himself, soaked through, his face blue, his bucket empty, the smashed eggs scattered across the road, his bicycle hurled down by the side of the bridge, to find his way home past the astonished and unsympathetic eyes of his fellow townspeople.

A message had been sent, but the *meaning* of that message and its precise target are harder to decipher. In attacking one member of the family, the attack can be seen as an attack on all. It may be significant that it was Roland, rather than the tougher Leonard, who was ambushed, a softer target, one less likely to escape or fight back – if, indeed, fight back they would. For this was the ultimate pacifist test: if attacked, would they attempt to defend themselves? It seems Roland did not defend himself, for if he had, that would have been trumpeted all over town and be bound to turn up, somewhere or other, in writing, which it does not. Like the dog in the night, the absence of evidence is the best evidence.

That the attack had a powerful personal motive seems clear enough, Jack Holland's presence as ringleader giving the evidence for that. Why might the son of the local police superintendent play such a leading role in what amounted to street violence and common assault, when his father had for months past been waging his own war against gangs of youths causing trouble in the town and blocking the highway? And the choice of the bridge as the site of the attack was also significant, not only for the obvious tactical reason, but also because it gave some privacy to the deed, just beyond the edge of the town. A few customers in 'The Fox' might have looked out to see what the commotion was about, but no one came to Roland's aid. This was both a personal and private settling of accounts.

The attack emerged from that close knit and exclusive community of young men, the school year group, who had grown up in the same small town, attended the same schools since childhood, sat in the same classes, been taught by the same teachers, remembered the same games, the same punishments; they had played the same games together in the schoolyard and out on the Recreation Ground, and the fields and woods about the town, gone to the same clubs, been members of the same football and rugby teams, played cricket together and believed in 'play up, play up and play the game!' These men shared the same beliefs, attitudes, values and memories and formed a community within the community. They formed a subculture within the wider culture of small town Lutterworth, and were entirely consonant with it. It was out of this tight knit family that the assault on Roland came, in defence of their own small community, its values and its members, for the Payne brothers had violated the most basic tenet of comradeship, the ideal which had persuaded thousands of their contemporaries to join up into their 'Pals' Battalions, and which many of those who served together later recalled as the most vital and lasting fact of their time in the trenches: the principle of sticking by your friends. The Paynes had, in their eyes, refused to do this.

Many years later, when talking about the event, Roland expressed surprise verging on disbelief that his attackers had been friends of his back to their shared school days. 'The people who attacked me down the road... were people that were at school with me... who I knew perfectly well. I had been friendly with them at school and yet they got hold of me and threw me in the river.'[6] He should not have been surprised. He had missed the point that he had been attacked by them, not in spite of the fact these were his former school mates, friends since childhood, who had grown up alongside him in small town Lutterworth, but because of it.

Jack Holland and his brother Fred had both been away to the war, willing volunteers, doing their bit as was appropriate to the sons of a senior police officer. But Jack was home, had been home since July 1916, a disabled cripple, invalided out due to his injuries, unable to hold his left arm above his head.[7] Jack would not return to the Front, his bit having been done: 'badly wounded and permanently disabled', 'incapacitated while on active service and unable to take any further active part in the war'.[8] He was clearly useless to the military, but just how 'incapacitated' he actually was is open to question, for in late November or early December 1916 he had broken his collar bone whilst playing football in Loughborough[9] and it would appear he was able-bodied enough to head a group of youths intent on dealing with Roland Payne the conscientious objector.

Jack Holland's brother, Fred, had been a conspicuous and popular member of the local community: at Christmas of 1916 Fred had joined with a young man called John Meacham, a former workhouse boy sent by the Guardians to the Royal Navy training ship *H.M.S. Exmouth*, and the two had entertained the inmates at the workhouse party.[10] Fred was wounded on July 31st 1917 leading his men towards the Westhoek Ridge outside Ypres on the opening day of the Third Battle of Ypres, better known as Passchendaele, and after three weeks of pain and suffering, and three weeks of nagging uncertainty, between hope and despair for his family at home in Lutterworth, he had died from his injuries in one of the many military hospitals outside Etaples near the French coast on August 22nd.[11] And by a twist of irony Fred Holland had been a Second Lieutenant in the 3rd Battalion of the Sherwood Foresters[12], the same Battalion which Leonard and Roland would have joined, had they put on khaki and accepted military discipline. Jack had been crippled and had come home, Fred had been killed and would never come home. To his gravestone – when eventually it was made – the family added the couplet:

> 'Only those who have loved and lost
> Can understand war's bitter cost.'

Perhaps by some perverse logic, Jack and his friends felt that it was unjust, or at the least unfair, that they and others from the town should have suffered and lost so much, 'war's bitter cost', when the Paynes ought also to have been there to sacrifice themselves and share in the loss. We can readily imagine their anger and distress when they saw Leonard and Roland Payne, who had not been to the war, still fit and well and living comfortably at home. In ambushing Roland Payne, Jack Holland was taking surrogate revenge against fate itself.

No complaint to the police was ever made by the Paynes about the attack on Roland. Perhaps the Paynes thought that the involvement of Superintendent Holland's son might prejudice their case or perhaps they preferred to allow sleeping dogs to lie where they were. That certainly would be John's way. So the Paynes did nothing to ease the situation: not to complain, not to seek police protection. And the stubborn intransigence which had sustained their dissent ensured that they would not now leave their home town, having taken so much trouble to return. But their silence allowed the situation to deteriorate as spring day succeeded to spring day.

★

The assault on Roland was, though, nothing more than the prelude to the much bigger, much more violent assault which was about to be launched against the whole of the Payne family. How could it be that a small rural town, described variously as 'somnolent' and 'dry', should come to produce such violence against one of its own families going about their lawful business? As always, the answer is to be found in the context. The later attack on the Paynes' shop belonged very precisely to one time – not before and not after – the evening of Tuesday May 28th 1918.

The community was under stress, verging on distress. The wartime population of Lutterworth had increased rapidly. It is difficult to be precise because of the lack of any census information during the war, but the Rural District Council was estimating a population of about 2,500 in 1917 and again in 1918.[13] If accurate, this would be an extraordinary increase, amounting to a growth since the 1911 census of almost a third. To put that in perspective, the *actual* rise in population between 1911 and the 1921 census was a little over 10%.[14] The council assumed a natural population increase of twelve persons per 1000 per year, a rate of increase which should have given a total population in 1917 or 1918 in the region of 2,055, far short of the 2,500 they were actually estimating.[15] This suggests a significant inward migration during the war which was not sustained once the war was over.

That this was putting pressure on amenities such as housing is clear from the council's assessment of the situation just after the end of the war: Lutterworth, it estimated, would require no less than 200 new homes, with a further hundred in the rest of the Rural District.[16] It would appear that the foundry was making the difference and even before the outbreak of war the Rural District Council recognised that its expansion would put pressure on the housing stock. New housing was built on the Gilmorton Road, but it was clear that the council would have to take a more proactive role. Twenty-three council houses had already been built by the end of 1915, though there the project came to a halt.[17] The large and lucrative war contracts which followed exacerbated the housing shortage in Lutterworth and as the foundry expanded so did its workforce, mainly males and those new to Lutterworth. So, as members of the town's established male population were moving out into the armed forces a new male population was moving in from the outside to do war work of national importance.

The wider climate was now turning heavily against the Paynes and those who thought like them. Something important had happened in English life in the first three and a half years of war: the destruction in the wider community of the nation (not just the conscientious objectors) of those liberal values which had informed so much of political and social life for the past decades and changed the lives of millions for the better.[18] They had been crushed by the overwhelming necessity of winning this war against German militarism, which showed no respect for those values. The draconian powers given to government by the Defence of the Realm Act, the introduction of conscription, press censorship and the powers allowed to the security services all contradicted those liberal values of individual freedom and voluntarism, the political values with which the Payne brothers had been brought up. 'War and the conduct of war threatened to eliminate liberalism as a coherent political position' in Britain.[19] Even far away in Russia, Lenin, who had other more pressing concerns at the time, noticed the change: 'Both England and America, the biggest and last representatives – in the whole world – of Anglo-Saxon "liberty", in the sense that they had no military cliques and bureaucracy, have today [August/September 1917] sunk into the all-European filthy, bloody morass of bureaucratic-military institutions which subordinate everything to themselves and trample everything underfoot.'[20] An overstatement, perhaps, but containing more than a germ of truth.

Then had come the massive German attack on the Western Front, known as the 'Spring Offensive' or the 'Ludendorff Offensive', launched on March 21st 1918. This had changed everything and, for the British, threatened to turn the fear of defeat into a reality. It 'rapidly became the all-encompassing fact of the war'.[21] This is not the place to rehearse in any great detail the events of March 21st 1918 and the following weeks except insofar as they help us to understand those extraordinary events in Lutterworth's Church Street just a few weeks later.[22]

At twenty to five on the morning of Thursday March 21st 1918 the German Army launched the biggest attack so far seen on the Western Front as 3,965 field guns, with 2,435 heavy guns and seventy-three super-heavy guns opened fire in a precisely targeted bombardment of the British lines with explosive and gas shells either side of St Quentin in northern France, while at closer range 3,532 trench mortars hit specific local positions. Winston Churchill was nearby: 'I woke up in complete silence at a few minutes past four [a.m.] and lay musing', he later wrote. 'Suddenly, after what seemed like half an hour, the silence was broken by six or seven very loud and very heavy explosions several miles away. I thought they were twelve-inch guns, but they were probably mines. And then, exactly as a pianist runs his hands across the keyboard from treble to bass, there rose in less than a minute the most tremendous cannonade I shall ever hear'.[23] To men who had heard artillery bombardments before, this was in a class of its own. William Carr heard it: 'Think of the loudest clap of thunder you have ever heard', he wrote, like so many Great War soldiers using meteorological imagery to try to convey something of the experience, 'then imagine what it would be like if it continued without stopping. That was the noise which woke us at 4:40 a.m. on Thursday 21st March. I have never before or since heard anything like it'.[24]

Then, at 9.40 a.m., after five hours of bombardment, the German guns fell silent and the storm troopers moved forward, 'without hurrahs', as their orders insisted, small groups of specially trained and well equipped soldiers advancing in leaps and bounds, taking every possible advantage of shell holes and craters and the lie of the land, unseen in the deadly fog which prevailed across the battlefield that morning saturated with thousands of gas shells. They slipped silently into the

British Forward Zone, infiltrating their defences, surrounding the 'blobs', the defensive strongholds which British military planners had so carefully positioned to exploit the lie of the land, each 'blob' helping defend each neighbouring 'blob', now made useless by the fog, bypassing the strongest British positions while the main German force, following up, attacked the redoubts and strongholds. On the first day the advanced German troops found themselves four and a half miles behind the original British front line, and with 21,000 prisoners to take care of. Nothing like this had happened since the first weeks of the war and it was now a new war of movement, with Paris itself ultimately threatened as the German advance rolled on. This German advance and the massive losses through death, injury or capture which came in its wake provoked another crisis which had a direct impact on events in small town Lutterworth: a crisis of manpower. Could the Germans be stopped with the troops available? The answer appeared to be 'no'.

In October 1917 Auckland Geddes had been drafted in as Minister of National Service to resolve the problem of how to meet the military's demands for ever more manpower without denuding essential industries of skilled workers. He had proposed a 'combing out' system by which men in key civilian occupations would be examined on an individual basis with a view to replacing them with women, boys and the physically unfit wherever possible, and, in addition, eighteen-year-olds could now be treated as reinforcements for the army.[25] Worse news was to follow as Geddes tried to assess the number of men available for military service and the result was truly 'shocking'.[26] The total number of males aged eighteen to twenty-five and fit for military service amounted to no more than 270,000. Of these, a third were employed in the mines, and about the same proportion in the shipyards and munitions factories, and some 70,000 were skilled workers, many in agriculture and transport. It was true that by extending the age range upwards, more men might be found, but no more than 700,000 could be considered as fit for active service, and again the great majority were engaged in vital war work. So it now seemed likely that even those who had believed themselves safe from the military call-up might lose their immunity. No more shocking or eloquent statement can be envisaged of the sheer murderous nature of the fighting for the Passchendaele ridge – nor for the Great War in general – than the simple, brutal fact that Britain was running short of men.

Meanwhile the Tribunals were still sitting in sceptical judgement on those who claimed exemption just as they had when conscription had first been introduced, but the cases were now different. There was a smattering of men claiming conscientious objection, as there always had been, but the men claiming exemption were now typically in their forties and in poor health. One such was the case, heard by the Rugby Tribunal, of a forty-one year old married taxi-cab proprietor who had already been rejected by the army three times, but had now been passed in the lowest order of fitness – but passed nonetheless. His plea tugs at the heartstrings: 'His health was so bad,' it was claimed, 'that he could not stand any exposure. Such a place would be too hard for [him], who had suffered considerably through the war. He lost all his capital when he was interned in Germany, and his health broke down owing to a shock he received consequent upon a murder being committed in the house in which he was living in Germany.' Evidently an unlucky man, his case was merely adjourned for a fortnight.[27]

Perhaps no single document better conveys the sense of crisis which suddenly gripped Britain in the days following the German Offensive than the minutes of the Cabinet meeting held on the morning of Monday March 25th 1918, as the scale of the actual and potential disaster sank in. Bullish as General Maurice's military report attempted to be, it could not disguise the fact that Ludendorff had 'effected a breach over a front of five miles'[28] – an event unprecedented since the trench line had first been dug and something which Haig had conspicuously failed to do in two bloody campaigns. So now, the sense of near panic trembling off the page, ministers fell over each other in trying to find new sources of men to fill the breach.

General Macready, the Adjutant General, offered 39,000 munitions workers against the advice of Winston Churchill as Minister of Munitions, who was already in the process of releasing 100,000.[29] The First Lord of the Admiralty resisted the call for him to 'loan' the Royal Marines to the army to help meet the crisis, arguing that 'with the United Kingdom now depleted of efficient army men, a far greater responsibility devolved on the navy for the protection of our shores' – a case which successfully defended his patch. Field Marshal French suggested that the volunteers might supply 'the best half-trained reserve we have', and Auckland Geddes wanted to persuade the Tribunals to cancel the exemptions already granted to fit men, going so far as to propose legislation to cancel all exemptions from military service. There was even talk of recalling men who had been wounded so badly as to be discharged from the army, an idea they did not pursue on the grounds not that the government had pledged it would not do this, but because it would haul in too few men to be worthwhile. It was reported that 'the Director General of Medical Services had recently been going into the question of the standard of eye-sight required by the troops and that a new test would shortly be instituted which would result in the number of "A" men for the army being increased.' 'The halt, the lame…' and now the blind as well.

Sooner or later, the question of the conscientious objectors was bound to be raised, and inevitably it was Lord Derby, Secretary of State for War, rather late in the meeting, who made the proposal:

'15. Lord Derby asked permission of the War Cabinet to send conscientious objectors abroad for labour work.

'It was pointed out by Sir Auckland Geddes that a pledge had been given by the late Prime Minister and others that this would not be done.

'The War Cabinet felt that as these men would be sent as a non-combatant corps, it was essential in the interests of the country under the present circumstances, that any pledge that had been given in this respect should be withdrawn.'

★

Ludendorff's ambition had been simple enough: to force a military solution on the Western Front before the Americans could arrive in numbers. But as alarming reports claimed headline attention in the press day after day in the last week of March, throughout April and into May, the impact on British public opinion was appalling. Could it be, after all, that this most terrible of wars might be lost at the last moment? John Buchan, as well-informed an observer as he was a thrilling novelist, writing in the wake of the German 1918 Offensive, talked of its aim to 'shake the nerve and confuse the judgement of our civilians'[30] – as neat a description of the *impact*, if not the objective, of the offensive as could be found.

In Leicestershire the police, aware of the dangers to civil order if morale collapsed or panic spread, acted to head off potential disaster. 'The chief constable impressed upon divisional officers the necessity of doing their best to keep alive a proper spirit in the public mind by their attitude, conversation, etc.', their minutes recorded.[31]

★

The losses kept mounting. Statistically, 1918 would be the worst year for the British Army in the First World War on the Western Front – its casualties were higher than in 1917 (including Passchendaele) and worse than 1916 (including the Somme).[32] And the killing and the loss shot through Lutterworth and south Leicestershire as much as anywhere else. As the German storm troopers had swept over the British lines either side of St Quentin in the first great rush of Ludendorff's Offensive, George Beales, formerly of Bitteswell Road, ex-Lutterworth Grammar School boy and on that day a Second Lieutenant in the 3rd Tyneside Scottish, was posted missing, then killed, as also was (probably) John Hubbard, a poor boy who had spent his childhood in Lutterworth Workhouse and in the Cottage Homes in Countesthorpe: the 'probably' is because no remains were ever found. Like so many on that day, he happened to be in a place where he could not have survived. Fred Buswell died, some way behind where the original front line had been, as the Germans continued their advance deep into Allied territory three days later, his parents receiving the dreaded letter in their druggist's shop on High Street. Two days after that Acting Captain Harry Evans died, his parents, Charles and Annie on George Street, receiving a telegram telling the news – Harry was an officer and so warranted a telegram, unlike Private Buswell's family who did not. And the wave of grief and despair flooded out through the surrounding villages as well. A random and incomplete search through local war memorials shows Robert Chedgey's name on Bitteswell's plaque, not killed in the great German advance, but dying a pointless death at sea, a purely random casualty of war. He was an officer's steward second class on board *H.M.S. Norman*, a destroyer on anti-U-Boat patrol off Rosyth. Robert was washed overboard while taking coffee to the captain on the bridge[33], a second tragedy for his parents William and Ellen, who had already lost a son, Percy, in March of 1917. Harold Lee's name is also to be found on Bitteswell's memorial: he found himself right in the centre of the sector against which the German Army launched its massive offensive of March 21st. The War Diary of his Battalion, the 2nd/4th Royal Berkshires, records that 'the enemy was encountered in overwhelming numbers' forcing a withdrawal 'under very heavy M.G. [machine gun] fire to Railway Cutting' near Ugny, west of St Quentin. The Battalion commander Lieutenant-Colonel J.H.S. Dimmer V.C., M.C. was killed there, bizarrely riding a white horse into battle, trying to rally his men for a futile counter-attack, 'and heavy casualties were sustained by the rank and file' – among them Harold Lee.[34] John Moore, from Walcote, was killed the next day, his widow Cicily left to fend as best she could. Francis Bartlett, from Broughton Astley, was killed two days after that, his wife Violet now a widow. Thirty-two year old Joseph Garner, from Broughton Astley, was killed in action three days later on March 28th, his younger brother John less than a month afterwards, their parents, Stephen and Mercy Jane, inconsolable. A Grenadier Guardsman, Lance Corporal A.S. Wood, also from Broughton Astley, was killed two days later. In April, Ullesthorpe lost William Lennard, leaving his wife Harriet a widow, and Walcote lost George Barnacle. It was the most concentrated period for local casualties in the whole of the First World War.

While it is difficult to prove a direct causal link between this litany of death in and around the German Spring Offensive which had begun on March 21st 1918, and the violence which exploded in Lutterworth towards the end of May, it seems inherently unlikely that those deaths of family, friends and neighbours, even (or perhaps especially) when many of them were simply listed as 'missing', did not have a powerful emotional impact on local people, affecting their attitudes and mentality. And we can readily suppose that this acceleration of deaths would increase the fears and anxieties of those with family, friends, neighbours or lovers still serving on the Western Front and who remained – as far as their families knew – fit and well. It does not seem improbable that these fears and anxieties would translate into resentment against and hostility towards these two young men who had suddenly turned up in their midst, cheerful, in the best of health and showing no inclination to change their own personal situation. And those fears and anxieties were wound up further when renewed German Offensives were anticipated at any moment.

★

The German successes in the spring of 1918 provoked a crisis mentality in government. Lloyd George, who had resisted Haig's demands for more men for a new British Offensive in Flanders in the spring of 1918, saying he would not act as a butcher's boy herding men to their deaths, now had to concede greater recruitment numbers for defence against the German Offensive. Already, in January, the government had proposed an enhanced call-up by extending the age limit and cancelling some exemptions, and this had received the Royal Assent on February 6th, but in light of the new emergency the War Cabinet on April 9th proposed a new Military Service Bill. Men up to fifty-one years of age could now be conscripted into the armed forces, with a provision that in a national emergency the limit could be raised to fifty-six. The young too were caught up in the net: 'every male who had attained the age of seventeen years but has not attained the age of eighteen years, shall be liable to perform such service in the Volunteer Force as may be prescribed'. Furthermore, all exemptions could be cancelled by government decree except those on conscientious grounds, clergy could be conscripted for all but combatant duties, and the prospect of extending conscription to Ireland was raised. It was this latter which aroused the greatest controversy – and was not pursued – and the Bill became law without it on April 18th 1918.[35] Only token opposition had been offered in Parliament. As the Labour M.P. and defender of the conscientious objectors, Philip Snowden explained: 'We offered practically no opposition to this measure on the grounds that conscription having been accepted, if the men were really needed for the effective prosecution of the war, no reasonable argument could be advanced against recruiting able-bodied men up to fifty-one, most of whom up to that time had confined their practical support of the war to "killing the Germans with their tongues"'.[36] Or, as David Marquand acidly commented, 'Once again, Labour's walls of Jericho had crumbled at the first blast of a ministerial trumpet'.[37] Not only could older men now be conscripted, men who had imagined themselves beyond military age, but also those in hitherto protected employment, such as munitions workers. It was a sign of the depth of the national crisis, which came in the wake of the German successes, and it must have sent shock waves through those who had thought themselves immune because of their work turning out shell casings for the war in Lutterworth's foundries.

★

So the war situation, increasingly threatening and frightening, had created its own atmosphere in Britain: nervous, edgy, hypersensitive. Much of the panic was directed against 'enemies within', anyone of foreign descent (not just German or Austrian) and, inevitably, pacifists and conscientious objectors. For weeks past, even before the German Offensives had been launched, the press had been filled with attacks on what they called as a form of insult 'pacifists'. It was into this atmosphere that the brothers had returned to their father's shop in Lutterworth trying to resume a normal life. The *Rugby Advertiser*, read by many in the town and by many of those who lived in Rugby but commuted by rail to work in the foundries, gave inches of column space to anti-'pacifist' propaganda, out of all proportion to the almost complete absence of coverage of the events of the war itself. Politicians, press and public opinion came together behind the Prime Minister's call for all out victory, the 'knock-out blow' against Germany, which became a quasi-official war aim, and even those who favoured a negotiated peace short of total victory found themselves attacked and abused.[38]

Typical was this, a fortnight before the attack on the Payne family's shop: Lloyd George, who had just visited the soldiers in France, was quoted as saying, 'I met no pacifists and pessimists among them', a subliminal linking of pacifism with defeatism. The author, an unnamed M.P., then wrote: 'There has been a good deal of gossip about an alleged Peace Offensive on the part of Germany... The pacifists were instantly all inquiries and curiosity. They thought they had scented out something which was likely to be to their advantage... These are the sort of rumours that come as God-sends to the pacifists, and, as they find wide-spread circulation, they are calculated to do much mischief. They divert attention from our supreme need, which is to prosecute the war with unabated intensity of purpose and unrelaxing pressure. A German peace we will not have, and this is all the Kaiser will offer us at the moment'.[39]

The Earl of Denbigh, Lutterworth's own personal aristocrat, was one who kept the patriotic pot boiling. 'Pacifists' were unpatriotic, muddle-headed and dangerous, threatening to throw away for nothing all the suffering of the past four years, all those lives lost. Addressing the Victoria Road Men's Meeting in Leicester at the beginning of December 1917 the Earl told his audience: 'Our very existence depends upon us "sticking it"… We must break the German military machine, in order to have a future for this country', he told his audience to loud applause[40], before switching the direction of his belligerence towards 'the pacifists'. At the beginning of May 1918 the *Leicester Daily Mercury* reported his most recent speech in the House of Lords, full of invective and abuse towards those deemed 'pacifists', 'cranks and curs' all of them.[41] A week later the Earl went so far as to move a resolution in the Lords 'regretting that stronger measures have not been taken to combat the various agencies in this country which are serving the interests of the enemy', a clear reference to the anti-war and pacifist organisations and individuals. It was reported in the press under the heading: 'Lord Denbigh on Mischievous Organisations'.[42]

He did not stop there. On Saturday May 18th the *Rugby Advertiser* reprinted a lengthy letter which had appeared in *The Times* on the previous Monday, written by the Earl on the subject of 'pacifist propoganda'.[43] This time he took the argument further: dark forces were at work in the form of 'professional and revolutionary pacifists', he told his readers, exploiting the ignorance of the 'man in the street' of Germany's true war aims – the destruction of Britain and the British Empire and the creation in the East of a great new German imperialism[44]; a claim given added veracity by the brutal Treaty of Brest-Litovsk forced upon the Bolshevik government in Moscow in March and depriving Russia of vast areas of land and huge material resources.[45]

The Earl's warnings might be seen as mere scaremongering, but coming from so distinguished a local figure and reproduced at length in local newspapers, their meaning could not have been lost on a local, Lutterworth, readership. If any man could claim the right to speak out it was the Earl. At Jutland, on May 31st 1916, his second son, Lieutenant Commander Hugh Feilding, a career naval officer, was serving on board *H.M.S. Defence*. His ship was caught unawares by the advancing German battleships and battle cruisers and suffered a direct hit: 'for a millisecond *Defence's* profile seemed to lose its definition, "her sides burst all ways", and the "entire ship was blown into the air, deckplates, bodies, and debris being plainly visible against the smoke"'.[46] And at Passchendaele the Earl had lost another son, Henry, killed at the point when the rain and the mud had rendered the battlefield impenetrable and when Haig's blind optimism foolishly saw an enemy on the point of collapse and ordered the continuation of the offensive.[47] As he said in a letter to the press, 'I hate this war… – haven't I reason, like too many others, to hate it? I don't, however, want to feel that all our sacrifices have been made in vain'.[48]

There is no doubting the sincerity of the Earl's views, repugnant as they were to those who fell victim to his eloquent tongue, and however far-fetched and 'wrong-headed' some of his ideas undoubtedly were.[49] The Earl was not one to say one thing in public and another in private. His personal letters to his wife whilst out on his crusade across the country read like lectures on the need to pursue the war. In Leeds, he complained to her that: 'absolutely nothing been done here in propaganda way – War Aims Committee non-existent and L. Mayor didn't know what such a thing meant!'[50] and 'It is appalling to see how this work has been neglected and what a dangerous situation might arise and may yet arise through the way this home propaganda has been mis-handled and neglected'.[51]

And the local newspapers joined in. 'One wonders,' wrote the *Leicester Daily Mercury*, 'what the feelings of the pacifist must be when he reads of deeds like those which have been told of our brave Leicesters who, even when it would have been no dishonour to surrender to a foe who had completely surrounded them, doggedly went on fighting – "Their's not to reason why, Their's but to do and die" [*sic*]. Today's local casualty list is the fitting answer of our Leicester soldiers to those who would have us bow the knee to German militarism'[52] – though the sense and implications of that last sentence are difficult to fathom.

More was to follow a week later when even greater coverage was given to the presence of a 'War Propaganda Van' in Rugby, manned by men fresh from the Front. The principal speaker, a Mr McKinnell, got the show started with a spirited exposition of the wickedness of the Germans, how they had planned and prepared for this war for years past, and how Britain had had no choice but to fight Germany in self-defence. 'We could not stand back and see a small nation threatened without putting out a hand to help. We could not see a big boy bully a small child without interfering,' he told his audience. It was, word for word, rhetoric straight out of 1914 and the enthusiasm surrounding the first declaration of war. Indeed, as Adrian Gregory points out, there was a continuous thread running through Britain's purposes in fighting this war, from the first day to the last: 'The British went to war in 1914 to curb and to punish German aggression in order to achieve a lasting peace. They pursued this goal with terrifying single-mindedness.'[53]

Next came Mr G. Teidman, a fitter by trade, a Trade Unionist and a man invalided out of the trenches after having been gassed. The voice of the common man! Or, as he put it, 'a voice from the trenches'. It was Teidman who launched into a frontal assault on the 'pacifists'. The press report continued: 'He had come to speak to them because there is a sense of danger in the country, not from the German lines – not from the lines where our boys are facing hell itself to keep them in safety – but from the people at home. He had travelled all over Wales and the greater part of the Midlands, and he had heard and seen signs of discontent. He had also seen a certain section of young men in this country banding themselves together and calling themselves "pacifists". He was sorry to have to say that certain gentlemen in responsible positions – and who had taken the oath of loyalty to their Flag and their King – were leading these young men whom the soldiers called "skin preservers", because they were afraid of their own skins. All this time they had been in good jobs, earning big money, and now, when they (the soldiers) were knocked out and came back and asked these young men to do their bit, they said they had either got a conscience, or else were pacifists...

'While men had been fighting there [in France and Flanders] for a bob a day the young men at home had been earning pounds a week, and because they were asked to give those at the front a rest and take their turn in the trenches, they said, "We are pacifists, and belong to the Noble Order of the I.O.P."[54] He felt he should like to get hold of them and take them to France. He was open to gamble', he continued, 'that they could cure them of their consciences and their pacifism'. And so, on and on... More atrocity stories, by now routine, of ravished and murdered women and babes – *And the pacifists say the Germans are our brothers*' (in italics, of course) – and a final swipe at those who were producing shoddy munitions for the men at the Front and so hampering Britain's final victory and a world where 'democracy at last would be safe for ever'.[55]

A sleight of hand had again been perpetrated and that word 'pacifist' used, as it had been used since the outbreak of war, as a term of abuse. It meant, unpatriotic, defeatist, cowardly, irrelevant and, even dangerous to Britain's war effort. Lord Denbigh, the Propaganda Van and the *Rugby Advertiser* in perfect harmony! So many ideas were jumbled together that it is not easy to disentangle them all and it becomes increasingly difficult to recognise genuine pacifists like the Payne brothers in the ways in which that word was being used as the war went on. 'Pacifists' had now also become the same as 'pessimists' and 'defeatists', undermining Britain's will to win by spreading gloomy predictions of defeat and catastrophe if the war continued. 'Pacifists' included anyone who questioned Lloyd George's doctrine that only a 'knock-out blow', total victory over Germany, would be enough as a war aim. Most violently castigated in this regard was Lord Lansdowne's 'peace by negotiation' slogan, but the attacks extended to anyone who sought even the most informal discussions to pave the way for a final settlement. 'Pacifists' were 'pro-German', enemies in our midst aiding the enemy, wittingly or unwittingly working towards a German victory. 'Pacifists' were unpatriotic at a time when the tide of patriotism was running high, men and women who cared nothing for their King or the Country, which had raised and protected them, or for their fellow-countrymen – which meant you and me. 'Pacifists' were traitors, cranks, curs, cowards, lunatics, dangerous – the abuse was interchangeable – and 'pacifist' had become a shorthand for them all.[56] This marked the prevailing mentality of the time, an attitude which as the twentieth century unfolded would become increasingly discredited but this was not so in 1918.

H.G. Wells, whose support for the war had never wavered and who inevitably had something to say on the matter, had taken time out in his 1917 book *War and the Future* to deal with the 'Yielding Pacifist and the Conscientious Objector', and did not pull his punches. Imagining himself explaining the British system to our foreign allies he wrote: 'Practically, of course, we offered to exempt anyone who conscientiously objected to fight or serve. Then the Pacifist and Pro-German people started to campaign to enrol objectors. Of course, every shirker, every coward and slacker in the country decided at once to be a conscientious objector. Anyone but a British legislator could have foreseen that. Then we started Tribunals to wrangle with the objectors about their *bona fides*. Then the Pacifists and the Pro-Germans issued little leaflets and started correspondence courses to teach people exactly how to lie to the Tribunals. Trouble about the freedom of the pamphleteer followed. I had to admit it – it had been a rather sloppy business.'[57] Wells' disingenuous identification of 'pacifists' with 'pro-German' does him no credit, but is typical of much anti-pacifist propaganda from the time, especially as German 'atrocities', real or imagined, created an atmosphere of genuine and widespread hatred for the enemy.

On the other hand, so overwhelming was the chorus of voices demanding the 'knock-out blow' as the only acceptable outcome of the war that we have to ask whether it did not contain more than a germ of wisdom. This was typical, a letter written to the *Leicester Daily Mercury* in October of 1917 accusing them of prolonging the war, its reasoning being: 'The pacifists are not at all a numerous body, [that] goes without saying, but their existence enables the German Government to quote from their speeches, to magnify their importance, and to rejoice exceedingly that such a body are *[sic]* at large in the country. This is a powerful stimulus to the German people, and so the war is prolonged.'[58] He had a point.

The Germans were certainly aware of British opponents of the war and the German military commander, Erich Ludendorff, was eager to exploit the British 'peace movement' when he thought it might bring him a military advantage. He later wrote: 'In January, 1918, I submitted a memorandum to the Chancellor of the Empire, Count von Hertling. I asked for the organisation of a dexterous, purposeful and consistent propaganda to support and further Lord Lansdowne's "patriotic peace movement" in England. This propaganda was to convince the English people that it was merely David Lloyd George's imperialistically ambitious "knock-out" policy that prolonged the war... I wrote the Imperial Chancellor: "... If we aim to enhance our chances for victory on the actual field of battle by victories behind the English front, our words must be chosen so as to make it possible for the English peace party to stand before their people and say: 'If you would let us guide you, the way for peace negotiations will be open and the honour and safety of England will be guaranteed.'" Unfortunately, Germany's weak and clumsy political administration hardly accomplished anything towards putting into effect these clear and concise ideas...'[59]

Ludendorff was deluded, of course, as well as cynical. Believing that 'public sentiment in the enemy countries could be effectually influenced in favour of peace negotiations if we succeeded in winning decisive battles', because 'the world always favours a winner', he had, at the height of Germany's successes in their Spring Offensives, urged again that 'the English peace movement should be urgently pressed now, in the hour of our greatest triumph, when the British Field-Marshal [Haig] publicly confessed that he was fighting in despair with his "back to the wall"'.[60] (This last was a reference to Douglas Haig's famous Order of the Day of April 11th 1918, which concluded with one of the Field Marshal's rare forays into what we might interpret as inspirational English: 'There is no other course open to us but to fight it out! Every position must be held to the last man: there must be no retirement. With our backs to the wall, and believing in the justice of our cause, each one of us must fight on to the end. The safety of our homes and the freedom of mankind alike depend on the conduct of each one of us at this critical moment.'[61]) Ludendorff's miscalculation in interpreting Haig's call as one of 'despair' merely underlines his ignorance of the British. If anything, the Germans' successes had had the opposite effect, rallying support for the war effort. One indicator of the mood in Britain, the number of workers' strikes, fell to almost nil while the crisis lasted and the Ministry of Munitions reported 'the magical disappearance of labour opposition' as workers rallied to the patriotic cause. 'There has been,' it continued, 'an almost entire cessation of public meetings to advocate an immediate peace.'[62] Not for the last time, as war crisis deepened, the British people re-doubled their determination to support their men in khaki and see the war through to victory.

There seems little doubt that the likes of Lloyd George and the Earl of Denbigh, Lord Northcliffe and most of the newspapers in Britain held the majority view: war to the finish, to final victory, to the 'knock-out blow' – the NCF, the Fellowship of Reconciliation, Ramsay MacDonald, Lord Lansdowne, the Quakers, a handful of disillusioned war poets, a small army of conscientious objectors and the Payne brothers notwithstanding.

When we try to put ourselves in the position of those in small town Lutterworth, who read their national and local newspapers day after day, we can see, as they saw, a demon, a monster, as powerfully drawn as the 'Beastly Hun', being fleshed out before them in all its menace and horror: the image of 'the pacifist'. This horrible picture was given legitimacy in its endorsement by figures of authority, not least the Earl of Denbigh himself. It was not, strictly speaking, an incitement to violence, but it does go some way to explain what was going on in the minds of those in Lutterworth who were outraged when two real life pacifists unexpectedly turned up in their town just as the war situation on the Western Front was approaching its last, most dangerous crisis.

★

In this atmosphere it is hardly surprising that ultra-patriotic nationalist groups like the British Empire Union, which was already firmly established in the Home Counties, and as close to Lutterworth as Market Harborough[63], shouted loudly enough to influence policy, though it was the eccentric M.P. Pemberton Billing who was setting the pace in the early months of 1918 through his newspaper, the *Vigilante*.[64] While the *Vigilante* had a tiny circulation, the influence of the Radical Right did not depend on numbers, but on powerful press support and the credulity of those who chose to listen. And while it may be true that 'the Radical Right played a major part in *directing* the attitudes of the populace'[65], it also *reflected* widespread public attitudes which were already there.

In true demagogue style Pemberton Billing had claimed the existence of a German 'Black Book' containing the names of 47,000 Britons in positions of influence who were, because of their unorthodox sexual practices, being blackmailed by the Germans to help them in the war. The myth of a 'Hidden Hand' at work in Britain was not new. The novels of William le Queux and John Buchan's pre-war classic *The Thirty-Nine Steps* had done much to popularise the idea, but Billing appeared convincing, claiming to hold evidence of German infiltration of the upper levels of the British Establishment and, more salacious and more appealing to some of his readers, evidence of 'sexual depravity' among those same pillars of the Establishment.[66] Matters came to a head after the *Vigilante* published an article in February 1918 under the remarkable title 'The Cult of the Clitoris', attacking the Canadian actress Maud Allan whose London stage performance as Salome in Oscar Wilde's erotic masterpiece had gone a great deal further than was expected on the stage at that time. Maud sued for libel. What gave the case its significance was that Billing's generalised claims of sexual and moral depravity among the ruling classes were now extended to named members of the family of the former Prime Minister Herbert Asquith and, of course, to the *bête noir* of the right, Lord Haldane. Playing on the homosexuality of the play's author, Pemberton Billing was able to paint a picture to send a horrified chill (or thrill) through the English public. When the case eventually came to trial, the Old Bailey jury, incredibly, found in favour of Billing, who was cheered from the court.[67] Billing's claims and the jury's response were more symptom than cause of the heightened emotional anxiety which gripped the British people in the first half of 1918. Fears about the outcome of the war were awakened: if God really was on the side of the righteous, and Britain's elite was really behaving in this godless manner, then who could be certain of final victory? Right may not triumph over might.

Thus the issue of 'manliness' was brought into sharper focus at this crucial juncture in the war. It was the same issue which Edward Williamson Mason had been confronted by at Catterick Camp when asked by a puzzled sergeant major: 'Surely, surely, Mason, you are not going to act the woman?' Humanity in their world was divided between men and women, male and female, and each was expected to behave in its own specific ways: 'gender confusion' was unknown to them, homosexuality still 'the Love that dare not speak its name'. So, confronted by war, 'men' were expected to behave like 'men', and when the gender stereotype was confounded bewilderment was left in its wake. The stereotype of the effeminate conscientious objector became the stuff of contemporary cartoons and lampoons. What was left was a perception that the conscientious objector, in not playing the 'man', was in some way 'unmanned', and was thus, in the eyes of the common man and woman, a figure of contempt who was fair game for all, whatever their motive.

★

In the midst of all the bluster, the distortions and the outright lies there lurked a valid concern. This had become Total War, a war which would be won or lost on the Home Front as easily (perhaps more easily) than on the battle front. The lesson of what had happened in Russia in 1917 was lost on nobody: how sudden and total the collapse of the Home Front, the economy, the political structure, the military, and the social system itself had been, not only when the Tsar was overthrown in March, but also by the destruction of Kerenski's Provisional Government in the Bolshevik coup of November.[68] *Weakness*, division and disunity at home, compounded by sheer exhaustion, *could* lead to disaster. And the massive mutinies in the French Army in the early summer of 1917 had appeared to bring the Allies within sight of defeat, mutinies blamed by the Generals (those truly to blame) on pacifists and feeble politicians at home.[69] Even though the general political, social, economic and cultural backgrounds of both Russia and France were entirely different from those of Britain, it could credibly be believed that 1917 and 1918 had the look of a civilisation on the brink of collapse.[70]

Lloyd George had clearly understood this: in his statement of British War Aims given on January 5th 1918 he had said, 'We have arrived at the most critical hour in this terrible conflict, and before any government takes the fateful decision as to the conditions under which it ought either to terminate or continue the struggle, it ought to be satisfied that the conscience of the nation is behind these conditions, for nothing else can sustain the effort which is necessary to achieve a righteous end to this war.'[71] Of course, Lloyd George, having already committed himself to the 'knock-out blow', would do everything he could to ensure that 'the conscience of the nation' was behind that policy and that policy alone, which meant marginalising or silencing those who disagreed.

The last word on the case at this point, a contrary view, will go to Ramsay MacDonald: 'What so many of our war cranks have never seen with their inflaming of hate and riotous immoral passion was that they were destroying the finer strands of the web of civilisation. When they joined the curs of the gutter in yelping at some of us, in judging us by wild passion, and when they added volume to the yelp, they were not attacking us but their own decency… It was a holiday in riff-raff – a demonstration of the ignorance, the prejudice and the brutality of the mob (not badly dressed or sans coulotte [sic]) which pretends to voice English sentiment at the present moment. It is a revelation for decent citizens to ponder over'. It might also pass as a comment on the dramatic and violent events about to unfold in Lutterworth.[72]

★

From the outset there had been plenty of precedents for violence. We have seen how, after the outbreak of war, there had been relatively minor local outbreaks of violence, or the threat of violence, against those seen as enemies: the Russian Jewish second-hand clothes dealer in Rugby whose shop was attacked by a drunken mob a week after the declaration of war, or the friends of Dr Krumbholz who had felt it necessary to publish his Englishness and that he had gone to join his British rather than German regiment. There had been violence offered to political opponents of the war, like the two Rugby socialists who had attempted to speak in the town's market place just after the war's outbreak and had had to be rescued from a hostile and violent crowd by the police.[73]

The violence of crowds was never far beneath the surface in First World War Britain. Professor Panikos Panayi has catalogued a horrific pattern of public violence against those seen as 'enemy aliens', chiefly (though not exclusively) in the working class districts of the big cities, and triggered by events in the war such as the atrocity stories which followed the German Army through Belgium, or the use of poison gas in the Second Battle of Ypres, or the sinking of the *Lusitania* in 1915.[74] The spring and summer of 1918 was such a time of xenophobic violence across Britain, with Belgians and Russian Jews targeted as well as anyone suspected of having German or Austrian origins, whether naturalised as British subjects or not. Some sections of the press – notably Lord Northcliffe's *Daily Mail* and *Weekly Dispatch*, as well as Horatio Bottomley's *John Bull* – worked relentlessly to stir up hostility towards hapless suspect civilians and demand that everyone of 'enemy alien' origin be interned.[75]

We might here pause for a moment and consider the striking parallels between press, public and government approaches towards 'enemy aliens' on the one hand and 'pacifists' on the other, during the First World War. Both were seen as 'the enemy within', undermining and betraying Britain's war effort. Both were victims of waves of hostility, leading in some cases and at certain times to riot and mob violence. In most cases property was the main target, though individual 'aliens' and 'pacifists' were also singled out for attack. In both cases the press was instrumental in whipping up public fury, supported by some populist and right-wing politicians.[76] In both cases the government found it politically necessary to take action, pushed forward by press and public opinion into steps they may not have wanted to take, seeking solutions which were as humane as could be found in the circumstances of war; and steps which, moreover, protected the vulnerable individual from public hysteria. In both cases the government resorted to a form of internment. 'Enemy aliens', like Jessie Seebach's husband in Cotesbach, found themselves interned in any one of twenty or so internment camps, prisons and prison ships all across the country – 23,000 of them in grim conditions at the Knockaloe camp on the Isle of Man alone[77], kept far away from their families and friends, while the conscientious objectors, for their part, were kept either under prison regimes (if they refused to co-operate) or in the laxer environment of the Work Centres (if they did), both usually far from their homes. The Work Centres provided little more than internment under another name, albeit an internment far more humane than was meted out to those of foreign birth.

★

That feelings were running high is evidenced by the extraordinary scenes in the market place in the centre of Leicester on the morning of Sunday May 5th 1918. The Left in Leicester used the occasion for their traditional May Day celebration, mounting a large rally in their usual venue, to be addressed by Ramsay MacDonald.

All might have passed off without undue incident had it not been for the fact that the War Aims Committee chose to meet in the same place at the same time. Though it was not known at the time, the National War Aims Committee was, in fact, a government organisation – 'officially unofficial'[78] – set up in August 1917 precisely to combat anti-war activity: it was financed from Secret Service funds (a real 'hidden hand') to combat the 'Hidden Hand' of popular imagination. The Home Office passed on information from local police forces and from the head of Special Branch, Basil Thomson, to the local War Aims Committees about forthcoming anti-war rallies and meetings, with the express intent that they be disrupted and broken up.[79] What MacDonald did not fully appreciate was that he

Leicester Market Place

was about to come under attack from the covert power of the British State. What ensued was one of the lesser known battles of the First World War: the Battle of Leicester Market.

In front of the arch outside the Corn Exchange, with its extraordinary double outside staircase, the Labour Party had set up two drays to act as a makeshift platform from which Ramsay MacDonald and Alderman Banton, among others, would address the gathering. On the fish market side of the market square the War Aims crowd was gathering, so as many as 7,000 people were packed into the market place, with a strong police presence of officers on horseback as well as on foot, the local police apparently unaware of the War Aims Committee's true colours.

The preliminary skirmishes were vocal. Ramsay, looking unwell, tried to speak to his half of the market square while the War Aims crowd endeavoured to drown him out by singing the national anthem and 'Rule Britannia', waving the flags of the Allies and cheering loudly. Though in body they were in Leicester, Ramsay said, 'in heart and soul they were over in the fighting line with the brave fellows'. It was a sentiment consistent with his view throughout the war, expressed during that Recruiting Rally in De Montfort Hall in 1914 when his words had been jeered and hooted by those who had not even heard them, and it cut no ice with his opponents now who refused to have any truck with his calls for a negotiated peace settlement. Then Alderman Banton, who had made that impassioned speech on August 2nd 1914 demanding that Britain not become involved in this war, spoke, intemperately accusing Sir Jonathan North, Leicester's Mayor, of inciting the counter-demonstration.

But phase two of the battle was already in motion as groups of War Aims men set out to physically attack the makeshift platform from which Alderman Banton was speaking. The fullest press report of the sortie claims it was led by men with experience of the trenches who, after some preliminary raids, launched a flanking attack designed to get round the crowd and through the open side of the archway behind the platform. 'The way they came on', reported the local press, 'showed they meant business.[80] For a minute it looked as if nothing could thwart their obvious intention of wrecking the platform', though what might then have become of those standing precariously on top of the platform is not clear.

It was now that the third element in the Sunday morning's events intervened – the police. What followed was described as a 'mad half-hour'[81] as a dozen police officers 'threw themselves' into the breach. 'At one time the attackers had actually reached the platform, and for a moment or so its fate hung in the balance.' In the melée that followed something close to 'general riot and disorder' occurred as the crowds jostled each other against the background of patriotic songs sung loudly, but probably artlessly. Whether the storming party lost its nerve when it realised that it might now have to decide what to do if it did reach its target, or whether the police were sufficiently sturdy in diverting the War Aims aggressors away from the Labour speakers is unclear, but the crisis passed and all three sides withdrew leaving the market place deserted, abandoned to a few children and stray dogs and, no doubt, the inevitable scattering of litter left by any crowd, until, bright and early on Monday morning, the market traders would set up their stalls and the more peaceable business of the place could recommence.

The leading local newspaper, the *Leicester Daily Mercury*, was in no doubt as to why the disturbance had occurred and did not see any need to explain. Its editorial said simply that 'in Leicester, rightly or wrongly, Labour meetings are chiefly regarded as "pacifist"'. No further explanation was needed: if the Labour Party was holding a public meeting, then it must be a pacifist meeting and there was no need to explain why a pacifist meeting would be attacked. Months of press distortions and slanders against those disloyal and traitorous 'pacifists' had had their effect. Nor did the *Mercury* condemn the attack on the Labour rally. Indeed it took as its principal target Alderman Banton. Commenting on his reaction to the trouble, the paper observed dryly that 'the sanest thing Alderman Banton said among some utterances that might otherwise be described was that Mr MacDonald and his supporters owed the Leicester Police a debt of gratitude for the protection they had afforded them'.[82] For weeks the Banton issue rumbled on through the press, centring round his charge that the mayor had incited the anti-Labour or anti-pacifist demonstration and thus the violence which had followed. It was a month before Banton withdrew his accusation, and then, in the *Mercury's* view, with bad grace. 'It is an old trick,' the paper commented, 'with a certain type of public men to abuse the Press when some "blazing indiscretion" had brought them to the bar of public opinion. But it is an amazing, not to say an impudent thing, for a man to take this course when in the same breath he is obliged to admit that he has been quite accurately reported.' The piece commented on the 'savage malignity' of Banton's attack on the *Mercury* and took exception to his suggestion that the paper's reporting was below standard because 'the best men… had gone to the war' – a crafty double-edged attack on the war and those who supported it. There would be no negotiated peace here either.[83]

A week or so after the battle in Leicester Market Place three men from the War Aims party appeared in the police court, charged with disorderly conduct. Albert Howarth, one of the three, was Secretary of the British Workers' League. He was unrepentant: 'I admit that I was pretty excited, but so bitter was the feeling against your present member for Leicester that I say that everybody in the market place was fully justified. The general opinion of those present was that the people on the platform were preaching sedition. If the same conditions arose I should do exactly the same next Sunday morning, and my justification is the sedition that is being preached week by week in the market place.' The magistrates dismissed all three cases.[84]

It would be easy to write off the 'Battle of Leicester Market' as a simple confrontation between groups of politically motivated men, some bent on violence. Banton's accusation that the mayor was behind the counter-demonstration by the War Aims Committee group appears to have been unfounded, but the attack on the platform holding the speakers, especially MacDonald and Banton, was clearly organised and led by violent men. However, it was more than that, for it spoke of something wider, the deeper fear, even panic, which the success of the Germans' Spring Offensive in northern France had created across Britain. Haig 'was exhibiting the nearest to panic of which he was capable'[85], though that did not stop him accusing the Prime Minister and even the King himself of 'funk' as the German Army advanced[86], or as A.J.P. Taylor put it: 'in these uneasy days nerves were on edge and few men judged sanely'.[87] It was during those 'uneasy days' that the Payne brothers returned from their time away and tried to settle back into their familiar daily routines, weaving baskets and running the shop on Church Street. The times were truly out of joint, in Lutterworth no less than anywhere else.

★

In such an atmosphere it might not take much to tip a volatile public opinion into outright terror – and direct enemy action against helpless civilians might achieve precisely that effect. And this was what happened as Britain now came under renewed bombardment from the air on the night of May 19th/20th 1918, as the massive fixed wing bombers of the 'England Squadron', Gothas and the appropriately named Giants, dropped over 14,000 kilograms of bombs on London, killing forty-nine and injuring 177 more. 'British airmen found the skies swarming with Germans' that night.[88] It is true that five of the Gothas were shot down and another forced to crash land, and that over the following days R.A.F bombers in retaliation attacked targets in Germany, hitting Koblenz, Metz and Thionville and a claimed poison gas factory in Mannheim, but the fact remained that the giant bombers had come, had reached their targets, and might yet come again. Memories of the 'Gotha Summer' of 1917 were still fresh: in the past twelve months the huge fixed wing bombers had mounted eight daylight and nineteen night raids against Britain, killing 835 people and injuring 1,935.[89]

The air raid of 19th/20th May was in reality the last time the bombers would fly over Britain in the First World War, but that was not known at the time. The threat and the anxiety were real enough. In London some deaths had been caused as crowds, terrified at the approach of the bombers, had stampeded in search of shelter: at Bishopsgate and Mile End in London fourteen had died, 'foreigners' being widely blamed for causing the tragedy, in this case not just the German pilots, but Russians in the crowd who it was said had barged women and children out of the way, the coroner condemning their conduct as 'entirely unworthy of men and nearly approaching the conduct of the lower animals'.[90] Appropriate, meaning foreign, non-British, scapegoats had been found.

If Leicestershire people assumed they were safe from Gotha or Zeppelin attack, there were manned 'Observation Posts' scattered across the region to watch for enemy aircraft, some with anti-aircraft guns at the ready. As long ago as September of 1917 the *Leicester Daily Mercury* had published advice on 'the importance of taking cover' during air raids and, in case the message was lost, the chief constable in January 1918 published posters advising every town and village in the county of what to do 'in the event of a visit by hostile Aircraft during DAYLIGHT'. In Lutterworth the hooter at George Spencer's works would give three blasts of fifteen seconds each if the planes came during the working week and on Sundays a church bell would ring for three twenty second bursts. The message was then underlined: 'As experience has clearly shown that the risk of serious casualties is greatly diminished by taking cover (even such cover as is afforded by an ordinary dwelling house), it is hoped the public will remain indoors until the danger has passed.'[91] To a newspaper reading public, all too familiar with photographs of demolished houses and bombed out buildings, it did little to reassure. There was, in fact, one further attempted Zeppelin raid against Britain, on the night of August 5th, but after one airship was shot down in flames off the Norfolk coast, the other four returned home. Their crews lived, but not to fight another day.[92] And if we might suspect that such terrors were remote from inland Lutterworth and its people, we can detect an echo of that last raid in the village of Gilmorton, three miles or so to the west of Lutterworth, when a zealous police officer, observing a house showing both downstairs and upstairs lights, used the fact that it was 'the night of the air raid' to identify the evening and to justify taking the family to court.[93]

★

But, though no German planes flew over Lutterworth after the first local Zeppelin scare in January 1916, Lutterworth was a damaged community in deeper, more profound and important ways. Fissures which had started to show themselves before the brothers had left had widened and cases referred to the magistrates' court in the latter part of the war were showing a more troubling side, the great and the good of the town all too aware of the impact the loss of so many fathers was having on their children. In January 1917 the Board of Guardians at the workhouse had issued an impassioned plea to the government that married men with families should not be conscripted ahead of single men[94] and Lupton Topham, in a case tried by him as magistrate in June of the same year, 'hoped the parents (where the father had not gone to the war) would deal more firmly' with the miscreants – a statement which assumed that mothers would be incapable of fulfilling that role themselves.[95]

Bored youths, too old for school and either working in munitions or not yet old enough for the army, were making a nuisance of themselves around the town. Some cases were trivial: sixteen year old Arthur Green appeared before the magistrates for the dastardly crime of ringing door bells and running away, his three alleged companions in crime apparently running fast enough to evade capture. On the same day six young men, ages ranging from twenty down to fifteen, appeared in court for causing an obstruction. They had gathered at 'the Narrows', that point at the top of High Street where the road narrowed alarmingly, and there was scarcely space to get one vehicle through at a time. The police officer who arrested them told the court that 'they kept making remarks on young ladies and others who passed by, some of an insulting nature, and persons passing by had to go in the road'. This had been a persistent problem going back several years, Superintendent Holland told the magistrates, and his patience had run out. When asked by the bench whether the youths were polite, the superintendent retorted: 'Politeness! They do not know what it means'. Yet the court was lenient: they were cautioned and made to pay 4d each in costs.[96] It was hardly a capital offence, but in law-abiding small town Lutterworth it was one nuisance too many and it did not end there, for in the summer two young men, both described as foundry hands, appeared in court for sitting on the window-sill of 'The Unicorn' pub in the middle of town swinging their legs out over the pavement. Superintendent Holland said that 'a great nuisance had been caused by youths sitting on window-sills, and if they were told to desist they went back to it again'. Or perhaps it was a matter of perception, the second half of the superintendent's comment more important than the first. Young men, foundry hands, doing important war work, earning good money, but with little to spend it on, bored in 'somnolent' Lutterworth, making a nuisance of themselves, going too far when they challenged the authority of those who told them to stop.[97] Again the magistrates were lenient: not wishing to record a conviction against them, they were ordered to pay three shillings in costs each.

It was the lack of deference, challenging authority, which was most worrying. Again, in that summer of 1917, four youths were in court for damaging a fence. There had been too much of this going on, Superintendent Holland told the court, and Lupton Topham agreed: 'A lot of boys in Lutterworth, like other places, seem to have got beyond parental control, and the amount of damage wantonly committed on hedges and fences during the past year far exceeded anything he had ever seen before'.[98] There was that nagging fear that social controls were failing, youths were running out of control and the very fabric of family life was under threat.

There was worse, things not expected in quiet, respectable Lutterworth or its even quieter satellite villages. In November of 1917, a munitions worker from Claybrooke, apparently invalided out of the army, assaulted his wife (not an uncommon occurrence at that time) and then set upon John Moore the Parish Constable when he tried to intervene.[99] In March of 1918, a foundry hand living in Ashby Magna attempted a (possibly minor) sexual assault against a female worker on her way home at the end of the day in a third class railway carriage and slapped another woman when she tried to stop him. In the view of the magistrates this went beyond horseplay.[100] He was given the choice of paying a thirty shillings fine or going to prison for fourteen days. In May a trivial quarrel between two shopkeepers over their respective dogs turned violent on High Street, right outside the Denbigh Arms Hotel, when one of them, Charles Whiston, was struck to the ground and kicked while he lay there by the other, George Kirby.[101] Shopkeepers brawling in the street in Lutterworth at ten o'clock on a Saturday morning! Such a thing had never been heard of.

The only bright spot was that fewer cases of drunkenness were reported as the war went on[102], following the national trend and linked to the restrictions on pub opening hours and huge increases in taxes on alcohol, the Church of England locally nevertheless congratulating itself on the success of its temperance campaign.[103]

★

War weariness is hard to quantify, but everywhere across the country the signs were clear that the war was taking its toll upon almost everyone and creating that public mood which would turn so powerfully against the Paynes. The daily casualty lists were grinding down morale, with no end – or at least no victory – in sight. Then had come the great German assaults of spring 1918 when the balance of the war seemed suddenly to be shifting away from the Allies.[104] Food Control Committees were set up, but a range of foodstuffs – sugar, tea, butter, lard, dripping, milk, bacon, pork, condensed milk, rice, currants, raisins, spirits and Australian wines – were all in short supply.[105] And, worst of all, margarine had taken over from butter. The minister in charge, Lord Rhondda, a coal mine owner – not a species normally associated with the common touch – did not help matters by talking of 'greedy growsers', by which he meant ordinary families struggling to cope.[106] Meat, fats and proteins were all scarce and it was only the restoration of higher bread quotas in February 1918 which brought hope that the end might be in sight, that the U-Boat threat may be over. On May 25th 1918, as the trouble in Lutterworth was coming to a head, the newspapers published the latest meat rationing restrictions: what an adult or child with a ration coupon was allowed to buy. The rations seem meagre enough.[107]

Then there were the taxes needed to pay for the war. The brothers' return to Lutterworth coincided with a sharp rise in Income Tax, a 20% increase to six shillings (30p.) in the £ for standard rate payers, while, more hurtful to some, duties on spirits and beer were doubled and duties on tobacco rose by 27%.[108]

★

In that early summer of 1918 the war seemed literally to hang in the balance, that Germany might, almost at the last gasp, seize victory from the jaws of defeat; and the signs from the war in the days leading up to the attack on the Payne family's shop were ominous indeed.

In the third week of May on the Western Front the tension was palpable as 'no news' day frustratingly followed 'no news' day, and as the Allies awaited what might be a massive, perhaps even a war winning, final German Offensive. 'No news' days they may have been, but they were certainly not 'all quiet'. British and French troops raided across No Man's Land in search of prisoners – and information. It was clear that the German commander Erich Ludendorff held the initiative in France and Flanders as the Allies, too weak themselves to launch an attack before the long awaited arrival of the Americans in large enough numbers, waited for the Germans to strike first. Apprehension was not misplaced, for the public understood the strategic position in the spring and early summer of 1918 well enough. The central fact was the Treaty of Brest-Litovsk, signed between the Germans and the new (and beleaguered) Bolshevik government in Russia in March, which had freed up the vast numbers of German troops used in the great Spring Offensive, and of which there seemed plenty left for whatever plans Ludendorff had in store now.[109]

On Wednesday May 22nd the *Leicester Daily Mercury* reported that 'as one glorious May day succeeds another, the question where and when the enemy will launch his second mighty blow becomes more and more engrossing. The solution of the problem must be near at hand'.[110] But days passed and there was no sign of the German Offensive. Speculation filled the gap. On Friday the 24th French reports were quoted suggesting mutinies in the German Army which were delaying the offensive, some reports suggested sickness in the enemy ranks, but on the same day less reassuring news came from the Central News Agency: 'There is no doubt, however, that during the past few days the enemy has been assembling a large number of shock troops at places convenient for using them to supplement the first great attack'.[111] Over the weekend nothing happened and people all across Britain and France waited, helpless and powerless, for the Germans to make their move.

★

Everything in Lutterworth was now coming together as May drew towards its close in 1918. The presence of the Payne brothers lay at its roots. The months of sustained propaganda against 'pacifists', the Earl of Denbigh's prominent voice and the *Rugby Advertiser* a strident propaganda vehicle, had demonised the 'pacifist' as much as it had the 'Hun', turning two young men whose religious conscience simply would not allow them to go out and kill into figures of hate. To some it must have been shameful, a source of humiliation, that Lutterworth should tolerate their presence. The war rested on a knife's edge with a string of German victories in the field, stretching back to March. Victory, or at the very least the avoidance of terrible defeat, was being jeopardised by the Payne brothers and their kind. Resentment was inevitable, especially now when middle-aged family men were being called up for active service, and were going, no matter how reluctantly, and with the prospect that even older men might be summoned and those in essential work making munitions might be dragged away to use the things they were making. While fathers were at the Front the moral and social fabric of the town – like the country at large – was being visibly damaged, some of the young disaffected, traditional authority failing to anchor society in its old and tested values. And there were plenty of demagogues ready to exploit the people's agony to their own advantage, from Pemberton Billing and his right-wing eccentrics to the chancer, Horatio Bottomley, the lowest common denominator, always ready to tell the public what it wanted to hear, and on to the embarrassingly jingoistic Arthur Winnington-Ingram, the (verbal) warrior Bishop of London – all of whom, it must be said, were able to read the mood of public opinion better than the professional politicians. So many of Lutterworth's menfolk had already been lost, wives made widows, children orphans, girls who would never marry because there would be too few men left to go round. In Leicester there had been serious lawlessness, something akin to all out riot in the market place, and in Lutterworth Roland Payne had been violently assaulted with no recompense in law.

All that was needed was a trigger. This was provided from far away when the German Army commander, Erich Ludendorff, at last decided to make his final, and possibly decisive, move. An extraordinary outburst of violence in Lutterworth followed soon after.

★

The blow on the Western Front fell early on the morning of Monday May 27th 1918 and when it came it was devastating. The target for Ludendorff's assault was a stretch of high ground in northern France, between Reims and Soissons, south of the area struck in March. It had been here, along the Chemin-des-Dames ridge, that the French in the previous April had attempted an ill-judged attack of their own, horribly bungled and contributing in large measure to the French Army mutinies of 1917. With enormous effort and the most appalling suffering, the French had managed to push the Germans back off the ridge and now they held the high ground. The Chemin-des-Dames, the 'Ladies' Road' ridge, named from the road which ran for twenty-three miles along its crest, a road built by Louis XV in more genteel days (for the rich at least) so his daughters might have an easier carriageway between their royal palace at Compiègne and the home of their friend, the Duchess of Nemours at the Château de la Bove, the charm of its name mocking the men who died here in 1917 and who would die here in 1918. 'Where are the butterfly ladies now?' asked one poet who was there.[112]

This had been a quiet sector of the front for months past, characterised as 'one of those backwaters where men slipped into the comfortable world of live and let live, developing more sympathy for their enemies a few metres to their front than the staff a dozen kilometres to the rear… it remained "the sanatorium of the Western Front", where both sides could send battered divisions to recover'.[113] So it was here that the shocked, exhausted and decimated IX Corps had been sent after their traumas further north when all but overrun by Ludendorff's aggression. And a good place it was: behind the churned up front lines 'the environment in which the British found themselves was very pleasant, if unmartial', as one historian has commented. 'An officer of the Devonshire Regiment observed that in some places there were rose-covered arbours, and another officer of the Middlesex Regiment compared their trenches to an underground Savoy Hotel. After the blasted wilderness of the Somme, Artois or Flanders, this must have seemed a paradise, and no more than they deserved.'[114]

All that changed suddenly and violently. Basil Liddell Hart summarised what happened on that Monday: 'At 1 a.m. on May 27th, 1918, a terrific storm of fire burst on the Franco-British front between Reims and north of Soissons, along the famous Chemin-des-Dames; at 4.30 a.m. an overwhelming torrent of Germans swept over the front trenches; by midday it was pouring over the many unblown bridges of the Aisne.'[115] The clipped language disguises a horrendous day of terror and horror for the French troops holding the line and for those British troops already exhausted by the fighting in the months following March 21st, who had been moved here to rest and recuperate, now finding themselves in the eye of the storm yet again. By 5.30 in the morning the Chemin-des-Dames ridge was lost as the events of March 21st seemed to be repeating themselves. While many were killed by the opening bombardment and others, surrounded and outnumbered, surrendered, many others fought on, resisting the German advance to the end. Martin Gilbert recounts how, at La-Ville-aux-Bois-les-Pontaverts, a British artillery battery did just that: in the nearby war cemetery 413 of the 540 graves are of men whose remains were unidentifiable, such was the ferocity of the fighting there.[116] The French Army again now suffered catastrophic losses on the Chemin-des-Dames as German troops poured through the Allied lines and seized it back. 'It was,' wrote Hew Strachan, 'the most significant defeat suffered by the French on the Western Front since 1914.'[117] The American military historian, Robert Asprey, went further: it was 'the greatest Allied crisis since the German drive on Paris in 1914'.[118] German forces streamed forward, crossing the Aisne, and by nightfall were on the Vesle and heading for the Marne – that touchstone of the first great German assault in 1914, that last line along which the Kaiser's invasion had been at last halted – and beyond the Marne... Paris.

What the spare official communiqués failed to convey was supplied by the journalists who witnessed the catastrophe. *The Times* correspondent waxed lyrical, but in doing so effectively conveyed the human significance of the appalling events unfolding on the Aisne:

'Today some way west of Reims and south of the battlefield, I watched for three or four hours a sight that was in its way even more painful and infuriating than the shameful story of the ruined Cathedral of Reims. It was a day of gorgeous sunlight and rich spring beauty. On either side the endless, hedgeless fields, golden with buttercups and white with swaying marguerites, or green with waist-high stretches of waving barley and rye, rose and fell to the meeting-place of the fathomless blue sky and distant hills. Far below in the valley the glittering Marne shone like a ribbon of silver laid on a cloth of green. And through it all – the work of the Germans contrasting with the work of God – along a white road for miles in front and behind, with hardly ever an interval, passed a slow-moving stream of humanity, old men and women and children and babies fleeing from the destruction to come.

'They were in carts and wagons; they pushed before them perambulators and rustic go-carts; they stumbled wearily along on foot. Every vehicle was piled high with their poor earthly belongings – chairs and tables, bedsteads, mattresses, quilts, pails, cooking pots, crockery, clocks – particularly bad things to leave behind when there are Germans about – bicycles, bundles, bandboxes – the whole simple machinery of their rustic lives. In many of the carts there were women and children, sometimes ten or a dozen in one wagon, stowed or perched somehow among the bundles.'[119]

Many Parisians fled from the city in panic as they had in 1914 and in March 1918. They had grown accustomed to bombardment from the air (the first German bomber had attacked Paris ten days after the outbreak of war[120]) and from long-range artillery, 'Big Bertha' opening its account on Good Friday 1918, causing death and damage from seventy miles away. In Paris, the spectre of a German Army at the gates raised another, more sinister spectre – the spectre of Communism. Within living memory a German Army had defeated the French in battle, laid siege to Paris and provoked the left-wing Paris Commune of 1871, arguably the world's first proletarian Communist Revolution. The Commune had been crushed with great violence and bloodshed, but the ideas which informed it had grown stronger, not weaker, in the intervening years, and with the overthrow of Tsar Nicholas in March 1917 and the subsequent Bolshevik coup in November, the prospect of a new Communist Revolution in Paris did not seem so far-fetched.[121]

The overwhelming German success on the first day left the Allied armies with a communications nightmare. It fell to a French staff officer, Jean de Pierrefeu, to compose the necessary press release. 'What were we to say in the communiqué?' he pondered. 'We could not very well admit, at the first mention of the battle, the loss of the Chemin des Dames and the crossing of the Aisne, which was the bitter truth, without the risk of striking panic into the public. But unless we prepared the way, what arrears might we not have to make up? Besides, if the enemy communiqué announced the true position, we should forfeit all faith in our veracity.'[122]

The results of Pierrefeu's deft handiwork were reflected in that evening's local *Leicester Daily Mercury*. 'Offensive Resumed. Battle in the Reims-Soissons Front' ran its headline. It was neutral enough stuff for Pierrefeu referred only to the night's bombardment, leaving the disastrous morning events to the bland phrase: 'The battle is in progress.' With nothing further to go on, the press could only report that 'The long-delayed Hun Offensive appears to have been resumed early this morning on a wide front between Reims and Soissons, where British troops are in line with the French. An attack has also developed against the French, between Locre and Voormézeele. The French communiqué describes this morning's attack as taking place on a very large front'.[123] No doubt even those who had grown used to following the war's movements in detail were sent off to search their maps anew, since these were unfamiliar names, unfamiliar places, previously firmly inside the French sector. And what they saw must have horrified them. This was indeed an attack along a 'very large front'. It stretched over twenty miles.

At 10.42 a.m. that same Monday a British communiqué reported that 'strong hostile attacks preceded by a bombardment of great intensity, developed early this morning on a wide front… There was considerable hostile artillery activity yesterday and last night on the British front'. A further French communiqué issued on that same morning gave no fresh news and little consolation: 'The French and British troops are resisting the German onset with their usual valour'.[124] To those as well versed in the coded language of such things as the British public were by 1918, the message would be read loud and clear: things were not going well. Not well at all. Usually some crumb of comfort was offered, some minor victory for the Allies or trivial setback for the enemy which might lighten the gloom. Here, there was nothing.

By Tuesday evening the local newspapers were carrying the shocking news in their headlines: 'Germans Across the Aisne'. As if in corroboration a German communiqué was quoted as saying that 'the troops of the Crown Prince [Rupprecht] have carried the Chemin-des-Dames ridge'. More scurrying to look at the maps, in disbelief. Few crumbs of reassurance could be offered, but crumbs were better than nothing: 'If [the Germans' intention] is to break our line at the first onset it has failed'; and 'the enemy pressed back the British to the second line of prepared positions', it was reported. A French communiqué reported Allied troops 'falling back gradually' as the Germans advanced. The matter was in hand: there were 'prepared positions', no need to panic.

These events in themselves were bad enough, but reports carried the threat of more. This attack may not even be the main one. The German breakthrough may be nothing more than a diversionary attack designed to draw French and British troops away from the real object of the German Offensive. The French were convinced this was what it was. The *Echo de Paris* that morning was quoted as saying that 'the question which is now to be answered is whether the enemy wishes by this colossal operation to cover his left flank with a view to a principal attack towards Amiens, and to draw our forces from that area'. Other French observers were more certain and the *Petit Journal* was reporting that 'it is the 'Picardy – Artois – Flanders front that remains the object of their chief preoccupation'. British journalists took the bait: under the headline 'Uncertainty of the Real Push', it was reported that: 'It appears possible that the Germans by this movement are endeavouring to attract the Allied reserves into the struggle while they themselves concentrate their forces for the main attack elsewhere'. 'The object of the enemy is still obscure', reported the *Leicester Daily Mercury*, but '…considered as a diversion, as French opinion holds, it is undertaken by astonishingly large forces'. If the Germans could deploy such 'astonishingly large forces' on a mere diversionary attack, what would a blow with their full strength be like?

★

Fear bordering on panic gripped the nation as the unthinkable threatened. This was far from the patriotic enthusiasm with which Lutterworth's townspeople had seen their young men off to the war in 1914. Then, what war enthusiasm there was had been motivated by thoughts of victory. Now, it was a perverse enthusiasm for the war, one born of fear of defeat. In Lutterworth, it was the specific event of the German successes on the Aisne which triggered the violent assault on the whole Payne family in their home and shop on Church Street.

That the Payne brothers' stand against the war was disapproved of by their neighbours is clear enough. The dunking of Roland in the River Swift by his former school friends gave a clear and tangible warning to the family that their presence in the town was not welcome to some, if not all. Even then, it is probably the case that they did not comprehend just how deep were the feelings in Lutterworth against them.[125] In retrospect the question appears not to have been whether there would be more, escalating trouble for them, but when and in what form it would strike.

Over half a century later the Payne brothers would claim that those who attacked their shop on the evening of May 28th 1918 were nothing more than 'a lot of drunken hooligans. They were not Lutterworth people, not in the strict sense. I think they were a lot of people who had come here in the munitions making game at the foundries and that sort of thing. I think that is what started it all off'.

They asserted that their shop was singled out because, 'A lot of these young fellows that were in munitions thought they were going to be called up for the army and they saw us coming back home free men which rather annoyed them'.[126]

Their account continued: 'We were all in the house and stones started coming through the windows. The first we knew about that trouble was, we saw a whole crowd of people coming from the Recreation Ground. They had had a meeting up there and organised everything. Before we knew what was happening stones were coming straight through the windows of the house... I remember we had the lights on at the time and we turned them off so they couldn't see what was going on. The next-door neighbour was a member of the local constabulary. He stood on the front door and kept them out of the house and he allowed us to go into his buildings to get out of the way because they tried to get hold of us. We hid in a shed for a long time and then the police actually came when they thought they had done enough damage. I think it was all very well organised because about midnight everybody disappeared and Leicestershire Police came and took possession of the place... We left the next morning.'[127]

As the brothers' spare account of what happened on that evening in May this is as much as we might hope for, given the distance in time and the peculiar circumstances, but it raises more questions than it answers and leaves much unsaid. For weeks past, ever since their return home, groups of people had gathered outside the Paynes' shop on Church Street each evening. Several weeks of pressure and verbal abuse, jeers, catcalls, hooting and the attack on Roland had not driven the brothers out. By now the nightly heckling had become almost a local routine.

It might be instructive to search further back into English social history to find precedents. There had long been a tradition in English life of active displays of public disapproval. In previous generations and in more normal times wife beaters and child molesters and the like had been the target of 'Rough Music', the cacophonous banging of, as one Leicestershire dialect dictionary explained, 'pokers and tongs, marrow-bones and cleavers, warming-pans and tin kettles, cherry-clacks and whistles, constables' rattles, and bladders with peas in them', topped off by 'yells and hisses'.[128] The treatment of the Paynes as described in the *Leicester Daily Mercury* or the *Rugby Advertiser* – groups hanging about outside the shop, yelling and hooting – was not a case of 'Rough Music' in the old sense, but it was certainly a case of public disapproval. And as in those earlier cases those who participated did not see themselves as in any way hooligans, but as decent, respectable people who were defending what was right.[129]

To some it was a matter of local pride, a matter of removing 'the stigma of harbouring C.O.s' and of Lutterworth's 'notoriety of possessing two C.O.s', as the local press put it.[13] They did not want their community polluted by the taint of 'pacifism'. To them the exorcising of the shame was a matter of local, literally of parochial, honour.

Perhaps we should see what was about to be unleashed against the Payne family as the expression of a release of pent-up fear and tension as the events of the war since the intoxicating August of 1914, through four long years of terrible loss and suffering, and its intensification in the last terrifying few months, exploded into a cleansing violence. For alongside that fracturing of the local community there had also been a great gathering together 'as people related by blood or by experience tried to draw strength from each other'[131] in the midst of their tribulation – and many, if not most of those, were women. Thus, the attack on the Paynes was a vehicle through which a fractured community could reaffirm its identity and its solidarity, its belongingness.

We might also see the violent rejection and expulsion of the Payne brothers as a bastardised memorialisation or commemoration of those who had died, as a form of paying respect to the dead, almost of acting on behalf of the dead in physically removing from the community those who had already removed themselves from it morally. As the Cambridge historian Jay Winter noted: 'After August 1914, commemoration was an act of citizenship. To remember was to affirm community, to assert its moral character, and to exclude from it those values, groups or individuals that placed it under threat. This form of collective affirmation in wartime identified individuals and their families with the community at large, understood both in terms of a localized landscape and a broader and more vaguely defined national entity under siege or threat.'[132] The Paynes were *not* attacked merely by a mob of 'drunken hooligans': it was their own community which turned against them.

Either way, the assault against the Paynes saw a great bringing together of a community torn by the loss (in many cases permanently) of so many of its menfolk, united by suffering and loss, a community like so many all over Britain feeling itself helpless and powerless as great and terrible events were unfolding on the Continent, entirely out of its control, but which would nevertheless decide its future and the futures of everyone in it. And the heightened patriotic fervour surrounding the rituals of Empire Day the previous Friday, May 24th, could have done nothing to calm the mood in the town. Nothing could be done in Lutterworth to halt Ludendorff's great advance over the Chemin-des-Dames and his inexorable advance towards Paris and victory in far-away France, but the presence of the Paynes was something they *could* do something about, something that would restore the balance of things.

Of course, we do not know how many people were involved in the harassment of the Paynes, nor whether the whole family fell victim. The press reports suggest the two girls were left alone, though here the press may not have reported the whole truth for fear of jeopardising the reputations of the protesters. However, it is clear that a tense and potentially dangerous situation had developed in the town and that no one did anything to stop it.

From eight o'clock that Tuesday evening a crowd had been gathering outside the Paynes' shop on Church Street. Probably this was a part of the by now routine harassment of the family, though it is possible that word had spread through the small town grapevine that something special was about to happen. Who was in this crowd? Even though it was eight or eight-thirty at night, there may well have been children among them, some of the older children at Sherrier School or the grammar school. There was little else for young people to do in Lutterworth on a weekday evening.

As for the Paynes, this was just another evening in which they found themselves under virtual siege. But they felt cosy and safe enough in the living room at the back of the shop on Church Street – John and his sons resting after a hard day's work trying hard to fulfil their contract to weave fruit baskets, doing their bit for the war effort. Jessie senior had spent her time preparing the family's evening meal from the rations she was allowed and, like mothers up and down the country, she no doubt showed great ingenuity in making ends meet. Jessie junior was there to help, home from her own day's work at Spencer's factory, pleased to see her brothers back home to relieve her of the necessity of making baskets herself during the evenings, looking after little Dora and perhaps helping her with her homework. It was a domestic scene like millions of others all over Britain, except perhaps for the presence of the two young men at table.

All accounts agreed that the attack was no spontaneous event. A group of men met on the town's Recreation Ground behind the churchyard and, agreed on what they would do, drew up their plan of action.[133] It is evident that the group decided that, once and for all, the problem of the conscientious objectors in their midst must be resolved. The Paynes, for their part, had shown the same stubborn determination which had seen them through their time in military camp, in prisons and in their work centres. It had been bad enough that the State authorities had forcibly removed them from their home and family: they were not now going to allow their neighbours to do it. So the confrontation was set.

It was evening, a little after nine o'clock. Lighting up time that night was 9.31 p.m. and the moon was three nights past full. It is also probable that the weather that early summer evening was dry, warm and balmy – a pleasant evening to get out of the house and wander down to Church Street to see what was going on. The pubs had just closed. It is possible that the conspirators had been drinking, or possibly they had not: it remains unclear. The Paynes' claim that they were 'drunken hooligans' remains unproven.[134]

Lutterworth's Recreation Ground – the 'Rec' – was a large area of land, almost seven acres [2.8 hectares], roughly triangular in shape, immediately to the west of the churchyard and the Rectory, an arm reaching away from the town into open country, bounded on the north by the Cricket Club grounds and the Coventry Road, and to the south by open fields, with the town's orchards and a corner of the garden of Lutterworth House where Lupton Topham lived.[135]

Why did the conspirators meet there? Outside the town proper, it gave a degree of privacy. Although it was hardly convenient, the path through the churchyard would take them on to the top of Churchgate and thence to Church Street where the Paynes lived. A short distance of a few hundred yards at most. We might wonder, if they had been drinking beforehand, why not hatch their plans in whatever pub in town they were patronising? As we have seen, there had been trouble on the Rec for months past, with groups of young people gathering there at night directing bad language towards 'respectable ladies' who were walking out: George Spencer had told the Parish Council he had 'not heard anything to equal it'.[136] It is possible then that they met on the Rec because they were those same foul-mouthed youths and that was where they had always met, where they felt secure, on home territory. This would suggest that perhaps the ringleaders in the attack on the Payne family came from local youths, now young men, possibly the same young men who had attacked Roland on the bridge a week before. It is even possible that they did not meet in a pub because some of them were too young to enter a pub.

Again, we have seen how the problem of groups of young men in the town had been a headache to the local police. Could the group who attacked the Paynes' shop simply be those disruptive young people seeking another target for their excess of energy? The six who had appeared before the Lutterworth Magistrates in January of 1917 charged with obstructing the pavement by the Narrows were, with the exception of one fifteen year old, all between eighteen and twenty.[137] We do not know their occupations. The two young men who were in court for sticking their legs across the pavement while sitting on the window sill of 'The Unicorn' were foundry workers, but their ages are not recorded.[138] The age of the first group raises the question of why they were in Lutterworth rather than in the army: they may have been home on leave, but if they were foundry workers, and thus doing genuine work of national importance, they could have been exempted from the call-up. The Payne brothers later alleged that the leaders among their attackers were foundry workers afraid that they might be conscripted, though this evidence is far from certain.[139]

Perhaps the brothers were merely reflecting a local prejudice against the foundry workers who had appeared in their midst, industrial workers reflecting a different ethic to that of small town Lutterworth, but there might be some plausibility to their version of events for foundry workers had been appearing as a disruptive and mildly lawless group of men with some regularity before the local magistrates for several months before the attack on the Paynes' shop. The charges were usually relatively minor – breaching the blackout regulations (as in the case of John Whyment of Station Road), or, paradoxically, riding their bicycles (or in one case, a horse and trap) at night without showing a light, but alcohol seems to have acted as a catalyst for trouble. Given the hot and dirty nature of foundry work this is hardly surprising. Alfred Rouse was one such, jailed for thirteen days in the summer of 1916, after holding up the work of the Lutterworth Foundry by refusing to leave the premises though so drunk he could hardly have known what he was doing.[140]

Whatever disruption was being caused in Lutterworth, there was a prevailing feeling in some of the surrounding villages that foundry workers were spending the hours of weekend darkness coming out into the countryside poaching game. Two workers, named George Perkins and Fred Wilson, late one Saturday night in early September 1916, had got into an argument with some villagers in Shawell, which had resulted in the violent assault of a villager called Charles Carter. The men's bicycles had been loaded down with rabbits and a gun was seen. Carter's sister said to the two men; 'I know who you are. You are from Lutterworth and work at the foundry'. She may also have described them as 'scum', though this was disputed in court, but another witness identified Perkins and Wilson as the 'dirty, low lot who came on Sundays poaching from Lutterworth'. In fact, on this point it was a case of mistaken identity, for both men came from Rugby, had settled jobs there and had no connection to Lutterworth Foundry, but the villagers had *assumed* that they did.[141] Relations with at least some of the foundry workers were evidently strained.

Alternatively, of course, the ringleaders could simply have been the same twelve or fifteen young men who had attacked Roland on the bridge a week before and thrown him in the river, the group led by Jack Holland, who, having failed in their first attempt to drive them out, decided to step up their campaign. This would be plausible, except for the presence of the superintendent's son, who we might suppose would not have appeared in such a public place carrying out an even more illegal assault than the one he had already perpetrated, one moreover which was bound to attract a police presence.

The group set off from the Rec to do its work, passing through the churchyard, past the scattering of Georgian and Victorian gravestones, and out through the gates which led in a very literal sense onto Churchgate, under the huge sycamore tree on their left that marked the edge of Sherrier School playground, past the sixteenth century timber framed 'Coach and Horses' on their right between Baker Street and Bank Street, and onto Church Street itself. It could not have taken them more than a few minutes to get there. Church Street must have presented something like a ghostly appearance, no lights showing because of the black-out, the kerbs and lampposts standing out painted in white[142], the whole scene lit by bright moonlight.

The Paynes' shop stood on the left at the far end of Church Street, a narrow and timeless building hemmed in by newer and grander shops, the end of Church Street giving at first sight the appearance of a cul-de-sac. Opposite was the massive 'Dalby's Buildings' completed in 1900, three storeys high and boasting the confidence of the town's revival after the coming of the railway. On the far side of the street, beyond John Payne's shop, there stood another Dalby shop, now demolished. At the end, High Street ran crosswise, but on its far side was another tall building, again now demolished. It has a closed in, claustrophobic look to it.

[Photo from Geoff Smith, 'Around Lutterworth', Chalford Books, 1997, p.51.]

A small motley crowd was already hanging about in the street in front of the Paynes' shop, much the same crowd which had been there every evening when the weather was decent, singing patriotic songs, hoping that one or more of the Paynes would come out onto the street so they could begin their chorus of shouts, jeers and yells. Perhaps they hoped that one of the brothers would emerge to cycle to their land out on the Rugby Road to gather eggs, though we suppose that after the attack on Roland this was a chore done by his sister Jessie or else done during the working day when the danger was less. These were a more or less random bunch of local people, some just passing by and watching what was happening, some of them more determined, gathered here because they could break the normal rules of behaviour given that the target of their hooliganism was the Paynes, the 'conchies'. It is quite possible that on this particular night there was a bigger than usual crowd, tipped off that something extraordinary was about to happen, something not to be missed. Perhaps there was the tension of expectancy in the air. What seems certain is that there was no one there sympathetic to the Paynes and their plight, no one who had turned up to support them.

It was when the leading group appeared, having marched from the Recreation Ground through the churchyard and down to the front of the shop, that the violence began. As they did see them approach, as Leonard later claimed, the Paynes wisely withdrew into their living rooms at the rear of the shop and switched off all the lights.[143] Normally, the shutters[144] which protected the front of the shop would have been up at night, but evidently the Paynes had been taken by surprise. The objective of the lead group, it immediately became clear, was to break into the shop: whether they also really wanted to get into the Paynes' living quarters at the rear is unclear. One evident eyewitness to what happened called them the 'storming party', a term which may have been colourful but certainly was not fanciful. To this end, the leaders made 'a determined attempt'[145] to break through the front door of the shop, smashing in one of its panels as they did.

This they could have done with ease, had it not been for the intervention of two courageous police officers, Sergeant Stapleton and P.C. Glover, one of whom fortuitously lodged next door, but was possibly also on the alert to prevent this kind of trouble. Stapleton was bundled to the ground in the first rush towards the shop door, but managed to regain his feet and block the way, while Glover drew his truncheon as a sign of his earnest. We can picture the two of them, Stapleton no doubt rattled by his treatment – not what was expected in Lutterworth – as they stood side by side while the 'storming party' tried to get round them and into the shop. The crowd gathered outside could never have seen anything like this before, but no one tried to stop it.

We cannot know exactly what the 'storming party' would have done had they broken through into the family's living quarters at the back of the shop and perhaps they did not know themselves. With the lights out in the shop and the family hiding silently in the back, they may not even have realised that they were at home at all. Their target was the two brothers, so we might suppose that if they had broken through Len and Roland would have been manhandled, beaten perhaps, dragged out of their home and possibly run out of town – frogmarched down High Street to the River Swift and hurled in, just as Roland had been the week before, and forcibly driven out along the Rugby Road with a warning not to return. But what of their father, John, or their mother, Jessie, or the two girls, Jessie and Dora? Perhaps John would have adopted the classic pacifist's answer to the question: what would you do if a German soldier threatened your wife? To which the reply was, 'I would put myself between him and her'. Perhaps he would have intervened in this passive way. In either case, it would have served no purpose except perhaps to draw the anger of the attackers towards John as well. As for the women, that is anybody's guess, though we can scarcely believe that either of the two Jessies would have stood idly by. We might at this point speculate on one rather obvious question: why did the crowd not go round to the back of the building? Access was not particularly difficult, so perhaps they did not think of it at the time, or if they were really outsiders they did not know, or perhaps they did not want to commit themselves to the potential for physical violence which an outflanking move like that might have produced.

Thus thwarted on the street side, the storming party began smashing the shop's windows and at this point some of those who had been loitering beforehand joined in, their expectant vigil in the street rewarded. 'Stones fell in showers'[146], one eyewitness reported, while another, in more military language, spoke of, 'a perfect fusillade of stones'.[147] Every window in the front of the building was shattered as the stones were hurled in. We might wonder where so many stones had come from: the streets in Lutterworth were tarmacked so either someone had come prepared or some of those in the crowd knew where they could lay their hands on so many missiles. The youngsters in the crowd may well have had specialist local knowledge in this regard. For the family cowering in the dark in the back of the building the very sound of this assault must have been terrifying, especially for little Dora. Before long there was not a sound window left in the front of the shop and even the windows of Vincent Ward, the cobbler who lived next door with his voluminous family, were shattered as well. Ten canaries Vincent kept in his shop were killed – the only deaths, but not the only casualties of the night.[148]

It was what did not happen next which defined the nature of the extraordinary event which was unfolding in the middle of somnolent little Lutterworth. Having smashed all the windows, the stone throwers did *not* run away. They stayed and they continued, even despite the police presence. This was no act of simple vandalism, no hit-and-run raid under cover of the black-out. This was something very different, of more serious intent, and much more dangerous in its possible outcomes. The windows smashed, it was then an easy matter for the 'storming party' to reach into the shop and drag out some of the Paynes' proudest examples of the basket maker's art, precious display basket ware, notably a beautiful child's crib. Everything was set ablaze in the darkened street, adding to the nightmare as the howling crowd swirled and milled by the light of the flickering flames. The police, normally so keen to prosecute anyone breaching the black-out regulations (as the magistrates' court reports week after week clearly showed), had, this time, other things on their mind.

Meanwhile, more and more people were gathering in Church Street, attracted by the noise and by word of mouth, as news spread through Lutterworth of the extraordinary scenes unfolding there. They came out from their homes in Bank Street and Baker Street, from the shops down High Street, or from Market Street and Station Road, from every part of the town. Church Street, Medieval in origin and never wide, rapidly filled up and we can imagine those coming from George Street, Bank Street or High Street having to jostle to see what was going on. For the crowd that grew outside the Paynes' shop was enormous, as many as a thousand people, reported one eyewitness, almost half the population of Lutterworth. Many of them were women.[149]

It would be easy to explain away the presence of such a huge crowd in terms of something extraordinary and exciting happening in small town, somnolent Lutterworth, rather like the circus coming to town or the local hunts in their scarlet coats, but clearly that will not do. We can think of most of these people as onlookers or bystanders, there to watch rather than to participate actively, but their attitude towards the Paynes was of positive hostility. There had been almost four years of catastrophic warfare, with the loss already of forty men[150] from a population of not much more than two thousand in Lutterworth, with many more from the surrounding villages, and the wounding and maiming of yet others; furthermore, the extension of conscription and the call-up in the last few days of older married men in the town with children, arguably too old already to be of much value. In addition, there had been the concerted campaign of hatred in sections of the national and local press against 'pacifists' as traitors who put their own safety ahead of the national need. Besides all that was simple fear: fear from air raids which brought the war home in a literal sense and the fear of defeat after all their sacrifices as the Germans' triumphs on the Western Front took their troops to within a few miles of Paris and victory in the Great War. All these factors converged to create an atmosphere of fear and tension and extreme anxiety, which approached hysteria. Lutterworth was far from 'somnolent' now. It had never seen anything like this before.

Far from being simply the behaviour of a few drunken hooligans, the attack on the Paynes' shop was a communal activity, in some senses resembling those earlier communal activities when the town had turned out to celebrate great national occasions such as the ending of the Crimean War, the Relief of Mafeking, victory in the Boer War or even more local carnivals like the great Foresters' Festival in August 1902 with its magnificent parade through all parts of the town, or the Yeomanry's annual displays of their military skills. While the crowd was brought together by their shared disgust of the Payne brothers and their behaviour, and they watched as the shop was attacked and smashed, there remained something of a carnival atmosphere about the whole affair. There was even a sense of humour: as the basket ware burned in the street they began to sing 'Keep the Home Fires Burning', which was presumably meant to be a witticism, vaguely ironic, and reinforcing what was now clearly a shared, community activity. When Constable Glover was hit in the eye by a stone 'the crowd was considerate enough to "cease fire" while the extent of the constable's injuries were being ascertained'. Once it was known that his injury was not serious, the barrage resumed.[151] Meanwhile, those who did not actively participate watched passively. No one in the crowd made any move to stop the violence.[152] The fact was that the Payne family, not just Leonard and Roland the conscientious objectors, had attracted such odium in the town that no one was prepared to lift a finger to help them.

There was another twist in the story of the Payne brothers, one which had haunted the two of them almost since the war's beginning. This was the issue of the shell baskets which was now raised again. How could the two of them claim to be genuine conscientious objectors if they had spent months before their call-up weaving baskets for the transportation of high explosive and gas shells en route to the Front? How could the family claim exemption for them when their workshop had been producing seats for war planes and baskets for observation balloons? These were war contracts making things to further the killing of other human beings, however indirect the connection might be. The accusation was reported directly in the *Leicester Daily Mercury* in its eyewitness report on the riot: 'At the beginning of the war, it is asserted, they worked upon war work, making shell baskets, and earned good wages.'[153]

Moreover, at a time of rationing and the hardships of war, they were apparently well paid. The word 'hypocrite' is nowhere written down in Lutterworth in the records of that time, but we can readily imagine it passing from mouth to ear throughout the community. So it was not simply a case of men of genuine religious conscience who refused to go out and kill others, a position difficult enough to defend publicly anyway in the context of the time, but they were credibly seen as hypocrites as well. For when called upon to go out and put their own lives on the line they had refused to go when so many others had volunteered to go and so many others had so reluctantly gone, answering the call-up, leaving wives and children behind.

To compound the problem, they had been allowed to return home for what some may regard as a less than honourable reason. It was true that John had declined the Dryad Company's offer of work making eighteen pounder shell baskets (although the suggestion from the Dryad management that this might help get his sons home quicker was probably not widely known in the town), this time he had accepted what was described as a 'big' government contract to weave fruit baskets in support of the government's forthcoming drive to pick fruit, which the children of Sherrier School – among others up and down the country – had been encouraged to go out and collect.[154] It is perhaps ironic that the Paynes had come under direct attack from their neighbours when they were actually doing work important to the nation and the war effort, for fruit picking was of national importance in 1918, rather than the time filling work of making doormats in the Wakefield Work Centre or toothpaste in Birmingham.

Ever since the first week of this war there had been a powerful public outcry against 'war profiteers'. This could extend from the biggest companies supplying the biggest contracts to the smallest shopkeeper and tradesman increasing prices to enhance his profits, and to farmers, described by one historian as 'the real kings of profit-making'.[155] Soon after the outbreak of war, it will be remembered, the local Rugby newspaper had published the letter of 'T.H.R.' attacking the 'class of people who have made a fetish of accumulating money by means of trading... Almost before the declaration of war was published certain wholesale traders raised their prices. This had the effect of starting the desired panic, and large dealers were enabled to dispose of their existing stock at a handsome profit by placing the new prices on the old stock. One shopkeeper is reported to have sunk so low in his greed for profit as to issue "revised" bills to purchasers who omitted to pay the first bill on the day the goods were delivered. The patriotism of this class of people who regard a national crisis as a means of filling their own pockets is nauseating in the extreme'.[156] Some, even those of the political right, were talking approvingly of 'wartime socialism' – society counting for more than the individual and all pulling together, rich and poor, side by side, helping each other in this time of crisis – and in this atmosphere the person who exploited the war for personal material gain had become a bogey; 'by 1917 profiteering had become a widespread term of abuse, a central concept of the discourse of the war'.[157]

But there was a fine line to be drawn between 'profiteering' and profiting from the war. Lutterworth as a town had, materially, done generally very well out of the Great War. The two foundries had been working flat out and paying high wages to meet the contracts for shell case making, attracting in the process workers from the surrounding villages, and George Spencer's Vedonis works, after a glitch mid-war, had been supplying the army's massive demands for clothing. It will be remembered that in Lutterworth and district some sixty extra men had had to be recruited to handle all the additional land to be ploughed as pastoral grazing was converted to arable land to make up the shortfall caused by the U-Boat campaign and the farmers gained from the change as food prices rose.[158] The Payne family business was doing nothing more than these, but of course the Payne boys were conscientious objectors and that made all the difference. Profiting from a war they would not join turned this into a moral issue and the moral indignation of their fellow townspeople was roused to quite extraordinary heights.

What happened next must have surprised all those gathered in Church Street as a goat and kid were ceremoniously paraded through their midst, driven from the Paynes' land out on the Rugby Road. As one of those involved said, they had been brought into town 'to see the fun'.[159] What had happened out of sight of the crowd was certainly not 'fun', for the Paynes' property there had been wrecked, their poultry turned loose, their beehives upturned, their fruit trees damaged.[160] This was a deliberate attack on their livelihood, inspired by rage and the desire to destroy. We do not know who was responsible. It could well have been the original 'storming party', frustrated in their first assault against the shop in Church Street but content to leave the much bigger crowd to finish the job, seeking out a new target for their aggression. Or this could have been the work of more local people, perhaps some of those who had been hanging around outside the shop earlier in the evening, now taking their lead from what they had seen the 'storming party' do. On the way there they had stopped off to smash the windows of the family's workshop off Regent Street. Others, meanwhile, had set off in the opposite direction, to the hut the Paynes owned on Bitteswell Road, where they wrenched the door off its hinges and scattered osiers onto the roof.[161] This has all the appearance of a concerted and determined assault against the Paynes and beneath it all there remained a deep and potentially lethal threat to the whole family. We might even surmise that it was the location of the Paynes' shop on Church Street, buildings adjoining it on both sides and right in the middle of town, that saved it from being set alight, with or without the family inside.

The riot had certainly run out of control although, apart from the minor injury to Constable Glover, no one so far had been hurt. With police help, the Paynes abandoned their home, moving out of the back of their house into the building next door.[162] In earlier occasions of riot in other parts of the country, mainly directed against Germans living in Britain, the local police forces had acted robustly, turning out mounted police and even the army when necessary, and the courts had dealt severely with those brought before them.[163] Did the police respond as firmly to the Lutterworth riot? There is no doubting the bravery of the two officers who put themselves in harm's way, defending the entrance to the shop, facing an increasingly hostile and threatening crowd, but one has to ask whether the police could have prevented the attack in the first place? Trouble had been clearly bubbling up for weeks past and yet there is no record of the police in Lutterworth taking any action to prevent its dangerous escalation. Nor is there any record of the Paynes asking for help from the police. Possibly John felt that an appeal to Walter Holland, one son killed another crippled in the war, would not have elicited the right result: he may have been right or he may have been wrong.

It was purely by coincidence that the Chief Constable of Leicestershire, Edward Holmes himself, happened to be in Lutterworth on the evening of the attack: he had arrived to attend the Petty Sessions to be held in the Town Hall the following morning. It must have been a matter of acute embarrassment to Superintendent Holland that a full-scale riot should have broken out on this very night. Only six weeks earlier the chief constable had impressed on his officers the need 'to keep alive a proper spirit in the public mind'[164] and the breakdown in law and order in Lutterworth must have been exactly the sort of thing he had wanted to prevent. The most likely place for such an august visitor to stay in Lutterworth was the Denbigh Arms, the oversized eighteenth century coaching inn near the bottom of High Street, a couple of hundred yards away from Church Street where the noise, the cheering and the singing throughout the latter part of the evening must have been clearly audible, the crowd heartily singing songs like 'When the Boys come Home' or 'Red, White and Blue' and, of course, 'Pack up your Troubles in your old Kit Bag'. [165] On their way to smashing up the Regent Street workshop, barely a hundred yards from the Denbigh, and letting loose the livestock on the Rugby Road, the rioters immediately passed the inn.

The immediate handling of the situation was left to Superintendent Holland though and it appears that he acted promptly once the seriousness of the breakdown in public order was understood. It may have been as early as nine-thirty or ten o'clock that he telephoned through to Leicester to call for reinforcements, supported no doubt by the presence of the chief constable. Until they could travel the fourteen miles or so from their headquarters in Leicester, it would be left to the local police to deal with the situation and this was something which was clearly beyond their ability. So Sergeant Stapleton and Constable Glover were left on their own to hold the crowd at bay, protect the Paynes and their property and get the family to a place of safety. There are no reports of other police officers coming to their assistance until much later in the evening.

There should have been several special constables Holland could have called out, but their role in the evening's events remains opaque. The following morning the chief constable felt the need to call them together in the Town Hall where he spoke to them behind closed doors, the only published word being that 'the chief constable (Mr E. Holmes) addressed the special constables on their duties in connection with the unfortunate occurrence in the town over the C.O. disturbances. All the constables present promised to take their full share in preserving the peace'.[166] The obvious inference is that on the Tuesday night their contribution to maintaining law and order had been deemed inadequate by the chief constable himself. Local people themselves, it is quite plausible to suggest that their loyalties were divided, their own attitude towards the Paynes overruling their oath to maintain the King's peace.

Much later, approaching 11 p.m., three car loads of police arrived from Leicester[167], by which time the Paynes' shop on Church Street had been wrecked, their properties on Rugby Road, Regent Street and Bitteswell Road all damaged and the family driven into hiding in the next door home of a police officer. Though some parts of the crowd hung about until one-thirty in the morning, by midnight the Lutterworth Riot was essentially over. The Paynes' livestock, still wandering about Church Street amidst the shattered glass and the detritus of a once proud shop display and the smouldering remains of burnt wickerwork, were rounded up by the police and driven into the yard at the back of 'The Hind Inn' until the animals could be herded back home to their shelters on the Rugby Road. No arrests were made, no one was charged, no one appeared in court, no one was punished. It was as though it had never happened.

Both the police and the Payne family then faced the decision of what to do next. No doubt on police advice, Len and Roland were persuaded that their presence in Lutterworth would pose a threat to law and order and to the other members of their family, and they must leave the town immediately. It must have been a bitter

Raids on "Conchies'" Home & Shop at Lutterwort

his picture shows the damage done to Mr. J. G. Payne's premises in Church-street.

The windows of the workshop off Regent-street were smashed by sto: by an angry crowd.

All that was left of a wooden structure in a garden on the Bitteswell road, after it had been set on fire. About £50 worth of osiers, which the shed contained, were also destroyed.

The attack on the Paynes property was reported in local newspapers

pill to swallow, but they were left with no realistic choice. Consequently, early on the following Wednesday morning Len and Roland cycled out of Lutterworth, under police escort, up the Leicester Road and out of town. After spending some time at a police station in Leicester, they went to stay with friends, most likely Thomas and Marion Harper in Syston, until they too became worried that their own house might be attacked. As Leonard later recalled, 'the next morning he said I am sorry but I have to ask you to go because my wife is an invalid and they might smash up our place here if we harbour you'. So for the first time the two brothers were split up, each going for a few days to a different friend's house in Leicester.[168] It was at that point Leonard and Roland Payne left Leicestershire.

But the 'crowd' had not done with the Paynes yet. The following afternoon, while they were meeting up with their friends in Leicester, the Lutterworth Fire Brigade was called out to a fire in a building out on the Bitteswell Road. By the time they got there the building was well ablaze, stuffed as it was with willow rods and osiers, valued at no less than £50, the raw materials of the Paynes' basket weaving craft, and nothing could be rescued save a few charred bundles. John had, we are told, only 'lightly insured' the building and so had to stand the loss.[169] If the anger of the Lutterworth people had been fired up by that big government contract for fruit baskets, which had been the occasion for bringing Len and Roland home and would have netted them a great deal of money, the brothers had now been driven into exile so the contract could not be fulfilled.

In Lutterworth's terms, justice had been done.

NOTES & REFERENCES

1. *Leicester Daily Mercury*, 29th May 1918.
2. *Rugby Advertiser*, 1st June 1918.
3. Jessie to Leonard and Roland, 31st October 1916.
4. Walter and Ada had married early in 1916. (Minutes of Superintendents' Meetings, 22nd February 1916. LRO DE5491/104.)
5. Roland to Mother and Dad, 29th June 1916.
6. Liddle interview, Brotherton Library, University of Leeds.
7. Mother to Leonard, 6th July 1916. 'He looks very bad,' she had written.
8. *Rugby Advertiser*, 1st and 3rd September 1917; *Leicester Daily Mercury*, 7th September 1917.
9. John to Leonard, 7th December 1916.
10. *Rugby Advertiser*, 30th December 1916; Workhouse Guardians' Minute Book. On John Meacham's background, see Board of Guardians Minutes, 27th May 1915. LRO.DE1909/353.
11. The Sherwood Foresters Roll, WFR Museum, Nottingham; *Rugby Advertiser*, 1st and 3rd September 1917. I am grateful to Dave Sands of the Worcestershire Regiment Museum, and Eddie Edwards of the WFR Museum (Sherwood Foresters Collection) for these references. W. Lockey of the 1st Sherwood Foresters left a graphic description of this attack, quoted in MacArthur (ed.), pp. 315-7.
12. At the time of his death he had been moved from the Reserve Battalion and was attached to the 1st Battalion. CWGC.
13. LRO.DE1379/826/1-6 (February 1917) and LRO.DE1379/446 (November 1918). It is unclear whether the council was including in its estimate of Lutterworth's population the 250 or so men who were away at the war, or the Payne brothers!
14. 2,531 had been Lutterworth's population at its height in 1841, before the long nineteenth-century decline had set in, and it was a population the town would not achieve again in a Census year until 1951, when it reached 3,197, though the 'missing' 1941 Census might have shown something in the region of 2,500.
15. Their estimate of a 12:1000 natural increase would have given Lutterworth 2,124 people by the time of the 1921 Census, when the actual figure was a little short of that at 2,092. It is again uncertain whether their calculation of natural increase allowed for the fact that some 250 men in the prime of their reproductive lives were away in the armed

forces: or perhaps it should be set against the estimated 150 'war weddings' across the Rural District.

16. 200 new homes in Lutterworth would have accommodated an additional 800 people or more: the houses to be built were to be of six rooms each, charging a rent of eight shillings per week. (Rural District Council General Committee Minutes, 29th November 1918. LRO.DE1379/446.)

17. See J.S. Dodge *The Leicester Road Council Estate, Lutterworth, 1913-2000*, privately published, Lutterworth, 2006, pp. 1-2.

18. In his brilliant 1935 book, *The Strange Death of Liberal England*, George Dangerfield argued persuasively that liberal England was dead even before the outbreak of war.

19. Wilson, p. 24.

20. Lenin, *The State and Revolution*, in *Selected Works of V.I. Lenin*, English edition, Foreign Languages Publishing House, Moscow, 1952, Vol. II, Part 1, reprinted Beijing, 1965. Perhaps this was the only point on which Lenin and the Payne brothers would have agreed!

21. Robin Prior and Trevor Wilson, *Passchendaele. The Untold Story*, Yale U.P., London, 1996, p. 195.

22. See J.E. Edmonds, *Military Operations: France and Belgium, 1918* (Official History), London, 1935. On the first day see Martin Middlebrook, *The Kaiser's Battle. 21 March 1918: The First Day of the German Spring Offensive*, Penguin Books, London, 1983. For the German Commander's retrospective view, see Erich von Ludendorff, *My War Memories*, Hutchinson, London, 1919, Vol. 2, p. 598.

23. Winston Churchill, *The World Crisis, 1916-1918*, Vol. 2, Thornton Butterworth, London, 1927, p. 411.

24. William Carr, *Time to Leave the Ploughshares. A Gunner Remembers 1917-1918*, Robert Hale, London, 1985, p. 98; Edmonds, *Military Operations: France and Belgium, 1918* (Official History), London, 1935, p.159. The artillery assault was master-minded by Lieutenant-Colonel Georg Bruchmüller. See John Tolland, *No Man's Land: The Story of 1918*, Methuen, London, 1982, p. 15. Peter Hart, *1918. A Very British Victory*, Phoenix Books, London, 2009, Chapter 3 makes extensive use of Imperial War Museum recorded interviews.

25. Adams and Poirier, pp. 208-9.

26. ibid., p. 214.

27. *Rugby Advertiser*, 15th June 1918.

28. TNA.CAB.23/5.

29. Male munitions workers in Britain who had believed themselves immune from conscription had reason to be anxious. Shortly after the First World War one economist summed up the situation thus: 'Military events had a drastic and immediate reaction

upon the labour situation. Before 1917 was out the defection of Russia had made necessary a complete re-examination of the position as to man-power; and during December and January conferences were in progress between the Minister of National Service (Sir Auckland Geddes) and the groups of trade unions with a view to an agreed revision of the schedules of protected occupations. Between 420,000 and 450,000 additional men were wanted for military service; and, broadly speaking, the government proposed to take them largely from the munitions shops by cancelling exemption certificates of the men under twenty-four... and since the leaving certificate had now been abolished, the two months' immunity allowed to the man ceasing work on munitions was cancelled... Between the institution of the schedule of protected occupations in May 1917, and the end of that year the munitions centres had given up nearly 68,000 men for military service. In the three months following the first Military Service Act of 1918, they gave 32,000 more; following the German offensive, they released 40,000 in five weeks.' (William Aylott Orton, *Labour in Transition. A Survey of British Industrial History since 1914*, Philip Allan, London, 1921, pp. 129 and 131.)

30. John Buchan, *Mr Standfast*, first published 1919, re-published by Penguin Books, Harmondsworth, 1956, p. 58.

31. Leicestershire Constabulary. Minutes of Superintendants' Meetings, 15th April 1918. LRO.DE 5491/104.

32. Tim Travers, *How the War was Won. Factors that Led to Victory in World War One*, Pen & Sword, Barnsley, 2005. Robin Prior and Trevor Wilson, *Passchendaele. The Untold Story*, Yale U.P., London, 1996, p. 200, argue that the crisis of 1918 might have been averted had the British Army still had the men lost in the ill-starred Passchendaele campaign of the previous year.

33. On Robert Chedgey, Ship's Log, *H.M.S. Norman*, 23rd February 1918, TNA.ADM53 52837. A detailed letter written by Frank Harrison of Frolesworth near Lutterworth gives a detailed account of the action in which Harry Evans died near Bucquoy on March 26th. (Paul Harrison, *A Leicestershire Boy Goes to War. A Look into his Diary with the West Yorks*, privately published, 2010, pp. 117-9. Copy in Lutterworth Library.)

34. War Diary, 2nd/4th Royal Berkshires, TNA.WO95 3065; and the enclosed copy of a letter from Captain A. Whitfield to Captain J. Carr describing the circumstances of Dimmer's death. For a narrative, see Middlebrook, *The Kaiser's Battle*, pp. 253-4.

35. See the minutes and report of the Committee under Sir George Cave to consider the proposed new Bill at TNA.CAB.24/5; Lloyd George, *War Memoirs*, Odhams, London, n.d., Vol. 2, pp. 1597 and 1600. Two days after the passage of the Bill a Royal Proclamation decreed that men aged between twenty-three and twenty-nine and who were the sole support of their disabled (for instance blind or crippled) parents could no longer claim exemption from military service. When challenged in Parliament, the

Minister replied that: 'the government deeply regrets that the present emergency forces them to exclude such cases… from the right to claim exemption… Unfortunately there are a very considerable number of peculiarly hard cases'. Hansard, Series 5, Vol. 106, col. 340. 15th May 1918. The government's position was not helped when it was revealed that the special committees set up to comb out men of military age from government departments contained Civil Servants of military age! ibid., cols. 955-6.

36. Quoted in Boulton, p.97.

37. David Marquand, *Ramsay MacDonald*, Jonathan Cape, 1977, p. 197. In fact, Marquand was commenting on Labour's acquiescence in the first Military Service Act in 1916, but the point is even more sharply made in 1918.

38. In an interview with the American press in September 1916 Lloyd George had said: 'In the British determination to carry the fight to a decisive finish there is something more than the natural demand for vengeance. The inhumanity and pitilessness of the fighting that must come before a lasting peace is possible is not comparable with the cruelty that would be involved in stopping the war while there remains the possibility of civilisation again being menaced from the same quarter. Peace now or at any time before the final and complete elimination of this menace is unthinkable.' (Quoted in David Lloyd George, *War Memoirs*, Vol. 1, Odhams, London, 1938, pp. 509-10.) Typical of those attacks is this, from a former major in the Sherwood Foresters: 'When the German failed in his much-vaunted supremacy in war… he called aloud for Peace… Now mark you, this is not a comic suggestion for the laughter of the inferior races! It is a solemn suggestion by the Statesmen of this valorous and superior breed, the German! And what is more – and what is vastly more incredible – there are large numbers of quite sincere and rather superior people in this country and other countries so lacking in all common sense, so hopelessly bereft of all strategic thinking, so fatuous a prey to what they believe to be the highest benevolence and humanitarianism, that they are ready to vote their governments into, and urge their Statesmen towards, accepting such a peace!' Haldane Macfall, *Germany at Bay*, American edn. published by George H. Doran, New York, n.d. (1917), p. 266. The tragedy of the situation was well summed up by James Sheehan: 'This was the vicious circle in which all the belligerents were trapped: the more sacrifices they demanded, the more essential victory became, which in turn required more sacrifices, and so on and on until one side finally collapsed.' *The Monopoly of Violence. Why Europeans Hate going to War*, Faber & Faber, London, 2010, p. 71.

39. *Rugby Advertiser*, 14th May 1918.

40. *Leicester Daily Mercury*, 3rd December 1917. We gain an insight into the Earl's approach from a letter he wrote to his wife from Chipping Norton on June 22nd 1918, describing the speech he had delivered that evening: 'I gave them a lurid account of what would

happen if C[hipping] N[orton] were a Belgian village invaded by Boche army – how the Mayor, the Vicar, Fr. Sole and the leading inhabitants would be made hostages, and then the shops and houses looted – then some[?] shots from drunken soldiers – then the civilians were firing on the troops – the shooting of the Mayor and party &c in rows while their families looked on. Still then the women and girls would be lucky if they escaped without being bayoneted; then the burning of the houses and the destruction of C.N.' (WRO.CR2017/C553/31.)

41. *Leicester Daily Mercury*, 1st May 1918. The Earl's attitude to the war had been put succinctly in a letter of his published in the *Rugby Advertiser* on April 5th 1918: 'I don't… want to feel that all our sacrifices have been made in vain, and I do not believe in the folly of trying to meet aggressive militarism with mere words'.

42. *Leicester Daily Mercury*, 9th May 1918.

43. *Rugby Advertiser*, 18th May 1918.

44. The Earl's pamphlet entitled *Why Germany Went to War* claimed that Germany planned to seize a European, African and Middle Eastern empire stretching in an unbroken line from Lapland to the borders of South Africa; pamphlet distributed by W.H. Smith, London, n.d. (1918). (WRO.CR2017/X33/2.) Almost identical claims had been published in Haldane Macfall, *Germany at Bay*, U.S. edn. pub. George H. Doran, New York, n.d. (1917), pp. 280ff.

45. Under the terms of the Treaty, the Bolsheviks were forced to give up all claims to the Baltic provinces, Poland, White Russia (later known as Byelorussia, now Belarus), Finland, Bessarabia, the Ukraine and the Caucasus. In one form or another, Russia lost 26% of its total population, 27% of its arable land, 32% of its average crops, 26% of its railway system, 33% of its manufacturing industries, 73% of its iron industry, and 75% of its coal fields. It lost almost all the territory, in fact, that had been added to the Tsarist dominions since the reign of Peter the Great more than 200 years earlier. (Martin Gilbert, *First World War*, Harper Collins, London, 1995, pp. 401-2; Nicholas V. Riasanovsky, *A History of Russia*, 2nd edn., O.U.P., Oxford, p. 529.) The lesson of what a German peace treaty imposed on the Western Allies might be like was not lost on the British public: what price the British Empire, then, following a German victory?

46. Andrew Gordon, *The Rules of the Game. Jutland and British Naval Command*. John Murray, London, 1996, pp. 444-5; H.W. Fawcett and G.W.W. Hooper, *The Fighting at Jutland. The Personal Experiences of Forty-five Officers and Men of the British Fleet*, Hutchinson, London, 1921, pp. 105-8; V.E. Tarrant, *Jutland: The German Perspective*, Brockhampton Press, London, 1999, pp. 127-9. A graphic account of the sinking of the 'Defence', given by Georg von Hase, First Gunnery Officer on the 'Derfflinger', is given in Appendix V of Richard Hallam and Mark Benyon (eds), *Scrimgoeur's Small Scribbling Diary, 1914-1916*, Conway Books, London, 2008, pp. 296-7. No one, of course,

survived. On 30th May 1918 the Earl reminded his wife: 'Two years tomorrow since the dear lad went at Jutland. It seems a long time ago.' (WRO.CR2017/C553/31.)

47. Prior and Wilson, pp. 165-6. Henry Feilding died on October 11th 1917.

48. *Rugby Advertiser*, 5th April 1918. The war took a heavy toll of those from the upper classes. Roughly 12% of British soldiers were killed in the Great War, though for peers and sons of peers the figure rose to 19%. 31% of those who graduated from Oxford in 1913 died in the war. (Adam Hochschild, *To End All Wars. How the First World War Divided Britain*, Macmillan, London, 2011, p. xiv.)

49. Such as his belief that the assassination of the Archduke Franz Ferdinand had been 'arranged by German agency or the result of a plot which they knew of but took no precautions against'. (*Why Germany Went to War*. WRO.CR2017/X33/2.)

50. Denbigh to his wife, 23rd April 1918. WRO.CR2017/C553/17.

51. Denbigh to his wife, 22nd April 1918. WRO.CR2017/C553/16.

52. *Leicester Daily Mercury*, 8th May 1918.

53. Gregory, p. 296.

54. 'International Order of Pacifists' (?)

55. *Rugby Advertiser*, 25th May 1918.

56. The application of such words and slogans has long been a chosen technique for politicians, as the Leicester secularist Chapman Cohen explained in a 1919 book: 'The skilled orator, playing on old feelings, using familiar terms, and invoking familiar ideas, finds a crowd quite plastic to his hands. It is for these reasons that there is so keen a struggle with political and social parties for a monopoly of good rallying cries, and a readiness to fix objectionable titles to their opponents. Patriotism, Little Englander, Jingo, The Church in Danger, Godless Education, [Pacifist], etc. etc. Causes are materially helped or injured by these means. There is little or no consideration given to their justice or reasonableness; it is the image aroused that does the work.' (Chapman Cohen, *Religion and Sex. Studies in the Pathology of Religious Development*, T.N. Foulis, London, 1919, p. 207.) Such words, slogans and images could be planted just as well in print as by the spoken word. By the same token, voices of reason and moderation were drowned out. One such voice belonged to Jan Smuts, the South African member of Lloyd George's War Cabinet, whose military and political qualifications were clearer than were the informal Quaker (and pacifist) influences upon his private life. On May 17th 1918 he delivered a speech in Glasgow in which he patiently and clearly explained that the 'knock-out blow' over Germany which Lloyd George favoured was not necessarily the best way in which to bring the war to an end. 'We have not gone into the war with any aggressive or offensive spirit,' he told his audience, setting the Allied position is sharp contrast with that of Germany whose motives throughout could be portrayed as aggressive. 'When this nation made its great choice in August, 1914, it

went into the war as a war of defence, of defence of the liberties of mankind, of the rights of small nations, and of the public law of Europe. That is what we are out for. That is our idea of victory. That is our war aim, and for that we will fight until we have succeeded and until we have won. We are not out to smash any country or government,' he went on. 'We are not making this war drag on uselessly in order to attain some impossible victory. We have a limited object… When we talk of victory we don't mean marching to the Rhine, we don't mean marching on Berlin, we don't mean going on with the war until we have smashed Germany and the German Empire, and are able to dictate peace to the enemy in his capital. We shall continue this war until the objects for which we set out are achieved, and we will continue on a defensive basis to the very end.' (Quoted in W.K. Hancock, 'Smuts', Vol. 1 *The Sanguine Years 1870-1919*, C.U.P., 1962, pp. 478-9.) Smuts' speech was not widely reported in the press, and his calm voice of reason was drowned out by those who saw only total victory for the Allies and total defeat for the Germans as the acceptable outcome of the war.

57. H.G. Wells, *War and the Future. Italy, France and Britain at War*, Cassell, London, 1917, p. 195.

58. Letter from C. Kirk of Leicester, *Leicester Daily Mercury*, 18th October 1917.

59. Ludendorff in Joffre, the Ex-Crown Prince of Germany, Foch and Ludendorff, *The Two Battles of the Marne*, Thornton Butterworth, London, 1927, pp. 224-5. It is clear that, in fact, it was not Ludendorff who came up with the scheme, but Lieutenant Colonel Hans von Haeften, though Ludendorff did give it his support. (Robert B. Asprey, *The German High Command at War*, Warner Books, 1994, p. 432.) For a devastating critique of Ludendorff's military and political abilities (or lack of them), see A.J.P. Taylor, *The Course of German History*, Methuen, London, 1961, pp. 197-201. Hindenburg also was aware of the British peace lobby, but offered his own analysis of its ineffectiveness: 'There was no sign of surrender on the enemy's part. On the contrary, each military defeat seemed only to strengthen the enemy's lust for destruction. This impression was in no wise diminished by the fact that here and there the voice of moderation was heard in the hostile camp. The dictatorial authority of the political organisms against which we were fighting was on the whole in no way injured. They held the wills and the resources of their nations together as if with iron bands, and by more or less autocratic methods suppressed the capacity for harm of all who dared to think differently from the tyrants in power. To me there was something very impressive in the working of these autocratic powers.' *The Great War*, Paul von Hindenburg, ed. Charles Messenger, Greenhill Books, London and St. Paul, 2006, pp. 181-2. Pots and kettles come to mind.

60. Joffre, et al., pp. 223 and 225.

61. Quoted, among other places, in John Terraine, *Douglas Haig. The Educated Soldier*, Leo Cooper, London, 1990, pp. 432-3.

62. Quoted Gregory, p.205. On the other hand, Tim Travers noted a 'noticeable drop in BEF morale' in France as the German Offensive rolled forward. (Travers, p. 106.)

63. Gregory, p. 234.

64. This example of Billing's style is from a House of Commons debate on the Government and the Press in March 1918: 'The point that does remain is this: Who elects the Press? Any rogue with a million of money — and most of the men who have millions are rogues — can get control of the Press, or a portion of it, at any minute; and so where is our democracy? Surely it is the duty of this House to stand between the capitalist Press and the people, and if we — I do not say we, I would not presume to say we — if the politicians and statesmen in this House are the slaves, from fear of political extinction, of a crowd of millionaires who have their money from whence they know best, and have invested it, instead of in ships, in newspapers, I say the very idea of democracy is a hollow dream. It simply means that the people are being governed by a servile House which is being dictated to by a capitalist Press, and the idea of democracy is a delusion.' (HC Deb, 11th March 1918, vol. 104, c. 138, via Hansard.millbanksystems.com.) The hypocrisy is breathtaking.

65. Panikos Panayi, *The Enemy in Our Midst. Germans in Britain During the First World War*, Berg, New York and London, 1991, p. 132, emphasis added.

66. Orlando Figes noted similar scurrilous attacks on the Russian Tsarina: 'Alexandra's "sexual corruption" became a kind of metaphor for the diseased condition of the tsarist regime. She was said to be a slut, the mistress of Rasputin and the lesbian lover of Anna Vyrubova, her lady-in-waiting, who was said to share her bed with Rasputin and the Tsar. None of these rumours had any basis in fact' any more than those carried by the *Vigilante*. (Orlando Figes, *A People's Tragedy. The Russian Revolution, 1891-1924*, Pimlico Books, 1997, p. 284.) Billing and his companions would never, though, have dared direct their overt attacks against members of the royal family, though their German ancestry might have given them cause – a significant point of difference.

67. The trial opened on May 29th, the day after the attack on the Paynes' shop. To show that it was not only the upper classes which were at risk from the wiles of the nation's enemies, Billing also warned: 'I had occasion the other day to refer to Bolshevism in this country, and to the fact that Frankfort Jews, through a Russian agency, are endeavouring to take advantage of the stupidity of our governing classes in order to set class against class in this country. I hope that the working men of this country will not be such fools as to try those methods.' (HC Deb, 11th March 1918, vol. 104, c. 141, via Hansard.millbanksystems.com)

68. 'Russian society had not stood the strain. The home front collapsed into class-war; the army at the front could not apparently be got to fight; while the army in the rear joined the forces of revolution. Virtually the whole of the country's working population went

on strike, although, with the German enemy at the gates, there was ostensibly every good cause for keeping a united front until the war had been won.' (Norman Stone, *The Eastern Front, 1914-1917*, Hodder and Stoughton, London, 1975, p. 282.)

69. Hew Strachan, *The First World War*, Pocket Books, London, 2006, pp. 242-3.

70. Though not directly relevant here – because it had not yet happened – it will be remembered that the German collapse on the home and military fronts at the end of October and the first weeks of November 1918 would come with equal suddenness and dramatic finality.

71. From 'World War One Document Archive', via wwi.lib.byu.edu, emphasis added.

72. *Leicester Pioneer*, 7th June 1918. The *Pioneer* made no mention of the events in Lutterworth: wrapped up in Leicester politics it seems to have been unaware.

73. *Rugby Advertiser*, 15th August 1914.

74. Panayi, pp. 229-231 and passim. Following the sinking of the *Lusitania* a hostile crowd gathered outside the shop of a naturalised German hairdresser called Meerholz on High Street in Rugby, but were successfully dispersed by the presence of the police after a couple of windows had been broken, and the following day at nearby Bilton the Warwickshire Police put a force of almost one hundred officers onto the streets to prevent a similar attack. Firm and timely police action could prevent trouble. (*Rugby Advertiser*, 18th May 1915.)

75. Panayi., pp. 216-7.

76. Rudolf Rocker, the German anarchist who spent much of the war in internment, commented that 'Upon a criminal undergoing his penalty, it is thought inhuman to heap abuse, and rightly so, but for the interned there is evidently another standard of moral conduct. It is thought necessary to institute whole press campaigns against them, and to fill papers for months on end with taunts regarding their condition' – another point of similarity. Panayi, p. 130.

77. ibid., Chapter 4, 'The Experience of Internment'. By the end of the war the daily bread ration had fallen from 1lb. 8oz. to just 5oz. with horse meat to eat.

78. Millman, p. 229.

79. Its executive committee included the leaders of the main political parties. When he investigated links between anti-war groups and German Intelligence, Thomson found no evidence. (Rose, pp. 53 and 66, n.34; Gregory, p.207.) The issue of how the British Government handled dissent in the First World War remains obscure. Professor Brock Millman: 'Perhaps part of the reason that measures to combat dissent have not received much attention is because crucial records have not been available. Consider the British case. Many of the most important files in the most important collections were to be closed for one hundred years. Much of this material has only recently been opened, and even at this late date it is obvious that many files are incomplete. Police

correspondence and reports, "black lists", Criminal Investigation Department (C.I.D.) surveillance records and domestic threat assessments may simply have been as embarrassing for the compilers after the war as for those then surveyed, or indeed, for those caught up in waging the war against internal enemies. Documents like these may have been purged; they may simply remain closed. Some important collections appear to have been almost completely sanitized.' And: 'We can, for instance, establish from the surviving correspondence that there were lists of those to be pre-emptively arrested in certain eventualities without being able to know who was on them because the lists themselves, in all probability, no longer exist. Similarly we can know that there was infiltration of suspect organizations – trade unions, and suspicious political and peace organisations for instance – without being able to establish the scale or effectiveness of such penetration. We know there were informers. Who they were and how they were recruited and selected remains a mystery. We know that, by 1917, information concerning the activities of dissenting organizations was being passed to civilian organizations for their pre-emption, without being able to establish the scale or global effectiveness of such co-ordination.' He comments that some government agencies had 'a selective memory and a bad conscience'. (Millman, pp. 3-4.)

80. *Leicester Daily Mercury*, 29th April 1918. See also the *Leicester Pioneer*, 17th May 1918.

81. *Leicester Daily Mercury*, 29th April 1918.

82. ibid.

83. *Leicester Daily Mercury*, 29th May 1918.

84. *Leicester Daily Mercury*, 15th May 1918; *Leicester Pioneer*, 17th May 1918. Some months earlier a group of leading local figures had written to Lord Hugh Cecil, who had just opposed in Parliament the disenfranchisement of conscientious objectors, asking him 'to address a Jubilee Meeting on the question [of the conscientious objectors] in Leicester.' (Draft letter at LRO.DE5508/76, dated 1st December 1917.) These were no war-rejectionists: Sydney Gimson was President of the Leicester Secular Society, a member of the leading local family in the Arts and Crafts movement, and a friend of William Morris; as Chairman of the Refugees Committee, it was Gimson who had personally organised and run the whole scheme for the relief of the Belgian refugees in Leicester; he had acted as Chairman of the District Munitions Committee, as Treasurer of the War Savings Committee for Leicester; and he and his wife had donated a farm for the Mayor's Scheme for Disabled Warriors. (See Armitage, pp. 37, 106, 119-21, 149 and 155.) Greater commitment to the war effort from a man of his age (he was fifty-seven) could hardly be imagined. James Kelly J.P. had left the I.L.P. when it had rejected all participation in the war, and joined instead the confusingly-named National Socialist Party which, as he explained 'believed in internationalism based upon nationality, believed in defending the country from aggression, and did not believe in

remaining neutral and seeing other nations crushed by Germany'. (*Leicester Daily Mercury*, 13th May 1918.) The third was J.T. Biggs, J.P.. Clearly well-intentioned, the invitation was firmly declined: 'I am afraid I think the question of conscientious objectors a very inappropriate subject for a public meeting at the present time,' wrote Lord Hugh. (LRO.DE5508/77, dated December 11th.) Evidently he was more in touch with public feeling than the more naïve local leaders.

85. Hew Strachan, *The First World War*, Pocket Books, London, 2006, p. 300.

86. Haig's diary entries 3rd April and 29th March 1918 respectively, in Sheffield and Bourne (eds.).

87. A.J.P. Taylor, *English History*, Penguin Books, Harmondsworth, p. 146.

88. Raymond H. Fredette, *The First Battle of Britain, 1917/18*, Cassell, London, 1966, pp. 207-211 and 266.

89. Fredette, pp. 181-2 and 263-6. See also C.M. White, *The Gotha Summer. The German daytime air raids on England, May to August 1917*, Robert Hale, London, 1986, passim.

90. Quoted in Neil Hanson, *First Blitz. The Secret Plan to Raze London to the Ground in 1918*, Corgi Books, London, p. 353. Deborah Thom, writing of the confusion between the two World Wars in the minds of some elderly contributors to oral history projects, asserts that 'the war of 1914-1918 had registered just as much fear of bombardment as had the much more serious raids' of the Second World War. (*Nice Girls and Rude Girls. Women Workers of World War 1*, I.B. Tauris, London, 2000, p. 17.) The threat from the air was more real, in fact, than the British public could have known, for the Germans had created a type of incendiary, the so-called 'Elektron' Fire Bomb, which was small enough and powerful enough to create widespread devastation when dropped in massive numbers from the heavy Gotha and Giant bombers. Paris and London were the chosen targets for destruction, aimed at the devastation not only of huge swathes of those cities but also of civilian morale. As it turned out, the weather, nervousness about British retaliatory raids on German cities, and the approaching ending of the war led to their cancellation, so this was one horror at least which they were spared, this time at least – none of which, of course, was known at the time. (Hanson, especially Chapters 17 and 18.) The Gothas and Giants never flew over Britain in anger again. Father Bernard Vaughan, the rabble-rousing Jesuit, had turned up in Leicester in October of 1917 addressing a large crowd in De Montfort Hall, calling for bombing raids against targets in Germany in reprisal for German bombing raids on England. (*Leicester Daily Mercury*, 12th October 1917.)

91. Police Notice: Hostile Aircraft, Parish of Bitteswell, LRO. DE759/130.

92. Fredette, pp. 212-3.

93. *Rugby Advertiser*, 8th August 1918.

94. *Rugby Advertiser*, 6th January 1917.

95. *Rugby Advertiser*, 23rd June 1917.

96. *Rugby Advertiser*, 27th January 1917.

97. *Rugby Advertiser*, 14th July 1917.

98. *Rugby Advertiser*, 23rd June 1917.

99. *Rugby Advertiser*, 3rd December 1917.

100. *Rugby Advertiser*, 16th March 1917.

101. The incident occurred on May 18th; the court case was reported in the *Rugby Advertiser*, 8th June 1918.

102. *Rugby Advertiser*, 16th February 1918.

103. Report on the Ruri-Decanal Conference in Lutterworth, *Rugby Advertiser*, 25th May 1918.

104. Adrian Gregory has written that 'the low point in public confidence was between October 1917 and February 1918. The prospects never seemed bleaker.' (Gregory p. 213.)

105. Arthur Marwick, *The Deluge. British Society and the First World War*, Penguin Books, Harmondsworth, 1967, p. 209.

106. Gregory, p. 218.

107. *Rugby Advertiser*, 25th May 1918.

108. *Leicester Journal*, 26th April 1918.

109. David Lloyd George, in his memoirs, said that 'Haig reported to the C.I.G.S. (Chief of the Imperial General Staff) that he anticipated in the near future an attack by about eighty divisions... Sir Henry Wilson reported to the War Cabinet ten days later that "by the second week in June the Germans would have reached their maximum available force, and might attack with at least 100 divisions which would be a larger force than that which took part in the offensive of 21st March."' (David Lloyd George, *War Memoirs*, Vol. 2, Odhams, London, n.d., pp. 1838-9.) The numbers were scarcely exaggerated, but this had much to do with political manoeuvring over the army's demand for more manpower: whatever the exact figures, a German attack in great force was still expected.

110. *Leicester Daily Mercury*, 22nd May 1918. 'The War Illustrated' devoted a whole page to Lovat Fraser's analysis of why the Germans delayed their offensive (8th June 1918 edition). It seems extraordinary that while the imminence of a German attack was common knowledge in Britain, most of the intelligence officers on the spot were convinced that no attack was coming, even on the day before it actually came. (Travers, p. 106.)

111. *Leicester Daily Mercury*, 24th May 1918.

112. Crosbie Garstin, 'Chemin des Dames', in Brian Gardner (ed.), *Up the Line to Death. The War Poets, 1914-1918*, Methuen, London, 1964, pp. 43-4.

113. Richard Holmes, *Fatal Avenue. A Traveller's History of Northern France and Flanders, 1346-1945*, Pimlico, London, 1993, p. 329.

114. Martin Marix Evans, *1918. The Year of Victories*, Capella Books, London, 2002, pp. 88-9.

115. Basil Liddell Hart, *History of the First World War*, Pan Books, London, 1972, p. 407. The incompetent French General Duchêne, commander along the Chemin, had failed to detect the German preparations along his front, had failed to organise a defence in depth as he had been ordered to do by Pétain and advised by the commander of the British forces alongside him, had ignored an American Army analysis which had warned of the Germans' intentions, had brushed aside evidence from German prisoners that a major offensive was in preparation in front of him, and had then packed his troops into the front line trenches where they were devastated by the German bombardment and easily over-run when the storm troopers moved in. See Asprey, pp. 413-4.

116. Martin Gilbert, *A History of the Twentieth Century*, Volume 1, Harper Collins, London, p. 496. A recent detailed account of the German Offensive based on many of the Imperial War Museum's taped interviews can be found in Peter Hart, *1918. A Very British Victory*, Phoenix Books, London, 2009, chapter 8.

117. Hew Strachan, *The First World War. An Illustrated History*, Simon and Schuster, London, 2003, p. 301.

118. Asprey, p. 414. The best account of the events of that day and the final stages of the war are in David Stevenson's masterly *With Our Backs to the Wall. Victory and Defeat in 1918*, Allen Lane, London, 2011, pp. 78-84.

119. Quoted in Newman Flower (ed.), *The History of the Great War*, Waverley Books, London, n.d. (1919/1920), Vol. XIII, p. 2,301.

120. Hanson, p. 19.

121. On the 1871 siege and Commune see Alistair Horne, *The Fall of Paris. The Siege and the Commune, 1870-71*, Macmillan, London, 1965. In Russia, Lenin drew inspiration from the Commune, comparing it with the abortive Revolution in Russia in 1905: 'In spite of all the differences between the aims and tasks confronting the Russian Revolution and those of the French Revolution of 1871, the Russian proletariat had to resort to the same means of struggle which the Paris Commune had initiated – civil war... Under certain conditions the class struggle assumes forms of armed struggle and civil war; there are times when the interest of the proletariat demand ruthless annihilation of its enemies in open battle. The French proletariat was the first to demonstrate this in the Commune...' (Quoted from Zagranichnaya Gazeta, March 1908, in V.I. Lenin, *The Paris Commune, The Little Lenin Library*, Vol. 5, Martin Lawrence, London, 1931, pp. 19-20.) In Britain there had already been talk of creating Soviets on the Russian model, at the Leeds Conference, while the abortive Spartakist

(Communist) Revolution in Germany was only a matter of months away. Hindenburg was very much aware of the potential instability of Parisian politics, writing in his memoirs that 'the sensitive point of the French front was the direction of Paris. At the time the political atmosphere of Paris seemed to be heavily charged. Our shells and attacks from the air had hitherto not produced the explosion, but we had reason to hope that there would be an explosion if we advanced our lines nearer to the city'. Hindenburg, ed. Charles Messenger, p. 180.

122. Quoted in John Toland, *No Man's Land. The Story of 1918*, Methuen, London, 1982, p. 253.

123. *Leicester Daily Mercury*, 27th May 1918.

124. ibid.

125. Given the Payne brothers' consistent exoneration of their neighbours in their 1973 interview, we can safely disregard their later reply when asked whether they had 'been cat-called in the streets', that 'No, we don't remember anybody saying anything to us at all'. Liddle interview, 1973.

126. Liddle interview.

127. ibid.

128. S. Evans, 'Leicestershire Words, Phrases and Proverbs', 1881, quoted in E.P. Thompson, *Rough Music*, in *Customs in Common*, Penguin Books, London, 1993, p. 469, n.1. Thompson quoted a case of ritual public disapproval regarding a wife-beater and his mother and sister from Berkshire as late as 1930, though by this time the custom had all but died out. ibid., p. 528.

129. Writing of crowds in the eighteenth century, when 'rough music' was at its most common, Thompson wrote that 'it is possible to detect in almost every eighteenth-century crowd action some legitimising notion. By the notion of legitimation I mean that the men and women in the crowd were informed by the belief that they were defending traditional rights or customs; and, in general, that they were supported by the wider consensus of the community. On occasion this popular consensus was endorsed by some measure of licence afforded by the authorities.' (E.P. Thompson, *The Moral Economy of the Crowd*, op. cit., p. 188. While this is not quite a description of the Lutterworth behaviour, these are enough similarities to be suggestive of an historical continuity. Clive Emsley, *Hard Men. The English and Violence since 1750*, Hambledon Continuum, London, 2005, pp. 97-99.

130. *Rugby Advertiser*, 1st June 1918, emphasis added.

131. The words are from Jay Winter, *Sites of Memory, Sites of Mourning. The Great War in European Cultural History*, C.U.P., 1996, p. 29.

132. ibid., p. 80.

133. *Leicester Daily Mercury*, 29th May 1918.

134. Liddle interview, 1973.

135. Today the land is occupied by an extension to the graveyard, a part of the Cricket Club's ground, and more recent housing.

136. See above, 'Home Front' n. 188. *Rugby Advertiser*, 2nd December 1916. 'Home Front' n. 189. Lutterworth Parish Council Minutes, 30th November 1914 and 31st May 1915. *Rugby Advertiser*, 5th September 1914.

137. *Rugby Advertiser*, 27th January 1917.

138. *Rugby Advertiser*, 14th July 1917.

139. Liddle interview, 1973.

140. *Rugby Advertiser*, 26th August 1916.

141. *Rugby Advertiser*, 9th September 1916.

142. *Leicester Daily Mercury*, 30th October 1917.

143. Liddle interview, 1973.

144. In a letter from Jessie to Len, dated 10th September 1916, she refers to four shutters covering the front of the shop, with two on each side.

145. *Leicester Daily Mercury*, 29th May 1918.

146. ibid.

147. *Rugby Advertiser*, 1st June 1918.

148. Vincent put in an unsuccessful claim for compensation from the Parish Council a month later, specifying his ten canaries, along with his windows, as a financial loss. (*Rugby Advertiser*, 29th June 1918.) Reports also said that 'a large plate glass window at Burton & Sons, grocers' was smashed. (*Rugby Advertiser*, 1st June 1918.)

149. *Leicester Daily Mercury*, 29th May 1918.

150. Lutterworth Local History Group, *Lutterworth War Memorial Names, 1914-1918, 1939-1945*, 2005. Thirty-eight deaths are identified before May 28th, with the subsequent addition of Wycliffe Sarson to the memorial. There are a further three deaths for which no date has been positively identified.

151. *Leicester Daily Mercury*, 29th May 1918.

152. Theories of crowd dynamics suggest several ways of understanding the Lutterworth riot. 'Contagion Theory', first advanced by Gustave Le Bon in 1896, proposes that people in a crowd will act very differently from the way they behave as individuals, being carried away by the emotion of the crowd, surrendering their sense of individual responsibility to the mass. His core ideas were ably summarised by Chapman Cohen: 'A crowd will do collectively what none of its constituent units would ever dream of doing singly. It becomes capable of deeds of heroism or of savage cruelty. It will sacrifice itself or others with indifference. Above all, the mere fact of moving in a mass gives the individual a sense of power, a certainty of being in the right that he can – save under exceptional circumstances – never acquire while alone. The intellect is subdued, inhibition is inoperative, the instincts are given free play, and their movement

is determined in turn by suggestions not unlike those with which a trained hypnotist influences his subject.' (Cohen, p. 206.) Much of the theory depends on the anonymity which the crowd offers to individuals, and since in small-town Lutterworth almost everyone was known to almost everyone else, this prerequisite would be missing, though if the brothers' account was correct and the ringleaders of the 'storming party' were foundry workers without roots in Lutterworth, they may have been unconcerned about being known and identifiable. The theory implies a degree of irrationality among the rioters. 'Convergence Theory', on the other hand, suggests that people come together in crowds because they already hold similar views or have similar objectives: their behaviour within the crowd is thus a rational expression of their feelings. In this case, those who came together on Church Street that night did so because they all shared a common sense of revulsion, anger, fear and frustration over the continued presence of the Payne brothers in Lutterworth, given the national and military context of the time. A third explanation of crowd behaviour comes from the work of Ralph Turner and Lewis Killian, who proposed 'Emergent-Norm Theory'. This states that those who come together in a crowd begin with a variety of different attitudes and beliefs, but develop their own rules and norms of behaviour as events develop. Thus, if one or two people begin to smash windows, others will join in as that becomes the norm of behaviour accepted by the members of that crowd. All three of these theories may have some relevance to the Lutterworth riot, as also may Simon Moore's 'Particle Model' of crowd behaviour which suggests that the presence of alcohol inhibits normal human interactions and leads to a greater risk of violence in crowds, such as happened on Church Street that night. The failure of witnesses to react to dramatic events was explored by American and British social scientists following the 1964 murder in New York of Kitty Genovese, when it is alleged that thirty-eight people walked by and failed to respond to her cries for help. Some social scientists identified the 'Bystander Effect', which suggests that most individuals will not react to a given situation, no matter how dramatic, unless others respond first. So, in the case of the attack on the Paynes' shop, since no one stepped in to try to stop what was happening (apart from the two police officers blocking the doorway), no one else in the crowd thought to do it themselves. See the summaries in www.experiencefestival.com. Dr. Simon Moore's work can be followed via www.scie-socialcareonline.org.uk or www.cardiff.ac.uk

153. *Leicester Daily Mercury*, 29th May 1918. John was by now all too aware of the problem. He had written to Roland in July of 1916 about another offered contract for work for the military, saying that 'I should not accept work of that sort (certainly no) the same trouble would take place as when we made the *shell Bas*.' (John to Roland 6th July 1916.)

154. Sherrier Girls' School Log Book, 3rd to 24th September 1918. LRO.DE3614/7.

155. Gregory, p. 141.

156. *Rugby Advertiser*, 29th August 1914.

157. Gregory, p. 139.

158. Lutterworth Rural District Council General Committee Minutes, 29th November 1918. LRO.DE1379/446.

159. *Leicester Daily Mercury*, 29th May 1918.

160. *Leicester Daily Mercury*, 30th May 1918.

161. *Leicester Daily Mercury*, 29th May 1918.

162. Liddle interview, 1973.

163. The anti-German rioting in Keighley in West Yorkshire in August 1914 and at Deptford in East London in October set the pattern for police responses to riots in the First World War. (See Panayi, Chapter 8.) Professor Panayi concludes that throughout the war 'the police, both regular and special constables, performed their tasks correctly' when dealing with anti-German rioters. (p. 257.) The case of the Paynes was, of course, rather different, the violence being directed not against those seen as 'outsiders', but against their own neighbours, 'insiders'.

164. Leicestershire Constabulary. Minutes of Superintendants' Meetings, 15th April 1918. LRO.DE5491/104/1.

165. *Leicester Daily Mercury*, 29th May 1918.

166. *Leicester Mail*, 31st May 1918. Holmes had already expressed his dislike of Special Constables, preferring Parish Constables instead. Perhaps what he saw in Lutterworth that night confirmed his prejudice. (Minutes of Superintendents' Meeting, 31st May 1915. LRO DE5491/104.)

167. *Rugby Advertiser*, 1st June 1918. Speaking many years later, the brothers said that 'the police actually came when they thought they had done enough damage', an expression of frustration that the police had not been able to do more to protect them, or perhaps a veiled reference to the possibly wilful failure of the specials?

168. Liddle interview, 1973.

169. *Leicester Daily Mercury*, 30th May 1918; *Rugby Advertiser*, 1st June 1918.

PART FIVE

THE LONG
ROAD HOME

The war ended at eleven o'clock in the morning of Monday, November 11th, 1918. The news had reached Lutterworth before noon and the town's first reaction was of unrestrained joy. Flags appeared, hung out of windows across the town 'as if by magic'; the workers in the factories and foundries left work to join in the celebrations; the bell ringers clambered up into the church tower to peal out the news while the town's brass band played and the Boy Scouts paraded in full kit. The parish church overflowed with those, Anglican and Non-Conformist, who rushed to give thanks to God, as a general day of joy and celebration marked the ending of the Great War.[1]

A group of youths celebrated the Armistice by hurling stones and brickbats at the Paynes' shop in Church Street.[2]

★

The Paynes' family fortunes lay in ruins. They had been plunged into crisis by the attack on their home, their shop, on their standing in local society and on their very livelihood. Thomas Harper tried to rally support for them, writing to *The Friend* to seek help from the Quaker community. A report of his letter was published a month after the event, on June 28th ,1918:

'Our Friend Thomas H. Harper, of Penelve, Wanlip Road, Syston, sends us an account of the shameful and lawless treatment of a Lutterworth basket-maker whose two sons, since May, 1916, have been in various prisons as conscientious objectors. In April the young men were released to work at home at their own trade on a large contract for fruit baskets. On May 28th a hostile crowd smashed the windows of their house and next day set fire to a valuable shed stacked full of their father's willows, doing nearly £200 worth of damage. During this attack – from 10 p.m. to nearly 2 a.m. – the crowd sang and cheered, and were then dispersed by police from Leicester. The father has been discharged from a twenty-seven years' public appointment, and his two daughters have also been discharged from their work. The damage done is not covered by insurance; and our Friend would be glad to receive any help that Friends may be willing to contribute towards the heavy losses sustained by this family.'[3]

What shocks most is the dismissal of the boys' father from his post as Assistant County Court Bailiff and the sacking of the girls.[4] It has not proved possible to discover any reason for their dismissal.

Thomas Harper's appeal brought a modest response from Britain's Quakers, though only the letters forwarded to the Paynes are in the collection, so there may have been others. Milton Arnold and his family from Suffolk sent £1[5], while sisters Josephine and Edith Theobald from Bath chipped in a ten shilling postal order 'to show our sympathy' for the way they had been 'so shamefully treated for conscience's sake', though, should a list of subscribers be published, they did not wish their names included. The Bentham Quakers from Lancaster, well known to the Harpers, managed an apologetic six shillings, all they could collect from the I.L.P. members there because 'you understand how many demands there are on the generosity of pacifists at this time'.[6] How far the generosity of socialists would extend to a small businessman may anyway be open to question. A cheque for £7–12 shillings came from 'Woodhouse friends', signed by J. Hale Todd, the brothers' Wakefield friend, Joe. He had just returned from his home town of Penrith, where he had met a Herbert Lester who had been a school friend of Thomas Harper in the high Pennines. More connections were forged[7], but that was all. It was hardly enough to start repairing the material damage. The moral damage was entirely another matter.

★

What of the brothers themselves? Len, in their 1973 interview with Peter Liddle, told how 'first of all we went to a big fruit merchant's in Stratford-upon-Avon and then we went to Bourneville to see the foreman at Cadbury's works, who we were very friendly with and he said come to me in the morning, I can find you jobs'. These useful contacts had been established while they had worked in the chemical works nearby, before their disastrous return home. 'So we went to see him the next morning and we were set on straight away but he said he couldn't let us start until he got permission from the government again. Well, then we had a few weeks waiting for this permission from the government to come through. So we went up to Joe Todd's up in Westmoreland to help on the farm until we got permission from the government. Then we got our permission from the government so we came back to Cadbury's and got some lodgings and started there'.[8]

Leonard described their work at Cadbury's many years later: 'We got on well at Cadbury's. They didn't question us about being conscientious objectors because they knew this. We were in the rooms at Cadbury's with the girls. What we were doing, we were collecting the chocolate from where it was made. It used to come up on lifts into these rooms and we had to collect all the various sorts of chocolates because when those girls were boxing chocolates they had perhaps seven or eight different types of chocolate for each box. So we had to take these all round to these girls for the boxing.' It was congenial work in comfortable surroundings and their family came to Bourneville to spend the first Christmas with them.[9] When interviewed decades later, Leonard reported that at no time while they were in Bourneville did they suffer any discrimination at all, at work or in their social lives there[10], though this is not true. In his written autobiographical notes to Peter Liddle, Leonard had already admitted that 'some of the workers were a little hostile, particularly amongst the females whose boys were at the Front, and I quite understood this'.[11] It is characteristic of Leonard that either he tried to disguise the degree of hostility directed towards him (as during his time in Wakefield or after his return home) or that he simply was not aware of it.

FOREIGN FIELDS

Ironically, some of the conscientious objectors did get to visit foreign parts, William Marwick helping the French to rebuild their shattered landscapes and re-house the dispossessed.[12] Joe Todd went further, doing harrowing relief work in the town of Zawiercie in far off Poland, overwhelmed by a population in desperate poverty, displaced persons returning from the east, some fleeing from the terrible civil war in Russia as Reds fought Whites for the soul of the country, families from Romania and the Ukraine bringing typhus with them. When a train load of 150 refugees from Romania had arrived at Joe's station in Zawiercie early in March, fifty were found to be dead from starvation, the Romanian border guards apparently so terrified of typhus that they had refused even to open the wagons. 'If you know of anyone,' he pleaded, 'who can possibly come out here show them this letter or tell them about it. We are in desperate need of workers, and if anyone can possibly get out, they are doing humanity a very good turn if they come out here. The work in France is certainly very useful but it is not nearly so useful as this. There is a great risk of typhus and the mortality among those who catch it is about 50%… but I think the risk is really worth the good done. If the typhus is not stopped it will decimate the whole of Europe, as it spreads so quickly.'[13] It would seem that Annie Dawson was now a distant memory. Appended to Joe's letter is a brief note in Leonard's handwriting, presumably written at the time of the 1973 interview with Peter Liddle: 'These papers refer to work abroad by C.O.s. My two friends J. Hall Todd and W.H. Marwick M.A. went out on this work. Unfortunately I could not get away, as my Father was ill at the time.'

But Leonard would get his trip abroad. The suggestion came from William Marwick, who recommended him to the Quakers' 'War Victims' Relief Committee', and appeared to want him to join him in France; it was another of the former Wakefield Work Centre residents, Howard Marten, who signed the invitation.[14] Accompanying it in the Payne papers is an application form and questionnaire, which had not been filled in. [Do you have] 'knowledge of French, German, Russian or other foreign language?' 'Experience of camp or open-air life?' 'Craft, trade or useful hobby?' 'Have you been inoculated against Typhoid? If not, are you willing to be, if necessary?'[15] The form makes clear that a volunteer's costs would be paid by the Quakers. ('Cost of outfit £15 to £20, and maintenance, about twenty-five shillings weekly… If you are in a position to contribute all or any part of these expenses, please say how much.') Whether Leonard was able pay his own way is not known, but it is doubtful whether he would want to burden his family further.

In June 1921 Leonard received a letter from the German Quakers in Berlin suggesting (again on William Marwick's recommendation) that he stay with the Friends in the coal and steel city of Dortmund in the Ruhr, a place as different from Lutterworth as it is possible to imagine. The legal and bureaucratic wheels churned forward through June and July, and the Quakers even had to appeal directly to the German Foreign Office when the Berlin Police refused to issue Leonard with the necessary clearances for his visit.[16] 'In consideration of the fact that our object in helping to arrange these visits was to contribute something towards promoting a better understanding between Germany and other countries, the Secretary of State has very kindly agreed to telegraph instructions to the German Passport Office,' wrote Hubert Kemp from the Quakers' office in Berlin. The visit went ahead, though we know nothing about what happened beyond an undated note (probably from 1973) in which Leonard wrote that: 'These [documents] are in connection with a Peace Mission to Germany during the after strain [?] of war. We were splendidly treated by the Germans. No trouble.' Leonard's mission to Germany was more a goodwill gesture than one of practical value, such as were William's work in rehousing the dispossessed in France or Joe's desperate work with the starving and disease-ridden in Poland. No mention was made of his visit in Leonard's autobiographical notes and the subject was not raised in the interview with Peter Liddle.

It would be interesting to know what Leonard made of the Germany he visited and equally interesting would be what the Germans made of Leonard and his 'Peace Mission'. It was not a good time to go. A British reporter in Germany told how 'the German people present, among many other contrasts, that of unmistakable prosperity and equally decided gloom, if not actual despondency', identifying 'the collapse of currencies' across Central Europe and 'the recent unprecedented depreciation in the German mark' as a major cause of tension, which had 'thoroughly unsettled the vast body of the German people'.[17] The increasingly acrimonious disputes over Germany's reparations payments under the Treaty of Versailles led to the Allied occupation of nearby Düsseldorf, Duisburg and Ruhrort in March, while Leonard was presumably still there, just a few miles away, in Dortmund.[18] While these events may well have encouraged German pacifists in their hatred of war, others may well have had an opposite reaction.

More positively, though, there is evidence that among many German ex-servicemen there was, by 1921, a feeling of revulsion against war itself, a rejection of the pre-1914 glorification of the military, a deep distrust of militarism and the old social structure which had underpinned it. While this did not signify any great pacifist movement in Germany (such as would develop in Britain in the 1930s), the anti-war Reichsbund could boast a membership of 830,000 in the early 1920s, twice as many as all the right-wing militarist Freikorps organisations put together.[19]

Perhaps there were two thoughts which might have crossed Leonard's mind had he contemplated the meaning of his German visit. The first concerns Lutterworth's own War Memorial, for it is instructive to put side by side Leonard's Quaker 'Peace Mission' to Germany, its aim to seek 'a better understanding between Germany and other countries', with the address given by the Earl of Denbigh – scourge of conscientious objectors during the war – at the unveiling of the town's War Memorial only a few weeks earlier. Whether Leonard had heard the speech or not is unknown, but it was widely reported in the local press.

There was no peace and reconciliation in the Earl's heart, only belligerence, enmity and infinite suspicion. 'They met that day [he said, as reported in one newspaper] to unveil a memorial to forty-nine men who showed heroism and self-sacrifice amid hardship and danger such as they had never before in this world had to face, and which had cost them their lives. It was this noble spirit of sacrifice in the protection of their country which had taken them out, and it should be a lesson to us all in the years to come to remind us, first of all, of the faults of the British nation, whose lamentable laxity was largely the cause of us having a war at all, in that we were unprepared and living in a state of fancied security. An isolated island, we thought there was no need to worry about what was happening on the Continent. It didn't seem to us to matter what other countries were involved if we were safe, the consequence being that when the blow came, it came as a thunder-clap and caught us quite unprepared and without adequate munitions. What was spoken of as our "contemptible little army" left our shores and proved an example of courage and endurance; but when they were gone, what a very little we had to take their place. We as a nation had taken no notice of how Germany was building herself up and intended humbling England to the dust, this idea having animated Germany for years before the war, and it was time the people of England were taught a lesson for its future good. This memorial would act as a warning for the future, and be a lasting monument of patriotism…' – a 'monument of patriotism', rather than a memorial to the lost men of Lutterworth. He ended in characteristic style: 'He reminded his hearers we are not out of the war zone yet, and our men would have died in vain if we didn't realise that our great watchwords are responsibility, duty, and self-sacrifice. If we only realised what our brave men died for, it would be our endeavour to make England what it had always been in the past.'[20]

The Earl had been invited to speak because of his local aristocratic status and because, as Lord of the Manor, no one else could be asked in his stead: we do not know what the Earl's audience, gathered in the hot sun on that Tuesday afternoon, made of what they heard. It gave meaning of sorts to the war, it validated the loss of so many lives, it gave a political message (appropriate to many of his hearers who saw Germany as the initiator of war), it contained a moral along the lines of 'all that is necessary for the triumph of evil is that good men do nothing', it linked the war to English values and English (not, notice, 'British') history and it was in keeping with much of the rhetoric of the 1920s. And yet... in retrospect, we are left with the feeling that it was not somehow appropriate.

It offered no concessions whatever to those who had had a conscientious objection to participation in the war, such as the Paynes. Though no one would expect someone like the Earl to modify his position by one iota, to someone like Leonard, preparing to set out on his Quaker 'Peace Mission' to Germany, it must have been a desperately disappointing occasion. The war against Germany had been won, but the war against war had not – not in Britain at least. There was another reflection too, a more positive one, and it came from those German ex-servicemen who had turned their backs on war. For in Britain, he found the same thing and it would be through Lutterworth's own returning ex-servicemen that Leonard and Roland Payne would make their first faltering steps on the long road home.

LUTTERWORTH RUGBY CLUB

The men who had been away returned home, too slowly for many of them, as Britain demobilised. Sport started up again. Sport would give the brothers their first entrée back into Lutterworth society. Their first steps were in Birmingham while working for Cadbury's: 'The Rugger team got going again, and I decided to join. I did not know what to expect, and I turned up for the first practice match, and discovered that most of the lads were ex-army officers. The next practice match I turned up for, and I was much surprised that my name appeared in the First Team for the opening game. I kept my place in the team all the time I was at Bourneville. They were a grand lot of chaps, and although they knew I was a C.O. I never heard one word said against me.'[21] Though again we need to allow for Leonard's positive gloss, this is far more credible than many of his other denials of hostility.

Leonard took up the story, the story of the beginning of his and Roland's first tentative rehabilitation: 'It was a very difficult time and no one had any idea what might happen on our return. So I decided to write to the [Lutterworth] Rugger Club Sec. who I had played with in the Boys' team years before. After a time he replied saying he had brought the matter up with the committee and players, and they had agreed that I should join the team.'[22] In his recorded interview, however, Leonard was more forthcoming about those arguments surrounding his return: 'I told him I was coming home at Christmas 1919, I should like to play for the club. Anyway a terrible argument went on in Lutterworth about this but eventually they agreed…'[23] 'The first Saturday match was at home and I was much surprised when several of the players called at my home to take me to the ground. I felt so confident because of this, and I knew that they had made up their minds to defend me if there was any trouble. This is the sportsmanship that I experienced both at Bourneville and Lutterworth, and I have never forgotten.'[24]

It is evident that some had different views, for there were threats to pull down the posts if the brothers played. It is significant, though not surprising in the context of that time, that most of their team mates were ex-servicemen. Both brothers

Leonard and Roland Payne in their rugby club kit, 1922

played in the team and later in the 1920s Leonard would go on to be Captain of the First XV for three consecutive seasons. Both brothers' names appear frequently in match reports during the 1920s – honourably mentioned in dispatches, as it were. 'We went on and got a wonderful team and won all the cups in Leicestershire,' he recalled with evident pride, 'and that was the finish.'[25]

DISENFRANCHISED

On May 20th, 1919, Leonard and Roland Payne were officially released from the restrictions placed upon them as conscientious objectors.[26] However, that did not mean they could return to civil life as free citizens like everyone else. The Representation of the People Act had become law in June 1918. It gave the vote to almost all men over twenty-one and, even more momentously, gave the vote to women over thirty. The electorate was almost trebled overnight. Those who had been conscientious objectors during the war, however, were deprived of the right to vote for five years in an act of petty spite. Leonard was already over twenty-one; Roland achieved his majority in 1918. Both were away in Bourneville when the 1918 Election was held and it is doubtful whether they had registered there as voters. On their permanent return though, the local Conservative Party became aware of their presence and their background, and just to make sure they did not slip through the electoral ban, one Herbert Grepe of South Wigston formally objected to both brothers' names appearing on the Electoral Register. 'That being a conscientious objector he is disqualified from being registered as a Parliamentary Elector for a period of five years from the legal date of the termination of the war,' he wrote on their forms of objection, dated 2nd February, 1924. (The Great War did not end formally, until the German delegation signed the Treaty of Versailles, in 1919.) The names of both Leonard and Roland Payne were duly struck from the register.[27]

It is clear that the issue of the conscientious objectors was still a political issue which some took very seriously indeed, stirred up in south Leicestershire in the neighbouring Parliamentary constituency of Market Bosworth in the General Election of December 1923. It was there in 1916 that the local Tribunal had rejected the claim of a conscientious objector while exempting the hunt servants from military service, a case which Philip Snowden had highlighted. That may be why the Labour Party put up as candidate Emrys Hughes, one of the first members of the No-Conscription Fellowship. The Tory candidate, Major Paget, a military man who used his army title and paraded in uniform at every opportunity, rose to the bait, referring to Hughes as 'this thing from Wales… well, I am not surprised that

426

they exported this rabbit to us'.[28] 'Thing' and 'rabbit' were straight from the First World War rhetoric book and made his meaning clear.

This attempt to play the 'C.O.' card drew a strong response from someone signing themselves 'Not a C.O.': 'As the local Conservative is endeavouring to prejudice Mr Emrys Hughes in the eyes of the electors by uncomplimentary references to his action during the war, may I be allowed to draw your readers' attention to a very significant recent happening'. The 'happening' for some was, no doubt, something of a damp squib, being the appointment of Leyton Richards, a member of the NCF's Executive during the war to the Carrs Lane Chapel in Birmingham. 'This shows,' wrote the correspondent, 'what a change there is in the minds of Christian people, to those men who were not able to reconcile warfare with Christian principles.'[29] It is doubtful whether this contributed significantly to Major Paget's loss of the election, but it is noticeable that Hughes almost pushed him into third place.[30]

How frustrating the Paynes found their new loss of civil rights is not known, but it came at a dramatic time in British political history for, in No. 10 Downing Street, was none other than Ramsay MacDonald, so recently 'the most hated man in Britain'. True, he only headed a minority government, kept in power by the votes of the Liberals in Parliament. And true also that his government lasted only nine months. It is also true that when he called a General Election in October the Conservatives won a resounding victory.[31] However, MacDonald had played his cards better than most at the time, for Labour was able to squeeze the Liberals' vote and MacDonald presented his own party as the only effective opposition to the Conservatives. It was a momentous shift in British politics, but not one to which the Payne brothers were able to contribute.

INDIFFERENCE

The Earl of Denbigh, Herbert Grepe and their kind certainly represented one strand of thought regarding the war and those who had fought – or not fought – in it. But it was not, by and large, the attitude of those who had actually fought in the war. They came back changed men, their perspective forever altered. Perhaps the greatest gulf in British society after the Great War was between those who had seen active service and had been in the trenches, and those who had not.

Priorities gradually began to shift as new influences, such as the great flu pandemic, came into play. If the war had respected little distinction between soldier and civilian, man, woman or child, the influenza strain which swept the world treated such humane distinctions with contempt. What had seemed so desperately urgent and important while the fighting was still going on, like Ludendorff's great Offensives of 1918 which had pushed the town's nerves over the edge of rationality, lost their urgency and their importance now peace had come. In Lutterworth what had appeared at first to be a desperately important priority at war's end, the need to organise peace celebrations and to memorialise the dead, slipped down the list. They never got round to organising 'peace rejoicings' as they had intended, partly because, when it came down to the details, no one was quite sure how they might do it or even on reflection, whether they ought to be doing it.[32]

What of a permanent war memorial for the town? The Parish Councillors seemed to have felt out of their depth. These were, of course, many of the same people who had sat on the conscription Tribunals where they had been equally out of their depth. There was no shortage of ideas, just a reluctance to commit to something so permanent. In this small town of shopkeepers, money also played its part. Thomas Buck the brewer, Chairman of the Parish Council, said of the war memorial plan in May of 1919 that 'he did not feel, in the face of high rates and ever-increasing expenditure, that it was an opportune time to go in for anything of a very elaborate or ambitious nature'.[33] It was still important, of course, that the town should have a war memorial, but somehow didn't seem quite so urgent anymore. Lutterworth would get its war memorial eventually, but, in that shocked period immediately following the Armistice[34], new priorities demanded attention.

The council had other things on its mind, which were newly urgent and important, and in March of 1919 a public meeting was convened to discuss the 'stupendous question of building houses for the working classes' in Lutterworth. Two hundred Lloyd George's 'homes fit for heroes' were needed but no one knew where or how to provide them.[35] In addition, a proportion of Lutterworth's existing housing was below standard. One anonymous writer to the local newspaper referred in sarcastic terms to 'those snug little houses off Station Road, with two sweet little rooms; or those around that quaint yard called Dixon Square; or, again, those dinky little places tucked behind Woodmarket, how secluded and mellow they are! No garden to till, scarcely any windows to clean, no absurd privacy, all life shared and its intimate details known to all'.[36] Many homes did not even have running water. What price a war memorial when there were families without decent homes?

★

At this time, most of the old guard of Lutterworth now departed the scene. James Darlington from 'The Hill' died in February 1918[37] and Charles Marriott from Cotesbach in July[38]. Arthur Massey, minister at the Congregational Chapel, had left Lutterworth to take up his work with the Pensions Ministry late in 1918[39] and the Rector, Montague Alderson, shortly after for Salisbury. Most significant of all, Lupton Topham sold his big house on Woodmarket and left the town late in 1920.[40] It took time, but a new energy invigorated the town and, as Lutterworth passed from the Armistice and into the 1920s, new ambitions emerged. For a time it looked as though Lutterworth might get its own public baths, standing as a war memorial – until Lupton Topham had scotched the idea in one of his last acts before leaving the town.[41] Lutterworth would not, in fact, get its swimming pool until the 1960s, but the ambition was there. And there was talk of building a new elementary school for the town to ease the overcrowding in the old Sherrier School building, a proposal which attracted the approval of the great William Brockington at the County Education department and which led to the creation of a new extension on the Bitteswell Road for the older children.[42] In 1923 it was proposed that Lutterworth, in order to avoid that bottleneck at the top of High Street called appropriately 'The Narrows', needed its own road bypass. Interestingly, local opinion was 'dead against any suggestion of side-tracking Lutterworth off the main road' and nothing came of it.[43] Others wondered if a branch line might be built from the Great Central Railway, leading from Lutterworth towards Coventry and

Birmingham. 'This would make Lutterworth an important junction, more industrial works would be established and more dwelling houses of all descriptions will have to be erected.'[44] Nothing came of that either, so why not 'turn Lutterworth into a health resort?' one local asked. During the war the cottage hospital and the Methodist schoolroom had, after all, been used to nurse wounded soldiers. 'Purity of atmosphere, coupled with pleasant surroundings of green fields' would provide an ideal setting, and Lutterworth still had lots of old coaching inns which might be adapted to use; and, it was argued, 'the experience gained [in nursing those soldiers] proved Lutterworth invaluable as a health resort'.[45] However, nothing came of these ideas.

It was not all negative. With the dead hand of the old guard lifted, new men could have their say. George Spencer continued as the leading progressive voice of the community and when the builder Peter Rourke suggested that a new night school teaching practical skills be created so youngsters could 'be better equipped to participate in [the country's] industrial and commercial life', the grammar school provided the facilities and the thing was up and running within weeks; a remarkable achievement.[46] Also on the positive side, Lutterworth's own 'Ex-Service and Working Men's Club' was opened on the Leicester Road in mid-October 1923[47], as clear a recognition as could be found of the town's acceptance of its semi-industrial status with its own embryonic working class. In 1919 a branch of the Labour Party had opened.

Lutterworth was becoming a different place, transforming itself from the 'somnolent' little town of shopkeepers ruled over by the watchful and paternalistic hand of Lupton Topham or James Darlington or Montague Alderson, which it had been in 1914. In retrospect, we might see that speech by the Earl of Denbigh at the unveiling of Lutterworth's War Memorial as the symbolic passing of an old age, one which now was being slowly left behind. In 1927, a young man called Leach, who lived in Broughton Astley, came to work in Lutterworth as a pharmacist's apprentice. Years later he wrote a brief typescript autobiography in which he described what he recalled about the shops and shopkeepers of the town. He remembered the Paynes: 'Conchi Paynes they were called as they had been conscientious objectors in the Great War.'[48] So this was what it had all come down to – an interesting local detail and a simple form of identification, a nickname. Their objection remained embedded in local memory, but the Payne brothers' Great War conscientious objection was becoming a matter of indifference.

CHANGING ATTITUDES AND A
NEW WORLD WAR

It was not just Lutterworth which adjusted its attitudes towards the Great War and to those who had been conscientious objectors, for feelings were gradually changing nationally. Broadly speaking, through the 1920s in Britain the received view that the war had been fought for honourable reasons prevailed: the loss of life a tragic, but necessary consequence. It was necessary to believe that, while wounds remained fresh. On the world stage the Treaty of Versailles and the other treaties with the other defeated nations, despite the reservations of some about the severity of punishments handed out, appeared a just settling of accounts. In the minds of some, 'Hang the Kaiser' extended to 'hang all Germans' as wartime hatreds continued unabated and the desire to expel all of German origin gathered temporary momentum.[49] Memories were too raw and it was too early for peace and reconciliation.

But the League of Nations brought new hope for lasting peace, created for the resolution of international disputes without the need for war. In 1928 the Kellogg-Briand Pact pledged the fifteen countries which signed it to abstain from war and hopes for the future rose again. Even Germany appeared, as the twenties went on, to be establishing a place among the civilised nations, guided by its new and progressive democratic republican government and the brilliant statesmanship of Gustav Stresemann. It joined the League in 1925, welcomed by, of all countries, France. As America withdrew into its shell of isolationism and Russia concentrated on building a communist society behind its own borders, the illusion was created of Britain's world dominance restored.

It was short-lived and, in 1929, it all came crashing down. The Great Crash was followed by the Great Depression and the rise of the Dictators. In Italy Mussolini tightened his grip on power and looked for foreign adventures for his 'New Roman Empire', using tanks, bombers and poison gas in 1935 to subdue the defenceless people of Abyssinia (Ethiopia). The Japanese too went on the rampage. Already, they had sought raw materials and new (forced) markets through their invasion of Manchuria and, in 1937, launched an all out attack on China, unspeakable cruelties coming in its wake. The League of Nations, repository of such grand hopes, looked on helpless. Later, of course, there was Hitler. The progress of Nazism in Germany and Hitler's ruthless policy of expansion need not be rehearsed here. They are well enough known.

Pacifist organisations, such as the No More War Movement (1921), which had developed out of the No-Conscription Fellowship, existed through the 1920s, but their size and influence were limited.[50] But paradoxically to some, the 1930s, that most dangerous and threatening of decades, saw the growth in Britain of a powerful Peace Movement. Novels such as Richard Aldington's *Death of a Hero* (1928), Siegfried Sassoon's *Memoirs of a Fox-hunting Man* (1928), Robert Graves' *Goodbye to all that* (1929), R.C. Sherriff's play *Journey's End* (1929), Ernest Hemingway's American *A Farewell to Arms* (1929), and the German Erich Maria Remarque's *All Quiet on the Western Front* (1929), filmed under Lewis Milestone's direction in America (1930), all echoed and created a widespread feeling of revulsion against war and a new determination among many to refuse to take up arms. The famous Oxford Union resolution that 'this House will in no circumstance fight for its King and Country', passed by 275 votes to 153 in February 1933, attracted massive publicity out of all proportion to its real significance, although its influence on public opinion is harder to gauge.[51] Neville Chamberlain's policy of appeasing the dictators was hugely popular, matching so closely the public mood and Chamberlain's own deepest personal feelings. Even *The Times*, so belligerent in 1914, joined in the rejoicing as Chamberlain brought 'peace in our time' back from Munich in 1938: 'The volume of applause for Mr Chamberlain, which continues to grow throughout the globe, registers a popular judgement that neither politicians nor historians are likely to reverse.'[52] It seemed that the pacifist philosophy had won the day. But such anti-war sentiment could be enjoyed only by the victors of 1914-1918. The losers could enjoy no such luxury, with tragic consequences.

By the later 1930s, Chamberlain's appeasement policy, which had offered such glorious hope in 1938, faltered and fell apart in 1939 and Europe slid towards inevitable war. Official attitudes to those who declined to take part in the armed conflict this time were more clearly defined from the outset. The Prime Minister, Neville Chamberlain, had declared that: 'In the view of the government, where scruples are conscientiously held, we desire that they should be respected and that there should be no persecution of those who hold them.'[53] A Tribunal member in the First World War, Chamberlain had learned the pointlessness of trying to compel conscientious objectors: 'It was a useless and exasperating effort to attempt to force such people to act in a manner contrary to their principles,' he said.[54] It was almost as though the ghost of Asquith's *'Ship of Liberal Values'* was resurrected from the depths, albeit in a different form, standing opposed to all that Nazism represented: militarism, the regimentation of society, the submersion of the individual and the exaltation of the mass, especially as defined by race and blood, the persecution of minorities, brutality, cruelty and aggressive war. Something resembling the old Liberal Values seemed now worth fighting for more than ever before.

In 1941 Churchill's Government introduced the National Service Bill. 'This Bill,' said Ernest Bevin, the Minister of Labour, in introducing it, 'proposes to make liable for Civil Defence service men who are liable to service in the armed forces of the Crown. It imposes similar liabilities upon men who are registered under the Act as conscientious objectors, on condition that they take up some specified work of a civilian nature and will continue to be under civilian control.' Bevin went out of his way to allay the fears of those who feared military conscription by the back door. 'Is Civil Defence a civilian job or is it a military job?' he asked. 'In this Bill we take the greatest care to keep it a civilian job.'[55] In these circumstances Leonard was not slow to come forward and offer his services, as he recounted many years later:

> 'The Second World War came, and I decided I would help in any way I could: ambulance work, fire fighting, etc, and as we were so near to Coventry and the terrible things that happened there, [most horrifically the Coventry blitz on the night of 14th November 1940] we were busy night after night for fear the bombs fell on the town. But we were lucky.'

However, their position changed in 1943. As Leonard again told it: 'The government decided to put all these operations under the Military Authorities. This meant that I had to take some sort of Oath and become part of the Military Authority. This I could not do, so they decided to take action against me.' Leonard received a form instructing him to attend for medical examination in Lutterworth under the Emergency Powers (Defence) Act. It is dated 21st July 1943. When Leonard failed to turn up, he was summoned to appear at the magistrates' court on October 7th 1943.[56] Leonard recalled, 'I was fined £25 or one month in prison. To their surprise I said I would take prison for a month. Someone paid the fine, and I was not bothered again.' It is not known who paid the fine, but shortly afterwards there was a brief tailpiece: 'A week or two after, the clerk of the court stopped me in the town and said how ashamed he was at what he had to do in the court and he hoped I would forgive him. We shook hands and parted good friends.'[57]

"Naturally, the common people don't want war, but after all, it is the leaders of a country who determine the policy, and it is always a simple matter to drag people along whether it is a democracy, or a fascist dictatorship, or a parliament, or a communist dictatorship. Voice or no voice, the people can always be brought to the bidding of the leaders. This is easy. All you have to do is to tell them they are being attacked, and denounce the pacifists for lack of patriotism and exposing the country to danger. It works the same in every country."

Hermann Goering, Hitler's Reich-Marshall
at the Nuremberg Trials after WWII

THE LONG ROAD TO
FORGETTING

Memories of that extraordinary night in 1918 when half the town lost its head gradually faded or were suppressed. Younger generations, born after the Great War, seem to have had little or no awareness of the events of May 28th, 1918, when that huge crowd had turned out to watch their neighbours attack two young men who were also their neighbours, whose crime was to refuse to do harm. The violence of that night was expunged from local legend and local history alike, as though it had never happened.

The physical attack on the Paynes was the product of extraordinary times of unprecedented fear, stress and pressure, when a population, ground down by almost four years of war, appeared to be facing defeat. The tide in the war turned on August 8th and gradually, after that, the Allied victory seemed more and more assured. The great scare of May was passed and with it the fear, stress and pressure which had exploded on the night of May 28th. After November 11th, there was no longer any real need to feel hatred for the Payne brothers for their refusal to put on uniform and go away to fight. The great Ludendorff Offensives of spring 1918 had passed into history and lost their power to terrify.

If memories of the attack died out, the memory of the hatred did not. Small towns have long memories and it is still possible in Lutterworth, speaking with those who have lived their own long lives in the town, to pick up the echoes of the town's feelings about the Payne brothers and their conscientious objection. 'Hated' is a word used by several older residents about the Paynes, a word they learnt from their parents who were of that Great War generation. One older resident, only recently, said: 'The Payne brothers. We don't talk about *them*'. It is not that this next generation shared that hatred, but more that they were taught about it. Interviews with a younger generation still – those born in the 1930s and 1940s – reveals little awareness of the Payne brothers' First World War experiences and no knowledge whatever of that extraordinary night in May 1918 when half the town turned out to assault them. Today in Lutterworth the events of that night are entirely forgotten.

★

The brothers remained in Lutterworth for the rest of their lives, building their own homes on the family's ground beyond the town, out on the Rugby Road. Roland remained a dedicated Quaker for the rest of his life, in large part through Edith's influence, and for many years was a Quaker Sunday School teacher. Whether his wife had taken the place of his brother as the dominating force in his life, or how far Leonard retained his grip, is uncertain. The brothers remained very close to each other for the rest of their lives. It was largely through Roland's industry in the family basket weaving business that the family's fortunes were restored: as a skilled craftsman there seemed little he could not make. If over subsequent years the family fell short of funds, they sold off properties in Lutterworth which their father had so carefully acquired. The 'homestead' out on the Rugby Road, with its bee hives and small-scale livestock rearing, yielded a modest income, but never enough to pay its way and it always ran at a loss. At times, Roland's son, Jack, had to bail them out financially. Roland himself died in 1986.

We have to ask how their First World War experiences, and especially of course that one night of violence, affected them in their many remaining years. Without some kind of scientific 'control sample' we cannot know. Both brothers were very enthusiastic practical jokers. Family legend has it that at a friend's wedding they made use of a builder's hoist to lift a, doubtless, terrified donkey onto the church roof. Whether the bride and groom, let alone the donkey, found this in any way amusing is not recorded, but we might imagine not. Nor again, when they spread itching powder in the wedding bed, possibly of the same couple. One writer has described practical jokes as 'the sadism of the jovial'[57], though sometimes one has to search hard to find much in the way of joviality. One should not get too dour about it, but practical jokes are intended to embarrass, ridicule and humiliate, to make fools of people. Thus, when they wrapped up a parcel filled with horse manure in fancy paper and left it in the street in Lutterworth to see who would pick it up and take it home, we might see the victim as the author of their own fate. Could there also be a darker element of revenge against their neighbours and fellow townspeople? Perhaps they would they have done this anyway. It is a childish prank, not one which might be expected from men in their mid-twenties or later. More difficult to understand are their protracted and unpleasant disputes with some members of their own family regarding the land where they had built their homes on the Rugby Road. What comes through is a meanness of spirit as well as of money.

A memorial to Conscientious Objectors 1995, Tavistock Square, London
(Photo by Author)

Leonard's life followed a different, possibly a darker, trajectory than Roland's. At first, while he was a star player for the Lutterworth RFC's First XI and then captain for three successive seasons, his life was moving back towards something resembling normality, his role in the family business helping to restore the family's fortunes. He appeared on the road to rehabilitation. Leonard liked the good life. That early interest in motorbikes was translated into a love of cars, the bigger the better. His life appeared to be back on track. Perhaps he should have been increasingly seen as an upright, even an honoured member of the local community, his Great War conscientious objection a mark of moral distinction.

And yet... something peculiar happened to Leonard Payne. His family is adamant that he was not religious. What had happened? Had he lost his Christian faith or his faith only in organised religion? Had his First World War experiences left him disillusioned and bitter? To answer those questions would involve us seeking to do what the Great War Tribunals tried and failed to do: hold up a mirror to men's souls.

His enthusiasm for sexual matters, over which he had suffered the teasing of his Wakefield friends and which had certainly contributed to the *Wakefield Express's* outrage at the conduct of the conscientious objectors and some Yorkshire females alike, continued into his later life. As he grew older, it became more and more inappropriate. Local rumour is not history and it may be untrue that Leonard exploited his sexual charms to the full and took advantage of the appalling excess of women over men, which those First World War casualty lists created. Rumour also said that he did not confine himself in the 1920s to unmarried women in the town and that he made his own significant personal contribution to Lutterworth's gene pool. In later life, as he grew old, he could not be left alone with women or girls, or so the family believed. Leonard Payne died in 1979.

★

This, then, was the story of the Payne brothers of Lutterworth. We can learn a great deal from their experiences in the hands of the State in the Great War, reminding ourselves that not all conscientious objectors were 'absolutists' refusing all compromise with the State, that not all conscientious objectors were sent to France and sentenced to death by firing squad (albeit the sentences commuted), that not all conscientious objectors were violently assaulted by army NCOs. Certainly, some conscientious objectors were treated in this way, and it is these cases which have quite rightly claimed the attention of historians and those concerned with the development of a 'civil rights' or a 'human rights' culture in modern Britain. However, that does not necessarily suggest that their experience was typical.

Here, we have to draw a distinction. The Payne brothers never published their letters, so meticulously kept during the Great War. The thought would never have occurred to them. At the outset of this essay it was suggested that they were not 'conscientious objectors' in some generic or abstract way, in the mould of Clifford Allen, Fenner Brockway or other luminaries of the No-Conscription Fellowship, or the other anti-conscription or pacifist groups set up during the war. Nor were they of the type of Henry Hobhouse, Howard Marten or Corder Catchpool and the others who published their own accounts of their experiences as conscientious objectors in the 1920s and '30s. However, those who made the most noise were not necessarily the most 'typical'. For the Payne brothers, like unknown numbers of other conscientious objectors, the right to hold a conscientious objection was not a fundamental human principle which had to be fought for in the interests of all mankind. To them, it was personal and individual. They could not take up arms, whatever the reason and at whoever's behest. It had been taken in with their mother's milk: they simply had no choice. It was others, the Clifford Allens and the Fenner Brockways, even the Hobhouses, the Martens and the Catchpools, who were fighting and suffering for them and their right to say 'No'. Not the other way round.

Contrary to so much that has been written about the Great War's conscientious objectors, the Payne brothers, whilst in the hands of the State, were treated with as much consideration and humanity as was possible, *at the time and in those precise circumstances*. It is utterly meaningless to condemn the authorities in the First World War for not holding the same sensibilities and sensitivity to human rights which are today held as commonplace. Just as today, they lived in their own time, their own contexts, and can be judged only by those standards. It was only when the brothers returned home that they came to understand that they had in fact been safer in the hands of the State than in the hands of the public, in the hands of their own neighbours. Perhaps 'Wyclif's town', with its multitude of places of worship and Christian denominations, should have done better when it came to charity and forgiveness, but Christian values and duty were open to differing interpretations and, 'at that time', fighting a crusading war against evil and in defence of your own country took precedence over Christian love and brotherhood. An attitude closer to St George than St Francis.

★

What then was the ultimate legacy of their conscientious objection? That remains hidden, unknown and unknowable, an 'inaccessible history', but it is possible that, somewhere in Germany today, a family is sitting round its dinner table in Stuttgart or Cologne, in Berlin or Munich, a family which would not have ever existed had the Payne brothers joined the army and killed the German family's grandfather or great-grandfather in a trench on the Somme or at Ypres or anywhere else on the Western Front. Perhaps their conscientious objection gave a German family life. That would be an honourable legacy, but that is unknowable. Perhaps their conscientious objection even took them a little closer to heaven. That too is unknowable.

★ ★ ★

NOTES & REFERENCES

1. An 'Armistice Service' was held in the Parish Church, date unspecified. There is a copy of the printed order of service in Lutterworth Museum. For a wider perspective on that day see Nicholas Best, *The Greatest Day in History. How the Great War Really Ended*, Weidenfeld and Nicolson, London, 2008.
2. *Rugby Advertiser*, 16th November 1918.
3. *The Friend*, 28th June 1918. In October the Parish Council tried to claim back from the Royal Insurance Company the cost incurred by the fire brigade in putting out the fire in the Bitteswell Road storage shed, but had to let the claim lapse because it had been the police and not John Payne who had called out the brigade. Parish Council Minutes, 28th October 1918. LRO DE2254/3.
4. Kelly's 1922 Directory shows John remaining as Deputy Registrar of Marriages, but not as Assistant County Court Bailiff. The 1936 edition indicates he had lost his role as Deputy Registrar of Marriages. Jessie and Dora may have been working for George Spencer.
5. Milton Arnold to Thomas Harper, 3rd July 1918.
6. Hinley Atkinson to Thomas Harper, 21st July 1918.
7. J. Hale Todd to Mr Harper, 9th July 1918. The handwriting is clearly Joe Todd's. There is no record of the £7 which Mr Lester said he had collected.
8. Leonard, MS autobiographical notes, Liddle Collection.
9. Family interview with Roland, Christmas 1971. From an anthropological point of view, their work alongside the women in the Cadbury's factory is highly suggestive. See footnote 126 to 'Away from Home'.
10. Liddle interview, 1973, transcript, Tape 44, pp.13-4.
11. Leonard, autobiographical MS, Liddle Collection, p. 10.
12. Marwick autobiographical typescript, Liddle Collection, Brotherton Library, University of Leeds, p. 5.
13. J. Hall Todd, typescript letter to 'Dear Friend', 8th and 12th March 1920. Liddle Collection, Brotherton Library, University of Leeds. Soon that part of Poland would be threatened by what some saw as another plague spreading in from the east, a full-scale invasion of Poland, the plan to make Poland Communist as a stepping stone to the Bolshevisation of Germany and then western Europe. A few months after Joe had told of such appalling

conditions in Zawiercie the Soviet Red Army was sweeping down across the plains of Poland, it seemed on the road to all-out victory. Only the so-called 'Miracle on the Vistula' in August of 1920, when the Red Army was halted and then driven out, saved both Poland and, arguably, western Europe from Communist invasion. Though the most desperate fighting took place further north, around Warsaw, the murderous brutality of the war sent fresh streams of terrified refugees fleeing westward towards Zawiercie. (See Norman Davies, *White Eagle, Red Star. The Polish-Soviet War 1919-1920 and the "Miracle on the Vistula"*, Macdonald, London, 1972; Adam Zamoyski, *Warsaw 1920. Lenin's Failed Conquest of Europe*, Harper Press, London, 2008.) We do not know whether Joe was still in Poland when the Polish-Russian War began in earnest in April 1920.

14. Payne documents in the Liddle Collection, Leeds.

15. This raises the question of whether Roland was involved as well. It is unlikely that Leonard would have been invited without Roland, nor that he would have gone without him, but no documents exist in any of the collections which include Roland.

16. File of five letters in the Liddle Collection, Leeds.

17. Leicester Mercury, 17th December 1921.

18. Gordon Craig, *Germany, 1866-1945*, OUP, 1978, p. 439.

19. Richard Bessel, *Germany after the First World War*, OUP, 1995, pp. 262 and 258. Germany's future did not, however, lie with the pacifist anti-war tendency. See, for example, Ludwig Bauer's scornful account of the failure of German pacifism in *War Again To-morrow*, trans. W. Horsfall Carter, Faber & Faber, London, 1932, pp. 65-9, written on the cusp of Germany's inter-war history.

20. *Rugby Advertiser*, 27th May 1921; also reported in the *Leicester Mercury*, same date.

21. Leonard, autobiographical MS, Liddle Collection, p. 10. As John Fox pointed out, 'ex-servicemen often respected and understood the objector better than many civilians. "Civilian" (often with "profiteer" in mind) was the veteran's real term of contempt.' John Fox, Forgotten *Divisions. The First World War from both sides of No man's Land*, Sigma Leisure, London, 1994, p. 174.

22. ibid., p. 11.

23. Liddle interview, Tape 44, transcript p. 15.

24. ibid., p. 11. In his recorded interview with Peter Liddle, Leonard said his first game had been away at the Glen Parva Barracks against an Army team.

25. Liddle interview, Tape 44, transcript p. 15. See the match reports in the *Lutterworth Guardian* and *South Leicestershire Advertiser*, 1923-1928, copies of which are held in Lutterworth Museum. I wish to record my thanks to Geoff Smith and the wonderful volunteers of Lutterworth Museum for allowing me access to this resource.

26. The original letter to Roland is in the Liddle Collection, Leeds.

27. Their names do not appear in the Harborough Division Electoral Register for spring

1924. Leonard believed it was local Conservatives who had objected, which is entirely plausible. Liddle interview transcript, 1973, Tape 44, p. 14.

28. *Lutterworth Guardian* and *South Leicestershire Advertiser*, 30th November 1923. Of impeccable socialist credentials, Hughes would marry Keir Hardie's daughter in the new year. He had to wait until 1946 before entering Parliament.

29. *Lutterworth Guardian*, 30th November 1923.

30. The 1923 Market Bosworth result was George Ward (Liberal) 11,526, Major Paget (Conservative) 8,430, and Emrys Hughes (Labour) 8,152. Lutterworth was in the Harborough constituency, where a Conservative majority of almost 3,000 was overturned in a straight fight with the Liberal (J.W. Black) who won a majority of 1,304 votes. *Lutterworth Guardian*, 14th December 1923.

31. See Christopher Andrew, The Defence of the Realm. *The Authorized History of MI5*, Allen Lane, London, 2009, pp. 148-152. Labour's chances were ruined by the so-called 'Zinoviev Letter', a forged document purporting to come from the leading Soviet politician, Gregory Zinoviev, encouraging Communist Revolution in Britain.

32. Lutterworth Parish Council Minutes, 25th November 1918 onwards. LRO.DE2254/3.

33. *Rugby Advertiser*, 30th May 1919. Lutterworth got its war memorial in 1921: It was built as a garden on the site of a demolished house in the middle of town, the bricks from the demolition being used to build a row of ten fine terraced houses. Four years after its completion the contractor who built the war memorial had still not been paid in full and was asking the public to chip in £100 to his own funds. *Lutterworth Guardian*, 26th June 1925.

34. See Juliet Nicolson. *The Great Silence, 1918-1920, Living in the Shadow of the Great War*, John Murray, London, 2009.

35. Minutes of Lutterworth Parish Meetings, p. 108, 17th March 1919. LRO.DE2254/13. Only 130 voters attended the meeting. Even before the First World War, as population had started to rise in the wake of the railway, housing had been a source of concern, and not just in Lutterworth. Dyke Acland's national survey in 1914 had highlighted the specific problems in Leicestershire: 'As soon as it is known that land is wanted for building, the price asked is unreasonable,' one witness told his committee. 'In many districts speculating builders would have built if the land could have been bought at a reasonable price.' (*The Land. The Report of the Land Enquiry Committee*, Vol. 2. Urban. Hodder and Stoughton, London, 1914, p. 322.) Having said that, the Rural District Council appears to have had mixed success in dealing with the issue. While the houses they did build were of good quality, some remained unoccupied. At a meeting of its Housing Central Committee towards the end of 1921 the chairman was puzzled that they had been unable to rent out the houses on Leicester Way at five or eight shillings per week, only to be told that 'They would have been let before this, but people cannot

afford to pay such rents'. (*Leicester Mercury*, 16th December 1921.) On the houses themselves, see Jim Dodge, *The Leicester Road Council Estate, Lutterworth, 1913-2000*, privately printed, Lutterworth, 2006, pp. 3-4.

36. *Lutterworth Guardian* and *South Leicestershire Advertiser*, 26th October 1923, letter by 'Noah'. A modest start at this small-scale slum-clearance had been made before the Great War: in 1910 ten cottages on Station Road were demolished, and seven new and presumably more spacious houses built on the site. (*Duties on Land Values ('Domesday') Book under the Finance Act 1910*, LRO.DE2972/149, entry dated 30th November 1910.) Seemingly unable to resolve the problem local councillors were still wringing their hands in 1925: 'Only those who had any experience of the conditions in which the people in some of the houses were living could realise the awful conditions,' said William Abbot. 'In several houses two or more families are living in one house, and it was against the health of the town that these conditions should continue.' *Lutterworth Guardian*, 6th February 1925. 'Take a view from the top of the church tower,' advised one observer later in the year, 'and you will scarcely see in and around Lutterworth one brick being laid upon another… The lack hits hardest the young people who want to get married. This makes the matter more than one of inconvenience, more than of economics, it becomes a matter affecting morals.' *Lutterworth Guardian*, 8th May 1925.

37. *Leicester Mercury*, 30th April 1918.

38. *Rugby Advertiser*, 13th July 1918.

39. *Leicester Mail*, 20th September 1918. LRO N/C/X/7. After working for the War Pensions Committee, he worked for the Leicestershire Education Department, moving then to a Congregational pastorate in Uppingham. In 1925 he was appointed full-time Secretary to the Leicestershire and Rutland Congregational Union. (*Lutterworth Guardian*, 1st May 1925.)

40. Lutterworth Parochial Church Council Minutes, 1st November 1920. LRO.DE4336/34.

41. Minute Book, Lutterworth Parish Meetings, LRO DE2254/13. The idea that Lutterworth needed a public baths and swimming pool was not new. Arthur Massey, the Congregational Minister, had suggested that 'a memorial of a permanent nature, whether a public baths, which could be utilised for meetings in winter… or whatever' would be a good way to mark the coronation of George V in 1911. (*Rugby Advertiser*, 8th April 1911.) At the Parish Meeting held on March 23rd 1914 the proposal had been put and rejected by the chairman. Perhaps Topham failed to understand the proposal, thinking it purely a leisure facility. Some years later, in 1925, the local newspaper asked: 'Where in this town or its neighbourhood can the majority of us practise thoroughly that virtue which is said to be next to Godliness? How many houses possess a bathroom or any convenience for a complete ablution?' (*Lutterworth Guardian*, 19th June 1925.) The problem of Lutterworth's inadequate water supply would remain an issue for

some time to come. Leeds Grammar School, by the way, did indeed build a swimming baths as its war memorial after the First World War, so Lutterworth would not have been on its own.

42. *Lutterworth Guardian*, 8th January and 30th May 1924. Whether this was needed because of an increase in the number of children born immediately following the ending of the war is uncertain.

43. *Lutterworth Guardian*, 26th October 1923. The M1 motorway would pass within a mile of Lutterworth forty years later!

44. *Lutterworth Guardian*, 5th October 1923.

45. *Lutterworth Guardian*, 12th October 1923.

46. *Lutterworth Guardian*, 28th September 1923.

47. *Lutterworth Guardian*, 12th October 1923.

48. C.E. Leach, *A Pharmaceutical Apprenticeship in the Late 1920s*, typescript, 1999, held by Lutterworth Library, p. 5.

49. See Nicolson, pp. 103-4.

50. These developments in the pacifist and anti-war lobbies are well summarised by Lyn Smith in *Voices against War*, Mainstream Publishing, Edinburgh and London, 2009, pp. 63-4.

51. See Charles Loch Mowat, *Britain between the Wars, 1918-1940*, Methuen, London, 1955, pp. 537 and 422.

52. *The Times*, 3rd October 1938.

53. Hansard, 4th May 1939, quoted in Rachel Barker, *Conscience, Government and War. Conscientious Objection in Great Britain, 1939-1945*, Routledge & Kegan Paul, London, 1988, p. 72.

54. Quoted in Peace Pledge Union website, www.ppu.org.uk/coproject.

55. Quoted Barker, pp. 55-57. On the outbreak of war all men between eighteen and forty were made liable for the call-up, the upper age limit being raised to fifty-one at the end of 1941. (PPU web-site.) At the outbreak of war Leonard was forty-four and Roland forty-two.

56. The Summons is also among the papers in the Liddle Collection.

57. Leonard's autobiographical MS, Liddle Collection, p. 11. Some 60,000 men and 1,000 women applied for conscientious objector status in the Second World War (as opposed to the 16,000 men in the First World War), with some 42,000 being accepted as genuine (70%). Among those who were refused conscientious objector status were members of Oswald Mosley's British Union of Fascists (the Blackshirts) who claimed the right not to fight against their ideological allies for a government 'which has deliberately raised the ideological issue by making one of its principal war aims the destruction of the political system of another great nation.' See Richard Griffiths, *A Note on Mosley,*

the *"Jewish War" and Conscientious Objection,* Journal of Contemporary History, October 2005, quotation from p. 678.

58. The phrase was used by Nathaniel Philbrick in *The Last Stand. Custer, Sitting Bull and the Battle of the Little Big Horn*, Bodley Head, London, 2010.

SELECT BIBLIOGRAPHY

Acland, Dyce, *The Land. The Report of the Land Enquiry Committee*, Vol. 2. Urban Hodder and Stoughton, London, 1914.

Adams, R.J.Q. and Philip Poirier, *The Conscription Controversy in Great Britain, 1900-1918*, Macmillan, London, 1987.

A German, *J'Accuse*, Hodder & Stoughton, London, 1915.

The Crime by the author of *J'Accuse*, Hodder & Stoughton, London, 1917.

Andrew, Christopher, *The Defence of the Realm. The Authorized History of MI5*, Allen Lane, London, 2009.

Angell, Norman, *The Great Illusion. A Study of the Relation of Military Power in Nations to their Economic and Social Advantage*, Heinemann, London, 1910.

Anon., *The Book[s] of Artemas*, W. Westall, London, 1918.

Arthur, Max (ed.), *Forgotten Voices of the Great War. A New History of WW1 in the Words of the Men and Women who were there*, Ebury Books, London, 2003.

-*The Road Home. The Aftermath of the Great War told by the Men and Women who Survived it*, Phoenix, London, 2010.

Asprey, Robert B., *The German High Command at War*, Warner Books, London, 1994.

Asquith, H.H., *Memories and Reflections, 1852-1927*, (2 Vols.) Cassell, London, 1928.

- *The Genesis of the War*, Cassell, London, 1923.

'B-2-15', *Among the Broad-Arrow Men of Leicester Gaol, 1920. A Plain Account of English Prison Life*, reprinted by David Dover, Loughborough, n.d. (2008).

Babington, Anthony, *For the Sake of Example: Capital Courts Martial, 1914-1920*, Paladin Books, London, 1985.

Bainton, Roland H., *Christian Attitudes toward War and Peace: A Historical and Critical Re-evaluation*, Abingdon Press, New York, 1960.

Barham, Peter, *Forgotten Lunatics of the Great War*, Yale, London, 2007.

Barker, Pat, *The Eye in the Door*, Penguin Books, Harmondsworth, 1993.

Rachel, Barker, *Conscience, Government and War. Conscientious Objection in Great Britain, 1939-1945*, Routledge & Kegan Paul, London, 1988.

Barker, W. (pub.), *For His Name's Sake: Being a Record of the Witness given by Members of Churches of Christ in Great Britain against Militarism during the European War, 1914-1918*, W. Barker, Heanor, 1921.

Baxter, Archibald, *We Will Not Cease. The Autobiography of a Conscientious Objector*, Victor Gallancz, London, 1939.

Beaverbrook, Lord, *Politicians and the War, 1914-1916*, Oldbourne Books, London, n.d.

Begbie, Harold, *Mr Sterling Sticks it Out*, Headley Bros., London, 1919.

Bell, Julian (ed.), *We Did Not Fight: 1914-1918 Experiences of War Resisters*, Cobden-Saunderson, London, 1935.

Richard, Bessel, *Germany after the First World War*, OUP, 1995.

Bibbings, Lois, *Telling Tales About Men. Conceptions of Conscientious Objectors to Military Service during the First World war*, Manchester University Press, 2009.

Birmingham Christadelphian Temperance Hall Ecclesia, *Constitution*, Birmingham, 1915.

Boulton, David, *Objection Overruled*, MacGibbon & Key, London, 1967.

Bristow, Adrian, *A Serious Disappointment. The Battle of Aubers Ridge, 1915 and the subsequent munitions scandal*, Leo Cooper, London, 1995.

Brock, Peter, (ed.), *These Strange Criminals. An Anthology of Prison Memoirs by Conscientious Objectors from the Great War to the Cold War*, Toronto, 2004.

Brockway, A. Fenner, *Inside the Left. Thirty Years of Platform, Press, Prison and Parliament*, George Allen & Unwin, London, 1942.

and Frederic Mullally, *Death Pays a Dividend*, Victor Gollancz, London, 1944.

A New Way with Crime, Williams & Norgate, London, 1928.

Brooke, Rupert, *1914 and other Poems*, Sidgwick & Jackson, London, 1916.

Brown, Malcolm, *The Imperial War Museum Book of the First World War*, Sidgwick & Jackson, London, 1991.

Brown, William, *War and the Psychological Conditions of Peace*, Adam & Charles Black, London, 1942.

Buchan, John, *Mr Standfast*, Hodder & Stoughton, London, 1919.

Bushaway, Bob, *Name upon Name. The Great War and Remembrance*, in Roy Porter (ed.), 'Myths of the English', Polity Press, London, 1993.

Carroll, Andrew, *Behind the Lines. Revealing and Uncensored Letters from our War-Torn World*, Ebury, London, 2005.

Catchpool, Corder, *On Two Fronts: Letters of a Conscientious Objector*, George Allen and Unwin, London, 1918, 3rd edn., 1940.

Childs, Major General Sir Wyndham, *Episodes and Reflections*, Cassell, London, 1930.

Church Congress, *The Official Report of the Church Congress held at Leicester on October 12th to 17th, 1919*, Nisbet, London, 1919.

Churchill, Winston S., *The World Crisis 1911-1918*, Odhams, London.

Clark, Christopher, *Kaiser Wilhem II. A Life in Power*, Penguin Books, London, 2009.

Clarke, I.F., *The Tale of the Next Great War, 1871-1914. Fictions of Future Warfare and Battles Still-to-come*, Liverpool University Press, Liverpool, 1995.

Clayton, Joseph, *The Rise and Decline of Socialism in Great Britain, 1884-1924*, London, 1926.

Codrington, George, *An Outline of the History of the Leicestershire (Prince Albert's Own) Yeomanry*, London, 1928.

Cohen, Chapman, *Religion and Sex. Studies in the Pathology of Religious Development*, T.N. Foulis, London, 1919.

Cooksley, Peter, *The Home Front. Civilian Life in World War One*, Tempus, London, 2006.

Corder, Herbert, *Compulsory Military Service in Australia and New Zealand*, published by Burtt Bros., Hull, n.d., catalogued in the Friends Library in London under 'Northern Friends Peace Board', Vol. 1, 1916-1928.

Corns, Cathryn & Hughes-Wilson, John, *Blindfold and Alone. Military Executions in the Great War*, Cassell, London, 2001.

Coulton, G.G., *The Case for Compulsory Military Service*, Macmillan, London, 1917.

Cromer, Earl of, et al., *After-War Problems*, George Allen & Unwin, London, 1917.

Cruttwell, C.R.M.F., *A History of the War, 1914-1918*, 1936, Granada Publishing, London, 1982.

Dangerfield, George, *The Strange Death of Liberal England*, Macgibbon & Key, London, 1966 edn.

Dennis, Peter, *The Territorial Army, 1907-1940*, Royal Historical Society, London, 1987.

Destree, Jules, *The Deportations of Belgian Workmen*, T. Fisher Unwin, London, 1917.

Dickinson, G. Lowes, *The International Anarchy, 1904-1914*, The Century Co, New York & London, 1926.

Dillon, E.J., *Ourselves and Germany*, Chapman & Hall, London, 1916.

Duckers, James Scott, *Handed Over. The Prison Experiences of Mr J. Scott Duckers, Solicitor of Chancery Lane, Under the Military Service Act, Written by Himself C.W. Daniel*, London, 1917.

Dyer, Geoff, *The Missing of the Somme*, Penguin Books, Harmondsworth, 1995.

Dyke, Henry van, *Fighting for Peace*, Charles Scribner, New York, 1917.

Ehrenreich, Barbara, *Blood Rites. The Origins and History of the Passions of War*, Granta, London, 2011.

Elliott, Malcolm, *Opposition to the First World War: The Fate of Conscientious Objectors in Leicester*, Transactions of the Leicestershire Archaelogical & Historical Society, 77, Leicester, 2003.

Ellsworth-Jones, Will, *We Will Not Fight. The Untold Story of World War One's Conscientious Objectors*, Aurum, London, 2007.

Emden, Richard van, *Boy Soldiers of the Great War*, Headline Books, London, 2006.

Emmott, A. (President), *The Nation's Morals. Proceedings of the Public Morals Conference held in London, 14th and 15th July 1910*, Cassell, London, 1910.

Emsley, Clive, *Hard Men. The English and Violence since 1750*, Hambledon Continuum, London, 2005.

- *The Great British Bobby. A History of British Policing from the 18th Century to the Present*, Quercus, London, 2009.

Ferguson, Niall, *The Pity of War*, Allen Lane, London, 1998.

Flower, Newman (ed.), *The History of the Great War*, Waverley Books, London, n.d. (1919/1920).

Foucault, Michel, *Discipline and Punish. The Birth of the Prison*, trans. Alan Sheridan, Peregrine Books, London, 1979.

Fox, Alan, *A History of the National Union of Boot and Shoe Operatives, 1874-1957*, Oxford, 1958.

Fox, John, *Forgotten Divisions. The First World War from both sides of No Man's Land*, Sigma Leisure, London, 1994.

Frantzen, Allen J., *Bloody Good: Chivalry, Sacrifice and the Great War*, Chicago University Press, Chicago, 2003.

Fredette, Raymond H., *The First Battle of Britain, 1917/18*, Cassell, London, 1966.

Freeman, Mark, *Muscular Quakerism? The Society of Friends and Youth Organisations in Britain, c. 1900-1950*, English Historical Review, cxxv, June 2010.

Freytag-Loringhoven, Baron von, *Deductions from the World War*, Constable, London, 1918.

Fromkin, David, *Europe's Last Summer. Why the World went to War in 1914*, Vintage Books, London, 2005.

Fussell, Paul, *The Great War and Modern Memory*, O.U.P., Oxford, 1975.

George, David Lloyd, *War Memoirs*, Odhams, London, 1938 edn.

Gilbert, Martin, *First World War*, Harper Collins, London, 1994.

Gliddon, Gerald, *The Aristocracy and the Great War*, Gliddon Books, Norwich, 2002.

Goebel, Stefan, *The Great War and Medieval Memory: War, Remembrance and Medievalism in Britain and Germany, 1914-1940*, C.U.P., 2007.

Goodall, Felicity, *A Question of Conscience. Conscientious Objection in the two World Wars*, Sutton, Stroud, 1997.

Graham, John W., *Conscription and Conscience: A History 1916-1919*, George Allen & Unwin, London, 1922.

Gregory, Adrian, *The Last Great War. British Society and the First World War*, C.U.P., 2008.

Grey, Sir Edward, *Twenty-Five Years, 1892-1916*, Hodder & Stoughton, London, 1925.

Griffiths, Richard, *A Note on Mosley, the "Jewish War" and Conscientious Objection*, Journal of Contemporary History, October 2005.

Gullace, Nicoletta, *"The Blood of Our Sons": Men, Women, and the Renegotiation of British Citizenship During the Great War*, Palgrave Macmillan, Basingstoke, 2002.

Haldane, Richard Burdon, *Richard Burdon Haldane: An Autobiography*, Hodder and Stoughton, London, 1929.

Hall, W. Arnold, *The Adult School Movement on the Twentieth Century*, Dept Adult Education, University of Nottingham, Nottingham, 1985.

Hallam, Andrew and Nicola (eds.), *Lady Under Fire on the Western Front. The Great War Letters of Lady Dorothie Feilding, M.M.*, Pen & Sword, Barnsley, 2011.

Halsalle, Henry de, *Degenerate Germany*, T. Werner Laurie, London, n.d. (1916).

Hammerton, Sir John, (ed) *World War 1914-1918. A Pictured History*, Amalgamated Press, London, n.d.

Hancock, W.K., 'Smuts', Vol. 1 *The Sanguine Years 1870-1919*, C.U.P., 1962.

Hanson, Neil, *First Blitz. The Secret Plan to Raze London to the Ground in 1918,* Corgi Books, London, 2009.

Hart, Peter, *1918. A Very British Victory*, Phoenix Books, London, 2009.

Higenbottam, S., *Our Society's History*, published by the Amalgamated Society of Woodworkers, Manchester, 1939.

Hiley, N., *Counter Espionage and Security in Great Britain during the First World War*, English Historical Review, London, 1986.

Hirst, Margaret E., *The Quakers in Peace and War*, Swarthmore Press, London, 1923.

Hendley, Matthew, *"Help us to Secure a Strong, Healthy, Prosperous and Peaceful Britain." The Social Arguments for Compulsory Military Service in Britain, 1899-1914*. Canadian Journal of History, August 1995.

Hiley, N., *Counter Espionage and Security in Great Britain during the First World War*, English Historical Review, 1986.

Hindenburg, Paul von, *The Great War*, ed. Charles Messenger, Greenhill Books, London and St. Paul, 2006.

Hinks, John, *Ramsay MacDonald. The Leicester Years, 1906-1918*, Privately printed, Leicester, 1996.

Hobhouse, Mrs Henry, *"I Appeal Unto Caesar". The Case of the Conscientious Objector*, George Allen and Unwin, London, 1917.

Hochschild, Adam, *To End All Wars. How the First World War Divided Britain*, Macmillan, London, 2011.

Holden, Wendy, *Shell Shock. The Psychological Impact of War*, Channel 4 Books, London, 1998.

Holman, Bob, *Good Old George. The Life of George Lansbury, best-loved leader of the Labour Party*, Lion publishing, London, 1990.

Holmes, Richard, *Fatal Avenue. A Traveller's History of Northern France and Flanders, 1346-1945*, Pimlico, London, 1993.

- *Tommy. The British Soldier on the Western Front 1914-1918*, Harper, London, 2004.

Howard, Michael (Introduced by), *A Part of History. Aspects of the British Experience of the First World War*, Continuum, London, 2008.

'Iconoclast' (Mary Agnes Hamilton), *The Man of Tomorrow: J. Ramsay MacDonald*, Independent Labour Party, London, 1923.

Jackson, Robert, *The Prisoners, 1914-1918*, Routledge, London, 1989.

Jannaway, Frank G., *Without the Camp. Being the Story of Why and How the Christadelphians were Exempted from Military Service*, Privately published, London, 1917.

Jehovah's Witnesses, *Jehovah's Witnesses. Proclaimers of God's Kingdom,* Watch Tower Bible and Tract Society, New York, 1993.

Joffre, the Ex-Crown Prince of Germany, Foch and Ludendorff, *The Two Battles of the Marne*, Thornton Butterworth, London, 1927.

Keegan, John, *A History of Warfare*, Hutchinson, London, 1993.

Kelman, John, *The War and Preaching*, Hodder & Stoughton, London, n.d.

Kennedy, Thomas, *The Hound of Conscience: A History of the No-Conscription Fellowship, 1914-1919*, University of Arkansas Press, Lafayetteville, 1987.

Kramer, Alan, *Dynamic of Destruction. Culture and Mass Killing in the First World War*, O.U.P., 2007.

Lee, John, *A Soldier's Life. General Sir Ian Hamilton, 1853-1947*, Macmillan, London.

Levine, Naomi B., *Politics, Religion and Love. The Story of H.H. Asquith, Venetia Stanley and Edwin Montagu, based on the Life and Letters of Edwin Samuel Montagu*, New York University Press, New York & London, 1991.

Liddle, Peter, *Home Fires and Foreign Fields*, Brassey, London, 1985.

Long, Walter (Viscount Long of Wraxall), *Memories*, Hutchinson, London, 1923.

MacArthur, Brian, *For King and Country. Voices from the First World War*, Abacus Books, London, 2008.

Macfall, Haldane, *Germany at Bay*, George H. Doran, New York, n.d. (1917).

March, Nora H., *Towards Racial Health. A Handbook for Parents, Teachers & Social Workers on the Training of Boys & Girls*, Routledge, London, 1915.

Marquand, David, *Ramsay MacDonald*, Jonathan Cape, London, 1977.

Martin, David A., *Pacifism. An Historical and Sociological Study*, Routledge and Kegan Paul, London, 1965.

Marwick, Arthur, *Clifford Allen. The Open Conspirator*, Oliver & Boyd, London, 1964.

Marwick, Arthur, *The Deluge. British Society and the First World War*, Penguin, Harmondsworth, 1967.

Mason, E. Williamson, *Made Free in Prison*, George Allen & Unwin, London, 1918.

Maurice, Sir Frederick, *Haldane, 1915-1928. The Life of Viscount Haldane of Cloan, K.T., O.M.*, Faber & Faber, London, 1939.

Middlebrook, Martin, *The Kaiser's Battle. 21 March 1918: The First Day of the German Spring Offensive*, Penguin Books, Harmondsworth, 1983.

Millman, Brock, *Managing Domestic Dissent in First World War Britain*, Cass, London, 2000.

- *HMG and the War against Dissent, 1914-18*, Journal of Contemporary History, July 2005.

Moran, Lord, *The Anatomy of Courage*, Sphere Books, London, 1968.

Morgan, J.H., *German Atrocities. An Official Investigation*, T. Fisher Unwin, London, 1916.

Morris, A.J. Anthony, 'Haldane's Army Reforms, 1906-8', in *History*, February 1971.

Mosse, George L., *Fallen Soldiers. Reshaping the Memory of the World Wars*, O.U.P., 1990.

Nevinson, Henry, *Fire of Life*, James Nisbet, London, 1935.

- *The Conscientious Objector*, typescript article in Friends' Library, London, Box L207/39.

Nicholson, Virginia, *Singled Out. How Two Million Women survived without men after the First World War*, Penguin Books, London, 2008.

Nicolson, Juliet, *The Perfect Summer. Dancing into Shadow. England in 1911*, John Murray, London, 2007.

- *The Great Silence. 1918-1920. Living in the Shadow of the Great War*, John Murray, London, 2010.

No-Conscription Fellowship, *The No-Conscription Fellowship. A Souvenir of its Work during the Years 1914-1919*, London, 1919.

Northampton Area Quaker Meeting, *Quaker Peace Stories*, pub. Northampton Area Quaker Meeting of the Religious Society of Friends, Northampton, 2010.

Northcliffe, Lord, *At the War*, Hodder & Stoughton, London, 1916.

Oram, Gerard, *Worthless Men. Race, Eugenics and the Death Penalty during the First World War*, Francis Boutle, London, 1998.

- *Death Sentences passed by Military Courts of the British Army, 1914-1924*, Francis Boutle, London, 1998.

Orr, Edgar W., *Christian Pacifism*, C.W. Daniel, Ashingdon, Essex, 1958.

Orton, William Aylott, *Labour in Transition. A Survey of British Industrial History since 1914*, Philip Allen, London, 1921.

Orwell, George, *Pacifism and the War*, 1942, via http://orwell.ru/library/articles/pacifism

Packer, Ian, *Religion and the New Liberalism. The Rowntree Family, Quakerism and Social Reform*, Journal of British Studies, April 2003.

Panayi, Panikos, *The Enemy in Our Midst. Germans in Britain During the First World War*, Berg, New York and London, 1991.

Parliament of Australia, *Conscientious Objection to Military Service in Australia*: Research Note no. 31, Canberra, 2002-03.

Pearce, Cyril, *Comrades in Conscience. The Story of an English Community's Opposition to the Great War*, Francis Boutle, London, 2001.

Pendlebury, Alyson, *Portraying "the Jew" in First World War Britain*, Vallentine Mitchell, London and Portland Oregon, 2006.

Politicus, *Viscount Grey of Fallodon*, Methuen, London, 1935.

Pugh, Martin, *We Danced All Night. A Social History of Britain Between the Wars*, Vintage Books, London, 2009.

Putkowski, Julian and Sykes, Julian, *Shot at Dawn. Executions in World War One by Authority of the British Army Act*, Leo Cooper, London, 1992.

Quaker Quest, *Twelve Quakers and Pacifism*, Quaker Quest Pamphlet 3, Hampstead, 2005.

Rae, John, *Conscience and Politics: The British Government and the Conscientious Objector to Military Service, 1916-1919*, OUP, London, 1970.

Reeder, Sybil, (compiled by), *Memories of Whitburn in Words and Pictures*, Whitburn, 2007.

Reilly, Catherine, *English Poetry of the First World War. A Bibliography*, George Prior, London, 1972.

Roberts, Earl of Kandahar, *Fallacies and Facts. An Answer to "Compulsory Service"*, John Murray, London, 1911.

Robbins, Keith, *The Abolition of War. The "Peace Movement" in Britain 1914-1919*, University of Wales Press, Cardiff, 1976.

Rose, Tania, *Aspects of Political Censorship, 1914-1918*, University of Hull Press, Hull, 1995.

Royle, Trevor, *The Flowers of the Forest. Scotland and the First World War*, Birlinn, Edinburgh, 2007.

Rumbold, Horace, *The War Crisis in Berlin, July-August 1914*, Constable, London, 1940.

Russell, Bertrand, *Why Men Fight*, Routledge Classics, London, 2010.

Rutenber, Culbert G., *The Dagger and the Cross: An Examination of Christian Pacifism*, Fellowship Publications, New York, 1958.

Salmon, Edward and James Worsfold (eds.), *The British Dominions Year Book 1916*, pub. The British Dominions General Insurance Co., London, 1916.

Seton-Watson, R.W., Wilson, J. Dover, Zimmern, Alfred E. and Greenwood, Arthur, *The War and Democracy,* Macmillan, London, 1914.

Searle, G.R., *Eugenics and Politics in Britain, 1900-1914*, Leyden, 1976.

Sheehan, James, *The Monopoly of Violence. Why Europeans Hate going to War*, Faber & Faber, London, 2007.

Sheffield, Gary, *Forgotten Victory. The First World War: Myths and Realities*, Review Books, London, 2002.

Shinwell, Emanuel, *The Labour Story*, Macdonald, London, 1963.

Smith, Lyn (ed.), *Voices against War. A Century of Protest*, Mainstream Publishing, Edinburgh & London, 2009.

Smith, M.K., 'Adult schools and the making of adult education', 2004, via www.infed.org/lifelonglearning/adult schools.htm

Stamp, Gavin, *The Memorial to the Missing of the Somme*, Profile Books, London, 2007.

Stationery Office, *War 1914: Punishing the Serbs*, Stationery Office, London, 1999.

Stevenson, David, *With Our Backs to the Wall. Victory and Defeat in 1918*, Allen Lane, London, 2011.

Strachan, Hew, *The First World War. A New Illustrated History*, Simon and Schuster, London, 2003.

Stromberg, Roland N., *Redemption by War. The Intellectuals and 1914*, The Regents Press of Kansas, 1982.

Tabili, Laura, *"Outsiders in the Land of their Birth": Exogamy, Citizenship and Identity in War and Peace*, Journal of British Studies, October 2005.

Tait, Fred, *Diary of a Conscientious Objector, 23 March 1918 to 26 April 1918*, Quaker Library, London, Temp. MSS 907.

Taylor, A.J.P., *The First World War. An Illustrated History*, Penguin, Harmondsworth, 1966.

– *English History, 1914-1945*, Penguin Books, Harmondsworth, 1970.

– *Beaverbrook,* Hamish Hamilton, London, 1972.

Taylor, Kate (ed.), *Aspects of Wakefield. Discovering Local History 3,* Wharncliffe Books, 2001.

Temple, William, *Christianity and the State*, Macmillan, London, 1928.

The Queen's Gift Book, published In aid of Queen Mary's Convalescent Auxiliary Hospitals for Soldiers and Sailors who have lost Limbs in the War, Hodder & Stoughton, London, 1916.

Thom, Deborah, *Nice Girls and Rude Girls. Women Workers in World War 1*, I.B. Tauris, London, 2000.

Thompson, E.P., *Customs in Common,* Penguin Books, London, 1993.

Tobias, Lily, *Eunice Fleet*, 1933, novel, republished Honno Classics, Wales, 2004.

Toland, John, *No Man's Land. The Story of 1918*, Methuen, London, 1982.

Toye, Richard*, Lloyd George and Churchill. Rivals for Greatness*, Macmillan, London, 2007.

Travers, Tim, *How the War was Won. Factors that Led to Victory in World War One*, Pen & Sword, Barnsley, 2005.

Trotter, Wilfred, *Speculations upon the Human Mind in 1915*, reprinted in *Instincts of the Herd in Peace and War, 1916-1919*, OUP, 1953.

War Office, *Manual of Military Law*, War Office, London, 1914.

Warren, Allen, *Sir Robert Baden-Powell, the Scout Movement and Citizen Training in Great Britain 1900-1920*, English Historical Review, 1986.

Wehberg, Hans, *The Outlawry of War*, Carnegie Endowment for International Peace, Washington, 1931.

Wells, H.G., *Will the War Change England?*, in *The War Illustrated Deluxe* volume II.

- *War and the Future. Italy, France and Britain at War*, Cassell, London, 1917.

Wickham Steed, Henry, *Through Thirty Years, 1892-1922. A Personal Narrative*, Vol. 2, Heinemann, London, 1924.

Wilson, H.W. & Hammerton, J.A. (eds.), *The Great War. The Standard History of the All-European Conflict*, Amalgamated Press, London, 1914-1919.

Wilson, Trevor, *The Downfall of the Liberal Party, 1914-1935*, Collins, London, 1968.

Winter, Denis, *Death's Men. Soldiers of the Great War*, Penguin Books, Harmondsworth, 1979.

Winter, Jay M., *Sites of Memory, Sites of Mourning. The Great Wear in European Cultural History*, Cambridge U.P., Cambridge, 1996.

Winter, Jay and Prost, Antoine, *The Great War in History. Debates and Controversies, 1914 to the Present*, CUP, Cambridge, 2005.

Winter, Jay (ed.), *The Legacy of the Great War Ninety Years On*, University of Missouri Press, Columbia and London, 2009.

Yoder, John H., *Nevertheless: The Varieties and Shortcomings of Religious Pacifism*, Herald Press, Ontario, 1971.

Zuber, Terence, *The Real German War Plan 1904-14*, The History Press, Stroud, 2011.

LOCAL HISTORY

Armitage, F.P., *Leicester 1914-1918: The War-Time Story of a Midland Town*, Edgar Backus, Leicester, 1933.

Bateman, J., *The Great Landowners of Great Britain and Ireland* (1883), ed. D. Spring, Leicester, 1971.

Beazley, Ben, *Four Years Remembered. Leicester During the Great War*, Breedon Books, Derby, 1999.

Bennett, J.D., *Members of Parliament for Leicester, 1832-1983*, Leicester, 1984.

Bevin, Hugh A., *The Book of Hinckley*, Barracuda Books, Buckingham, 1983.

Boyd-Hope, Gary and Sargent, Andrew, *Railway and Rural Life. S.W.A. Newton and the Great Central Railway*, English Heritage and Leicestershire County Council, 2007.

Burn, Ian, et al, *A Brief History of Leire*, part 2, Leire History Group, 2000.

Clarke, K.C., *Blaby Parish Council: The First Hundred Years, 1894-1994*, no imprint, 1995.

Clayton, Michael, *Foxhunting in Paradise*, John Murray, London, 1993.

Coleman, Sidney E., *Leicester as I Remember it*, in *The Leicestershire Historian*, 1978-9.

Crompton, James, *John Wyclif. A Study in Mythology*, Transactions of the Leicestershire Archaelogical & Historical Society, Leicester, 1966-7.

Davies, J.C., *Town Affairs: The Making of Modern Market Harborough*, Market Harborough U.D.C., 1974.

Deacon, C.W., *The Court Guide & County Blue Book of Derbs., Notts., Leics, Rutland and N'ants, 1908*, C.W. Deacon , London, 1908.

Dodge, J.S., *A Look at Lutterworth 2000, or Thereabouts*, Privately printed, Lutterworth, 1999.

Dodge, J.S., 'Lutterworth Banks', in *Lutterworth Local History Group Journal*, 2002.

Dodge, J.S., *The Leicester Road Council Estate, Lutterworth, 1913-2000*, Lutterworth, 2006.

Dodge, J.S. & Spencer, Peter, *Notes for a Brief Life of George Spencer, 1868-1946*, Lutterworth, 2001.

Dyson, A.H., (ed. Hugh Goodacre), *Lutterworth: John Wycliffe's Town*, Methuen, London, 1913.

Dyson, A.H. and Skillington, S.H., *Lutterworth Church and its Associations with a Chapter on John Wycliffe*, C.H. Gee, Leicester, 1916.

Edensor, Dennis, *In Grateful Memory. The War Memorial at North Kilworth*, Diamond D Publishing, 2009.

Ellis, Colin B., *Leicestershire and the Quorn Hunt,* Leicester, 1951.

Foster, Michael, *The Railway at Ullesthorpe*, in Ullesthorpe, Ullesthorpe Book Group, n.d.

Gates, R., *History of Lutterworth United Reformed Church 1689-1997*, compiled by Ron Gates, researched by Peter Bruce, edited by Barbara Gates.

Gimson, J. Mentor, *A Guide to Leicester and District*, Brit. Ass. Adv. of Science, Leicester, 1907.

Gräf, Holger Th., *Leicestershire Small Towns and Pre-Industrial Urbanisation*, Transactions of the Leicestershire Archaelogical and Historical Society, 68, 1994.

Goodacre, John, *The Transformation of a Peasant Economy. Townspeople and villagers in the Lutterworth area, 1500-1700*, Scolar Press, London, 1994.

Gregory, Chris, *Syston as I Remember it*, Leicestershire Library & Information Service, Leicester, 1992.

Harrison, Fred M.W., *It All Began Here. The Story of the East Midlands Baptist Association*, London, 1986.

Henderson, Evelyn, *Milestones of Hinckley, 1640-1981*, Hinckley, 1981.

Healy, John, *Great Central Memories*, Baton Transport, London, 1987.

Herbertson, A.J. and O.J.R. Howarth (eds), *The Oxford Survey of the British Empire: The British Isles*, Clarendon Press, Oxford, 1914.

Hill, Lynda and Bailey, Roz, *Lutterworth High Street in the Nineteenth Century*, Mulberry Press, Lutterworth, 2000.

- *Butchers, Baker and Candlestick Makers. Trades in a Victorian Street, Lutterworth, Leicestershire*, Volcano publishing, Dunton Bassett, 1995.

Holliman, L. Lynch, B. & Pitcher, G., *Braybrooke. Jubilee to Jubilee*, Matador, Market Harborough, 2003.

Howes, Chas (ed), *Leicester. Its Civic, Industrial, Institutional and Social Life*, Midland Service Agencies, Leicester, 1927.

Husbands Bosworth Historical Society, *Bygone Bosworth*, No. 9, September 1986.

Irving, George, *Lutterworth Grammar School Anniversary Book*, 1956, p. 39. Reprinted and extended, Lutterworth GS & CC, Lutterworth, 1980.

Kendall, Ernest E., *Doing and Daring. The Story of Melbourne Hall Evangelical Free Church, Leicester*, Rushden, n.d. (1955).

Keogh, Jean, *Feilding Palmer Cottage Hospital, 1899-1999*, Privately printed, Lutterworth, 1999.

Lancaster, Bill, *Radicalism, Cooperation and Socialism, Leicester Working Class Politics, 1860-1906,* Leicester, 1987.

Leacroft, Helen and Richard, *The Theatre in Leicestershire. A History of Entertainment in the County from the 15th Century to the 1960s*, Leicestershire Libraries and Information Service, Leicester, 1986.

Leicester Museums, *The Last Main Line. An Illustrated History of the Building of the Great Central Railway*, 2nd edn., 1973.

Little, Roger (ed.), Lutterworth 1891 Census Name Index, Lutterworth Local History Group, Lutterworth, 2001.

Lund, Brian, *Leicestershire Railway Stations in Old Picture Postcards*, Yesterday's Leicestershire Series No. 2, pub. Keyworth, Notts, 1996.

Lucas, Duncan, Tricia Berry and Peter Mastin, *Pocket Images: Wigston Magna and South*, Nonsuch, Stroud, 2006.

Lutterworth Local History Group, *Lutterworth War Memorial Names, 1914-1918, 1939-1945: A Preliminary Study*, Lutterworth, 2005.

Lutterworth Wyclif Memorial Chapel, *200 Years of Methodism in Lutterworth*, published by the Lutterworth Wyclif Memorial Chapel, 2004.

Mitchell, Sheila, *Not Disobedient: A History of the United Baptist Church, Leicester, including Harvey Lane 1760-1845, Belvoir Street 1845-1940 and Charles Street 1831-1940*, no imprint, Leicester, 1984.

Nash, David and Reeder, David (eds.), *Leicester in the Twentieth Century*, Alan Sutton with Leicester City Council, Stroud, 1993.

Nuttall, G. Clarke, *Guide to Leicester and Neighbourhood*, Edward Shardlow, Leicester, 1905

Paget, Guy and Irvine, Lionel, *Leicestershire*, Robert Hale, London, 1950.

Paget, J. Otho, *Memories of the Shires*, London, 1920.

Richardson, Matthew, *The Tigers. 6th, 7th, 8th and 9th (Service) Battalions of the Leicestershire Regiment*, Pen & Sword Books, Barnsley, 2000.

Rimmington, Gerald, *Congregationalism and Society in Leicestershire and Rutland, 1916-1966*, Transactions of the Leicestershire Archaeological and Historical Society, Volume 8, Leicester, 2007.

Rolt, L.T.C., *The Making of a Railway*, Hugh Evelyn, London, 1971.

Rugby Local History Group, *Hospital of St. Cross, Rugby, 1884-1984*, published by Rugby Health Authority (1984). See also typescript in Rugby Library.

Schultka, Henrietta, *Lost Lives. The War Dead of Countesthorpe, Kilby, Peatling Magna, P. Parva and Shearsby, 1914-18 and 1939-45*, published by the author, Countesthorpe, 2007.

Simmons, Jack, *Leicester Past and Present*, vol. 2, London, 1974.

Thorpe, George, *A Sketch of Lutterworth*, typescript in Lutterworth Library, 1969.

Simpson, Charles, *The Harboro' Country*, John Lane the Bodley Head, London, 1927.

Smith, Geoff, *Around Lutterworth*, Chalfont, Stroud, 1997.

- *Around Lutterworth. A Second Selection* Tempus, Stroud, 2002.

Steppler, Glenn, *Britons to Arms! The Story of the British Volunteer Soldier and Volunteer Tradition in Leicestershire and Rutland*, Alan Sutton, Stroud, 1992.

Victoria County History of Warwickshire, Vol. 2, ed. William Page, Archibald Constable, London, 1908.

Victoria County History of Leicestershire, ed. W.G. Hoskins and R.A. McKinley, Dawsons, London, Vol. 3, 1955.

Williams, Daniel (ed.), *The Adaptation of Change. Essays in the History of 19th Century Leicester and Leicestershire*, Leics. Museums Publication No. 18, Leicester, 1980.

ACKNOWLEDGEMENTS

In the circumstances, it is impossible to include everyone who Andy contacted during the course of his research, although I know he would wish to acknowledge the wide range of information and help he received from various sources all over the country. However, I would like to give particular thanks to Nancy and Dick Lord and family, who gave Andy access to the letters, the Payne family, Amanda McHugh, Marilyn Brown whose expertise in reprographics enabled Andy to create early drafts of the work, Jim Dodge and Jean Soden, Staff at the Quaker Library, National Archives, Durham Library and Leicestershire Record Office and other centres. Andy would also be grateful to Mandy Cutler for her suggestions, and Viv Weller for the invaluable support she has given in enabling the book to come to print.